W9-ACY-215

LITERARY AND LIBRARY PRIZES

LITERARY AND LIBRARY PRIZES

10TH EDITION

Revised and Edited by
Olga S. Weber & Stephen J. Calvert

R. R. BOWKER COMPANY
New York & London 1980

Published by R. R. Bowker Company
1180 Avenue of the Americas, New York, N.Y. 10036
Copyright © 1980 by Xerox Corporation
All rights reserved.
International Standard Book Number: 0-8352-1249-1
International Standard Serial Number: 0075-9880
Library of Congress Catalog Card Number: 59-11370
Printed and bound in the United States of America

Contents

Preface

Since 1935, when Bessie Graham's *Famous Literary Prizes and Their Winners* was first published—later titled *Literary Prizes and Their Winners* and then, with the addition of library awards in 1959, *Literary and Library Prizes*—the R. R. Bowker Company has made available throughout ten editions of this book invaluable information on about 675 literary and library prizes and over 10,000 winners of these prizes. Historians, thereby, can chart the success authors have attained through the receipt of literary awards during their careers.

It can be learned through these editions that John Steinbeck, for example, first established his reputation with the publication of *Tortilla Flat*, which won the California Literature Medal Award in 1936. The following year, his *In Dubious Battle* was again honored with a California Literature Medal Award. *Of Mice and Men*, dramatized in the year of its publication, won the New York Drama Critics Circle Award in 1938. In that same year, his short story "The Promise" was awarded third prize in the O. Henry Memorial Awards. *The Grapes of Wrath*, probably Steinbeck's greatest work, received three awards in 1940: the California Literature Medal Award, the A.B.A. National Book Award (no longer given), and the prestigious Pulitzer Prize. In 1962, Steinbeck received international literary recognition when he was presented with the Nobel Prize for Literature for the body of his work. Before his death in 1968, one more award accorded him is recorded in *Literary and Library Prizes*: the *Bestsellers* Paperback of the Year Award (no longer given) in 1964 for *Travels with Charley*.

Though many may be short-lived, the number of literary and library awards offered annually is ever increasing. The tenth edition of *Literary and Library Prizes* lists 454 awards, including 97 that are new to this edition. This volume is not to be considered comprehensive, however, since it does not include those prizes that are little known nor those that are of only local importance. Awards to subprofessionals are generally excluded; very few drama awards are listed, and most journalism awards are omitted; only a few awards for short stories or articles in periodicals are included. The editors have tried to weigh carefully all factors in introducing new awards into this edition—not necessarily in terms of the monetary value of an award but the subject matter honored, recognition of regional literary talent, and prominence of the organization sponsoring an award.

The book is divided into four major sections: International Prizes, American Prizes, British Prizes, and Canadian Prizes. Awards listed under International Prizes are made to writers of any nationality. The section American Prizes is subdivided into General, Publishers', Juvenile, Poetry, Drama, Short Story, and Library Prizes.

Most annual awards are given for published books or for achievements in the previous calendar year, although some prizes are offered in recognition of a life's work. It has been our intention to list the date of the award as the year in which it was *presented* rather than the year in which the work was published. The name of the original publisher is given, but no attempt has been made to determine whether or not the book is in print. For awards made outside of the United States, the American publisher is given when known; otherwise, the foreign publisher's name appears. Awards discontinued since the last edition are included in this edition with winners up to the last year of award. Other discontinued awards are noted in the index with the year of the edition in which they last appeared.

Every effort has been made to make the listings of winners as current as possible. We have attempted in the compilation of this volume to verify all information sent to us by sponsoring organizations. However, should any errors or omissions be detected, the editors will appreciate having these called to their attention, and announcements of new prizes will be welcomed.

The editors wish to acknowledge with thanks the cooperation of award-sponsoring organizations in responding to our request for information.

Olga S. Weber
Stephen J. Calvert

December 1979

International Prizes

International Prizes

African Roots Award

The International African Institute, the Alex Haley Roots Foundation, Holmes & Meier (Africana Publishing Company), and Hutchinson Publishing Group are the sponsors of this annual award established in 1979. A gold medal and £500 are offered for the best original, factual contribution to the knowledge, understanding, and strengthening of cultural bonds between the peoples of Africa and peoples of African descent elsewhere in the world. Entries may include historical research on African cultural and linguistic survivals in the New World, as well as works that present and interpret African societies and civilizations to a general audience outside Africa. The award is open to nationals of any country, writing in any language. Entries must be works published or accepted for publication during the preceding calendar year. The deadline for submission of entries is March 31, and the award winner is announced in August. Full details and submission forms are available from the Assistant Director, Administration, International African Institute, 210 High Holborn, London WC1V 7BW, England.

1979
  Albert J. Raboteau
  Slave Religion: The "Invisible" Institution of the Antebellum South (Oxford Univ. Press)

Bennett Award

The *Hudson Review,* 65 East 55 Street, New York, New York 10022, established this biennial award in 1975 in memory of Joseph Bennett, an editor of the literary quarterly, who died in 1972. The award honors a writer whose work has not received full recognition, or a writer who is at a critical stage where a substantial grant would be particularly beneficial in furthering creative development. The first award of $12,500 was awarded May 3, 1976, at the Grolier Club, New York.

1976
  Jorge Guillén (Spain)
1978
  Andrei Sinyavsky (USSR)

English-Speaking Union Book Award

This award was established in 1973 by the English-Speaking Union, 16 East 69 Street, New York, New York 10021, for the best book of belles lettres published in the English language by an African or Asian author whose native language is not English. The award, $2,000 and travel expenses to the United States for the presentation ceremony, is given annually in May in Washington, D.C., or in New York City.

1974
  Kamala Markandaya
  Two Virgins (John Day)
1975
  R. K. Narayan
  My Days (Viking)

1976
  T. Obinkaram Echewa
  The Land's Lord (Lawrence Hill)
1977–1979
  No awards

European Cortina *Ulisse* Prize

The Italian magazine *Ulisse* has instituted this prize of one million lire (approximately $1,225) with a view to encouraging the idea that "culture ought to be a common instrument of civilization and not the privilege of the few." The members of the jury are representatives from the Accademia Nazionale dei Lincei, the National Council for Research, and the Italian UNESCO Delegation; the Editor of *Ulisse* and delegates from the other institutes and organizations contribute to the prize. Address inquiries to the Editor, *Rivista Ulisse*, Sezione Premio Europeo Cortina Ulisse, Via Po, I-00198 Rome, Italy.

1949
  John Read (United Kingdom)
  A Direct Entry to Organic Chemistry (Methuen)
1950
  Carlo Morandi (Italy)
  L'Idea dell'Unità Politica d'Europa nel XIX e XX Secolo
  Pierre Belperron (France)
  La Guerre de Sécession (Librairie Académique Perrin)
1951
  Lionello Venturi (Italy)
  Come Si Comprende la Pittura
1952
  Ernest Baldwin (United Kingdom)
  Dynamic Aspects of Biochemistry (Cambridge Univ. Press)
1953
  No award

1954
  Graham Hutton (United Kingdom)
  We Too Can Prosper: The Promise of Productivity (Macmillan)
1955
  Eduard Spranger (Germany)
  Pädagogische Perspektiven (Quelle & Meyer)
1956
  Luigi Preti (Italy)
  Le Lotte Agrarie nella Valle Padana (Einaudi)
1957
  No award
1958
  G. Löwenthal and J. Hausen (Germany)
  Wir Werden durch Atome Leben

1959
  Georges Elgozy (France)
  La France devant le Marché Commun (Flammarion)
1960
  No award
1961
  Felice Ippolito (Italy)
  L'Italia e l'Energia Nucleare (Neri Pozza)
1962
  Werner Holzer (Germany)
  Das Nackte Antlitz Afrikas
1963
  No award
1964
  Hans Herbert Goetz (Germany)
  Weil Alle Besser Leben Wollen
1965
  Ladislao Mittner (Italy)
  Storia della Letteratura Tedesca dal Pietismo al Romanticismo (Einaudi)
1966
  No award
1967
  Giulio Carlo Argan (Italy)
  Progetto e Destino
1968
  André Martinet (France)
  La Considération Fonctionnelle du Langage
1969
  No award

1970
  Edouard Bonnefous (France)
  Le Monde Est-Il Surpeuplé? (Hachette)
1971
  Edward Max Nicholson (United Kingdom)
  The Environmental Revolution (Hodder & Stoughton)
1972
  No award
1973
  George Steiner (United Kingdom)
  Language and Silence
  Ezio Raimondi (Italy)
  Tecniche della Critica Letteraria (Einaudi)
1974
  Andrew Shonfield (United Kingdom)
  Europe: Journey to an Unknown Destination (Allen Lane)
1975
  No award
1976
  Paul Bairoch (France)
  Le Tiers-Monde dans l'Impasse: Le Démarrage Économique du 18e au 20e Siècle (Gallimard)
1977
  No award
1978
  Piero Angela (Italy)
  Da Zero a Tre Anni (Garzanti)

Clarence L. Holte Prize

The Twenty-First Century Foundation announced in 1979 the creation of the international Clarence L. Holte Prize in recognition of significant and lasting contributions to the cultural heritage of Africans and of the "African diaspora" made through published writings of excellence in literature and the humanities. The prize, given biennially in February, is awarded by a jury of five scholars of international repute. Nominations should be made before July 1 in the year prior to the award. The prize will include the biennial income from a fund of $50,000 in perpetuity, $5,000 in 1979. Inquiries concerning the prize should be sent to Mary Walker, Twenty-First Century Foundation, 112 West 120 Street, New York, New York 10027.

1979
    Chancellor Williams
    The Destruction of Black Civilization: Great Issues of a Race from 4500 B.C. to 2000 A.D., enlarged and revised edition (Third World)

I.L.A.B. Prize for Bibliography

The International League of Antiquarian Booksellers, c/o Dr. Frieder Kocher-Benzing, Rathenaustrasse 21, Stuttgart, Federal Republic of Germany, established an international bibliographic prize in 1963. The triennial award of $1,000 is given to the author of the best work of learned bibliography or of research into the history of the book or of typography, unpublished or printed. Anyone is eligible to enter. Entries must be submitted in a language that is universally used.

1964
    No award

1967
    Jean Peeters-Fontainas
    Bibiographie des Impressions Espagnoles des Pays-Bas Méridionaux (Adler)

1970
    Wytze Hellinga and Lotte Hellinga
    The Fifteenth Century Printing Types of the Low Countries (Menno Hertzberger, Amsterdam)
    I. C. Koeman
    Atlantes Neerlandici (Theatrum Orbis Terrarum, Amsterdam)

1973
    Claus Nissen
    Die Zoologische Buchillustration: Ihre Bibliographie und Geschichte (A. Hiersemann, Stuttgart)

1976
    C. William Miller
    Benjamin Franklin's Philadelphia Printing 1728–1766: A Descriptive Bibliography (American Philosophical Society)

1979
    Blanche Henrey
    British Botanical and Horticultural Literature before 1800 (Oxford Univ. Press)

International Book Award

The International Book Award was established in 1973 by the International Book Committee to recognize outstanding services rendered by a person or institution to the cause of books in such fields as authorship, publishing, production, book design, translation, library services, bookselling, encouragement of the reading habit, and promotion of international cooperation. The award testifies to the dedication of the book professions to the UNESCO aim of furthering the use of books in the service of mutual understanding. Selection of the recipient is made by the International Book Committee on the basis of a majority vote of its members. The same procedure is employed to determine the place and date of the presentation. The chairperson of the International Book Committee is Theodore Waller, Executive Vice President, Grolier Inc., Danbury, Connecticut 06816. Inquiries concerning the award should be directed to Cilia Zaher, International Book Committee, UNESCO, 7 place de Fontenoy, F-75700 Paris, France.

1973
    Herman Liebaers
    Chairperson, International Book Year Support Committee; President, IFLA; Royal Librarian of Belgium

1974
    Shoichi Noma
    President, Japanese Publishers Association; President, Kodansha Ltd.

1975
    USSR National Committee for International Book Year
    For its initiative in having 1972 proclaimed International Book Year

1976
    Ronald Baker
    Director, Publishing Association, United Kingdom
1977
    Julian Behrstock
    Director, Division of Free Flow of Information and Communication Policies, UNESCO
1978
    Virginia Betancourt
    Director, National Library of Venezuela
1979
    Léopold Sédar Senghor
    President of Senegal

Irish-American Cultural Institute Literary Awards

The Irish-American Cultural Institute, 683 Osceola Avenue, St. Paul, Minnesota 55105, established the Butler Family Awards in Irish Literature (renamed the Irish-American Cultural Institute Literary Awards) in 1966 for the purpose of recognizing and encouraging excellence among writers who write in the Irish language. Any creative work—fiction, poetry, or drama—written in Irish is eligible and may be submitted from any country in the world. Prizes are awarded irregularly in the amounts of $5,600, $2,800, and $1,400. Winners of the awards are chosen by a panel of judges in Dublin, Ireland, and the awards are officially presented there as well. Winners since 1975 were not available at press time.

The Institute is currently in the process of establishing a $7,500 grant to be awarded annually to a U.S. author of a novel dealing with Irish-American life. Announcement of the details of the grant is expected in 1980. Further information about these literary awards, as well as about the Institute's awards for the visual arts ($10,000), music ($5,000), and ballet and theater ($10,000), is available from Eoin McKiernan of the Irish-American Cultural Institute.

1967
    Máirtin Ó Cadhain
    An tSraith ar Lar

1969
    Frank O'Brien
    Litríocht Nua

1971
  Seosamh Mac Grianna
  'An Druma Mor ($5,600)
  Sean Ó Luing
  O'Donnabhain Rosa ($2,800)
  Diarmaid Ó Suilleabhain
  Ar Uain Bheo ($1,400)
  Seán Ó Riordain
  Collected Works ($1,400) Special
  O'Shaughnessy Family Award

1975
  Michael Hartnett, poet
  For work in progress, in English
  ($5,000)
  Breandán Ó hEithir, novelist and journalist
  For work in progress, in Irish ($5,000)

The Jerusalem Prize

This award, offered by the Jerusalem Municipality, was established at the first Jerusalem International Book Fair in 1963. The biennial prize is $3,000 and a citation from the Jerusalem Municipality at the opening of the Book Fair. Its purpose is to honor an author who has contributed to the world's understanding of "the freedom of the individual in society." For further information, contact the Jerusalem International Book Fair, 22 Jaffa Street, Jerusalem 91000, Israel.

1963
  Bertrand Russell (United Kingdom)
1965
  Max Frisch (Switzerland)
1967
  André Schwarz-Bart (France)
1969
  Ignazio Silone (Italy)
1971
  Jorge Luis Borges (Argentina)

1973
  Eugene Ionesco (France)
1975
  Simone de Beauvoir (France)
1977
  Octavio Paz (Mexico)
1979
  Isaiah Berlin (United Kingdom)

Kalinga Prize

This prize, awarded annually by UNESCO, 7 place de Fontenoy, F-75700 Paris, France, to a science writer selected by an international jury, was established in 1952 by the Kalinga Foundation Trust, founded by Biju Patnaik of Cuttack, Orissa, India, for the dual purpose of recognizing outstanding interpretation of science to the general public and of strengthening scientific and cultural links between India and other nations. The winner receives a prize of £1,000 and a gold medal. The winner is also invited to the annual meeting of the Indian Science Congress and to spend a month visiting and lecturing in India. The award takes its name from an ancient empire of the Indian subcontinent that was conquered in the third century B.C. by the Emperor

Asoka, who was so appalled by the cost of his conquest in terms of human life and suffering that he swore never to wage war again.

1952
   Louis de Broglie (France)
1953
   Julian Huxley (United Kingdom)
1954
   Waldemar Kaempffert (United States)
1955
   Augusto Pi-Suner (Venezuela)
1956
   George Gamow (United States)
1957
   Bertrand Russell (United Kingdom)
1958
   Karl von Frisch (Germany)
1959
   Jean Rostand (France)
1960
   Ritchie Calder (United Kingdom)
1961
   Arthur C. Clarke (United Kingdom)
1962
   Gerard Piel (United States)
1963
   Jagjit Singh (India)
1964
   Warren Weaver (United States)
1965
   Eugene Rabinowitch (United States)

1966
   Paul Couderc (France)
1967
   Fred Hoyle (United Kingdom)
1968
   Gavin de Beer (United Kingdom)
1969
   Konrad Lorenz (Austria)
1970
   Margaret Mead (United States)
1971
   Pierre Auger (France)
1972
   Philip H. Abelson (United States)
   Nigel Calder (United Kingdom)
1973
   No award
1974
   Luis Estrada (Mexico)
   José Reis (Brazil)
1975
   No award
1976
   A. I. Oparin (USSR)
   George Porter (United Kingdom)
1977
   Fernand Seguin (Canada)

Neustadt International Prize for Literature

Offered by *World Literature Today* (formerly *Books Abroad*), University of Oklahoma, Norman, Oklahoma 73019, this award was established September 15, 1969, and endowed by the Neustadt family in 1972. It is an award for distinguished and continuing artistic achievement in the fields of poetry, drama, or fiction. A new international jury of twelve is appointed for each successive award by the editor in consultation with the Editorial Board. Each member of the jury may present one candidate. A majority (seven) of the jury must be present for the deliberations and the final voting in Norman. Representative selections of a candidate's work must be available to the jury in either French or English translation. Announcement of the winner is made in February, and the award is officially presented every other year at the University of Oklahoma, Norman. The prize is an award certificate, a silver eagle feather, and a minimum of $10,000. *World Literature Today* dedicates one issue to the laureate. The University of Oklahoma Press will seriously consider the publication of a book by or about the recipient.

1970
  Giuseppe Ungaretti (Italy)
1972
  Gabriel García Márquez (Colombia)
1974
  Francis Ponge (France)

1976
  Elizabeth Bishop (United States)
1978
  Czeslaw Milosz (Poland)

Nobel Prize for Literature

Of all the literary prizes, the Nobel Prize for Literature is the highest in value and honor. It is one of the five prizes founded by Alfred Bernhard Nobel (1833–1896), the other four awards being for physics, chemistry, medicine, and peace. By the terms of Nobel's will, the prize for literature is to be given to the person "who shall have produced in the field of literature the most distinguished work of an idealistic tendency." It consists of a gold medal bearing an inscription suitable to the recipient and a sum of money, which originally amounted to $40,000. This sum has fluctuated through the years; in 1979 it amounted to $190,000. The award is administered by the Swedish Academy in Stockholm, and official presentation is made on December 10, the anniversary of Nobel's death. No one may apply for the Nobel Prize; it is not for competition. It is awarded to an author for his or her total literary output and not for any single work.

1901
  Sully Prudhomme, French poet
1902
  Theodor Mommsen, German historian
1903
  Björnstjerne Björnson, Norwegian dramatist, poet, and novelist
1904
  Frédéric Mistral, Provençal poet and philologist, and José Echegaray y Eizaguirre, Spanish dramatist
1905
  Henryk Sienkiewicz, Polish novelist
1906
  Giosuè Carducci, Italian poet
1907
  Rudyard Kipling, English novelist and poet

1908
  Rudolf Eucken, German philosopher
1909
  Selma Lagerlöf, Swedish novelist and poet
1910
  Paul von Heyse, German novelist, playwright, and poet
1911
  Maurice Maeterlinck, Belgian dramatist, poet, and essayist
1912
  Gerhart Hauptmann, German dramatist, poet, and novelist
1913
  Rabindranath Tagore, Hindu essayist and poet
1914
  No award

1915
Romain Rolland, French novelist and dramatist
1916
Verner von Heidenstam, Poet Laureate of Sweden
1917
Karl Gjellerup, Danish novelist and poet
Henrik Pontoppidan, Danish novelist
1918
No award
1919
Carl Spitteler, Swiss novelist and poet
1920
Knut Hamsun, Norwegian novelist
1921
Anatole France, French novelist, poet, and playwright
1922
Jacinto Benavente y Martínez, Spanish dramatist
1923
William Butler Yeats, Irish poet and dramatist
1924
Władysław Stanisław Reymont, Polish novelist
1925
George Bernard Shaw, Irish dramatist and novelist
1926
Grazia Deledda, Italian novelist
1927
Henri Louis Bergson, French philosopher
1928
Sigrid Undset, Norwegian novelist
1929
Thomas Mann, German novelist
1930
Sinclair Lewis, American novelist
1931
Erik Axel Karlfeldt, Swedish lyric poet. Posthumous award. Karlfeldt had refused the award ten years before on the grounds that he was an official of the Academy
1932
John Galsworthy, English novelist and dramatist
1933
Ivan Alekseevich Bunin, Russian novelist and poet
1934
Luigi Pirandello, Italian novelist and dramatist
1935
No award
1936
Eugene O'Neill, American dramatist
1937
Roger Martin Du Gard, French novelist
1938
Pearl S. Buck, American novelist
1939
Frans Eemil Sillanpää, Finnish novelist
1940–1943
No awards
1944
Johannes V. Jensen, Danish novelist and poet
1945
Gabriela Mistral, Chilean poet
1946
Hermann Hesse, Swiss (born in Germany) novelist, poet, and essayist
1947
André Gide, French novelist, essayist, philosopher, and poet
1948
T. S. Eliot, English (born in the United States) poet and critic
1949
No award
1950
William Faulkner, American novelist (award held over from 1949), and Bertrand Russell, English philosopher and mathematician

1951
Pär Lagerkvist, Swedish novelist, poet, essayist, and philosopher
1952
François Mauriac, French novelist, journalist, and poet
1953
Winston Churchill, English historian and statesman
1954
Ernest Hemingway, American novelist
1955
Halldór Kiljan Laxness, Icelandic novelist
1956
Juan Ramón Jiménez, Spanish poet
1957
Albert Camus, French novelist and playwright
1958
Boris Pasternak, Russian poet and novelist (prize declined)
1959
Salvatore Quasimodo, Italian poet and critic
1960
Saint-John Perse, French poet
1961
Ivo Andrić, Yugoslavian novelist
1962
John Steinbeck, American novelist
1963
George Seferis, Greek poet
1964
Jean-Paul Sartre, French philosopher, novelist, and playwright (prize declined)

1965
Mikhail Sholokhov, Russian novelist
1966
S. Y. Agnon, Israeli novelist, and Nelly Sachs, German poet
1967
Miguel Angel Asturias, Guatemalan novelist
1968
Yasunari Kawabata, Japanese novelist
1969
Samuel Beckett, Irish novelist and playwright
1970
Aleksandr I. Solzhenitsyn, Russian novelist
1971
Pablo Neruda, Chilean poet
1972
Heinrich Böll, German novelist
1973
Patrick White, Australian novelist
1974
Harry Martinson and Eyvind Johnson, Swedish authors
1975
Eugenio Montale, Italian poet
1976
Saul Bellow, American novelist
1977
Vicente Aleixandre, Spanish poet
1978
Isaac Bashevis Singer, Yiddish author
1979
Odysseus Elytis, Greek poet

Peace Prize

Established in 1950, this prize is awarded annually by the Börsenverein des Deutschen Buchhandels (Federation of German Publishers and Booksellers) to a writer, artist, or scientist for his or her contribution to the cause of world peace. The prize jury, composed of publishers, booksellers, columnists, university professors, and so on, is elected by the Annual Conference of the members of the Börsenverein. Each prize winner receives DM25,000 (about $13,735) and a certificate, presented at St. Paul's Church in Frankfurt-am-Main during the week of the Frankfurt Book Fair. For further information, write to the Director, Press and Information, Börsenverein des Deutschen Buchhandels e.V., Grosser Hirschgraben 17/21, Postfach 2404, D-6000 Frankfurt-am-Main, Federal Republic of Germany.

1950
  Max Tau
1951
  Albert Schweitzer
1952
  Romano Guardini
1953
  Martin Buber
1954
  Carl J. Burckhardt
1955
  Hermann Hesse
1956
  Reinhold Schneider
1957
  Thornton Wilder
1958
  Karl Jaspers
1959
  Theodor Heuss
1960
  Victor Gollancz
1961
  Sarvepalli Radhakrishnan
1962
  Paul Tillich
1963
  Carl Friedrich von Weizsäcker
1964
  Gabriel Marcel
1965
  Nelly Sachs

1966
  Augustin Bea
  Willem A. Visser 't Hooft
1967
  Ernst Bloch
1968
  Léopold Sédar Senghor
1969
  Alexander Mitscherlich
1970
  Alva Myrdal
  Gunnar Myrdal
1971
  Marion, Countess Dönhoff
1972
  Janusz Korczak
1973
  Club of Rome
1974
  Frère Roger, Prior of Taize
1975
  Alfred Grosser
1976
  Max Frisch
1977
  Leszek Kolakowski
1978
  Astrid Lindgren
1979
  Yehudi Menuhin

Remembrance Award

Established in 1964, this award is given to an author of a literary work of high merit— novel, essay, drama, poetry, history, or memoir—that was inspired by the experience of the Nazi holocaust and that most effectively presents this experience for the benefit of our own and future generations. The ultimate aim of the award is the establishment of a new humanism and a more enlightened vision of the world we live in. The award consists of $2,500 and is given annually by the World Federation of Bergen-Belsen Associations, Box 333, Lenox Hill Station, New York, New York 10021. Published works and manuscripts are judged by an international jury of leading contemporary writers.

1965
  Eliezer Wiesel (United States)
  Town beyond the Wall, trans. by Stephen Becker (Atheneum) and other writings
1967
  Manès Sperber (Austria)
  Wie eine Träne im Ozean: Romantrilogie (Europa Verlags)
1968
  Arthur Morse (United States)
  While Six Million Died: A Chronicle of American Apathy (Random)
1969
  Chaim Grade (United States)
  Seven Little Lanes
  Jean Cayrol (France)
  Poetry
  Joshua Wygodski (Israel)
  Collected works
1970
  The City of Jerusalem
1971
  Abba Kovner (Israel)
  Little Sister of Mine
1972
  Uri Zvi Greenberg (Israel)
  Collected works
1973
  Michel Borwicz (France)
  Jewish Resistance of Nazi-Occupied Europe

  Leon Eitinger (Norway)
  Psychological Studies of Concentration Camp Survivors
  Leon Lenemen (France)
  The Tragedy of Soviet Jewry
  Mendel Mann (France)
  Collected works
  Yitzchak Mer (Israel)
  Stalemate with Death
  Jacob Robinson (United States)
  Historical research
  Leib Rochman (Israel)
  In Your Blood You Shall Live
  S. L. Shneiderman (United States)
  When the Vistula Spoke Yiddish
  Daniel Stern (United States)
  Who Shall Live, Who Shall Die (Crown)
  Abraham Sutzkever (Israel)
  Poems of the Holocaust
  Mordchai Tzanim (Israel)
  Collected works
1974
  George Steiner (England)
  Language of Silence
1975
  Andre Ne'her
  Collected philosophical works
Discontinued

American Prizes

General Prizes

ARLIS/NA Art Publishing Awards

These awards were established in 1973 by the Art Libraries Society of North America (ARLIS/NA), 7735 Old Georgetown Road, Suite 4444, Washington, D.C. 20014, to single out one or two of the best art books of the year and to encourage the publishing in North America of art books that embody good design and layout, good materials and workmanship, sound binding, good quality illustrations, and reliable scholarly/ research apparatus, such as indexes, bibliographies, and so on. The awards are presented at the business meeting of the Art Libraries Society of North America during its annual conference, usually in late January. Trade books released initially by publishers in the United States and Canada are eligible. In the case of concurrent foreign and North American editions, the awards are limited to those books for which the executive functions are based primarily in North America. Translations, reprints, and successive editions are eligible only when significantly altered, improved, or redeveloped.

1974
   Jonathan Green, ed.
   Camera Work: A Critical Anthology (Aperture)
   Coy Ludwig
   Maxfield Parrish (Watson-Guptill)
1975
   Lincoln Kirstein
   Elie Nadelman (Eakins)
   Pierpont Morgan Library Curators
   Major Acquisitions of the Pierpont Morgan Library, 1924–1974, 4 vols. (Pierpont Morgan Library)
1976
   Dan Burne Jones
   The Prints of Rockwell Kent (Univ. of Chicago Press)
1977
   Robert A. Sobieszek and Odette M. Appel

The Spirit of Fact: Daguerreotypes of Southworth and Hawes, 1843–1862 (Godine)
1978
   Detroit Institute of Arts and St. Louis Art Museum
   Henri Matisse Paper Cut-Outs (Abrams)
1979
   David Robertson
   Sir Charles Eastlake and the Victorian Art World (Princeton Univ. Press)
   Metropolitan Museum of Art
   Georgia O'Keeffe: A Portrait by Alfred Stieglitz (Metropolitan Museum of Art)
   Sebastian Serlio, On Domestic Architecture (Architectural History Foundation)

ASCAP – Deems Taylor Awards

The American Society of Composers, Authors and Publishers (ASCAP) offers these awards, which were established in 1967, to honor the memory of Deems Taylor, distinguished composer-critic-commentator and president of ASCAP (1942–1948) who died in 1966. Any nonfiction book or newspaper or magazine article about music or those who create it, published in the United States in English during the calendar year preceding the presentations, is eligible. Writers, publishers, or editors may submit entries to the ASCAP – Deems Taylor Awards, American Society of Composers, Authors and Publishers, One Lincoln Plaza, New York, New York 10023. Four copies of each entry are required. The books and articles submitted are judged by six gifted, well-known members of ASCAP. Cash prizes are awarded in each of the two categories (books and articles). The awards are given annually—in May, whenever possible—and are presented in the ASCAP board room. Listed below are first place winners for the years 1968 – 1972. Thereafter the awards are no longer qualified as first place, second place, and so on. Therefore all winners are named from 1973 on.

BOOKS

1968
   George T. Simon
   The Big Bands (Macmillan)
1969
   Gunther Schuller
   Early Jazz: Its Roots and Musical Development (Oxford Univ. Press)
1970
   Alan Rich
   Music: Mirror of the Arts (Praeger and Ridge)
1971
   Lee Eliot Berk
   Legal Protection for the Creative Musician (Berklee)
1972
   Charles Rosen
   The Classical Style: Haydn, Mozart, Beethoven (Viking)
1973
   Lehman Engel
   Words with Music (Macmillan)
   Lillian Libman
   And Music at the Close: Stravinsky's Last Years (Norton)
   Richard A. Peterson and R. Serge Denisoff

Sounds of Social Change (Rand McNally)
Boris Schwartz
Music and Musical Life in Soviet Russia, 1917–1970 (Norton)
Alec Wilder
American Popular Song: The Great Innovators, 1900–1950 (Oxford Univ. Press)

1974
   Duke Ellington
   Music Is My Mistress (Doubleday)
   Myra Friedman
   Buried Alive (Morrow)
   Philip Hart
   Orpheus in the New World (Norton)
   Henry-Louis de La Grange
   Mahler (Doubleday)
   Max Wilk
   They're Playing Our Song (Atheneum)

1975
   Edward T. Cone
   The Composer's Voice (Univ. of California Press)
   Howard Dietz
   Dancing in the Dark (Quadrangle)

BOOKS (cont.)

Hampton Hawes and Don Asher
Raise Up Off Me (Coward)

Joseph H. Kwabena Nketia
The Music of Africa (Norton)

Ned Rorem
The Final Diary (Holt)

1976

Philip S. Foner
American Labor Songs of the Nineteenth Century (Univ. of Illinois Press)

Vera Brodsky Lawrence
Music for Patriots, Politicians, and Presidents (Macmillan)

Charles Rosen
Arnold Schoenberg (Viking)

Frank R. Rossiter
Charles Ives and His America (Liveright)

Leonard Stein
Style and Idea (St. Martin's)

1977

Leo Kraft
Gradus (Norton)

Dan Morgenstern
Jazz People (Abrams)

Albert Murray
Stomping the Blues (McGraw)

Larry Sandberg and Dick Weissman
The Folk Music Sourcebook (Knopf)

Geoffrey Stokes
Starmaking Machinery (Bobbs)

1978

John Hammond
John Hammond on Record (Ridge)

Edward Lowinsky, ed.
Josquin des Pres (Oxford Univ. Press)

Howard S. Smither
A History of the Oratorio (Univ. of North Carolina Press)

Maynard Solomon
Beethoven (Schirmer)

Jeff Todd Titon
Early Downhome Blues: A Musical and Cultural Analysis (Univ. of Illinois Press)

1979

Paul F. Berliner
The Soul of Mbira (Univ. of California Press)

Mercer Ellington and Stanley Dance
Duke Ellington in Person (Houghton)

James Haskins and Kathleen Benson
Scott Joplin: The Man Who Made Ragtime (Doubleday)

Richard H. Hoppin
Medieval Music (Norton)

H. C. Robbins Landon
Haydn: Chronicle and Works (Indiana Univ. Press)

Claude V. Palisca, ed.; trans. by Warren Babb
Hucbald, Guido and John on Music: Three Medieval Treatises (Yale Univ. Press)

Arnold Shaw
Honkers and Shouters: The Golden Years of Rhythm and Blues (Macmillan)

ARTICLES

1968

James Ringo
Reviews published in *The American Record Guide*

1969

Joan Peyser
Article published in *The New York Times*

1970

Ralph J. Gleason
Article published in *Lithopinion*

1971

Boris E. Nelson
Nineteen articles published in the *Toledo Blade*

ARTICLES (cont.)

1972

Elliott W. Galkin
Articles published in the Baltimore *Sun*

1973

Martin Bernheimer
Articles in the *Los Angeles Times*

Robert Finn
Articles in the *Cleveland Plain Dealer*

Bruce Pollock
Articles in *Rock Magazine*

Alan Rich
Articles in *New York Magazine*

1974

Ben Fong-Torres
Articles in *Rolling Stone*

Jack O'Brian
Articles distributed by King Features

Alan Rich
Articles in *New York Magazine*

Hubert Saal
Articles in *Newsweek*

1975

Ralph Gleason
Articles in the Baltimore *Sun*

Richard Franko Goldman
"American Music: 1918–1960" in *The New Oxford History of Music* (Oxford Univ. Press)

David Hamilton
Articles in *The New Yorker*

Andrew Porter
Articles in *The New Yorker*

1976

Robert Commanday
Articles in the *San Francisco Chronicle*

Richard Dyer
Articles in the *Boston Globe*

Robert Finn
Articles in the *Cleveland Plain Dealer*

Gary Giddins
Articles in *The Village Voice*

Jack O'Brian
Articles distributed by King Features

1977

John Ardoin
Articles in the *Dallas Morning News*

Paul Baratta
Articles in *Songwriter Magazine*

Richard Dyer
Articles in the *Boston Globe*

Gary Giddins
Articles in *The Village Voice*

Samuel Lipman
Articles in *Commentary*

Irving Lowens
Articles in the *Washington Star*

Karen Monson
Articles in the *Chicago Daily News*

Maureen Orth
Articles in *Newsweek*

1978

Martin Bernheimer
Articles in the *Los Angeles Times*

David Burge
Articles in *Contemporary Keyboard*

Douglas M. Green
Articles in the *International Alban Berg Society Newsletter*

Joe Klein
Articles in *Rolling Stone*

Gene Lees
Articles in *High Fidelity*

George Perle
Articles in the *International Alban Berg Society Newsletter*

Andrew Porter
Articles in *The New Yorker*

1979

David Burge
Articles in *Contemporary Keyboard*

Robert Finn
Articles in the *Cleveland Plain Dealer*

ARTICLES (cont.)

Bernard Holland
Articles in *Pittsburgher Magazine*

Leighton Kerner
Articles in *The Village Voice*

Michael Nelson
Article in *Baltimore Magazine*

Paul Nelson
Article in *Rolling Stone*

Jack O'Brian
Articles distributed by King Features

Tony Schwartz
Article in *Newsweek*

Arthur A. Allen Award

This award is offered by the Laboratory of Ornithology, 159 Sapsucker Woods Road, Cornell University, Ithaca, New York 14850. Candidates are nominated by a committee of the administrative board and the final vote is taken by an assembled board. A medal is awarded to an ornithologist, amateur or professional, who has made an outstanding contribution to widening popular interest in birds. The award is presented annually in September or October at an award banquet at Cornell University.

1967
Roger Tory Peterson
1968
James Fisher
1969
George Miksch Sutton
1970
Alexander Wetmore
1971
Peter Scott
1972
Allan D. Cruickshank
1973
Elizabeth Austin
Oliver L. Austin, Jr.

1974
Olin Sewall Pettingill, Jr.
1975
Walter J. Breckenridge
1976
Joseph J. Hickey
1977
Jean T. Delacour
1978
Karl H. Maslowski
1979
Chandler S. Robbins

American Academy and Institute of Arts and Letters

In 1976, after seventy-two years of separate though related existence, the National Institute of Arts and Letters and the American Academy of Arts and Letters voted for a merger that made them one institution with a single board of directors, committee structure, and budget. The amalgamated institution is known as the American Academy and Institute of Arts and Letters and retains jointly all the privileges granted by their charters from Congress. The history of the two constituent societies can be found in the ninth edition of this book (p. 156).

The main function of the Academy-Institute, which is to stimulate and encourage the arts, is carried out by conferring honors and awards for works of high merit. A description of these awards and lists of the recipients may be found in the pages following. No applications may be submitted for any of the awards.

American Academy and Institute of Arts and Letters Awards in Literature

In 1941 the National Institute of Arts and Letters established a program of conferring awards on nonmembers of the Institute for creative achievement in art, music, and literature. Originally in the sum of $500, the awards in recent years have been raised to $4,000 each. Awards are conferred on writers for published works of distinction and may not be applied for. The winners receive their prizes and citations at the Annual Ceremonial of the American Academy and Institute of Arts and Letters.

1941
  Mary M. Colum
  Jesse Stuart
1942
  Hermann Broch
  Norman Corwin
  Edgar Lee Masters
  Muriel Rukeyser
1943
  Virgil Geddes
  Carson McCullers
  José García Villa
  Joseph Wittlin
1944
  Hugo Ignotus
  Jeremy Ingalls
  Thomas Sancton
  Karl J. Shapiro
  Eudora Welty
  Tennessee Williams
1945
  Kenneth Fearing
  Feike Feikema
  Alexander Greendale
  Norman Rosten
  Jean Stafford
  Marguerite Young

1946
  Gwendolyn Brooks
  Kenneth Burke
  Malcolm Cowley
  Peter DeVries
  Langston Hughes
  Arthur Laurents
  Marianne Craig Moore
  Arthur Schlesinger, Jr.
  Irwin Shaw
1947
  Nelson Algren
  Eleanor Clark
  Lloyd Frankenberg
  Robert Lowell
  Elizabeth Parsons
  James Still
1948
  Bertolt Brecht
  Dudley Fitts
  Harry Levin
  James F. Powers
  Genevieve Taggard
  Allen Tate
1949
  Léonie Adams
  James Agee
  Joseph Campbell

Alfred Kazin
Vincent McHugh
James Stern
1950
John Berryman
Paul Bowles
Maxwell David Geismar
Caroline Gordon
Shirley Graham
Hyam Plutzik
1951
Newton Arvin
Elizabeth Bishop
Louise Bogan
Brendan Gill
Randall Jarrell
Vladimir Nabokov
1952
Saul Bellow
Alfred Hayes
Theodore Roethke
Elizabeth Spencer
Peter Taylor
Yvor Winters
1953
Eric Bentley
Isabel Bolton
Richard Chase
Francis Fergusson
Paul Goodman
Delmore Schwartz
1954
Hannah Arendt
Ray Bradbury
Richmond Lattimore
David Riesman
Ruthven Todd
C. Vann Woodward
1955
Richard Eberhart
Robert Horan
Chester Kallman
William Krasner
Milton Lott
Morton D. Zabel
1956
James Baldwin

John Cheever
Henry Russell Hitchcock
Joseph Kerman
Josephine Miles
Priscilla Robertson
Frank Rooney
1957
Leslie Fiedler
Robert Fitzgerald
Mary McCarthy
W. S. Merwin
Flannery O'Connor
Robert Pack
1958
Joseph Frank
Herbert Gold
R. W. B. Lewis
William Maxwell
William Meredith
James Purdy
Francis Steegmuller
1959
Truman Capote
Leon Edel
Charles Jackson
Stanley Kunitz
Conrad Richter
Isaac Bashevis Singer
James Wright
1960
Irving Howe
Norman Mailer
Wright Morris
Adrienne Rich
Philip Roth
W. D. Snodgrass
May Swenson
1961
Edward Dahlberg
Jean Garrigue
Mark Harris
David McCord
Warren Miller
Brian Moore
Howard Nemerov
1962
Daniel Fuchs

John Hawkes
Galway Kinnell
Edwin O'Connor
Frank O'Connor
Joan Williams
John Williams
1963
Richard Bankowsky
William Gaddis
Joseph Heller
John Hollander
William Humphrey
Peter Matthiessen
Richard Yates
1964
Lionel Abel
Dorothy Baker
Norman Fruchter
Thom Gunn
Eric Hoffer
David Ignatow
Kenneth Rexroth
1965
Ben Belitt
Robert Bly
J. V. Cunningham
Denise Levertov
Joseph Mitchell
P. M. Pasinetti
Henry Roth
Harvey Swados
1966
William Alfred
John Barth
James Dickey
Shirley Hazzard
Josephine Herbst
Edwin Honig
Gary Snyder
M. B. Tolson
1967
Philip Booth
Hortense Calisher
Daniel Hoffman
Stanley Edgar Hyman
Bernard Knox

Walker Percy
David Wagoner
1968
John Malcolm Brinnin
Fred Chappell
Reuel Denney
Howard Moss
John Frederick Nims
Julia Randall
Richard G. Stern
Eleanor Ross Taylor
1969
John Ashbery
George P. Elliott
Allen Ginsberg
Hugh Kenner
L. E. Sissman
1970
Brewster Ghiselin
Gordon S. Haight
Richard Howard
Pauline Kael
Jerzy Kosinski
James McPherson
N. Scott Momaday
Grace Paley
F. D. Reeve
Kurt Vonnegut, Jr.
1971
Wendell Berry
Stanley Burnshaw
Martin Duberman
Ronald L. Fair
Charles Gordone
Barbara Howes
Arthur Kopit
Leonard Michaels
Leonard Nathan
Reynolds Price
Wilfrid Sheed
1972
Harry Crews
Peter Davison
Paula Fox
Penelope Gilliatt
Pauline Hanson
Michael S. Harper

Israel Horovitz
Walter Kerr
Gilbert Rogin
Ann Stanford
1973
  Marius Bewley
  Maeve Brennan
  Irving Feldman
  Frances FitzGerald
  Dorothy Hughes
  Philip Levine
  Daniel P. Mannix
  Cynthia Ozick
  Jonathan Schell
  Austin Warren
1974
  Ann Cornelisen
  Stanley Elkin
  Elizabeth Hardwick
  Josephine Johnson
  Donald Justice
  David Rabe
  Charles Rosen
  Sam Shepard
  James Tate
  Henry Van Dyke
  Lanford Wilson
1975
  William S. Burroughs
  J. P. Donleavy
  John Gardner
  William H. Gass
  Terrence McNally
  Tillie Olsen
  John Peck
  Mark Strand
  Colin M. Turnbull
  Helen Hennessy Vendler
1976
  Robert Coover

Robert Craft
E. L. Doctorow
Eugene D. Genovese
Kenneth Koch
Charles Simic
John Simon
Louis Simpson
Susan Sontag
Louis Zukofsky
1977
  A. R. Ammons
  Walter J. Bate
  Cynthia Macdonald
  Joseph McElroy
  John McPhee
  James Schuyler
  Paul Theroux
  Anne Tyler
  Robert Watson
  Charles Wright
1978
  Renata Adler
  William Arrowsmith
  Lerone Bennett, Jr.
  Terrence DesPres
  Leslie Epstein
  Michael Herr
  Murray Kempton
  Alison Lurie
  Toni Morrison
  Page Smith
1979
  Arlene Croce
  Barry Hannah
  James McConkey
  John N. Morris
  Robert M. Pirsig
  Richard Poirier
  Philip Schultz
  Dave Smith

Award of Merit Medal

The American Academy of Arts and Letters established in 1940 the Award of Merit Medal. The medal and a prize of $1,000 are given annually to a highly outstanding person in one field of the arts, alternately in this order: novel, poetry, drama, painting, and sculpture. The award is officially presented at the Annual Ceremonial of the American Academy and Institute of Arts and Letters. Members of the Academy-Institute are not eligible. Listed below are the prizes awarded for novel, poetry, and drama.

1944
    Theodore Dreiser, Novel
1945
    Wystan Hugh Auden, Poetry
1946
    John Van Druten, Drama
1949
    Thomas Mann, Novel
1950
    Saint John Perse, Poetry
1951
    Sidney Kingsley, Drama
1954
    Ernest Hemingway, Novel
1955
    Jorge Guillén, Poetry
1956
    Enid Bagnold, Drama
1959
    Aldous Huxley, Novel
1960
    Hilda Doolittle, Poetry

1961
    Clifford Odets, Drama
1964
    John O'Hara, Novel
1965-1966
    No awards, Poetry and Drama
1969
    Vladimir Nabokov, Novel
1970
    Reed Whittemore, Poetry
1971
    No award, Drama
1974
    Nelson Algren, Novel
1975
    Galway Kinnell, Poetry
1976
    No award, Drama
1979
    William Gass, Novel

Marc Blitzstein Award for the Musical Theatre

In 1965 the friends of Marc Blitzstein set up a fund in his memory for an award of $2,500 to be given from time to time to a composer, lyricist, or librettist to encourage the creation of works of merit for the musical theatre. Presentation is made at the Annual Ceremonial of the American Academy and Institute of Arts and Letters.

1965
    William Bolcom
1966-1967
    No awards
1968
    Jack Beeson

1969-1975
    No awards
1976
    John Olon-Scrymgeour
1977-1979
    No awards

E. M. Forster Award

The distinguished English author E. M. Forster bequeathed the American publication rights and royalties of his posthumous novel Maurice to Christopher Isherwood, who transferred them to the National Institute of Arts and Letters for the establishment of an E. M. Forster Award, to be given from time to time to a young English writer for a stay in the United States.

1972
  Frank Tuohy
1973
  Margaret Drabble
1974
  Paul Bailey
1975
  Seamus Heaney

1976
  Jon Stallworthy
1977
  David Cook
1978
  No award
1979
  Bruce Chatwin

Gold Medal Awards

The American Academy and Institute of Arts and Letters annually awards the Gold Medal for distinguished achievement in various categories of the arts, given in a six-year rotation: Architecture (including landscape architecture) and Poetry; Drama and Graphic Art; Belles Lettres, Criticism, and Painting; Biography and Music; the Novel and Sculpture; and the Short Story and History. The list below indicates only those winners in the field of letters.

1910
  James Ford Rhodes, History
1911
  James Whitcomb Riley, Poetry
1913
  Augustus Thomas, Drama
1915
  William D. Howells, Fiction
1916
  John Burroughs, Essays and Belles Lettres
1918
  William R. Thayer, History and Biography
1922
  Eugene G. O'Neill, Drama
1924
  Edith Wharton, Fiction
1925
  William C. Brownell, Essays and Belles Lettres
1927
  William M. Sloane, History and Biography

1929
  Edwin A. Robinson, Poetry
1931
  William Gillette, Drama
1933
  Booth Tarkington, Fiction
1935
  Agnes Repplier, Essays and Belles Lettres
1937
  Charles M. Andrews, History and Biography
1939
  Robert Frost, Poetry
1941
  Robert E. Sherwood, Drama
1943
  Stephen Vincent Benét, Literature
1944
  Willa Cather, Fiction
1946
  Van Wyck Brooks, Essays and Criticism

1948
   Charles Austin Beard, History and Biography
1950
   Henry L. Mencken, Essays and Criticism
1952
   Thornton Wilder, Fiction
   Carl Sandburg, History and Biography
1953
   Marianne Craig Moore, Poetry
1954
   Maxwell Anderson, Drama
1955
   Edmund Wilson, Essays and Criticism
1957
   John Dos Passos, Fiction
   Allan Nevins, History and Biography
1958
   Conrad Aiken, Poetry
1959
   Arthur Miller, Drama
1960
   E. B. White, Essays and Criticism
1962
   William Faulkner, Fiction
   Samuel Eliot Morison, History and Biography
1963
   William Carlos Williams, Poetry
1964
   Lillian Hellman, Drama

1965
   Walter Lippmann, Essays and Criticism
1967
   Katherine Anne Porter, Fiction
   Arthur Schlesinger, Jr., History and Biography
1968
   Wystan Hugh Auden, Poetry
1969
   Tennessee Williams, Drama
1970
   Lewis Mumford, Belles Lettres
1972
   Eudora Welty, Novel
   Henry Steele Commager, History
1973
   John Crowe Ransom, Poetry
1975
   Kenneth Burke, Belles Lettres and Criticism
1976
   Leon Edel, Biography
1977
   Saul Bellow, Novel
1978
   Barbara W. Tuchman, History
   Peter Taylor, Short Story
1979
   Archibald MacLeish, Poetry

Howells Medal

This award was established in 1921 by the American Academy of Arts and Letters to honor William Dean Howells, president of the Academy from 1908 to 1920. Given once every five years for the most distinguished work of American fiction published during the preceding five years, the award, in the form of a gold medal, is presented at the Annual Ceremonial of the American Academy and Institute of Arts and Letters.

1925
   Mary E. Wilkins Freeman
   For her entire work

1930
   Willa Cather
   Death Comes for the Archbishop
   (Knopf)

1935
   Pearl S. Buck
   The Good Earth (John Day)
1940
   Ellen Glasgow
   For her entire work
1945
   Booth Tarkington
   For his entire work
1950
   William Faulkner
   For his entire work
1955
   Eudora Welty
   The Ponder Heart (Harcourt)

1960
   James Gould Cozzens
   By Love Possessed (Harcourt)
1965
   John Cheever
   The Wapshot Scandal (Harper)
1970
   William Styron
   The Confessions of Nat Turner (Random)
1975
   Thomas Pynchon
   For his entire work

Sue Kaufman Prize for First Fiction

The Sue Kaufman Prize for First Fiction, $1,000, will be given annually for the best published first novel or collection of short stories of the preceding year. This prize was established by Dr. Jeremiah A. Barondess in 1979 in memory of his wife, Sue Kaufman, a novelist and short story writer.

Loines Award for Poetry

This award was established by the friends of Russell Loines, who presented the fund to the National Institute of Arts and Letters. The $2,500 award is given from time to time to an American or English poet, not as a prize but as a recognition of value, preferably of value not widely recognized.

1931
   Robert Frost
1933
   Edward Doro
1939
   Joy Davidman
1942
   Horace Gregory
1948
   William Carlos Williams
1951
   John Crowe Ransom
1954
   David Jones

1956
   John Betjeman
1957
   Edwin Muir
1958
   Robert Graves
1960
   Abbie Huston Evans
1962
   I. A. Richards
1964
   John Berryman
1966
   William Meredith

1968
  Anthony Hecht
1970
  Robert Hayden
1972
  William Jay Smith

1974
  Philip Larkin
1976
  Mona Van Duyn

Richard and Hinda Rosenthal Foundation Awards

The Richard and Hinda Rosenthal Foundation Award was established in 1957 for that work of fiction published during the preceding twelve months, which, although not a commercial success, is a considerable literary achievement. The award, formerly $1,000 but recently raised to $3,000, is given annually at the Annual Ceremonial of the American Academy and Institute of Arts and Letters. An award in the same amount is also conferred on young, gifted painters.

1957
  Elizabeth Spencer
  The Voice at the Back Door (McGraw)
1958
  Bernard Malamud
  The Assistant (Farrar)
1959
  Frederick Buechner
  The Return of Ansel Gibbs (Knopf)
1960
  John Updike
  The Poorhouse Fair (Knopf)
1961
  John Knowles
  A Separate Peace (Macmillan)
1962
  Paule Marshall
  Soul Clap Hands and Sing (Atheneum)
1963
  William Melvin Kelley
  A Different Drummer (Doubleday)
1964
  Ivan Gold
  Nickel Miseries (Viking)
1965
  Thomas Berger
  Little Big Man (Dial)

1966
  Tom Cole
  An End to Chivalry (Little)
1967
  Thomas Pynchon
  The Crying of Lot 49 (Lippincott)
1968
  Joyce Carol Oates
  A Garden of Earthly Delights (Vanguard)
1969
  Frederick Exley
  A Fan's Notes (Harper)
1970
  Jonathan Strong
  Tike and Five Stories (Little)
1971
  Christopher Brookhouse
  Running Out (Little)
1972
  Thomas McGuane
  The Bushwhacked Piano (Simon & Schuster)
1973
  Thomas Rogers
  Confessions of a Child of the Century (Simon & Schuster)

1974
Alice Walker
In Love and Trouble (Harcourt)
1975
Ishmael Reed
The Last Days of Louisiana Red (Random)
1976
Richard Yates
Disturbing the Peace (Delacorte)

1977
Spencer Holst
Spencer Holst Stories (Horizon)
1978
Douglas Day
Journey of the Wolf (Atheneum)
1979
Diane Johnson
Lying Low (Knopf)

Traveling and Residential Fellowships

The American Academy in Rome and the American Academy of Arts and Letters collaborated from 1951 to 1962 in giving fellowships to young writers of promise for residence at the Academy in Rome. From 1963 until 1969 the American Academy of Arts and Letters established its own fellowship for a year's residence and travel abroad. These fellowships were discontinued, but in 1976 the Academy in Rome reinstated an annual residential fellowship in literature and requested the American Academy of Arts and Letters to select the annual recipients.

ROME FELLOWSHIPS

1951
Anthony Hecht
1952
William Styron
1953
Sigrid de Lima
1954
Richard Wilbur
1955
Ralph Ellison
1956
Ralph Ellison (renewal) and John Ciardi
1957
Robert Francis
Louis Simpson
1958
Robert Bagg
George Garrett
1959
Harold Brodkey

Edmund Keeley
1960
Harold Brodkey (renewal) and Walter Clemons
1961
Walter Clemons (renewal) and George Starbuck
1962
George Starbuck (renewal) and Alan Dugan
1976
Miller Williams
1977
Daniel Mark Epstein
1978
John Peck
1979
Joseph Caldwell

TRAVELING FELLOWSHIPS

1963
Anne Sexton

TRAVELING FELLOWSHIPS (cont.)

1964
   Edward Hoagland
1965
   Cormac McCarthy

1966
   H. E. F. Donahue
1967
   A. R. Ammons
1969
   Robert Stone

Marjorie Peabody Waite Award

Established in 1956 by a gift from Elizabeth Ames in memory of her sister, the Marjorie Peabody Waite Award, originally $1,000, is conferred annually on an older person for continuing achievement and integrity in his or her art, and is given in rotation to an artist, a composer, and a writer. Beginning in 1963, the amount of the award was raised to $1,500. Presentation is made at the Annual Ceremonial of the American Academy and Institute of Arts and Letters. Awards for writers are listed below.

1958
   Dorothy Parker
1961
   Edward McSorley
1964
   Dawn Powell
1967
   Stringfellow Barr

1970
   Ramon Guthrie
1973
   A. Hyatt Mayor
1976
   René Wellek
1979
   James Still

The Morton Dauwen Zabel Award

In 1966 the National Institute of Arts and Letters received a bequest from Morton Dauwen Zabel for a prize to be given each year in rotation to an American poet, a writer of fiction, and a critic, the recipients to be writers of progressive, original, and experimental tendencies rather than of academic and conservative tendencies. The winner is determined by a qualified jury or board of three members of the Academy-Institute.

1970
   George Steiner
1971
   Charles Reznikoff
1972
   Donald Barthelme
1973
   Marjorie Hope Nicolson
1974
   John Logan

1975
   Charles Newman
1976
   Harold Rosenberg
1977
   David Shapiro
1978
   Joan Didion
1979
   Richard Gilman

The American Book Awards (TABA)

The American Book Awards (TABA) is a new industry-wide program to recognize the best of both hardcover and paperback publishing in the United States. TABA was created in 1979 by the Association of American Publishers (AAP), under whose auspices the awards will be made. The AAP was also the administrator of the National Book Awards—the predecessor of TABA—which was discontinued after the 1979 awards. TABA has four goals: to acknowledge and reward the very best writing; to increase awareness of books and their authors; to increase interest in reading generally; and to reach new audiences for books.

The American Book Awards will be given annually for the best books written or translated by American authors and published in the United States during the previous calendar year. Two awards will be made in each of the following 13 categories, one to a hardcover book and one to a paperback: (1) General Fiction, (2) Science Fiction, (3) Mystery, (4) Biography, (5) Autobiography, (6) Children's Books, (7) Science, (8) History, (9) General Nonfiction (criticism, essays, humor, contemporary thought), (10) Religion and Inspiration, (11) Art and Illustrated Books, (12) Current Interest (lifestyles, sports, self-improvement, crafts, hobbies, cooking), and (13) Reference Books. One award will be made in each of the following four categories regardless of whether the book is hardcover or paperback: First Novel, Western, Poetry, and Translation. There will be three technical achievement awards: Best Book Design, Best Jacket (hardcover), a Best Cover Design (paperback). At the discretion of TABA's board of directors, an award may also be given for the collected works of a single author or to any specialized book that does not fit into an established category but, in the board's opinion, merits recognition.

The awards procedure has three steps: titles will be submitted by publishers for consideration (a $25 fee will be charged for each title); five nominated titles will be chosen in each category; and members of the Academy of the American Book Awards, composed of various national organizations within the industry, will vote to choose the winners. Committees of eleven to thirty people for each category will be responsible for the nominating. These committees will represent the Academy membership and will also include individuals or representatives of groups having special expertise in particular categories. For voting purposes, the Academy's membership is divided into five general groups: authors, booksellers, critics, librarians, and publishers. Votes will be distributed in a "representative manner" among the membership. There will also be a small number of votes accorded to member organizations that do not fall naturally into any of the five groups. Balloting will be handled by an independent accounting organization. If nominating committee members feel that there are fewer than five books that fit the criteria in any category, fewer will be nominated.

Books submitted for the three technical achievement awards and for the categories Art and Illustrated Books, Reference Books, and Translation will be judged by nominating committees of five to seven people who have expertise in those areas. These committees will also decide the winners.

The deadline for the submission of titles by publishers for consideration by the nominating committees is October 1. The $1,000 awards will be presented at a spring ceremony in New York City. For further information concerning the awards, contact

Joan Cunliffe, Director, The American Book Awards, Association of American Publishers, One Park Avenue, New York, New York 10016.

American Catholic Historical Association

Peter Guilday Prize

Established in 1971, this award of $100 is given annually in order to stimulate interest in the field of church history among young scholars. It is awarded to the writer whose article is his or her first scholarly publication and is judged to be the best of those in its category accepted for publication in any given year by the editors of *The Catholic Historical Review*. The article must deal with some aspect of the history of the Catholic Church broadly considered. The prize is named in honor of the American Catholic Historical Association's principal founder and secretary of many years, as well as editor of the *Review*. Manuscripts and inquiries should be sent to the Editor, *Catholic Historical Review*, Catholic University of America Press, 620 Michigan Avenue N.E., Washington, D.C. 20064. The outcome of each year's competition is announced at the Association meeting, December 28–30.

1972
James P. Gaffey
"The Changing of the Guard: The Rise of Cardinal O'Connel of Boston," *Catholic Historical Review*, July 1973

1973
No award

1974
B. Robert Kreiser
"Religious Enthusiasm in Early 18th Century Paris," *Catholic Historical Review*, July 1975

1975
No award

1976
J. Dean O'Donnell, Jr.
"Cardinal Charles Lavigerie: The Politics of Getting a Red Hat," *Catholic Historical Review*, April 1977

1977
Mark A. Gabbert
"Bishop Avant Tout: Archbishop Sibour's Betrayal of the Second Republic," *Catholic Historical Review*, April 1978

1978
Virginia W. Leonard
"Education and the Church-State Clash in Argentina, 1945–1955," *Catholic Historical Review*, April 1979

Howard R. Marraro Prize

Named in honor of the late professor of Columbia University who bequeathed a permanent trust fund to the American Catholic Historical Association, this award is restricted to a book or essay dealing with Italian history or Italo-American history or relations. The award is $500 for a book and a lesser sum for an article. The work must be published and the author must be a citizen or permanent resident of the United

States or Canada. Three copies of the work, if possible, should be sent together with a brief curriculum vitae and bibliography of the author to the American Historical Association, 400 A Street S.E., Washington, D.C. 20003. Inquiries may be addressed to the Secretary, American Catholic Historical Association, Catholic University of America, Washington, D.C. 20064. The winner is announced at the Association's annual meeting, December 28–30.

1974
Eric W. Cochrane
Florence in the Forgotten Centuries, 1527–1800 (Univ. of Chicago Press)
1975
Silvano Tomasi
Piety and Power: The Role of Italian Parishes in the New York Metropolitan Area, 1880–1930 (Center for Migration Studies, Staten Island, New York)
1976
No award

1977
Sarah Lubin Blanshei
Perugia, 1260–1340: Conflict and Change in a Medieval Italian Urban Society (American Philosophical Society)
1978
Paul F. Grendler
The Roman Inquisition and the Venetian Press 1540–1605 (Princeton Univ. Press)

John Gilmary Shea Prize

At the silver jubilee meeting of the American Catholic Historical Association in December 1944, the John Gilmary Shea Prize was instituted. The prize is given to encourage research and writing in the history of the Catholic Church, and it is named for the father of American Catholic history, John Gilmary Shea (1824–1892), who by his numerous writings created this specialized field of American history. The committee of judges for the prize consists of the president and the secretary, as well as three qualified members of the Association, representing three distinct fields of history. Only books published within the twelve-month period beginning on October 1 of the previous year will be considered; three copies of each entry must be received by the judges by October 15. Books entered in the competition must deal with the history of the Catholic Church broadly considered, and authors must be citizens or permanent residents of the United States or Canada. Should the committee judge the books or manuscripts submitted in any single year as not meeting all the standards of the award, no prize will be awarded that year. The award of $300 is given at the annual luncheon conference of the American Catholic Historical Association during Christmas week. All correspondence relating to the prize should be addressed to the Secretary, American Catholic Historical Association, Catholic University of America, Washington, D.C. 20064.

1946
Carlton J. H. Hayes
Wartime Mission in Spain (Macmillan)

1947–1949
No awards

1950
John H. Kennedy
Jesuit and Savage in New France
(Yale Univ. Press)

1951
George Paré
The Catholic Church in Detroit, 1701–1888 (Gabriel Richard)

1952–1953
No awards

1954
Philip Hughes
The Reformation in England (Macmillan)

1955
Annabelle M. Melville
John Carroll of Baltimore (Scribner)

1956
John Tracy Ellis
American Catholicism (Univ. of Chicago Press)

1957
Thomas T. McAvoy
The Great Crisis in American Catholic History, 1895–1900 (Univ. of Chicago Press)

1958
John M. Daley
"Georgetown University: Origin and Early Years"

1959
Robert A. Graham
Vatican Diplomacy: A Study of Church and State on the International Plane (Princeton Univ. Press)

1960
Maynard J. Geiger
The Life and Times of Junípero Serra (Academy of American Franciscan History)

1961
John Courtney Murray
We Hold These Truths: Catholic Reflections on the American Proposition (Sheed)

1962
Francis Dvornik
The Slavs in European History and Civilization (Rutgers Univ. Press)

1963
Oscar Halecki
The Millennium of Europe (Univ. of Notre Dame)

1964
Helen C. White
Tudor Books of Saints and Martyrs (Univ. of Wisconsin Press)

1965
John T. Noonan, Jr.
Contraception: A History of Its Treatment by the Catholic Theologians and Canonists (Harvard Univ. Press)

1966
Robert Ignatius Burns
The Jesuits and the Indian Wars of the Northwest (Yale Univ. Press)

1967
Robert Ignatius Burns
The Crusader Kingdom of Valencia: Reconstruction on a Thirteenth-Century Frontier (Harvard Univ. Press)

1968
Edward Surtz
The Works and Days of John Fisher, 1469–1535, Bishop of Rochester, in the English Renaissance and the Reformation (Harvard Univ. Press)

1969
Robert Brentano
Two Churches: England and Italy in the Thirteenth Century (Princeton Univ. Press)

1970
David M. Kennedy
Birth Control in America: The Career of Margaret Sanger (Yale Univ. Press)

1971
Jaroslav Pelikan
The Emergence of the Catholic Tradition (100–600) (Univ. of Chicago Press)

1972
John T. Noonan, Jr.
Power to Dissolve: Lawyers and Marriages in the Courts of the Roman Curia (Belknap)
1973
Robert E. Quirk
The Mexican Revolution and the Catholic Church, 1910–1929 (Indiana Univ. Press)
1974
Thomas W. Spalding
Martin John Spalding: American Churchman (Catholic Univ. of America Press)
1975
Jay P. Dolan
The Immigrant Church. New York's Irish and German Catholics, 1815–1865 (Johns Hopkins)

1976
Emmet Larkin
The Roman Catholic Church and the Creation of the Modern Irish State, 1878–1886 (American Philosophical Society)
1977
Timothy Tackett
Priest and Parish in Eighteenth-Century France: A Social and Political Study of the Curés in a Diocese of Dauphiné 1750–1791 (Princeton Univ. Press)
1978
Charles W. Jones
Saint Nicholas of Myra, Bari, and Manhattan: Biography of a Legend (Univ. of Chicago Press)

American Historical Association

The American Historical Association awards are designed particularly to encourage those scholars who have not published extensively or established a wide reputation. A published entry must not bear a publication date earlier than one, two, or five years (depending on the award's frequency) prior to June 1 of the year in which the award is given. Further information concerning the prizes may be obtained from the American Historical Association, 400 A Street S.E., Washington, D.C. 20003.

Herbert Baxter Adams Prize

The Herbert Baxter Adams Prize of $300, originally offered biennially in 1938, became an annual award in 1971. It is awarded for the best book on European history by an American citizen. The entry must be the author's first substantial book.

1938
Arthur McCandless Wilson
French Foreign Policy during the Administration of Cardinal Fleury, 1726–1743 (Harvard Univ. Press)
1940
John Shelton Curtiss
Church and State in Russia, 1900–1917 (Columbia Univ. Press)

1942
E. Harris Harbison
Rival Ambassadors at the Court of Queen Mary (Princeton Univ. Press)

1944
R. H. Fisher
The Russian Fur Trade, 1550–1700 (Univ. of California Press)

1946
A. W. Salomone
Italian Democracy in the Making
(Univ. of Pennsylvania Press)

1948
Raymond de Roover
The Medici Bank: Its Organization, Management, Operations, and Decline (New York Univ. Press)

1950
Hans W. Gatzke
Germany's Drive to the West (Johns Hopkins Univ. Press)

1952
Arthur J. May
The Hapsburg Monarchy, 1867–1914 (Harvard Univ. Press)

1954
W. C. Richardson
Tudor Chamber Administration, 1485–1547 (Louisiana State Univ. Press)

1956
Gordon Craig
Politics of the Prussian Army, 1640–1945 (Oxford Univ. Press)

1958
Arthur Wilson
Diderot: The Testing Years (Oxford Univ. Press)

1960
Caroline Robbins
The Eighteenth Century Commonwealthman (Harvard Univ. Press)

1962
Jerome Blum
Lord and Peasant in Russia (Princeton Univ. Press)

1964
Archibald S. Foord
His Majesty's Opposition, 1714–1830 (Oxford Univ. Press)

1966
Gabriel Jackson
The Spanish Republic and the Civil War, 1931–39 (Princeton Univ. Press)

1968
Arno J. Mayer
Politics and Diplomacy of Peacemaking: Containment and Counterrevolution at Versailles 1918–1919 (Knopf)

1970
John P. McKay
Pioneers for Profit: Foreign Entrepreneurship and Russian Industrialization, 1885–1913 (Univ. of Chicago Press)

1971
Edward E. Malefakis
Agrarian Reform and Peasant Revolution in Spain, Origins of the Civil War (Yale Univ. Press)

1972
Richard Hellie
Enserfment and Military Change in Moscovy (Univ. of Chicago Press)

1973
Martin Jay
The Dialectical Imagination: A History of the Frankfurt School and the Institute for Social Research, 1923–1950 (Little)

1974
Joan Wallach Scott
The Glassworkers of Carmaux: French Craftsmen and Political Action in a Nineteenth-Century City (Harvard Univ. Press)

1975
James S. Donnelly, Jr.
The Land and the People of Nineteenth-Century Cork (Routledge & Kegan Paul)

1976
Frederick H. Russell
The Just War in the Middle Ages (Cambridge Univ. Press)

1977

Charles S. Maier
Recasting Bourgeois Europe: Stabilization in France, Germany and Italy in the Decade after World War I (Princeton Univ. Press)

1978

A. N. Galpern
The Religions of the People in Sixteenth-Century Champagne (Harvard Univ. Press)

George Louis Beer Prize

The George Louis Beer Prize of $300 is awarded annually for the best book by an American scholar on European international history since 1895.

1930

Bernadotte Everly Schmitt
The Coming of the War, 2 vols. (Scribner)

1931

Oran James Hale
Germany and the Diplomatic Revolution: A Study in Diplomacy and the Press, 1904–1906 (Univ. of Pennsylvania Press)

1932

Oswald H. Wedel
Austro-German Diplomatic Relations, 1908–1914 (Stanford Univ. Press)

1933

Robert Thomas Pollard
China's Foreign Relations, 1917–1931 (Macmillan)

1934

Ross J. S. Hoffman
Great Britain and the German Trade Rivalry, 1875–1914 (Univ. of Pennsylvania Press)

1935 –1936

No awards

1937

Charles Wesley Porter
The Career of Théophile Declassé (Univ. of Pennsylvania Press)

1938

René Albrecht-Carrié
Italy at the Paris Peace Conference (Columbia Univ. Press)

1939

Pauline Relyea Anderson
Background of Anti-English Feeling in Germany, 1890–1902 (American Univ. Press)

1940

Richard Heathcote Heindel
The American Impact on Great Britain, 1898–1914 (Univ. of Pennsylvania Press)

1941

Arthur J. Marder
The Anatomy of British Sea Power (Knopf)

1942

No award

1943

Arthur Norton Cook
British Enterprise in Nigeria (Univ. of Pennsylvania Press)

1944–1951

No awards

1952

Robert H. Ferrell
Peace in Their Time: The Origins of the Kellogg-Briand Pact (Yale Univ. Press)

1953

Russell Fifield
Woodrow Wilson and the Far East (Cornell Univ. Press)

1954

Wayne S. Vucinich
Serbia between East and West: The

Events of 1903–1908 (Stanford Univ. Press)

1955
Richard Pipes
The Formation of the Soviet Union (Harvard Univ. Press)

1956
Henry Cord Meyer
Mitteleuropa in German Thought and Action, 1815–1945 (Batsford)

1957
Alexander Dallin
German Rule in Russia, 1941–1945 (St. Martin's)

1958
Vincent Marmety
The United States and East Central Europe (Princeton Univ. Press)

1959
Ernest R. May
The World War and American Isolation, 1914–17 (Harvard Univ. Press)

1960
Rudolph Binion
Defeated Leaders: The Political Fate of Caillaux, Jouvenel and Tardieu (Columbia Univ. Press)

1961
Charles F. Delzell
Mussolini's Enemies: The Italian Anti-Fascist Resistance (Princeton Univ. Press)

1962
Piotr S. Wandycz
France and Her Eastern Allies, 1919–1925 (Univ. of Minnesota Press)

1963
Edward W. Bennett
Germany and the Diplomacy of the Financial Crisis, 1931 (Harvard Univ. Press)

Hans A. Schmitt
The Path to European Union (Louisiana State Univ. Press)

1964
Ivo J. Lederer
Yugoslavia at the Paris Peace Conference (Yale Univ. Press)

Harold I. Nelson
Land and Power: British and Allied Policy on Germany's Frontiers, 1916–1919 (Univ. of Toronto Press)

1965
Paul Spencer Guinn, Jr.
British Strategy and Politics 1914 to 1918 (Oxford Univ. Press/Clarendon)

1966
No award

1967
George A. Brinkley
The Volunteer Army and the Revolution in South Russia (Univ. of Notre Dame Press)

Robert Wohl
French Communism in the Making (Stanford Univ. Press)

1968
No award

1969
Richard H. Ullman
Britain and the Russian Civil War, November 1918–February 1920 (Princeton Univ. Press)

1970
Samuel R. Williamson, Jr.
The Politics of Grand Strategy: Britain and France Prepare for War, 1904–1914 (Harvard Univ. Press)

1971
Gerhard L. Weinberg
The Foreign Policy of Hitler's Germany, Diplomatic Revolution in Europe, 1933–36 (Univ. of Chicago Press)

1972
Jon Jacobson
Locarno Diplomacy: Germany and the West (Princeton Univ. Press)

1973 –1975
No awards

1976

Charles S. Maier
Recasting Bourgeois Europe: Stabilization in France, Germany and Italy in the Decade after World War I (Princeton Univ. Press)

1977

Stephen A. Schuker
The End of French Predominance in Europe: The Financial Crisis of Nineteen Twenty Four and the Adoption of the Dawes Plan (Univ. of North Carolina Press)

1978

No award

Albert J. Beveridge Award

The Albert J. Beveridge Award consists of $5,000 from income provided by the Albert J. Beveridge Fund. It is awarded for the best book in English on American history (the United States, Latin America, and Canada) from 1492 to the present. Offered biennially from 1939 to 1945, it has since then been an annual award.

1939

John T. Horton
James Kent: A Study in Conservatism (Appleton)

1941

Charles A. Barker
The Background of the Revolution in Maryland (Yale Univ. Press)

1943

Harold Whitman Bradley
The American Frontier in Hawaii: The Pioneers, 1789–1843 (Stanford Univ. Press)

1945

John Richard Alden
John Stuart and the Southern Colonial Frontier (Univ. of Michigan Press)

1946

Arthur E. Bestor
Backwoods Utopias: The Sectarian and Owenite Phases of Communitarian Socialism in America, 1663–1829 (Univ. of Pennsylvania Press)

1947

Lewis Hanke
The Struggle for Justice in the Spanish Conquest of America (Univ. of Pennsylvania Press)

1948

Donald Fleming
John William Draper and the Religion of Science (Univ. of Pennsylvania Press)

1949

Reynold M. Wik
Steam Power on the American Farm: A Chapter in Agricultural History, 1850–1920 (Univ. of Pennsylvania Press)

1950

Glyndon G. Van Deusen
Horace Greeley: Nineteenth Century Crusader (Univ. of Pennsylvania Press)

1951

Robert Twymann
History of Marshall Field and Co., 1852–1906 (Univ. of Pennsylvania Press)

1952

Clarence Versteeg
Robert Morris, Revolutionary Financier (Univ. of Pennsylvania Press)

1953

George R. Bentley
A History of the Freedman's Bureau (Univ. of Pennsylvania Press)

1954

Arthur M. Johnson
The Development of American Petroleum Pipelines: A Study in Enterprise and Public Policy (Cornell Univ. Press)

1955

Ian C. C. Graham
Colonists from Scotland: Emigration to North America, 1707–1783 (Cornell Univ. Press)

1956

Paul Schroeder
The Axis Alliance and Japanese-American Relations, 1941 (Cornell Univ. Press)

1957

David Fletcher
Rails, Mines, and Progress: Seven American Promoters in Mexico (Cornell Univ. Press)

1958

Paul Conkin
Tomorrow a New World: The New Deal Community Program (Cornell Univ. Press)

1959

Arnold M. Paul
Free Conservative Crisis and the Rule of Law: Attitudes of Bar and Bench, 1887–1895 (Cornell Univ. Press)

1960

C. Clarence Clendenen
The United States and Pancho Villa (Cornell Univ. Press)

Nathan Miller
The Enterprise of a Free People: Canals and the Canal Fund in the New York Economy, 1792–1838 (Cornell Univ. Press)

1961

Calvin DeArmond Davis
The United States and the First Hague Peace Conference (Cornell Univ. Press)

1962

Walter LaFeber
The New Empire: An Interpretation of American Expansion, 1860–1898 (Cornell Univ. Press)

1963

No award

1964

Linda Grant De Pauw
The Eleventh Pillar: New York State and the Federal Constitution (Cornell Univ. Press)

1965

Daniel M. Fox
The Discovery of Abundance (Cornell Univ. Press)

1966

Herman Belz
Reconstructing the Union: Conflict of Theory and Policy during the Civil War (Cornell Univ. Press)

1967

No award

1968

Michael Paul Rogin
The Intellectuals and McCarthy: The Radical Specter (M.I.T. Press)

1969

Sam Bass Warner, Jr.
The Private City: Philadelphia in Three Periods of Its Growth (Univ. of Pennsylvania Press)

1970

Sheldon Hackney
Populism to Progressivism in Alabama (Princeton Univ. Press)

Leonard L. Richards
"Gentlemen of Property and Standing": Anti-Abolition Mobs in Jacksonian America (Oxford Univ. Press)

1971

Carl N. Degler
Neither Black nor White: Slavery and Race Relations in Brazil and the United States (Macmillan)

David J. Rothman
The Discovery of the Asylum: Social Order and Disorder in the New Republic (Little)
1972
James T. Lemon
The Best Poor Man's Country (Johns Hopkins Univ. Press)
1973
Richard L. Slotkin
Regeneration through Violence: The Mythology of the American Frontier, 1600–1850 (Wesleyan Univ. Press)
1974
Peter H. Wood
Black Majority (Knopf)
1975
David Brion Davis
The Problem of Slavery in the Age of Revolution, 1700–1823 (Cornell Univ. Press)
1976
Edmund S. Morgan
American Slavery–American Freedom: The Ordeal of Colonial Virginia (Norton)
1977
Henry F. May
The Enlightenment in America (Oxford Univ. Press)
1978
John Leddy Phelan
The People and the King: The Comunero Revolution in Colombia, 1781 (Univ. of Wisconsin Press)

Albert B. Corey Prize in Canadian-American Relations

The Corey Prize was awarded for the first time in 1967. It is awarded biennially for the best book on the history of Canadian-American relations or on the history of both countries. The $1,000 prize is awarded jointly by the Canadian Historical Association and the American Historical Association.

1967
Gustave Lanctot
Canada and the American Revolution (Harvard Univ. Press)

1969
Kenneth Bourne
Britain and the Balance of Power in North America, 1815–1908 (Univ. of California Press)

1971
No award

1972
Charles P. Stacey
Arms, Men and Governments: The War Policies of Canada 1939–45 (The Queen's Printer, Ottawa)

1974
Lester B. Pearson
Mike, The Memoirs of the Right Honourable Lester B. Pearson, 2 vols. (Univ. of Toronto Press and Quadrangle)
1976
Robert H. Babcock
Gompers in Canada: A Study in American Continentalism before the First World War (Univ. of Toronto Press)
1978
Michael B. Katz
The People of Hamilton, Canada West: Family and Class in a Mid-Nineteenth-Century City (Harvard Univ. Press)

John H. Dunning Prize

The John H. Dunning Prize of $300 has been awarded biennially since 1929 for a published work on any subject relating to American history.

1929
Haywood J. Pearce, Jr.
Benjamin H. Hill: Secession and Reconstruction (Univ. of Chicago Press)
1931
Francis B. Simkins and R. H. Woody
South Carolina during Reconstruction (Univ. of North Carolina Press)
1933
Amos A. Ettinger
The Mission to Spain of Pierre Soule (Yale Univ. Press)
1935
Angie Debo
The Rise and Fall of the Choctaw Republic (Univ. of Oklahoma Press)
1937
No award
1938
Robert A. East
Business Enterprise in the American Revolutionary Era (Columbia Univ. Press)
1940
Richard W. Leopold
Robert Dale Owen (Harvard Univ. Press)
1942
Oscar Handlin
Boston's Immigrants (Harvard Univ. Press)
1944
Elting E. Morison
Admiral Sims and the Modern American Navy (Houghton)
1946
David Ellis
Landlords and Farmers in the Hudson Mohawk Region (Cornell Univ. Press)
1948
William E. Livezey
Mahan and Seapower (Univ. of Oklahoma Press)
1950
Henry Nash Smith
Virgin Land: The American West as Symbol and Myth (Harvard Univ. Press)
1952
Louis C. Hunter and Beatrice J. Hunter
Steamboats on the Western Rivers: An Economic and Technological History (Harvard Univ. Press)
1954
Gerald Carson
The Old Country Store (Oxford Univ. Press)
1956
John Higham
Strangers in the Land: Patterns of American Nativism (Rutgers Univ. Press)
1958
Marvin Meyers
The Jacksonian Persuasion (Stanford Univ. Press)
1960
Eric L. McKitrick
Andrew Johnson and Reconstruction (Univ. of Chicago Press)
1962
E. James Ferguson
The Power of the Purse: A History of American Public Finance, 1776–1790 (Institute of Early American History and Culture by the Univ. of North Carolina Press)
1964
John H. Cox and LaWanda Cox
Politics, Principle, and Prejudice, 1865–1866 (Free Press)

1966
John Willard Shy
Toward Lexington: The Role of the British Army in the American Revolution (Princeton Univ. Press)

1968
Robert L. Beisner
Twelve against Empire: The Anti-Imperialists, 1898–1900 (McGraw)

1970
Gordon S. Wood
The Creation of the American Republic, 1776–1787 (Institute of Early American History and Culture by the Univ. of North Carolina Press)

1972
John P. Diggins
Mussolini and Fascism: The View from America (Princeton Univ. Press)

1974
Paul Boyer and Stephen Nissenbaum
Salem Possessed: The Social Origins of Witchcraft (Harvard Univ. Press)

1976
Thomas S. Hines
Burnham of Chicago: Architect and Planner (Oxford Univ. Press)

1978
J. Mills Thornton
Politics and Power in a Slave Society: Alabama, 1800–1861 (Louisiana State Univ. Press)

John K. Fairbank Prize in East Asian History

The Fairbank Prize was established in 1968 by friends of John K. Fairbank and was first awarded in 1969. The prize of $500 is awarded biennially for an outstanding book on the history of China, Vietnam, Chinese Central Asia, Mongolia, Korea, or Japan, since 1800.

1969
Tetsuo Najita
Hara Kei in the Politics of Compromise, 1905–1915 (Harvard Univ. Press)
Harold Schiffrin
Sun Yat-sen and the Origins of the Chinese Revolution (Univ. of California Press)
1971
Jerome B. Greider
Hu Shih and the Chinese Renaissance: Liberalism in the Chinese Revolution, 1917–1937 (Harvard Univ. Press)

1973
W. G. Beasley
The Meiji Restoration (Stanford Univ. Press)

1975
Jen Yu-wen
The Taiping Revolutionary Movement (Yale Univ. Press)

1977
Gail Lee Bernstein
Japanese Marxist: A Portrait of Kawakami Hajime, 1879–1946 (Harvard Univ. Press)

Leo Gershoy Award

Commencing in 1977, this award is offered biennially for the most outstanding work published in English on any aspect of seventeenth- and eighteenth-century European history. It includes a cash award of $1,000.

1977
  Simon Schama
  Patriots and Liberators: Revolution in the Netherlands, 1780–1813 (Knopf)

Clarence H. Haring Prize

The Clarence H. Haring Prize of $500 is awarded every five years to the Latin American who, in the opinion of the Judging Committee, has written the most outstanding book on Latin American history during the preceding five years.

1966
  Daniel Cosío Villegas
  Historia Moderna de México
1971
  Luis González
  Pueblo en Vilo (El Colegio de México, Centro de Estudios Históricos)

1976
  Tulio Halperin-Donghi
  Politics, Economics, and Society in Argentina in the Revolutionary Period (Cambridge Univ. Press)

Howard R. Marraro Prize in Italian History

The Marraro Prize was awarded for the first time in 1973. It is given annually for the best book or article that deals with either Italian cultural history or Italian-American relations. Competitors must be resident citizens of the United States or Canada. The award is $500.

1973
  Edward R. Tannenbaum
  The Fascist Experience: Italian Society and Culture, 1922–1945 (Basic Books)
1974
  Benjamin F. Brown
  The Complete Works of Sidney Sonnino (Univ. Press of Kansas)
1975
  Robert Brentano
  Rome before Avignon: A Social History of Thirteenth Century Rome (Basic Books)

1976
  Richard A. Webster
  Industrial Imperialism in Italy, 1908–1915 (Univ. of California Press)
1977
  Gene A. Brucker
  The Civic World of Early Renaissance Florence (Princeton Univ. Press)
1978
  Virginia Yans-McLaughlin
  Family and Community: Italian Immigrants in Buffalo, 1880–1930 (Cornell Univ. Press)

Robert Livingston Schuyler Prize

The Robert Livingston Schuyler Prize of $500 was established by the Taraknath Das Foundation to be awarded at five-year intervals for the best work published in the field of modern British, British imperial, and British Commonwealth history written by an American citizen. Entries must be submitted by June 1 of the year in which the award is made.

1951
    Howard Robinson
    Britain's Post Office (Oxford Univ. Press)
1956
    David Harris Willson
    King James VI and I (Jonathan Cape)
1961
    Mark H. Curtis
    Oxford and Cambridge in Transition, 1558–1642 (Oxford Univ. Press)
1966
    Philip D. Curtin
    The Image of Africa: British Ideas and Action, 1780–1850 (Univ. of Wisconsin Press)
1971
    W. K. Jordan
    Edward VI: The Young King and *The Threshold of Power*, 2 vols. (Belknap)
1976
    John Clive
    Macaulay: The Shaping of the Historian (Knopf)

Watumull Prize

The Watumull Prize of $1,000 is awarded biennially, since 1954 in even-numbered years, for the best works on the history of India originally published in the United States.

1945
    Ernest J. H. Mackay
    Chanhu-Daro Excavations, 1935–36 (American Oriental Society)
1947
    No award
1949
    Holden Furber
    John Company at Work (Harvard Univ. Press)
    Gertrude Emerson Sen
    The Pageant of India History, Vol. I (Longmans)
1951
    Louis Fischer
    The Life of Mahatma Gandhi (Harper)
    T. Walter Wallbank
    India in the New Era (Scott, Foresman)
1954
    D. Mackenzie Brown
    The White Umbrella: Indian Political Thought from Manu to Gandhi (Univ. of California Press)
    W. Norman Brown
    The United States and India and Pakistan (Harvard Univ. Press)
1956
    No award
1958
    William de Bary, ed.
    Sources of the Indian Tradition (Columbia Univ. Press)

1960

Michael Brecher
Nehru: A Political Biography (Oxford Univ. Press)

1962

George D. Bearce
British Attitudes toward India, 1784–1858 (Oxford Univ. Press)

Stanley A. Wolpert
Tilak and Gokhale: Revolution and Reform in the Making of Modern India (Univ. of California Press)

1964

Charles A. Drekmeier
Kingship and Community in Early India (Stanford Univ. Press)

Charles H. Heimsath
Indian Nationalism and Hindu Social Reform (Princeton Univ. Press)

1966

Thomas R. Metcalf
The Aftermath of Revolt: India, 1857–1870 (Princeton Univ. Press)

B. R. Nayar
Minority Politics in the Punjab (Princeton Univ. Press)

1968

John Broomfield
Elite Conflict in a Plural Society: Twentieth-Century Bengal (Univ. of California Press)

Myron Weiner
Party Building in a New Nation (Univ. of Chicago Press)

1970

Stephen N. Hay
Asian Ideas of East and West: Tagore and His Critics in Japan, China, and India (Harvard Univ. Press)

Eugene F. Irschick
Politics and Social Conflict in South India: The Non-Brahman Movement and Tamil Separatism, 1916–1929 (Univ. of California Press)

David Kopf
British Orientalism and the Bengal Renaissance: The Dynamics of Indian Modernization, 1773–1835 (Univ. of California Press)

1972

Elizabeth Whitcombe
Agrarian Conditions in Northern India, Vol. 1: The United Provinces under British Rule, 1860–1900 (Univ. of California Press)

1974

Leonard A. Gordon
Bengal: The Nationalist Movement, 1876–1940 (Columbia Univ. Press)

1976

Michael Pearson
Merchants and Rulers in Gujarat: The Response to the Portuguese in the Sixteenth Century (Univ. of California Press)

1978

John R. McLane
Indian Nationalism and the Early Congress (Princeton Univ. Press)

American Medical Writers Association Book Award

The American Medical Writers Association, 5272 River Road, Suite 290, Bethesda, Maryland 20016, has been presented since 1973 to outstanding publications in the field of medicine in one or more of the following categories: physicians, allied health professionals, sex education, lay/trade, and special awards. The award, a cube with seal, is presented annually in October at the awards luncheon of the Association.

1973

Edward M. Brecher
Licit and Illicit Drugs (Little)

Howard F. Conn
Current Therapy (Saunders)

Walter Brown Shelley
Consultations in Dermatology (Saunders)

William J. Turtle
Doctor Turtle's Babies (Saunders)

1974

Meyer Friedman and Ray H. Rosenman
Type A Behavior and Your Heart (Knopf)

James F. Holland and Emil Frei III
Cancer Medicine (Lea & Febiger)

Keith L. Moore
The Developing Human (Saunders)

David R. Zimmerman
RH (Macmillan)

1975

Spyros Andreopoulos
Primary Care (Wiley)

Sanford Chan-Palay and Victoria Chan-Palay
Cerebellar Cortex (Springer-Verlag)

Guido Majno
The Healing Hand (Harvard Univ. Press)

Robert Massie and Suzanne Massie
Journey (Knopf)

Gilles R. G. Monif
Obstetrics and Gynecology (Harper)

David G. Nathan and Frank A. Oski
Hematology in Infancy (Saunders)

1976

Abraham I. Braude
Antimicrobial Drug Therapy (Saunders)

Alfred W. Crosby, Jr.
Epidemic and Peace, 1918 (Greenwood)

David G. Delvin
The Book of Love (St. Martin's)

David Malikin and Herbert Rusalem
Contemporary Vocational Rehabilitation (New York Univ. Press)

1977

Irene Mortenson Burnside
Nursing and the Aged (McGraw)

Alfred S. Evans
Viral Infections of Humans (Plenum)

David Hendin
Life Givers (Morrow)

1978

Ancel Blaustein
Pathology of the Female Genital Tract (Springer-Verlag)

H. V. Crock and H. Yoshizawa
The Blood Supply of the Vertebral Column and Spinal Cord in Man (Springer-Verlag)

Robert H. Pantell, James F. Fries, and Donald M. Vickery
Taking Care of Your Child (Addison-Wesley)

Robert M. Veatch
Case Studies in Medical Ethics (Harvard Univ. Press)

David Werner
Where There Is No Doctor (Hesperian Foundation)

American Psychiatric Association

The American Psychiatric Association (APA), 1700 18 Street N.W., Washington, D.C. 20009, offers three annual awards for outstanding contributions in the field of psychiatry. These awards are presented each year during the annual meeting of the Association.

Manfred S. Guttmacher Award

The American Psychiatric Association established this award in 1967 to honor the memory of Dr. Manfred S. Guttmacher. It is given for outstanding contributions to the literature of forensic psychiatry in the form of a book, monograph, paper, or any other work, including audiovisual presentations submitted to or presented at any professional meeting or published in the preceding calendar year. The Award Board selects a recipient every two years; the next award will be presented at the Convocation of Fellows at the 1981 annual meeting of the Association. The award consists of $500 and a bronze plaque. The recipient is invited to present a lecture during the annual meeting, for which an honorarium of $250 is provided.

1972
David B. Wexler and coauthors
"The Administration of Psychiatric Justice: Theory and Practice in Arizona"

1973
Morton Birnbaum
"The Right to Treatment: Some Comments on Implementation," *Duquesne Law Review*, vol. 10, 1972

1974
Ralph Slovenko
Psychiatry and Law (Little)

1975
Alexander D. Brooks
Law, Psychiatry, and the Mental Health System (Little)

1976
Alan A. Stone

"Mental Health and Law: A System in Transition," *DHEW Publication no. (ADM) 75-176*

1977
Frank W. Miller, Robert O. Dawson, George E. Dix, and Raymond I. Parnas
The Mental Health Process (Foundation Press)

1978
Sidney Bloch and Peter Reddaway
Psychiatric Terror: How Soviet Psychiatry Is Used to Suppress Dissent (Basic Books)

1979
J. K. Wing
Reasoning about Madness (Oxford Univ. Press)

Agnes Purcell McGavin Award

This award was established in 1964 by the estate of Dr. Agnes P. McGavin to honor a psychiatrist who has done outstanding work in the previous year related to the preventive aspects of the emotional disorders of childhood. The recipient is selected by the McGavin Award Board of the APA on a noncompetitive basis, although suggestions may be submitted to the McGavin Award Board, American Psychiatric Association, 1700 18 Street N.W., Washington, D.C. 20009. The board reserves the right to withhold the award in any year in which appropriate and important work in the preventive field is not available. The presentation of the award, $500 and a plaque, is made at the convocation of the annual meeting of the Association.

1964
Dr. Edith B. Jackson, Denver, Colorado

1965
Dr. David M. Levy, New York, New York

1966
Dr. René Spitz, Geneva, Switzerland

1967
Dr. Leo Kanner, Baltimore, Maryland

1968
Dr. George E. Gardner, Boston, Massachusetts

1969
Dr. Lauretta Bender, Queens Village, New York

Dr. Margaret Mahler, New York, New York

Dr. Howard Potter, Tomkins Cove, New York

1970
Dr. Milton J. E. Senn, New Haven, Connecticut

1971
Dr. Marion E. Kenworthy, New York, New York

1972
Dr. Irene M. Josselyn, Phoenix, Arizona

1973
Dr. William S. Langford, Professor of Psychiatry Emeritus, Columbia University, New York, New York

1974
Dr. Reginald S. Lourie, Professor of Child Health and Human Development and Psychiatry, George Washington University, and Director, Department of Psychiatry, Children's Hospital, and Medical Director, Hillcrest Children's Center, Washington, D.C.

1975
Dr. Othilda Krug, Cincinnati, Ohio

1976
Dr. Eleanor Pavenstedt, Tiverton, Rhode Island

Dr. Eveoleen N. Rexford, Divisional Professor, Harvard University, Cambridge, Massachusetts

1977
Dr. Viola Bernard, Clinical Professor Emeritus, College of Physicians and Surgeons, Columbia University, New York, New York

1978
Dr. George Tarjan, Professor of Psychiatry, School of Medicine, University of California, Los Angeles, California

1979
Dr. E. James Anthony, Ittleson Professor of Psychiatry, Director of the Eliot Division of Child Psychiatry and the Edison Child Development Research Center, School of Medicine, Washington University, St. Louis, Missouri

Isaac Ray Award in Memory of Margaret Sutermeister

The Isaac Ray Award was created in 1951 to promote better understanding between members of the legal and medical professions. The award was named in honor of Dr.

Isaac Ray, one of the original founders and fourth president of the Association. For the first fifteen years the award provided an honorarium of $1,000 to the grantee, funded through the generosity of the Aquinas Fund. In June 1973, a bequest of $20,000 was made to the APA in memory of Margaret Sutermeister by her mother Bertha B. Sutermeister. This gift was identified as unrestricted and accepted for use in furthering the Isaac Ray Award. The award is now known as the Isaac Ray Award in Memory of Margaret Sutermeister. An honorarium of $1,500 is presented biennially (annually until 1978) to a psychiatrist, attorney, or professional in the field of human behavior who has made outstanding contributions to forensic psychiatry or to the psychiatric aspects of jurisprudence. The recipient assumes the responsibility to deliver a lecture or series of lectures on psychiatry and the law and to present a manuscript for publication. The award is presented at the convocation of the annual meeting of the Association.

1952
Dr. Winfred Overholser, Superintendent, St. Elizabeth's Hospital, Washington, D.C.

1953
Dr. Gregory Zilboorg, Professor of Psychiatry, New York State University Medical College, New York, New York

1954
The Honorable John Biggs, Jr., Chief Judge of U.S. Court of Appeals for the Third Judicial Circuit, Wilmington, Delaware

1955
Professor Henry Weihofen, Professor of Law, University of New Mexico, Albuquerque, New Mexico

1956
Dr. Philip Roche, Associate in Psychiatry, University of Pennsylvania Medical School, Philadelphia, Pennsylvania

1957
Dr. Manfred Guttmacher, Psychiatrist and Chief Medical Officer of the Supreme Bench of Baltimore, Maryland

1958
Dr. Alistair William McLeod, Assistant Professor of Psychiatry, McGill University, Montreal, Canada

1959
Dr. Maxwell Jones, Director, Social Rehabilitation Unit, Belmont Hospital, Sutton, Surrey, England

1960
Judge David L. Bazelon of the U.S. Court of Appeals, Washington, D.C.

1961
Dr. Sheldon Glueck, Roscoe Pound Professor of Law, Harvard University, Cambridge, Massachusetts

1962
Dr. Karl A. Menninger, The Menninger Foundation, Topeka, Kansas

1963
Judge Morris Ploscowe, Associate Professor of Law, New York University, New York, New York

1964
Judge Justine Wise Polier, New York, New York

1965
Dr. Georg K. Sturup, Hellerup, Denmark

1966–1967
No awards

1968
Dr. Bernard Diamond, University of California, Berkeley, California

1969–1974
No awards

1975
Dr. Jay Katz, Professor Adjunct of Law and Psychiatry, Yale University, New Haven, Connecticut

1976
Dr. Jonas Robitscher, Henry R. Luce Professor of Law and Behavioral Sciences, Emory University School of Law, Atlanta, Georgia

1977
Dr. Bruno M. Cormier, Professor, Department of Psychiatry, and Director, Clinic in Forensic Psychiatry, McGill University, Montreal, Canada

1978
Dr. Andrew S. Watson, Professor of Psychiatry, Medical School, and Professor of Law, Law School, University of Michigan, Ann Arbor, Michigan

1979
No award

American Psychological Foundation National Media Awards

Since 1956 the American Psychological Foundation annually has presented awards to those individuals who during the year have best presented psychology to the general public. The purpose of the awards is to recognize and encourage outstanding, accurate reporting that increases the public's knowledge and understanding of psychology. Awards are made in five categories: television/film, radio, newspaper reporting, magazine writing, and books/monographs. Winners in each category receive a special citation and $1,000 at the annual convention of the American Psychological Association. Convention travel expenses are paid by the Foundation. Nominations for the books/monographs category may be made by anyone and should be submitted with two copies of the material to be judged no later than May 5. Address inquiries to Kathleen Holmay, Information Officer, American Psychological Association, 1200 17 Street N.W., Washington, D.C. 20036. Below are listed the winners of the books/monographs category.

1956–1966
No awards

1967
Gay Gaer Luce and Julius Segal
Sleep (Coward)

1968–1970
No awards

1971
Richard I. Evans
Gordon Allport: The Man and His Ideas (Dutton)

1972
No award

1973
Elliott Aronson
The Social Animal (Freeman)

1974
Maya Pines
The Brain Changers (Harcourt)

1975
Lee Edson and the editors of Time-Life
How We Learn (Time-Life)

1976
Jonathan L. Freedman
Crowding and Behavior (Freeman)

1977
Peter Chew
The Inner World of the Middle-Aged Man (Macmillan)

1978
   Robert M. Stern and William J. Ray
   Biofeedback (Dow Jones-Irwin)

1979
   Elaine Walster and G. William Walster
   A New Look at Love (Addison-Wesley)

American Revolution Round Table Award

The Round Table established this annual award in 1958 to encourage research and writing on the American Revolution. It honors the author of the book published in the previous year on any aspect of the Revolution that is deemed by the Board of Governors the best combination of scholarship and literary merit. Each winner receives a bronze plaque at a ceremony at Fraunces Tavern, New York City, each January. Recent award winners are listed below. Information on the award and earlier award winners (1958–1972) is available from the Chairman, American Revolution Round Table, Box 654, Times Square Station, New York, New York 10036.

1973
   John Brooke
   George III (McGraw)

1974
   Catherine S. Crary
   The Price of Loyalty: Tory Writings from the Revolutionary Era (McGraw)

1975
   David Freeman Hawke
   Paine (Harper)

1976
   Thomas Fleming
   1776: Year of Illusions (Norton)

1977
   Charles Bracelen Flood
   Rise, and Fight Again (Dodd)

1978
   Philip Young
   Revolutionary Ladies (Knopf)

1979
   Michael Kammen
   A Season of Youth (Knopf)

American-Scandinavian Foundation/ P.E.N. Translation Prizes

The American-Scandinavian Foundation and the P.E.N. American Center established these prizes in 1979 to bring the best of contemporary Scandinavian literature to American readers. The prizes will be given annually, beginning in May 1980, for translations into English works of fiction and poetry by Danish, Finnish, Icelandic, Norwegian, or Swedish authors born after 1880. The two prizes will consist of $500 each and publication of the winning manuscripts in a special literary issue of ASF's *Scandinavian Review*. Entries will be judged by the P.E.N. American Center. The deadline for the first award is February 15, 1980. Further information on entry requirements can be obtained from Kathleen Madden, American-Scandinavian Foundation, 127 East 73 Street, New York, New York 10021.

Joseph L. Andrews Bibliographical Award

The American Association of Law Libraries presents a certificate to the person who has made the most significant contribution to legal bibliographic literature. The main criteria are creativity, evaluative elements, and the extent to which judgment was a factor in its formulation. The award is for a single publication or publications in a given year as opposed to the cumulative efforts of a career. It is usually presented at the annual meeting of the American Association of Law Libraries. For further information, contact the American Association of Law Libraries, 53 West Jackson Boulevard, Chicago, Illinois 60604.

1967
Anthony Grech
The Dominican Crisis (Oceana) and *The Southeast Asia Crisis* (Oceana)

1968
Stojan A. Bayitch
Latin America and the Caribbean (Oceana)

Beatrice S. McDermott and Freda A. Coleman
Government Regulation of Business (Gale)

Jacob Robinson
International Law and Organization: General Sources of Information (Humanities)

1969
Ralph E. McCoy
Freedom of the Press (Southern Illinois Univ. Press)

1970
Richard Sloane
Recommended Law Books (ABA)

1971
Harry Bitner and Meira Pimsleur
For contributions to *Law Books Recommended for Libraries* (Rothman)

1972
Dorothy C. Tompkins
Sentencing the Offender (Institute of Governmental Studies) and *The Prison and the Prisoner* (Institute of Governmental Studies)

1973
Wybo P. Heere
Air Law Bibliography (Oceana)

Lilly Melchior Roberts
Bibliography of Legal Festschriften (Nijhoff)

1974
No award

1975
Helena P. von Pfeil
Juvenile Rights since 1967 (Rothman)

1976
Fannie J. Klein
The Administration of Justice in the Courts (Oceana)

1977
Leon Radzinowicz
Criminology and the Administration of Criminal Justice (Mansell)

1978
Marija Matich Hughes
The Sexual Barrier (Hughes)

1979
Beatrice J. Kalisch
Child Abuse and Neglect (Greenwood)

Animal Rights Writing Award

This award was established in 1972 to encourage writing on the moral and ethical concepts of animal rights. It is given annually by the Board of Directors, Society for Animal Rights, 421 South State Street, Clarks Summit, Pennsylvania 18411, to the author of an exceptionally meritorious published book or article in the field of animal rights. Each award winner receives $300 and a brass plaque at a ceremony held in the winter or spring. The first two awards were presented in the U.S. embassies in Bern and London.

1972–1977
   No awards
1978
   Hans Ruesch
   Slaughter of the Innocent (Bantam)
   Peter Singer
   Animal Liberation: A New Ethics for Our Treatment of Animals (Avon)
1979
   Jeanie Blake
   "Animal Rights," newspaper series (New Orleans *Times-Picayune*)

Anisfield-Wolf Award

This award was established in 1934 by Edith Anisfield Wolf in memory of her father, John Anisfield. It was originally sponsored by the *Saturday Review*, but it is currently offered by the Cleveland Foundation, National City Bank Building, Cleveland, Ohio 44114. The award was originally given for scholarly books published in the field of race relations; since 1942, it has been given to the best books concerned with racial problems in the field of creative literature. Works of fiction, drama, poetry, biography, or autobiography are eligible. A copy of the book in published form is submitted to each of three judges. The awards, which originally consisted of $1,000 for each of the two books chosen, are now in the amount of $1,500.

1935
   Harold Gosnell
   Negro Politicians: The Rise of Negro Politics in Chicago (Univ. of Chicago Press)
1936
   Julian Huxley and A. C. Haddon
   We Europeans: A Survey of "Racial" Problems (Harper)
1937–1938
   No awards
1939
   E. Franklin Frazier
   The Negro Family in the United States (Univ. of Chicago Press)

1940
   No award

1941
   Leopold Infeld
   Quest (Doubleday)
   James G. Leyburn
   The Haitian People (Yale Univ. Press)

1942
   Zora Neale Hurston
   Dust Tracks on a Road (Lippincott)
   Donald Pierson
   Negroes in Brazil (Univ. of Chicago Press)

1943
Roi Ottley
New World A-Coming (Houghton)
Maurice Samuel
The World of Sholom Aleichem
(Knopf)
1944
Gwethalyn Graham
Earth and High Heaven (Lippincott)
Gunnar Myrdal
An American Dilemma (Harper)
1945
St. Clair Drake and Horace Cayton
Black Metropolis (Harcourt)
Wallace Stegner and the editors of
Look
One Nation (Houghton)
1946
Sholem Asch
East River (Houghton)
Pauline R. Kibbe
Latin Americans in Texas (Univ. of
New Mexico Press)
1947
John Collier
The Indians of the Americas (Norton)
Worth Tuttle Hedden
The Other Room (Crown)
1948
J. C. Furnas
Anatomy of Paradise (Sloane)
Alan Paton
Cry the Beloved Country (Scribner)
1949
S. Andhil Fineberg
Punishment without Crime (Double-
day)
Shirley Graham
Your Most Humble Servant (Messner)
1950
Henry Gibbs
Twilight in South Africa (Philosophical
Lib.)
John Hersey
The Wall (Knopf)

1951
Brewton Berry
Race Relations (Houghton)
Laurens van der Post
Venture to the Interior (Morrow)
1952
Farley Mowat
People of the Deer (Little)
Han Suyin
A Many-Splendored Thing (Little)
1953
Vernon Bartlett
Struggle for Africa (Praeger)
Langston Hughes
Simple Takes a Wife (Simon & Schus-
ter)
1954
Oden Meeker
Report on Africa (Scribner)
Lyle Saunders
Cultural Difference and Medical Care
(Russell Sage Foundation)
1955
John P. Dean and Alex Rosen
A Manual of Intergroup Relations
(Univ. of Chicago Press)
George W. Shepherd, Jr.
They Wait in Darkness (John Day)
1956
Gilberto Freyre
*The Masters and the Slaves: A Study
in the Development of Brazilian Civ-
ilization* (Knopf)
Trevor Huddleston
Naught for Your Comfort (Doubleday)
1957
Jessie B. Sams
White Mother (McGraw)
South African Institute of Race Rela-
tions
Handbook on Race Relations (Oxford
Univ. Press)
1958
Martin Luther King, Jr.
Stride toward Freedom (Harper)

George Eaton Simpson and J. Milton Yinger
Racial and Cultural Minorities (Harper)

1959

Basil Davidson
The Lost Cities of Africa (Little)

John Haynes Holmes
I Speak for Myself (Harper)

1960

E. R. Braithwaite
To Sir, with Love (Prentice)

Louis E. Lomax
The Reluctant African (Harper)

1961

Gina Allen
The Forbidden Man (Chilton)

Dwight L. Dumond
Antislavery (Univ. of Michigan Press)

John Howard Griffin
Black Like Me (Houghton)

1962

Theodosius Dobzhansky
Mankind Evolving (Yale Univ. Press)

1963

Nathan Glazer and Daniel P. Moynihan
Beyond the Melting Pot (M.I.T. Press)

Harold R. Isaacs
The New World of Negro Americans (John Day)

Bernhard E. Olson
Faith and Prejudice (Yale Univ. Press)

1964

Milton M. Gordon
Assimilation in American Life (Oxford Univ. Press)

James M. McPherson
The Struggle for Equality: Abolitionists and the Negro in the Civil War and Reconstruction (Princeton Univ. Press)

Abram L. Sachar
A History of the Jews (Knopf)

James W. Silver
Mississippi: The Closed Society (Harcourt)

1965

H. C. Baldry
Unity of Mankind in Greek Thought (Cambridge Univ. Press)

Claude Brown
Manchild in the Promised Land (Macmillan)

Malcolm X and Alex Haley
Autobiography of Malcolm X (Grove)

Amram Scheinfeld
Your Heredity and Environment (Lippincott)

1966

David Brion Davis
The Problem of Slavery in Western Culture (Cornell Univ. Press)

Oscar Lewis
La Vida (Random)

1967

Norman Cohn
Warrant for Genocide: The Myth of the Jewish World Conspiracy and the Protocols of the Elders of Zion (Harper)

Robert Coles
Children of Crisis: A Study of Courage and Fear (Atlantic-Little)

Raul Hilberg
The Destruction of European Jews (Quadrangle)

1968

E. Earl Baughman and W. Grant Dahlstrom
Negro and White Children (Academic)

Gwendolyn Brooks
In the Mecca (Harper)

Leonard Dinnerstein
The Leo Frank Case (Columbia Univ. Press)

Stuart Levine and Nancy O. Lurie

The American Indian Today (Everett Edwards)
1969
Dan T. Carter
Scottsboro (Louisiana State Univ. Press)
Vine Deloria, Jr.
Custer Died for Your Sins (Macmillan)
Florestan Fernandes
The Negro in Brazilian Society (Columbia Univ. Press)
Audrie Girdner and Anne Loftis
The Great Betrayal (Macmillan)
1970–1971
No awards
1972
Pat Conroy
The Water Is Wide (Houghton)
Betty Fladeland
Men and Brothers (Univ. of Illinois Press)
Lee Rainwater
Behind Ghetto Walls (Aldine)
1973
Charles Duguid
Doctor and the Aborigines (Rigby)
Michel Fabre
The Unfinished Quest of Richard Wright (Morrow)
Naboth Mokgatle
The Biography of an Unknown South American (Univ. of California Press)
Albie Sachs

Justice in South Africa (Univ. of California Press)
Louis L. Snyder
The Dreyfus Case (Rutgers Univ. Press)
1974
Eugene D. Genovese
Roll, Jordan, Roll (Pantheon)
Leon Poliakov
The Aryan Myth (Basic Books)
1975
Lucy S. Dawidowicz
The War against the Jews (Bantam)
Thomas Kiernan
The Arabs (Little, Brown)
Raphael Patai and Jennifer Wing
The Myth of the Jewish Race (Scribner)
1976
Richard Kluger
Simple Justice (Knopf)
Michi Weglyn
Years of Infamy (Morrow)
1977
Allan Chase
The Legacy of Malthus: The Social Costs of the New Scientific Racism (Knopf)
Maxine Hong Kingston
Woman Warrior (Knopf)
1978
No award

Athenaeum Literary Award

This award, sponsored by The Athenaeum of Philadelphia, East Washington Square, Philadelphia, Pennsylvania 19106, was established in 1950 in recognition and encouragement of the literary achievements of authors who were "bona fide residents of Philadelphia or Pennsylvania within a radius of 30 miles of City Hall" at the time their book was written or published. Any volumes of general literature (fiction, history, biography, drama, belles lettres) written by a Philadelphian (as determined by geographical residence above) are eligible. Technical, scientific, exclusively educational, and juvenile books are not included. Books are considered on the basis of their significance and importance to the general public as well as for literary excellence.

1949
John L. LaMonte
The World of the Middle Ages (Appleton)
1950
Henry N. Paul
The Royal Play of Macbeth (Macmillan)
1951
Arthur Hobson Quinn
The Literature of the American People (Appleton)
1952
Nicholas B. Wainwright
A Philadelphia Story (Philadelphia Contributionship for the Insuring of Houses from Loss of Fire)
1953
Lawrence Henry Gibson
The Culmination, 1760-1763 (Knopf)
1954
Davis Grubb
The Night of the Hunter (Harper)
1955
Conyers Read
Mr. Secretary Cecil and Queen Elizabeth (Knopf)
1956
Livingston Biddle, Jr.
The Village Beyond (Lippincott)
Samuel Noah Kramer
From the Tablets of Sumer (Falcon's Wing)
1957
Catherine Drinker Bowen
The Lion and the Throne (Little)
Bettina Linn
A Letter to Elizabeth (Lippincott)
1958
Loren Eiseley
Darwin's Century (Doubleday)
1959
John Canaday

Mainstreams of Modern Art: David to Picasso (Simon & Schuster)
1960
David Taylor
Storm the Last Rampart (Lippincott)
Edwin Wolf II, with John F. Fleming
Rosenbach: A Biography (World)
1961
Roy F. Nichols
The Stakes of Power, 1845-1887 (Hill & Wang)
Lauren R. Stevens
The Double Axe (Scribner)
1962
Curtis Bok
Maria (Knopf)
Carleton S. Coon
The Origin of Races (Knopf)
Richard S. Dunn
Puritans and Yankees (Princeton Univ. Press)
1963
Daniel Hoffman
The City of Satisfactions (Oxford Univ. Press)
Samuel Noah Kramer
The Sumerians (Univ. of Chicago Press)
1964
Kristin Hunter
God Bless the Child (Scribner)
Elizabeth Gray Vining
Take Heed of Loving Me (Lippincott)
Dorothy Shipley White
Seeds of Discord (Syracuse Univ. Press)
1965
Laurence Lafore
The Long Fuse (Lippincott)
1966
Edward S. Gifford, Jr.
Father against the Devil (Doubleday)

1967
Edmund N. Bacon
Design of Cities (Viking)
Daniel P. Mannix
The Fox and the Hound (Dutton)
1968
Ernest Earnest
Expatriates and Patriots (Duke Univ. Press)
Robert C. Smith
The Art of Portugal (Weidenfeld)
1969
Henry C. Pitz
The Brandywine Tradition (Houghton)
1970
No award
1971
Loren Eiseley
The Night Country (Scribner)

1972
Jerre Mangione
The Dream and the Deal (Little)
1973
John Maass
The Glorious Enterprise (American Life Foundation)
1974
John Royston Coleman
Blue Collar Journal (Lippincott)
1975
Martin P. Snyder
City of Independence (Praeger)
1976
No award
1977
Seymour Adelman
The Moving Pageant (Sutter)

The Emily Clark Balch Prizes

These prizes were established in 1955 through the bequest of Emily Clark Balch to the University of Virginia for the purpose of "stimulating appreciation and creation of American literature." The $500 prizes are awarded annually by the *Virginia Quarterly Review*, One West Range, Charlottesville, Virginia 22903, for the best short story (stories) and the best poem(s) published that calendar year in the *Review*. (Prior to 1978, the form of writing that received the prize and the frequency and amount of the cash award varied.) An announcement of the winners appears in the Winter issue; there is no official presentation.

POETRY

1956
Carlos Baker
"On Getting Back to Airplane Spotting after Ten Years"
1959
Elizabeth Jackson Barker
"Yes and No Stories," "The Names of the Rose, or, What the Word Said," and "Nocturne"
1962
Reed Whittemore
"The Music of Driftwood"

1964
Hayden Carruth
"North Winter"
1966
Jean Garrigue
"Moon," "The Water by the River Sorgue," and "A Dream"
1968
John Berryman
"Eleven Dream Songs"
1970
Rudy Shackelford
"Life Cycle of the Snowman," "An Old Timepiece," "Icarus II," "The Exten-

POETRY (cont.)

sion," "Site of Future Construction," "Taper's Progress," "Harvest Scene," and "Waltzes for Mechanical Piano"
1972
Felix Stefanile
"The Weather Didn't Do Us Any Good," "American Legend," and "Riding the Storm"
1974
Wendell Berry
"The Bed" and "From the Crest"
1976
Donald Hall
"Maple Syrup"

Lisel Mueller
"The Triumph of Life: Mary Shelley"
1978
Carolyn Forché
"San Onofre"

Sandford Lyne
"Armadillo"

SHORT STORY

1956
Siegel Fleisher
"The Old Man's Up and Around"
1958
Helga Sandburg
"Witch Chicken"

1961
Bige Hammons
"The Breath of a Man"
1963
Helen Hudson
"Thy Servant"
1967
William Moseley
"The Preacher and Margery Scott"
1969
Olivia Davis
"A Girl Bathing"
1971
Ann Jones
"In Black and White"
1973
Burke Davis III
"Points of Intersection"
1975
Kent Nelson
"The Humpbacked Bird"
1977
Margaret Edwards
"The Fountain of Milk"

Mary Heath
"Grace Abounding"

Richard Lyons
"The Woman"
1978
H. E. Francis
"Naming Things"

Bancroft Prizes

Established under the will of Frederic Bancroft and offered by Columbia University, New York, New York 10027, the first award was given in April 1948 for books published in 1947. Provision is made for two annual prizes of $4,000 each to be awarded to the authors of distinguished works in either American history (including biography) or American diplomacy or both. (Prior to 1978, a third $4,000 prize was sometimes awarded for the category international relations of the United States.) The word "American" is interpreted to include all the Americas, North, Central, and South; however, the award is confined to works originally written in English or of which there is a published translation in English. Volumes of papers, letters, and speeches of famous

Americans, unless edited by the author, are not eligible. Autobiographies are eligible, but books reporting on recent personal experiences of Americans, within a limited area both in time and geography, cannot be considered. The decision is made by trustees of Columbia University upon nomination by the Bancroft Prize Committee. Awarded in the spring each year to books first published the preceding year, it is officially presented to the authors of the winning volumes at a dinner given by the Friends of the Libraries, Columbia University.

Communications in regard to the Bancroft Prizes and works submitted in competition may be sent to the Bancroft Prize Committee, 202A, Low Library, Columbia University, New York, New York 10027, as published, but in no case later than November 1 for books published the preceding year. It is requested that four copies be furnished—three for the members of the Prize Committee and one for the Libraries of Columbia University. The address should state that the books are for the Bancroft Prize Competition.

1948

Bernard De Voto
Across the Wide Missouri (Houghton)

Allan Nevins
Ordeal of the Union (Scribner)

1949

Samuel Eliot Morison
The Rising Sun in the Pacific (Little)

Robert E. Sherwood
Roosevelt and Hopkins (Harper)

1950

Herbert E. Bolton
Coronado (Whittlesey and Univ. of New Mexico Press)

Lawrence H. Gipson
The Victorious Years, 1758-1760, Vol. 7 of the series The Great War for the Empire (Knopf)

1951

Arthur N. Holcombe
Our More Perfect Union (Harvard Univ. Press)

Henry N. Smith
Virgin Land (Harvard Univ. Press)

1952

Merlo J. Pusey
Charles Evans Hughes (Macmillan)

C. Vann Woodward
Origins of the New South, 1877-1913 (Louisiana State Univ. Press)

1953

George Dangerfield
The Era of Good Feelings (Harcourt)

Eric F. Goldman
Rendezvous with Destiny (Knopf)

1954

William L. Langer and S. Everett Gleason
The Undeclared War (Harper)

Clinton Rossiter
Seedtime of the Republic (Harcourt)

1955

Paul Horgan
Great River, the Rio Grande (Rinehart)

Leonard D. White
The Jacksonians (Macmillan)

1956

J. G. Randall and Richard N. Current
Lincoln the President (Dodd)

Elizabeth Stevenson
Henry Adams (Macmillan)

1957

George F. Kennan
Russia Leaves the War (Princeton Univ. Press)

Arthur S. Link
Wilson: The New Freedom (Princeton Univ. Press)

1958

Frank Luther Mott
History of American Magazines (Belknap)

Arthur M. Schlesinger, Jr.
Crisis of the Old Order (Houghton)

1959

Daniel J. Boorstin
The Americans: The Colonial Experience (Random)

Ernest Samuels
Henry Adams: The Middle Years (Belknap)

1960

Margaret Leech
In the Days of McKinley (Harper)

R. R. Palmer
The Age of the Democratic Revolution: A Political History of Europe and America, 1760-1800 (Princeton Univ. Press)

1961

Arthur S. Link
Wilson: The Struggle for Neutrality, 1914-1915 (Princeton Univ. Press)

Merrill D. Peterson
The Jefferson Image in the American Mind (Oxford Univ. Press)

1962

Lawrence A. Cremin
The Transformation of the School (Knopf)

Martin B. Duberman
Charles Francis Adams, 1807-1886 (Houghton)

Felix Gilbert
To the Farewell Address: Ideas of Early American Foreign Policy (Princeton Univ. Press)

1963

Page Smith
John Adams (Doubleday)

John G. Stoessinger
The Might of Nations: World Politics in Our Time (Random)

Roberta Wohlstetter
Pearl Harbor: Warning and Decision (Stanford Univ. Press)

1964

William E. Leuchtenburg
Franklin D. Roosevelt and the New Deal, 1932-1940 (Harper)

Paul Seabury
Power, Freedom and Diplomacy: The Foreign Policy of the United States of America (Random)

John L. Thomas
The Liberator: William Lloyd Garrison (Little)

1965

Dorothy Borg
The United States and the Far Eastern Crisis of 1933-1938 (Harvard Univ. Press)

Bradford Perkins
Castlereagh and Adams: England and the United States, 1812-1823 (Univ. of California Press)

William B. Willcox
Portrait of a General: Sir Henry Clinton in the War of Independence (Knopf)

1966

Theodore W. Friend III
Between Two Empires: The Ordeal of the Philippines, 1926-1946 (Yale Univ. Press)

Richard B. Morris
The Peacemakers: The Great Powers and American Independence (Harper)

1967

William W. Freehling
Prelude to Civil War: The Nullification Controversy in South Carolina, 1816-1836 (Harper)

Charles Sellers
James K. Polk, Continentalist, 1843-1846, Vol. II (Princeton Univ. Press)

James Sterling Young
The Washington Community, 1800–1828 (Columbia Univ. Press)

1968

Bernard Bailyn
The Ideological Origins of the American Revolution (Belknap)

Henry Allen Bullock
A History of Negro Education in the South from 1619 to the Present (Harvard Univ. Press)

Richard L. Bushman
From Puritan to Yankee: Character and the Social Order in Connecticut, 1690–1765 (Harvard Univ. Press)

1969

Winthrop D. Jordan
White over Black: American Attitudes toward the Negro, 1550–1812 (Univ. of North Carolina Press)

N. Gordon Levin, Jr.
Woodrow Wilson and World Politics: America's Response to War and Revolution (Oxford Univ. Press)

Rexford Guy Tugwell
The Brains Trust (Viking)

1970

Dan T. Carter
Scottsboro: A Tragedy of the American South (Louisiana State Univ. Press)

Charles Coleman Sellers
Charles Wilson Peale (Scribner)

Gordon S. Wood
The Creation of the American Republic, 1776–1787 (Univ. of North Carolina Press)

1971

Erik Barnouw
The Image Empire: A History of Broadcasting in the United States, Volume III–From 1953 (Oxford Univ. Press)

David M. Kennedy
Birth Control in America: The Career of Margaret Sanger (Yale Univ. Press)

Joseph Frazier Wall
Andrew Carnegie (Oxford Univ. Press)

1972

Carl N. Degler
Neither Black nor White (Macmillan)

Robert Middlekauff
The Mathers: Three Generations of Puritan Intellectuals, 1596–1728 (Oxford Univ. Press)

Samuel Eliot Morison
The European Discovery of America: The Northern Voyages (Oxford Univ. Press)

1973

Frances FitzGerald
Fire in the Lake: The Vietnamese and the Americans in Vietnam (Atlantic-Little)

John Lewis Gaddis
The United States and the Origins of the Cold War (Columbia Univ. Press)

Louis R. Harlan
Booker T. Washington (Oxford Univ. Press)

1974

Ray Allen Billington
Frederick Jackson Turner: Historian, Scholar, Teacher (Oxford Univ. Press)

Townsend Hoopes
The Devil and John Foster Dulles (Atlantic)

Stephen Thernstrom
The Other Bostonians: Poverty and Progress in the American Metropolis, 1880–1970 (Harvard Univ. Press)

1975

Robert William Fogel and Stanley L. Engerman
Time on the Cross: The Economics of American Negro Slavery and *Time on*

the Cross: Evidence and Methods, A Supplement (Little)

Eugene Genovese
Roll, Jordan, Roll (Pantheon)

Alexander L. George and Richard Smoke
Deterrence in American Foreign Policy: Theory and Practice (Columbia Univ. Press)

1976

David Brion Davis
The Problem of Slavery in the Age of Revolution, 1770-1823 (Cornell Univ. Press)

R. W. B. Lewis
Edith Wharton: A Biography (Harper)

1977

Alan Dawley
Class and Community: The Industrial Revolution in Lynn (Harvard Univ. Press)

Robert A. Gross
The Minutemen and Their World (Hill & Wang)

Barry W. Higman
Slave Population and Economy in Jamaica, 1807-1834 (Cambridge Univ. Press)

1978

Alfred D. Chandler, Jr.
The Visible Hand: The Managerial Revolution in American Business (Harvard Univ. Press)

Morton J. Horwitz
The Transformation of American Law, 1780-1860 (Harvard Univ. Press)

1979

Christopher Thorne
Allies of a Kind: The United States, Britain, and the War against Japan, 1941-1945 (Oxford Univ. Press)

Anthony F. C. Wallace
Rockdale: The Growth of an American Village in the Early Industrial Revolution (Knopf)

Stuart L. Bernath Prize

The Society for Historians of American Foreign Relations, University of Akron, Department of History, Akron, Ohio 44325, offers two annual awards to recognize and to encourage distinguished research and writing by scholars of American foreign relations during the calendar year. An award of $500 has been given annually since 1972 for a book on any aspect of American foreign relations. It must be the author's first or second book. A second award of $200 was established in 1976 for an article on American foreign relations or foreign policy. The article chosen should be among the author's first five. Articles having more than two authors are not eligible. Presentation of both awards is made annually at the April meeting of the Organization of American Historians. Listed below are the book award winners.

1972

Kenneth E. Shewmaker
American and Chinese Communists, 1927-1945 (Cornell Univ. Press)

Joan Hoff Wilson
American Business and Foreign Policy, 1920-1933 (Univ. Press of Kentucky)

1973

John Gaddis
The United States and the Origins of the Cold War, 1941–1947 (Columbia Univ. Press)

1974

Michael H. Hunt
Frontier Defense and the Open Door: Manchuria and Chinese-American Relations, 1895–1911 (Yale Univ. Press)

1975

Frank D. McCann, Jr.
The Brazilian-American Alliance, 1937–1945 (Princeton Univ. Press)

Stephen E. Pelz
Race to Pearl Harbor: The Failure of the Second London Naval Conference and the Onset of World War II (Harvard Univ. Press)

1976

Martin Sherwin
A World Destroyed: The Atomic Bomb and the Grand Alliance (Knopf)

1977

Roger V. Dingman
Power in the Pacific: The Origins of Naval Arms Limitation, 1914–1922 (Univ. of Chicago Press)

1978

James R. Leutze
Bargaining for Supremacy: Anglo-American Naval Collaboration, 1937–1941 (Univ. of North Carolina Press)

1979

Phillip J. Baram
The Department of State in the Middle East, 1919–1945 (Univ. of Pennsylvania Press)

Howard W. Blakeslee Awards

To encourage attainment of the highest standards of reporting on the heart and circulatory diseases, the American Heart Association, 7320 Greenville Avenue, Dallas, Texas 75231, established these awards in 1952. The awards honor the achievements of the late Howard W. Blakeslee, Science Editor of the Associated Press and a founder of the National Association of Science Writers. To be eligible, entries must have been printed or broadcast in a recognized national or local medium of mass communication including press, magazine, radio, television, film, or books, and must convey information about the heart and blood vessel diseases. A minimum of $500 is presented to the winner of each award selected by the Blakeslee Awards Committee at the Association's annual meeting and scientific sessions each year in varying cities. Listed below are winners in the category of books.

1954

William A. Brams
Managing Your Coronary (Lippincott)

1960

Isaac Asimov
The Living River (Abelard)

H. M. Marvin
Your Heart: A Handbook for Laymen (Doubleday)

1961

Douglas Ritchie
Stroke (Doubleday)

1962

Bernard Seeman
The River of Life (Norton)

1964

Alton Blakeslee and Jeremiah Stamler

Your Heart Has Nine Lives (Prentice)
Eric Hodgins
Episode: Report on the Accident inside My Skull (Atheneum)
1965
Francis D. Moore
Give and Take: The Development of Tissue Transplantation (Doubleday)
1969
Cameron Hawley
The Hurricane Years (Little)

1975
JoAnn Stichman and Jane Schoenberg
How to Survive Your Husband's Heart Attack (McKay)
1977
William A. Nolen
Surgeon under the Knife (Coward)

Brandeis University Creative Arts Awards

In 1956, the Brandeis University Creative Arts Awards Commission was established as an expression of the university's conviction that educational institutions should play an important role in the encouragement and development of the artistic and cultural life of America.

Medals and citations are presented annually in four major fields—Fine Arts, Literature, Music and Dance, and Theater Arts and Film—by professional juries selected by the Creative Arts Awards Commission. Applications are not accepted for these awards. Medals are awarded to established artists in recognition of a lifetime of distinguished achievement, and citations are conferred on particularly talented artists actively engaged in mid-career. Since 1964, the Creative Arts Awards Commission has presented a special award for Notable Achievement in Creative Arts. A $1,000 honorarium accompanies each award. The offices of the Creative Arts Awards Commission are at 12 East 77 Street, New York, New York 10021. The award winners in the Literature and Theater Arts and Film categories are listed below.

POETRY-FICTION-NONFICTION

1957
William Carlos Williams, medal
Katherine Hoskins, citation
1958
John Crowe Ransom, medal
Barbara Howes, citation
1959
"H. D." [Hilda Doolittle], medal
Hayden Carruth, citation
1960
Yvor Winters, medal
John Berryman, citation

1961
Allen Tate, medal
Louis O. Coxe, citation
1962
Louise Bogan, medal
Ben Belitt, citation
1963
Marianne Moore, medal
Howard Nemerov, citation
1964
Vladimir Nabokov, medal
Richard Yates, citation
1965
Stanley Kunitz, medal
Anthony Hecht, citation

POETRY-FICTION-NONFICTION (cont.)

1966
Eudora Welty, medal
John Barth, citation
1967
Conrad Aiken, medal
May Swenson, citation
1968
Lionel Trilling, medal
Elizabeth M. Thomas, citation
1969
Léonie Adams, medal
Galway Kinnel, citation
1970
Isaac Bashevis Singer, medal
Robert Coover, citation
1971
Richard Wilbur, medal
James Wright, citation
1972
Katherine Anne Porter, medal
Edward Hoagland, citation
1973
Alfred Kazin, medal
Theodore Solotaroff, citation
1974
Robert Francis, medal
John Frederick Nims, citation
1975
Christopher Isherwood, medal
Harold Brodkey, citation
1976
Irving Howe, medal
Susan Sontag, citation
1977
Robert Lowell, medal
Theodore Weiss, citation
1978
Saul Bellow, medal
Grace Paley, citation
1979
Jeremy Bernstein, medal
Peter Matthiessen, citation

THEATER AND FILM

1957
Hallie Flanagan Davis, medal
The Shakespearewrights, citation
1958
Stark Young, medal
Paul Shyre, citation
1959
George Kelly, medal
Richard Hayes, citation
1960
Thornton Wilder, medal
William Alfred, citation
1961
Lillian Hellman, medal
Julian Beck and Judith Malina, citation
1962
Samuel N. Behrman, medal
James P. Donleavy, citation
1963
Jo Mielziner, medal
Joseph Papp, citation
1964
Cheryl Crawford, medal
Jack Richardson, citation
1965
Tennessee Williams, medal
Michael Smith, citation
1966
Eva LeGallienne, medal
Alvin Epstein, citation
1967
Jerome Robbins, medal
Ellen Stewart, citation
1968
Richard Rodgers, medal
Tom O'Horgan, citation
1969
Boris Aronson, medal
The Negro Ensemble Company, citation
1970
Arthur Miller, medal
The Open Theater, citation

THEATER AND FILM (cont.)

1971
Charles Chaplin, medal
Bruce Baillie, citation
1972
Alfred Lunt and Lynn Fontanne, medal
The New Dramatists, citation
1973
John Ford, medal
Stan Brakhage, citation
1974
Helen Hayes, medal
Arena Stage, citation
1975
King Vidor, medal
Jordan Belson, citation
1976
Harold Clurman, medal
Sam Shepard, citation
1977
Howard Hawks, medal
John Hancock, citation
1978
Jessica Tandy and Hume Cronyn, medal
Long Wharf Theatre, citation
1979
George Cukor, medal
Bruce Conner, citation

NOTABLE ACHIEVEMENT IN CREATIVE ARTS

1964
R. Buckminster Fuller

1965
Alfred H. Barr, Jr.
1966
Meyer Schapiro
1967
Kenneth Burke
1968
Martha Graham
1969
Lewis Mumford
1970
Lloyd Goodrich
1971
George Balanchine
1972
I. A. Richards
1973
Leonard Bernstein
1974
No award
1975
Aaron Copland
1976
Isaac Stern
1977
Alfred A. Knopf
1978
No award
1979
Edwin Denby

Bread Loaf Writers' Conference Endowment Fund

The Bread Loaf Writers' Conference Endowment Fund, established by friends of Bread Loaf, makes possible the award of fellowships and scholarship assistance.

These awards are either provided by the Fund or supported from year to year. Further inquiries about the following awards should be directed to the Bread Loaf Writers' Conference, Middlebury College, Middlebury, Vermont 05753.

John Atherton Awards

These fellowships and scholarships are awarded annually in memory of John Atherton, artist and writer. They have been endowed by Maxine B. Wyckoff.

FELLOWS

1966
   F. M. Esfandiary
1967
   Stephen Walton
1968
   Harry Crews
   Roy Friedman
1969
   Rodger Kingston
   Charles Newman
   Dan Potter
1970
   Bennett Kremen
   Glenn A. Meeter
   Hilma Wolitzer
1971
   Barry Hannah
   Elaine Kraf
1972
   Julie Goldsmith Gilbert
1973
   Christopher Brookhouse
   Calvin Forbes
1974
   David Black
   Judith Minty
   Linda Pastan
1975
   Dave Smith
1976
   Carol Muske
1977
   Joe DiPrisco
   Ellen Voigt

1978
   James Applewhite
1979
   Sydney Lea

SCHOLARS

1975
   Jack Porter
   Muriel Spanier
   Connie Stapleton

1976
   Alice Hoffman
   David Milofsky

1977
   Margaret Edwards
   Dannye Romine

1978
   Anthony Abbott
   Jane Butler
   Joan Johnson
   John Morgan
   Candice Ward

1979
   Linsey Abrams
   Julia Alvarez
   Lynn Emanuel
   Robert Hedin

Margaret T. Bridgman Awards

These awards are two fellowships—or scholarship assistance—given to writers of prose or poetry from a special fund endowed as a memorial by John M. Bridgman and the friends of Margaret T. Bridgman.

FELLOWS

1976
David St. John
1977
Alicia Ostriker
1978
Gail Mazur
1979
Carol Frost

SCHOLARS

1975
Tess Gallagher

Marianne Gingher
Judy Moyer
1976
James Atlas
Edward Mooney
1977
Jane Smiley
Dona Stein
1978
Arlene Biggs
Emily Lambert
1979
Meg Dodds
Marilyn Coffey

Jane Tinkham Broughton Fellowship in Writing for Children

This fellowship has been given by William Broughton as a memorial to his mother.

1975
Nancy Winslow Parker
1976
Leon Shtainmets
1977
Marilynne Roach

1978
Charlotte Koplinka
1979
Carolyn Polese

Alan Collins Fellowship in Prose

This fellowship was established by Catherine Collins in memory of her husband, Alan Collins, who was for many years a Conference staff member.

1969
Alan Weiss
1970
Bernard Kaplan
1971
William Crawford Woods

1972
David Freeman
1973
Francine Prose
1974
Ira Sadoff

1975
  Kelly Cherry
1976
  Susan Shreve
1977
  Ronni Sandroff

1978
  Craig Nova
1979
  Robert Houston

Bernard De Voto Fellowship in Prose

This fellowship is provided in alternate years by the Houghton Mifflin Company in memory of the late Bernard De Voto, a longtime member of the Conference staff.

1956
  Wilbur Cross III
1957
  Dan Wakefield
1958
  Vii Putnam
1959
  No award
1960
  Martin Dibner
1961
  Milton White
1962
  Robert Hutchinson
1963
  Alan Levy
1964
  Mary Bacon Durant
1965
  Kristin Hunter
1966
  Jay Neugeboren
1967
  Arona McHugh

1968
  Robert E. Mueller
1969
  Nora Levin
1970
  Elizabeth Scott
1971
  Charles Flowers
1972
  Donald St. George Reeves
1973
  Andrew Goldstein
1974
  Thomas Patrick Nugent
1975
  Bryan Wooley
1976
  Donald Bredes
1977
  Donald Chankin
1978
  Meredith Sue Willis
1979
  David Milofsky

Robert Frost Fellowship in Poetry *see* Poetry Prizes

Mary Louise Kennedy–*Weekly Reader* Children's Book Club Fellowship in Writing for Children

This fellowship has been fully endowed by the *Weekly Reader* Children's Book Club and Wesleyan University.

1975
  Doris B. Smith
1976
  Sue Ellen Bridgers
1977
  Blanche Willoughby

1978
  Gregory Maguire
1979
  John Barrett
  Mally Cox-Chapman

National Arts Club Scholarships

These scholarships in prose or poetry have been provided by the National Arts Club to students from colleges or universities in the New York City area. (The National Arts Club also supports the Tennessee Williams Fellowship, q.v.)

1975
  Askold Melnyczuk
  Susan Mitchell
  Mary Morris

1976
  Wendy Lamb
  Pam Lambert
  Kevin Lowry
  Jill Ryan

1977
  Joseph G. Glover
  Richard Grayson
  Tom Nevins
1978
  Robert Bedick
  Joseph Donohue
  Amber Spence
1979
  Diane Stevenson

Fletcher Pratt Fellowship in Prose

This fellowship was first awarded in 1957 and is endowed with funds given by friends of the late Fletcher Pratt in memory of his long service at Bread Loaf.

1957
  Jane Mayhall
1958
  Bernard Asbell
1959
  George Lea
1960
  Anthony Robinson
1961
  Frank Hercules
1962
  George Cuomo
1963
  Edward P. Stafford
1964
  Romulus Linney

1965
  Ralph Lee Smith
1966
  Marvin Schiller
1967
  William V. Caldwell
1968
  Roger Hall
1969
  No award
1970
  James Lee Burke
1971
  Michael Stephens
1972
  William Amidon

1973
Alan Goldfein
1974
Maureen Mylander
1975
Tim O'Brien
1976
Richard Ford

1977
Gail Kessler
1978
Allen Weir
1979
Harry Heinemann

William Raney Award in Prose

First given in 1967, this award, one fellowship or two scholarships, commemorates William Raney's devotion to Bread Loaf. It is made possible by contributions of his friends and colleagues.

FELLOWS

1967
Gerald C. Zeigerman
1968
Paul Tyner
1969
Jonathan Strong
1970
Michael Mewshaw
1971
Eleanor Glaze
1972
David Madden
1973
Scott Spencer
1974
Robert Seigel

1975
Tom Gavin
1977
David Huddle

SCHOLARS

1976
Priscilla Price
Margaret Robinson
1978
Philip Cioffari
Anneliese Schultz
1979
Alan Hines
Joann Kobin

William Sloane Fellowship in Prose

This fellowship is a memorial to William Sloane, who served the Bread Loaf Conference as a staff member for 27 years. It is supported by a fund in the Conference endowment.

1976
Terrence Des Pres

1977
George R. R. Martin

1978
Don Hendrie
1979
Sara Ann Friedman
Sanford Smoller

Shane Stevens Fellowship in Fiction

This fellowship, endowed by Shane Stevens, is awarded to a writer of fiction who has had a first book published within the preceding year.

1978
  Ellen Schwamm

1979
  Mary Robinson

Shane Stevens Fellowship in the Novel

This fellowship, endowed by Shane Stevens, is awarded to a writer who has published a first novel within the preceding year.

1979
  Ron Hansen

Time, Inc., Awards

These awards—fellowships and scholarship assistance—are endowed by Time, Inc.

FELLOWS

1978
  Dorothy Gallagher
1979
  Michael Angelella
  Ron Powers

Scott Edelstein
Douglas Pike
Todd Strasser

1979
  Mary Ellen Donovan
  Karen Petrovich
  Nancy Rubin

SCHOLARS

1978
  Mary Beth Brown

Transatlantic Review Awards

These awards to writers of prose or poetry have been made possible by the Henfield Foundation.

FELLOWS

1975
  Stephen Dunn

1976
  Gregory Orr

FELLOWS (cont.)

1977
  Laura Gilpin
1978
  Steve Orlen
1979
  Christopher Bursk

SCHOLARS

1978
  Carol Henrickson
  Robert Louthan
1979
  Bernard Meredith

Tennessee Williams Fellowship

This fellowship in prose or poetry is supported by the National Arts Club.

1976
  Carolyn Forché

1977
  Raymond Sokolov

1978
  Judith Moffett
1979
  Donald E. Axinn
  Carole Oles

Bross Foundation Decennial Prize

This cash prize is offered for the book or manuscript by any author that best relates the humanities, social sciences, biological sciences, or any other branch of knowledge to the Christian religion. The Bross Foundation was planned by William Bross, leading Chicago churchman and onetime lieutenant governor of Illinois, in memory of the death of an infant son. It was established in 1879 to become effective upon the donor's death. The amount of the award depends upon the accumulation of simple interest on the principal sum of the original gift. It is currently $20,000. The prize is administered by the trustees of Lake Forest College, North Hall, Lake Forest, Illinois 60045. The winner is selected by an advisory group of scholars chosen by the college. Official presentation of the prize is made every ten years at Lake Forest College, the next to be awarded in 1980.

1880
  Mark Hopkins
  "The Evidence of Christianity"

1903
  Marcus Dodds
  "The Bible, Its Origins and Nature"

1906
  James Orr
  The Problem of the Old Testament (Scribner)

1907
  J. Arthur Thomson
  The Bible of Nature (Scribner)
1908
  Frederick Bliss
  "Religions of Modern Syria and Palestine"
1911
  Josiah Royce
  The Sources of Religious Insight (Scribner)

1915
Thomas J. Thoburn
"The Mystical Interpretation of the Gospels"

1916
Henry Wilkes Wright
Faith Justified by Progress (Scribner)

1920
Christianity and Problems of Today (Scribner)

1921
John P. Peters
Bible and Spade (Scribner)

1923
Moses Bross Thomas
The Biblical Idea of God (Scribner)

1925
Douglas Clyde McIntosh
The Reasonableness of Christianity (Scribner)

1929
James G. K. McClure
The Supreme Book of Mankind: The Origin and Influence of the English Bible (Scribner)

1940
Harris Franklin Rall
Christianity: An Inquiry into Its Nature and Truth (Scribner)

1950
Amos N. Wilder
Modern Poetry and the Christian Traditions (Scribner)

1960
John A. Hutchison
Language and Faith: An Essay in Sign, Symbol and Meaning (Westminster)

1967
Kenneth A. Cragg
"The Event of the Qur'an"

Michael Novak
The Experience of Nothingness (Harper)

Charles C. West
The Power to Be Human: Toward a Secular Theology (Macmillan)

1970
Claude Welch
Protestant Thought in the Nineteenth Century, Vol. 1, 1799–1870 (Yale Univ. Press)

Brotherhood Awards

Annually since 1954 the National Conference of Christians and Jews, 43 West 57 Street, New York, New York 10019, has given an award in fourteen categories of the mass media including books (both fiction and nonfiction), newspapers, and magazines (editorials, articles, and fiction). Under the terms of the award, the winning entry must contribute to increased enlightenment, understanding, and respect for religious, racial, and nationality differences and the strengthening of a free and democratic society, based on the fundamental moral and ethical principles of all great religions. The awards consist of gold medallions encased in Lucite, with Certificates of Recognition for runners-up. Anyone is eligible and may submit his or her own or another individual's material. In 1969, new categories for fiction and nonfiction books for children were created, but they are not awarded annually. Listed below are the winners in the categories of fiction and nonfiction books.

FICTION

1955
Lillian Smith
The Journey (World)
1956
Jo Sinclair
The Changelings (McGraw)
1957
Sikes Johnson
The Hope of Refuge (Little)
Edwin O'Connor
The Last Hurrah (Little)
1958
Bernard Malamud
The Assistant (Farrar)
1959
No award
1960
Morris L. West
The Devil's Advocate (Morrow)
1961
Harper Lee
To Kill a Mockingbird (Lippincott)
Keith Wheeler
Peaceable Lane (Simon & Schuster)
1962
Alan Paton
Tales from a Troubled Land (Scribner)
Patrick White
Riders in the Chariot (Viking)
1963–1967
No awards
1968
Elliott Arnold
A Night of Watching (Scribner)
1969–1979
No awards

FICTION (CHILDREN AND YOUTH)

1969
Kristin Hunter
The Soul Brothers and Sister Lou (Scribner)
1970–1979
No awards

NONFICTION

1955
Pearl S. Buck
My Several Worlds (John Day)
Oscar Handlin
The American People in the 20th Century (Harvard Univ. Press)
Oden Meeker
Report on Africa (Scribner)
1956
Kenneth Seeman Giniger
The Compact Treasury of Inspiration (Hawthorn)
Edwin N. Griswold
The Fifth Amendment Today (Harvard Univ. Press)
John Lord O'Brian
National Security and Individual Freedom (Harvard Univ. Press)
Boyd C. Shafer
Nationalism: Myth and Reality (Harcourt)
Lillian Smith
Now Is the Time (Viking)
Walter White
How Far the Promised Land? (Viking)
1957
Marian Anderson
My Lord, What a Morning (Viking)

NONFICTION (cont.)

David Daiches
Two Worlds (Harcourt)

Will Herberg
Protestant, Catholic, Jew (Double-day)

Kathryn Hulme
The Nun's Story (Little)

Samuel J. Konefsky
The Legacy of Holmes and Brandeis (Macmillan)

Barbara Miller Solomon
Ancestors and Immigrants (Harvard Univ. Press)

Adele Wiseman
The Sacrifice (Viking)

1958
Jessie Bennett Sams
White Mother (McGraw)

1959
James McBride Dabbs
The Southern Heritage (Knopf)

1960
Kyle Haselden
The Racial Problem in Christian Perspective (Harper)

Martin E. Marty
The New Shape of American Religion (Harper)

1961
Robert McAfee Brown and Gustave Weigel
An American Dialogue (Doubleday)

Jacob Javits
Discrimination—U.S.A. (Harcourt)

Marguerite Rush Lerner
Red Man, White Man, African Chief (Medical Books for Children)

1962
James Baldwin
Nobody Knows My Name (Dial)

Oscar Lewis
Children of Sanchez (Random)

1963
Paul G. Kauper
Civil Liberties and the Constitution (Univ. of Michigan Press)

Alfred J. Marrow
Changing Patterns of Prejudice (Chilton)

1964
Mathew Ahmann, ed.
Race: Challenge to Religion (Regnery)

Bernhard E. Olson
Faith and Prejudice (Yale Univ. Press)

1965
Milton M. Gordon
Assimilation in American Life (Oxford Univ. Press)

Charles E. Silberman
Crisis in Black and White (Random)

1966
Edward H. Flannery
The Anguish of the Jews (Macmillan)

Philip A. Johnson
Call Me Neighbor, Call Me Friend (Doubleday)

1967
Steve Allen
The Ground Is Our Table (Doubleday)

David Brion Davis
The Problem of Slavery in Western Culture (Cornell Univ. Press)

Roland de Corneille
Christians and Jews: The Tragic Past and the Hopeful Future (Harper)

Martin Luther King, Jr.
Where Do We Go from Here? (Harper)

1968
Mrs. Medgar Evers (with William Peters)
For Us, the Living (Doubleday)

William L. Katz
Eyewitness: The Negro in American History (Pitman)

NONFICTION (cont.)

Arthur D. Morse
While Six Million Died (Random)
1969
Arthur Gilbert
The Vatican Council and the Jews
(World)
Stuart Levine and Nancy O. Lurie, eds.
The American Indian Today (Everett Edwards)
Anne Moody
Coming of Age in Mississippi (Dial)
Leon H. Sullivan
Build Brother Build (Macrae Smith)
1970-1977
No awards
1978
Robert F. Drinan

Honor the Promise: America's Commitment to Israel (Doubleday)
Dr. and Mrs. Thomas P. Melady
Idi Amin Dada: Hitler in Africa (Andrews & McMeel)
1979
Samuel Sandmel
Anti-Semitism in the New Testament? (Fortress)

NONFICTION
(CHILDREN AND YOUTH)

1970
Bradford Chambers, ed.
Chronicles of Negro Protest (Parents' Magazine)
1971-1979
No awards

John Burroughs Medal

Offered by the John Burroughs Memorial Association, Inc., American Museum of Natural History, 79 Street at Central Park West, New York, New York 10024, the first bronze medal was given in 1926. It is awarded annually for "a foremost literary work in the field so eminently occupied during his lifetime by John Burroughs," who called himself a "literary naturalist." Books of nature, eligible for consideration, should combine literary quality with accuracy of statement, should be based on originality of observations and conclusions of the author, and should be written somewhat in the style of John Burroughs's writings. The selection is made by a jury of five. Announcement of the award is made in April at the annual meeting of the Association, if a suitable book has been published within six years preceding presentation of the award. The entire works of an author are taken into consideration when determining the recipient of the award.

1926
William Beebe
For his entire work
1927
Ernest Thompson Seton
Lives of Game Animals (Scribner)
1928
John Russel McCarthy
Nature poems

1929
Frank M. Chapman
Handbook of Birds (Appleton)
1930
Archibald Rutledge
Peace in the Heart (Doubleday)
1931
No award

1932
   Frederick S. Dellenbaugh
   A Canyon Voyage (Putnam)
1933
   Oliver P. Medsgar
   For a series of books on spring, summer, autumn, winter (Wayne)
1934
   W. W. Christman
   Wild Pasture Pine (Argus)
1935
   No award
1936
   Charles Crawford Ghorst
   For recorded bird songs
1937
   No award
1938
   Robert Cushman Murphy
   Oceanic Birds of South America (Macmillan)
1939
   T. Gilbert Pearson
   Adventures in Bird Protection (Appleton)
1940
   Arthur Cleveland Bent
   For series of Life Histories of North American Birds (Smithsonian Institution)
1941
   Louis J. Halle, Jr.
   Birds against Men (Sloane)
1942
   Edward Armstrong
   Birds of the Grey Wind (Oxford Univ. Press)
1943
   Edwin Way Teale
   New Horizons (Dodd)
1944
   No award
1945
   Rutherford Platt
   This Green World (Dodd)
1946
   Francis Lee and Florence P. Jacques
   Snowshoe Country (Univ. of Minnesota Press)
1947
   No award
1948
   Theodora Stanwell-Fletcher
   Driftwood Valley (Little)
1949
   Allan D. Cruickshank and Helen G. Cruickshank
   Flight into Sunshine (Macmillan)
1950
   Roger Tory Peterson
   Birds over America (Dodd)
1951
   No award
1952
   Rachel L. Carson
   The Sea around Us (Oxford Univ. Press)
1953
   Gilbert Klingel
   The Bay (Dodd)
1954
   Joseph Wood Krutch
   The Desert Year (Bobbs)
1955
   Wallace Byron Grange
   Those of the Forest (Devin-Adair)
1956
   Guy Murchie
   Song of the Sky (Houghton)
1957
   Archie Carr
   Windward Road (Knopf)
1958
   Robert Porter Allen
   On the Trail of Vanishing Birds (McGraw)
1959
   No award
1960
   John Kieran
   A Natural History of New York City (Houghton)

1961
Loren C. Eiseley
The Firmament of Time (Random)

1962
George Miksch Sutton
Iceland Summer (Univ. of Oklahoma Press)

1963
Adolph Murie
A Naturalist in Alaska (Devin-Adair)

1964
John Hay
The Great Beach (Doubleday)

1965
Paul Brooks
Roadless Area (Knopf)

1966
Louis Darling
The Gull's Way (Morrow)

1967
Charlton Ogburn, Jr.
The Winter Beach (Morrow)

1968
Hal Borland
Hill Country Harvest (Lippincott)

1969
Louise deKiriline Lawrence
The Lovely and the Wild (McGraw)

1970
Victor V. Scheffer
The Year of the Whale (Scribner)

1971
John K. Terres
From Laurel Hill to Siler's Bog (Knopf)

1972
Robert Arbib
The Lord's Wood (Norton)

1973
Elizabeth Barlow
The Forests and Wetlands of New York City (Little)

1974
Sigurd F. Olson
Wilderness Days (Knopf)

1975
No award

1976
Ann Haymond Zwinger
Run, River, Run (Harper)

1977
Aldo Leopold
Sand County Almanac (Tamarack and Oxford Univ. Press)

1978
Ruth Kirk
Desert: The American Southwest (Houghton)

California Literature Medal Award

Offered by the Commonwealth Club of California, Monadnock Arcade, 681 Market Street, San Francisco, California 94105, the award was established in 1931 to encourage California authors in writing good literature. The rules require that an author must have been a registered voter in California at the date the manuscript was delivered to a publisher or that he or she must have lived within the boundaries of California for not less than approximately three-fourths of the three years preceding delivery of manuscript. Both fiction and nonfiction books on any subject are eligible for consideration, and entrants are not restricted to California themes. The annual awards consist of two gold medals and up to six silver medals. One gold medal is awarded for a work of fiction and the other for a work of nonfiction. Three silver medals are awarded to the next best entries, regardless of classification. There are also the optional awards of one special silver medal each for the best book of poetry, the best juvenile, the best first novel, and the best book dealing with California. A jury of seven makes the decisions, and the awards are usually presented in June in San Francisco.

1932
Herbert Eugene Bolton
Outpost of Empire (Knopf) Gold Medal

1933
Sara Bard Field
Barabbas (Boni) Gold Medal

1934
B. P. Kurtz
Pursuit of Death (Oxford Univ. Press) Gold Medal

1935
Ruth Eleanor McKee
The Lord's Anointed (Doubleday) General Literature Gold Medal

George D. Lyman
Saga of the Comstock Lode (Scribner) Scholarship and Research Gold Medal

1936
John Steinbeck
Tortilla Flat (Grosset) General Literature Gold Medal

Albert Léon Guérard
Literature and Society (Lothrop) Scholarship and Research Gold Medal

1937
John Steinbeck
In Dubious Battle (Viking) General Literature Gold Medal

Herbert Eugene Bolton
Rim of Christendom (Macmillan) Scholarship and Research Gold Medal

1938
Hans Otto Storm
Pity the Tyrant (Longmans) General Literature Gold Medal

E. T. Bell
Men of Mathematics (Simon & Schuster) Scholarship and Research Gold Medal

1939
George R. Stewart, Jr.
East of the Giants (Holt) General Literature Gold Medal

Herbert I. Priestley
France Overseas (Appleton) Scholarship and Research Gold Medal

1940
John Steinbeck
Grapes of Wrath (Viking) General Literature Gold Medal

Franklin Walker
San Francisco's Literary Frontier (Knopf) Scholarship and Research Gold Medal

Robin Lampson
Death Loses a Pair of Wings (Scribner) Poetry Silver Medal

Mary Virginia Provines
Bright Heritage (Longmans) Juvenile Silver Medal

1941
Stewart Edward White
Wild Geese Calling (Doubleday) General Literature Gold Medal

Carl Thurston
The Structure of Art (Univ. of Chicago Press) Scholarship and Research Gold Medal

Kenneth Rexroth
In What Hour (Macmillan) Poetry Silver Medal

Doris Gates
Blue Willow (Viking) Juvenile Silver Medal

1942
Joseph Henry Jackson
Anybody's Gold (Appleton) General Literature Gold Medal

Lesley Byrd Simpson
Many Mexicos (Putnam) Scholarship
and Research Gold Medal

1943

Oscar Lewis
I Remember Christine (Knopf) General Literature Gold Medal

James Westfall Thompson
History of Historical Writing (Macmillan) Scholarship and Research Gold Medal

H. L. Davis
Proud Riders (Harper) Poetry Silver Medal

Hildegarde Hawthorne
Long Adventure (Appleton) Juvenile Silver Medal

1944

Dorothy Baker
Trio (Houghton) General Literature Gold Medal

Frank Munk
The Legacy of Nazism (Macmillan) Scholarship and Research Gold Medal

Katherine Wigmore Eyre
Spurs for Antonia (Oxford Univ. Press) Juvenile Silver Medal

1945

Sally Carrighar
One Day on Beetle Rock (Knopf) General Literature Gold Medal

Thomas Bailey
Woodrow Wilson and the Lost Peace (Macmillan) Scholarship and Research Gold Medal

Kenneth Rexroth
Phoenix and the Tortoise (New Directions) Poetry Silver Medal

Howard Pease
Thunderbolt House (Doubleday) Juvenile Silver Medal

1946

Adria Locke Langley

A Lion Is in the Streets (McGraw)
General Literature Gold Medal

Laura L. Hinkley
Charlotte and Emily—The Brontës (Hastings House) Scholarship and Research Gold Medal

Margaret Leighton
The Singing Cave (Houghton) Juvenile Silver Medal

1947

Royce Brier
Western World (Doubleday) General Literature Gold Medal

John A. Crow
The Epic of Latin America (Doubleday) Scholarship and Research Gold Medal

E. H. Staffelbach
Towards Oregon (Macrae Smith) Juvenile Silver Medal

Edward Weismiller
The Faultless Shore (Houghton) Poetry Silver Medal

1948

Louis Booker Wright
The Atlantic Frontier (Knopf) Scholarship and Research Gold Medal

Janet Lewis
The Trial of Sören Qvist (Doubleday) General Literature Gold Medal

Allen R. Bosworth
Sancho of the Long, Long Horns (Doubleday) Juvenile Silver Medal

Hazel Zimmerman
Journey to Victory (Humphries) Poetry Silver Medal

1949

Dixon Wecter
Age of the Great Depression (Macmillan) Scholarship and Research Gold Medal

Hollister Noble
Woman with a Sword (Doubleday) General Literature Gold Medal

Holling C. Holling
Seabird (Houghton) Juvenile Silver Medal

1950

William Irvine
The Universe of G. B. S. (McGraw) Nonfiction Gold Medal

Robert Carver North
The Revolt in San Marcos (Houghton) Fiction Gold Medal

Helen Rand Parish
At the Palace Gates (Viking) Juvenile Silver Medal

Harry Brown
The Beast in His Hunger (Knopf) Poetry Silver Medal

1951

Vina Delmar
About Mrs. Leslie (Harcourt) Fiction Gold Medal

Henry H. Hart
Sea Road to the Indies (Macmillan) Nonfiction Gold Medal

Marion Garthwaite
Thomas and the Red Headed Angel (Messner) Juvenile Silver Medal

Phillips Kloss
Dominant Seventh (Caxton) Poetry Silver Medal

1952

William Saroyan
Tracy's Tiger (Doubleday) Fiction Gold Medal

Eric Hoffer
The True Believer (Harper) Nonfiction Gold Medal

Mildred N. Anderson
Sandra and the Right Prince (Oxford Univ. Press) Juvenile Silver Medal

Leon J. Richardson
Old Cronies (Feathered Serpent) Poetry Silver Medal

1953

H. L. Davis

Winds of Morning (Morrow) Fiction Gold Medal

Walton Bean
Boss Ruef's San Francisco (Univ. of California Press) Nonfiction Gold Medal

Rutherford G. Montgomery
Wapiti the Elk (Little) Juvenile Silver Medal

Stanton A. Coblentz
Time's Traveler (Wings) Poetry Silver Medal

1954

Ray Bradbury
Fahrenheit 451 (Ballantine) Fiction Gold Medal

Ruby B. Goodwin
It's Good to Be Black (Doubleday) Nonfiction Gold Medal

Bill Brown
Roaring River (Coward) Juvenile Silver Medal

1955

Louise A. Stinetorf
Beyond the Hungry Country (Lippincott) Fiction Gold Medal

Everett Carter
Howells and the Age of Realism (Lippincott) Nonfiction Gold Medal

Leonard Wibberley
Epics of Everest (Farrar) Juvenile Silver Medal

1956

C. S. Forester
The Good Shepherd (Little) Fiction Gold Medal

Alan Temko
Notre-Dame of Paris (Viking) Nonfiction Gold Medal

Frederick A. Lane
Westward the Eagle (Holt) Juvenile Silver Medal

Delina Margot-Parle
Symphony (Humphries) Poetry Silver Medal

1957

Elizabeth Linington
The Long Watch (Viking) Fiction Gold Medal

Kathryn Hulme
The Nun's Story (Little) Nonfiction Gold Medal

Harlan Thompson
Spook the Mustang (Doubleday) Juvenile Silver Medal

1958

C. Y. Lee
The Flower Drum Song (Farrar) Fiction Gold Medal

Lu Emily Pearson
Elizabethans at Home (Stanford Univ. Press) Nonfiction Gold Medal

Nicholas E. Wyckoff
The Braintree Mission (Macmillan) Silver Medal

William Rawle Weeks
Knock and Wait a While (Houghton) Silver Medal

Phyllis Gordon Demarest
Wilderness Brigade (Doubleday) Silver Medal

Edward Ormondroyd
David and the Phoenix (Follett) Juvenile Silver Medal

1959

J. Christopher Herold
Mistress to an Age (Bobbs) Nonfiction Gold Medal

Dennis Murphy
The Sergeant (Viking) Fiction Gold Medal

David Lavender
Land of Giants (Doubleday) Silver Medal

Fred Blackburn Rogers
Montgomery and the Portsmouth

(Howell-North) Californiana Silver Medal

Ann Stanford
Magellan (Talisman) Poetry Silver Medal

George E. Mowry
The Era of Theodore Roosevelt (Harper) Silver Medal

Oakley Hall
Warlock (Viking) Silver Medal

Edward A. Herron
First Scientist of Alaska: William Healy Dall (Messner) Juvenile Silver Medal

1960

Eugene Vale
The Thirteenth Apostle (Scribner) Fiction Gold Medal

John C. Miller
Alexander Hamilton, Portrait in Paradox (Harper) Nonfiction Gold Medal

Henry F. May
The End of American Innocence (Knopf) Unclassified Silver Medal

Elliott Arnold
The Flight from Ashiya (Knopf) Unclassified Silver Medal

Fawn M. Brodie
Thaddeus Stevens, Scourge of the South (Norton) Unclassified Silver Medal

William Bronson
The Earth Shook, the Sky Burned (Doubleday) Californiana Silver Medal

Philip H. Ault
This is the Desert (Dodd) Juvenile Silver Medal

1961

Allan Nevins
The War for the Union, 2 vols. (Scribner) Nonfiction Gold Medal

George Dangerfield
Chancellor Robert R. Livingston of New York 1746–1813 (Harcourt) Unclassified Silver Medal

Chloe Gartner
The Infidels (Doubleday) Unclassified
Silver Medal

Helen Bauer
Hawaii, the Aloha State (Doubleday)
Juvenile Silver Medal

1962

Irving Stone
The Agony and the Ecstasy (Doubleday) Fiction Gold Medal

Leon Uris
Mila 18 (Doubleday) Unclassified Silver Medal

Dale Van Every
Forth to the Wilderness (Morrow) Unclassified Silver Medal

Theodora Kroeber
Ishi in Two Worlds: A Biography of the Last Wild Indian in North America (Univ. of California Press) Californiana Silver Medal

Eric Barker
A Ring of Willows (New Directions) Poetry Silver Medal

Gordon D. Shirreffs
The Gray Sea Raiders (Chilton) Juvenile Silver Medal

1963

Jonreed Lauritzen
The Everlasting Fire (Doubleday) Fiction Gold Medal

Page Smith
John Adams (Doubleday) Nonfiction Gold Medal

Heinz Politzer
Franz Kafka: Parable and Paradox (Cornell Univ. Press) Unclassified Silver Medal

Robert E. Stewart and Mary Stewart
Adolph Sutro (Howell-North) Unclassified Silver Medal

John Upton Terrell
Journey into Darkness (Morrow) Unclassified Silver Medal

Chet Schwarzkopf
Heart of the Wild (Doubleday) Californiana Silver Medal

Iris Noble
First Woman Ambulance Surgeon: Emily Barringer (Messner) Juvenile Silver Medal

1964

Geddes MacGregor
The Hemlock and the Cross (Lippincott) Nonfiction Gold Medal

Virginia Lee
The House That Tai Ming Built (Macmillan) Fiction Gold Medal

Arnold T. Schwab
James Gibbons Huneker (Stanford Univ. Press) Unclassified Silver Medal

Leonard Wibberley
Ah, Julian! (Washburn) Unclassified Silver Medal

Nicholas Riasanovsky
A History of Russia (Oxford Univ. Press) Unclassified Silver Medal

Frank M. Stanger
South from San Francisco (San Mateo County Historical Association) Californiana Silver Medal

Maryhale Woolsey
The Keys and the Candle (Abingdon) Juvenile Silver Medal

1965

Leon Uris
Armageddon (Doubleday) Fiction Gold Medal

Dale Van Every
The Final Challenge: The American Frontier, 1804–1845 (Morrow) Nonfiction Gold Medal

Wallace Stegner
A Gathering of Zion (McGraw) Unclassified Silver Medal

Irving Wallace
The Man (Simon & Schuster) Unclassified Silver Medal

C. D. O'Malley
Andreas Vesalius of Brussels (Univ. of California Press) Unclassified Silver Medal

Eleanor Cameron
A Spell Is Cast (Little) Juvenile Silver Medal

Julia Altrocchi
Girl with Ocelot and Other Poems (Humphries) Poetry Silver Medal

Robert Kroninger
Sarah and the Senator (Howell-North) Californiana Silver Medal

1966

Michael Blankfort
Behold the Fire (New American Library) Fiction Gold Medal

Richard Dillon
Meriwether Lewis (Coward) Nonfiction Gold Medal

John Beatty and Patricia Beatty
Campion Towers (Macmillan) Juvenile Silver Medal

1967

Herbert Wilner
All the Little Heroes (Bobbs) Fiction Gold Medal

Wilfred Stone
The Cave and the Mountain: A Study of E. M. Forster (Stanford Univ. Press) Nonfiction Gold Medal

Melba Berry Bennett
The Stone Mason of Tor House: The Life and Times of Robinson Jeffers (Ward Ritchie) Unclassified Silver Medal

Robert Allen Rutland
The Ordeal of the Constitution: The Antifederalists and the Ratification Struggle of 1787–1788 (Univ. of Oklahoma Press) Unclassified Silver Medal

Jack Kisling
The Crow Flies Crooked (McKay) Unclassified Silver Medal

Leonard Pitt
Decline of the Californios: A Social History of the Spanish-Speaking Californians, 1846–1890 (Univ. of California Press) Californiana Silver Medal

Albert Sidney Fleischman
Chancy and the Grand Rascal (Little) Juvenile Silver Medal

1968

Wallace Stegner
All the Little Live Things (Viking) Fiction Gold Medal

Margaret Sanborn
Robert E. Lee: The Complete Man (Lippincott) Nonfiction Gold Medal

Elliott Arnold
A Night of Watching (Scribner) Unclassified Silver Medal

Herbert Gold
Fathers (Random) Unclassified Silver Medal

Edward Ellis Smith
The Young Stalin (Farrar) Unclassified Silver Medal

Richard Dillon
Fools Gold: The Biography of John Sutter (Coward) Californiana Silver Medal

Robb White
Silent Ship, Silent Sea (Doubleday) Juvenile Silver Medal

Brother Antoninus [William Everson]
Rose of Solitude (Doubleday) Poetry Silver Medal

1969

Arthur Hailey
Airport (Doubleday) Fiction Gold Medal

William Weber Johnson
Heroic Mexico: The Violent Emergence of a Modern Nation (Doubleday) Nonfiction Gold Medal

Andrew F. Rolle
Immigrant Upraised: Italian Adventurers and Colonists in an Expanding

America (Univ. of Oklahoma Press) Unclassified Silver Medal

Geraldine Joncich
The Sane Positivist: A Biography of Edward L. Thorndike (Wesleyan Univ. Press) Unclassified Silver Medal

Ralph J. Roske
Everyman's Eden (Macmillan) Californiana Silver Medal

1970

Carl Landauer
Germany: Illusions and Dilemmas (Harcourt) Nonfiction Gold Medal

Audrie Girdner and Anne Loftis
The Great Betrayal (Macmillan) Silver Californiana Medal

Theodore Taylor
The Cay (Doubleday) Juvenile Silver Medal

Adrien Stoutenburg
A Short History of the Fur Trade (Houghton) Poetry Silver Medal

Eleanor Cameron
The Green and Burning Tree (Little) Unclassified Silver Medal

M. F. K. Fisher
With Bold Knife and Fork (Putnam) Unclassified Silver Medal

Irving S. Michelman
Business at Bay (Kelley) Unclassified Silver Medal

1971

Will Durant and Ariel Durant
Interpretations of Life (Simon & Schuster) Nonfiction Gold Medal

Ferol Egan
The El Dorado Trail (McGraw) Californiana Silver Medal

Clyde Robert Bulla
Jonah and the Great Fish (Crowell) Juvenile Silver Medal

Kay Boyle
Testament for My Students (Doubleday) Poetry Silver Medal

Stephen N. Hay
Asian Ideas of East and West (Harvard Univ. Press) Unclassified Silver Medal

Immanuel C. Y. Hsu
The Rise of Modern China (Oxford Univ. Press) Unclassified Silver Medal

Jessamyn West
Crimson Ramblers of the World, Farewell (Harcourt) Unclassified Silver Medal

1972

Ernest J. Gaines
The Autobiography of Miss Jane Pittman (Dial) Fiction Gold Medal

William Dickey
More under Saturn (Wesleyan Univ. Press) Poetry Silver Medal

Miska Miles
Annie and the Old One (Atlantic) Silver Juvenile Medal

Alexander Saxton
The Indispensable Enemy (Univ. of California Press) Californiana Silver Medal

William Peter Blatty
The Exorcist (Harper) Unclassified Silver Medal

Harold L. Kahn
Monarchy in the Emperor's Eyes (Harvard Univ. Press) Unclassified Silver Medal

Marion P. Ireland
Textile Art in the Church (Abingdon) Unclassified Silver Medal

1973

Clair Huffaker
The Cowboy and the Cossack (Trident) Fiction Gold Medal

Kevin Starr
Americans and the California Dream 1850–1915 (Oxford Univ. Press) Nonfiction Gold Medal

Edgar Bowers
Living Together (Godine) Poetry Silver Medal

Jay Monaghan
Chile, Peru and the California Gold Rush of 1849 (Univ. of California Press) Californiana Silver Medal

John Niven
Gideon Welles (Oxford Univ. Press) Unclassified Silver Medal

Judith Rascoe
Yours and Mine (Little) Unclassified Silver Medal

Celeste Turner Wright
A Sense of Place (Golden Quill) Unclassified Silver Medal

Steven Crouch
Steinbeck Country (American West) Unclassified Silver Medal

1974
Jacob Bronowski
The Ascent of Man (Little) Nonfiction Gold Medal

Ella Leffland
Love Out of Season (Atheneum) Fiction Gold Medal

Ray Raphael
An Everyday History of Somewhere (Knopf) Californiana Silver Medal

Don Freeman
The Paper Party (Viking) Juvenile Silver Medal

Leonard W. Levy
Against the Law (Harper) Unclassified Silver Medal

Vina Delmar
A Time for Titans (Harcourt) Unclassified Silver Medal

Evan S. Connell, Jr.
The Connoisseur (Knopf) Unclassified Silver Medal

1975
Michael Crichton

The Great Train Robbery (Knopf) Fiction Gold Medal

Brian Fagan
Rape of the Nile (Scribner) Nonfiction Gold Medal

David Lavender
Nothing Seemed Impossible (American West) Californiana Silver Medal

Leonard Nathan
Returning Your Call (Princeton Univ. Press) Poetry Silver Medal

Harold E. Thomas
Coyotes: Last Animals on Earth (Lothrop) Juvenile Silver Medal

Will Durant and Ariel Durant
The Age of Napoleon (Simon & Schuster) Unclassified Silver Medal

Peter Ward Fay
The Opium War (Univ. of North Carolina Press) Unclassified Silver Medal

Robert A. Rosenstone
Romantic Revolutionary (Knopf) Unclassified Silver Medal

1976
Page Smith
A New Age Now Begins (McGraw) Nonfiction Gold Medal

Wallace Stegner
The Spectator Bird (Doubleday) Fiction Gold Medal

Thom Gunn
Jack Straw's Castle (Farrar) Poetry Silver Medal

Karl Shapiro
Adult Bookstore (Random) Poetry Silver Medal

Nancy Huddleston Packer
Small Moments (Univ. of Illinois Press) Unclassified Silver Medal

Eugen Weber
Peasants into Frenchmen: The Modernization of Rural France, 1870–1914 (Stanford Univ. Press) Unclassified Silver Medal

1977

Ferol Egan
Fremont: Explorer for a Restless Nation (Doubleday) Nonfiction Gold Medal

Ingrid Rimland
The Wanderers (Concordia) First Novel Silver Medal

Louis Irigaray and Theodore Taylor
A Shepherd Watches, a Shepherd Sings (Doubleday) Juvenile Silver Medal

Ann Stanford
In Mediterranean Air (Doubleday) Poetry Silver Medal

Henry Evans
Botanical Prints (Freeman) Unclassified Silver Medal

Brooke Hayward
Haywire (Doubleday) Unclassified Silver Medal

1978

Gordon A. Craig
Germany, 1866–1945 (Oxford Univ. Press) Nonfiction Gold Medal

David Rains Wallace
The Dark Range (Sierra Books) Californiana Silver Medal

Elizabeth Forsythe Hailey
A Woman of Independent Means (Viking) First Novel Silver Medal

Sheila Moon
Songs for Wanderers (Golden Quill) Poetry Gold Medal

Dale Fife
North of Danger (Dutton) Juvenile Gold Medal

Charles W. Jones
Saint Nicholas of Myra, Bari, and Manhattan (Univ. of Chicago Press) Unclassified Silver Medal

A. Scott Berg
Max Perkins: Editor of Genius (Dutton) Unclassified Silver Medal

Campion Award

The Campion Award, established in 1955, is given for long and distinguished service in the cause of Christian letters. It recognizes an author's entire literary output rather than an individual volume. The actual award is an enamel plaque and scroll in honor of Blessed Edmund Campion, Catholic martyr under Elizabeth I of England. Any author, not necessarily Catholic, in the field of literature is eligible. The decision is made by a vote of the Editorial Board of the Catholic Book Club, 106 West 56 Street, New York, New York 10019.

1955
Jacques Maritain
1956
Helen Constance White
1957
Paul Horgan
1958
James Brodrick
1959
Sister Mary Madeleva

1960
Frank Sheed and Maisie Ward
1961
John LaFarge
1962
Harold C. Gardiner
1963
Thomas Stearns Eliot
1964
Barbara Ward

1965
  Msgr. John Tracy Ellis
1966
  John C. Murray
1967
  Phyllis McGinley
1968
  George N. Shuster
1969
  No award

1970
  G. B. Harrison
1971
  Walter Kerr and Jean Kerr
1972–1973
  No awards
1974
  Karl Rahner
1975–1978
  No awards

Chicago Book Clinic Award

The Chicago Book Clinic, 54 East Erie Street, Chicago, Illinois 60611, holds an annual exhibit of top honor books for the purpose of commending and encouraging excellent work in planning, supervision, and execution of the physical and visual aspects of books published, manufactured, or designed in the sixteen midwestern states: Arkansas, Illinois, Indiana, Iowa, Kansas, Kentucky, Michigan, Minnesota, Missouri, Nebraska, North Dakota, Ohio, Oklahoma, South Dakota, Tennessee, and Wisconsin. Honor books are selected, a catalog is printed, and the show tours libraries throughout the United States. The awards, certificates of excellence, are presented at the show opening on the first Tuesday in May in Chicago. The archive of approximately 800 books is housed at Loyola University Press.

Child Study Association of America/Wel-Met Family Life Book Award

The Family Life Book Award was given by the Child Study Association of America/Wel-Met, 853 Broadway, New York, New York 10003, for an outstanding contribution in the fields of family life and mental health education. The Association is now defunct; it has been absorbed by the Jewish Board of Family and Children's Services (JBFCS), 120 West 57 Street, New York, New York 10019. The Family Life Book Award has been discontinued, although the JBFCS may establish a new award in the future. The Child Study Association of America/Wel-Met also gave a Children's Book Award, which is now sponsored by the Child Study Children's Book Committee at Bank Street College.(see Juvenile Prizes).

1960
  Selma H. Fraiberg
  The Magic Years (Scribner)
1961
  Beatrice M. Wright

Physical Disability—A Psychological Approach (Harper)
1962
  Oscar Lewis
  The Children of Sanchez (Random)

1963
Benjamin Spock
Problems of Parents (Houghton)
1964
Erik H. Erikson
Youth: Change and Challenge (Basic Books)
Roma Gans
Common Sense in Teaching Reading: A Practical Guide (Bobbs)
1965
Martin L. Hoffman and Lois Waldis Hoffman, eds.
Review of Child Development Research (Russell Sage Foundation)
1966
Claude Brown
Manchild in the Promised Land (Macmillan)
1967
Robert Coles
Children of Crisis (Little)
Eleanor Pavenstedt, ed.
The Drifters (Little)
1968–1969
No awards
1970
American Friends Service Committee
Who Shall Live? Man's Control over Birth and Death (Hill & Wang)

T. Brazelton
Infants and Mothers: Differences in Development (Delacorte-Dell)
1971
Robert Coles
Erik H. Erikson (Atlantic)
1972–1973
No awards
1974
Stella Chess and Jane Whitbread
How to Help Your Child Get the Most out of School (Doubleday)
Anne Steinmann and David Fox
The Male Dilemma (Jason Aronson)
1975
No award
1976
Helene S. Arnstein
The Roots of Love (Bobbs)
James P. Comer and Alvin F. Poussaint
Black Child Care (Simon & Schuster)
1977
James Levine
Who Will Raise the Children? New Options for Fathers (and Mothers) (Lippincott)
Discontinued

Christopher Book Awards

The Christophers, 12 East 48 Street, New York, New York 10017, established the Christopher Awards in 1949. The annual Christopher book, film, and television awards are given to writers, producers, and directors whose works are representative of the best achievements in their fields. Works are judged on the bases of their affirmation of the highest values of the human spirit, artistic and technical proficiency, and a significant degree of public acceptance. Formerly, all books and short stories and articles from newspapers and magazines were eligible; now only books qualify. Entries may be submitted, but anything in print may be honored by the judges. In 1949 and 1950 the awards were monetary. Now they consist of a bronze medallion engraved with the Christopher motto, "Better to light one candle than to curse the darkness." The awards, discontinued in 1962, were reinstated in 1970 to mark the twenty-fifth anniversary of the Christophers. Listed below are the books that have received the Christopher Award. Although awards were sometimes offered for juvenile books between 1949 and 1961, juveniles are listed separately beginning in 1970.

1949
George Howe
Call It Treason (Viking)

Marie L. Nowinson
The Martels (Dutton)

Charles O'Neal
Three Wishes (Messner)

1950
Houston Harte, ed.
In Our Image (Oxford Univ. Press)

Betty Martin
Miracle at Carville (Doubleday)

Karl Stern
Pillar of Fire (Harcourt)

1951
Fulton Oursler
The Greatest Book Ever Written (Doubleday)

1952
Marie Killilea
Karen (Prentice)

Clare Boothe Luce
Saints for Now (Sheed)

H. F. M. Prescott
Man on a Donkey (Macmillan)

Rev. Mark Tennien
No Secret Is Safe (Farrar)

1953
April Oursler Armstrong
The Greatest Faith Ever Known (Doubleday)

R. C. V. Bodley
The Warrior Saint (Little)

Charles Lindbergh
Spirit of St. Louis (Scribner)

1954
Anne Fremantle
Treasury of Early Christianity (Viking)

Heinrich Harrer
Seven Years in Tibet (Dutton)

Lillian Roth, Mike Connolly, and Gerold Frank
I'll Cry Tomorrow (Fell)

George N. Shuster
Religion behind the Iron Curtain (Macmillan)

1955
Anne M. Lindbergh
Gift from the Sea (Pantheon)

Phyllis McGinley
The Love Letters of Phyllis McGinley (Viking)

Frances Gray Patton
Good Morning, Miss Dove (Dodd)

Carlos Romulo
Crusade in Asia (John Day)

John Schindler
How to Live 365 Days a Year (Prentice)

Marion Sheehan
The Spiritual Woman, Trustee of the Future (Harper)

Karl Stern
The Third Revolution (Harcourt)

Barbara Ward
Faith and Freedom (Norton)

1956
Ira Avery
The Five Fathers of Pepi (Bobbs)

Adele Comandini
Doctor Kate (Rinehart)

Ruth Cranston
The Miracle of Lourdes (McGraw)

Thomas Dooley
Deliver Us from Evil (Farrar)

Rumer Godden
An Episode of Sparrows (Viking)

John F. Kennedy
Profiles in Courage (Harper)

George Mardikian
Song of America (McGraw)

Budd Schulberg
Waterfront (Random)

Agnes Turnbull
Golden Journey (Houghton)

1957

Eric Wollencott Barnes
The Man Who Lived Twice (Scribner)

George N. Shuster
In Silence I Speak (Farrar)

Irving Stone
Men to Match My Mountains (Doubleday)

Edwin Teale
Autumn across America (Dodd)

Don Whitehead
The F.B.I. Story: A Report of the People (Random)

1958

J. Donald Adams
Triumph over Odds (Duell)

Charles Ferguson
Naked to Mine Enemies (Little)

Oscar Handlin
Al Smith and His America (Little)

J. Edgar Hoover
Masters of Deceit (Holt)

W. A. Swanberg
First Blood—The Story of Fort Sumter (Scribner)

1959

Leonard Bernstein
The Joy of Music (Simon & Schuster)

R. L. Bruckberger
Image of America (Viking)

Eugene Kinkead
In Every War but One (Norton)

Alfred Lansing
Endurance: Shackleton's Incredible Voyage (McGraw)

Barrett McGurn
Decade in Europe (Dutton)

Harold R. Medina
The Anatomy of Freedom (Holt)

Samuel Eliot Morison
John Paul Jones (Atlantic-Little)

Cornelius Ryan
The Longest Day—June 6, 1944 (Simon & Schuster)

Eugene Vale
The Thirteenth Apostle (Scribner)

Barbara Ward
Five Ideas That Change the World (Norton)

1960

James Patrick Derum
Apostle in a Top Hat (Hanover)

Thomas Dooley
My Story (Farrar)

Marie Killilea
Treasure on the Hill (Dodd)

John Courtney Murray
We Hold These Truths (Sheed)

G. B. Stern
Bernadette (Thomas Nelson)

1961

Bruce Catton
The Coming Fury (Doubleday)

Roland de Vaux
Ancient Israel (McGraw)

John Gardner
Excellence (Harper)

William Harbaugh
Power and Responsibility (Farrar)

Jacques Maritain
On the Use of Philosophy (Princeton Univ. Press)

Marion Mill Preminger
The Sands of Tamanrasset (Hawthorn)

M. L. Shrady
In the Spirit of Wonder (Pantheon)

1970

Jeannette Eyerly
Escape from Nowhere (Lippincott)

Thomas Fleming
The Man from Monticello (Morrow)
Rollo May
Love and Will (Norton)
Louis M. Savary
Listen to Love (Regina)
Gay Talese
The Kingdom and the Power (World)
Whitney Young
Beyond Racism (McGraw)

1971
Raymond E. Brown
The Gospel According to St. John (Doubleday)
René Dubos
Reason Awake (Columbia Univ. Press)
John W. Gardner
Recovery of Confidence (Norton)
Joanne Greenberg
In This Sign (Holt)
John Hemming
Conquest of the Inca (Harcourt)
Philip B. Kunhardt, Jr.
My Father's House (Random)
Peter Matthiessen
Sal Si Puedes—César Chávez and the New American Revolution (Random)
Charles E. Silberman
Crisis in the Classroom: The Remaking of American Education (Random)

1972
Anonymous
Go Ask Alice (Prentice)
Dee Brown
Bury My Heart at Wounded Knee: An Indian History of the American West (Holt)
Ernesto Cardenal
The Psalms of Struggle and Liberation (Herder)

Henry Clark
Ministries of Dialogue (Association Press)
Avery Dulles
The Survival of Dogma (Doubleday)
Elaine Goodman and Walter Goodman
The Rights of People: The Major Decisions of the Warren Court (Farrar)
Samuel Eliot Morison
The European Discovery of America: The Northern Voyages, A.D. 500–1600 (Oxford Univ. Press)
Malcolm Muggeridge
Something Beautiful for God (Harper)
Eudora Welty
One Time, One Place (Random)
Gordon C. Zahn, ed.
Thomas Merton on Peace (McCall)

1973
Dorothy Day
On Pilgrimage: The 60's (Curtis)
Frances FitzGerald
Fire in the Lake (Atlantic-Little)
Russell Kirk
Eliot and His Age (Random)
Trina Paulus
Hope for the Flowers (Paulist-Newman)
Peter Reddaway
Uncensored Russia (American Heritage-McGraw)
Dennis Smith
Report from Engine Co. 82 (Saturday Review)
William Edgett Smith
We Must Run While They Walk: A Portrait of Africa's Julius Nyerere (Random)
Ernest van den Haag
Political Violence and Civil Disobedience (Harper)
Barbara Ward and René Dubos
Only One Earth (Norton)

Richard Wheeler
Voices of 1776 (Crowell)

1974

Erma Brenner
A New Baby! A New Life (McGraw)

Hope Chamberlin
A Minority of Members: Women in the U.S. Congress (Praeger)

Sharon R. Curtin
Nobody Ever Died of Old Age (Atlantic-Little)

Allen F. Davis
American Heroine: The Life and Legend of Jane Addams (Oxford Univ. Press)

Barbara Howes, ed.
The Eye of the Heart: 42 Great Short Stories by Latin American Writers (Bobbs)

Kenneth Koch
Rose, Where Did You Get That Red? (Random)

A. W. Reed
Myths and Legends of Australia (Taplinger)

Dougal Robertson
Survive the Savage Sea (Praeger)

Ronald B. Taylor
Sweatshops in the Sun: Child Labor on the Farm (Beacon)

1975

Lester R. Brown and Erik P. Eckholm
By Bread Alone (Praeger)

Lynn Caine
Widow (Morrow)

John R. Coleman
Blue-Collar Journal: A College President's Sabbatical (Lippincott)

Adele Faber and Elaine Mazlish
Liberated Parents/Liberated Children (Grosset)

James Thomas Flexner
Washington, the Indispensable Man (Little)

Lawrence LeShan
How to Meditate: A Guide to Self-Discovery (Little)

Charles H. Percy
Growing Old in the Country of the Young (McGraw)

Theodore Rosengarten
All God's Dangers: The Life of Nate Shaw (Knopf)

Jonathan D. Spence
Emperor of China (Knopf)

Hiltgunt Zassenhaus
Walls: Resisting the Third Reich— One Woman's Story (Beacon)

1976

Maggie Cavagnaro and David Cavagnaro
Almost Home (American West)

Loren Eiseley
All the Strange Hours (Scribner)

Frank Gibney
Japan: The Fragile Superpower (Norton)

Dagfinn Gronoset
Anna, trans. by Ingrid B. Josephson (Knopf)

Paul Horgan
Lamy of Santa Fé (Farrar)

Phillip Lopate
Being with Children (Doubleday)

Robert Massie and Suzanne Massie
Journey (Knopf)

Robin Prising
Manila, Goodbye (Houghton)

Edward Weisband and Thomas M. Franck
Resignation in Protest (Grossman/Viking)

Tom Wicker
A Time to Die (Quadrangle)

David R. Zimmerman
To Save a Bird in Peril (Coward)

1977
Joseph John Deacon
Joey (Scribner)
Alex Haley
Roots (Doubleday)
Irving Howe
World of Our Fathers (Harcourt)
Yousuf Karsh
Karsh Portraits (New York Graphic Society)
George Kirkham
Signal Zero (Lippincott)
Ron Kovic
Born on the Fourth of July (McGraw)
Glenn T. Miller
Religious Liberty in America (Westminster)
Hedrick Smith
The Russians (Quadrangle)
William W. Warner
Beautiful Swimmers, illus. by Consuelo Hanks (Atlantic-Little)
1978
Will D. Campbell
Brother to a Dragonfly (Seabury/Continuum)
Peter Forbath
The River Congo (Harper)
Archie Hill
Closed World of Love (Simon & Schuster)
John McPhee
Coming into the Country (Farrar)
Stephen B. Oates
With Malice toward None: The Life of Abraham Lincoln (Harper)
Richard K. Taylor
Blockade (Orbis)
1979
Robert C. Alberts
Benjamin West: A Biography (Houghton)
Robert Coles and Jane Hallowell Coles

Women of Crisis: Lives of Struggle and Hope (Delacorte/Seymour Lawrence)·
Ivan Doig
This House of Sky: Landscapes of a Western Mind (Harcourt)
Josephine Whitney Duveneck
Life on Two Levels: An Autobiography (William Kaufmann)
Josh Greenfield
A Place for Noah (Holt)
Pierre-Jakez Hélias
The Horse of Pride: Life in a Breton Village, trans. by June Guicharnaud (Yale Univ. Press)
Barray Holstun Lopez
Of Wolves and Men (Scribner)
Malcolm Muggeridge
A Twentieth Century Testimony (Thomas Nelson)
Gordon Parks
Flavio (Norton)
Tim Severin
The Brendan Voyage, illus. by Trondur Patursson (McGraw)

JUVENILES

1970
Leo Lionni
Alexander and the Wind-up Mouse (Pantheon)
Milton Meltzer
Brother, Can You Spare a Dime? (Knopf)
George Selden
Tucker's Countryside, illus. by Garth Williams (Farrar)
1971
John Christopher
The Guardians (Macmillan)
Pierre Janssen
A Moment of Silence, trans. by William R. Tyler (Atheneum)

JUVENILES (cont.)

William I. Kaufman
UNICEF Book of Children's Legends,
UNICEF Book of Children's Poems,
UNICEF Book of Children's Prayers,
and *UNICEF Book of Children's Songs* (Stackpole)

Zilpha Keatley Snyder
The Changeling (Atheneum)

Peter Spier
The Erie Canal (Doubleday)

Philip Sterling
Sea and Earth: The Life of Rachel Carson (Crowell)

1972

Clyde Robert Bulla
Pocahontas and the Strangers (Crowell)

Russell Hoban
Emmet Otter's Jug-Band Christmas (Parents' Magazine)

Arnold Lobel
On the Day Peter Stuyvesant Sailed into Town (Harper)

Miska Miles
Annie and the Old One (Atlantic-Little)

Zilpha Keatley Snyder
The Headless Cupid (Atheneum)

1973

Griffing Bancroft
Vanishing Wings (Franklin Watts)

Sylvia L. Engdahl
This Star Shall Abide (Atheneum)

David L. Harrison
The Book of Giant Stories (American Heritage-McGraw)

Mary Rodgers
Freaky Friday (Harper)

Howard G. Smith
Tracking the Unearthly Creatures of Marsh and Pond (Abingdon)

William Steig
Dominic (Farrar)

Brinton Turkle
The Adventures of Obadiah (Viking)

1974

Martha Alexander
I'll Protect You from the Beasts (Dial)

N. M. Bodecker
It's Raining, Said John Twaining (Atheneum)

Carol Fenner
Gorilla, Gorilla, illus. by Symeon Shimin (Random)

Michael Fox
The Wolf, illus. by Charles Fracé (Coward)

Kristin Hunter
Guests in the Promised Land (Scribner)

Robert A. Liston
The Right to Know: Censorship in America (Franklin Watts)

1975

Helen Coutant
First Snow, illus. by Vo-Dinh (Knopf)

Mary Rodgers
A Billion for Boris (Harper)

Uri Shulevitz
Dawn (Farrar)

Ann E. Weiss
Save the Mustangs (Messner)

Charlotte Zolotow
My Grandson Lew, illus. by William Pène du Bois (Harper)

1976

Cora Annett
How the Witch Got Alf, illus. by Steven Kellogg (Franklin Watts)

Mitsumasa Anno
Anno's Alphabet: An Adventure in Imagination (Crowell)

Natalie Babbitt
Tuck Everlasting (Farrar)

Walter D. Edmonds
Bert Breen's Barn (Little)

David Macauley
Pyramid (Houghton)

JUVENILES (cont.)

1977

N. M. Bodecker
Hurry, Hurry, Mary Dear! and Other Nonsense Poems (McElderry/Atheneum)

Roger W. Drury
The Champion of Merrimack County, illus. by Fritz Wegner (Little)

Mildred Kantrowitz
Willy Bear, illus. by Nancy Winslow Parker (Parents' Magazine)

Arnold Lobel
Frog and Toad All Year (Harper)

Norma Fox Mazer
Dear Bill, Remember Me and Other Stories (Delacorte)

1978

Dale Carlson
Where's Your Head? Psychology for Teenagers, illus. by Carol Nicklaus (Atheneum)

Julia Cunningham
Come to the Edge (Pantheon)

Ashok Davar
The Wheel of King Asoka, illus. by the author (Follett)

Peter Spier
Noah's Ark, trans. and illus. by the author (Doubleday)

Jane Yolen
The Seeing Stick, illus. by Remy Charlip and Demetra Maraslis (Crowell)

1979

M. E. Kerr
Gentlehands (Harper)

Katherine Paterson
The Great Gilly Hopkins (Crowell)

Rosalie Seidler
Panda Cake (Parents' Magazine)

Barbara Williams
Chester Chipmunk's Thanksgiving, illus. by Kay Chorao (Dutton)

The Civil War Round Table of New York

Benjamin Barondess Lincoln Award

The Civil War Round Table of New York, Inc., 289 New Hyde Park Road, Garden City, New York 11530, established this award in memory of the late Benjamin Barondess, author, New York attorney, Lincoln student, and one-time vice-president of the society. The award is presented at the February meeting of the Round Table to a person or institution for the best literary or other contribution to the greater appreciation of the life and works of Abraham Lincoln. The award consists of a copy of the Volk bust of Abraham Lincoln with an inscription and $100 contributed by the family of the late Benjamin Barondess.

1962

Neil Harris
"Philosophy of Abraham Lincoln"

1963

Adele Gutman Nathan
Lincoln's America (Grosset)

When Lincoln Went to Gettysburg (Aladdin)
Two Lincoln pageants

1964

Lloyd Ostendorf and Charles Hamilton

Lincoln in Photographs (Univ. of Oklahoma Press)

1965

Louis A. Warren
Lincoln's Gettysburg Declaration (Lincoln National Life Foundation)

1966

Della Crowder Miller
Abraham Lincoln (Christopher)

1967

Kenneth A. Bernard
Lincoln and the Music of the Civil War (Caxton)

1968

Richard Allen Heckman
Lincoln vs. Douglas (Public Affairs Press)

1969

Paul M. Angle
A Portrait of Abraham Lincoln in Letters by His Oldest Son (Chicago Historical Society)

1970

Victor Searcher
Lincoln Today (Yoseloff)

1971

David Plowden and Bryan Holme
Lincoln and His America (Viking)

1972

Michael Davis
The Image of Lincoln in the South (Univ. of Tennessee Press)

1973

Mrs. Frankie Hewitt, Founder of the Ford's Theatre Society
For her work in presenting appropriate plays at the historic theater

1974

Arnold Gates
For his work as literary editor of *Lincoln Herald* since 1956

1975

Lincoln Memorial University, Harrogate, Tennessee
For furthering the Lincoln story

1976

Floyd E. Risvold, ed.
A True History of the Assassination of Abraham Lincoln and of the Conspiracy of 1865, by Louis J. Weichmann (Knopf)

1977

Mabel Kunkel
Abraham Lincoln: Unforgettable American (Delmar)

1978

Stephen B. Oates
With Malice toward None: The Life of Abraham Lincoln (Harper)

1979

Louis A. Warren Lincoln Library and Museum, Fort Wayne, Indiana
For its contribution to the greater appreciation of the life and works of Abraham Lincoln

Fletcher Pratt Award

The Civil War Round Table of New York established this award in 1957 to honor the late Fletcher Pratt, author, historian, and onetime president of the society. An award committee selects the winning book. The award, which consists of a bronze plaque, is given annually in May for the best nonfiction book on the Civil War for the past year or for contributions to the study of Civil War history. Anyone is eligible, and presentation is made in New York City.

1957

Bruce Catton
This Hallowed Ground (Doubleday)

1958

Burke Davis
The Last Cavalier (Rinehart)

1959
Philip Van Doren Stern
An End to Valor (Houghton)
1960
Allan Nevins
The War for the Union: War Becomes Revolution, 1862–1863 (Scribner)
1961
R. Ernest Dupuy and Trevor N. Dupuy
The Compact History of the Civil War (Hastings House)
1962
Glenn Tucker
Chickamauga (Bobbs)
1963
Harry Hansen
The Civil War (Duell)
1964
Shelby Foote
The Civil War: A Narrative (Random)
1965
Clifford Dowdey
The Seven Days: The Emergence of Lee (Little)
1966
James V. Murfin
The Gleam of Bayonets (Yoseloff)
1967
Charles B. Dew
Ironmaker to the Confederacy: Joseph R. Anderson and the Tredegar Iron Works (Yale Univ. Press)
1968
Glyndon G. Van Deusen
William Henry Seward (Oxford Univ. Press)
1969
Edwin B. Coddington

The Gettysburg Campaign: A Study in Command (Scribner)
1970
Bruce Catton
Grant Takes Command (Little)
1971
Frank E. Vandiver
Their Tattered Flags (Harper's Magazine)
1972
Robert Manson Myers
The Children of Pride (Yale Univ. Press)
1973
John Y. Simon, ed.
The Papers of Ulysses S. Grant (Southern Illinois Univ. Press)
1974
Shelby Foote
The Civil War: A Narrative, 3 vols. (Random)
1975
David H. Donald, ed.
Gone for a Soldier: The Civil War Memoirs of Private Alfred Bellard (Little)
1977
Richard Wheeler
Voices of the Civil War (Crowell)
1978
William C. Davis
For his contribution to Civil War history
1979
Rowena Reed
Combined Operations in the Civil War (Naval Institute)

Council for Wisconsin Writers Awards

Originally, this was an annual award announced in September. It was established in 1964 by representatives of writers' organizations in Wisconsin with the support of the Johnson Foundation, Racine, Wisconsin, to recognize outstanding literary work by living resident Wisconsin writers published between January 1 and December 31 of the year for which the award was made. Three $500 awards were offered in the categories fiction, nonfiction, and juvenile (book length); and four $250 awards were offered in the categories fiction and nonfiction (less than book length), play, and collected poetry. Decision was by a panel of judges chosen annually by the Council.

1965
Chad Walsh. Poetry
1966
Beverly Butler. Novel
1967
John Barker. Nonfiction
1968
August Derleth. Poetry
Mel Ellis. Nonfiction
Donald Emerson. Novel
Hope Dahle Jordan. Juvenile
Jack Ritchie. Short Story
Robert W. Wells. Short Nonfiction
1969
Marion Fuller Archer. Juvenile
Ludmilla Bollow. Play
Mel Ellis. Short Nonfiction
Dion Henderson. Short Fiction
Ruth Fouts Pochmann. Nonfiction
Waldon Porterfield. Fiction
Raymond E. Vils. Poetry
1970
Jill Weber Dean and Larry Servais. Short Nonfiction
Mel Ellis. Fiction
Dion Henderson. Fiction
Hope Dahle Jordan. Juvenile
Herbert Kubly. Nonfiction
Thomas P. Ramirez. Short Fiction
Celeste Raspanti. Play
Chad Walsh. Poetry
1971
Marjorie Bitker. Fiction

Paul Covert. Fiction
Mel Ellis. Juvenile
Roger Mitchell. Poetry
Celeste Raspanti. Play
Harold Rolseth. Short Fiction
Robert W. Wells. Nonfiction
1972
Marion Fuller Archer. Juvenile
David Crowe. Short Nonfiction
Warren Fine. Fiction
Edward Krug. Scholarly Book
Joseph McBride. Nonfiction
S. J. Poulter. Poetry
Jack Tichie. Short Fiction
1973
Mel Ellis. Nonfiction
John Fogarty. Short Nonfiction
Kathryn Lamboley. Short Fiction
James Olson. Fiction
Felix Pollack. Poetry
Alice E. Smith. Scholarly Book
Beatrice E. Smith. Juvenile
1974
Marcia A. Conta. Picture Book
Steven Feierman. Scholarly Book
Robert E. Gard. Short Fiction
Arthur Hove. Short Nonfiction
Tony Hozeny. Fiction
Leon McClinton. Juvenile
Gwen Schultz. Nonfiction
Kathleen Wiegner. Poetry
Discontinued

The Count Dracula Society Awards

The Count Dracula Society has established the following three awards to honor outstanding achievement in gothic literature. Although most think of Count Dracula as only a creature of fiction, a historical Count Dracula did exist. The fictional Dracula was based on a fifteenth-century count of Wallachia whose defiance of invading Turks led to his being hailed as a Christian knight. Further information on each award can be obtained from Donald A. Reed, President, Count Dracula Society, 334 West 54 Street, Los Angeles, California 90037.

Mrs. Ann Radcliffe Awards

Established in 1962, this award is given annually for outstanding achievements in television, cinema, and literature. The award, a scroll and a medal, is presented at the Mrs. Ann Radcliffe Awards Dinner held in Hollywood every April. Only recipients of literature awards are listed here.

1963
   Forrest J. Ackerman
1964
   Russell Kirk
   Donald A. Reed
1965
   Ray Bradbury
1966
   Forrest J. Ackerman
1967
   August Derleth
1968
   A. E. Van Vogt
1969
   Robert Bloch
1970
   Fritz Leiber
1971
   Ray Bradbury

1972
   Henry Eichner
1973
   Devendra P. Varma
1974
   Thomas Tryon
1975
   Arthur Lennig
1976
   Leonard Wolf
1977
   Robert Cremer
1978
   C. L. Moore
1979
   Raymond McNally

Reverend Dr. Montague Summers Memorial Award

This award, established in 1962, is given annually for outstanding achievement in gothic literature. A gold trophy is presented to the winner at the Mrs. Ann Radcliffe Awards Dinner in Hollywood every April.

1969
   Donald A. Reed
1970
   Frank H. Cunningham
1971
   Devendra P. Varma
1972
   William Crawford

1973
   Bob Clampett
1974
   E. B. Murray
1975
   Raymond McNally
1976
   Don Glut

1977
   Stephan Kaplan

1979
   Bramwell Young

1978
   Edward Ansara

Horace Walpole Gold Medal

This award is given annually for individual achievements in fantasy, horror, terror, and science fiction literature and films. The gold medal is presented at the Mrs. Ann Radcliffe Awards Dinner in Hollywood each April.

1968
   Donald A. Reed

1969
   Vincent Price

1970
   Rouben Mamoulian
   Devendra P. Varma

1971
   George Pal
   Barbara Steele

1972
   Christopher Lee
   Rod Serling

1973
   Radu Florescu
   Raymond McNally

1974
   W. S. Lewis
   Manuel Weltman

1975
   Devendra P. Varma

1976
   Margaret L. Carter

1977
   Devendra P. Varma

1978
   Frank Langella

1979
   Christopher Lee

Dartmouth Medal

The Reference and Adult Services Division (RASD) of the American Library Association (ALA), 50 East Huron Street, Chicago, Illinois 60611, established this award in 1974 to "honor achievement in creating reference works outstanding in quality and significance." "Creating" reference works may include, but is not necessarily limited to, writing, compiling, editing, or publishing books or the provision of information in other forms for reference use, e.g., a data bank. The award, a bronze medal designed by Rudolph Ruzicka, is donated by Dartmouth College, Hanover, New Hampshire 03755. The medal is oval and features on its obverse, against a filigree of olive branches, the head of Athena with the words "Dartmouth Medal" above and below.

The recipient, selected by a committee of the ALA Reference and Adult Services Division, may be an individual, a group, a firm, or other organization. Presentation is made during the ALA annual conference at the RASD membership meeting.

1975
New England Board of Higher Education, for establishing NASIC, Northeast Academic Science Information Center, a regional experiment in the brokerage of information services

1976
No award

1977
Atlas of Early American History: The Revolutionary Era, 1760-1790, Lester J. Cappou, ed. (Princeton Univ. Press, for the Newberry Library and the Institute of Early American History and Culture)

1978
International Encyclopedia of Psychiatry, Psychology, Psychoanalysis, and Neurology, Benjamin B. Wolman, ed.-in-chief (Van Nostrand, for Aesculapius)

1979
The Encyclopedia of Bioethics, Warren Reich, ed.-in-chief (Free Press)

Delta Kappa Gamma Society Educator's Award

The Delta Kappa Gamma Society presents an annual Educator's Award (biennial, (1946-1968) to the author of a book that may influence future directions in the teaching profession. The contribution may be in the fields of research, philosophy, or any other area of learning that is stimulating and creative. The author must be a woman from a country in which the Society is established (United States, Canada, Norway, Sweden, Finland, Iceland, Great Britain, the Netherlands, El Salvador, Guatemala, and Mexico), and the book must be published or translated into English within a prescribed one-year period. The award of $1,000 is presented at the international convention of the Society in even-numbered years and at the four regional conferences in odd-numbered years.

1946
Dorothy Canfield Fisher
Our Young Folks (Harcourt)

1948
Kate Wofford
Modern Education in the Small Rural School (Macmillan)

1950
Louise Hall Tharp
The Peabody Sisters of Salem (Little)

1952
Catherine Drinker Bowen
John Adams and the American Revolution (Atlantic-Little)

1954
Agnes Meyer
Out of These Roots (Atlantic-Little)

1956
Kate Hevner Mueller
Educating Women for a Changing World (Univ. of Minnesota Press)

1958
Dorothy Rogers
Mental Hygiene in Elementary Education (Houghton)

1960
Blanche Jefferson
Teaching Art to Children: The Values of Creative Expression (Allyn & Bacon)
1962
Marianne Besser
Growing Up with Science (McGraw)
1964
Roma Gans
Common Sense in Teaching Reading: A Practical Guide (Bobbs)
1966
Jessie Bernard
Academic Women (Pennsylvania State Univ. Press)
1968
Maya Pines
Revolution in Learning (Harper)
1969
Helaine Dawson
Outskirts of Hope (McGraw)
1970
Lisa Richette
Throwaway Children (Lippincott)
1971
Muriel Beadle
A Child's Mind (Doubleday)
1972
Elizabeth Janeway

Man's World, Woman's Place (Morrow)
1973
Rosalind Loring and Theodora Wells
Breakthrough: Women into Management (Van Nostrand)
1974
Maxine Greene
Teacher as Stranger: Educational Philosophy for the Modern Age (Wadsworth)
1975
Diane Ravitch
The Great School Wars (Basic Books)
1976
Carole Klein
The Myth of the Happy Child (Harper)
1977
Ellen Moers
Literary Women (Doubleday)
1978
Kate Long
Johnny's Such a Bright Boy, What a Shame He's Retarded (Houghton)
1979
Evelyne Accad
Veil of Shame (Editions Naaman)
Helen Gouldner
Teachers' Pets, Troublemakers, and Nobodies (Greenwood)

Dexter Prize

In 1968, the Society for the History of Technology first awarded the Dexter Prize, established to honor the author of an outstanding book on the history of technology published during the previous three years. The annual award is determined by the Awards Committee of the Society. The prize of $1,000 and a plaque, donated by the Dexter Chemical Corporation, is presented at a banquet, usually in October. Inquiries should be sent to the Society for the History of Technology, c/o History Department, University of California, Santa Barbara, California 93106.

The names of the winning authors are listed below; the titles and publishers of the winning books were not available.

1968
Hans Eberhard Wulff

1969
Gotz Quarh

1970
  Lynn White, Jr.
1971
  Edwin T. Layton, Jr.
1972
  Thomas Parke Hughes
1973
  Donald S. L. Cardwell
1974
  Daniel J. Boorstin
  Donald R. Hall

1975
  Bruce Sinclair
1976
  Hugh G. J. Aitken
1977
  Richard W. Bulliet
1978
  Reese V. Jenkins

Alfred Einstein Award

Established in 1967 and offered annually by the American Musicological Society, 201 South 34 Street, Philadelphia, Pennsylvania 19104, this award is named for the renowned scholar and member of the Society. It is given to a young scholar who has published an article on a musicological subject in the preceding year. The award carries a stipend of $400, given by Eva H. Einstein.

1967
  Richard L. Crocker
  "The Troping Hypothesis," *Musical Quarterly*, vol. LII, 1966
1968
  Ursula Kirkendale
  "The Ruspoli Documents on Handel," *Journal of the American Musicological Society*, vol. XX, 1967
1969
  Philip Gossett
  "Rossini in Naples: Some Major Works Recovered," *Musical Quarterly*, vol. LIV, 1968
1970
  Lawrence Gushee
  "New Sources for the Biography of Johannes de Muris," *Journal of the American Musicological Society*, vol. XXII, 1969
1971
  Lewis Lockwood
  "The Autograph of the First Movement of Beethoven's Sonata for Vio-

loncello and Pianoforte, Opus 69," *Music Forum*, vol. II, 1970
1972
  Sarah Fuller
  "Hidden Polyphony—A Reappraisal," *Journal of the American Musicological Society*, vol. XXIV, 1971
1973
  Rebecca A. Baltzer
  "Thirteenth-Century Illuminated Miniatures and the Date of the Florence Manuscript," *Journal of the American Musicological Society*, vol. XXV, 1972
1974
  Lawrence F. Bernstein
  "La Courone et Fleur des Chansons à Troys: A Mirror of the French Chanson in Italy in the Years between Ottaviano Petrucci and Antonio Gardano," *Journal of the American Musicological Society*, vol. XXVI, 1973
1975
  Eugene K. Wolf and Jean K. Wolf

"A Newly Identified Complex of Manuscripts from Mannheim," *Journal of the American Musicological Society*, vol. XXVII, 1974
1976
Craig Wright
"Dufay at Cambrai: Discoveries and Revisions," *Journal of the American Musicological Society*, vol. XXVIII, 1975
1977
James Webster

"Violoncello and Double Bass in the Chamber Music of Haydn and His Viennese Contemporaries, 1750-1780," *Journal of the American Musicological Society*, vol. XXIX, 1976
1978
Charles M. Atkinson
"The Earliest Agnus Dei Melody and Its Tropes," *Journal of the American Musicological Society*, vol. XXX, 1977

Emerson-Thoreau Medal

The Emerson-Thoreau Medal is offered by the American Academy of Arts and Sciences, 165 Allandale Street, Jamaica Plain, Massachusetts 02130. Established in 1956, the medal and honorarium of $1,000 are given in recognition of distinguished achievement in the broad field of literature. The award is not made on the basis of any single work, but for the overall body of the recipient's works. The winner is selected by the Academy and presentation is made at the Academy.

1959
    Robert Frost
1960
    T. S. Eliot
1961
    Henry Beston
1962
    Samuel Eliot Morison
1963
    Katherine Anne Porter
1964
    Mark Van Doren
1965
    Lewis Mumford
1966
    Edmund Wilson
1967
    Joseph Wood Krutch

1968
    John Crowe Ransom
1969
    Hannah Arendt
1970
    Ivor Armstrong Richards
1971-1974
    No awards
1975
    Robert Penn Warren
1976
    No award
1977
    Saul Bellow
1978
    No award
1979
    James T. Farrell

Explicator Award

This annual award was established in 1956 by the *Explicator* and is now given by the Explicator Literary Foundation, 3241 Archdale Road, Richmond, Virginia 23235, for the purpose of encouraging *explication de texte*, that is, critical or analytic writing, in English and American literature. Any work in this field is eligible for a $300 prize and a bronze plaque, which are awarded in the fall each year.

1956
Hyatt H. Waggoner
Hawthorne: A Critical Study (Harvard Univ. Press)
1957
Robert B. Heilman
Magic in the Web: Action and Language in Othello (Univ. of Kentucky Press)
1958
Harold S. Wilson
On the Design of Shakespearian Tragedy (Univ. of Toronto Press)
1959
Bernice Slote
Keats and the Dramatic Principle (Univ. of Nebraska Press)
1960
Isabel Gamble MacCaffrey
Paradise Lost as "Myth" (Harvard Univ. Press)
1961
John Russell
Henry Green: Nine Novels and an Unpacked Bag (Rutgers Univ. Press)
1962
Samuel Hynes
The Pattern of Hardy's Poetry (Univ. of North Carolina Press)
1963
Robert Martin Adams
Surface and Symbol: The Consistency of James Joyce's Ulysses (Oxford Univ. Press)
1964
Reuben A. Brower
The Poetry of Robert Frost (Oxford Univ. Press)
1965
E. D. Hirsch, Jr.
Innocence and Experience (Yale Univ. Press)

1966
Joseph N. Riddel
The Clairvoyant Eye: The Poetry and Poetics of Wallace Stevens (Louisiana State Univ. Press)
1967
Kathleen Williams
Spenser's World of Glass (Univ. of California Press)
1968
Paul J. Alpers
The Poetry of the Faerie Queene (Princeton Univ. Press)
1969
Barbara H. Smith
Poetic Closure: A Study of How Poems End (Univ. of Chicago Press)
1970
Helen Hennessy Vendler
On Extended Wings: Wallace Stevens' Longer Poems (Harvard Univ. Press)
1971
Rosalie L. Colie
"My Echoing Song": Andrew Marvell's Poetry of Criticism (Princeton Univ. Press)
1972
Richard L. Levin
The Multiple Plot in English Renaissance Drama (Univ. of Chicago Press)
1973
Raymond M. Olderman
Beyond the Waste Land: A Study of the American Novel in the Nineteen Sixties (Yale Univ. Press)
1974
Barbara Kiefer Lewalski
Donne's Anniversaries and the Poetry of Praise: The Creation of a Symbolic Mode (Princeton Univ. Press)

1975
  No award
1976
  No contest held
1977
  Avrom Fleishman

Virginia Woolf: A Critical Reading
(Johns Hopkins Univ. Press)
1978
  A. Dwight Culler
  The Poetry of Tennyson (Yale Univ. Press)

R. T. French Tastemaker Award

This award is offered by the R. T. French Company, One Mustard Street, Box 23450, Rochester, New York 14692. It was established in 1966 to give recognition to the outstanding cookbooks of the year, due to the feeling that cookbook authors have great influence as "tastemakers" and should be recognized as such. Cookbooks must be nominated by publishers. Only original works published and distributed during the year previous to the award are eligible; updatings and revisions are not eligible. A Nominating Committee composed of senior cookbook editors, authors, and food editors makes the final determination on eligibility of entries. Books are currently judged in nine categories: (1) Best of Show, (2) Basic/General, (3) Foreign/Regional, (4) Specialty/Novelty, (5) Soft Cover, (6) Entertaining, (7) Organic/Natural, (8) Special Diet, (9) Best First Cookbook. Entries approved by the Nominating Committee are listed on ballots and sent to a list of 1,600 food editors of magazines and newspapers, senior cookbook editors at publishing houses, and cookbook authors. A Judges Committee selects the winners on the basis of the votes each receives. The Tastemaker Award, a crystal champagne bucket engraved with the winner's name and $500 for Best of Show, is presented annually in April at a luncheon in New York City. The 1979 award luncheon was held at the Park Lane Hotel.

1967
  Gloria Bley Miller
  The Thousand Recipe Chinese Cookbook (Atheneum)
1968
  Anne Seranne
  America Cooks (Putnam) Best of Show

  José Wilson
  House and Garden's New Cook Book (Simon & Schuster) Basic

  Elizabeth Lambert Ortiz
  The Complete Book of Mexican Cooking (Evans) Foreign

  Helen McCully
  Nobody Ever Tells You These Things about Food and Drink (Holt) Specialty

Clementine Paddleford
Clementine Paddleford's Cook Book (Essandess) Soft Cover
1969
  Jean Hewitt
  New York Times Large Type Cookbook (Golden) Best of Show and Basic

  Dale Brown
  American Cooking (Time-Life) Regional

  Annemarie Huste
  Annemarie's Personal Cookbook (Universal) Specialty

  Better Homes and Gardens Editors
  Better Homes and Gardens Cooking for Two (Meredith) Specialty

Sunset Editors
Sunset Cook Book of Desserts (Lane)
Soft Cover

1970

Craig Claiborne
Kitchen Primer (Knopf) Basic

Jean Hewitt
The New York Times Main Dish Cookbook (Golden) Soft Cover

Ada Boni
Italian Regional Cooking, trans. by Maria Langdale and Ursula Whyte (Dutton) Foreign

Better Homes and Gardens Editors
Better Homes and Gardens Ground Meat Cook Book (Meredith) Specialty

1971

Albert Stockli
Splendid Fare (Knopf) Best of Show and Basic

Jeanne Voltz
California Cookbook (Bobbs) Regional

Sunset Editors
Sunset Oriental Cook Book (Lane) Soft Cover

1972

Craig Claiborne
The New York Times International Cookbook (Harper) Best of Show and Foreign

Charlotte Adams
The Four Seasons Cookbook (Holt) Basic

Jean Hewitt
The New York Times Natural Foods Cookbook (Quadrangle) Specialty

Helen Worth
Hostess without Help (Westover) Entertaining

Alan Hooker
Herb Cookery (101 Productions) Soft Cover

1973

James Beard
American Cookery (Little) Best of Show and Basic

Craig Claiborne and Virginia Lee
The Chinese Cookbook (Lippincott) Foreign

Dorothy Ivens
Pâtés and Other Marvelous Meat Loaves (Lippincott) Specialty

Marian Burros and Lois Levine
Summertime Cookbook (Macmillan) Entertaining

Beatrice Trum Hunter
The Natural Foods Primer (Simon & Schuster) Organic/Natural

Nancy Bryal
Better Homes and Gardens Low-Calorie Desserts (Meredith) Special Diet

Diana Kennedy
The Cuisines of Mexico (Harper) Best First Cookbook

Sunset Editors
Cooking with Wine (Lane) Soft Cover

1974

Perla Myers
The Seasonal Kitchen (Holt) Best of Show, Basic, and Best First Cookbook

Marcella Hazan
The Classic Italian Cookbook (Harper) Foreign

Madeleine Kamman
Dinner against the Clock (Atheneum) Specialty

Paul Rubinstein
Feasts for Two (Macmillan) Entertaining

Diana Collier and Joan Wiener
Bread: Making It the Natural Way (Lippincott) Organic/Natural

Anne Seranne
Anne Seranne's Good Food without Meat (Morrow) Special Diet

Sunset Editors
Sunset Ideas for Cooking Vegetables
(Lane) Soft Cover

1975

Nika Hazelton
I Cook as I Please (Grosset) Basic

Richard Olney
Simple French Food (Atheneum)
Best of Show and Foreign

Bernard Clayton, Jr.
The Complete Book of Breads (Simon & Schuster) Specialty and Best
First Cookbook

Helen Corbitt
Helen Corbitt Cooks for Company
(Houghton) Entertaining

Beryl M. Marton
Diet for One, Dinner for All (Western)
Health and Diet

Daphne Metaxas
Classic Greek Cooking (Nitty Gritty
Productions) Soft Cover

1976

Jean Anderson and Elaine Hanna
Doubleday Cookbook (Doubleday)
Best of Show and Basic

Nancy Morton
*Better Homes and Gardens Heritage
Cookbook* (Meredith) Foreign/Regional

Craig Claiborne
*Craig Claiborne's Favorites from the
New York Times* (Quadrangle) Specialty

Jean Hewitt
The New York Times Weekend Cookbook (Quadrangle) Entertaining

June Roth
*Salt-Free Cooking with Herbs and
Spices* (Regnery) Natural and Special
Diet

Mable Hoffman
Crockery Cookery (HP Books) Soft
Cover

Evan Jones
*American Food, the Gastronomic
Story* (Dutton) Best First Cookbook
Settlement Cookbook (Simon &
Schuster) Cookbook Hall of Fame

1977

Michel Guérard
Michel Guérard's Cuisine Minceur
(Morrow) Best of Show, Foreign, and
Best First Cookbook

Carol Cutler
*The Six-Minute Soufflé and Other
Culinary Delights* (Potter) Basic

Nika Hazelton
The Unabridged Vegetable Cookbook (Evans) Specialty

Diana von Welanetz and Paul von
Welanetz
The Pleasure of Your Company (Atheneum) Entertaining

Barbara Gibbon
The Slim Gourmet (Harper) Health
and Nutrition

Mable Hoffman
Crêpe Cookery (HP Books) Soft Cover

1978

James Beard
*James Beard's Theory and Practice
of Good Cooking* (Knopf) Best of
Show and Basic

Jeanne A. Voltz
The Flavor of the South (Doubleday)
Regional

Anne Willan
*Great Books and Their Recipes:
From Traillevent to Escoffier* (McGraw) European

Irene Kuo
The Key to Chinese Cooking (Knopf)
International

Robert Ackart
A Celebration of Vegetables (Atheneum) Natural/Special Diet

Sonia Uvezian
The Book of Salads (101 Productions)
Soft Cover

Maida Heather
Books of Great Cookies (Knopf) Specialty

1979
Julia Child
Julia Child and Company (Knopf)
Best of Show

Time-Life Editors
The Time-Life American-Regional Cookbook (Little) Regional

Marcella Hazan
More Classic Italian Cookery (Knopf)
Foreign

Ann Seranne
The Joy of Giving Homemade Food (McKay) Specialty

Craig Claiborne and Pierre Franey
Veal Cookery (Harper) Single Subject

Marion Burros
Pure and Simple: Delicious Recipes for Additive-Free Cooking (Morrow)
Natural

Barbara Gibbons
The International Slim Gourmet Cookbook (Harper) Special Diet

Sunset Editors
Cooking for Two . . . Or Just for You (Lane) Soft Cover

Friends of American Writers Award

The Friends of American Writers is an organization of Chicago women formed "to encourage and promote high standards and ideals among American writers." If a book is to be eligible for the award, one of three conditions must be fulfilled: the author must be a native of Arkansas, Illinois, Indiana, Iowa, Kansas, Kentucky, Michigan, Minnesota, Missouri, Nebraska, North Dakota, Ohio, Oklahoma, South Dakota, Tennessee, or Wisconsin; he or she must currently reside in one of the aforementioned states or previously have lived in the Midwest for a considerable period of time; or the locale of the book must be the aforementioned region. Details concerning the award may be obtained from Mrs. Norman A. Parker, 840 William, River Forest, Illinois 60305.

Between 1928 and 1938 prizes ranging between $100 and $500 were awarded to nineteen authors, among whom were Carl Sandburg, Harriet Monroe, Vincent Sheehan, Donald Culross Peattie, and John Gunther. In 1938, a $1,000 prize was given to a single author. After that a smaller sum was sometimes given, but since 1948, the annual award has been $1,000. In 1960, an award of $100 for juvenile books was established.

1938
William Maxwell
They Came Like Swallows (Harper)
1939
Herbert Krause
Wind without Rain (Bobbs)
1940
Elgin Groseclose
Ararat (Carrick)

1941
Marcus Goodrich
Delilah (Farrar)
1942
Paul Engle
West of Midnight (Random)
1943
Kenneth S. Davis
In the Forests of the Night (Houghton)

1944
    Paul Hughes
    Retreat from Rostov (Random)
1945
    Warren Beck
    Final Score (Knopf)
1946
    Dorothy Langley
    Dark Medallion (Simon & Schuster)
1947
    Walter Havighurst
    Land of Promise (Macmillan)
1948
    A. B. Guthrie, Jr.
    The Big Sky (Sloane)
1949
    Michael De Capite
    The Bennett Place (John Day)
1950
    Edward Nicholas
    The Hours and the Ages (Sloane)
1951
    Leon Statham
    Welcome Darkness (Crowell)
1952
    Vern Sneider
    The Teahouse of the August Moon
    (Putnam)
1953
    Leonard Dubkin
    The White Lady (Putnam)
1954
    Alma Routsong
    A Gradual Joy (Houghton)
1955
    Harriette Arnow
    The Dollmaker (Macmillan)
1956
    Carol Brink
    The Headland (Macmillan)
1957
    Thomas Belden and Marva Belden
    So Fell the Angels (Little)
1958
    William F. Steuber, Jr.
    The Landlooker (Bobbs)

1959
    Paul Darcy Boles
    Parton's Island (Macmillan)
1960
    Otis Carney
    Yesterday's Hero (Houghton)
1961
    James McCague
    Fiddle Hill (Crown)
1962
    A. E. Johnson [Annabel Johnson and
    Edgar Johnson]
    The Secret Gift (Doubleday)
1963
    Lois Phillips Hudson
    The Bones of Plenty (Little)
1964
    Harry Mark Petrakis
    The Odyssey of Kostas Volakis
    (McKay)
1965
    William H. A. Carr
    The du Ponts of Delaware (Dodd)
1966
    Jamie Lee Cooper
    Shadow of a Star (Bobbs)
1967
    Frederick J. Lipp
    Rulers of Darkness (World)
1968
    Allan W. Eckert
    Wild Season and *The Frontiersman*
    (Little)
1969
    Ellis K. Meacham
    The East Indiaman (Little)
1970
    Richard Marius
    The Coming of Rain (Knopf)
1971
    Edward Robb Ellis
    A Nation in Torment (Coward)
1972
    Keyes Beech
    Not without the Americans (Double-
    day)

1973
Thomas Rogers
The Confession of a Child of the Century by Samuel Heather (Simon & Schuster)
1974
Robert Boston
A Thorn for the Flesh (Harper)
1975
Wendell Berry
A Memory of Old Jack (Harcourt)
1976
Margot Peters
Unquiet Soul (Doubleday)
1977
William Brashler
City Dogs (Harper)
1978
John Hassler
Staggerford (Atheneum)
1979
Bette Howland
Blue in Chicago (Harper)

JUVENILE

1960
Clifford B. Hicks
First Boy on the Moon (Winston)
1961
Dorothea J. Snow
Sequoyah, Young Cherokee Guide (Bobbs)
1962
Mary Evans Andrews
Hostage to Alexander (Longmans)
1963
Nora Tully MacAlvay
Cathie and the Paddy Boy (Viking)
1964
Ruth Painter Randall
I Jessie (Little)
1965
Rebecca Caudill
The Far-Off Land (Viking)

1966–1968
No awards
1969
Charles Raymond
Jud (Houghton)
1970
Jean Maddern Pitrone
Trailblazer (Harcourt)
1971
Anne E. Neimark
A Touch of Light (Harcourt)
1972
Zibby Oneal
War Work (Viking)
1973
Howard Knotts
The Winter Cat (Harper)
Peter Z. Cohen
Foal Creek (Atheneum)
1974
Betty Biesterveld
Six Days from Sunday (Rand McNally)
1975
Eric A. Kimmel
The Tartar's Sword (Coward)
1976
Anne Snyder
First Step (Holt)
1977
Robbie Branscum
Toby, Granny and George (Doubleday)
Robert Remini
The Revolutionary Age of Andrew Jackson (Harper)
1978
Audree Distad
The Dream Runner (Harper)
Carol Farley
Loosen Your Ears (Atheneum)
1979
Jamie Gilson
Harvey, the Beer Can King (Lothrop)
Gloria Whelan
A Clearing in the Forest (Putnam)

Friends of Literature Awards

The Friends of Literature (Robert Adelsperger, President, Circle Campus, Box 8198, Chicago, Illinois 60680) is a Chicago organization founded to study literature and to honor those who create it; to bring book lovers more closely together; to encourage the reading of good books; and to crystallize the literary spirit of Chicago into effective organization. Every April, at the Shakespeare Birthday Program and Award Dinner of the Chicago Foundation for Literature, prizes are given to authors or other literary personalities who are residents of the Chicago area or are strongly identified with the city. The following awards are given: Friends of Literature Award, $500, established in 1931 and given for fiction or nonfiction; Grace Thayer Bradley Award for Poetry, given 1951–1958; Robert F. Ferguson Memorial Award, $100, established in 1953 and usually, but not exclusively, given for poetry; Cliff Dwellers Arts Foundation Award, $200, established in 1973 and given for fiction, nonfiction, poetry, etc.; Vicki Penziner Matson Memorial Award, $200, established in 1974 and given for fiction, nonfiction, poetry, etc.; and Friends of Literature Award for Poetry, $100, given for a volume of published poetry. Citations are also awarded for various contributions to the civic and cultural life of Chicago, such as distinguished service to letters. The funds for the prizes come from voluntary contributions and may vary from year to year; winners are chosen by the Friends of Literature Committee on Awards.

1931
Henry Justin Smith
Joslyn (Washington) Fiction
George Dillon
Boy in the Wind. Poetry

1932
Harriet Monroe
Distinguished service to poetry

1933
No award

1934
Carl Sandburg
Lincoln—The Prairie Years (Harcourt) Prose
Lew Sarett
Wings against the Moon (Holt) Poetry
Howard Vincent O'Brien
"All Things Considered" (newspaper column) Journaiism

1935
Helena Carus
Artemis Fare Thee Well (Little) Fiction
Elder Olson
Things of Sorrow (Macmillan) Poetry

1936
T. V. Smith
The Promise of American Politics (Univ. of Chicago Press) Prose
Marion Strobel
Lost City (Houghton) Poetry

1937
No awards

1938
Alice Gerstenberg
For contribution to little theater movement (dramatic writing and production)

1939
Uptown Players
For contribution to cultural life of Chicago

1940
Louis Zara
This Land Is Ours (Houghton) Fiction
Alexander Saxton
Poetry

1941
Percy H. Boynton
Distinguished service to literature

Martin Stevers
Mind through the Ages (Doubleday)
Nonfiction
Robert Abbott
Poetry
1942
Preston Bradley
Distinguished service to literature
Vincent Starrett
Books Alive (Random) Nonfiction
Rachel Albright
Poetry
1943
John T. Frederick
Distinguished service to literature
Jessica Nelson North
Poetry and fiction
Phyllis A. Whitney
Juvenile fiction
1944
LaMar Warrick
Yesterday's Children (Crowell) Fiction
Cecil B. Williams
In Time of War (Torch) Poetry
Otto Eisenschiml
Distinguished service to literature
Bookfellows
In commemoration of twenty-fifth year
of distinguished service to literature
Flora Warren Seymour and George
Steele Seymour
"Cultural Heritage of America" (news-
paper column) Journalism
1945
Dorothy Sparks
Nothing as Before (Harper) Fiction
Edith Lovejoy Pierce
Poetry
Frank Whitmore
Distinguished service to literature
Marshall Field
Freedom Is More Than a Word (Univ.
of Chicago Press) Contribution to
world peace

1946
Marguerite Henry
Justin Morgan Had a Horse (Wilcox &
Follett) Fiction
Herma Clark
"When Chicago Was Young" (news-
paper column) Journalism
John Drury
Old Chicago Houses (Univ. of Chi-
cago Press) Contribution to cultural
life of Chicago
1947
John Frederick Nims
Iron Pastoral (Sloane) Poetry
Poetry magazine
Help and encouragement to poets
Adolph H. Kroch
Contribution to the cultural life of Chi-
cago
Florence Marvyn Bauer
Behold Your King (Bobbs) Fiction
1948
Robert E. Merriam
Dark December (Ziff-Davis) Non-
fiction
Carl B. Roden and Stanley Pargellis
Contribution to the cultural life of Chi-
cago
1949
Leonard Dubkin
Murmur of Wings (McGraw) and *En-
chanted Streets* (Little) Nonfiction
Frank O'Hara
Distinguished service in the field of
drama
Alice Manning Dickey
Founder and director of the Mid-
western Writers' Conference
1950
Ralph Korngold
Two Friends of Man (Little) Nonfiction
Elizabeth Fontaine
Founder and moving spirit of the Hos-
pitalized Veterans' Writers Project

Ralph B. Henry
Distinguished service to literature

Carl I. Henrikson
Co-founder of the Friends of Literature

Harry Hansen
Distinguished service to literature and contribution to Chicago's literary renaissance

1951

Keith Wheeler
The Reef (Dutton) Fiction

Poetry magazine
Grace Thayer Bradley Award for Poetry

Anita Libman Lebeson
Pilgrim People (Harper) and other writings. Nonfiction

1952

Poetry magazine
Commemoration of its fortieth anniversary

Hiram Powers Dilworth
Grace Thayer Bradley Award for Poetry

Rabbi Louis M. Binstock
The Power of Faith (Prentice) Nonfiction

Fanny Butcher
Distinguished service to literature

1953

Branding Iron Press
Entrepreneur in publishing

Sigrid Sittig
"Remember My Love." Grace Thayer Bradley Award for Poetry

Harold L. Bowman
Distinguished service to literature and contribution to the cultural life of Chicago

Frederic Babcock
Commemorating tenth anniversary as editor of *Magazine of Books* and distinguished service to literature

Bernard Jacobs and Rita Jacobs
Adventures in cultural broadcasting

Poetry magazine
Help and encouragement to poets

1954

Ruth Moore
Man, Time and Fossils (Knopf) Nonfiction

Reuel Denney
Grace Thayer Bradley Award for Poetry

Poetry magazine
Robert F. Ferguson Memorial Award

Winifred C. Boynton
Faith Builds a Chapel (Reinhold) Distinguished service to literature

Clara Ingram Judson
Distinguished service to literature for young readers

Philip Maxwell
Commemorating twenty-fifth anniversary as director, Chicagoland Music Festival, and contribution to the cultural life of the Midwest

1955

Leonard Nathan
A Wind Like a Bugle (Macmillan) Fiction

Poetry magazine
Grace Thayer Bradley Award for Poetry

Isabella Gardner
Birthdays from the Ocean (Houghton)
Robert F. Ferguson Memorial Award

Agatha L. Shea
Distinguished service to literature for young readers

Chicago magazine
Contribution to the cultural life of our day

Playwrights Theatre Club
Contribution to the cultural life of Chicago

1956

Julia Siebel
Narrow Covering (Harcourt) Fiction

Adrienne Cecile Rich
The Diamond Cutters (Harper) Grace Thayer Bradley Award for Poetry

Poetry magazine
Robert F. Ferguson Memorial Award

Christopher Janus and J. Patrick Lannan
Distinguished service to poetry

Van Allen Bradley
Distinguished service to letters

Myrtle Dean Clark
Contribution to the cultural life of Chicago

Marjorie Barrows
Distinguished service to literature for young readers

1957

Ruth Stephan
The Flight (Knopf) Fiction

Ruth Herschberger
Grace Thayer Bradley Award for Poetry

Walter Rideout
The Radical Novel in the United States (Harvard Univ. Press) Robert F. Ferguson Memorial Award

Wright Howes
Distinguished bibliography

Herman Kogan
Distinguished service to letters

Frederic E. Faverty
Contribution to "Our Literary Heritage" (newspaper column) Journalism

1958

Gordon N. Ray
The Uses of Adversity and *Age of Wisdom*, 2 vols. (Harvard Univ. Press) Nonfiction

Sydney J. Harris
"Strictly Personal" (newspaper column) Robert F. Ferguson

Memorial Award

Frederick Bock
Grace Thayer Bradley Award for Poetry

Poetry magazine
Mary Hastings Bradley
Contribution to the cultural heritage of Chicago

Ruth H. Harshaw
Contribution to young readers through "Carnival of Books" (radio program)

Henry Regnery
Contribution to the literary prestige of Chicago

1959

Daniel J. Boorstin
The Americans: The Colonial Experience (Random) Nonfiction

Lillian Budd
April Harvest (Duell) Fiction

Marcia Lee Masters
"Impressions of My Father" and other writings. Robert F. Ferguson Memorial Award

Genevieve Foster
Distinguished service to literature for young readers

The Musarts Club
Contribution to the cultural life of Chicago

1960

Richard Ellmann
James Joyce (Viking) Nonfiction

Saul Bellow
Henderson, the Rain King (Viking) Fiction

Helen Singer
"Nine Poems" and other writings. Robert F. Ferguson Memorial Award

Marjorie R. Hopkins
Distinguished service to the theater arts

Gertrude Gscheidle
Distinguished service to literature

1961

Don Russell
The Lives and Legends of Buffalo Bill: A Biography of William F. Cody (Univ. of Oklahoma Press) Nonfiction

Henry Rago
For distinguished service to poetry. Robert F. Ferguson Memorial Award

John Reich
Distinguished service to the theater arts

Andrew McNally III
Distinguished service to creative publishing

1962

Muriel Beadle
These Ruins Are Inhabited (Doubleday) Nonfiction

Norris Lloyd
A Dream of Mansions (Random) Fiction

TV station WTTW
Robert F. Ferguson Memorial Award

Eloise Requa
Distinguished service to world understanding

Rudolph Ganz
Distinguished service to the cultural life of Chicago through music

Emily M. Hilsabeck
Excellence in editing *Book Ink*

1963

Richard Stern
In Any Case (McGraw) Fiction

John P. McPhaul
Deadlines and Monkeyshines (Prentice) Nonfiction

Demetrious Michalaros
Contribution to Greek-American letters. Robert F. Ferguson Memorial Award

Regina Z. Kelly
Literature for young readers

Mildred Bruder
Distinguished service to literature

Studs Terkel
Contribution to the cultural life of Chicago
Poetry magazine

1964

Harry Mark Petrakis
The Odyssey of Kostas Volakis (McKay) Fiction

Arthur H. Nethercot
The Last Four Lives of Annie Besant (Univ. of Chicago Press) Nonfiction

Gwendolyn Brooks
Selected Poems (Harper) and other writings. Robert F. Ferguson Memorial Award

Robert Cromie
Distinguished service to letters

Jessie Orton Jones
Distinguished service to literature, especially for the young reader
Poetry magazine

1965

John Stewart Carter
Full Fathom Five (Houghton) Fiction

Ernest Samuels
Henry Adams: The Major Phase (Belknap) Nonfiction

Maurice English
Midnight in the Century (Prairie School) Robert F. Ferguson Memorial Award

Nicholas von Hoffman
Mississippi Notebook (David White) Journalism

Polly Goodwin
Distinguished service to literature for the young reader

Ralph Newman
For the preservation and perpetuation of Civil War history

Roscoe B. Thomas
Distinguished service to Friends of Literature
Poetry magazine

1966

Vincent Starrett
Born in a Bookshop (Univ. of Oklahoma Press) Nonfiction

Bessie Louise Pierce
History of Chicago, 4 vols. (Knopf)

Lisel Mueller
Dependencies (Univ. of North Carolina Press) Robert F. Ferguson Memorial Award

Al N. Oikonomides and Alyce Cresap
Entrepreneurs in the revival of classical studies (Argonaut)

Edward B. Hungerford
Distinguished service to young readers through historical novels
Poetry magazine

1967

Langdon Gilkey
Shantung Compound (Harper) Nonfiction

Alexander Karanikas
Tillers of a Myth (Univ. of Wisconsin Press) Nonfiction

Frederick Sweet
Miss Mary Cassatt (Univ. of Oklahoma Press) Robert F. Ferguson Memorial Award

David Etter
Go Read the River (Univ. of Nebraska Press) Poetry

Louis Sudler
Contribution to the cultural life of Chicago
Poetry magazine

1968

Laura Fermi
Illustrious Immigrants: Intellectual Migration from Europe, 1930–41 (Univ. of Chicago Press) Nonfiction

Joseph Haas and Gene Lovitz
Carl Sandburg: A Pictorial Biography (Putnam) Robert F. Ferguson Memorial Award

Archibald MacLeish
A Continuing Journey (Houghton) and other writings. Poetry

Susan Reidichs
Spring Mud on Patent Leather Shoes. Young poets

Myrtle R. Walgreen
Distinguished service to the cultural life of Chicago

Beatrice T. Spachmen
Distinguished service to the performing arts
Poetry magazine

1969

Richard Bradford
Red Sky at Morning (Lippincott) Fiction

Anne Emery
Literature for young readers

Philip Appleman
Summer Love and Surf (Vanderbilt Univ. Press) Robert F. Ferguson Memorial Award

Hope Abelson
Distinguished service to The Living Theatre

Louis Marder
Distinguished service to Shakespearian letters

1970

Hoke Norris
It's Not Far but I Don't Know the Way (Swallow) Fiction

Fairfax Cone
With All Its Faults (Little) Nonfiction

Mark Perlberg
The Burning Field (Morrow) Robert F. Ferguson Award

Jonathan Strong
Tike, and Five Stories (Little) Roscoe and Helen Thomas Memorial Award

Mary Lynn McCree and Allen F. Davis
80 Years at Hull House (Quadrangle)

Contribution to the historical heritage of Chicago

Joseph R. Shapiro
Contribution to the cultural life of Chicago for founding and sustaining the Museum of Contemporary Art
Poetry magazine

1971

James Sherburne
Hacey Miller (Houghton) Fiction

Samuel Schoenbaum
Shakespeare's Lives (Oxford Univ. Press) Nonfiction

Cyrus Colter
Beach Umbrella (Swallow) Robert F. Ferguson Memorial Award

John Hough, Jr.
A Peck of Salt (Atlantic-Little) Roscoe and Helen Thomas Memorial Award

Irene Hunt
No Promises in the Wind (Follett) Literature for young readers

Michael Anania
The Color of Dust (Swallow) Poetry

Harold Blake Walker
Distinguished service to mankind
Poetry magazine

1972

Virginia Matson
Abba Father (Moody) Fiction

Fanny Butcher
Many Lives, One Love (Viking) Nonfiction

Eloise Bradley
The River Remembers. Robert F. Ferguson Memorial Award

Helen Thomson
Murder at Harvard (Houghton) Roscoe and Helen Thomas Memorial Award

George Keathley
Contribution to the performing arts of Chicago

Stanley M. Freehling
Contribution to the cultural heritage of Chicago
Poetry magazine

1973

James P. Sloan
The Case History of Comrade V (Houghton) Fiction

Justin G. Turner and Linda Levitt Turner
Mary Todd Lincoln: Her Life and Letters (Knopf) Nonfiction

Gail Burket
From the Prairies. Robert F. Ferguson Memorial Award

Marcel Weinberg
Spots of Time (Macmillan) Roscoe and Helen Thomas Memorial Award

Charles Newman
Northwestern Tri-Quarterly. Cliff Dwellers Arts Foundation Award

Margaret Hillis
Contribution to the cultural life of Chicago through music

John Maxon
Contribution to the cultural life of Chicago through art

1974

Elmer Gertz
To Life (McGraw) Nonfiction

Jane Howard
A Different Woman (Dutton) Nonfiction

Robert Short
A Time to Be Born—A Time to Die (Harper) Robert F. Ferguson Memorial Award

Fran Podulka
The Wonder Jungle (Putnam) Vicki Penziner Matson Memorial Award

Robert Siegel
The Beasts and the Elders (Univ. Press of New England) Cliff Dwellers Arts Foundation Award

Daniel MacMaster
Contribution to the cultural heritage of Chicago through history

Elisa Bialk
Distinguished writing for young readers
Poetry magazine

1975

Susan Fromberg Schaeffer
Anya (Macmillan) Fiction

Robert M. Pirsig
Zen and the Art of Motorcycle Maintenance (Morrow) Nonfiction

Betty Madden
Arts, Crafts, and Architecture in Early Illinois (Univ. of Illinois Press) Nonfiction

Harry Barnard
Forging of an American Jew: The Life and Times of Judge Julian W. Mack (Herzl) Nonfiction

Lucien Stryk
Awakening (Swallow) Robert F. Ferguson Memorial Award

Archie Lieberman
Farm Boy (Abrams) Vicki Penziner Matson Memorial Award

Leo Rosten
Dear Herm (McGraw) Cliff Dwellers Arts Foundation Award

Ann Ida Gannon
Contribution to the cultural life of Chicago through education

Patrick Henry
Contribution to the cultural life of Chicago through theater
Poetry magazine

1976

Richard Warrington Baldwin Lewis
Edith Wharton: A Biography (Harper) Nonfiction

Lacey Baldwin Smith
Elizabeth Tudor: Portrait of a Queen (Little) Nonfiction

William Hunt
Of the Map That Changes (Swallow) Robert F. Ferguson Memorial Award

Gladys Moon Cook
Vashti and the Strange God (David C. Cook) Vicki Penziner Matson Memorial Award

David Lowe
Lost Chicago (Houghton) Cliff Dwellers Arts Foundation Award

Preston Bradley
Distinguished service to the cultural life of Chicago and to the Friends of Literature

Leslie Cross
Distinguished service to literature and to the Friends of Literature
Poetry magazine

1977

Morris Philipson
The Wallpaper Fox (Scribner) Fiction

Gene Wolfe
Peace. Fiction

Sam Hamod
The Famous Boating Party (Cedar Creek) Robert F. Ferguson Memorial Award

Norman Maclean
A River Runs through It (Univ. of Chicago Press) Cliff Dwellers Arts Foundation Award

Herman Kogan and Rick Kogan
Yesterday's Chicago (Seemann) Vicki Penziner Matson Memorial Award

Thomas Reninger
Hair Story. North Shore Creative Writers Memorial Award

Carol Fox
Contribution to the cultural life of Chicago through opera

Otto Loeser
Special recognition for service to the Friends of Literature

1978
John Bartlow Martin
Adlai Stevenson and the World (Doubleday) Nonfiction
Michael Murphy
Hemingsteen. Fiction
Naomi Lazard
The Moonlit Upper Deckerina. Robert F. Ferguson Memorial Award
Eugenia Price
Maria (Lippincott) Vicki Penziner Matson Memorial Award
Barbara C. Schaaf
Mr. Dooley's Chicago (Doubleday) Cliff Dwellers Arts Foundation Award
W. Clement Stone
Contribution to the civic life of Chicago
David Mamet
Contribution to the cultural life of Chicago through theater
1979
James Carroll
Mortal Friends (Little) Fiction

Shirley Nelson
The Last Year of the War (Harper) Fiction
Harold Blake Walker
Days Demanding Courage (Rand McNally) Hazel R. Ferguson Memorial Award
Norbert Blei
The House of the Sunshine Now. Cliff Dwellers Arts Foundation Award
Jean Block
Hyde Park Houses. Special Chicago Foundation for Literature Award
Richard Jensen
Illinois: A Bicentennial History. Vicki Penziner Matson Memorial Award
Harry Zelzer
Contribution to the cultural life of Chicago through the musical and performing arts
Georg Solti
Contribution to the cultural life of Chicago through music

Gavel Award

The American Bar Association, 1155 East 60 Street, Chicago, Illinois 60637, inaugurated the Gavel Award in 1958 to accord national recognition to U.S. information and entertainment media for outstanding contributions "to public understanding of the American legal and judicial systems." Any general circulation newspaper, wire service, news syndicate, magazine, book publisher, radio or television station or network, and film producing or theatrical company in the United States is eligible. Awards for the literary category began in 1964. The award, a gavel, is given in August at the annual meeting of the American Bar Association. The winners of the literary category are listed below.

1964
Herbert Mitgang
The Man Who Rode the Tiger (Lippincott)
1965
A. L. Todd
Justice on Trial (McGraw)

1966 –1970
No book awards
1971
Fred P. Graham
The Self-Inflicted Wound (Macmillan)
1972
Arthur R. Miller

The Assault on Privacy: Computers, Data Banks, and Dossiers (Univ. of Michigan Press)

1973

No award

1974

James F. Simon

In His Own Image: The Supreme Court in Richard Nixon's America (McKay)

1975

J. P. MacKenzie

The Appearance of Justice (Scribner)

1976

Alexander M. Bickel

The Morality of Consent (Yale Univ. Press)

1977

Archibald Cox

The Role of the Supreme Court in American Government (Oxford Univ. Press)

1978

Raoul Berger

Government by Judiciary: The Transformation of the Fourteenth Amendment (Harvard Univ. Press)

1979

A. Leon Higginbotham

In the Matter of Color: Race and the American Legal Process: The Colonial Period (Oxford Univ. Press)

Our Legal Heritage (Silver Burdett)

Geographic Society of Chicago Publication Award

Established in 1951 by the Geographic Society of Chicago, 7 South Dearborn Street, Chicago, Illinois 60603, the award is made to the individual whose book, monograph, or article, of a popular nature, does most to encourage a broader public interest in the field of geography. The publication may be fictional or nonfictional and is considered on its scientific merit as well as its popular appeal. The award is made annually, in April or May, at the discretion of the Committee on Medals and Awards. At the annual dinner of the Society in Chicago, an illuminated scroll or a framed certificate is presented to the winner.

1952

Rachel L. Carson

The Sea around Us (Oxford Univ. Press)

1953

William O. Douglas

Beyond the High Himalayas (Doubleday)

1954

No award

1955

Container Corp. of America

World Geo-Graphic Atlas: A Composite of Man's Environment

1956

Wallace Stegner

Beyond the Hundredth Meridian: John Wesley Powell and the Second Opening of the West (Houghton)

1957

Life Editors, Lincoln Barnett, and Jane W. Watson

The World We Live In (Golden)

1958

American Heritage Editors and Richard M. Ketchum

American Heritage magazine and *The American Heritage Book of Great*

Historic Places (American Heritage and Simon & Schuster)
1959
John Gunther
Inside Russia Today, Inside Africa, Inside U.S.A., Inside Latin America, Inside Asia, and *Inside Europe* (Harper)
Herman Kogan and Lloyd Wendt
Chicago: A Pictorial History (Dutton)
1960
Fred W. Foster, ed., and James A. Bier, cartographer
Atlas of Illinois Resources: Section II, Mineral Resources (Illinois Division of Industrial Planning and Development)
David Lowenthal
George Perkins Marsh: Versatile Vermonter (Columbia Univ. Press)
1961
John A. Shimer
This Sculptured Earth: The Landscape of America (Columbia Univ. Press)
1962
Time, Inc., and Rand McNally & Co. Editors
The Life Pictorial Atlas of the World (Rand McNally)
1963
Jean Gottmann
Megalopolis: The Urbanized Northeastern Seaboard of the United States (Twentieth Century)
Alan Moorehead
The White Nile and
The Blue Nile (Harper)
1964
D. Van Nostrand Co. Editors
The Searchlight series
1965
Kirtley F. Mather
The Earth beneath Us (Random)
1966
Leslie Brown
Africa: A Natural History (Random)

Pierre Deffontaines, ed.
The Larousse Encyclopedia of World Geography (Odyssey)
1967
American Heritage Editors
The American Heritage Pictorial Atlas of United States History (McGraw)
1968
No award
1969
Charles Bricker
Landmarks of Mapmaking (Elsevier)
James A. Michener
Iberia, Spanish Travels and Reflections (Random)
1970
Harold M. Mayer and Richard C. Wade
Chicago: Growth of a Metropolis (Univ. of Chicago Press)
1971
Hodding Carter and Dan Guravich
Man and the River: The Mississippi (Rand McNally)
Charles Steinhacker
Superior (Harper)
1972
Calvin Kentfield and Ray Atkeson
The Pacific Coast (Rand McNally)
May Theilgaard Watts
Reading the Landscape of Europe (Harper)
1973
Alice Taylor, ed.
Focus series and Focus Books (American Geographical Society)
1974
National Wildlife Federation and International Wildlife Federation
Bimonthly publications
David Muench and N. Scott Momaday
Colorado (Rand McNally)
1975
Goode's World Atlas (Rand McNally)
James A. Michener
Centennial (Random)

Walter Sullivan
Continents in Motion: The New Earth Debate (McGraw)

1976

William Carter
Middle West Country (Houghton)

George A. Davis and O. Fred Donaldson
Blacks in the United States: A Geographic Perspective (Houghton)

Eric Newby
The Magnificent Continent (Rand McNally)

1977

Ronald Abler and John S. Adams, eds.
A Comparative Atlas of America's Great Cities: Twenty Metropolitan Regions (Univ. of Minnesota Press)

Lester J. Cappon
Atlas of Early American History, Vol. 2: The Revolutionary Era, 1760–1790 (Princeton Univ. Press)

Evelyn Oppenheimer and Bill Porterfield, eds.
The Book of Dallas (Doubleday)

Bill Thomas
The Swamp (Norton)

1978

Michael Frome
The National Parks (Rand McNally)

Uwe George
In the Deserts of This Earth, trans. by Richard Winston and Clara Winston (Harcourt)

1979

Barry Goldwater and David Muench
Arizona (Rand McNally)

Benjamin F. Richason, Jr., ed.
Introduction to Remote Sensing of the Environment (Kendall/Hunt)

Margaret Sedeen, ed.
National Geographic Picture Atlas of Our Fifty States (National Geographic Society)

Gold Medallion Book Awards

The Evangelical Christian Publishers Association (ECPA), Box 35, La Habra, California 90631, established these awards in 1978 for the purpose of encouraging a trend toward excellence in evangelical Christian book publishing. The Association annually presents five gold medallions for the best religious books in the following categories: Inspirational, Biography, Fiction, Bible Study/Theology, and Juvenile. Selected bookstore operators serve as first-round judges, and book review editors of selected religious periodicals serve as final judges. Nominated books must have been published between September 1 and August 31 of the following year. The prizes, plaques bearing gold medallions, are then awarded the next year at the ECPA Presidents' Banquet, held just prior to the Christian Booksellers Convention in July.

1978

Tim Dowley
Eerdmans' Handbook to the History of Christianity (Eerdmans)
Jesus: Friend of Children (David C. Cook)

Joyce Landorf
I Came to Love You Late (Revell)

Sheldon Vanauken
A Severe Mercy (Harper)

Phillip Yancy
Where Is God When It Hurts? (Zondervan)

1979

F. F. Bruce

Paul: Apostle of the Heart Set Free (Eerdmans) Biography
Joni Eareckson
A Step Further (Zondervan) Inspirational
Elgin Groseclose
The Kiowa (David C. Cook) Fiction

Alvera Mickelsen and Berkley Mickelsen
The Family Bible Encyclopedia, 2 vols. (David C. Cook) Juvenile
Edith Schaeffer
Affliction (Revell) Bible Study/Theology

The Horace Gregory Award

This award was offered by the Horace Gregory Foundation, c/o Joseph Campbell, 136 Waverly Place, New York, New York 10014. It was established in 1969 to honor those who had retired from teaching careers but were engaged in writing and required encouragement to continue their writing by giving them support for research and creative writing. Residents or citizens of the United States who had careers in letters and teaching and were engaged in writing were eligible. The prize of $2,000 was presented annually in early June in New York City.

1969   Discontinued
  Horace Gregory
1974
  William York Tindall

John Simon Guggenheim Memorial Fellowships

In order to improve the quality of education and the practice of arts and professions in the United States, to foster research, and to promote better international understanding, Simon Guggenheim, the late U.S. senator, and his wife established in 1925 the John Simon Guggenheim Memorial Foundation in memory of a son who died in 1922.

Three million dollars was devoted to the establishment of this foundation, which provides grants for men and women of high intellectual and personal qualifications who have already demonstrated unusual capacity for productive scholarship or unusual ability in the fine arts. The Foundation's present endowment is about $100,000,000. The fellowships are offered to further the development of scholars and artists by assisting them to engage in research in any field of knowledge and artistic creation. Citizens and permanent residents of the United States, the other American republics, the Philippines, Canada, and the Caribbean are eligible. Fellowships are awarded by the trustees upon nominations made by a committee of selection. The amount of each grant is adjusted to the needs of the fellows, after consideration of their other resources and the purpose and scope of their studies. The fellowships are given annually and are usually announced in March. Applications must be made in writing on or before October 1 of the preceding year to the John Simon Guggenheim Memorial Foundation, 90 Park Avenue, New York, New York 10016. Fellows who seek further assistance must apply before October 15; immediate renewals are not offered.

About 10,000 persons have received fellowships so far, among them several hundred poets, playwrights, novelists, and writers in such fields as literary criticism, history, biography, and science. Listed below are those who have received grants for creative writing in fiction, drama, and poetry.

1926
Stephen Vincent Benét
1927
Odell Shepard
Walter White
1928
Léonie Adams
Countee Cullen
Paul Green
Lynn Riggs
Allen Tate
Eric Derwent Walrond
1930
Walter Stanley Campbell
Ellsworth Prouty Conkle
Jonathan Daniels
Edward Davison
Helen Rose Hull
Joseph Wood Krutch
Nella Larson
Jacques Le Clercq
Phelps Putnam
Stanley Vestal
Thomas Wolfe
1931
Emjo Basshe
Kate Clugston
Hart Crane
Maurice Hindus
Katherine Anne Porter
John Crowe Ransom
Genevieve Taggard
1932
Louis Adamic
H. L. Davis (Mexico)
George Dillon
J. Frank Dobie

Evelyn Scott
Caroline Gordon Tate
1933
Louise Bogan
e. e. cummings
Leonard Ehrlich
Matthew Josephson
Younghill Kang
Glenway Wescott
1934
Conrad Aiken
Kay Boyle
Albert Halper
Alexander Laing
George Milburn
Isidor Schneider
1935
Alvah Cecil Bessie
Jack Conroy
Harvey Fergusson
Langston Hughes
Lola Ridge
Edmund Wilson
1936
Leopold Atlas
Albert Bein
Edward Doro
James Thomas Farrell
Kenneth Flexner Fearing
Jacob Hauser
Josephine Herbst
Granville Hicks
Kenneth Patchen
Robert Turney
1937
Sterling Allen Brown
Harold Lewis Cook

Frederic Prokosch
Sonia Raiziss
Jesse Hilton Stuart

1938
Arthur Arent
August William Derleth
Clifford Shirley Dowdey, Jr.
Rolfe Humphries
Carlyle Ferren MacIntyre

1939
John Dos Passos
Harold Augustus Sinclair
Robert Penn Warren
Richard Wright

1940
Hermann J. Broch
Ward Allison Dorrance
Lloyd Frankenberg
Lewis Galantière
Edwin Moultrie Lanham
Andrew Nelson Lytle
Delmore Schwartz
Christine Weston

1941
Wilbur Joseph Cash
Brainard Cheney
Edwin Corle
Reuel Nicholas Denney
Oliver La Farge
Norman Rosten
Ramon Sender (Mexico)
James Still

1942
Wystan Hugh Auden
Dorothy Baker
Alexander Greendale
Carson McCullers
Wright Morris
Eudora Welty
George Zabriskie

1943
Jeremy Ingalls
Hugh MacLennan (Canada)
Vladimir Nabokov
Vladimir Pozner
Muriel Rukeyser

José García Villa
Edward Ronald Weismiller

1944
Howard Baker
Marie Campbell
Israel James Kapstein
Jay Saunders Redding
Karl J. Shapiro

1945
Ben Belitt
Hodding Carter
Paul G. Horgan
Stanley Jasspon Kunitz
Marianne Moore
Robert Pick
Theodore Roethke
Jean Stafford
William E. Wilson

1946
Gwendolyn Brooks
Sam Byrd
Everett Howard Hunt, Jr.
Randall Jarrell
Roger Lemelin (Canada)
Alan Lomax
Virginia Eggertsen Sorensen
Arthur Ranous Wilmurt

1947
Ralph Bates
Elizabeth Bishop
Eleanor Clark
John Richard Humphreys
Robert Traill Spence Lowell, Jr.
Isaac Rosenfeld

1948
Agustí Lleonart Bartra (Mexico)
Saul Bellow
Elizabeth Bruce Hardwick
Douglas Valentine Le Pan (Canada)
James Farl Powers
Kenneth Rexroth
Peter Robert Viereck
Theodore Ward
William Woods
Marguerite Vivian Young

1949
  Brother Antonius [William Everson]
  Eleanor Green
  John Latouche
  Mary McCarthy
  Jean Paul Malaquais
  Wallace Earle Stegner
  Jay Williams
1950
  Lincoln Barnett
  Rosalie Moore
  Peter Hillsman Taylor
  Janet Lewis Winters
1951
  Charles Edward Butler
  John Cheever
  William Goyen
  Pierre Marcelin (Haiti)
  Olaf Arnold Sundgaard
  Philippe Thoby-Marcelin (Haiti)
1952
  John Berryman
  Hortense Calisher
  André Giroux (Canada)
  Edgar Austin Mittelholzer (Barbados)
  Bryon Herbert Reece
  Adrienne Rich
  Richard Purdy Wilbur
1953
  Godfrey Blunden
  Edgar Collins Bogardus
  Oliver Vincent Dodson
  Paul Hamilton Engle
  Thomas Hal Phillips
  Elizabeth Spencer
1954
  James Arthur Baldwin
  Stephen Becker
  Jorge Guillén
  Anthony Evan Hecht
  Julius Horwitz
  W. Denis Johnston
  George Lamming (Barbados)
  René Marqués (Puerto Rico)
  May Sarton
1955
  Barbara Gibbs Golffing

Barbara Howes
Kermit Houston Hunter
André Langevin (Canada)
Samuel Selvon (British Caribbean)
Edilberto K. Tiempo (Philippines)
1956
  Margaret Kirkland Avison (Canada)
  David Karp
  Harry Miles Muheim
  Edward Charles O'Gorman
  Frank Rooney
  David Russell Wagoner
  Donald Earl Wetzel
1957
  Holger Cahill
  Aldred Chester
  Lucy Cathcart Daniels
  Borden Deal
  Herbert Gold
  Robert Conroy Goldston
  Errol John (Trinidad)
  Marcia Nardi
  Alistair Reid
  Mary Lee Settle
  Adele Wiseman (Canada)
1958
  Lionel Abel
  Doris Betts
  Philip Booth
  Edgar Bowers
  Margaret Currier Boylen
  Daniel Curley
  Katherine Hoskins
  Errol John (Trinidad)
  Loften Mitchell
  James Otis Purdy
  Josephine Carson Rider
1959
  Emigdio Alvarez Enriquez (Philippines)
  William Blackwell Branch
  Rosa Chacel (Argentina)
  James V. Cunningham
  Peter Steinam Feibleman
  Edward James Hughes
  Edmund LeRoy Keeley
  Mary Lavin

William Manchester
Brian Moore (Canada)
Victor Stafford Reid (British West Indies)
Philip Roth
May Swenson
John Updike
Bianca Van Orden
1960
John Berry
Jane Marvel Cooper
Jean Garrigue
Joshua Joseph Greenfeld
Bienvenido N. Santos (Philippines)
David Derek Stacton
Harvey Swados
Donald Windham
1961
Wendell Erdman Berry
James Dickey
George Paul Elliott
Curtis Arthur Harnack
Kenneth Koch
Paule Burke Marshall
Grace Paley
Mordecai Richler (Canada)
George Edwin Starbuck
1962
Evan Shelby Connell, Jr.
John C. B. Hawkes, Jr.
Galway Kinnell
Denise Levertov
Louis Simpson
Edward Lewis Wallant
Thomas Alonzo Williams, Jr.
Clara Brussel Winston
Richard Yates
María Concepción Zardoya
1963
Marie-Claire Blais (Canada)
Henry W. Butler
Emilio Díaz Valcárcel (Puerto Rico)
Alan Dugan
Robert Duncan
Edward Field
Jack Gelber
Alberto Girri (Argentina)

Ivan Gold
John Alexander Graves III
Donald Hall
Anne Hébert (Canada)
1964
Robert Bly
Robert Creeley
Jack Gilbert
Jan A. S. Hartman
Edward M. Hoagland
Herbert H. Lieberman
Robie Macauley
Alan R. Marcus
Larry McMurtry
Reynolds Price
Kit Reed
Jack C. Richardson
Robert Sward
James A. Wright
Samuel Yellen
1965
Albert Bermel
Kenneth H. Brown
Hayden Carruth
Seymour Epstein
Allen Ginsberg
John Haines
Mark Harris
David Ignatow
LeRoi Jones [Imamu Amiri Baraka]
Richard E. Kim
Alison Lurie
Wallace Markfield
Hardie St. Martin
Lore Segal
Arnold Weinstein
1966
A. R. Ammons
Homero Aridjis (Mexico)
Max Aub (Mexico)
Donald Barthelme
Cecil Dawkins
Stanley Elkin
Donald Finkel
Jesse Hill Ford
Richard J. Howard
Tom Mayer

Terrence McNally
Gabriela Roepke Bahamonde (Chile)
Susan Sontag
William E. Stafford
1967
John Ashbery
Paul Blackburn
Charles J. Dizenzo
Maureen Howard
Adrienne Kennedy
Arthur Kopit
Jerzy Kosinski
Vicente Leñero (Mexico)
Thomas McGrath
Marco Antonio Montes de Oca (Mexico)
Héctor Alvarez Murena (Argentina)
Alden Nowlan (Canada)
Joyce Carol Oates
Tomás Segovia (Mexico)
Kurt Vonnegut, Jr.
1968
R. V. Cassill
José Donoso (Chile)
Salvador Elizondo (Mexico)
Leon Gillen
Thomas Kinsella
Howard Nemerov
Alejandra Pizarnik (Argentina)
Juan Rulfo (Mexico)
Sam Shepard
L. E. Sissman
Mark Richard Smith
Gary S. Snyder
Robert Anthony Stone
Jesús Urzagasti Aguilera (Bolivia)
1969
José Carlos Becerra Ramos (Mexico)
Carlos Germán Belli de la Torre
(Peru)
Michael Benedikt
William Howard Gass
Diane Giguère (Canada)
James Thomas Harrison
Juan José Hernández (Argentina)
Jorge Ibargüengoitia (Mexico)
Cormac McCarthy

James Rodney McConkey
Thomas H. Rogers
Anne Sexton
1970
Robert Boles
Guillermo Cabrera Infante (Cuba)
Benjamin Caldwell
Rosalyn Drexler
George P. Elliott
Thomas Eyen
Leonard Gardner
Leo Litwak
Leonard Michaels
José Emilio Pacheco (Mexico)
Fernando del Paso (Mexico)
James D. Reed
Ronald Ribman
Augusto Roa Bastos (Paraguay)
William Pitt Root
Raphael Rudnick
Louis Simpson
1971
Julie Bovasso
Edward Brathwaite (Jamaica)
Ed Bullins
Lonnie Carter
Tom Clari
Robert Coover
Robert Creeley
Robert Fitzgerald
Thom Gunn
Thomas Kinsella
Victor Kolpacoff
Charles Ludlam
Marco Antonia Montes de Oca (Mexico)
Daniel Moyano (Argentina)
Rochelle Owens
Wilfrid Sheed
Sam Shepard
Ruth Stone
Henry Van Dyke
Larry Woiwode
1972
Peter S. Beagle
Kenneth Bernard
Robert Bly

Donald Davie
Christopher Davis
E. L. Doctorow
Alan Dugan
Maria Irene Fornes
Paula Fox
Ernest J. Gaines
Juan García Ponce (Mexico)
Wilford Leach
James Alan McPherson
Jerome Max
Robert S. Montgomery
José Ricardo Morales (Chile)
H. A. Murena (Argentina)
Nicanor Parra (Chile)
Charles Simic
W. D. Snodgrass
Mona Van Duyn
Diane Wakoski
James Whitehead
Lanford Wilson
Geoffrey Wolff
Sol Yurick

1973
John Ashbery
Brock Brower
Antonio Di Benedetto (Argentina)
José Donoso (Chile)
Salvador Elizondo (Mexico)
Irving Feldman
Isabel Fraire (Mexico)
Frederick E. Gaines
John Gardner
Charles F. Gordon
William Harrison
David Ignatow
Madison Jones
X. J. Kennedy
Myrna Lamb
Philip Levine
Michael McClure
Hector Manjarrez (Mexico)
Murray Mednick
W. S. Merwin
Barton Midwood
Joseph Papaleo
Stanley Plumly

Barry Reckford (Jamaica)
James Scully
Gilbert Sorrentino
Richard G. Stern
Ronald Tavel
Frederic Tuten
Jean-Claude van Itallie
Joseph A. Walker
Theodore Weesner

1974
Stephen W. Berg
José Bianco (Argentina)
Alfredo Bryce Echenique (Peru)
Robert Coover
Russell Edson
Paul Foster
Frank Gagliano
George P. Garrett
Juan José Gurrola (Mexico)
Shirley Hazzard
Jill Hoffman
William M. Hoffman
Galway Kinnell
Etheridge Knight
Tom McHale
Jack Matthews
Mark Medoff
J. Christopher Middleton
Charles Newman
Richard Rhodes
Jerome Rothenberg
Javier Sologuren (Peru)
Mark Strand
Alexander L. Theroux
Charles K. Williams
Jay Wright
Susan Yankowitz
Al Young
John Alonzo Yount

1975
Edward Abbey
Ai
Marvin Bell
Augusto Boal (Brazil)
L. J. Davis
Peter P. Everwine
Ronald Fair

Richard Foreman
Louise Glück
Gail Godwin
Edward Hoagland
Albert F. Innaurato
Philip Magdalany
William Meredith
Tillie Olsen
Ishmael Reed
Gustavo Sainz (Mexico)
J. R. Salamanca
Severo Sarduy (Cuba)
Tomás Segovia (Mexico)
Susan Sontag
Ruth Stone
Jeff Weiss
Joy Williams
Charles Wright

1976
Jon Anderson
James Applewhite
Russell Banks
Rosellen Brown
Ed Bullins
Henri Coulette
Alberto Cousté (Argentina)
Andre Dubus
Michael S. Harper
John Clellon Holmes
John W. Irving
Ruth Prawer Jhabvala
Donald Justice
Alan Lelchuk
Cormac McCarthy
Joseph P. McElroy
Sandra McPherson
Czesław Miłosz
Leonard Nathan
Silvina Ocampo (Argentina)
David Rabe
Ronald Sukenick
James Tate
Jean Valentine
Enrique Verástegui (Peru)
Hilma Wolitzer
Lorees Yerby

1977
José Agustín (Mexico)
Thomas Babe
Ann Beattie
Joseph Brodsky
Francisco Cervantes (Mexico)
Norman Dubie
Leslie Epstein
Richard Ford
Charles Fuller
William Heyen
Israel Horovitz
Richard Hugo
Crispin Larangeria
Enrique Andreés Lihn (Chile)
James McMichael
Robert Mezey
Jay Neugeboren
Craig Nova
Gregory Orr
Jonathan Penner
David St. John
Megan Terry
Mauricio Wacquez (Chile)
Derek Alton Walcott (Trinidad)
Alice Walker
Sylvia Jean Wilkinson

1978
Alice Adams
Jonathan Baumbach
Elizabeth Bishop
Raymond Carver
Antonio Cisneros (Peru)
Jorge Eduardo Eielson (Peru)
Clayton Eshleman
Thomas Farber
Andrew Fetler
Carolyn Forché
Tess Gallagher
William Hauptman
Bette Howland
David Huerta (Mexico)
Leonard Melfi
John Morris
Bharati Mukherjee
Shiva Naipaul (Trinidad)
Darcy O'Brien

Dennis Schmitz
Wallace Shawn
Ellen Voigt
James Wright
David Young
1979
Homero Aridjis (Mexico)
Héctor Bianciotti (Argentina)
Frank Bidart
Hayden Carruth
John Casey
Don DeLillo
Robert C. S. Downs
Christopher Durang
John Engels
Frederick Feirstein

Dick Goldberg
Robert Hass
Sam Koperwas
John B. Logan
John Montague
Howard Frank Mosher
Raúl Navarrete (Mexico)
Augusto Roa Bastos (Paraguay)
Gonzalo Rojas (Venezuela)
Luis Rafael Sánchez (Puerto Rico)
Thomas Savage
Susan Richards Shreve
Roberta Silman
Gary Soto
Allen Wier

Sarah Josepha Hale Award

To honor Sarah Josepha Hale, poet, novelist, editor, and crusader for women's rights, the Friends of the Richards Free Library in her birthplace, Newport, New Hampshire, established this award in 1957. Each August a medal is given to someone distinguished in the field of literature and letters whose work reflects New England atmosphere or influence. A committee of distinguished men and women of the book world makes the decision. The first medal was awarded retroactively for 1956 to Robert Frost.

1956
Robert Frost
1957
John P. Marquand
1958
Archibald MacLeish
Dorothy Canfield Fisher (Special Award)
1959
Mary Ellen Chase
1960
Mark Van Doren
1961
Catherine Drinker Bowen
1962
David McCord
1963
John Hersey

1964
Ogden Nash
1965
Louis Untermeyer
Raymond Holden (Special Award)
1966
Robert Lowell
1967
John Kenneth Galbraith
1968
Richard Wilbur
1969
Lawrance Thompson
1970
Elizabeth Yates
1971
Norman Cousins

1972
  May Sarton
1973
  Henry Steele Commager
1974
  Nancy Hale
1975
  Edwin Way Teale

1976
  John Ciardi
1977
  Roger Tory Peterson
1978
  No award

James A. Hamilton–Hospital Administrators' Book Award

This award is offered by the American College of Hospital Administrators (ACHA), 840 North Lake Shore Drive, Chicago, Illinois 60611, a professional society, in cooperation with the Alumni Association of the Program in Hospital and Health Care Administration at the University of Minnesota. The award was created by the Alumni Association to pay tribute to James Hamilton, founder and director of the graduate program between 1945 and 1965. Books must have meaning to the whole field of administration, have made a valuable contribution to the literature on administration, and give promise of making a significant impact on the advancement of administration as a science. Only books published two years before the date of presentation are eligible. Selection is made by a special Committee on the Book of the Year Award composed of faculty members from schools of business and management, directors of graduate programs in hospital and health services administration, and practicing administrators. The prize consists of $500, a special medallion, and a framed certificate. It is presented annually at a luncheon held during an ACHA-sponsored Congress on Administration, a three-day management-oriented educational meeting held in Chicago in February.

1958
  Herbert A. Simon
  Administrative Behavior (Macmillan)
1959
  Chris Argyris
  Personality and Organization (Harper)
1960
  Harold Leavitt
  Managerial Psychology (Univ. of Chicago Press)
1961
  Melville Dalton
  Men Who Manage (Wiley)

1962
  Douglas McGregor
  The Human Side of Enterprise (McGraw)
1963
  Rensis Likert
  New Patterns of Management (McGraw)
1964
  Basil S. Georgopoulos and Floyd C. Mann
  The Community General Hospital (Macmillan)

1965

Richard A. Johnson, Fremont E. Kast, and James E. Rosenzweig
The Theory and Management of Systems (McGraw)

1966

Alfred P. Sloan, Jr.
My Years with General Motors (Doubleday)

1967

Robert T. Golembiewski
Men, Management and Morality: Toward a New Organizational Ethic (McGraw)

1968

Daniel Katz and Robert L. Kahn
The Social Psychology of Organizations (Wiley)

1969

Paul R. Lawrence and Jay W. Lorsch
Organization and Environment: Managing Differentiation and Integration (Harvard Business School)

1970

Harry Levinson
The Exceptional Executive (Harvard Univ. Press)

1971

Clarence C. Walton
Ethos and the Executive: Values in Managerial Decision Making (Prentice)

1972

John P. Campbell, Marvin D. Dunnette, Edward E. Lawler III, and Karl E. Weick, Jr.
Managerial Behavior, Performance and Effectiveness (McGraw)

1973

Anne Ramsay Somers
Health Care in Transition: Directions for the Future (American Hospital Association)

1974

Basil S. Georgopoulos
Organization Research on Health Institutions (Institute for Social Research, Univ. of Michigan)

1975

Peter F. Drucker
Management: Tasks, Responsibilities, Practices (Harper)

1976

William F. Christopher
The Achieving Enterprise (AMACOM)

1977

Robert N. Anthony and Regina E. Herzlinger
Management Control in Nonprofit Organizations (Irwin)

1978

Frederick I. Herzberg
The Managerial Choice: To Be Efficient and to Be Human (Dow Jones/Irwin)

1979

George A. Steiner and John B. Miner
Management Policy and Strategy (Macmillan)

Sidney Hillman Foundation Awards

Every year since 1950 the Sidney Hillman Foundation, Inc., 15 Union Square West, New York, New York 10003, has offered awards for outstanding contributions on such themes as civil liberties, race relations, social and economic welfare, and world understanding and related problems in the daily press, magazines, books, radio, and television. The General Executive Board of the Amalgamated Clothing Workers of America established the Foundation to honor the memory and perpetuate the ideals of Sidney Hillman, its first president. A prize of $750, together with a scroll, is given to each winner, usually at a luncheon in New York City early in May. There are no restrictions on eligibility. Submissions may be made by anyone, and decisions are made by three outside judges whose determination is final. Entries must have been published or produced under professional auspices during the year for which an award is sought. No unpublished manuscripts are considered. Only book awards are listed below.

1950
John Hersey
The Wall (Knopf)

1951
Alan Barth
The Loyalty of Free Men (Viking)

1952
Herbert Block
The Herblock Book (Beacon)

1953
Theodore H. White
Fire in the Ashes (Sloane)

1954
Henry Steele Commager
Freedom, Loyalty and Dissent (Oxford Univ. Press)

1955
John Lord O'Brian
National Security and Individual Freedom (Harvard Univ. Press)

1956
Walter Gelhorn
Individual Freedom and Governmental Restraints (Louisiana State Univ. Press)

1957
Wilma Dykeman and James Stokely
Neither Black nor White (Rinehart)

1958
John Kenneth Galbraith
The Affluent Society (Houghton)

1959
Harold M. Hyman
To Try Men's Souls (Univ. of California Press)

1960
Davis McEntire
Residence and Race (Univ. of California Press)

William L. Shirer
The Rise and Fall of the Third Reich (Simon & Schuster) Special award

1961
Jane Jacobs
Death and Life of Great American Cities (Random)

1962
Michael Harrington
The Other America (Macmillan)

1963
Richard Hofstadter
Anti-Intellectualism in American Life (Random)

1964
James W. Silver
Mississippi: The Closed Society (Harcourt)

Bernard D. Nossiter
The Mythmakers (Houghton)

1965
Kenneth B. Clark
Dark Ghetto (Harper)

1966
Joseph P. Lyford
The Airtight Cage (Harper)

1967
Ronald Steel
Pax Americana (Viking)

Alan F. Westin
Privacy and Freedom (Atheneum)

1968
George R. Stewart
Not So Rich as You Think (Houghton)

1969
Richard D. McCarthy
Ultimate Folly (Knopf)

1970
Ramsey Clark
Crime in America (Simon & Schuster)

1971
Morton Mintz and Jerry S. Cohen
America, Inc. (Dial)
1972
Frances FitzGerald
Fire in the Lake (Atlantic-Little)
1973
Jervis Anderson
A. Philip Randolph: A Biographical Portrait (Harcourt)
Arthur M. Schlesinger, Jr.
The Imperial Presidency (Houghton)
Aleksandr Solzhenitsyn
Special award
1974
Noel Mostert

Supership (Knopf)
Richard Barnet and Ronald Müller
Global Reach (Simon & Schuster)
1975
E. J. Kahn, Jr.
The China Hands (Viking)
1976
Richard Kluger
Simple Justice (Knopf)
1977
Philip Caputo
A Rumor of War (Holt)
1978
Charles E. Silberman
Criminal Violence, Criminal Justice (Random)

Alice Davis Hitchcock Book Award

The Society of Architectural Historians, 1700 Walnut Street, Suite 716, Philadelphia, Pennsylvania 19103, established the Alice Davis Hitchcock Book Award in 1949. A framed Wedgwood plaque is given for the most distinguished work of scholarship in the history of architecture published in the two preceding years by a North American Scholar. Books to be considered for the award should be sent to each member of the Book Award Committee (names furnished to publishers), as well as to the central office of the Society. The award is presented at the annual spring meeting of the Society of Architectural Historians.

1950
Harold Wethey
Colonial Architecture and Sculpture in Peru (Harvard Univ. Press)
1951
Rexford Newcomb
Architecture of the Old Northwest Territory (Univ. of Chicago Press)
1952
Anthony N. B. Garvan
Architecture and Town Planning in Colonial Connecticut (Yale Univ. Press)
1953
Antoinette Downing and Vincent Scully

The Architectural Heritage of Newport, R.I. (Harvard Univ. Press)
1954
Thomas Howarth
Charles Rennie Mackintosh and the Modern Movement (Wittenborn)
1955
Henry-Russell Hitchcock
Early Victorian Architecture in Britain, 2 vols. (Yale Univ. Press)
1956
Talbot Hamlin
Benjamin H. Latrobe (Oxford Univ. Press)
1957
Carroll L. V. Meeks

The Architecture of the Railroad Station (Yale Univ. Press)

1958
Frederick D. Nichols
The Early Architecture of Georgia (Univ. of North Carolina Press)

1959
Marcus Whiffen
The Public Buildings of Williamsburg (Colonial Williamsburg)

1960
Kenneth J. Conant
Carolingian and Romanesque Architecture: 800–1200 (Penguin)

1961
David R. Coffin
The Villa d'Este at Tivoli (Princeton Univ. Press)

1962
James Ackerman
The Architecture of Michelangelo, 2 vols. (Viking)

1963
George Kubler
The Art and Architecture of Ancient America (Penguin)

1964
Robert Branner
La Cathédrale de Bourges (Wittenborn)

1965
Alan Gowans
Images of American Living (Lippincott)

1966
John McAndrew
The Open Air Churches of Sixteenth-Century Mexico (Harvard Univ. Press)

1967
Richard Krautheimer
Early Christian and Byzantine Architecture (Penguin)

1968
Richard Pommer
Eighteenth-Century Architecture in Piedmont (New York Univ. Press)

1969
Barbara Miller Lane
Architecture and Politics in Germany, 1918–1945 (Harvard Univ. Press)

1970
Phyllis Williams Lehmann
Samothrace, Vol. III: The Hieron (Princeton Univ. Press)

1971
Franklin Toker
The Church of Notre-Dame in Montreal (McGill-Queens Univ. Press)

1972
No award

1973
H. Allen Brooks
The Prairie School (Univ. of Toronto Press)
Thomas F. Mathews
The Early Churches of Constantinople: Architecture and Liturgy (Pennsylvania State Univ. Press)

1974
Marvin Trachtenberg
The Campanile of Florence Cathedral: Giotto's Tower (NYU Press)

1975
Laura Wood Roper
FLO: A Biography of Frederick Law Olmsted (Johns Hopkins Univ. Press)

1976
Rudolf Wittkower
Gothic vs. Classic: Architectural Projects in Seventeenth-Century Italy (Braziller)

1977
No award

1978
Mary Louise Christovich, Sally Kittredge Evans, Betsy Swanson, and Roulhac Toledano
The Esplanade Ridge, vol. V in New Orleans Architecture series (Pelican)

1979
Myra Nan Rosenfeld
Sebastiano Serlio on Domestic Architecture (Architectural History Fdn.)

Hugo Awards

Initiated in 1953 by the World Science Fiction Convention, but given annually only since 1955, these awards are named after Hugo Gernsback, the "founder" of science fiction. Winners are selected by the Convention members by mail ballot, and the award, a silver rocket ship, is presented at the Award Banquet of the Convention over Labor Day weekend. Science fiction and fantasy writers, artists, and professional and amateur publishers are eligible for awards. Nominations are required. The Convention address changes yearly, but inquiries regarding the award may be sent to Howard DeVore, 4705 Weddel Street, Dearborn, Michigan 48125. DeVore has published *A History of the Hugo, Nebula, and International Fantasy Awards,* which contains complete listings of nominees and winners from 1952 to 1975. Awards are given for novel, novelette, short fiction, illustrator, professional magazine, amateur publication, fact articles, new science fiction author or artist, feature writer, critic, dramatic presentation, and professional artist. Occasionally, awards are provided for best movies, television shows, and live dramatic performances. The John W. Campbell Award is given to an author whose first professional story was published during the two years preceding presentation of the award. The Gandalf Award is given to a writer who, in the course of his or her career, has contributed to the advancement of fantasy or heroic fantasy. Listed below are winners of the Hugo Award novel category, the John W. Campbell Award, and the Gandalf Award.

John W. Campbell Award

1973
  Jerry Pournelle
1974
  Spider Robinson
  Lisa Tuttle
1975
  P. J. Plauger
1976
  Tom Reamy
1977
  C. J. Cherryl
1978
  Orson Scott Card
1979
  Stephen Donaldson

Gandalf Award

1974
  J. R. R. Tolkien
1975
  Fritz Leiber

1976
  L. Sprague de Camp
1977
  Andre Norton
1978
  Poul Anderson
1979
  Ursula K. LeGuin

Hugo Award for Novels

1953
  Alfred Bester
  The Demolished Man (New American Library)
1954
  No award
1955
  Mark Clifton and Frank Riley
  They'd Rather Be Right (Gnome)
1956
  Robert A. Heinlein
  Double Star (Doubleday)

1957
No award
1958
Fritz Leiber
The Big Time (Ace)
1959
James Blish
A Case of Conscience (Ballantine)
1960
Robert A. Heinlein
Starship Troopers (Putnam)
1961
Walter M. Miller, Jr.
A Canticle for Leibowitz (Bantam)
1962
Robert A. Heinlein
Stranger in a Strange Land (Putnam)
1963
Phillip K. Dick
The Man in the High Castle (Putnam)
1964
Clifford Simak
Way Station (Macfadden)
1965
Fritz Leiber
The Wanderer (Ballantine)
1966
Frank Herbert
Dune (Ace)
Roger Zelazny
This Immortal (Ace)
1967
Robert A. Heinlein
The Moon Is a Harsh Mistress (Putnam)
1968
Roger Zelazny
Lord of Light (Doubleday)

1969
John Brunner
Stand on Zanzibar (Doubleday/Ballantine)
1970
Ursula K. LeGuin
The Left Hand of Darkness (Ace)
1971
Larry Niven
Ringworld (Walker)
1972
Philip Jose Farmer
To Your Scattered Bodies Go (Putnam)
1973
Isaac Asimov
The Gods Themselves (Doubleday)
1974
Arthur C. Clarke
Rendezvous with Rama (Harcourt)
1975
Ursula K. LeGuin
The Dispossessed (Harper)
1976
Joe Haldeman
The Forever War (St. Martin's)
1977
Kate Wilhelm
Where Late the Sweet Birds Sang (Harper)
1978
Frederik Pohl
Gateway (St. Martin's)
1979
Vonda N. McIntyre
Dreamsnake (Houghton)

JWB Jewish Book Council

Gerrard and Ella Berman Award

The JWB Jewish Book Council, 15 East 26 Street, New York, New York 10010, established this award in the name of Bernard H. Marks for a work dealing with the whole or some aspect of Jewish history, past or present, which in the opinion of the judges combines scholarship and literary merit. In 1978, the name of the award was changed to the Gerrard and Ella Berman Award for Jewish history. The books to be considered must have been originally written in English, Hebrew, or Yiddish by residents or citizens of the United States or Canada. Books on the holocaust or Israel are not eligible. The award, $500 and a citation, usually will be for a book published in the year preceding the annual presentation ceremony in May.

1973
Arthur J. Zuckerman
A Jewish Princedom in Feudal France (Columbia Univ. Press)

1974
Bernard D. Weinryb
The Jews of Poland: A Social and Economic History of the Jewish Community in Poland from 1100 to 1800 (Jewish Publication Society)

1975
Solomon Zeitlin
For cumulative contributions to Jewish history

1976
Raphael Patai and Jennifer Patai Wing

The Myth of the Jewish Race (Scribner)

1977
Irving Howe
World of Our Fathers (Harcourt)

1978
Celia S. Heller
On the Edge of Destruction (Columbia Univ. Press)

1979
Salo W. Baron
For contributions to Jewish historical research and thought

Frank and Ethel S. Cohen Award

The JWB Jewish Book Council established the Frank and Ethel S. Cohen Award to be given to the author of a work dealing with some aspect of Jewish thought, past or present, which in the opinion of the judges combines knowledge, clarity of thought, and literary merit. The award of $500 and a citation will be given to the author of a book published during the preceding calendar year. The books to be considered must have been originally written in English by residents of the United States or Canada. The announcement of the winner is made at the annual meeting of the JWB Jewish Book Council, which generally takes place in May.

1963
Moses Ricshin
The Promised City (Harvard Univ. Press)

1964
Ben Zion Bokser
Judaism: Profile of a Faith (Burning Bush/Knopf)

1965
Israel Efros
Ancient Jewish Philosophy (Wayne State Univ. Press)

1966
David Polish
The Higher Freedom, A New Turning Point in Jewish History (Quadrangle)

1967
Nahum M. Sarna
Understanding Genesis: The Heritage of Biblical Israel (United Synagogue Book Service)
1968
Michael A. Mayer
Origins of the Modern Jew (Wayne State Univ. Press)
1969
Emil L. Fackenheim
Quest for Past and Future: Essays in Jewish Theology (Univ. of Indiana Press)
1970
Abraham Joshua Heschel
Israel: An Echo of Eternity (Farrar)
1971
Mordecai M. Kaplan
The Religion of Ethical Nationhood: Judaism's Contribution to World Peace (Macmillan)
1972
Abraham E. Millgram
Jewish Worship (Jewish Publication Society)
1973
Samuel Sandmel
Two Living Traditions: Essays on Religion and the Bible (Wayne State Univ. Press)
Elie Wiesel
Souls on Fire: Portraits and Legends of Hasidic Masters (Random)
1974
Eugene B. Borowitz
The Mask Jews Wear: The Self-Deceptions of American Jewry (Simon & Schuster)
1975
Eliezer Berkovits
Major Themes in Modern Philosophies of Judaism (Ktav)
1976
Solomon B. Freehof
Contemporary Reform Responsa (Hebrew Union College Press)
1977
David Hartman
Maimonides: Torah and Philosophic Quest (Jewish Publication Society)
1978
Raphael Patai
The Jewish Mind (Scribner)
1979
Robert Gordis
Love and Sex: A Modern Jewish Perspective (Women's League for Conservative Judaism/Farrar)

William and Janice Epstein Award

The JWB Jewish Book Council established the William and Janice Epstein Award in 1949 (known as the Harry and Ethel Daroff Memorial Fiction Award until 1972) to encourage fictional writing on Jewish themes and to give recognition to the authors of such books. The award is made for a book of fiction on a Jewish theme published during the preceding year or for the cumulative contribution of an author. A citation and $500 are presented to the winner in May at the annual meeting of the JWB Jewish Book Council.

1950
John Hersey
The Wall (Knopf)
1951
Soma Morgenstern
The Testament of the Lost Son (Jewish Publication Society)
1952
Zelda Popkin
Quiet Street (Lippincott)
1953
Michael Blankfort
The Juggler (Little)

1954
  Charles Angoff
  In the Morning Light (Beechhurst)
1955
  Louis Zara
  Blessed Is the Land (Crown)
1956
  Jo Sinclair
  The Changelings (McGraw)
1957
  Lion Feuchtwanger
  Raquel: The Jewess of Toledo (Messner)
1958
  Bernard Malamud
  The Assistant (Farrar)
1959
  Leon Uris
  Exodus (Doubleday)
1960
  Philip Roth
  Goodbye, Columbus (Houghton)
1961
  Edward L. Wallant
  The Human Season (Harcourt)
1962
  Samuel Yellen
  The Wedding Band (Atheneum)
1963
  Isaac Bashevis Singer
  The Slave (Farrar)
1964
  Joanne Greenberg
  The King's Persons (Rinehart)
1965
  Elie Wiesel
  The Town beyond the Wall (Atheneum)
1966
  Meyer Levin
  The Stronghold (Simon & Schuster)

1967
  No award
1968
  Chaim Grade
  The Well (Jewish Publication Society)
1969
  Charles Angoff
  Memory of Autumn (Yoseloff/Barnes)
1970
  Leo Litwak
  Waiting for the News (Doubleday)
1971
  No award
1972
  Cynthia Ozick
  The Pagan Rabbi and Other Stories (Knopf)
1973
  Robert Kotlowitz
  Somewhere Else (Charterhouse)
1974
  Francine Prose
  Judah the Pious (Atheneum)
1975
  Jean Karsavina
  White Eagle, Dark Skies (Scribner)
1976
  Johanna Kaplan
  Other People's Lives (Knopf)
1977
  Cynthia Ozick
  Bloodshed and Three Novellas (Knopf)
1978
  Chaim Grade
  The Yeshiva, 2 vols. (Bobbs)
1979
  Gloria Goldreich
  Leah's Journey (Harcourt)

Rabbi Jacob Freedman Award

The JWB Jewish Book Council established this award, presented in the name of Rabbi Jacob Freedman, for a book that is considered by the judges to be a Jewish classic and whose English translation has literary merit. The books to be considered must have been translated (from any language) by residents or citizens of the United States or Canada. Only books originally written before 1920 are eligible. The award, $500 and a citation, is given to the translator of a book published in the preceding two calendar years. The presentation ceremony generally takes place in May.

1975
Jewish Publication Society Committee of Translators of the Prophets
The Book of Isaiah (Jewish Publication Society)

1976
William G. Braude and Israel J. Kapstein
Pesikta de-Rab Kahana: R. Kahana's Compilation of Discourses for Sabbaths and Festal Days (Jewish Publication Society)

1977
Zvi L. Lampel
Maimonides' Introduction to the Talmud (Judaica)

1978
No award

1979
William M. Brinner
An Elegant Composition concerning Relief after Adversity, by Nissim ben Jacob ibn Shahin (Yale Univ. Press)

Leon Jolson Award

Established in 1966, the Leon Jolson Award is given for the best book on the Nazi holocaust. A committee of judges selects the winner of the $500 prize, which is presented annually in May at the meeting of the JWB Jewish Book Council in New York.

1966
Zosa Szajkowski
Analytical Franco-Jewish Gazetteer, 1939–45 (Frydman)

1967
Abraham Kin, Mordecai Kosover, and Isaiah Trunk, eds.
Algemeyne Entisklopedye: Yidn VII (Dubnow Fund & Encyclopedia Committee)

1968
Jacob Robinson
And the Crooked Shall Be Made Straight (Macmillan)

1969
Judah Pilch
The Jewish Catastrophe in Europe (American Association for Jewish Education)

Nora Levin
The Holocaust: The Destruction of European Jewry (Crowell)

1970
Zalman Zylbercweig
Lexicon of the Yiddish Theater: Martyrs Volume (Hebrew Actors Union of America)

1971
Ephraim Oshry
Sheelot u-Teshuvot: Mi-Maamakim

1972
Henry L. Feingold
The Politics of Rescue: The Roosevelt Administration and the Holocaust, 1938–1945 (Rutgers Univ. Press)

1973
Aaron Zeitlin
Vaiterdike Lider fun Hurban un Lider

fun Gloiben in Yanish Korshaks Letze Gang (Bergen Belsen Memorial Press)
1974
No award
1975
Isaiah Trunk
Judenrat: The Jewish Councils in Eastern Europe under Nazi Occupation (Macmillan)
1976
Leyzer Ran
Yerushalayim de Lite: Jerusalem of Lithuania

1977
Ephraim Oshry
Sefer Sheelot U-Teshuvot Mi-Maamakim: Part 4: Book of Questions and Answers from the Depths
1978
Terrence Des Pres
The Survivor: An Anatomy of Life in the Death Camp (Oxford Univ. Press)
1979
Michael Selzer
Deliverance Day: The Last Hours at Dachau (Lippincott)

Morris J. Kaplun Memorial Award

The JWB Jewish Book Council established the Morris J. Kaplun Award, presented by the Morris J. and Betty Kaplun Foundation, for a book dealing with the whole or some aspect of Israel. The award of $500 and a citation is given to the author of a book published during the preceding year. The books to be considered must have been originally written in English, Hebrew, or Yiddish by residents of the United States or Canada. The presentation ceremony generally takes place in May of each year.

1974
Isaiah Friedman
The Question of Palestine, 1914–1918: British-Jewish-Arab Relations (Schocken)
1975
Arnold Krammer
The Forgotten Friendship: Israel and the Soviet Bloc, 1947–1953 (Univ. of Illinois Press)
1976
Melvin I. Urofsky
American Zionism from Herzl to the Holocaust (Doubleday)

1977
Howard M. Sachar
A History of Israel (Knopf)
1978
Hillel Halkin
Letters to an American Jewish Friend (Jewish Publication Society)
1979
Ruth Gruber
Raquela: A Woman of Israel (Coward)

Harry and Florence Kovner Memorial Awards

In 1950, the Harry Kovner Memorial Awards (called the Harry and Florence Kovner Memorial Awards since 1959) for English-Jewish, Hebrew, and Yiddish poetry were established by the JWB Jewish Book Council. Annually in May, a citation and $500 award (formerly $100 and $250) are presented at the meeting of the JWB Jewish

Book Council. The awards are currently given for books of poetry published during the preceding three years (once every three years for English, Hebrew, and Yiddish), or for cumulative contributions by American citizens or residents, as described by a committee of judges.

ENGLISH POETRY

1951
  Judah Stampfer
  Jerusalem Has Many Faces (Farrar)
1952
  A. M. Klein
  Cumulative contributions to English-Jewish poetry
1953
  Isidore Goldstick
  For translation of *Poems of Yehoash*
1954
  Harry H. Fein
  Cumulative contributions to English-Jewish poetry
1955–1958
  No awards
1959
  Grace Goldin
  Come under the Wings: A Midrash on Ruth (Jewish Publication Society)
1960
  Amy K. Blank
  The Spoken Choice (Hebrew Union College Press)
1961
  No award
1962
  Irving Feldman
  Work and Days and Other· Poems (Little)
1963
  Charles Reznikoff
  By the Waters of Manhattan (New Directions)
1964–1965
  No awards
1966
  Ruth Finer Mintz
  The Darkening Green (Big Mountain)

1967–1968
  No awards
1969
  Ruth Whitman
  The Marriage Wig and Other Poems (Harcourt)
1971
  Ruth Finer Mintz
  Traveler through Time (Jonathan David)
1974
  Harold Schimmel, trans.
  Songs of Jerusalem and Myself, by Yehuda Amichai (Harper)
1977
  Myra Sklarew
  From the Backyard of the Diaspora (Dryad)

HEBREW POETRY

1951
  Aaron Zeitlin
  Shirim U'Poemot (Songs and Poems)
1952
  Hillel Bavli
  Cumulative contributions to Hebrew poetry
1953
  A. S. Schwartz
  Cumulative contributions to Hebrew poetry
1954
  Ephraim E. Lisitzky
  Be-Ohalei Kush (In Negro Tents)
1955
  Gabriel Preil
  Ner Mul Kochavin (Candle under the Stars)

HEBREW POETRY (cont.)

1956
Hillel Bavli
Aderet Ha-Shanim (Mantle of Years)
1957
Moshe Feinstein
Avraham Abulafia
1958
Aaron Zeitlin
Bein Ha-Esh Veha-Yesha (Yavneh)
1959
Moshe Ben Meir
Tzlil va Tzel
1960
Eisig Silberschlag
Kimron Yamai
1961
Ephraim E. Lisitzky
K'Mo Hayom Rad (Medhberot)
1962
Gabriel Preil
Mapat Erev (Dvir)
1963
Arnold Band
Ha-Rei Boer ha-Esh (Ogen)
1964–1965
No awards
1966
Simon Halkin
Crossing the Jabbok (Am Oved)
1967
Leonard D. Friedland
Shirim be-Sulam Minor (M. Newman)
1968
No award
1969
Reuven Ben-Yosef
Derech Eretz (Hakebutz Hameuchad)
1972
Eisig Silberschlag
Igrotai El Dorot Aherim (Letters to Other Generations) (Kir yat Sefer)
1975
Reuven Ben-Yosef
Metim ve-Ohavim (Massada)

1978
T. Carmi
El Eretz Aheret (To Another Land) (Dvir)

YIDDISH POETRY

1951
Ber Lapin
Der Fuller Krug (The Brimming Jug)
1952
Mordicai Jaffe
For editing and translation of *Anthology of Hebrew Poetry*
1953
Mark Schwaid
For collected poems
1954
Eliezer Greenberg
Banachtiger Dialog (Night Dialogue)
1955
Alter Esselin
Lider fun a Midbarnik (Poems of a Hermit)
1956
Naphtali Gross
Posthumously, for cumulative contributions to Yiddish poetry
1957
Jacob Glatstein
Fun Mein Gantzer Mei
1958
I. J. Schwartz
For cumulative contributions to Yiddish poetry
1959
Benjamin Bialostotzky
Lid Tzu Lid (CYCO)
1960
Ephraim Auerbach
Gildene Shekiah
1961
Joseph Rubinstein
Megilath Russland (CYCO)

YIDDISH POETRY (cont.)

1962
Israel Emiot
In Nigun Eingehert

1963
Chaim Grade
Det Mentsh fun Fier (CYCO)

1964
Aaron Glanz-Leyeles
Amerika un Ich (CYCO)

1965
Aleph Katz
Di Emesse Hasunah (CYCO)

1966
Kadia Molodowsky
Licht fun Dorenboim (Kiyum)

1967
Jacob Glatstein
A Yid fun Lublin (CYCO)

1968
Aaron Zeitlin
Lider fun Hurban un Lider fun Gloiben
(World Federation of Bergen-Belsen
Associations)

1969
Rachel H. Korn
Di Gnod fun Vort (Hemenora)

1970
Eliezer Greenberg
Eibiker Dorsht (Eternal Thirst)

1973
Meir Sticker
Yidishe Landshaft (Teretz)

1976
M. Husid
A Shotn Tragt Main Kroin (Book Committee, Montreal)

1979
Moishe Steingart
In Droisen fun der Velt (Shulsinger Bros.)

Charles and Bertie G. Schwartz Award *see* Juvenile Prizes

Joseph Henry Jackson Award

The Joseph Henry Jackson Award, administered by the San Francisco Foundation, Room 1602, 425 California Street, San Francisco, California 94104, was established as a memorial to the distinguished San Francisco literary critic. It is designed to continue and develop the sort of encouragement and recognition of fine literary work by young writers long provided by Joseph Henry Jackson himself. The annual grant-in-aid, first awarded in 1957, consists of an award of $2,000 to a young writer, age twenty through thirty-five, who is a resident of northern California or Nevada for three consecutive years immediately prior to the deadline. The competition is open to unpublished works of fiction, nonfictional prose, or poetry.

1957
Dennis Murphy
The Sergeant (Viking)

1958
William C. Wiegand
The Treatment Man (McGraw)

1959
Ernest J. Gaines
"Comeback"

1960
James Fetler
"The Seen and Not Seen"

1961
   Philip Levine
   "Berenda Slough and Other Poems"
1962
   James Leigh
   "What Can You Do?"
1963
   Leonard Gardner
   "Fat City"
1964
   Floyd Francis Salas
   "The Star, the Cross and the Broad-
   sword"
1965
   Frank Chew Chin, Jr.
   "A Chinese Lady Dies"
1966
   Louis Dell Logan
   "Alligator's Hopes in a Tadpole Town"
1967
   James D. Houston
   Gig (Dial)
1968
   Stanley T. Rice, Jr.
   "Eye"
1969
   Al Young
   "California Dancing"
1970
   Ernest Brawley
   "In the Shadow of Thy Wings"

1971
   Richard Lourie
   "Sagittarius in Warsaw"
1972
   Raymond Kingsley
   "Rehabilitation"
1973
   Russell Brandon
   Untitled collection of short stories
1974
   Mark F. Jarman
   Untitled collection of poetry
1975
   Fredric Matteson
   "Seeing the Ocean for the First Time"
1976
   Stephen M. Tracy
   "The Potatoe Baron and the Line,"
   "Charlie the Magician and the Day
   Care Center," and "The Meagerest of
   Disciplines"
1977
   Stephanie Mines
   "Poems and Prose Poems by a Soli-
   tary Woman"
1978
   John Thomas Lescroart
   "Sunburn"
1979
   Mindy Eunsoo Pennybacker
   "Fallings from Us, Vanishings" and
   "Chang in Granada"

The Jamestown Manuscript Prize

In 1974, the Institute of Early American History and Culture established an entirely
new manuscript award to supersede the Jamestown Award (1962–1972) and the Institute Manuscript Award (1952–1967). The new prize covers the entire chronological
span of early American history and the related history of the British Isles, Europe,
West Africa, and the Caribbean, and provides a $1,500 cash prize and publication by
the Institute and the University of North Carolina Press. The prize competition is open
only to authors of scholarly manuscripts who have not previously published a book.
Manuscripts may only be submitted between August 1 and September 30. Authors
should write to the Editor of Publications, Institute of Early American History and Culture, Box 220, Williamsburg, Virginia 23185, for detailed instructions for submitting
entries.

1975
James H. Kettner
The Development of American Citizenship, 1608–1870
1976
David G. Allen
In English Ways: The Movement of Societies and the Transferal of English Local Law and Custom to Massachusetts Bay, 1600–1690
1977–1979
No awards

John H. Jenkins Award for Bibliography

This annual award of $500 was established in 1972 by John H. Jenkins, an antiquarian bookseller in Austin, Texas, and Union College, Schenectady, New York. Jenkins—at considerable personal risk—caught and turned over to the FBI the thief who had stolen from the Schaffer Library of Union College the first volume of Audubon's *Birds of America*, bought by Union in 1840 from Audubon himself. Jenkins generously returned the reward money to Union, which matched the sum to found this award. The aim of the award is to recognize the best bibliography published during the previous two years. Selection of the winner is made by a panel of five judges in the autumn. Announcement of the award winner is made in June at a ceremony on the day before the Union College Commencement. Inquiries should be sent to Professor Carl Niemeyer, Schaffer Library, Union College, Schenectady, New York 12308.

1973
G. Thomas Tanselle
Guide to the Study of United States Imprints, 2 vols. (Belknap)
1974
Philip Gaskell
A New Study of Bibliography (Oxford Univ. Press)
1975
Jacob N. Blanck
Bibliography of American Literature, Vol. 6: Augustus Baldwin Longstreet to Thomas William Parsons (Yale Univ. Press)
1976
Ronald Burt DeWaal
The World Bibliography of Sherlock Holmes and Dr. Watson (New York Graphic Society)
1977
D. F. Foxon
English Verse, 1701–1750, 2 vols. (Cambridge Univ. Press)
1978
H. J. Hanham, ed.
Bibliography of British History, 1851–1914 (Oxford Univ. Press)
1979
G. E. Bentley, Jr.
Blake Books (Oxford Univ. Press)

Jewish Heritage Award for Excellence in Literature

This award was established in 1966 to honor an author for a body of work on aspects of Jewish life or thought. It is offered by the Commission on Adult Jewish Education,

B'nai B'rith, 1640 Rhode Island Avenue N.W., Washington, D.C. 20036. The winner is announced annually in late fall, and in early spring a $1,000 prize is presented at a public Jewish Heritage Award Luncheon, usually in New York City. A board of judges makes the decision. Applications are not accepted. The Commission also gave the B'nai B'rith Book Award from 1970 to 1972.

1966
  Elie Wiesel
1967
  Maurice Samuel
1968
  Saul Bellow
1969
  Salo W. Baron
1970
  Isaac Babel (posthumous)
1971
  Abraham J. Heschel
1972
  Jacob Glatstein (posthumous)

1973
  Nahum N. Glatzer
1974
  Gershom Scholem
1975
  Eliezer Greenberg
  Irving Howe
1976
  Chaim Grade
1977
  Bernard Malamud
1978
  No award
1979
  Abraham Sutzkever

Janet Heidinger Kafka Prize

The Kafka Prize, sponsored by the English Department and the Writers' Workshop of the University of Rochester, was established in 1976 as a memorial to Janet Heidinger Kafka, a young Random House editor, who was killed in an accident. Contributors to the fund that supports the prize include family, friends, and colleagues. The prize is awarded annually to a woman citizen of the United States who has written the best published work of fiction, whether a novel, short story collection, or experimental writing, but excluding children's books. Entries will be evaluated by a panel of five jurors, one of whom is either a member of the publishing industry, a book critic, or an author, and who is not associated with the University of Rochester. Five copies of each entry should be submitted for consideration before December 31 of the year in which the book is published. Collections of short stories must have been assembled for the first time, or at least one-third of the material must be previously unpublished. The prize, a cash award that varies from year to year, is presented to the winner in July at the conclusion of the Writers' Workshop on the University of Rochester campus. Inquiries should be directed to Anne Ludlow, Assistant Dean, University College, University of Rochester, Rochester, New York 14627.

1976
  Jessamyn West
  Massacre at Fall Creek (Harcourt)
1977
  Judith Guest
  Ordinary People (Viking)

1978
  Toni Morrison
  Song of Solomon (Knopf)
1979
  Mary Gordon
  Final Payments (Random)

Coretta Scott King Award

Established in 1969 at the American Library Association (ALA) convention in Atlantic City, New Jersey, this award has four purposes: to commemorate the life and works of the late Dr. Martin Luther King, Jr.; to honor Mrs. King for her courage to continue to fight for peace and world brotherhood; to encourage creative artists and authors to promote the cause of peace and brotherhood through their works; and to inspire children and youth to dedicate their talents and energies to help achieve these goals. The most important criterion is the inspirational quality that links the book to the future. The award, presented at the annual ALA convention, consists of an honorarium, a plaque, and a set of the *Encyclopaedia Britannica*. Further information may be obtained from Howard G. Ball, Dean, School of Library Media, Box 223, Alabama A&M University, Normal, Alabama 35762.

1970
Lille Patterson
Martin Luther King Jr.: Man of Peace (Garrard)
1971
Charlemae Rollins
Black Troubadour: Langston Hughes (Rand McNally)
1972
Elton C. Fax
Seventeen Black Artists (Dodd)
1973
Alfred Duckett
I Never Had It Made: The Autobiography of Jackie Robinson (Putnam)
1974
Sharon Bell Mathis, author, and George Ford, illus.
Ray Charles (Crowell).

1975
Dorothy W. Robinson, author, and Herbert Temple, illus.
Legend of Africania (Johnson)
1976
Pearl Bailey
Duey's Tale (Harcourt)
1977
James Haskins
The Story of Stevie Wonder (Lothrop)
1978
Eloise Greenfield and Carol Byard
Africa Dream (John Day)
1979
Ossie Davis
Escape to Freedom (Viking)
Tom Feelings, illus.
Something on My Mind, by Nikki Grimes (Dial)

Otto Kinkeldey Award

Established in 1967 and offered annually by the American Musicological Society, 201 South 34 Street, Philadelphia, Pennsylvania 19104, this award is named for the scholar-librarian who was the first president and later the honorary president of the American Musicological Society. It is given to a U.S. or Canadian author of the most notable full-length study in any branch of musicology published during the previous year. Selection is made by a specially appointed committee. A scroll and $400 are presented to each of the winners at the annual meeting of the American Musicological Society.

1967
William W. Austin
Music in the Twentieth Century (Norton)

1968
Rulan Chao Pian
Sonq Dynasty Musical Sources and Their Interpretation (Harvard Univ. Press)

1969
Edward Lowinsky
The Medici Codex of 1518 (Univ. of Chicago Press)

1970
Nino Pirrotta
Li Due Orfei, da Poliziano a Monteverdi (Edizioni RAI)

1971
Daniel Heartz
Pierre d'Attaignant, Royal Printer of Music (Univ. of California Press)

Joseph Kerman
Ludwig van Beethoven, Autograph Miscellany from ca. 1786 to 1799. British Museum add. ms. 19801 (The Kafka Sketchbook) (Oxford Univ. Press)

1972
Albert Seay
Jacobus Arcadelt, Opera Omnia, Vol. II (American Institute of Musicology)

1973
H. Colin Slim
A Gift of Madrigals and Motets (Univ. of Chicago Press)

1974
Robert L. Marshall
The Compositional Process of J. S. Bach (Princeton Univ. Press)

1975
Vivian Perlis
Charles Ives Remembered: An Oral History (Yale Univ. Press)

1976
David P. McKay and Richard Crawford
William Billings of Boston: Eighteenth-Century Composer (Princeton Univ. Press)

1977
H. C. Robbins Landon
Haydn: Chronicle and Works, Vol. III: Haydn in London, 1791–1795 (Indiana Univ. Press)

1978
Richard L. Crocker
The Early Medieval Sequence (Univ. of California Press)

The Kosciuszko Foundation Doctoral Dissertation Award

This award, offered by the Kosciuszko Foundation, 15 East 65 Street, New York, New York 10021, was established to commemorate the millennium in 1966 of Poland's conversion to Christianity and to enable the publication of the doctoral dissertation written on a Polish subject that in the opinion of the Foundation has made the most significant contribution to the development of Polish studies. All disciplines are included: literature, linguistics, history, art, music, etc. Studies relating to the Poles in America or other countries are also included. Manuscripts must be submitted no later than July 15 of any given year. Awards are announced on or before October 1. A $1,000 grant is given to the publisher who will agree to publish the dissertation. The winner is notified by letter.

1964
J. U. Niemcewicz and Metchie Budka, trans.
Under Their Vine and Fig Tree (New Jersey Historical Society)

1965
Victor Greene
The Slavic Community on Strike (Univ. of Notre Dame Press)

1966
Joseph Wieczerzak
A Polish Chapter in Civil War America (Twayne)

1967
Jerzy Maciuszko
The Polish Short Story in English Translation (Wayne State Univ. Press)

1968
Robert Ferring
The Accomplished Ambassador of Christopher Varsavius

1969
Eugene Obidinski
The Poles of Buffalo

Frank Renkiewicz
The Poles of St. Joseph County

1970–1971
Winners unavailable

1972
Janina Cottam
Biography of Baleslaw Limanowski

Neil C. Sandberg
Ethnic Identity and Assimilation: The Polish-American Community; Case Study of Metropolitan Los Angeles (Praeger)

Joan Skurniewicz
The Polish National Ideal in the Life and Works of Joachim M. Lelewel

1973
John J. Kulczycki
Polish Society in Poznania and the School Strikes of 1901–1907

Anthony Joseph Kuzniewski
Faith and Fatherland: An Intellectual History of the Polish Immigrant Community in Wisconsin, 1838–1918

Maria J. Swiecicka
The Memoirs of Jan C. Pasek

1974
Stanislaus Blejwas
Warsaw Positivism, 1864–1890: Organic Work as an Expression of National Survival in Nineteenth-Century Poland

James S. Pula
The Life and Times of Wlodzimierz Krzyzanowski: Polish Immigrant, Civil War General, Federal Agent

Paul Wrobel
An Ethnographic Study of a Polish American Parish and Neighborhood

1975
Harry E. Dembkowski
Polish Federalism in the Golden Age

Laetare Medal

Established in 1883, this historic award honors American Catholics who have distinguished themselves in such fields of endeavor as the arts and sciences, government, or the professions. Although it is not a literary prize, a number of its recipients have been literary figures. The gold medal is awarded yearly by the University of Notre Dame, Notre Dame, Indiana 46556, and the winner is selected by a faculty committee headed by the president of the university. Announcement of the award is made on Laetare Sunday, the fourth Sunday of Lent. Its presentation is usually made at the convenience of the winner, either at his or her city of residence or on the Notre Dame campus. Since 1968 priests and religious have also been eligible for the medal. The following list includes only those awards given for distinguished contributions in the field of literature.

1883
John Gilmary Shea, historian
1888
Patrick V. Hickey, founder and editor, *Catholic Review*
1889
Anna Hansen Dorsey, novelist
1892
Henry F. Brownson, philosopher and author
1893
Patrick Donohue, founder, the Boston *Pilot*
1895
Mary A. Sadlier, novelist
1907
Katherine Eleanor Conway, journalist and author
1909
Frances Tiernan [Christian Reid], novelist
1910
Maurice Francis Egan, author and diplomat
1911
Agnes Repplier, author
1913
Charles B. Herberman, editor, *Catholic Encyclopedia*
1916
James Joseph Walsh, physician and author
1935
Francis Hamilton Spearman, novelist
1936
Richard Reid, lawyer and journalist
1941
William Thomas Walsh, journalist and author

1942
Helen Constance White, author and teacher
1943
Thomas Francis Woodlock, editor
1944
Anne O'Hare McCormick, journalist
1946
Carlton J. H. Hayes, historian and diplomat
1947
William G. Bruce, publisher
1957
Clare Boothe Luce, author and diplomat
1960
George N. Shuster, author and educator
1961
John F. Kennedy, president of the United States, author, and Pulitzer Prize winner
1964
Phyllis McGinley, poet
1971
Jean Kerr, author
Walter Kerr, drama critic
1972
Dorothy Day, founder of the Catholic Worker Movement, journalist, and author
1973
John A. O'Brien, author
1974
James A. Farley, U.S. postmaster general, businessman, and author
1975
Ann Ida Gannon, president, Mundelein College

1976
Paul Horgan, author

1978
John Tracy Ellis, historian

D. H. Lawrence Fellowship

This annual award was first given in 1958 by the University of New Mexico, Albuquerque, to encourage writers of fiction, poetry, and drama. The university provides residence at the Lawrence ranch near Taos, New Mexico, for eight to ten weeks in June, July, and August, as well as a stipend of $700. The ranch is Lawrence's memorial. His ashes rest in a chapel near his house, and his widow, Frieda Lawrence Ravagli, who gave the ranch to the University of New Mexico, is buried nearby. Selection is made by a committee of authorities in these fields, with announcement of the award made annually in April. Inquiries should be addressed to the Department of English, University of New Mexico, Albuquerque, New Mexico 87131.

1958
    Alfred Alvarez
1959
    Douglas Nichols
1960
    Robert Creeley
1961
    Jascha Kessler
1962
    George P. Elliott
1963
    Charles Tomlinson
1964
    John Verrall
1965
    Ann Quin
1966
    Robert S. Sward
1967
    Henry Rago
1968
    Henry Roth

1969
    Edward Dorn
1970
    Sean Hignett
1971
    Howard McCord
1972
    Keith Wilson
1973
    Glenna Luschei
1974
    Alan Friedman
1975
    Charlotte Painter
1976
    Robert Ecker
1977
    Alan Kapelner
1978
    Karen Hillier
1979
    Joseph McElroy

Pierre Lecomte du Noüy
Foundation Award

Two Pierre Lecomte du Noüy Foundations, one in the United States and one in France, were created in 1954 by Mme. Lecomte du Noüy in memory of her husband

Pierre (1883–1947), a French scientist and author. The American Foundation award, given every other year, consists of a silver medal and $2,000. It is presented to the author of an outstanding essay, biography, autobiography, or other work that reveals a special concern both for the spiritual life of the age and for the defense of human dignity. The French Foundation award, 5,000 francs, is given in alternate years. Books published within the preceding two years are eligible for the prize. They must be published in the language of the respective country, but may be translations from other languages. Further information is available from the Association Lecomte du Noüy, 15 avenue Elysée, F-75007 Paris, France.

1954
Marcel Sendrail
Le Serpent et le Miroir (Plon)
1955
C. A. Coulson
Science and Christian Belief (Univ. of North Carolina Press)
1956
Maurice Vernet
L'Homme Maitre de Sa Destinée (Grasset)
1957
William E. Hocking
The Coming World Civilization (Harper)
1958
No award
1959
Michael Polanyi
Personal Knowledge (Routledge) and *The Study of Man* (Univ. of Chicago Press)
1960
Henri Breuil
For his entire work
Rémy Chauvin
Dieu des Savants, Dieu de l'Experience (Mame)
1961
Loren Eiseley
Firmament of Time (Atheneum)
1962
Henri Gouhier
Bergson et le Christ des Evangiles (Fayard)

Marie-Noël
Notes Intimes (Stock)
1963
Theodosius Dobzhansky
Mankind Evolving (Yale Univ. Press)
Charles Hartshorne
The Logic of Perfection (Open Court)
1964
Olivier Costa de Beauregard
Le Second Principe de la Science du Temps (Seuil)
1965–1966
No awards
1967
Bernard d'Espagnat
Conceptions de la Physique Contemporaine (Hermann)
1968
Alister Hardy
The Living Stream (Collins)
1969
No award
1970
Jean Dorst
Avant que Nature Meure (Delachaux & Niestlé)
Stanley L. Jaki
Brain, Mind and Computers (Herder)
1971
Pierre-Henri Simon
Questions aux Savants (Seuil)
1972
No award
1973
René Barjavel
La Faim du Tigre (Denoël)

A. R. Peacocke
Science and the Christian Experience
(Oxford Univ. Press)

1974–1975
No awards
Discontinued

David D. Lloyd Prize

The Harry S. Truman Library Institute for National & International Affairs, Independence, Missouri 64050, established the David D. Lloyd Prize in 1963 to recognize the best book on the presidency of Harry S. Truman. The book must deal with some aspect of the social and political development of the United States primarily between April 12, 1945, and January 20, 1953, or must be directly associated with the public career of Harry S. Truman. The award of $1,000 is biennial, for the period ending December 31 of odd-numbered years. The winner is announced at the annual meeting of the Board of Directors of the Harry S. Truman Library Institute in April or May. Two copies of each book to be entered must be submitted to the Chairman of the Lloyd Prize Committee, Department of Political Science, 210 Barrows Hall, University of California, Berkeley, California 94720.

1964
No award
1966
Earl Latham
The Communist Controversy in Washington: From the New Deal to McCarthy (Harvard Univ. Press)
1968
Irwin Ross
The Loneliest Campaign: The Truman Victory of 1948 (New American Library)
1970
Dean Acheson
Present at the Creation (Norton)
Richard G. Hewlett and Francis Duncan
Atomic Shield 1947/1952 (Pennsylvania State Univ. Press)

1972
Susan M. Hartman
Truman and the 80th Congress (Univ. of Missouri Press)
1974
Alonzo L. Hamby
Beyond the New Deal: Harry S. Truman and American Liberalism (Columbia Univ. Press)
1976
Lynn Etheridge Davis
The Cold War Begins: Soviet-American Conflict over Eastern Europe (Princeton Univ. Press)
1978
David S. McLellan
Dean Acheson: The State Department Years (Dodd)

Locus Awards

Locus Publications, Box 3938, San Francisco, California 94119, established these annual awards in 1971 to honor the year's best novel, short fiction, collection, anthology, artist, magazine, illustrated or art book, and reference work in the field of science fiction and fantasy. The winners are selected through a poll of the readers of *Locus* magazine. Each winner receives a trophy at the annual West Coast Science Fiction Convention (Westercon) in July. Winners of the novel category are listed below.

1971
  Larry Niven
  Ringworld (Ballantine)
1972
  Ursula K. LeGuin
  The Lathe of Heaven (Scribner)
1973
  Isaac Asimov
  The Gods Themselves (Doubleday)
1974
  Arthur C. Clarke
  Rendezvous with Rama (Harcourt)
1975
  Ursula K. LeGuin
  The Dispossessed (Harper)

1976
  Joe Haldeman
  The Forever War (St. Martin's)
1977
  Kate Wilhelm
  Where Late the Sweet Birds Sang (Harper)
1978
  Frederik Pohl
  Gateway (St. Martin's)
1979
  Vonda N. McIntyre
  Dreamsnake (Houghton)

Loubat Prizes

The Loubat Prizes were instituted in 1893 by a grant from Joseph Florimond, Duc de Loubat. They consist of a first prize of $1,200 and a second prize of $600 for the best work printed and published in the English language on the history, geography, ethnology, philology, or numismatics of North America. The fund is administered by Columbia University, New York, and the jury of awards is chosen from eminent men and women of learning. The awards are made every five years at the commencement exercises of Columbia University. The competition for the prizes is open to all persons. The applicant need not be connected with Columbia or be a resident of the United States. In the list below, first award winners precede second award winners.

1893
  Henry Adams
  History of the United States of America during the Administrations of Jefferson and Madison (Scribner)
  A. F. Bandelier
  Report of Investigations among the Indians of the Southwestern States (Archeological Institute, Boston)
1898
  William Henry Holmes
  Stone Implements of the Potomac-

Chesapeake Tide Water Provinces (Smithsonian Institution)
  Franz Boas
  The Growth of Children (U.S. Government Printing Office)
1903
  No awards
1908
  Herbert Levi Osgood
  The American Colonies in the Seventeenth Century (Columbia Univ. Press)

Thomas Aloysius Hughes
The History of the Society of Jesus in North America (Longmans)
1913
George Louis Beer
The Old British Colonial System (Macmillan)
John Reed Swanton
The Indian Tribes of the Lower Mississippi Valley (Smithsonian Institution)
1918
Clarence Walworth Alvord
The Mississippi Valley in British Politics (A. H. Clark)
Herbert I. Priestley
José de Gálvez, Visitor-General of New Spain: 1765–1771 (Univ. of California Press)
1923
Justin Harvey Smith
The War with Mexico (Macmillan)
William Henry Holmes
Handbook of Aboriginal American Antiquities
1928
Herbert Levi Osgood
The American Colonies in the Eighteenth Century (Columbia Univ. Press)
Herbert J. Spinden
The Reduction of Maya Dates (Peabody Museum, Cambridge, Mass.)
1933
Charles Oscar Paullin and John Kirtland Wright
An Atlas of the Historical Geography of the United States (American Geographical Society)
Walter Prescott Webb
The Great Plains (Houghton/Ginn)

1938
Samuel Eliot Morison
The Founding of Harvard College and *Harvard College in the Seventeenth Century* (Harvard Univ. Press)
Samuel Kirkland Lothrop
Coclé: An Archaeological Study of Central Panama, Pt. 1 (Peabody Museum, Cambridge, Mass.)
1943
Sylvanus Griswold Morley
The Inscriptions of Peten (Carnegie Institution)
Edmund Cody Burnett
The Continental Congress (Macmillan)
1948
Lawrence Henry Gipson
The British Empire before the American Revolution (Knopf)
Hans Kurath
Linguistic Atlas of New England
1953
Mitford M. Mathews, ed.
A Dictionary of Americanisms (Univ. of Chicago Press)
James Garfield Randall
Midstream: Lincoln the President (Dodd)
Ralph Hall Brown
Historical Geography of the United States (Harcourt)
1958
Douglas Southall Freeman
George Washington (Scribner)
Henry Pochmann
German Culture in America, 1600–1900 (Univ. of Wisconsin Press)
1963, 1968, 1973, 1978
No awards

Louisiana Literary Award

This award was established in 1948 to focus attention and interest on published materials about Louisiana and to encourage writers and publishers to produce more and better literature about the state. It is given by the Louisiana Library Association, Louisiana State Library, Baton Rouge, Louisiana 70803, for a book published during the year dealing with a Louisiana subject. The book must provide a sound interpretation of the unique Louisiana heritage and must contribute to the permanent record of the state. It may be adult or juvenile, fiction or nonfiction, and it may be in any literary medium. The award, a bronze medallion, is presented each year at the annual convention of the Louisiana Library Association.

1949
Hewitt Ballowe
Creole Folk Tales (Louisiana State Univ. Press)
1950
John Chase
Frenchmen, Desire, Good Children, and Other Streets of New Orleans (Crager)
1951
Carlyle Tillery
Red Bone Woman (Longmans)
1952
Robert Tallant
The Pirate Lafitte and the Battle of New Orleans (Random)
1953
John Kendall
The Golden Age of the New Orleans Theater (Louisiana State Univ. Press)
1954
R. G. McWilliams, trans. and ed.
Fleur de Lys and Calumet; Being the Penicaut Narrative of French Adventure in Louisiana (Louisiana State Univ. Press)
1955
No award
1956
George Hines Lowery
Louisiana Birds (Louisiana State Univ. Press)
1957
Allan P. Sindler
Huey Long's Louisiana (Johns Hopkins Univ. Press)
1958
Charles P. Roland
Louisiana Sugar Plantations During

the Civil War (E. J. Brill, Leiden, Netherlands)
1959
John Duffy
The Rudolf Matas History of Medicine in Louisiana, Vol. I (Louisiana State Univ. Press)
1960
No award
1961
Isidore B. Cohn and Herman B. Deutsch
Rudolph Matas (Doubleday)
1962
Charles B. Brooks
The Siege of New Orleans (Univ. of Washington Press)
1963
Lauren C. Post
Cajun Sketches (Louisiana State Univ. Press)
1964
John Winters
Civil War in Louisiana (Louisiana State Univ. Press)
1965
Vincent H. Cassidy and Amos E. Simpson
Henry Watkins Allen of Louisiana (Louisiana State Univ. Press)
1966
Jack D. L. Holmes
Gayoso: The Life of a Spanish Governor in the Mississippi Valley, 1789–1799 (Louisiana State Univ. Press)
1967
John Percy Dyer
Tulane, The Biography of a University (Harper)

1968
Al Rose and Edmond Souchon
New Orleans Jazz (Louisiana State Univ. Press)
1969
No award
1970
T. Harry Williams
Huey Long (Knopf)
1971
Dorothea McCants
They Came to Louisiana (Louisiana State Univ. Press)
1972
Ernest J. Gaines
The Autobiography of Miss Jane Pittman (Dial)
1973
Clair A. Brown
Wildflowers of Louisiana (Louisiana State Univ. Press)
1974
Peter S. Feibelman
The Bayous (Time-Life)

1975
George H. Lowery
Mammals of Louisiana and Adjacent Waters (Louisiana State Univ. Press)
1976
Joe Gray Taylor
Louisiana Reconstructed, 1863–1877 (Louisiana State Univ. Press)
1977
Mary Alice Fontenot and Paul B. Freeland
Acadia Parish, Louisiana: A History to 1900 (Claitors)
1978
Gary Mills
The Forgotten People (Louisiana State Univ. Press)
Walker Percy
Lancelot (Farrar)
1979
Don Marquis
In Search of Buddy Bolden (Louisiana State Univ. Press)

Edward MacDowell Medal

A painter, sculptor, composer, or writer who has made an outstanding contribution to the arts is honored annually in August by The MacDowell Colony, Inc., 680 Park Avenue, New York, New York 10021. The award, established in 1960, is an appropriately inscribed bronze medal, officially presented at The MacDowell Colony in Peterborough, New Hampshire. The award is given alternately to visual artists, writers, and composers selected by an independent committee of peers in each of the disciplines.

1960
Thornton Wilder
1961
Aaron Copland
1962
Robert Frost
1963
Alexander Calder
1964
Edmund Wilson

1965
Edgard Varèse
1966
Edward Hopper
1967
Marianne Moore
1968
Roger Sessions
1969
Louise Nevelson

1970
  Eudora Welty
1971
  William Schuman
1972
  Georgia O'Keeffe
1973
  Norman Mailer
1974
  Walter Piston
  Martha Graham (Special Award)

1975
  Willem de Kooning
1976
  Lillian Hellman
1977
  Virgil Thomson
1978
  Richard Diebenkorn
1979
  John Cheever

Marian Library Medal

The Marian Library of the University of Dayton, Dayton, Ohio 45469, originally established the award of a gold medal to promote the writing of better books in English on the Blessed Virgin Mary. Each year from 1953 through 1967, a national committee of five judges selected that book originally published in the United States in English that would best promote a knowledge and love of the Blessed Virgin. Works published first in England or Ireland were also considered. In 1959, 1962, and 1965 the award was given to works either wholly or partially translated from other languages. Starting in 1971, the medal has been given once every four years at the time of the International Mariological Congress. An international panel is asked to recommend that scholar whose work since the last Congress has done the most to advance scientific research in Mariology.

1953
  Fulton J. Sheen
  The World's First Love (McGraw)
1954
  John S. Kennedy
  Light on the Mountain (McMullen)
1955
  William G. Most
  Mary in Our Life (Kenedy)
1956
  Ruth Cranston
  The Miracle of Lourdes (McGraw)
1957
  Juniper B. Carol
  Fundamentals of Mariology (Benziger)
1958
  Don Sharkey and Joseph Debergh
  Our Lady of Beauraing (Hanover)

1959
  Edward O'Connor
  The Dogma of Immaculate Conception (Univ. of Notre Dame Press)
1960
  John J. Delaney
  A Woman Clothed with the Sun (Hanover)
1961
  Sister Mary Pierre
  Mary Was Her Life (Benziger)
1962
  Marion A. Habig
  Marian Era, Vol. 2 (Franciscan Herald)
1963
  Titus F. Cranny
  Our Lady and Reunion (Graymoor)

1964
  Hilda Graef
  Mary: A History of Doctrine and Devotion (Sheed)
1965
  Edward Schillebeeckx
  Mary Mother of the Redemption (Sheed)
1966
  Cyril Vollert
  A Theology of Mary (Herder)
1967
  Thomas A. O'Meara
  Mary in Protestant and Catholic Theology (Sheed)

1968–1970
  No awards
1971
  Charles Balić
  Numerous publications and work in organizing international Mariological congresses
1975
  Giuseppe M. Besutti
  Contributions to work in international Marian bibliography

Mayflower Cup

This engraved cup has been offered annually since 1931 by the Society of Mayflower Descendants in North Carolina, through the North Carolina Literary and Historical Association, 109 East Jones Street, Raleigh, North Carolina 27611. In making the award, the Society hopes to promote interest in the writings of North Carolinians, particularly within their home state. The cup is awarded each November for an outstanding published work of nonfiction by any resident of North Carolina. Entries must represent initial publication. Neither reissues nor subsequent editions of a work are eligible nor are purely scientific or technical studies. The cup is usually given for a single work, but at the discretion of the Society's Board of Awards, it may be given in recognition of exceptional literary achievement over a period of years.

1931
  M. C. S. Noble
  History of the Public Schools in North Carolina (Univ. of North Carolina Press)
1932
  Archibald Henderson
  Bernard Shaw: Playboy and Prophet (Appleton)
1933
  Rupert P. Vance
  Human Geography of the South (Univ. of North Carolina Press)

1934
  Erich W. Zimmermann
  World Resources and Industries (Harper)

1935
  James Boyd
  Roll River (Scribner)

1936
  Mitchell B. Garrett
  The Estates General of 1789 (Appleton)

1937
Richard H. Shryock
The Development of Modern Medicine (Univ. of Pennsylvania Press)
1938
Jonathan Daniels
A Southerner Discovers the South (Macmillan)
1939
Bernice Kelly Harris
Purslane (Univ. of North Carolina Press)
1940
David L. Cohn
The Good Old Days (Simon & Schuster)
1941
Wilbur J. Cash
The Mind of the South (Knopf)
1942
Elbert Russell
The History of Quakerism (Macmillan)
1943
J. Saunders Redding
No Day of Triumph (Harper)
1944
Adelaide L. Fries
The Road to Salem (Univ. of North Carolina Press)
1945
Josephus Daniels
The Wilson Era: Years of Peace, 1910–1917 (Univ. of North Carolina Press)
1946
Josephina Niggli
Mexican Village (Univ. of North Carolina Press)
1947
Robert E. Coker
This Great and Wide Sea (Univ. of North Carolina Press)
1948
Charles S. Sydnor
The Development of Southern Sectionalism, 1819–1848 (Louisiana State Univ. Press)

1949
Phillips Russell
The Woman Who Rang the Bell (Univ. of North Carolina Press)
1950
Max Steele
Debby (Harper)
1951
Jonathan Daniels
The Man of Independence (Lippincott)
1952
John P. McKnight
The Papacy (Rinehart)
1953
LeGette Blythe and Mary T. Martin Sloop
Miracle in the Hills (McGraw)
1954
Hugh T. Lefler and Albert Ray Newsome
North Carolina (Univ. of North Carolina Press)
1955
Jay B. Hubbell
The South in American Literature, 1607–1900 (Duke Univ. Press)
1956
Glenn Tucker
Tecumseh, Vision of Glory (Bobbs)
1957
Archibald Henderson
George Bernard Shaw: Man of the Century (Appleton)
1958
Ben Dixon MacNeill
The Hatterasman (Blair)
1959
Burke Davis
The Road to Appomattox (Rinehart)
1960
Richard Bardolph
The Negro Vanguard (Rinehart)
1961
LeGette Blythe
Thomas Wolfe and His Family (Doubleday)

1962

Bill Sharpe

For outstanding literary achievement over a period of years

1963

Ethel Stephens Arnett

William Swain, Fighting Editor: The Story of O. Henry's Grandfather (Piedmont)

1964

Glenn Tucker

Dawn Like Thunder (Bobbs)

1965

John Ehle

The Free Men (Harper)

1966

Glenn Tucker

Zeb Vance, Champion of Personal Freedom (Bobbs)

1967

Joel Colton

Leon Blum: Humanist in Politics (Knopf)

1968

George B. Tindall

The Emergence of the New South, 1913–1945 (Louisiana State Univ. Press)

1969

John R. Alden

History of the American Revolution (Knopf)

1970

James H. Brewer

The Confederate Negro, 1861–1865 (Duke Univ. Press)

1971

Jonathan Daniels

Ordeal of Ambition: Jefferson, Hamilton, Burr (Doubleday)

1972

John F. Bivins, Jr.

The Moravian Potters in North Carolina (Univ. of North Carolina Press)

1973

Lionel Stevenson

The Pre-Raphaelite Poets (Univ. of North Carolina Press)

1974

Helen Smith Bevington

For outstanding literary achievement over a period of years

1975

C. Hugh Holman

The Loneliness at the Core (Louisiana State Univ. Press)

1976

Eleanor S. Godfrey

The Development of English Glassmaking, 1560–1640 (Univ. of North Carolina Press)

1977

Lawrence Goodwyn

Democratic Promise: The Populist Movement in America (Oxford Univ. Press)

1978

Lewis D. Rubin, Jr.

The Wary Fugitives: Four Poets and the South (Louisiana State Univ. Press)

Mediaeval Academy of America

The Mediaeval Academy of America, 1430 Massachusetts Avenue, Cambridge, Massachusetts 02138, offers three prizes for publications in medieval studies: the John Nicholas Brown Prize, the Elliott Prize, and the Haskins Medal. All three awards are presented at the annual meeting of the Academy. The Elliott Prize was established in 1972 in honor of Van Courtlandt Elliott. It consists of $300 awarded annually to a young scholar publishing a first article. Articles appearing in any journal (American or foreign) will be welcomed for consideration, provided their authors are residents of the United States or Canada. At the discretion of the judges, the award may be a single prize of $300 or two prizes of $150 each.

The Brown Prize and the Haskins Medal are described below.

John Nicholas Brown Prize

This prize was established in 1978 in honor of John Nicholas Brown, one of the founders of the Mediaeval Academy and its treasurer for fifty years (1926–1975). It consists of $500 awarded annually for a first book or monograph on a medieval subject judged to be of outstanding quality. The author must be a resident of North America.

1979
Claiborne W. Thompson
Studies in Upplandic Runography
(Univ. of Texas Press)

Haskins Medal

This prize was established in 1940 in honor of Charles Homer Haskins, distinguished historian of the Middle Ages, one of the founders of the Mediaeval Academy, and the Academy's second president. A gold medal is given for a distinguished book in the field of medieval studies by a scholar having professional residence in the United States or Canada.

1940
Bertha H. Putnam
Proceedings before the Justice of the Peace in the Fourteenth and Fifteenth Centuries, Edward III to Richard III
(Harvard Univ. Press)

1941
W. E. Lunt
Financial Relations of the Papacy with England to 1327 (Mediaeval Academy)

1942
John M. Manly and Edith Rickert
Text of the Canterbury Tales (Univ. of Chicago Press)

1943
D. D. Egbert
The Tickhill Psalter and Related Manuscripts (New York Public Library)

1944
No award

1945
George E. Woodbine
Bracton de legibus et consuetudinibus angliae, Vol. IV (Yale Univ. Press)

1946
J. Burke Severs
The Literary Relationships of Chaucer's Clerk's Tale (Yale Univ. Press)

1947–1948
No awards

1949
George Sarton
Introduction to the History of Science, Vol. III (Williams & Wilkins)

1950
Raymond De Roover
Money, Banking, and Credit in

Mediaeval Bruges (Mediaeval Academy)
1951
Roger Sherman Loomis
Arthurian Tradition and Chrétien de Troyes (Columbia Univ. Press)
1952
Alexander A. Vasiliev
Justin the First (Harvard Univ. Press)
1953
Millard Meiss
Painting in Florence and Siena after the Black Death (Princeton Univ. Press)
1954
No award
1955
George H. Forsyth, Jr.
The Church of St. Martin at Angers: The Architectural History of the Site from the Roman Empire to the French Revolution (Princeton Univ. Press)
1956
Ernest A. Moody
Truth and Consequence in Medieval Logic (Humanities)
1957
Elias Avery Lowe
Codices latini antiquiores (Oxford Univ. Press)
1958
Ernest Hatch Wilkins
Studies in the Life and Works of Petrarch (Mediaeval Academy)
1959
Ernst H. Kantorowicz
The King's Two Bodies: A Study in Mediaeval Theology (Princeton Univ. Press)
1960
Francis Dvornik
The Idea of Apostolicity in Byzantium and the Legend of the Apostle Andrew (Harvard Univ. Press)
1961
Gerhart B. Ladner
The Idea of Reform: Its Impact on

Christian Thought and Action in the Age of the Fathers (Harvard Univ. Press)
1962
Erwin Panofsky
Renaissance and Renascences in Western Art (Almqvist & Wiksell)
1963
Paul Frankl
The Gothic: Literary Sources and Interpretations through Eight Centuries (Princeton Univ. Press)
1964
Pearl Kibre
Scholarly Privileges in the Middle Ages: The Rights, Privileges, and Immunities of Scholars and Universities at Bologna, Padua, and Oxford (Mediaeval Academy)
1965
Morton W. Bloomfield
Piers Plowman as a Fourteenth-Century Apocalypse (Rutgers Univ. Press)
1966
Gaines Post
Studies in Medieval Thought, Public Law and the State, 1100–1322 (Princeton Univ. Press)
1967
O. B. Hardison, Jr.
Christian Rite and Christian Drama in the Ages: Essays in the Origin and Early History of Modern Drama (Johns Hopkins Univ. Press)
1968
Marshall Clagett
Archimedes in the Middle Ages: The Arabo-Latin Tradition (Univ. of Wisconsin Press)
1969
Giles Constable
The Letters of Peter the Venerable (Harvard Univ. Press)
1970
Robert Brentano
Two Churches; England and Italy in

the Thirteenth Century (Univ. of California Press)
1971
S. Harrison Thomson
Latin Bookhands of the Later Middle Ages, 1100–1500 (Cambridge Univ. Press)
1972
Kenneth J. Conant
Cluny: Les Eglises et la Maison du Chef d'Ordre (Mediaeval Academy)
1973
Shelomo D. Goitein
A Mediterranean Society, 2 vols. (Univ. of California Press)
1974
Kurt Weitzmann
Studies in Classical and Byzantine Manuscript Illumination, ed. by Herbert L. Kessler (Univ. of Chicago Press)
1975
Speros Vryonis, Jr.
The Decline of Medieval Hellenism in Asia Minor and the Process of Islamization from the Eleventh through the Fifteenth Century (Univ. of California Press)
1976
Robert Ignatius Burns
Islam under the Crusaders: Colonial Survival in the Thirteenth Century of Valencia (Princeton Univ. Press)
1977
Charles S. Singleton, ed.
Boccaccio's Autograph Manuscript of The Decameron (Decameron: Edizione Diplomatico-Interpretativa dell'Autografo Hamilton 90) (Johns Hopkins Univ. Press)
1978
George Kane and E. Talbot Donaldson, eds.
Edition of the B-Text of Piers Plowman (Athlone)
1979
George Cuttino
Gascon Register A (Oxford Univ. Press)

Frederic G. Melcher Book Award

Frederic G. Melcher, Unitarian/Universalist layman, suggested to his denomination that honor be paid to the book published in America during the past calendar year that made the most significant contribution to religious liberalism. Originally called the Channing-Ballou Award, the name was changed after Melcher's death. Anybody is eligible and any literary form is eligible—fiction, nonfiction, drama, or poetry—as long as the work is written in the tradition of free inquiry. Decision is made by five judges. The award consists of a cash prize of $1,000 plus a bronze medallion. Formal presentation is made annually at the General Assembly of the denomination. For further details, contact Melcher Book Award, 25 Beacon Street, Boston, Massachusetts 02108.

1964
Herbert J. Muller
Religion and Freedom in the Modern World (Univ. of Chicago Press)

1965
Rolf Hochhuth
The Deputy (Grove)

1966
No award
1967
Peter Gay
The Enlightenment (Knopf)
1968
Alan Westin
Privacy and Freedom (Atheneum)
1969
Donald Cutler, ed.
The Religious Situation (Beacon)
1970
Erik H. Erikson
Gandhi's Truth (Norton)
1971
Daniel Berrigan
Trial Poems and *The Trial of the Catonsville Nine* (Beacon) and *No Bars to Manhood* (Doubleday)
1972
William G. McLoughlin
New England Dissent, 1630–1883 (Harvard Univ. Press)
1973
Dorothy Day
On Pilgrimage in the Sixties (Curtis)

1974
Robert Jewett
The Captain America Complex (Westminster)
1975
Eugene Genovese
Roll, Jordan, Roll (Pantheon)
1976
Joseph Campbell
The Mythic Image (Princeton Univ. Press)
1977
James Luther Adams
On Being Human, Religiously: Selected Essays in Religion and Society, ed. by Max L. Stackhouse (Beacon)
1978
Michael Walzer
Just and Unjust Wars (Basic Books)
1979
Sissela Bok
Lying: Moral Choice in Public Life (Pantheon)

C. Wright Mills Award

The Society for the Study of Social Problems established this annual award in 1964 to honor the author(s) of the book published during the previous year that best exemplifies social science scholarship in the tradition of C. Wright Mills. Nominations are made by publishers or by individual members of the Society, and winners are selected by a committee of distinguished social science scholars appointed by the president of the Society. A $500 award is presented to the winning author(s) at the Society's annual meeting in August. Inquiries concerning the award should be sent to the Society for the Study of Social Problems, 208 Rockwell Hall, State University College, 1300 Elmwood Avenue, Buffalo, New York 14222.

1965
David Matza
Delinquency and Drift (Wiley)

1966
Robert Boguslaw
The New Utopians (Prentice)

1967
Jerome H. Skolnick
Justice without Trial (Wiley)
1968
Travis Hirschi and Hanan C. Selvin
Delinquency Research: An Appraisal of Analytic Methods (Free Press)

Elliot Liebow
Talley's Corner: A Study of Negro Street Corner Men (Little)

1969

Gerald D. Suttles
The Social Order of the Slum (Univ. of Chicago Press)

1970

Laud Humphreys
Tearoom Trade: Impersonal Sex in Public Places (Aldine)

1971

Jacqueline P. Wiseman
Stations of the Lost: The Treatment of Skid Row Alcoholics (Prentice)

1972

Frances Fox Piven and Richard A. Cloward
Regulating the Poor: The Functions of Public Welfare (Pantheon)

1973

David M. Gordon
Theories of Poverty and Unemployment: Orthodox, Radical, and Dual Labor Market Perspectives (Lexington)

1974

Isaac D. Balbus
The Dialectics of Legal Repression: Black Rebels before the American Courts (Russell Sage Foundation)

James B. Rule
Private Lives and Public Surveillance: Social Control in the Computer Age (Penguin)

1975

Harvey Braverman
Labor and Monopoly Capital: The Degradation of Work in the Twentieth Century (Monthly Review)

1976

Mary O. Furner
Advocacy and Objectivity (Univ. of Kentucky Press)

1977

Janice E. Perlman
The Myth of Marginality: Urban Power and Politics in Rio de Janeiro (Univ. of California Press)

1978

Rosabeth Moss Kantor
Men and Women in the Corporation (Basic Books)

1979

Walter Korpi
The Working Class in Welfare Capitalism: Work, Unions and Politics in Sweden (Routledge & Kegan Paul)

Modern Language Association of America

James Russell Lowell Prize

This award was established in 1968 by the Modern Language Association (MLA) of America, 62 Fifth Avenue, New York, New York 10011. It is open only to members of MLA. The prize is limited to "an outstanding literary or linguistic study, a critical edition of an important work, or a critical biography by a member of the Modern Language Association." Seven copies of the book must be submitted to Lowell Prize, c/o MLA, by January 31 of the year following publication. A letter giving the book's title and date of publication and affirming that the author is a member in good standing of the MLA should be mailed separately. Selection is made by a committee of distinguished members of the Association. The winner is announced annually in March or April, and the award, a certificate and $1,000, is presented at the MLA annual convention held the following December.

1970
Helen H. Vendler
On Extended Wings: Wallace Stevens' Longer Poems (Harvard Univ. Press)

1971
Bruce A. Rosenberg
The Art of the American Folk Preacher (Oxford Univ. Press)

1972
Meyer H. Abrams
Natural Supernaturalism: Tradition and Revolution in Romantic Literature (Norton)

1973
Theodore Ziolkowski
Fictional Transfiguration of Jesus (Princeton Univ. Press)

1974
Leslie A. Marchand
Byron's Letters and Journals (Harvard Univ. Press)

1975
Josephine Miles
Poetry and Change (Univ. of California Press)

1976
Jonathan Culler
Structuralist Poetics (Cornell Univ. Press)

1977
Joseph Frank
Dostoevsky: The Seeds of Revolt, 1821-1849 (Princeton Univ. Press)

1978
Stephen Booth
Shakespeare's Sonnets (Yale Univ. Press)

Howard R. Marraro Prize for an Outstanding Scholarly Study in Italian Literature or in Comparative Literature involving Italian

This prize was instituted in 1973 by the MLA for a distinguished scholarly study of book or essay length on any phase of Italian literature, comparative literature involving Italian, or for scholarly contributions over a lifetime to the same disciplines. It carries a $500 award and a citation, presented annually at the MLA convention held each December 26-29. Those wishing to propose nominees should write to the Howard R. Marraro Prize, Office of Research and Special Publications, Modern Language Association, 62 Fifth Avenue, New York, New York 10011.

1973
Bernard Weinberg
Tratti di Poetica e Retorica del Cinquecento (Laterza)

1974
Thomas G. Bergin
For his career as translator, scholar, and teacher of contemporary and classical Italian literature

1975
Beatrice Corrigan
For her career as a pioneer of Italian studies in Canada and her achieve-

ments as author, editor, translator,
and teacher

1976-1977

No awards

1978

Franco Fido

Guida a Goldoni: Teatro e Società nel Settecento (Einaudi)

The James Mooney Award

Established in 1972 by the Southern Anthropological Society (SAS), this award is given to encourage distinguished writing in the field of anthropology. The award is given annually and consists of $1,000 and publication within a year by the University of Tennessee Press. It is named for the anthropologist James Mooney (1861-1921), who was particularly known for his work on the Ghost Dance religion and on the history and mythology of the Cherokee Indians. The competition is open to any student of New World cultures and societies, including ethnography, linguistics, archeology, physical anthropology, history, folklore, and sociology. Inquiries should be sent to the Chairman, SAS Awards Committee, Department of Geography and Anthropology, Louisiana State University, Baton Rouge, Louisiana 70803.

1973

Dickson D. Bruce, Jr.

And They All Sang Hallelujah: Plain-Folk Camp-Meeting Religion, 1800-1845

1974-1976

No awards

1977

James M. Crawford

The Mobilian Trade Language

1978

Charles L. Briggs

The Wood-Carvers of Cordova

1979

F. Carlene Bryant

We're All Kin: A Cultural Study of an East Tennessee Mountain Neighborhood

Thomas More Association Medal

The Thomas More Association Medal was established in 1954 by the Thomas More Association, 180 North Wabash Avenue, Chicago, Illinois 60601. Although it was formerly given to a publisher, it is now given to an author for "the most distinguished contribution to Catholic literature." The award, announced annually in February in Chicago, consists of a bronze medal on a plaque. Nominations by publishers of individual books or series published during any single year should be submitted by December 1 of that year to the president of the Association. The winner is selected by the Board of Directors of the Association.

1955

Doubleday & Co.

Image Books series

1956

Alfred A. Knopf, Inc.

The Cypresses Believe in God, by Jose Maria Gironella

1957

P. J. Kenedy & Sons

Butler's Lives of the Saints, ed. by Donald Attwater

1958
Farrar, Straus & Cudahy, Inc.
Vision Books series
1959
Hawthorn Books
The Twentieth Century Encyclopedia of Catholicism, ed. by Henri Daniel-Rops
1960
J. B. Lippincott Co.
For publishing the fiction of Muriel Spark
1961
Doubleday & Co.
Dictionary of Catholic Biography, ed. by James Tobin and John J. Delaney
1962
Random House, Inc.
A Man for All Seasons, by Robert Bolt
1963
Wm. Morrow & Co., Inc.
The Birthday King, by Gabriel Fielding
1964
Harper & Row, Inc.
The Future of Man, by Pierre Teilhard de Chardin
1965
Farrar, Straus & Giroux, Inc.
Everything That Rises Must Converge, by Flannery O'Connor
1966
Doubleday & Co.
The Jerusalem Bible
1967
Herder & Herder
A New Catechism
1968
Hans Küng
The Church (Sheed)

1969
John L. McKenzie
The Roman Catholic Church (Holt)
1970
Daniel Callahan
Abortion: Law, Choice and Morality (Macmillan)
1971
Daniel Berrigan
The Dark Night of the Resistance (Doubleday)
1972
Andrew Greeley and Eugene Kennedy
For distinguished contributions to Catholic literature
1973
Graham Greene
The Honorary Consul (Simon & Schuster)
1974
Piers Paul Read
Alive (Lippincott)
1975
John J. Delaney
For five decades of distinguished contribution to Catholic literature
1976
Tom McHale
School Spirit (Doubleday)
1977
Andrew Greeley
The American Catholic (Basic Books)
1978
Eugene Kennedy
Himself: The Life and Times of Mayor Richard J. Daley (Viking)
Temporarily suspended

Morey Award

The Charles Rufus Morey Book Award is offered by the College Art Association of America, 16 East 52 Street, New York, New York 10022. The annual award, established in 1953, is purely honorary and is given without remuneration to an outstanding book in the field of the history of art, written by a scholar residing in the United States or in Canada and published during the two years preceding the announcement of the award.

1954
H. W. Janson
Apes and Ape Lore in the Middle Ages and the Renaissance (Abrams)

1955
Erwin Panofsky
Early Netherlandish Painting (Harvard Univ. Press)

1956
Henry Russell Hitchcock
Early Victorian Architecture (Yale Univ. Press)

1957
Vincent Scully
The Shingle Style (Yale Univ. Press)

1958
Richard Krautheimer
Lorenzo Ghiberti (Princeton Univ. Press)

1959
H. W. Janson
Sculpture of Donatello (Princeton Univ. Press)

1960
Henry Russell Hitchcock
Architecture, 19th and 20th Centuries (Penguin)

1961
No award

1962
Erwin Panofsky
Renaissance and Renascences in Western Art (Harper)

1963
James S. Ackerman
The Architecture of Michelangelo (Viking)

1964
George Kubler
The Art and Architecture of Ancient America (Penguin)

1965
Sydney J. Freedberg
Andrea del Sarto (Harvard Univ. Press)

1966
Erwin Panofsky
Tomb Sculpture (Abrams)

1967
Richard Offner
The Corpus of the Florentine Paintings (Augustine)

1968
Paul A. Underwood
The Kariye Djami (Princeton Univ. Press)

1969
Millard Meiss
French Painting in the Time of Jean de Berry (Praeger)

1970
Gisela M. A. Richter
Engraved Gems of the Greeks and Etruscans (Praeger)

1971
Charles Ilsley Minott
"The Theme of the Nerode Altarpiece," *Art Bulletin*, 1969

1972
Seymour Slive
Frans Hals (Phaidon/Praeger)

1973
Donald Posner
Annibale Carracci: A Study in the Reform of Italian Paintings around 1590 (Phaidon)

1974
Ilene H. Forsyth
The Throne of Wisdom (Princeton Univ. Press)

John Rupert Martin
The Decorations for the Pompa Introitus Ferdinandi (Schram)

1975
No award
1976
Alessandra Comini
Egon Schiele's Portraits (Univ. of California Press)
Millard Meiss
The Limbourges and Their Contemporaries (Braziller)
1977
Marilyn Aronberg Lavin
Seventeenth-Century Barberini Docu-
ments and Inventories of Art (New York Univ. Press)
1978
Kurt Weitzmann
The Monastery of Saint Catherine at Mount Sinai, The Icons, Vol. I: From the Sixth to the Tenth Century (Princeton Univ. Press)
1979
Anne Coffin Hanson
Manet and the Modern Tradition (Yale Univ. Press)

Frank Luther Mott–Kappa Tau Alpha Award

Kappa Tau Alpha, scholarship society in the field of education for journalism, established this award in 1944. The award is given to the author of the printed book that, in the opinion of a special committee appointed by the national president of the society, represents the best research in the field of communications for the preceding year. On April 1 of each year the winner is announced. Since 1958 the award has consisted of a decorative plaque plus $250. The Kappa Tau Alpha national office is at the School of Journalism, University of Missouri, Columbia, Missouri 65201.

1945
Thomas E. Dabney
One Hundred Great Years: A History of the New Orleans Times-Picayune (Louisiana Univ. Press)
1946
Neil Borden
National Advertising in Newspapers (Harvard Univ. Press)
1947
Harold D. Lasswell, Bruce Lannes Smith, and Ralph D. Casey
Propaganda, Communications, and Public Opinion: A Comprehensive Reference Guide (Princeton Univ. Press)
1948
Clarence S. Brigham
History and Bibliography of American
Newspapers, 1690–1820 (American Antiquarian Society)
1949
Paul Lazarsfeld and Patricia Kendall
Radio Listening in America (Prentice)
1950
Herbert Brucker
Freedom of Information (Macmillan)
1951
Alex Inkeles
Public Opinion in Soviet Russia (Harvard Univ. Press)
1952
Meyer Berger
The Story of the New York Times (Simon & Schuster)
1953
Frederick S. Siebert
Freedom of the Press in England, 1476–1775 (Univ. of Illinois Press)

1954
Harold L. Cross
The People's Right to Know (Columbia Univ. Press)
1955
James W. Markham
Bovard of the Post-Dispatch (Louisiana State Univ. Press)
1956
J. Cutler Andrews
The North Reports the Civil War (Univ. of Pittsburgh Press)
1957
Frederick S. Siebert, Theodore Peterson, and Wilbur Schramm
Four Theories of the Press (Univ. of Illinois Press)
1958
Frank Luther Mott
A History of American Magazines, 1885–1905 (Harvard Univ. Press)
1959
Arthur M. Schlesinger, Sr.
Prelude to Independence: The Newspaper War on Britain, 1764–1776 (Knopf)
1960
Leonard W. Levy
Legacy of Suppression (Harvard Univ. Press)
1961
W. A. Swanberg
Citizen Hearst (Scribner)
1962
Theodore E. Kruglak
The Two Faces of TASS (Minnesota Univ. Press)
1963
Peter Lyon
Success Story: The Life and Times of S. S. McClure (Scribner)
1964
Wilbur Schramm
Mass Media and National Development (Stanford Univ. Press)

1965
Elmer E. Cornwell, Jr.
Presidential Leadership of Public Opinion (Indiana Univ. Press)
1966
Edward W. Scripps
I Protest (Univ. of Wisconsin Press)
1967
James W. Markham
Voices of the Red Giant (Iowa State Univ. Press)
1968
Bryce W. Rucker
The First Freedom (Southern Illinois Univ. Press)
1969
Calder Pickett
Ed Howe: Country Town Philosophy (Univ. of Kansas Press)
1970
J. Cutler Andrews
The South Reports the Civil War (Univ. of Pittsburgh Press)
1971
Charles H. Brown
William Cullen Bryant, A Biography (Scribner)
1972
William E. Ames
History of the National Intelligencer (Univ. of North Carolina Press)
1973
Marion K. Sanders
Dorothy Thompson (Houghton)
1974
Merlo S. Pusey
Eugene Meyer (Knopf)
1975
Claude-Anne Lopez and Eugenia W. Herbert
The Private Franklin: The Man and His Family (Norton)
1976
William E. Porter
Assault on the Media: The Nixon Years (Univ. of Michigan Press)

1977

Chalmers M. Roberts
The Washington Post: The First 100 Years (Houghton)

1978
Keven M. McAuliffe
The Great American Newspaper: Rise and Fall of The Village Voice (Scribner)

National Book Awards

The annual National Book Awards were established in 1950 by the Association of American Publishers (formerly the American Book Publishers' Council), the American Booksellers Association, and the Book Manufacturers Institute. The $1,000 awards were established to give recognition to the most distinguished books of fiction, nonfiction, and poetry of the previous year.

In 1964, the Nonfiction category was discontinued and awards were given in its stead for Arts and Letters (discontinued in 1976), History and Biography, and Science, Philosophy, and Religion; in 1967, a Translation category was added; and in 1969, the category Children's Literature was added. The Science, Philosophy, and Religion category was discontinued after the 1970 award and replaced by The Sciences (1971–1975) and Philosophy and Religion (1972–1975). History and Biography was split into separate categories in 1972, the latter becoming Biography and Autobiography in 1977. The category Contemporary Affairs was established in 1972 and became Contemporary Thought in 1967.

The National Book Committee administered the awards until 1975, when the American Academy and Institute of Arts and Letters took them over for two years. The Association of American Publishers then administered the awards from 1977 to 1979, at which time the awards were discontinued. In 1980, the National Book Awards will be replaced by The American Book Awards (TABA) (q.v.), which are also administered by the Association of American Publishers.

FICTION

1950
Nelson Algren
The Man with the Golden Arm (Doubleday)
1951
William Faulkner
The Collected Stories of William Faulkner (Random)
Brendan Gill
The Trouble of One House (Doubleday) Special citation

1952
James Jones
From Here to Eternity (Scribner)
1953
Ralph Ellison
Invisible Man (Random)
1954
Saul Bellow
The Adventures of Augie March (Viking)
1955
William Faulkner
A Fable (Random)

FICTION (cont.)

1956
   John O'Hara
   Ten North Frederick (Random)
1957
   Wright Morris
   The Field of Vision (Harcourt)
1958
   John Cheever
   The Wapshot Chronicle (Harper)
1959
   Bernard Malamud
   The Magic Barrel (Farrar)
1960
   Philip Roth
   Goodbye, Columbus (Houghton)
1961
   Conrad Richter
   The Waters of Kronos (Knopf)
1962
   Walker Percy
   The Moviegoer (Knopf)
1963
   J. F. Powers
   Morte D'Urban (Doubleday)
1964
   John Updike
   The Centaur (Knopf)
1965
   Saul Bellow
   Herzog (Viking)
1966
   Katherine Anne Porter
   The Collected Stories of Katherine Anne Porter (Harcourt)
1967
   Bernard Malamud
   The Fixer (Farrar)
1968
   Thornton Wilder
   The Eighth Day (Harper)
1969
   Jerzy Kosinski
   Steps (Random)

1970
   Joyce Carol Oates
   Them (Vanguard)
1971
   Saul Bellow
   Mr. Sammler's Planet (Viking)
1972
   Flannery O'Connor
   Flannery O'Connor: The Complete Stories (Farrar)
1973
   John Barth
   Chimera (Random)

   John Williams
   Augustus (Viking)
1974
   Isaac Bashevis Singer
   A Crown of Feathers and Other Stories (Farrar)

   Thomas Pynchon
   Gravity's Rainbow (Viking)
1975
   Robert Stone
   Dog Soldiers (Houghton)

   Thomas Williams
   The Hair of Harold Roux (Random)
1976
   William Gaddis
   J R (Knopf)
1977
   Wallace Stegner
   The Spectator Bird (Doubleday)
1978
   Mary Lee Settle
   Blood Tie (Houghton)
1979
   Tim O'Brien
   Going after Cacciato (Delacorte/Seymour Lawrence)

NONFICTION

1950
   Ralph L. Rusk
   Ralph Waldo Emerson (Scribner)

NONFICTION (cont.)

1951
Newton Arvin
Herman Melville (Sloane)
1952
Rachel L. Carson
The Sea around Us (Oxford Univ. Press)
1953
Bernard De Voto
The Course of Empire (Houghton)
1954
Bruce Catton
A Stillness at Appomattox (Double-day)
1955
Joseph Wood Krutch
The Measure of Man (Bobbs)
1956
Herbert Kubly
American in Italy (Simon & Schuster)
1957
George F. Kennan
Russia Leaves the War (Princeton Univ. Press)
1958
Catherine Drinker Bowen
The Lion and the Throne (Little)
1959
J. Christopher Herold
Mistress to an Age: A Life of Madame de Staël (Bobbs)
1960
Richard Ellmann
James Joyce (Oxford Univ. Press)
1961
William L. Shirer
The Rise and Fall of the Third Reich (Simon & Schuster)
1962
Lewis Mumford
The City in History (Harcourt)
1963
Leon Edel
Henry James: The Conquest of Lon-don; Henry James: The Middle Years (Lippincott)

ARTS AND LETTERS

1964
Aileen Ward
John Keats: The Making of a Poet (Viking)
1965
Eleanor Clark
The Oysters of Locmariaquer (Pantheon)
1966
Janet Flanner (Genêt)
Paris Journal (1944–1965) (Atheneum)
1967
Justin Kaplan
Mr. Clemens and Mark Twain (Simon & Schuster)
1968
William Troy
Selected Essays (Rutgers Univ. Press)
1969
Norman Mailer
The Armies of the Night (World)
1970
Lillian Hellman
An Unfinished Woman (Little)
1971
Francis Steegmuller
Cocteau (Little)
1972
Charles Rosen
The Classical Style: Haydn, Mozart, Beethoven (Viking)
1973
Arthur M. Wilson
Diderot (Oxford Univ. Press)
1974
Pauline Kael
Deeper into the Movies (Atlantic)

ARTS AND LETTERS (cont.)

1975
Roger Shattuck
Marcel Proust (Viking)
Lewis Thomas
The Lives of a Cell: Notes of a Biology Watcher (Viking)
1976
Paul Fussell
The Great War and Modern Memory (Oxford Univ. Press)

HISTORY AND BIOGRAPHY

1964
William H. McNeill
The Rise of the West (Univ. of Chicago Press)
1965
Louis Fischer
The Life of Lenin (Harper)
1966
Arthur M. Schlesinger, Jr.
A Thousand Days (Houghton)
1967
Peter Gay
The Enlightenment (Knopf)
1968
George F. Kennan
Memoirs: 1925–1950 (Atlantic-Little)
1969
Winthrop D. Jordan
White over Black: American Attitudes toward the Negro, 1550–1812 (Univ. of North Carolina Press)
1970
T. Harry Williams
Huey Long (Knopf)
1971
James MacGregor Burns
Roosevelt: The Soldier of Freedom (Harcourt)

SCIENCE, PHILOSOPHY, AND RELIGION

1964
Christopher Tunnard and Boris Pushkarev
Man-Made America: Chaos or Control? (Yale Univ. Press)
1965
Norbert Wiener
God and Golem, Inc. (M.I.T. Press)
1966
No award
1967
Oscar Lewis
La Vida (Random)
1968
Jonathan Kozol
Death at an Early Age (Houghton)
1969
R. J. Lifton
Death in Life: Survivors of Hiroshima (Random)
1970
Erik H. Erikson
Gandhi's Truth: On the Origins of Militant Nonviolence (Norton)

POETRY

1950
William Carlos Williams
Paterson III and *Selected Poems* (New Directions)
1951
Wallace Stevens
The Auroras of Autumn (Knopf)
1952
Marianne Moore
Collected Poems (Macmillan)
1953
Archibald MacLeish
Collected Poems: 1917–1952 (Houghton)

POETRY (cont.)

1954
Conrad Aiken
Collected Poems (Oxford Univ. Press)
1955
e. e. cummings
Poems: 1923–1954 (Harcourt) Special Citation
Wallace Stevens
Collected Poems of Wallace Stevens (Knopf)
1956
W. H. Auden
The Shield of Achilles (Random)
1957
Richard Wilbur
Things of This World (Harcourt)
1958
Robert Penn Warren
Promises: Poems, 1954–1956 (Random)
1959
Theodore Roethke
Words for the Wind (Doubleday)
1960
Robert Lowell
Life Studies (Farrar)
1961
Randall Jarrell
The Woman at the Washington Zoo (Atheneum)
1962
Alan Dugan
Poems (Yale Univ. Press)
1963
William Stafford
Traveling through the Dark (Harper)
1964
John Crowe Ransom
Selected Poems (Knopf)
1965
Theodore Roethke
The Far Field (Doubleday)

1966
James Dickey
Buckdancer's Choice (Wesleyan Univ. Press)
1967
James Merrill
Nights and Days (Atheneum)
1968
Robert Bly
The Light around the Body (Harper)
1969
John Berryman
His Toy, His Dream, His Rest (Farrar)
1970
Elizabeth Bishop
The Complete Poems (Farrar)
1971
Mona Van Duyn
To See, to Take (Atheneum)
1972
Howard Moss
Selected Poems (Atheneum)
Frank O'Hara
The Collected Poems (Knopf)
1973
A. R. Ammons
Collected Poems: 1951–1971 (Norton)
1974
Allen Ginsberg
The Fall of America: Poems of These States, 1965–1971 (City Lights)
Adrienne Rich
Diving into the Wreck (Norton)
1975
Marilyn Hacker
Presentation Piece (Viking)
1976
John Ashbery
Self-Portrait in a Convex Mirror (Viking)
1977
Richard Eberhart
Collected Poems: 1930–1976 (Oxford Univ. Press)

POETRY (cont.)

1978
 Howard Nemerov
 The Collected Poems (Univ. of Chicago Press)
1979
 James Merrill
 Mirabell: Books of Number (Atheneum)

TRANSLATION

1967
 Gregory Rabassa
 Hopscotch, by Julio Cortazar (Pantheon)
 Willard Trask
 History of My Life, by Casanova (Harcourt)
1968
 Howard Hong and Edna Hong
 Søren Kierkegaard's Journals and Papers, Vol. 1 (Indiana Univ. Press)
1969
 William Weaver
 Cosmicomics, by Italo Calvino (Harcourt)
1970
 Ralph Manheim
 Castle to Castle, by Louis-Ferdinand Céline (Delacorte)
1971
 Frank Jones
 Saint Joan of the Stockyards, by Bertolt Brecht (Indiana Univ. Press)
 Edward G. Seidensticker
 The Sound of the Mountain, by Yasunari Kawabata (Knopf)
1972
 Austryn Wainhouse
 Chance and Necessity: An Essay on the Natural Philosophy of Modern Biology, by Jacques Monad (Knopf)

1973
 Allen Mandelbaum
 The Aeneid of Virgil (Univ. of California Press)
1974
 Karen Brazell
 The Confessions of Lady Nijo (Doubleday/Anchor)
 Helen Lane
 Alternating Currents, by Octavio Paz (Richard Seaver/Viking)
 Jackson Mathews
 Monsieur Teste, by Paul Valéry (Princeton Univ. Press)
1975
 Anthony Kerrigan
 The Agony of Christianity and Essays on Faith, by Miguel de Unamuno (Princeton Univ. Press)
1977
 Li-Li Ch'en
 Master Tung's Western Chamber Romance: A Chinese Chantefable (Cambridge Univ. Press)
1978
 Richard Winston and Clara Winston
 In the Deserts of This Earth, by Uwe George (Harcourt)
1979
 Clayton Eshleman and José Rubia Barcia
 The Complete Posthumous Poetry, by César Vallejo (Univ. of California Press)

CHILDREN'S LITERATURE

1969
 Meindert DeJong
 Journey from Peppermint Street (Harper)
1970
 Isaac Bashevis Singer
 A Day of Pleasure: Stories of a Boy Growing Up in Warsaw (Farrar)

CHILDREN'S LITERATURE (cont.)

1971
Lloyd Alexander
The Marvelous Misadventures of Se-bastian (Dutton)
1972
Donald Barthelme
The Slightly Irregular Fire Engine or the Hithering Thithering Djinn (Farrar)
1973
Ursula K. LeGuin
The Farthest Shore (Atheneum)
1974
Eleanor Cameron
The Court of the Stone Children (Dutton)
1975
Virginia Hamilton
M. C. Higgins the Great (Macmillan)
1976
Walter D. Edmonds
Bert Breen's Barn (Little)
1977
Katherine Paterson
The Master Puppeteer (Crowell)
1978
Judith Kohl and Herbert Kohl
The View from the Oak: The Private Worlds of Other Creatures (Sierra Club/Scribner)
1979
Katherine Paterson
The Great Gilly Hopkins (Crowell)

THE SCIENCES

1971
Raymond Phineas Stearns
Science in the British Colonies of America (Illinois Univ. Press)
1972
George L. Small
The Blue Whale (Columbia Univ. Press)

1973
George B. Schaller
The Serengeti Lion: A Study of Preda-tor-Prey Relations (Univ. of Chicago Press)
1974
S. E. Luria
Life: The Unfinished Experiment (Scribner)
1975
Silvano Arieti
Interpretation of Schizophrenia (Basic Books)

BIOGRAPHY

1972
Joseph P. Lash
Eleanor and Franklin: The Story of Their Relationship Based on Eleanor Roosevelt's Private Papers (Norton)
1973
James Thomas Flexner
George Washington: Anguish and Farewell (1793–1799) (Little)
1974
Douglas Day
Malcolm Lowry (Oxford Univ. Press)
1975
Richard Sewall
The Life of Emily Dickinson (Farrar)
1976
No award

BIOGRAPHY AND AUTOBIOGRAPHY

1977
W. A. Swanberg
Norman Thomas: The Last Idealist (Scribner)
1978
W. Jackson Bate
Samuel Johnson (Harcourt)

BIOGRAPHY AND AUTOBIOGRAPHY
(cont.)

1979
   Arthur M. Schlesinger, Jr.
   Robert Kennedy and His Times
   (Houghton)

CONTEMPORARY AFFAIRS

1972
   Stewart Brand
   The Last Whole Earth Catalog: Access to Tools (Portola/Random)
1973
   Frances FitzGerald
   Fire in the Lake: The Vietnamese and the Americans in Vietnam (Little)
1974
   Murray Kempton
   The Briar Patch: The People of the State of New York vs. Lumumba Shakur et al. (Dutton)
1975
   Theodore Rosengarten
   All God's Dangers: The Life of Nate Shaw (Knopf)
1976
   Michael J. Arlen
   Passage to Ararat (Farrar)

CONTEMPORARY THOUGHT

1977
   Bruno Bettelheim
   The Uses of Enchantment: The Meaning and Importance of Fairy Tales (Knopf)
1978
   Gloria Emerson
   Winners and Losers: Battles, Retreats, Gains, Losses and Ruins from a Long War (Random)

1979
   Peter Matthiessen
   The Snow Leopard (Viking)

HISTORY

1972
   Allan Nevins
   Ordeal of the Union series—Vol. 7, *The War for the Union: The Organized War, 1863-64;* Vol. 8, *The War for the Union: The Organized War to Victory, 1864-65* (Scribner)
1973
   Robert Manson Myers
   The Children of Pride (Yale Univ. Press)
   Isaiah Trunk
   Judenrat (Macmillan)
1974
   John Clive
   Macauley: The Shaping of the Historian (Knopf)
1975
   Bernard Bailyn
   The Ordeal of Thomas Hutchinson (Harvard Univ. Press)
1976
   David B. Davis
   The Problem of Slavery in an Age of Revolution: 1770-1823 (Cornell Univ. Press)
1977
   Irving Howe
   World of Our Fathers (Harcourt)
1978
   David McCullough
   The Path between the Seas: The Creation of the Panama Canal, 1870-1914 (Simon & Schuster)
1979
   Richard Beale Davis
   Intellectual Life in the Colonial South, 1585-1763 (Univ. of Tennessee Press)

PHILOSOPHY AND RELIGION

1972
 Martin E. Marty
 Righteous Empire: The Protestant Experience in America (Dial)
1973
 Sydney E. Ahlstrom
 A Religious History of the American People (Yale Univ. Press)
1974
 Maurice Natanson
 Edmund Husserl: Philosopher of Infinite Tasks (Northwestern Univ. Press)
1975
 Robert Nozick
 Anarchy, State and Utopia (Basic Books)

National Book Critics Circle Awards

In 1975, the National Book Critics Circle (NBCC), Box 6000, Radio City Station, New York, New York 10019, established four awards to encourage excellence in criticism, fiction, nonfiction, and poetry. The winner in each category is presented with a scroll at the NBCC's annual conference in New York City in January. Books published during the previous year by American writers are eligible. The recipients are selected by the advisory board members and officers of the National Book Critics Circle.

CRITICISM

1976
 Paul Fussell
 The Great War and Modern Memory (Oxford Univ. Press)
1977
 Bruno Bettelheim
 The Uses of Enchantment: The Meaning and Importance of Fairy Tales (Knopf)
1978
 Susan Sontag
 On Photography (Farrar)
1979
 Meyer Schapiro
 Modern Art: Nineteenth and Twentieth Centuries (Selected Papers, vol. 2) (Braziller)

FICTION

1976
 E. L. Doctorow
 Ragtime (Random)
1977
 John Gardner
 October Light (Knopf)
1978
 Toni Morrison
 Song of Solomon (Knopf)
1979
 John Cheever
 The Stories of John Cheever (Knopf)

NONFICTION

1976
 R. W. B. Lewis
 Edith Wharton (Harper)
1977
 Maxine Hong Kingston
 The Woman Warrior: Memoirs of a Girlhood among Ghosts (Knopf)
1978
 W. Jackson Bate
 Samuel Johnson (Harcourt)
1979
 Maureen Howard
 Facts of Life (Little)

NONFICTION (cont.)

Garry Wills
Inventing America: Jefferson's Declaration of Independence (Doubleday)

POETRY

1976
John Ashbery
Self-Portrait in a Convex Mirror (Viking)

1977
Elizabeth Bishop
Geography III (Farrar)
1978
Robert Lowell
Day by Day (Farrar)
1979
Peter Davison, ed.
Hello, Darkness: The Collected Poems of L. E. Sissman (Atlantic)

National Endowment for the Arts Grants

In late 1965, the National Endowment for the Arts, 1800 F Street N.W., Washington, D.C. 20506, was established by an act of Congress to help develop the country's cultural resources. Allocations are made to 54 state and territorial arts councils and in the fields of architecture, planning and design; dance; education; literature; music and opera; public media; theater; and the visual arts. Most of the grants are available only on a matching basis; some are outright grants.

In the field of creative writing, the following persons received grants to enable them to complete works in progress or conduct research essential to their continuing work. Beginning in 1977, grants are awarded biennially. For the names of recipients prior to 1976, consult the ninth edition of *Literary and Library Prizes*.

1976

POETRY
Thomas D. Absher
Diane Ackerman
S. Keith Althaus
John Beecher
Beth Bently
Stephen Berg
Mei-Mei Berssenbrugge
Harvey S. Bialy
Frank Bidart
Harold Bond
John Carpenter
Marisha Chamberlain
Henry Charlile
David L. Curry
James D. Den Boer
Ann Darr
Michael Davidson
Russell Edson
Ted Enslin
Constance Urdang Finkel
Tess Gallagher
Virginia L. Gilbert
Gary Gildner
Patricia Goedicke
Patricia M. Hampl
Kenneth Hanson
C. G. Hanzlicek
Marie Harris
Richard Harteis
Robert Hedin
Michael Hogan

POETRY (cont.)

Anne Hussey
Thomas Johnson
David M. Kelly
Robert Kelly
Theodore Kooser
Philip Levine
Thomas Lux
James McAfee
David McElroy
James Martin
Peter Michelson
Gary L. Miranda
James Masao Mitsui
Carole Oles
Alicia Ostriker
Ron Overton
Jerold Ramsey
William Ransom
Shreela Ray
Jerome Rothenberg
Michael Ryan
David St. John
Reginald Saner
Leslie Scalopino
Dennis Schmitz
James Scully
Richard Shelton
John Skoyles
David Smith
Kim Stafford
Gerald Stern
Floyd Stuart
Nancy Sullivan
Barbara Szerlip
John Taggart
Dennis Trudell
Leslie Ullman
Arthur Vogelsang
Ellen Voigt
Nancy Willard
Eleanor Wilner
William Witherup
Charles David Wright
John Yau
Ray Young Bear

Wayne Zade
Christie Zawadiwsky

FICTION

Chester Aaron
Alice Adams
Calvin Anderson
Max Apple
Linda Arking
John Barry
Audrey Borenstein
Malcolm Bosse
J. Alan Broughton
Janet G. Burroway
Frederick Busch
Jane Casey
Mary E. Counselman
Max Crawford
George Cuomo
Cecil Daukins
Rick Demarinis
Stephan R. Dunn
Andrew Fetler
Gary Goss
Allan Gurganus
Josephine Haxton
Pati Hill
Richard F. Hill
William Hjortsberg
William Hoffman
James Houston
Edward Hower
Gayl Jones
Steve Katz
Yong Ik Kim
James McCartin
Frederick Manfred
Arthenia Millican
John Milton
Stephan Minot
Daniel O'Brian
William O'Brian
Jonathan Penner
John Rechy
C. W. Smith
Pat Staten

FICTION (cont.)

Barry Targan
Harry Taylor
John Yount

DRAMA

Anna Marie Barlow
Lennox Brown
George Codegan
Raymond Coreil
Charles Fuller
Lloyd Gold
Charles Gregory
Susan Griffin
James Harris
William Hoffman
Momoko Iko
Tim Kelly
Cleveland Kurtz
Lance Lee
Cornel Lengyel
Jack Marlando
Tim Mason
Susan Miller
Michael Moody
Robert Mullen
Morna Murphy
Ronnie Paris
Richard Plattz
Harold Stuart
Sharon Vogel
Edgar White

OTHER

Nelson Algren
Helen Barolini
Richard Grossinger
W. Lewis Hyde
Elinor Langer
Grover Lewis
Howard McCord
Peter Marin
James Mersmann

Margaret Newlin
Shaun O'Connell
Michael Rossman
Peter Schrag
Edward Snow
Richard Taylor

1977–1978

Robert H. Abel
Jonis Agee
Jody Aliesan
Paula Gunn Allen
Ray Aranha
Sandra F. Asher
John Balaban
Russell E. Banks
Jim W. Barnes
Peter S. Beagle
Marvin H. Bell
Kenneth Bernard
David A. Berry
Alvah Bessie
Corinne Demas Bliss
Victor F. Bockris
Paul F. Bowles
Thomas Boyle
Chandler Brossard
Olga C. Broumas
Rita Mae Brown
Michael Dennis Browne
Mary P. Cable
Robert O. Callahan
James Campbell
Alvaro Cardona-Hine
Lorna D. Cervantes
David Ulysses Clark
William Cobb
L. Keith Cohen
James A. Coleman
Jack W. Conroy
Clark Coolidge
Barbara A. Corcoran
Mary E. Corrigan
Henri Coulette
Louis O. Coxe
Allen Davis III

1977–1978 (cont.)

James L. de Jongh
William Dickey
Pietro Di Donato
John A. Domini
D. W. Donzella
Rita F. Dove
Andre J. Dubus
Jeffrey L. Duncan
Margaret F. Edwards
George Garrett Epps
Welch D. Everman
Thomas David Farber
James T. Farrell
Harrison M. Fisher
Jane Flanders
Carolyn Forché
Kathleen J. Fraser
Virginia W. Furtwangler
James A. Galvin
Eugene K. Garber
John R. Gardiner
Barbara Garson
Patricia J. Gibson
John C. Gilhooley
Joseph G. Glover
Jaimy M. Gordon
Delcie S. Gourdine
Douglas W. Gower
Stephen R. Grecco
Hannah Green
Jonathan Edward Greene
Debora J. Greger
Patricia B. Griffith
James Leland Grove
Lee Gutkind
Oakley Hall III
Robert D. Harbison
Naomi Joy Harjo
Michael S. Harper
William N. Harrison
William T. Hauptman
Marianne Hauser
Julie Hayden
Anne Hebson
Michael J. Heffernan

Jack L. Heifner
Robert W. Hemenway
Don F. Hendrie, Jr.
Roberta J. Hill
Edward Honig
David R. Huddle
Mary Gray Hughes
Harvey J. Jacobs
Mark F. Jarman
Catherine H. Jones
Jerry Kamstra
Barbara J. Keiler
Tamara J. Kennelly
Richard E. Kim
Galway Kinnell
Milton Klonsky
Hans Koning
Henry J. Korn
Wayne Banks Lanier, Jr.
Larry M. Levinger
James F. Lewisohn
Morton J. Lichter
Renee B. Lieberman
Lucy Lim
Ronald W. Loewinsohn
Barbara A. Long
Phillip Lopate
Glenna B. Luschei
Mekeel McBride
Susan MacDonald
Colleen J. McElroy
Donna B. Mack
Janet McReynolds
James L. Magnuson
Joseph C. Maiolo
Freya F. Manfred
Paule B. Marshall
Mary W. Marvin
Gail B. Mazur
Ifeanyi A. Menkiti
William S. Merwin
Deena P. Metzger
Dorothy Monet
Fred T. Morgan
Mary Morris
Sena J. Naslund
Kent S. Nelson

1977–1978 (cont.)

Paul S. Nelson, Jr.
Michael D. Neville
Susan S. Neville
Hugh Nissenson
James E. Nolan
Louis D. Ohle
Eve Olitsky
Sally A. Ordway
Gregory S. Orr
Greg L. Pape
Jeff L. Pate
Quintin Peterson
Catherine Petroski
Ann L. Petry
Roger C. Pfingston
Jayne Anne Phillips
Marge Piercy
Allen J. Planz
Stanley R. Plumly
Nancy A. Potter
Frederic Prokosch
Leroy V. Quintana
Eugene B. Redmond
Louis A. Reile
Kenneth Rexroth
Richard L. Rhodes
Noel Rico
John L. Robinson
Leon Rooke
Ned Rorem
David A. Rounds
Michael Rubin
J. R. Salamanca
Floyd F. Salas
Sonia B. Sanchez
Thomas R. Sanchez
Teo Savory
Nora C. Sayre
Carolynne B. Scott
Richard O. Shaw
Jane Shore
Roger D. Skillings, Jr.
Jane G. Smiley

Ebbe R. Smith
Mark R. Smith
Robert T. Sorrells
Kathleen D. Spivack
Claude I. Stanush
Bradford Stark
Jack Steele
Meredith L. Steinbach
Robert Steiner
John Stewart
Milan Stitt
Mark Strand
Jean Strouse
Brian Swann
Stephen J. Tapscott
Henry S. Taylor
Patricia E. Taylor
James W. Thomas
Tom Thomas
Gary R. Thompson
Jean Louise Thompson
Nancy Price Thompson
Robert S. Thompson
Frederick W. Turner III
Sara A. Vogan
John von Hartz
Diane Vreuls
Alice Walker
Granville Walker, Jr.
Gerald L. Wallace
Martin L. Wampler
Igor M. Webb
Edward G. Williams
John A. Williams
Jonathan C. Williams
Meredith Sue Willis
Edward D. Wilson
Joyce M. Winslow
William Wiser
Jack C. Wolf
Tobias Wolff
Hilma Wolitzer
Robert A. Wrigley
Geoffrey M. Young
Ahmos Zu-Bolton

National Medal for Literature

The National Medal for Literature, one of the nation's most prestigious awards in the field, is conferred annually on a living American author for his or her total contribution to American letters. Each recipient of the bronze medal, designed by Leonard Baskin, also receives $15,000 ($10,000 from 1965 to 1977). The medal is endowed by the Guinzburg Fund in memory of Harold K. Guinzburg, founder of Viking Press and an organizer of the National Book Committee. The award was sponsored by the National Book Committee from 1965 to 1973. Sponsorship was then assumed in 1976 by the National Institute of Arts and Letters/American Academy of Arts and Letters (now the American Academy and Institute of Arts and Letters). In 1978, the New York Public Library conferred the medal. It has not yet been decided by the trustees of the Guinzburg Fund whether the medal will be awarded in 1979 or, if it is, who the sponsor will be.

1965
    Thornton Wilder
1966
    Edmund Wilson
1967
    W. H. Auden
1968
    Marianne Moore
1969
    Conrad Aiken
1970
    Robert Penn Warren
1971
    E. B. White

1972
    Lewis Mumford
1973
    Vladimir Nabokov
1974-1975
    No awards
1976
    Allen Tate
1977
    Robert Lowell
1978
    Archibald MacLeish

National Religious Book Awards

The *Religious Book Review*, Box 1331, Roslyn Heights, New York 11577, and Omni Communications, Box 6001, Grand Rapids, Michigan 49506, cosponsor these annual awards, established in 1977, to acknowledge the contributions religious publishing makes to American life. Publishers nominate titles from their own lists. Independent committees of booksellers, librarians, editors, and book reviewers select one winner and two or three outstanding titles for each of four (in 1978, three) categories: Inspirational, Scholarly, Community Life and Social Awareness, and Children and Youth. Special awards may also be given from time to time. Each winner receives a trophy and each finalist a plaque, presented in March in New York City. Only winners are listed below.

1978
Sheldon Vanauken
A Severe Mercy (Harper) Popular
Peter Spier
Noah's Ark (Doubleday) Children
E. P. Sanders
Paul and Palestinian Judaism: A Comparison of Patterns of Religion (Fortress) Scholarly
The Book of Common Prayer (Seabury) Special Award for Outstanding Publication in Religion
Tim Dowley, ed.
Eerdman's Handbook to the History of Christianity (Eerdmans) Special Award for Outstanding Publication in Religion
1979
Joseph G. Donders
Jesus the Stranger: Reflections on the Gospels (Orbis) Inspirational
Albert J. Raboteau
Slave Religion (Oxford Univ. Press) Scholarly
Donald B. Kraybill
The Upside-Down Kingdom (Herald) Community Life/Social Awareness
Walter Wangerin, Jr.
The Book of the Dun Cow (Harper) Children/Youth
Hans Bouma, author, and Rien Poortvliet, illustrator
He Was One of Us: The Life of Jesus of Nazareth (Doubleday) Special Award
Abba Eban, author, and Gordon Wetmore, illustrator
Promised Land (Thomas Nelson) Special Award

Nebenzahl Prize

The Nebenzahl Prize was established in 1978 by the Hermon Dunlap Smith Center for the History of Cartography at the Newberry Library to encourage independent scholarly research in the history of cartography. The prize will be awarded annually in December for an original, scholarly, book-length manuscript on any aspect of the history of cartography. The winning author will receive $1,500 from a fund established by Mr. and Mrs. Kenneth Nebenzahl, and the manuscript will be published by the University of Chicago Press. Manuscripts will be judged by a committee of five: the director of the Hermon Dunlap Smith Center, a University of Chicago Press editor, and three independent judges. Complete manuscripts should be submitted to the Director, Hermon Dunlap Smith Center for the History of Cartography, Newberry Library, 60 West Walton Street, Chicago, Illinois 60610.

1978
No award

Nebula Awards

Offered by the Science Fiction Writers of America (SFWA), 68 Countryside Apartments, Hackettstown, New Jersey 07840, this annual award was established in 1965, with the first awards given in 1966 for the best novel, novella, novelette, and short story published in the previous year in the field of science fiction. An additional category—dramatic presentation—was established in 1974, but the award is not given annually. Grand Master Nebula Awards are also given from time to time, and, in 1979, a special SFWA President's Award was given. Any science fiction or fantasy story that has been published by an American trade publisher or in an American magazine of national distribution is eligible: short story, to 7,500 words; novelette, 7,500–17,500 words; novella, 17,500–40,000 words; novel, over 40,000 words. Ballots are distributed to the active worldwide SFWA membership of over 500 to choose winners in each category. The award is a Lucite trophy with a clear top in which a "galaxy" hangs suspended over a rock crystal embedded in the black base. Each trophy is unique. The awards are presented at the annual SFWA Award Banquet held in April in New York City (odd-numbered years) and alternately in San Francisco and Los Angeles (even-numbered years).

BEST NOVEL

1966
   Frank Herbert
   Dune (Chilton)
1967
   Samuel R. Delany
   Babel 17 (Ace)

   Daniel Keyes
   Flowers for Algernon (Longmans)
1968
   Samuel R. Delany
   The Einstein Intersection (Ace)
1969
   Alexei Panshin
   Rite of Passage (Ace)
1970
   Ursula K. LeGuin
   The Left Hand of Darkness (Ace)
1971
   Larry Niven
   Ringworld (Ballantine)
1972
   Robert Silverberg
   A Time of Changes (New American Library)
1973
   Isaac Asimov
   The Gods Themselves (Doubleday)
1974
   Arthur C. Clarke
   Rendezvous with Rama (Harcourt)

1975
   Ursula K. LeGuin
   The Dispossessed (Harper)
1976
   Joe Haldeman
   The Forever War (St. Martin's)
1977
   Frederik Pohl
   Man Plus (Random)
1978
   Frederik Pohl
   Gateway (Random)
1979
   Vonda N. McIntyre
   Dreamsnake (Houghton)

BEST NOVELLA

1966
   Brian Aldiss
   "The Saliva Tree"
   Roger Zelazny
   "He Who Shapes"
1967
   Jack Vance
   "The Last Castle"
1968
   Michael Moorcock
   "Behold the Man"
1969
   Anne McCaffrey
   "Dragonrider"

BEST NOVELLA (cont.)

1970
  Harlan Ellison
  "A Boy and His Dog"
1971
  Fritz Leiber
  "Ill Met in Lankhmar"
1972
  Katherine MacLean
  "The Missing Man"
1973
  Arthur C. Clarke
  "A Meeting with Medusa"
1974
  Gene Wolfe
  "The Death of Dr. Island"
1975
  Robert Silverberg
  "Born with the Dead: Three Novellas about the Spirit of Man"
1976
  Roger Zelazny
  "Home Is the Hangman"
1977
  James Tiptree, Jr.
  "Houston, Houston, Do You Read?"
1978
  Spider Robinson and Jeanne Robinson
  "Stardance"
1979
  John Varley
  "The Persistence of Vision"

1969
  Richard Wilson
  "Mother to the World"
1970
  Samuel R. Delany
  "Time Considered as a Helix of Semi-Precious Stones"
1971
  Theodore Sturgeon
  "Slow Sculpture"
1972
  Poul Anderson
  "The Queen of Air and Darkness"
1973
  Poul Anderson
  "Goat Song"
1974
  Vonda McIntyre
  "Of Mist, and Grass, and Sand"
1975
  Gregory Benford and Gordon Eklund
  "If the Stars Are Gods"
1976
  Tom Reamy
  "San Diego Lightfoot Sue"
1977
  Isaac Asimov
  "The Bicentennial Man"
1978
  Raccoona Sheldon
  "The Screwfly Solution"
1979
  Charles L. Grant
  "A Glow of Candles"

BEST NOVELETTE

1966
  Roger Zelazny
  "The Doors of His Face, the Lamps of His Mouth"
1967
  Gordon R. Dickson
  "Call Him Lord"
1968
  Fritz Leiber
  "Gonna Roll Them Bones"

BEST SHORT STORY

1966
  Harlan Ellison
  " 'Repent, Harlequin,' Said the Ticktockman"
1967
  Richard McKenna
  "The Secret Place"
1968
  Samuel R. Delany
  "Aye, and Gomorrah"

BEST SHORT STORY (cont.)

1969
  Kate Wilhelm
  "The Planners"
1970
  Robert Silverberg
  "Passengers"
1971
  No award
1972
  Robert Silverberg
  "Good News from the Vatican"
1973
  Joanna Russ
  "When It Changed"
1974
  James Tiptree, Jr.
  "Love Is the Plan, the Plan Is Death"
1975
  Ursula K. LeGuin
  "The Day before the Revolution"
1976
  Fritz Leiber
  "Catch That Zeppelin"
1977
  Charles L. Grant
  "A Crowd of Shadows"
1978
  Harlan Ellison
  "Jeffty Is Five"

1979
  Edward Bryant
  "Stone"

DRAMATIC PRESENTATION

1974
  Stanley R. Greenberg
  Soylent Green, from the novel *Make Room, Make Room*, by Harry Harrison
1975
  Woody Allen
  Sleeper
1976
  Mel Brooks, Gene Wilder, and Mary Wollstonecraft Shelley
  Young Frankenstein

GRAND MASTER NEBULA AWARDS

  L. Sprague de Camp
  Robert A. Heinlein
  Clifford D. Simak
  Jack Williamson

PRESIDENT'S AWARD

1979
  Jerry Siegel and Joe Shuster
  Superman (DC Comics)

New York State Historical Association Awards

Dixon Ryan Fox Memorial Award

When Dixon Ryan Fox died in 1945, a memorial fund of approximately $10,000 was raised to support the publication of books about New York State. This was seen as a revolving fund that would continue its usefulness long after the amount of the original fund was expended, in the hope of encouraging the publication of sound, readable, useful books that might be difficult to publish without the support of the New York State Historical Association, Cooperstown, New York 13326. Given intermittently at the New York State Historical Association offices, the award consists of financial support of varying amounts. Rigid rules have never been drawn up; the trustee committee treats each application and its needs as a special case.

1947
David M. Ellis, James A. Frost, Harry Carman, and Harold C. Syrett
A Short History of New York State (Cornell Univ. Press)

1951
Jared van Wagenen, Jr.
The Golden Age of Homespun (Cornell Univ. Press)

1952
Edward Deming Andrews
The People Called Shakers (Oxford Univ. Press)
C. Elta VanNorman
"A Bibliography of New York State History"

1955
Lawrence H. Leder
Robert Livingston and the Politics of Colonial New York (Univ. of North Carolina Press)

1963
David C. Huntington
A biography of Frederic C. Church

1972
Alice Kenny and Leslie J. Workman
"Medieval Traditions in American Culture"

Kerr History Prize

Endowed in 1969 by Paul S. Kerr and named for him by the New York State Historical Association's Board of Trustees, the prize was established to encourage scholarship and to recognize the exceptional quality of particular articles published in the quarterly journal *New York History*. The prize is awarded each year to the best article appearing in *New York History*, as judged by the Trustees Publication Committee. It consists of a $200 award and a handsome scroll.

Manuscript Award

Established in 1973 to encourage and reward scholarship relating to the history of New York State, the award consists of a prize of $1,000 presented annually to the best unpublished manuscript dealing with the history of New York State, as judged by a special editorial committee. In addition to granting the prize, the Association assists the prize winner in obtaining a publisher. Manuscripts must be received by February 1 of each year to be considered for the award, which is announced in July. If in any given year no manuscript of superior quality is submitted, the award will not be made. Address inquiries to Wendell Tripp, New York State Historical Association, Cooperstown, New York 13326.

1974
Douglas Greenberg
" 'Persons of Evil Name and Fame': Crime and Law Enforcement in the Colony of New York, 1691-1776"

1975

Robert C. Ritchie

"The Duke's Province: A Study of New York Politics and Society, 1664–1691"

1976

Leslie E. Fishbein

"Radical Renaissance: The Ideological Conflict of the Radicals Associated with *The Masses*"

1977

Edward K. Spann

"The New Metropolis: New York City, 1840–1857"

1978

Hendrik Booraem V

"Conscience and Politics: The Republican Party of New York State, 1854–1856"

1979

Richard L. McCormick

"Shaping Republican Strategy: Political Change in New York State, 1893–1910"

Thomas Newcomen Award in Business History

The Newcomen Society in North America, Downingtown, Pennsylvania 19335, with the cooperation of the *Business History Review*, 214-16 Baker Library, Soldiers Field, Boston, Massachusetts 02163, established the Thomas Newcomen Award in Business History to help promote the writing of books on the history of business in the United States and Canada. This award is given not only for the history of firms or industries but also for books tracing interactions of businessmen, analyses of business philosophy or behavior, and studies of the adjustment of businesses and businessmen to their economic, political, and social environments. A selected committee representing the Newcomen Society and the *Business History Review* chooses a winner based on the book's contribution to knowledge, depth of analysis, soundness of reasoning, clarity of style and organization, and general readability and format. The award of $1,000 and a scroll is presented once every three years at one of the Newcomen Society's meetings.

1964

Alfred D. Chandler, Jr.

Strategy and Structure: Chapters in the History of the Industrial Enterprise (M.I.T. Press)

1967

Sidney Pollard

The Genesis of Modern Management: A Study of the Industrial Revolution in Great Britain (Harvard Univ. Press)

1970

Robert W. Ozanne

A Century of Labor-Management Relations at McCormick and International Harvester (Univ. of Wisconsin Press) and *Wages in Practice and Theory: McCormick and International Harvester, 1860-1960* (Univ. of Wisconsin Press)

1973

Thomas C. Cochran

Business in American Life: A History (McGraw)
1976
Irvine H. Anderson, Jr.
The Standard-Vacuum Oil Company

and United States East Asian Policy, 1933–1941 (Princeton Univ. Press)

Ohioana Book Awards

The Martha Kinney Cooper Ohioana Library Association, 1105 Ohio Departments Building, 65 South Front Street, Columbus, Ohio 43215, established these awards in 1941 to carry out the three purposes of the library: to honor Ohio writers, to acquaint the public with their books, and to collect these books in one place, thereby preserving the culture and traditions of the state. The Ohioana Library has been developed mainly by private subscription and carries on a variety of projects to promote the books of Ohio authors. At the annual meeting, held in Columbus in October or November, a ceramic medal designed by Paul Bogatay is given to those Ohio writers judged to have written the best books during the previous year. Medals have been awarded in a wide variety of categories through the years, but in recent years they have most often been awarded in the categories Fiction, Nonfiction, Juvenile, Poetry, Biography, History, and Ohio Scene. The winners in these categories are listed below. Other Ohioana Book Awards have been given on an irregular basis in the special categories Books about the War, Critical and Scholarly, Humor, Literary History and Criticism, Natural History, Personal Experiences, Philosophy and Religion, Popular Novels, Social History, and Social Studies. The award winners in these categories can be found in the 1967 edition of *Literary and Library Prizes*. For the purposes of this edition, three other special categories have been combined with related categories: Autobiography with Biography, Teen-Age Books with Juvenile, and Historical Narrative with History. Also in this edition, for the first time, is a list of winners of the annual Florence Roberts Head Memorial Award, first given in 1963.

In addition to these literary awards, the Ohioana Library Association has given over the years a variety of other awards, medals, fellowships, and citations to Ohio authors, composers, scientists, educators, and citizens. Lists of all award winners can be obtained from the Ohioana Library Association.

In 1942, at the thirteenth annual meeting of the Association, the first presentations were made for the books that "contributed most to the understanding of present-day America." A $50 war bond went to James B. Reston for *Prelude to Victory* (Knopf), with honorable mention going to Walter Havighurst for *Long Ships Passing* (Macmillan) and to W. M. Kiplinger for *Washington Is Like That* (Harper).

FICTION

1943
Martin Joseph Freeman
Bitter Honey (Macmillan)

1944
Ann Steward
Take Nothing for Your Journey (Macmillan)

FICTION (cont.)

1945
  Henrietta Buckmaster
  Deep River (Harcourt)
1946
  Dorothy James Roberts
  A Durable Fire (Macmillan)
1947
  Janet Hart Diebold
  Mandrake Root (Holt)
1948
  George Freitag
  The Lost Land (Coward)
1949
  Virgil Scott
  The Hickory Stick (Morrow)
1950
  Robert Kossuth Marshall
  Little Squire Jim (Duell)
1951
  No award
1952
  William Fridley
  A Time to Go Home (Dutton)
1953
  William Donohue Ellis
  The Bounty Lands (World)
1954
  No award
1955
  Agatha Young
  Clown of the Gods (Random)
1956
  Jo Sinclair
  The Changelings (McGraw)
1957
  Herbert Gold
  The Man Who Was Not with It (Atlantic-Little)
1958
  Charles O. Locke
  The Hell Bent Kid (Norton)
1959
  Anne Chamberlain
  The Darkest Bough (Bobbs)

1960
  Peter Taylor
  Happy Families Are All Alike (McDowell, Obolensky)
1961
  Jo Sinclair
  Anna Teller (McKay)
1962
  Raymond De Capite
  A Lost King (McKay)
1963
  Hiram Haydn
  The Hands of Esau (Harper)
1964
  Josephine W. Johnson
  The Dark Traveler (Simon & Schuster)
1965
  Jack Matthews
  Bitter Knowledge (Scribner)
1966
  Fletcher Knebel
  The Night of Camp David (Harper)
1967
  William Harrington
  Yoshar the Soldier (Dial)
1968
  Bentz Plagemann
  The Heart of Silence (Morrow)
1969
  James McConkey
  Crossroads (Dutton)
1970
  Robert L. Fish
  The Xavier Affair (Putnam)
1971–1972
  No awards
1973
  Hannah Green
  The Dead of the House (Doubleday)
1974
  No award
1975
  Toni Morrison
  Sula (Knopf)
1976–1977
  No awards

FICTION (cont.)

1978
  John Jakes
  The American Bicentennial series (Jove/Harcourt)
1979
  Nicholas Guild
  The Summer Soldier (Seaview Books)

NONFICTION

1943
  Clarence A. Mills
  Climate Makes the Man (Harper)
1944
  No award
1945
  Foster Rhea Dulles
  The Road to Teheran —1789–1943 (Princeton Univ. Press)
1946–1954
  No awards
1955
  Arthur Loesser
  Men, Women and Pianos (Simon & Schuster)
1956
  John F. Cady
  The Roots of French Imperialism in Eastern Asia (Cornell Univ. Press)
1957
  Bruce Catton
  This Hallowed Ground (Doubleday)
1958
  Arthur M. Schlesinger, Jr.
  The Crisis of the Old Order, 1919–1933 (Houghton)
1959
  Sally Carrighar
  Moonlight at Midday (Knopf)
1960
  Nelson Glueck
  Rivers in the Desert (Farrar)

Harry V. Jaffa
Crisis of the House Divided (Doubleday)
1961
  Louis Filler
  The Crusade against Slavery (Harper)
1962
  Bruce Catton
  The Coming Fury (Doubleday)
1963
  Paul Murray Kendall
  The Yorkist Age (Norton)
1964
  Lucy Lilian Notestein
  Hill Towns of Italy (Little)
1965
  Sherman E. Lee
  A History of Far Eastern Art (Abrams)
1966
  Rutherford Platt
  The Great American Forest (Prentice)
1967
  John Bartlow Martin
  Overtaken by Events (Doubleday)
1968
  No award
1969
  Nelson Glueck
  The River Jordan (McGraw)
1970
  Charles G. Rousculp
  Chalk Dust on My Shoulder (Merrill)
1971–1972
  No awards
1973
  J. Allen Hynek
  The UFO Experience (Regnery)
1974
  No award
1975
  Algis Ruksenas
  Day of Shame (McKay)
1976 –1977
  No awards

NONFICTION (cont.)

1978
Paul Colinvaux
Why Big Fierce Animals Are Rare
(Princeton Univ. Press)
1979
No award

JUVENILE AND YOUNG ADULT

1943
Anna Bird Stewart
Bibi: The Baker's Horse (Lippincott)
1944
Lois Lenski
Bayou Suzette (Stokes)
1945
Florence Mary Fitch
One God: The Ways We Worship Him
(Lothrop)
1946
James Grover Thurber
The White Deer (Harcourt)
1947
Harriet Torrey Evatt
The Snow Owl's Secret (Bobbs)
1948
Carolyn Treffinger
Li Lun, Lad of Courage (Abingdon)
1949
Robert McCloskey
Blueberries for Sal (Viking)
1950
Walter Havighurst and Marion Ha-
vighurst
Song of the Pines (Winston)
1951
No award
1952
Anna Bird Stewart
Enter David Garrick (Lippincott)
1953
No award

1954
Bertha C. Anderson
Tinker's Tim and the Witches (Little)
1955
William E. Scheele
Prehistoric Animals (World)
1956
James Flora
The Fabulous Firework Family (Har-
court)
1957
Edward Eager
Knight's Castle (Harcourt)
1958
Robert McCloskey
Time of Wonder (Viking)
1959
Jeanette Eaton
America's Own Mark Twain (Morrow)
1960
Carol Kendall
The Gammage Cup (Harcourt)
1961
Jack Warner Schaefer
Old Ramon (Houghton)
1962
Suzanne de Borhegyi
Ships, Shoals and Amphoras (Holt)
1963
Edward Eager
Seven-Day Magic (Harcourt)
1964 –1966
No awards
1967
Dale Hollerback Fife
Walk a Narrow Bridge (Coward)
1968
Elisabeth Hamilton Friermood
Focus the Bright Land (Doubleday)
1969
Virginia Hamilton
The House of Dies Drear (Macmillan)
1970
Jan Whal
The Norman Rockwell Storybook
(Windmill/Simon & Schuster)

JUVENILE AND YOUNG ADULT
(cont.)

1971
   Robert McKay
   Dave's Song (Meredith)
   Marion Renick
   Ohio (Coward)
1972
   Mary O'Neill
   Winds (Doubleday)
1973–1975
   No awards
1976
   Mary Jo Stephens
   Witch of the Cumberlands (Houghton)
1977
   Brinton Turkle
   Deep in the Forest (Dutton) and illustrations for *Island Time*, by Bette Lamont (Lippincott)
1978
   Jane Louise Curry
   Poor Tom's Ghost (Atheneum)
1979
   No award

POETRY

1944
   Kenneth Patchen
   Cloth of the Tempest (Harper)
1945
   No award
1946
   Alice Monk Mears
   Brief Enterprise (Dutton)
1947–1959
   No awards
1960
   James Wright
   Saint Judas (Wesleyan Univ. Press)
1961
   Ralph Hodgson
   The Skylark and Other Poems (St. Martin's)

1962–1964
   No awards
1965
   George Dell
   Written on Quail and Hawthorn Pages (Capital Univ. Press)
1966–1967
   No awards
1968
   Hollis Summers
   The Peddler and Other Domestic Matters (Rutgers Univ. Press)
1969–1972
   No awards
1973
   Mary Oliver
   The River Styx, Ohio (Harcourt)
1974
   Kenneth Koch
   Rose, Where Did You Get That Red? (Random)
1975–1979
   No awards

BIOGRAPHY AND AUTOBIOGRAPHY

1944
   Fred Charters Kelly
   The Wright Brothers (Harcourt)
1945
   No award
1946
   Carl Frederick Wittke
   Against the Current: The Life of Karl Heinzen (Univ. of Chicago Press)
1947
   James M. Cox
   Journey through My Years: An Autobiography (Simon & Schuster)
1948
   George Crile
   George Crile: An Autobiography (Lippincott)
1949
   Ridgley Torrence
   The Story of John Hope (Macmillan)

BIOGRAPHY AND AUTOBIOGRAPHY
(cont.)

1950
Andrew Denny Rodgers III
Liberty Hyde Bailey (Princeton Univ. Press)
1951
Amy Kelly
Eleanor of Aquitaine and the Four Kings (Harvard Univ. Press)
1952
Ernest G. Schwiebert
Luther and His Times (Concordia)

Norman Thomas
A Socialist's Faith (Norton)
1953
Howard Swiggett
The Extraordinary Mr. Morris (Doubleday)
1954
Rollo Walter Brown
The Hills Are Strong (Beacon)
1955 –1957
No awards
1958
Paul Murray Kendall
Warwick the Kingmaker (Norton)
1964
Charles Allen Smart
Viva Juarez! (Lippincott)
1965
Randolph C. Randall
James Hall: Spokesman of the New West (Ohio State Univ. Press)
1966
Alpheus Thomas Mason
William Howard Taft: Chief Justice (Simon & Schuster)
1967
Louis Filler
The Unknown Edwin Markham (Antioch)
1968
Richard O'Connor
Ambrose Bierce (Little)

1969
Charles Sawyer
Concerns of a Conservative Democrat (Southern Illinois Univ. Press)
1970
Robert M. Crunden
A Hero in Spite of Himself: Brand Whitlock in Art, Politics, and War (Knopf)
1971
William Manners
TR and Will: A Friendship That Split the Republican Party (Harcourt)

Jesse Owens
Black Think (Morrow)
1972
Charles M. Cummings
Yankee Quaker Confederate General (Fairleigh Dickinson Univ. Press)
1973
James T. Patterson
Mr. Republican: A Biography of Robert A. Taft (Houghton)
1974
Donald Smythe
Guerrilla Warrior: The Early Life of John J. Pershing (Scribner)
1975
No award
1976
Nancy Lenz Harvey
The Rose and the Thorn (Macmillan)

Ruby V. Redinger
George Eliot: The Emergent Self (Knopf)
1977
Robert Canzoneri
A Highly Ramified Tree (Viking)
1978
No award
1979
Allan Peskin
Garfield (Kent State Univ. Press)

D. G. Sanders
The Brasspounder (Hawthorn)

HISTORY

1946
Arthur M. Schlesinger, Jr.
The Age of Jackson (Little)
1947
Walter Havighurst
Land of Promise (Macmillan)
1948
No award
1949
Howard Robinson
The British Post Office (Princeton Univ. Press)
1950–1951
No awards
1952
Bruce Catton
Mr. Lincoln's Army (Doubleday)
1953
No award
1954
Clarence Edward Macartney
Grant and His Generals (McBride)
1955 –1958
No awards
1959
Arthur M. Schlesinger, Sr.
Prelude to Independence: The Newspaper War on Britain, 1764–1776 (Knopf)
1960–1967
No awards
1968
Allan Eckert
The Frontiersman (Little)
1969 –1972
No awards
1973
Kenneth E. Davison
The Presidency of Rutherford B. Hayes (Greenwood)
1974 –1976
No awards
1977
Walter C. Langsam and L. D. Warren
The World and Warren's Cartoons (Exposition)

Terry Waldo
This Is Ragtime (Hawthorn)
1978
Thomas H. Smith
The Mapping of Ohio (Kent State Univ. Press)
1979
John D. Unruh, Jr.
The Plains Across (Univ. of Illinois Press)

OHIO SCENE

1944
Philip Dillon Jordan
Ohio Comes of Age (Ohio State Archaeological & Historical Society)
1945–1956
No awards
1957
Thomas Graham Belden and Marva Robins Belden
So Fell the Angels (Little)
1958
No award
1959
Alfred Byron Sears
Thomas Worthington: Father of Ohio Statehood (Ohio State Univ. Press for the Ohio Historical Society)
1960
Margaret Leech
In the Days of McKinley (Harper)
1961–1962
No awards
1963
Walter Sutton
The Western Book Trade (Ohio State Univ. Press for the Ohio Historical Society)
1964
H. Wayne Morgan
William McKinley and His America (Syracuse Univ. Press)
1965
No award

OHIO SCENE (cont.)

1966
Leslie C. Peltier
Starlight Nights (Harper)
1967–1969
No awards
1970
Lawrence A. Frost
The Thomas Edison Album (Superior)
1971
John Unterecker
Voyager: A Life of Hart Crane (Farrar)
1972
John M. Taylor
Garfield of Ohio —The Available Man
(Norton)

1973
No award
1974
Donald F. Anderson
William Howard Taft (Cornell Univ.
Press)
1975
George E. Condon
Stars in the Water (Doubleday)
1976
Polk Laffoon IV
Tornado (Harper)
1977–1979
No awards

Florence Roberts Head Memorial Award

1963
Ellen Bromfield Geld
The Heritage (Harper)
1964
Helen Hooven Santmyer
Ohio Town (Ohio State Univ. Press)
1965
Randolph C. Randall
*James Hall: Spokesman of the New
West* (Ohio State Univ. Press)
1966
Florence Ellinwood Allen
To Do Justly (Western Reserve Univ.
Press)
1967
Conrad Richter
The Awakening Land (Knopf) and *A
Country of Strangers* (Knopf)
1968
Jack Matthews
Hanger Stout, Awake (Harcourt)
1969
Jacob H. Dorn
Washington Gladden (Ohio State
Univ. Press)

1970
Jean Gould
*The Poet and Her Book: Edna St. Vin-
cent Millay* (Dodd)
1971
Alberta Pierson Hannum
Look Back with Love (Vanguard)
1972
James M. Merrill
William Tecumseh Sherman (Rand
McNally)
1973
Charles Holmes
The Clocks of Columbus (Atheneum)
1974
Josephine Johnson
Seven Houses (Simon & Schuster)
1975
Patricia Penton Leimbach
A Thread of Blue Denim (Prentice)
1976
William B. Thomas
The Country in the Boy (Thomas Nel-
son)

1977
  John Baskin
  *New Burlington: The Life and Death
  of an American Village* (Norton)
1978
  John I. Kolehmainen
  From Lake Erie's Shores to the Ma-

honing and Monongahela Valleys
(Ohio Finnish-American Historical So-
ciety)
1979
  Janet Hickman
  Zoar Blue (Macmillan)

Organization of American Historians

Five literary awards are currently offered by the Organization of American Historians,
112 North Bryan, Bloomington, Indiana 47401, and a sixth award will be offered for the
first time in 1981. The winners of the six awards described below are announced at
the Organization's annual meeting held in April.

Ray Allen Billington Award

This biennial award—established in honor of a former president of the Organization—
will be presented for the first time in April 1981 for a book on American frontier history
published in 1979 or 1980. Frontier history is defined broadly to include the pioneer
periods of all geographical areas, as well as comparisons between American and
other frontiers. The award consists of $500 and a medal.

Binkley–Stephenson Award

This annual $500 award, honoring two past editors of the *Journal of American History*,
is for the best scholarly article published in the *Journal* during the preceding year.
Inquiries should be sent to Lewis Perry, Editor, *Journal of American History*, Ballantine Hall 702, Indiana University, Bloomington, Indiana 47405.

Merle Curti Award

This award, first presented in 1977 and now given annually, is given alternately for a
book on American intellectual history and for a book on social history published during
the two preceding years. The prize is $500, a medal, and a certificate. The deadline
for submission is October 1.

1977
  Henry F. May
  Enlightenment in America (Oxford
  Univ. Press)

1979
  Gary Wills
  *Inventing America: Jefferson's Decla-
  ration of Independence* (Doubleday)

Louis Pelzer Memorial Award

Established in 1946, this award is presented annually to a graduate student for the winning essay on American history submitted to the Award Committee. January 1 is the entry deadline. The award consists of $500, a medal, and publication of the essay in the *Journal of American History*. Inquiries should be directed to Lewis Perry, Editor, *Journal of American History*, Ballantine Hall 702, Indiana University, Bloomington, Indiana 47405.

Charles Thomson Prize

This annual prize was established in 1975 and is cosponsored by the Organization of American Historians and the National Archives, Washington, D.C., to honor Thomson, the first secretary of the Continental Congress. It is given to an author of a previously unpublished essay on any aspect of American history that reflects significant research in the National Archives, regional archives, or in one of the presidential libraries. The prize consists of $250 and publication in *Prologue*. Entries should not exceed 7,500 words and should be submitted before August 1 to the Editor, *Prologue*, U.S. National Archives Records and Services, Washington, D.C. 20408.

Frederick Jackson Turner Award

Established in 1958 as the Prize Studies Award of the Mississippi Valley Historical Association, the award was redefined in 1977. It is now awarded annually to the author of a significant book on American history who has not previously published a book-length study of history. Only manuscripts accepted for publication by university presses are eligible. The deadline each year is July 1. The author's prize consists of $500, a medal, and a certificate. In addition, the university press that publishes the book will be given a $3,000 subsidy for the publication of another manuscript on American history.

1977
Merritt Roe Smith
Harpers Ferry Armory and the New Technology: The Challenge of Change (Cornell Univ. Press)
1978
Daniel T. Rodgers
Work Ethic in Industrial America, 1850–1920 (Univ. of Chicago Press)

1979
Charles F. Fanning, Jr.
Peter Finley Dunne and Mr. Dooley: The Chicago Years (Univ. Press of Kentucky)

P.E.N. American Center

P.E.N. American Center, 47 Fifth Avenue, New York, New York 10003, currently offers five annual awards, one biennial award, and one annual special citation, described below.

Goethe House –P.E.N. Translation Prize

This prize was first presented by the P.E.N. American Center for the best book-length translation from German into English, donated by Goethe House, New York. It is presented annually for a work published in the preceding year or, in the case of drama, performed in the year preceding the award. The winner receives a cash award of $500.

1974
Sophie Wilkins
The Lime Works, by Thomas Bernhard (Knopf)
1975
Peter Sander
Ice Age (play), by Tankred Dorst
1976
Ralph Manheim
A Sorrow Beyond Dreams, by Peter Handke (Farrar)
1977
Douglas Parmée
An Exemplary Life, by Siegfried Lenz (Hill & Wang)

1978
Joachim Neugroschel
For cumulative contributions to the translation of German literature, including Dolf Sternberger's *Panorama of the 19th Century* (Urizen) and Reiner Kunze's *The Wonderful Years* (Braziller)
1979
Leila Vennewitz
And Never Said a Word, by Heinrich Böll (McGraw), as well as in recognition of her thirteen other translations of works by Böll

Calouste Gulbenkian –P.E.N. Translation Prize

Beginning in 1979, this biennial prize of $500 is awarded for a distinguished translation from Portuguese into English, donated by the Gulbenkian Foundation of Lisbon.

1979
Helen R. Lane
The Three Marias: New Portuguese Letters (Doubleday)

Ernest Hemingway Foundation Award

Beginning in 1976, the P.E.N. American Center established the annual Ernest Hemingway Foundation Award of $6,000 for the best first novel or short story collection by an American published during the previous year. The new award is donated by the Ernest Hemingway Foundation, established by P.E.N. member Mary Hemingway in memory of her husband. First novels or collections of short stories in the English language are eligible. Mysteries or Westerns will not be considered unless their genre is deemed secondary to their overall literary purpose and quality. Submission of one copy each of books that meet the requirements of the award may be sent to the Ernest Hemingway Foundation Award in care of the P.E.N. American Center. The deadline is December 31 of each year.

1976
  Lloyd Little
  Parthian Shot (Viking)
1977
  Renata Adler
  Speedboat (Random)

1978
  Darcy O'Brien
  A Way of Life, Like Any Other (Norton)
1979
  Reuben Bercovitch
  Hasen (Knopf)

Lucille J. Medwick Memorial Award

This annual award, established in 1975, was donated by the Medwick Foundation in memory of Lucille J. Medwick, poet and associate editor of the *New York Quarterly*. The award of $500 is given for distinguished service to the literary community and for the commitment to serve the young, the unrecognized, and the unpopular.

1975
  Grace Schulman
1976
  Harry Smith
1977
  Alice S. Morris

1978
  David R. Godine
1979
  Ted Solotaroff

P.E.N. Publisher Citation

In 1976, the P.E.N. American Center established the annual P.E.N. Publisher Citation for "distinctive and continuous service to international letters, to the freedom and dignity of writers, and to the free transmission of the printed word across the barriers of poverty, ignorance, censorship, and repression." The recipient of this citation is chosen by the Center's Executive Board; no nominations are accepted.

1976
  Victor Weybright
1977
  Helen Wolff

1978
  James Laughlin

P.E.N. Translation Prize

P.E.N. American Center, the international writers' organization, established this annual prize in 1962. The prize of $1,000, which is donated by the Book-of-the-Month Club, is awarded for the best translation of a book into English from any language. The work must be published in the United States in the current calendar year; technical, scientific, and reference works are not eligible. Three judges are appointed to read the books submitted to the Translation Committee. The deadline for submission of books is December 31. The prize is presented at the annual dinner meeting of the American Center of P.E.N. in May. Submissions should be made to the Chairman, Translation Committee, P.E.N. American Center.

1963
Archibald Colquhoun
The Viceroys, by Federico di Roberto (Harcourt)

1964
Ralph Manheim
The Tin Drum, by Günter Grass (Fawcett)

1965
Joseph Barnes
The Story of a Life, by Konstantin Paustovsky (Pantheon)

1966
Geoffrey Skelton and Adrian Mitchell
The Persecution and Assassination of Jean-Paul Marat, as Performed by the Inmates of the Asylum of Charenton under the Direction of the Marquis de Sade, by Peter Weiss (Atheneum)

1967
Harriet de Onis
Sagarana, by J. Guimarães Rosa (Knopf)

1968
Vladimir Markov and Merrill Sparks
Modern Russian Poetry (Bobbs)

1969
W. S. Merwin
Selected Translations 1948–68 (Atheneum)

1970
Sidney Alexander
The History of Italy, by Francesco Guicciardini (Macmillan)

1971
Max Hayward
Hope against Hope, by Nadezhda Mandelstam (Atheneum)

1972
Richard Winston and Clara Winston
Letters of Thomas Mann (Knopf)

1973
J. P. McCulloch
The Poems of Sextus Propertius (Univ. of California Press)

1974
Hardie St. Martin and Leonard Mades
The Obscene Bird of Night, by José Donoso (Knopf)

1975
Helen R. Lane
Count Julian, by Juan Goytisolo (Viking)

1976
Richard Howard
A Short History of Decay, by E. M. Cioran (Viking)

1977
Gregory Rabassa
The Autumn of the Patriarch, by Gabriel García Marquez (Harper)

1978
Adrienne Foulke
One Way or Another, by Leonardo Sciascia (Harper)

1979
Charles Wright
The Storm and Other Poems, by Eugenio Montale (Oberlin College Field Translation series)

P.E.N. Writing Awards for Prisoners

Established in 1973, these annual awards are given for the best unpublished manuscripts submitted by prisoners in U.S. federal, state, or county prisons. Awards are granted in three categories: Poetry (not to exceed 100 lines), Fiction (not to exceed 5,000 words), and Nonfiction (not to exceed 5,000 words). Entries for the current competition may be submitted between September 1, 1979, and March 1, 1980. Winners will be announced in late spring, 1980. Cash awards will be made for each category: $100 first prize, $50 second prize, and $25 third prize.

Pfizer Award

The Pfizer Award, in the amount of $500, was established in 1958 by the History of Science Society for presentation to the American author of the best book on the history of science. The award winner is usually announced in December at the annual meeting of the Society. The present secretary of the Society is Professor Sally Gregory Kohlstedt, Maxwell School, Syracuse University, Syracuse, New York 13210.

1959
Marie Boas Hall
Robert Boyle and Seventeenth Century Chemistry (Cambridge Univ. Press)

1960
Marshall Clagett
The Science of Mechanics in the Middle Ages (Univ. of Wisconsin Press)

1961
Cyril Stanley Smith
History of Metallography (Univ. of Chicago Press)

1962
Henry Guerlac
Lavoisier: The Crucial Year (Cornell Univ. Press)

1963
Lynn T. White
Medieval Technology and Social Change (Oxford Univ. Press/Clarendon)

1964
Robert E. Schofield
The Lunar Society of Birmingham (Oxford Univ. Press/Clarendon)

1965
C. D. O'Malley
Andreas Vesalius of Brussels, 1514–1564 (Univ. of California Press)

1966
L. Pearce Williams
Michael Faraday, A Biography (Basic Books)

1967
Howard B. Adelmann
Marcello Malpighi and the Evolution of Embryology (Cornell Univ. Press)

1968
Edward Rosen
Kepler's Somnium (Univ. of Wisconsin Press)

1969
Margaret T. May
Galen on the Usefulness of the Parts (Cornell Univ. Press)

1970
Michael Ghiselin
The Triumph of the Darwinian Method (Univ. of California Press)

1971
David Joravsky
The Lysenko Affair (Harvard Univ. Press)

1972

Richard S. Westfall
Force in Newton's Physics (American Elsevier)

1973

Joseph S. Fruton
Molecules and Life (Wiley)

1974

Susan Schlee
Edge of an Unfamiliar World (Dutton)

1975

Frederic L. Holmes
Claude Bernard and Animal Chemistry (Harvard Univ. Press)

1976

Otto Neugebauer
A History of Ancient Mathematical Astronomy (Brown Univ. Press)

Keith M. Baker
Condorcet: From Natural Philosophy to Social Mathematics (Univ. of Chicago Press) Citation of Outstanding Merit

1977

Stephen G. Brush
The Kind of Motion We Call Heat: A History of the Kinetic Theory of Gases in the Nineteenth Century (North Holland)

1978

Allen Dubus
The Chemical Philosophy: Paracelsian Science and Medicine in the Sixteenth and Seventeenth Century (Neale Watson Academic Publications)

Merritt Roe Smith
Harpers Ferry Armory and the New Technology: The Challenge of Change (Cornell Univ. Press)

Phi Beta Kappa

The Phi Beta Kappa Book Awards, offered by Phi Beta Kappa, 1811 Q Street N.W., Washington, D.C. 20009, are made annually in December and carry a prize of $2,500 to each winning author. A description of each award follows.

Christian Gauss Award

The Christian Gauss Award was established by the Phi Beta Kappa Senate in 1950 to be awarded annually to the best book of literary scholarship or criticism published in the United States as an initial step in the recognition of advanced scholarship in the liberal arts. The name was established by the honor society when it announced the first award in 1951, in memory of the distinguished scholar and former president of the United Chapters of ΦBK, who had been a prime mover in establishing the prize. Books in the field of literary scholarship or criticism published in the United States between July 1 of the preceding year and June 30 of the year in which the award is made are eligible. Entries must be original publications. Translations and republished or revised works, even with considerable changes or additions, will not be considered; however, this stipulation does not exclude books that contain chapters or sections previously published as articles in magazines, newspapers, or learned journals. Except in rare instances involving a small and integrated "team" of writers, entries should be the work of a single author. A literary work must contain an introduction amounting to a critical or historical estimate that might have been published independently. If a book has been published abroad before the date of its American publication, it is ineligible, unless either its foreign publication is by arrangement with the American publisher or, in the case of books published by the American affiliate of a foreign press, publication in the United States follows within sixty days of publication abroad. Seven copies of each entry are required for distribution to the Award Committee. A committee of six scholars appointed by the ΦBK Senate makes its recommendations to the Senate for the winning entry.

1951
Ruth Wallerstein
Studies in Seventeenth-Century Poetic (Univ. of Wisconsin Press)
1952
Jerome Hamilton Buckley
The Victorian Temper (Harvard Univ. Press)
1953
Francis Fergusson
Dante's Drama of the Mind: A Modern Reading of the Purgatorio (Princeton Univ. Press)
1954
Meyer Howard Abrams
The Mirror and the Lamp: Romantic Theory and the Critical Tradition (Oxford Univ. Press)
1955
Louis L. Martz
The Poetry of Meditation (Yale Univ. Press)
1956
Walter Jackson Bate
The Achievement of Samuel Johnson (Oxford Univ. Press)
1957
Walter E. Houghton
The Victorian Frame of Mind (Yale Univ. Press)
1958
Cedric H. Whitman
Homer and the Heroic Tradition (Harvard Univ. Press)
1959
Margaret Gilman
The Idea of Poetry in France (Harvard Univ. Press)

1960
Reuben Arthur Brower
Alexander Pope: The Poetry of Allusion (Oxford Univ. Press)
1961
Charles R. Anderson
Emily Dickinson's Poetry: Stairway of Surprise (Holt)
1962
Wayne C. Booth
The Rhetoric of Fiction (Univ. of Chicago Press)
1963
Joan Webber
Contrary Music: The Prose Style of John Donne (Univ. of Wisconsin Press)
1964
Walter Jackson Bate
John Keats (Harvard Univ. Press)
1965
Geoffrey H. Hartman
Wordsworth's Poetry, 1787–1814 (Yale Univ. Press)
1966
Wilfred Stone
The Cave and the Mountain: A Study of E. M. Forster (Stanford Univ. Press)
1967
Larzer Ziff
The American Eighteen Nineties: Life and Times of a Lost Generation (Viking)
1968
Barbara Herrnstein Smith
Poetic Closure: A Study of How Poems End (Univ. of Chicago Press)

1969
  Louis Crompton
  Shaw the Dramatist (Univ. of Nebraska Press)
1970
  Walter Jackson Bate
  The Burden of the Past and the English Poet (Harvard Univ. Press)
1971
  Carl Woodring
  Politics in English Romantic Poetry (Harvard Univ. Press)
1972
  Hugh Kenner
  The Pound Era (Univ. of California Press)
1973
  Gwyn Jones
  Kings, Beasts and Heroes (Oxford Univ. Press)

1974
  Clarence Brown
  Mandelstam (Cambridge Univ. Press)
1975
  Robert Gittings
  Young Thomas Hardy (Atlantic-Little)
1976
  Elisabeth W. Schneider
  T. S. Eliot: The Pattern in the Carpet (Univ. of California Press)
1977
  Joseph Frank
  Dostoevsky: The Seeds of Revolt, 1821–1849 (Princeton Univ. Press)
1978
  Charles R. Anderson
  Person, Place, and Thing in Henry James's Novels (Duke Univ. Press)

The Phi Beta Kappa Award in Science

This award was established in 1958 to encourage more literate and scholarly interpretations of the physical and biological sciences and mathematics by scientists themselves.

1959
  Loren Eiseley
  Darwin's Century: Evolution and the Men Who Discovered It (Doubleday)
1960
  Marston Bates
  The Forest and the Sea (Random)
1961
  Martin Lindauer
  Communication among Social Bees (Harvard Univ. Press)
1962
  James L. Dyson
  The World of Ice (Knopf)
1963
  René Dubos
  The Unseen World (Rockefeller Institute Press in association with Oxford Univ. Press)

1964
  Verne Grant
  The Origin of Adaptations (Columbia Univ. Press)

1965
  Donald R. Griffin
  Bird Migration (Natural History Press-Doubleday/Anchor)

1966
  René Dubos
  Man Adapting (Yale Univ. Press)

1967
  Haig P. Papazian
  Modern Genetics (Norton)

1968
  Alister Hardy
  Great Waters (Harper)

1969
G. J. V. Nossal
Antibodies and Immunity (Basic Books)
1970
John Teal and Mildred Teal
The Life and Death of a Salt Marsh (Atlantic-Little)
1971
Linus Pauling
Vitamin C and the Common Cold (Freeman)
1972
Barry Commoner
The Closing Circle: Nature, Man and Technology (Knopf)
1973
Herman H. Goldstine
The Computer from Pascal to von Neumann (Princeton Univ. Press)
1974
Howard E. Gruber and Paul H. Barrett
Darwin on Man (Dutton)

1975
Guido Majno
The Healing Hand: Man and Wound in the Ancient World (Harvard Univ. Press)
1976
William W. Warner
Beautiful Swimmers: Watermen, Crabs and the Chesapeake Bay (Atlantic)
1977
Gerard K. O'Neil
The High Frontier: Human Colonies in Space (Morrow)
1978
Colin Blakemore
Mechanics of the Mind (Cambridge Univ. Press)

The Phi Beta Kappa Ralph Waldo Emerson Award

This award was established by the Phi Beta Kappa Senate in 1959 to honor interpretive historical, philosophical, and religious studies in the great tradition of humane learning. History and philosophy are conceived in as broad terms as possible in order to include appropriate works in political science, economics, sociology, and cultural anthropology. Limited or purely technical studies do not qualify.

1960
Albert William Levi
Philosophy and the Modern World (Indiana Univ. Press)
1961
W. T. Stace
Mysticism and Philosophy (Lippincott)
1962
Herbert J. Muller
Freedom in the Ancient World (Harper)

1963
Richard Hofstadter
Anti-Intellectualism in American Life (Knopf)
1964
Thomas F. Gossett
Race: The History of an Idea in America (Southern Methodist Univ. Press)
1965
Howard Mumford Jones
O Strange New World: American Culture—The Formative Years (Viking)

1966
  John Herman Randall, Jr.
  The Career of Philosophy: From the German Enlightenment to the Age of Darwin (Columbia Univ. Press)
1967
  Robert Coles
  Children of Crisis: A Study of Courage and Fear (Atlantic-Little)
1968
  Winthrop D. Jordan
  White over Black: American Attitudes toward the Negro, 1550-1812 (Univ. of North Carolina Press)
1969
  Peter Gay
  Weimar Culture: The Outsider as Insider (Harper)
1970
  Rollo May
  Love and Will (Norton)
1971
  Charles A. Barker
  American Convictions: Cycles of Public Thought 1600-1850 (Lippincott)
1972
  John Rawls
  A Theory of Justice (Belknap)

1973
  Barrington Moore, Jr.
  Reflections on the Causes of Human Misery and upon Certain Proposals to Eliminate Them (Beacon)
1974
  Frederic C. Lane
  Venice: A Maritime Republic (Johns Hopkins Univ. Press)
1975
  Marshall G. S. Hodgson
  The Venture of Islam (Univ. of Chicago Press)
1976
  Paul Fussell
  The Great War and Modern Memory (Oxford Univ. Press)
1977
  Eugen Weber
  Peasants into Frenchmen: The Modernization of Rural France, 1870-1914 (Stanford Univ. Press)
1978
  Bruce Kuklick
  The Rise of American Philosophy: Cambridge, Massachusetts, 1860-1930 (Yale Univ. Press)

Henry M. Phillips Prize

The Henry M. Phillips Prize was made available by the American Philosophical Society through a gift in 1888 from Emily Phillips of Philadelphia in memory of her brother, Henry M. Phillips. The income from this fund is used to award a prize for the best essay or book on the science and philosophy of jurisprudence. Recent awards have been given for published books, but in earlier years essays were considered before publication. At irregular intervals an honorarium of $1,500 to $2,000 and a certificate are presented to the winner at the American Philosophical Society, 104 South Fifth Street, Philadelphia, Pennsylvania 19106.

1895
  George H. Smith
  "The Theory of State"

1900
  W. H. Hastings
  "The Development of Law as Illus-

trated by the Decisions Relating to the Police Power of the State"

1912

Charles H. Burr
"The Treaty-Making Power of the United States and the Methods of Its Enforcement as Affecting the Police Powers of the States"

1921

Quincy Wright
"The Relative Rights, Duties, and Responsibilities of the President, of the Senate and the House, and the Judiciary in Theory and Practice"

1935

Lon L. Fuller
"American Legal Realism"

1942

Edward S. Corwin
The President: Office and Powers (New York Univ. Press) and his articles on American constitutional law

1950

Philip C. Jessup
Modern Law of Nations (Macmillan)

1955

Edmond Cahn
The Sense of Injustice (New York Univ. Press) and his contribution to

Supreme Court and Supreme Law (Indiana Univ. Press)

1957

Catherine Drinker Bowen
The Lion and the Throne (Little)

1960

Roscoe Pound
"Jurisprudence"

1962

Karl Nickerson Llewellyn
The Common Law Tradition: Deciding Appeals (Little)

1963–1973

No awards

1974

John Rawls
A Theory of Justice (Belknap)

1975

No award

1976

Wolfgang G. Friedmann
Legal Theory (Columbia Univ. Press) and *Law in a Changing Society* (Columbia Univ. Press)

Harry W. Jones
The Efficacy of Law (Northwestern Univ. Press) and "An Invitation to Jurisprudence," *Columbia Law Review*, 1974

Edgar Allan Poe Awards

In 1945, the Mystery Writers of America, Inc., 105 East 19 Street, New York, New York 10003, established the Edgar Allan Poe Awards to "recognize outstanding contributions to various categories of mystery, crime, and suspense writing." The awards, ceramic statuettes of Edgar Allan Poe known as "Edgars," are given annually in April in the following ten categories: Novel, First Novel, Fact Crime, Paperback Original, Critical/Biographical Study, Juvenile Novel, Short Story, Motion Picture, Television Program, and Television Program in Series. The winners in the first six categories are listed below, along with the Grand Master award winners. Winners in the four other categories cited, as well as winners of "Ravens" for best book cover illustration, Edgar winners in discontinued categories—Mystery Criticism (1945–1966), Foreign Film (1958–1965), and Radio Drama (1945–1958)—and Special Award winners (1948–1977) can be obtained from the Mystery Writers of America.

NOVEL

1954
Charlotte Jay
Beat Not the Bones (Harper)
1955
Raymond Chandler
The Long Goodbye (Houghton)
1956
Margaret Millar
Beast in View (Random)
1957
Charlotte Armstrong
A Dram of Poison (Coward)
1958
Ed Lacy
Room to Swing (Harper)
1959
Stanley Ellin
The Eighth Circle (Random)
1960
Celia Fremlin
The Hours before Dawn (Lippincott)
1961
Julian Symons
Progress of a Crime (Harper)
1962
J. J. Marric
Gideon's Fire (Harper)
1963
Ellis Peters
Death of the Joyful Woman (Crime Club)
1964
Eric Ambler
The Light of Day (Knopf)
1965
John le Carré
The Spy Who Came In from the Cold (Coward)
1966
Adam Hall
The Quiller Memorandum (Simon & Schuster)
1967
Nicolas Freeling
King of the Rainy Country (Harper)

1968
Donald Westlake
God Save the Mark (Random)
1969
Jeffery Hudson
A Case of Need (World)
1970
Dick Francis
Forfeit (Harper)
1971
Maj Sjöwall and Per Wahlöö
The Laughing Policeman (Pantheon)
1972
Frederick Forsyth
The Day of the Jackal (Viking)
1973
Warren Kiefer
The Lingala Code (Random)
1974
Tony Hillerman
Dance Hall of the Dead (Harper)
1975
Jon Cleary
Peter's Pence (Morrow)
1976
Brian Garfield
Hopscotch (Evans)
1977
Robert Parker
Promised Land (Houghton)
1978
William Hallahan
Catch Me: Kill Me (Bobbs)
1979
Ken Follett
The Eye of the Needle (Arbor House)

FIRST NOVEL

1946
Julius Fast
Watchful at Night (Farrar)
1947
Helen Eustis
The Horizontal Man (Harper)

FIRST NOVEL (cont.)

1948
Fredric Brown
The Fabulous Clipjoint (Dutton)
1949
Mildred Davis
The Room Upstairs (Simon & Schuster)
1950
Alan Green
What a Body (Simon & Schuster)
1951
Thomas Walsh
Nightmare in Manhattan (Little)
1952
Mary McMullen
Strangle Hold (Harper)
1953
William Campbell Gault
Don't Cry for Me (Dutton)
1954
Ira Levin
A Kiss before Dying (Simon & Schuster)
1955
Jean Potts
Go, Lovely Rose (Scribner)
1956
Lane Kauffmann
The Perfectionist (Lippincott)
1957
Douglas McNutt Douglas
Rebecca's Pride (Harper)
1958
William R. Weeks
Knock and Wait a While (Houghton)
1959
Richard Martin Stern
The Bright Road to Fear (Ballantine)
1960
Henry Slesar
The Grey Flannel Shroud (Random)
1961
John Holbrook Vance
The Man in the Cage (Random)

1962
Suzanne Blanc
The Green Stone (Harper)
1963
Robert L. Fish
The Fugitive (Simon & Schuster)
1964
Cornelius Hirschberg
The Florentine Finish (Harper)
1965
Harry Kemelman
Friday the Rabbi Slept Late (Crown)
1966
John Ball
In the Heat of the Night (Harper)
1967
Ross Thomas
The Cold War Swap (Morrow)
1968
Michael Collins
Act of Fear (Dodd)
1969
E. Richard Johnson
Silver Street (Harper)
1970
Joe Gores
A Time for Predators (Random)
1971
Lawrence Sanders
The Anderson Tapes (Putnam)
1972
A. H. Z. Carr
Finding Maubee (Putnam)
1973
R. H. Shimer
Squaw Point (Harper)
1974
Paul E. Erdman
The Billion Dollar Sure Thing (Scribner)
1975
Gregory McDonald
Fletch (Bobbs)
1976
Rex Burns
The Alvarez Journal (Harper)

FIRST NOVEL (cont.)

1977
James Patterson
The Thomas Berryman Number (Little)
1978
Robert Ross
A French Finish (Putnam)
1979
William L. DeAndrea
Killed in the Ratings (Harcourt)

FACT CRIME

1948
Edward D. Radin
Twelve against the Law (Duell)
1949
Marie Rodell, ed.
Regional Murder series
1950
Joseph Henry Jackson
Bad Company: The Story of California's Legendary and Actual Stage-Robbers, Bandits, Highwaymen and Outlaws from the Fifties to the Eighties (Harcourt)
1951
Edward D. Radin
Twelve against Crime (Putnam)
1952
St. Clair McKelway
True Tales from the Annals of Crime and Rascality (Random)
1953
Erle Stanley Gardner
Court of Last Resort (Sloane)
1954
John Bartlow Martin
Why Did They Kill? (Ballantine)
1955
Charles Boswell and Lewis Thompson
The Girl with the Scarlet Brand

1956
Manly Wade Wellman
Dead and Gone (Univ. of North Carolina Press)
1957
Charles Samuels and Louise Samuels
Night Fell on Georgia (Dell)
1958
Harold R. Danforth and James D. Horan
The D.A.'s Man (Crown)
1959
Wenzell Brown
They Died in the Chair (Popular Library)
1960
Thomas Gallager
Fire at Sea (Rinehart)
1961
Miriam Allen deFord
The Overbury Affair (Chilton)
1962
Barrett Prettyman, Jr.
Death and the Supreme Court (Harcourt)
1963
Francis Russell
Tragedy in Dedham (McGraw)
1964
Gerold Frank
The Deed (Simon & Schuster)
1965
Anthony Lewis
Gideon's Trumpet (Random)
1966
Truman Capote
In Cold Blood (Random)
1967
Gerold Frank
The Boston Strangler (New American Library)
1968
Victoria Lincoln
A Private Disgrace (Putnam)

FACT CRIME (cont.)

1969
John Walsh
Poe, the Detective (Rutgers Univ. Press)
1970
Herbert B. Ehrmann
The Case That Will Not Die (Little)
1971
Mildred Savage
A Great Fall (Simon & Schuster)
1972
Sandor Frankel
Beyond a Reasonable Doubt (Stein & Day)
1973
Stephen Fay, Lewis Chester, and Magnus Linkletter
Hoax (Viking)
1974
Barbara Levy
Legacy of Violence (Prentice)
1975
Vincent Bugliosi and Curt Gentry
Helter Skelter (Norton)
1976
Tom Wicker
A Time to Die (Quadrangle)
1977
Thomas Thompson
Blood and Money (Doubleday)
1978
George Jonas and Barbara Amiel
By Persons Unknown (Grove)
1979
Vincent Bugliosi and Ken Hurwitz
Til Death Do Us Part (Norton)

PAPERBACK ORIGINAL

1971
Dan J. Marlowe
Flashpoint (Gold Medal)

1972
Frank McAuliffe
For Murder I Charge More (Ballantine)
1973
Richard Wormser
The Invader (Gold Medal)
1974
Will Perry
Death of an Informer (Pyramid)
1975
Roy Winsor
The Corpse That Walked (Fawcett)
1976
John R. Feegal
Autopsy (Avon)
1977
Gregory McDonald
Confess, Fletch (Avon)
1978
Mike Jahn
The Quark Maneuver (Ballantine)
1979
Frank Bandy
Deceit and Deadly Lies (Charter)

CRITICAL/BIOGRAPHICAL STUDY

1977
Chris Steinbrunner, Otto Penzler, Marvin Lachman, and Charles Shibuk
Encyclopedia of Mystery and Detection (McGraw)
1978
John J. McAleer
Rex Stout (Little)
1979
Gwen Robins
The Mystery of Agatha Christie (Doubleday)

JUVENILE NOVEL

1961
Phyllis A. Whitney
The Mystery of the Haunted Pool (Westminster)

JUVENILE NOVEL (cont.)

1962
Edward Fenton
The Phantom of Walkaway Hill (Doubleday)

1963
Scott Sorbett
Cutlass Island (Little)

1964
Phyllis A. Whitney
Mystery of the Hidden Hand (Westminster)

1965
Marcella Thum
Mystery of Crans Landing (Dodd)

1966
Leon Ware
The Mystery of 22 East (Westminster)

1967
Kin Platt
Sinbad and Me (Chilton)

1968
Gretchen Sprague
Signpost to Terror (Dodd)

1969
Virginia Hamilton
The House of Dies Drear (Macmillan)

1970
Winifred Finlay
Danger in Black Dyke (S. G. Phillips)

1971
John Rowe Townsend
The Intruder (Lippincott)

1972
Joan Aiken
Nightfall (Holt)

1973
Robb White
Deathwatch (Doubleday)

1974
Jay Bennett
The Long Black Coat (Delacorte)

1975
Jay Bennett
The Dangling Witness (Delacorte)

1976
Robert C. O'Brien
Z for Zachariah (Atheneum)

1977
Richard Peck
Are You in the House Alone? (Viking)

1978
Eloise Jarvis McGraw
A Really Weird Summer (Atheneum)

1979
Dana Brookins
Alone in Wolf Hollow (Seabury)

Pulitzer Prizes in Letters

The Pulitzer Prizes in Letters were established in 1917 by the terms of the will of Joseph Pulitzer (1847–1911), newspaper genius of the New York *World* who is also remembered for his endowment of the Columbia University School of Journalism. Currently six prizes of $1,000 each are awarded annually as follows:

1. For distinguished fiction published in book form during the year by an American author, preferably dealing with American life.

2. For a distinguished play by an American author, preferably original in its source and dealing with American life.

3. For a distinguished book of the year on the history of the United States.

4. For a distinguished biography or autobiography by an American author published during the year.

5. For a distinguished volume of verse published during the year by an American author.

6. For a distinguished book of nonfiction by an American author, giving prime consideration to high literary quality and originality.

The award of Pulitzer Prizes and Fellowships is made by Columbia University on the recommendation of the Pulitzer Prize Board. The Pulitzer Prize Board meets annually in April.

Nominating jurors are appointed by the university in each category. They are invited to exercise their independent and collective judgment and submit from three to five nominations. The nominating jurors are advised that their nominations are for the information and advice of the Pulitzer Prize Board only inasmuch as the Board is charged with the responsibility and authority under the will of Joseph Pulitzer to select, accept, substitute, or reject these nominations, and may in extraordinary circumstances offer its own. Jurors are permitted to make additional prize nominations in further jury reports to the Pulitzer Prize Board, particularly in such fields as letters, drama, and music, where specialized expertise is required.

Entries must be submitted in writing and addressed to the Secretary of the Pulitzer Prize Board, Professor Richard T. Baker, 702 Journalism, Columbia University, New York, New York 10027. Entries for letters awards must be submitted on or before November 1 to cover books published during the year between January 1 and December 31.

Competition for prizes is limited to work done during the calendar year ending December 31, except in drama and music. For the drama prize, works produced during the twelve months from April 1 through March 31 are considered. For the music award, works performed between March 15 in one year and March 14 of the subsequent year are considered. Entries should be received by the Prize Board by March 1, if possible.

For the prizes in letters, four copies of each book shall be sent to the Secretary of the Pulitzer Prize Board within a month of publication up to November 1, except for books scheduled for publication in November and December, which may be submitted in galley proof. For the prize in drama, entries shall be made while the work is being performed together with up to four published or manuscript copies of each work, where requested, and an agreement from the producer to permit the purchase of tickets by the Secretary of the Pulitzer Prize Board for those concerned in the judging, not to exceed two each. For the prize in music, entries similarly shall be accompanied by an agreement from performing organizations to submit scores and recordings or, when necessary, to make arrangements for the judging in the same manner as the drama prize.

If in any one year no book, play, or musical composition entered for a prize shall be of sufficient excellence in the opinion of the Pulitzer Prize Board, or if in any other subject of competition all the competitors shall fall below the standard of excellence fixed by the Pulitzer Prize Board, then in that case the amount of such prize or prizes may be withheld in such year.

Any author, composer, or journalist, including previous prize winners, is eligible for consideration each year for any award.

On the recommendation of the faculty of the Graduate School of Journalism, three fellowships of $3,000 each are made to enable three of its outstanding graduates to travel and study abroad. Competition for these fellowships is not necessarily restricted to those who are graduated from the School of Journalism in the year when the award is made.

NOVEL

1917
No award
1918
Ernest Poole
His Family (Macmillan)
1919
Booth Tarkington
The Magnificent Ambersons (Doubleday)
1920
No award
1921
Edith Wharton
The Age of Innocence (Appleton)
1922
Booth Tarkington
Alice Adams (Doubleday)
1923
Willa Cather
One of Ours (Knopf)
1924
Margaret Wilson
The Able McLaughlins (Harper)
1925
Edna Ferber
So Big (Doubleday)
1926
Sinclair Lewis
Arrowsmith (Harcourt)
1927
Louis Bromfield
Early Autumn (Stokes)
1928
Thornton Wilder
The Bridge of San Luis Rey (Boni)
1929
Julia Peterkin
Scarlet Sister Mary (Bobbs)

1930
Oliver La Farge
Laughing Boy (Houghton)
1931
Margaret Ayer Barnes
Years of Grace (Houghton)
1932
Pearl S. Buck
The Good Earth (John Day)
1933
T. S. Stribling
The Store (Doubleday)
1934
Caroline Miller
Lamb in His Bosom (Harper)
1935
Josephine Winslow Johnson
Now in November (Simon & Schuster)
1936
Harold L. Davis
Honey in the Horn (Harper)
1937
Margaret Mitchell
Gone with the Wind (Macmillan)
1938
John Phillips Marquand
The Late George Apley (Little)
1939
Marjorie Kinnan Rawlings
The Yearling (Scribner)
1940
John Steinbeck
The Grapes of Wrath (Viking)
1941
No award
1942
Ellen Glasgow
In This Our Life (Harcourt)

NOVEL (cont.)

1943
   Upton Sinclair
   Dragon's Teeth (Viking)
1944
   Martin Flavin
   Journey in the Dark (Harper)
1945
   John Hersey
   A Bell for Adano (Knopf)
1946
   No award
1947
   Robert Penn Warren
   All the King's Men (Harcourt)

FICTION

1948
   James A. Michener
   Tales of the South Pacific (Macmillan)
1949
   James Gould Cozzens
   Guard of Honor (Harcourt)
1950
   A. B. Guthrie, Jr.
   The Way West (Sloane)
1951
   Conrad Richter
   The Town (Knopf)
1952
   Herman Wouk
   The Caine Mutiny (Doubleday)
1953
   Ernest Hemingway
   The Old Man and the Sea (Scribner)
1954
   No award
1955
   William Faulkner
   A Fable (Random)
1956
   MacKinlay Kantor
   Andersonville (World)

1957
   No award
1958
   James Agee
   A Death in the Family (McDowell, Obolensky)
1959
   Robert Lewis Taylor
   The Travels of Jaimie McPheeters (Doubleday)
1960
   Allen Drury
   Advise and Consent (Doubleday)
1961
   Harper Lee
   To Kill a Mockingbird (Lippincott)
1962
   Edwin O'Connor
   The Edge of Sadness (Little)
1963
   William Faulkner
   The Reivers (Random)
1964
   No award
1965
   Shirley Ann Grau
   The Keepers of the House (Random)
1966
   Katherine Anne Porter
   The Collected Stories of Katherine Anne Porter (Harcourt)
1967
   Bernard Malamud
   The Fixer (Farrar)
1968
   William Styron
   The Confessions of Nat Turner (Random)
1969
   N. Scott Momaday
   House Made of Dawn (Harper)
1970
   Jean Stafford
   Collected Stories (Farrar)
1971
   No award

FICTION (cont.)

1972
Wallace Stegner
Angle of Repose (Doubleday)
1973
Eudora Welty
The Optimist's Daughter (Random)
1974
No award
1975
Michael Shaara
The Killer Angels (McKay)
1976
Saul Bellow
Humboldt's Gift (Viking)
1977
No award
1978
James Alan McPherson
Elbow Room (Atlantic)
1979
John Cheever
The Stories of John Cheever (Knopf)

DRAMA

1917
No award
1918
Jesse Lynch Williams
Why Marry? (Scribner)
1919
No award
1920
Eugene O'Neill
Beyond the Horizon (Random)
1921
Zona Gale
Miss Lulu Bett (Appleton)
1922
Eugene O'Neill
Anna Christie (Random)
1923
Owen Davis
Icebound (Little)

1924
Hatcher Hughes
Hell-Bent fer Heaven (Harper)
1925
Sidney Howard
They Knew What They Wanted (Doubleday)
1926
George Kelly
Craig's Wife (Little)
1927
Paul Green
In Abraham's Bosom (McBride)
1928
Eugene O'Neill
Strange Interlude (Random)
1929
Elmer L. Rice
Street Scene (French)
1930
Marc Connelly
The Green Pastures (Farrar)
1931
Susan Glaspell
Alison's House (French)
1932
George S. Kaufman, Morrie Ryskind, and Ira Gershwin
Of Thee I Sing (Knopf)
1933
Maxwell Anderson
Both Your Houses (French)
1934
Sidney Kingsley
Men in White (Covici-Friede)
1935
Zoë Akins
The Old Maid (Appleton)
1936
Robert E. Sherwood
Idiot's Delight (Scribner)
1937
Moss Hart and George S. Kaufman
You Can't Take It with You (Farrar)
1938
Thornton Wilder
Our Town (Coward)

DRAMA (cont.)

1939
Robert E. Sherwood
Abe Lincoln in Illinois (Scribner)
1940
William Saroyan
The Time of Your Life (Harcourt)
1941
Robert E. Sherwood
There Shall Be No Night (Scribner)
1942
No award
1943
Thornton Wilder
The Skin of Our Teeth (Harper)
1944
No award
1945
Mary Chase
Harvey (Dramatists Play Service)
1946
Russel Crouse and Howard Lindsay
State of the Union (Random)
1947
No award
1948
Tennessee Williams
A Streetcar Named Desire (New Directions)
1949
Arthur Miller
Death of a Salesman (Viking)
1950
Richard Rodgers, Oscar Hammerstein II, and Joshua Logan
South Pacific (Random)
1951
No award
1952
Joseph Kramm
The Shrike (Random)
1953
William Inge
Picnic (Random)

1954
John Patrick
The Teahouse of the August Moon (Putnam)
1955
Tennessee Williams
Cat on a Hot Tin Roof (New Directions)
1956
Albert Hackett and Frances Goodrich
Diary of Anne Frank (Random)
1957
Eugene O'Neill
Long Day's Journey into Night (Yale Univ. Press)
1958
Ketti Frings
Look Homeward, Angel (Scribner)
1959
Archibald MacLeish
J.B. (Houghton)
1960
Jerome Weidman and George Abbott (book), Jerry Bock (music), Sheldon Harnick (lyrics)
Fiorello! (Random)
1961
Tad Mosel
All the Way Home (Obolensky)
1962
Frank Loesser and Abe Burrows
How to Succeed in Business without Really Trying
1963 –1964
No awards
1965
Frank D. Gilroy
The Subject Was Roses (Random)
1966
No award
1967
Edward Albee
A Delicate Balance (Atheneum)
1968
No award

DRAMA (cont.)

1969
Howard Sackler
The Great White Hope (Dial)
1970
Charles Gordone
No Place to Be Somebody (Bobbs)
1971
Paul Zindel
The Effect of Gamma Rays on Man-in-the-Moon Marigolds (Harper)
1972
No award
1973
Jason Miller
That Championship Season (Atheneum)
1974
No award
1975
Edward Albee
Seascape (Atheneum)
1976
James Kirkwood and Nicholas Dante (book), Michael Bennett (choreography), Marvin Hamlisch (music), and Edward Kleban (lyrics)
A Chorus Line
1977
Michael Cristofer
The Shadow Box
1978
Donald L. Coburn
The Gin Game
1979
Sam Shepard
Buried Child

HISTORY

1917
J. J. Jusserand
With Americans of Past and Present Days (Scribner)

1918
James Ford Rhodes
A History of the Civil War, 1861–1865 (Macmillan)
1919
No award
1920
Justin H. Smith
The War with Mexico (Macmillan)
1921
William Sowden Sims, in collaboration with Burton J. Hendrick
The Victory at Sea (Doubleday)
1922
James Truslow Adams
The Founding of New England (Little)
1923
Charles Warren
The Supreme Court in United States History (Little)
1924
Charles Howard McIlwain
The American Revolution—A Constitutional Interpretation (Macmillan)
1925
Frederic L. Paxson
A History of the American Frontier (Houghton)
1926
Edward Channing
The History of the United States (Macmillan)
1927
Samuel Flagg Bemis
Pinckney's Treaty (Johns Hopkins Univ. Press)
1928
Vernon Louis Parrington
Main Currents in American Thought (Harcourt)
1929
Fred Albert Shannon
The Organization and Administration of the Union Army, 1861–1865 (A. H. Clark)

HISTORY (cont.)

1930
   Claude H. Van Tyne
   The War of Independence (Houghton)
1931
   Bernadotte E. Schmitt
   The Coming of the War: 1914 (Scribner)
1932
   John J. Pershing
   My Experiences in the World War (Stokes)
1933
   Frederick J. Turner
   The Significance of Sections in American History (Holt)
1934
   Herbert Agar
   The People's Choice (Houghton)
1935
   Charles McLean Andrews
   The Colonial Period of American History (Yale Univ. Press)
1936
   Andrew C. McLaughlin
   The Constitutional History of the United States (Appleton)
1937
   Van Wyck Brooks
   The Flowering of New England (Dutton)
1938
   Paul Herman Buck
   The Road to Reunion, 1865–1900 (Little)
1939
   Frank Luther Mott
   A History of American Magazines (Harvard Univ. Press)
1940
   Carl Sandburg
   Abraham Lincoln: The War Years (Harcourt)

1941
   Marcus Lee Hansen
   The Atlantic Migration, 1607–1860 (Harvard Univ. Press)
1942
   Margaret Leech
   Reveille in Washington (Harper)
1943
   Esther Forbes
   Paul Revere and the World He Lived In (Houghton)
1944
   Merle Curti
   The Growth of American Thought (Harper)
1945
   Stephen Bonsal
   Unfinished Business (Doubleday)
1946
   Arthur M. Schlesinger, Jr.
   The Age of Jackson (Little)
1947
   James Phinney Baxter III
   Scientists against Time (Little)
1948
   Bernard DeVoto
   Across the Wide Missouri (Houghton)
1949
   Roy Franklin Nichols
   The Disruption of American Democracy (Macmillan)
1950
   Oliver W. Larkin
   Art and Life in America (Rinehart)
1951
   R. Carlyle Buley
   The Old Northwest, Pioneer Period 1815–1840 (Towers)
1952
   Oscar Handlin
   The Uprooted (Little)
1953
   George Dangerfield
   The Era of Good Feelings (Harcourt)

HISTORY (cont.)

1954
Bruce Catton
A Stillness at Appomattox (Double-day)
1955
Paul Horgan
Great River: The Rio Grande in North American History (Rinehart)
1956
Richard Hofstadter
Age of Reform (Knopf)
1957
George F. Kennan
Russia Leaves the War (Princeton Univ. Press)
1958
Bray Hammond
Banks and Politics in America —From the Revolution to the Civil War (Princeton Univ. Press)
1959
Leonard D. White
The Republican Era: 1869–1901 (Macmillan)
1960
Margaret Leech
In the Days of McKinley (Harper)
1961
Herbert Feis
Between War and Peace: The Potsdam Conference (Princeton Univ. Press)
1962
Lawrence H. Gipson
The Triumphant Empire, Thunder-Clouds Gather in the West (Knopf)
1963
Constance McLaughlin Green
Washington, Village and Capital, 1800–1878 (Princeton Univ. Press)
1964
Sumner Chilton Powell
Puritan Village: The Formation of a New England Town (Wesleyan Univ. Press)

1965
Irwin Unger
The Greenback Era (Princeton Univ. Press)
1966
Perry Miller
The Life of the Mind in America: From the Revolution to the Civil War (Harcourt)
1967
William H. Goetzmann
Exploration and Empire (Knopf)
1968
Bernard Bailyn
The Ideological Origins of the American Revolution (Harvard Univ. Press)
1969
Leonard W. Levy
The Origins of the Fifth Amendment (Oxford Univ. Press)
1970
Dean Gooderham Acheson
Present at the Creation: My Years in the State Department (Norton)
1971
James MacGregor Burns
Roosevelt, the Soldier of Freedom (Harcourt)
1972
Carl N. Degler
Neither Black nor White (Macmillan)
1973
Michael Kammen
People of Paradox: An Inquiry Concerning the Origins of American Civilization (Knopf)
1974
Daniel J. Boorstin
The Americans: The Democratic Experience (Random)
1975
Dumas Malone
Jefferson and His Time, Vols. 1–4 (Little)
1976
Paul Horgan
Lamy of Santa Fé (Farrar)

HISTORY (cont.)

1977
David M. Potter
The Impending Crisis (manuscript finished by Don E. Fehrenbacher) (Harper)
1978
Alfred D. Chandler, Jr.
The Visible Hand: The Managerial Revolution in American Business (Harvard Univ. Press)
1979
Don E. Fehrenbacher
The Dred Scott Case (Oxford Univ. Press)

BIOGRAPHY AND AUTOBIOGRAPHY

1917
Laura E. Richards and Maude Howe Elliott, assisted by Florence Howe Hall
Julia Ward Howe (Houghton)
1918
William Cabell Bruce
Benjamin Franklin, Self-Revealed (Putnam)
1919
Henry Adams
The Education of Henry Adams (Houghton)
1920
Albert J. Beveridge
The Life of John Marshall (Houghton)
1921
Edward Bok
The Americanization of Edward Bok (Scribner)
1922
Hamlin Garland
A Daughter of the Middle Border (Macmillan)

1923
Burton J. Hendrick
The Life and Letters of Walter H. Page (Houghton)
1924
Michael Idvorsky Pupin
From Immigrant to Inventor (Scribner)
1925
M. A. DeWolfe Howe
Barrett Wendell and His Letters (Little)
1926
Harvey Cushing
The Life of Sir William Osler (Oxford Univ. Press)
1927
Emory Holloway
Whitman (Knopf)
1928
Charles Edward Russell
The American Orchestra and Theodore Thomas (Doubleday)
1929
Burton J. Hendrick
The Training of an American: The Earlier Life and Letters of Walter H. Page (Houghton)
1930
Marquis James
The Raven (Bobbs)
1931
Henry James
Charles W. Eliot (Houghton)
1932
Henry F. Pringle
Theodore Roosevelt (Harcourt)
1933
Allan Nevins
Grover Cleveland (Dodd)
1934
Tyler Dennett
John Hay (Dodd)
1935
Douglas S. Freeman
R. E. Lee (Scribner)

BIOGRAPHY AND AUTOBIOGRAPHY
(cont.)

1936
Ralph Barton Perry
The Thought and Character of William James (Little)
1937
Allan Nevins
Hamilton Fish (Dodd)
1938
Odell Shepard
Pedlar's Progress (Little)
Marquis James
Andrew Jackson (Bobbs)
1939
Carl Van Doren
Benjamin Franklin (Viking)
1940
Ray Stannard Baker
Woodrow Wilson, Life and Letters, Vols. VII–VIII (Doubleday)
1941
Ola Elizabeth Winslow
Jonathan Edwards (Macmillan)
1942
Forrest Wilson
Crusader in Crinoline (Lippincott)
1943
Samuel Eliot Morison
Admiral of the Ocean Sea (Little)
1944
Carleton Mabee
The American Leonardo: The Life of Samuel F. B. Morse (Knopf)
1945
Russel Blaine Nye
George Bancroft: Brahmin Rebel (Knopf)
1946
Linnie Marsh Wolfe
Son of the Wilderness (Knopf)
1947
William Allen White
The Autobiography of William Allen White (Macmillan)

1948
Margaret Clapp
Forgotten First Citizen: John Bigelow (Little)
1949
Robert E. Sherwood
Roosevelt and Hopkins (Harper)
1950
Samuel Flagg Bemis
John Quincy Adams and the Foundations of American Foreign Policy (Knopf)
1951
Margaret Louise Coit
John C. Calhoun: American Portrait (Houghton)
1952
Merlo J. Pusey
Charles Evans Hughes (Macmillan)
1953
David J. Mays
Edmund Pendleton, 1721–1803 (Harvard Univ. Press)
1954
Charles A. Lindbergh
The Spirit of St. Louis (Scribner)
1955
William S. White
The Taft Story (Harper)
1956
Talbot Faulkner Hamlin
Benjamin Henry Latrobe (Oxford Univ. Press)
1957
John F. Kennedy
Profiles in Courage (Harper)
1958
John A. Carroll and Mary W. Ashworth
George Washington, Vol. VII (Scribner)
Douglas S. Freeman
George Washington, Vols. I–VI (Scribner)
1959
Arthur Walworth
Woodrow Wilson, American Prophet (Longmans)

BIOGRAPHY AND AUTOBIOGRAPHY
(cont.)

1960
Samuel Eliot Morison
John Paul Jones (Little)
1961
David Donald
Charles Sumner and the Coming of the Civil War (Knopf)
1962
No award
1963
Leon Edel
Henry James (Lippincott)
1964
Walter Jackson Bate
John Keats (Harvard Univ. Press)
1965
Ernest Samuels
Henry Adams, 3 vols. (Harvard Univ. Press)
1966
Arthur M. Schlesinger, Jr.
A Thousand Days: John F. Kennedy in the White House (Houghton)
1967
Justin Kaplan
Mr. Clemens and Mark Twain (Simon & Schuster)
1968
George F. Kennan
Memoirs 1925–1950 (Little)
1969
Benjamin L. Reid
The Man from New York: John Quinn and His Friends (Oxford Univ. Press)
1970
T. Harry Williams
Huey Long (Knopf)
1971
Lawrence Thompson
Robert Frost: The Years of Triumph, 1915–1938 (Holt)
1972
Joseph P. Lash
Eleanor and Franklin (Norton)

1973
W. A. Swanberg
Luce and His Empire (Scribner)
1974
Louis Sheaffer
O'Neill, Son and Artist (Little)
1975
Robert Caro
The Power Broker: Robert Moses and the Fall of New York (Knopf)
1976
R. W. B. Lewis
Edith Wharton: A Biography (Harper)
1977
John E. Mack
A Prince of Our Disorder: The Life of T. E. Lawrence (Little)
1978
Walter Jackson Bate
Samuel Johnson (Harcourt)
1979
Leonard Baker
Days of Sorrow and Pain: Leo Baeck and the Berlin Jews (Macmillan)

POETRY

1922
Edwin Arlington Robinson
Collected Poems (Macmillan)
1923
Edna St. Vincent Millay
The Ballad of the Harp-Weaver; A Few Figs from Thistles (Harper); Eight sonnets in *American Poetry, 1922; A Miscellany*
1924
Robert Frost
New Hampshire: A Poem with Notes and Grace Notes (Holt)
1925
Edwin Arlington Robinson
The Man Who Died Twice (Macmillan)

POETRY (cont.)

1926
   Amy Lowell
   What's O'Clock (Houghton)
1927
   Lenora Speyer
   Fiddler's Farewell (Knopf)
1928
   Edwin Arlington Robinson
   Tristram (Macmillan)
1929
   Stephen Vincent Benét
   John Brown's Body (Farrar)
1930
   Conrad Aiken
   Selected Poems (Scribner)
1931
   Robert Frost
   Collected Poems (Holt)
1932
   George Dillon
   The Flowering Stone (Viking)
1933
   Archibald MacLeish
   Conquistador (Houghton)
1934
   Robert Hillyer
   Collected Verse (Knopf)
1935
   Audrey Wurdemann
   Bright Ambush (John Day)
1936
   Robert P. Tristram Coffin
   Strange Holiness (Macmillan)
1937
   Robert Frost
   A Further Range (Holt)
1938
   Marya Zaturenska
   Cold Morning Sky (Macmillan)
1939
   John Gould Fletcher
   Selected Poems (Farrar)
1940
   Mark Van Doren
   Collected Poems (Holt)

1941
   Leonard Bacon
   Sunderland Capture (Harper)
1942
   William Rose Benét
   The Dust Which Is God (Dodd)
1943
   Robert Frost
   A Witness Tree (Holt)
1944
   Stephen Vincent Benét
   Western Star (Farrar)
1945
   Karl Shapiro
   V-Letter and Other Poems (Reynal)
1946
   No award
1947
   Robert Lowell
   Lord Weary's Castle (Harcourt)
1948
   W. H. Auden
   The Age of Anxiety (Random)
1949
   Peter Viereck
   Terror and Decorum (Scribner)
1950
   Gwendolyn Brooks
   Annie Allen (Harper)
1951
   Carl Sandburg
   Complete Poems (Harcourt)
1952
   Marianne Moore
   Collected Poems (Macmillan)
1953
   Archibald MacLeish
   Collected Poems: 1917–1952
   (Houghton)
1954
   Theodore Roethke
   The Waking (Doubleday)
1955
   Wallace Stevens
   Collected Poems (Knopf)
1956
   Elizabeth Bishop
   Poems—North & South (Houghton)

POETRY (cont.)

1957
Richard Wilbur
Things of This World (Harcourt)
1958
Robert Penn Warren
Promises: Poems 1954–1956 (Random)
1959
Stanley Kunitz
Selected Poems: 1928–1958 (Little)
1960
W. D. Snodgrass
Heart's Needle (Knopf)
1961
Phyllis McGinley
Times Three: Selected Verse from Three Decades (Viking)
1962
Alan Dugan
Poems (Yale Univ. Press)
1963
William Carlos Williams
Pictures from Breughel (New Directions)
1964
Louis Simpson
At the End of the Open Road (Wesleyan Univ. Press)
1965
John Berryman
77 Dream Songs (Farrar)
1966
Richard Eberhart
Selected Poems (1930–1965) (New Directions)
1967
Anne Sexton
Live or Die (Houghton)
1968
Anthony Hecht
The Hard Hours (Atheneum)
1969
George Oppen
Of Being Numerous (New Directions)

1970
Richard Howard
Untitled Subjects (Atheneum)
1971
William S. Merwin
The Carrier of Ladders (Atheneum)
1972
James Wright
Collected Poems (Wesleyan Univ. Press)
1973
Maxine W. Kumin
Up Country (Harper)
1974
Robert Lowell
The Dolphin (Farrar)
1975
Gary Snyder
Turtle Island (New Directions)
1976
John Ashbery
Self-Portrait in a Convex Mirror (Viking)
1977
James Merrill
Divine Comedies (Atheneum)
1978
Howard Nemerov
Collected Poems (Univ. of Chicago Press)
1979
Robert Penn Warren
Now and Then: Poems, 1976–1978 (Random)

SPECIAL AWARDS AND CITATIONS

1944
Richard Rodgers and Oscar Hammerstein II
Oklahoma!
1957
Kenneth Roberts
For his historical novels
1960
Garrett Mattingly
The Armada (Houghton)

SPECIAL AWARDS AND CITATIONS
(cont.)

1961
American Heritage Picture History of the Civil War (Doubleday)
1973
James Thomas Flexner
George Washington, Vols. I—IV (Little)
1977
Alex Haley
Roots (Doubleday)
1978
E. B. White
For the full body of his work

GENERAL NONFICTION

1962
Theodore H. White
The Making of the President 1960 (Atheneum)
1963
Barbara W. Tuchman
The Guns of August (Macmillan)
1964
Richard Hofstadter
Anti-Intellectualism in American Life (Random)
1965
Howard Mumford Jones
O Strange New World (Viking)
1966
Edwin Way Teale
Wandering through Winter (Dodd)
1967
David Brion Davis
The Problem of Slavery in Western Culture (Cornell Univ. Press)
1968
Will Durant and Ariel Durant
Rousseau and Revolution (Simon & Schuster)

1969
René Dubos
So Human an Animal (Scribner)
Norman Mailer
The Armies of the Night (World)
1970
Erik H. Erikson
Gandhi's Truth (Norton)
1971
John Toland
The Rising Sun (Random)
1972
Barbara W. Tuchman
Stilwell and the American Experience in China, 1911–1945 (Macmillan)
1973
Robert Coles
Children of Crisis, Vols. II and III (Little)
Frances FitzGerald
Fire in the Lake: The Vietnamese and Americans in Vietnam (Little)
1974
Ernest Becker
The Denial of Death (Free Press)
1975
Annie Dillard
Pilgrim at Tinker Creek (Harper's Magazine)
1976
Robert N. Butler
Why Survive? Being Old in America (Harper)
1977
William W. Warner
Beautiful Swimmers (Atlantic-Little)
1978
Carl Sagan
The Dragons of Eden (Random)
1979
Edward O. Wilson
On Human Nature (Harvard Univ. Press)

Sir Walter Raleigh Award for Fiction

A statuette of Sir Walter Raleigh is the award offered by the Historical Book Club of North Carolina through the North Carolina Literary and Historical Association, 109 East Jones Street, Raleigh, North Carolina 27611. The award, established in 1951 for North Carolina writers of fiction, including the novel, drama, short story, and poetry, is announced in November and is presented at the annual meeting of the North Carolina Literary and Historical Association in Raleigh. To be eligible for the award, the author or authors shall have maintained legal residence, actual residence, or a combination of both in the state of North Carolina for the three years immediately preceding the close of the contest period. All works from which the Club's Board of Awards makes its selection must have been previously published. If it chooses, the Board may base its decision on the writer's overall career rather than a particular title.

1952
Paul Green
For outstanding literary achievement

1953
Inglis Fletcher
For series of books
Frances Gray Patton
The Finer Things of Life (Dodd)

1954
Ovid Pierce
The Plantation (Doubleday)

1955
Frances Gray Patton
Good Morning, Miss Dove (Dodd)

1956
Frances Gray Patton
A Piece of Luck (Dodd)

1957
Doris Betts
Tall Houses in Winter (Putnam)

1958
Betty Smith
Maggie—Now (Harper)

1959
Ernest Frankel
Band of Brothers (Macmillan)

1960
Ovid Pierce
On a Lonesome Porch (Doubleday)

1961
Frank Borden Hanes
The Fleet Rabble (Farrar)

1962
Reynolds Price
A Long and Happy Life (Atheneum)

1963
Richard McKenna
The Sand Pebbles (Harper)

1964
John Ehle
The Land Breakers (Harper)

1965
Doris Betts
The Scarlet Thread (Harper)

1966
Heather Ross Miller
Tenants of the House (Harcourt)

1967
John Ehle
The Road (Harper)

1968
Sylvia Wilkinson
A Killing Frost (Houghton)

1969
Bynum Shaw
The Nazi Hunter (Norton)

1970
Guy Owen
Journey for Joedel (Crown)

1971
  John Ehle
  Time of Drums (Harper)
1972
  Daphne Athas
  Entering Ephesus (Viking)
1973
  Fred Chappell
  The Gaudy Place (Harcourt)
1974
  Doris Betts
  Beasts of the Southern Wild (Harper)

1975
  John Ehle
  The Changing of the Guard (Random)
1976
  Reynolds Price
  The Surface of Earth (Atheneum)
1977
  Sylvia Wilkinson
  Shadow of the Mountain (Houghton)
1978
  Mary Sheppard
  All Angels Cry (Moore)

Religious Book Awards

The Religious Book Awards were an outgrowth of the National Catholic Book Awards sponsored from 1964 to 1975 by the Catholic Press Association. Then cosponsored by the Catholic Press Association (CPA) and the Associated Church Press (ACP), 119 North Park Avenue, Rockville Centre, New York 11570, these awards were established to honor outstanding religious book publishing and to stimulate reading of religious books. Nominations of books were made by the publishing companies, not by authors or agents. Original hardcover and paperback books published in the United States during the calendar year before the year of presentation were eligible. Distinguished experts in the religious book reviewing field selected a winner in each category. Titles and publishers of the winners were announced before presentation of the Religious Book Awards at the Book Awards Luncheon during the joint CPA-ACP convention in the spring. The awards were discontinued in 1978.

1976
  John McHugh
  The Mother of Jesus in the New Testament (Doubleday) Scripture

  Malcolm Muggeridge
  Jesus: The Man Who Lives (Harper) History/Biography

  John Macquarrie
  Thinking about God (Harper) Theology

  André Feuillet
  The Priesthood of Christ and His Ministers, trans. by Matthew J. O'Connell (Doubleday) Theology

  Edward R. Dufresne
  Partnership: Marriage and the Committed Life (Paulist) Personal/Family

  Jacques Ellul
  The New Demons (Seabury) Community life

  Leo Suenens
  A New Pentecost? (Seabury) Community life

  Arthur Simon
  Bread for the World (Paulist-Eerdmans) Religion/Society

  Anne Arnott
  The Secret Country of C. S. Lewis (Eerdmans) Youth

  Peter Milward and Raymond Schoder
  Landscape and Inscape (Eerdmans) Illustrated books

Eugen Weiler
Jesus, Son of God (Franciscan Herald) Illustrated books

Dorothy Gilman
A Nun in the Closet (Doubleday) Fiction

The Zondervan Pictorial Encyclopedia of the Bible (Zondervan) Special award

1977

Walther von Loewenich
Luther's Theology of the Cross (Augsburg) Theology

Bernard Cooke
Ministry of Word and Sacraments (Fortress) Theology

Hans Küng
On Being a Christian (Doubleday) Theology

William R. Hutchison
The Modernist Impulse in American Protestantism (Harvard Univ. Press) History/Biography

T. H. L. Parker
John Calvin: A Biography (Westminster) History/Biography

Samuel Sandmel, M. Jack Suggs, and Arnold Tkacik
The New English Bible with the Apocrypha (Oxford Univ. Press) Scripture

Michael Avi-Yonah
Encyclopedia of Archeological Excavations in the Holy Land, Vols. 1–2 (Prentice) Scripture

Marvin J. Taylor
Foundation for Christian Education in an Era of Change (Abingdon) Religious education

Iris V. Cully
New Life for Your Sunday School (Hawthorn) Religious education

Gloria Durka and Joanmarie Smith
Emerging Issues in Religious Education (Paulist) Religious education

R. M. Rummery
Catechesis and Religious Education in a Pluralist Society (Our Sunday Visitor) Religious education

Joseph Gremillion
Gospel of Peace and Justice (Orbis) Pastoral/Counselling

Gary Collins
How to Be a People Helper (Vision) Pastoral/Counselling

Ran Shechori
Art in Israel (Schocken) Pictorial books

Charles Colson
Born Again (Chosen Books) Inspirational

1978

J. C. Wynn
Christian Education for Liberation and Other Upsetting Ideas (Abingdon) Religious education

Michael Warren
Youth Ministry (Paulist) Religious education

Avery Dulles
The Resilient Church: The Necessity and Limits of Adaptation (Doubleday) Theology

John A. T. Robinson
Redating the New Testament (Westminster) Theology

Nicholas Wolterstorff
Reason within the Bounds of Religion (Eerdmans) Theology

Mary Lukas and Ellen Lukas
Teilhard: The Man, the Priest, the Scientist (Doubleday) History/Biography

Simone Pétrement
Simone Weil, trans. by Raymond Rosenthal (Pantheon) History/Biography

Raymond E. Brown
The Birth of the Messiah: A Commentary on the Infancy Narratives in Matthew and Luke (Doubleday) Scripture

Joseph Blenkinsopp
Prophecy and Canon (Notre Dame Univ. Press) Scripture

E. P. Sanders
Paul and Palestinian Judaism (Fortress) Scripture

J. M. Robinson, ed.
The Nag Hammadi Library (Harper) Scripture

Ronald S. Sider
Rich Christians in an Age of Hunger (Paulist) Pastoral/Counselling

Francis A. Schaeffer
How Should We Then Live? The Rise and Decline of Western Thought and Culture (Revell) Inspirational

Erwin Weber
Illustrated Works: From Luther to 1580 (Concordia) Inspirational

Discontinued

Mary Roberts Rinehart Foundation Award

This award was established in 1958 to perpetuate the memory of the writer Mary Roberts Rinehart and offered by the Mary Roberts Rinehart Foundation, 516 Fifth Avenue, New York, New York 10036. Its purpose is to aid and assist writers of creative ability who lack financial means to complete their work, and preference is given to new and relatively unknown writers. Applicants for the grants-in-aid of approximately $500 each must fill out an application form, which is available on request. Each application form should be accompanied by at least 25 percent of the project plus a plan or outline. Writers receiving grants-in-aid are notified by letter.

1960
  Roy Bongartz
  "Rose Monday"
  Dudley Duane Unkefer
  "The Color Is Good-Bye"
  Dorothy West
  "The Wedding"
1961
  Richard Kim
  The Martyred (Braziller)
1962
  Robert P. Dana
  "Collected Poems" (published by Norton as *Some Versions of Silence*)
  Charlotte Painter
  "The Three Angels" (published by Random as *Seeing Things*)
1964
  Jean McCrae Ross
  Untitled collection of short stories

  C. William Wiser
  "Short Sketches of Bohemia" (published by Doubleday as *K* and by Harcourt as *The Wolf Is Not Native to the South of France*)
1965
  Samuel Birnkrant
  "Instant in the Wind"
1966
  Audrey Lee
  Untitled collection of short stories
  Leslie Hua-Ling Nieh
  "The Lost Golden Bell"
1967
  Paul R. Butler
  Untitled novel
  Barbara Reid
  "Moon in the Yellow River" (published by Morrow as *Miguel and His Racehorse*, by Macmillan as *The Cobbler's*

Reward, and by Apple-Wood as *The Tears of San Lorenzo: Two Novellas*)

Wendell N. Rollason
"One Man's Effort"

1968

Jean Byers McCormick
"The World Changers"

1969

Sol Battle
Untitled dramas

E. Michael Desilets
"A Long Time on Campus"

Marek Hlasko
"The Rice Burners"

1970

Gwyneth Cravens
"Pigmeat" and untitled novel (published by Dutton as *The Black Death*)

David Michael
"Columbine" (published by Houghton as *A Blow to the Head*)

1971

Peter Dunham
Magazine articles

Jerome Lesser
"Winter Kept Us Warm"

Jerome Lord
"Teresa, Teresa" and "The Election"

Philip O'Connor
Old Morals, Small Continents, Darker Times (Univ. of Iowa Press) and *Stealing Home* (Knopf)

1972

Stephan Ajay
Collected Poems (New Rivers)

James Files
"The Testing Ground"

William Harris
Untitled novel

Stephen Herman
Untitled collection of poems

Howard P. Hildreth
"Southern Phase of the American Revolution"

Stephen Kline
"The Americans: A Random Sample"

1973

Yvonne Chism-Peace
"Quiet as Ice"

Eric Edson
"The Emperor of Ice-Cream"

Wendell Evan Golder
"Comes the Moment: Accounts of Contemporary Conscience Decisions"

Michael Neville
"Marvin's Mourning Meadows" (produced by Manhattan Theater Club as *Ballymurphy*)

Richard Price
The Wanderers (Houghton) and *Ladies' Man* (Houghton)

Lee Riordan
Untitled history-memoir about the Japanese earthquake of 1923

Bjorn Rye
The Expatriate (Bobbs)

1974

Ray Young Bear
Untitled collection of poems

David Dwyer
Ariana Olisvos, Last Works and Days (Univ. of Massachusetts Press)

Emanuel Evans, Jr.
"Spark of Hate, Ray of Hope"

Julia Older
"The Appalachian Trail: A Nature Narrative in Poetry and Prose"

Jeffrey Robinson
"All the Rivers Run into the Sea"

Joseph Shaw
"Indian Summer and Other Stories"

Shawn Hsu Wong
"Night Driver"

1975

Raymond Abbott
The Axing of Leo White Hat (Apple-Wood) and *That Day in Gordon* (to be published by Harcourt)

William Oscar Boggs
Untitled collection of poems

Michael Durkin
"George III"

Edward Grinnan
"Gabriel's Horn" (produced at Ann Arbor Medieval Festival)

Stephen Policoff
"The Powers of Light and Darkness"

Michael Ryan
Untitled collection of poems

William Schuster
"Clearings"

Norman Solomon
"Mind Reader in Washington"

Jeffrey Talmadge
Untitled collection of poems

1976

Barbara Dunning
"Murder Takes a Spin"

John Bart Gerald
Untitled collection of short stories

Candace Glass
Untitled collection of short stories

David Holmstrom
"The Boy from Hell"

Kathleen Kimball
"The Chinese Question"

James Thomas
"Stories at Sea and Other Places"

Patricia Van Olinda
"When Mara Came"

Roger Warner II
"Freight Train Blues"

Judith Weiss
"Vermont Diary"

Samuel Wheat
"Bill Wright"

Meredith Sue Willis
"Five Galatians"

1977

Richard Anderson
"Curious Souls"

Michael Andryc
"Montana Roadhouse"

Edward Cohen
Untitled drama

Charles Ghigna
Untitled collection of poems

Jeffrey Greene
Untitled collection of poems

Philip Meyer
Untitled collection of novellas

Patricia Montley
"Mother Jones"

Quintin Peterson
"Changes"

Stephanie Schulsinger
"Lost Presidents"

Donald Stap
Untitled collection of poems

William Turner
"Van Zandt Dead"

Richard Vetere
Trilogy of dramas

Joel Weishaus
Untitled collection of poems

Nina Winter
"Incarnations"

1978

Harry Fincken
"Life Wishes"

Harold Jewell
"Galea and the Glowing Square"

Lurey Khan
Untitled history/biography

Brad Leithauser
Untitled collection of poems

Robert Lietz, Jr.
Untitled collection of poems

Sarah Hamilton Maines
"The Secret of the Sho-Dog Rose"

Vincent Nicolosi
"In a Kingdom"

Don Nigro
"Terre Haute"

Meir Ribalow
"Minor Miracles"
Bernard Rollins
"The Dragonmakers"
Carroll Dale Short
Untitled novel
1979
David Bain
"Refugees"
Kathy Callaway
"The Outsider"

Joseph Campbell
"The Weight"
Elizabeth Hinchliffe
"The Descent of Ariel"
Patricia Orvis
Untitled novel
Miriam de Uriarte
Untitled collection of poems

SAMLA Studies Award

This award is offered by the South Atlantic Modern Language Association (SAMLA), Drawer CA, University of Alabama, University, Alabama 35486, and the University of Georgia Press. It was established in 1967 to encourage distinguished scholarly writing and is open to all SAMLA members. Manuscripts must be scholarly works in languages and literatures, exclusive of bibliographies and editions, written in English, and prepared according to accepted scholarly standards. No substantial part can have been published previously, and dissertations in their original form are not eligible. While no specific length is demanded, manuscripts should be approximately 60,000 to 100,000 words, including notes and bibliographical essay. Only typed double-spaced ribbon copies will be considered. Manuscripts may be submitted anytime between January 1 and April 1 to the Chairman, SAMLA Studies Award Committee, whose name and address are available from the SAMLA Executive Director. Manuscripts are judged by members of this committee, which consists of seven professors on the faculties of universities in the SAMLA region. The winner is announced at the annual meeting of SAMLA in November. The award is $500 and publication by the University of Georgia Press. (From 1967 to 1971 winning books were published by the University Press of Kentucky.)

1967
  Robert Hunter West
  Shakespeare and the Outer Mystery
  (Univ. of Kentucky Press)
1968
  Paul Ramsey
  The Art of John Dryden (Univ. of Kentucky Press)
1969
  George C. Herndl
  The High Design: English Renais-

sance Tragedy and the Natural Law
(Univ. Press of Kentucky)
1970
  Claude Kurt Abraham
  Enfin Malherbe: The Influence of Malherbe on French Lyric Prosody, 1605–1674 (Univ. Press of Kentucky)
1971
  David Brown Morris
  The Religious Sublime: Christian Poetry and Critical Tradition in Eigh-

teenth-Century England (Univ. Press of Kentucky)

William H. Shurr
The Mystery of Iniquity: Melville as Poet, 1857-1891 (Univ. Press of Kentucky)

1972
Joseph Allen Bryant
The Compassionate Satirist: Ben Jonson and His Imperfect World (Univ. of Georgia Press)

1973
Blue Calhoun
The Pastoral Vision of William Morris: The Earthly Paradise (Univ. of Georgia Press)

1974
No award

1975
Elsa Nettels
James and Conrad (Univ. of Georgia Press)

1976
Ronald Arthur Horton
The Unity of "The Faerie Queene" (Univ. of Georgia Press)

1977
Jeffrey Helterman
"Symbolic Action in the Plays of the Wakefield Master"

1978
Walter E. Meyers
"Aliens and Linguists: Language Study and Science Fiction"

1979
Brian McCrea
"Henry Fielding and the Politics of Mid-Eighteenth-Century England"

Science-Writing Award in Physics and Astronomy

The American Institute of Physics (AIP) and the United States Steel Foundation established this annual award in 1968 "to stimulate and recognize distinguished writing that improves public understanding of physics and astronomy." Two prizes are given each year—one to a physicist, astronomer, or member of AIP member and affiliated societies and the other to a journalist—for an article (or series), a booklet, or a book published during the previous year (June 1 to May 31). Entries must be available to and intended for the general public; textbooks and materials from professional-level scientific, technical, or trade publications are not eligible. Authors must be citizens or residents of the United States, Canada, or Mexico, and entries must be published in one of these countries. Entries are judged by a committee selected by the AIP Governing Board. Winners of the two annual prizes each receive $1,500, a certificate, and an inscribed stainless steel Moebius strip. A certificate is also presented to the publisher of the winning entry. The awards to journalists are conferred at a luncheon of the AIP/National Association of Science Writers, Washington Group, in Washington, D.C., during the spring meeting of the American Physical Society. The awards to scientists are conferred at the annual meeting of Corporate Associates of the American Institute of Physics in the autumn. Further information concerning the award can be obtained from the American Institute of Physics, Public Relations Division, 335 East 45 Street, New York, New York 10017.

SCIENTISTS

1968
No award

1969
Kip S. Thorne
"The Death of a Star," in *Science Year: The World Book Science Annual* (World Book)

1970
Jeremy Bernstein
The Elusive Neutrino (Atomic Energy Commission)

1971
Robert H. March
Physics for Poets (McGraw)

1972
Dietrich Schroeer
Physics and Its Fifth Dimension: Society (Addison-Wesley)

1973
Banesh Hoffmann and Helen Dukas
Albert Einstein: Creator and Rebel (Viking)

1974
Robert D. Chapman
Comet Kohoutek (NASA/Goddard Space Flight Center)

1975
Robert H. March
"The Quandary over Quarks," in *Science Year: The World Book Science Annual* (World Book)

1976
Jeremy Bernstein
"Physicist: I. I. Rabi," *The New Yorker*

1977
Steven Weinberg
The First Three Minutes: A Modern View of the Origin of the Universe (Basic Books)

1978
Edwin C. Krupp, ed.
In Search of Ancient Astronomies (Doubleday)

1979
Hans C. von Baeyer
"The Wonder of Gravity," *College of William and Mary Alumni Magazine*

JOURNALISTS

1968
William J. Perkinson
"ABM Primer: Physics for Defense," Baltimore *Evening Sun*

1969
Walter Sullivan
"Flight of Apollo 8," *New York Times*

1970
C. P. Gilmore
"Can We Stop Earthquakes from Happening?" *Popular Science*

1971
Kenneth Weaver
"Voyage to the Planets," *National Geographic*

1972
Jerry E. Bishop
"Celestial Clue," *Wall Street Journal*

1973
Edward Edelson
"The Mystery of Space," New York *Daily News*

1974
Patrick Young
"A Quake Is Due At . . . ," *National Observer*

1975
Tom Alexander
"Ominous Changes in the World's Weather," *Fortune*

1976
Frederic Golden
"Forecast: Earthquake," *Time*

1977
William D. Metz
"Fusion Research," *Science*

JOURNALISTS (cont.)

1978
Timothy Ferris
The Red Limit: The Search for the Edge of the Universe (Morrow)

1979
Robert Cowen
"The New Astronomy," *Christian Science Monitor*

Scribes Award

The Scribes Award was established at the 1960 meeting of Scribes as an annual award for the author of the fiction or nonfiction book written by either a lawyer or a layperson and published during the preceding year that best conveys to the lay reader the true spirit and meaning of the legal profession. It is presented at the annual meeting of the Scribes at the same time and in the same city as the annual meeting of the American Bar Association. The home office of Scribes is Wake Forest University, School of Law, Winston-Salem, North Carolina 27109.

1961
Charles L. Black, Jr.
The People and the Court: Judicial Review in a Democracy (Macmillan)
Helen Shirley Thomas
Felix Frankfurter: Scholar on the Bench (Johns Hopkins)

1962
Barrett Prettyman
Death and the Supreme Court (Harcourt)

1963
Daniel M. Berman
A Bill Becomes a Law (Macmillan)

1964
David Mellinkoff
The Language of the Law (Little)

1965
James B. Donovan
Strangers on a Bridge (Atheneum)

1966
No award

1967
Louis Nizer
The Jury Returns (Doubleday)

1968
Martin Mayer
The Lawyers (Harper)

1969
Paul Freund
On Law and Justice (Harvard Univ. Press)

1970
No award

1971
Leon Friedman and Fred Israel, eds.
The Justices of the Supreme Court (Chelsea/Bowker)

1972
F. Lee Bailey
The Defense Never Rests (Stein)

1973
Robert Shogan
A Question of Judgment (Bobbs)

1974
Lawrence Friedman
A History of American Law (Simon & Schuster)

1975
Robert A. Leflar
Appellate Judicial Opinions (West)

1976
Richard Kluger
Simple Justice: The History of Brown v. Board of Education and Black America's Struggle for Equality (Knopf)

1977
   Arthur T. Vanderbilt II
   Changing Law: A Biography of Arthur T. Vanderbilt (Rutgers Univ. Press)
1978
   Laurence H. Tribe
   American Constitutional Law (Foundation Press)

1979
   Gerald T. Dunne
   Hugo Black and the Judicial Revolution (Simon & Schuster)

Constance Lindsay Skinner Award

This award has been given since 1940 by the Women's National Book Association (WNBA) (Ann Heidbreder Eastman, National President, 716 Burress Drive N.W., Blacksburg, Virginia 24060) in memory of Constance Lindsay Skinner, editor of the Rivers of America series, who made a highly creative contribution to American letters. Its purpose is to recognize and commend women who have made imaginative and outstanding contributions to the world of books or to our culture through books. The award is given for a sustained contribution of unusual worth over a period of time or for a single great achievement. In order to be eligible for the award, a woman must be a resident of the United States and derive part or all of her income from books and the allied arts. Nominations for the award are made and voted upon each year by the entire national membership of WNBA—now about 1,000. Presentation of a citation and gift is made at the Constance Lindsay Skinner Ceremony, usually in the spring. Although this is primarily a book-trade award, it has been awarded to authors and librarians.

1940
   Anne Carroll Moore, librarian
1941
   Blair Niles, author
1942
   Irita Van Doren, book review editor
1943
   Mary Graham Bonner, author
1944
   Mildred C. Smith, editor
1945
   Lillian Smith, author
1946
   Amy Loveman, editor
1947
   Emily P. Street, book sales and advertising director
1948
   May Lamberton Becker, book reviewer

1949
   Lucile Pannell, bookseller
1950
   May Massee, children's book editor
1951
   Dorothy Canfield Fisher, author
1952
   Margaret C. Scoggin, young people's librarian
1953
   Lilian C. Gurney, bookseller
1954
   Elizabeth Gray Vinning, author and teacher
1955
   Fanny Butcher, book reviewer
   Bertha Mahony Miller, editor
1956
   Mary Ellen Chase, author

1957
Anne J. Richter, editor
1958
Edith Hamilton, author
1959
May Hill Arbuthnot, educator and critic
Marchette Chute, author
1960
Pearl Buck, author
1961
Eleanor Roosevelt, author
1962
Catherine Drinker Bowen, author
1963
Rachel Carson, author
1964
Polly Goodwin, children's book reviewer
1965
Virginia Mathews, school and library consultant
1966
Blanche W. Knopf, president, Alfred A. Knopf, Inc.
1967
Mildred L. Batchelder, children's librarian
1968
Ruth Hill Viguers, author and librarian
1969
Victoria S. Johnson, public relations

1970
Charlemae Hill Rollins, librarian and author
1971
Augusta Baker, school and public librarian
1972
Ursula Nordstrom, publisher, Harper & Row
1973
Mary V. Gaver, librarian and author
1974
No award
1975
Margaret K. McElderry, children's book editor
1976
Frances Neal Cheney, Professor Emeritus, Peabody Library School
Helen Honig Meyer, President, Dell Publishing Company
Barbara Ringer, Register of Copyrights, Library of Congress
1977
No award
1978
Mary Stahlman Douglas, former editor, book page, Nashville *Banner*

The Society of American Historians

Allan Nevins Prize

In order to promote better writing of serious history, the Society of American Historians, Inc., 610 Fayerweather Hall, Columbia University, New York, New York 10027, established this prize in 1961 to honor the best-written scholarly doctoral dissertation on a topic of American history. The Society defines history broadly and accepts manuscripts dealing historically with American arts, literature, science, and biographical studies of Americans. Only one entry can be submitted by each chairperson of a department of history or a related field. The authors of all entries must grant an option for publication of the work to one of the seven major publishing houses that currently support the Nevins Prize. Named in honor of Allan Nevins, longtime professor of history at Columbia University and distinguished author, an award of $1,000 is presented at an annual banquet in New York City. The winner is announced in early spring.

1961
Waldo Heinrichs, Jr.
American Ambassador: Joseph C. Grew and the Development of the U.S. Diplomatic Tradition (Little)

1962
John L. Thomas
Liberator: William Lloyd Garrison (Little)

1963
Willie Lee Rose
Rehearsal for Reconstruction (Bobbs)

1964
Joanne Loewe Neel
Phineas Bond: A Study in Anglo-American Relations, 1786-1812 (Univ. of Pennsylvania Press)

1965
William Freehling
Prelude to Conflict: The Nullification Controversy in South Carolina, 1816-1836 (Harper)

1966
Robert L. Beisner
Twelve against the Empire: The Anti-Imperialists, 1898-1900 (McGraw)

1967
Richard Alan Lawson
The Failure of Independent Liberalism, 1930-1941 (Putnam)

1968
Jerome Sternstein
Nelson Aldrich, the Early Years (Knopf)

1969
Steven A. Channing
Crisis of Fear: Secession in South Carolina, 1859-1860 (Simon & Schuster)

1970
Mary Beth Norton
The British-Americans: The Loyalist Exiles in England, 1774-1789 (Little)

1971
Edward H. McKinley
The Lure of Africa: The American Interest in Tropical Africa, 1919-1939 (Bobbs)

1972
Heath Twitchell, Jr.
The Biography of General Henry T. Allen (Rutgers Univ. Press)

1973
George B. Forgie
"Father Past and Child Nation: The Romantic Imagination and the Origins of the American Civil War"

1974
James L. Roark
Masters without Slaves: Southern Planters in the Civil War and Reconstruction (Norton)

1975
Gary May
"The China Service of John Carter Vincent, 1924-1953"

1976
Robert Dawidoff
The Education of John Randolph (Norton)

1977
John McCardell, Jr.
The Idea of a Southern Nation: Southern Nationalists and Southern Nationalism, 1830-1860 (Norton)

1978
Mark Schwehn
"The Making of Modern Consciousness in America: The Works and Careers of Henry Adams and William James"

1979
John Ettling
"The Germ of Laziness: The Rockefeller Sanitary Commission in the Southern States, 1909-1914"

Francis Parkman Prize

Offered by the Society of American Historians, the prize consists of $500 and a bronze medal awarded annually to the book that best epitomizes Parkman's combination of literary and scholarly distinction. Any book on American history or biography published during the calendar year is eligible. In September or October the Society sends notices to all major publishing houses inviting them to submit as many entries as they wish. The judges' decision is announced at an awards banquet early in the following year.

1957
George Frost Kennan
Russia Leaves the War (Princeton Univ. Press)

1958
Arthur M. Schlesinger, Jr.
The Crisis of the Old Order: 1919–1933 (Houghton)

1959
Ernest Samuels
Henry Adams: The Middle Years, 1877–1891 (Belknap)

1960
Matthew Josephson
Edison: A Biography (McGraw)

1961
Elting E. Morison
Turmoil and Tradition: A Study of the Life and Times of Henry L. Stimson (Houghton)

1962
Leon Wolff
Little Brown Brother (Doubleday)

1963
James T. Flexner
That Wilder Image: The Painting of America's Native School from Thomas Cole to Winslow Homer (Little)

1964
William E. Leuchtenburg
Franklin D. Roosevelt and the New Deal, 1932–1940 (Harper)

1965
Willie Lee Rose
Rehearsal for Reconstruction: The Port Royal Experiment (Bobbs)

1966
Daniel J. Boorstin
The Americans: The National Experience (Random)

1967
William H. Goetzmann
Exploration and Empire (Knopf)

1968
No award

1969
Winthrop D. Jordan
White over Black: American Attitudes toward the Negro, 1550–1812 (Univ. of North Carolina Press)

1970
Theodore A. Wilson
The First Summit: Roosevelt and Churchill at Placentia Bay, 1941 (Houghton)

1971
James MacGregor Burns
Roosevelt: The Soldier of Freedom, 1940–1945 (Harcourt)

1972
Joseph P. Lash
Eleanor and Franklin (Norton)

1973
Kenneth S. Davis
FDR: The Beckoning of Destiny, 1882–1928 (Putnam)

1974
Robert W. Johannsen
Stephen A. Douglas (Oxford Univ. Press)

1975
Robert A. Caro
The Power Broker: Robert Moses and the Fall of New York (Knopf)
1976
Edmund S. Morgan
American Slavery, American Freedom (Norton)
1977
Irving Howe
World of Our Fathers (Harcourt)

1978
David McCullough
The Path between the Seas: The Creation of the Panama Canal, 1870–1914 (Simon & Schuster)
1979
R. David Edmunds
The Potawatomis: Keepers of the Fire (Univ. of Oklahoma Press)

Society of Colonial Wars in the State of New York Citation of Honour

The Citation of Honour was established in 1951 by the Society of Colonial Wars in the State of New York to be presented annually in recognition of outstanding contributions on any phase of American colonial history produced during the preceding calendar year in the fields of literature, drama, music, or art. The purpose of the award is twofold: to promote a wider knowledge of the era in which the Society has a vital and hereditary interest and to encourage the production of worthwhile material concerned with early America. The citation, administered by a special awards committee of the Society, is engrossed upon a parchment scroll of appropriate design, encased in a leather portfolio, and accompanied by a suitable bronze medallion. The citations are announced and presented at the Annual Court of the Society held each December in New York City. All materials and communications should be addressed to the Awards Committee, Society of Colonial Wars, 122 East 58 Street, New York, New York 10022. The following list includes only winners of the Citation of Honour for literature. The Society also bestows Citations of Honourable Mention, which are not included here.

1952
Douglas Southall Freeman
Planter and Patriot (Scribner)
1953
Nathaniel Claiborne Hale
Virginia Adventurer (Dietz)
1954
Bradford Smith
Captain John Smith (Lippincott)
1955
John J. Vrooman
The Massacre (Baronet Litho)

1956
Carl Bridenbaugh
Cities in Revolt (Knopf)
1957
No award
1958
Anya Seton
The Winthrop Woman (Houghton)
1959
Elizabeth George Speare
The Witch of Blackbird Pond (Houghton)

1960
    F. van Wyck Mason
    The Young Titan (Doubleday)
1961
    Richard L. Morton
    Colonial Virginia (Univ. of North Carolina Press)
1962
    Dale Van Every
    Forth to the Wilderness (Morrow)
1963
    Edward P. Hamilton
    The French and Indian Wars (Doubleday)
1964
    Ivor Noel Hume
    Here Lies Virginia (Knopf)
1965
    Philip Barbour
    The Three Worlds of Captain John Smith (Houghton)
1966
    Robert C. Alberts
    The Most Extraordinary Adventures of Major Robert Stobo (Houghton)
1967
    David Hawke
    The Colonial Experience (Bobbs)
1968
    Phillip Viereck
    The New Land (John Day)
1969
    Walter D. Edmonds
    The Musket and the Cross (Little)
1970
    Clifford K. Shipton
    National Index of American Imprints through 1800 (Barre)

1971
    Ann Leighton
    Early American Gardens (Houghton)

1972
    No award

1973
    Leonard W. Labaree, ed.
    The Papers of Benjamin Franklin (American Philosophical Society and Yale Univ. Press)
    David Sherman Lovejoy
    The Glorious Revolution in America (Harper)

1974
    Douglas Edward Leach
    Arms for Empire (Macmillan)

1975
    Thomas Elliot Norton
    The Fur Trade in Colonial New York (Univ. of Wisconsin Press)

1976
    Michael Kammen
    Colonial New York: A History (Scribner)

1977
    Ian R. Christie and Benjamin W. Labaree
    Empire or Independence, 1760–1776 (Norton)

1978
    Phinizy Spalding
    Oglethorpe in America (Univ. of Chicago Press)

The Sorokin Award

Offered by the American Sociological Association, 1722 N Street N.W., Washington, D.C. 20036, the Sorokin Award is presented to the author of the publication that, in the opinion of the Selection Committee, contributed outstandingly to the progress of sociology during the two preceding years. Members of the American Sociological Association or other interested parties may nominate publications of any kind (theoretical essay, empirical report, book, or article) that are distinguished by their excellence. The award of $500 is announced at the annual meeting.

1968
Peter Blau, Otis Dudley Duncan, and Andrea Tyree
The American Occupational Structure (Wiley)

1969
William A. Gamson
Power and Discontent (Dorsey)

1970
Arthur L. Stinchcombe
Constructing Social Theories (Harcourt)

1971
Robert W. Friedrichs
A Sociology of Sociology (Free Press)
Harrison C. White
Chains of Opportunity: Systems Models of Mobility in Organization (Harvard Univ. Press)

1972
Eliot Freidson
Profession of Medicine: A Study of the Sociology of Applied Knowledge (Dodd)

1973
No award

1974
Clifford Geertz
The Interpretation of Cultures (Basic Books)
Christopher Jencks
Inequality (Basic Books)

1975
Immanuel Wallerstein
The Modern World System (Academic)

1976
Robert Bellah
The Broken Covenant: American Civil Religion in Time of Trial (Seabury)
Jeffrey Paige
Agrarian Revolution: Social Movements and Export Agriculture in the Underdeveloped World (Free Press)

1977
Perry Anderson
Considerations on Western Marxism (NLB, London)
Kai T. Erikson
Everything in Its Path (Simon & Schuster)

1978
No award

Southern Historical Association

Francis Butler Simkins Award in Southern History

The Southern Historical Association together with the Longwood College (Virginia) History Department established in 1977 the Francis Butler Simkins Award for a first book by an author or authors in the field of Southern history, published in the biennial period preceding the presentation of the award. The award consists of a certificate and $200. Inquiries should be addressed to Bennett H. Wall, Secretary-Treasurer,

Southern Historical Association, Department of History, Tulane University, New Orleans, Louisiana 70118.

1977
   Virginia Spencer Carr
   The Lonely Hunter: A Biography of Carson McCullers (Doubleday)

Charles S. Sydnor Prize

The Charles S. Sydnor Prize, named after the Southern historian, was established in 1954 by the Southern Historical Association, History Department, Tulane University, New Orleans, Louisiana 70118. A committee of three, appointed by the Association, chooses the most distinguished book in the field of Southern history to receive the award of $500. Books are considered over two-year periods.

1956
   Joseph H. Parks
   General Edmund Kirby Smith (Louisiana State Univ. Press)
1958
   Arlin Turner
   George W. Cable (Duke Univ. Press)
1960
   Dewey W. Grantham
   Hoke Smith (Louisiana State Univ. Press)
1962
   C. Vann Woodward
   The Burden of Southern History (Louisiana State Univ. Press)
1964
   Albert D. Kirwan
   John J. Crittenden: The Struggle for the Union (Univ. of Kentucky Press)
1966
   Willie Lee Rose
   Rehearsal for Reconstruction: The Port Royal Experiment (Bobbs)
1968
   George B. Tindall
   The Emergence of the New South, 1913–1945 (Louisiana State Univ. Press)

1970
   Sheldon Hackney
   Populism to Progressivism in Alabama (Princeton Univ. Press)
1972
   Allen W. Trelease
   White Terror: The Ku Klux Klan Conspiracy and Southern Reconstruction (Harper)
1974
   Thomas B. Alexander and Richard E. Berringer
   The Anatomy of the Confederate Congress (Vanderbilt Univ. Press)
1976
   Edmund S. Morgan
   American Slavery, American Freedom: The Ordeal of Colonial Virginia (Norton)
1978
   Thomas C. Holt
   Black over White: Negro Political Leadership in South Carolina during Reconstruction (Univ. of Illinois Press)

Southwestern Literary Award

In 1972 the Southwestern Press Associates formed the National Library Council to administer the biennial Southwestern Literary Award of $2,500 for an outstanding work of fiction by a resident of southern California, Arizona, or New Mexico. Its purpose was to encourage writers under the age of forty to further their commitment to the field of creative writing.

1973–1974
  No award
1975–1976
  John Gilmore

Blowout
Discontinued

Spingarn Medal

This gold medal is awarded annually by the National Association for the Advancement of Colored People (NAACP), 1790 Broadway, New York, New York 10019, to an outstanding American black. It was instituted in 1914 by J. E. Spingarn, then chairman of the board of directors of the NAACP. The Committee of Awards to whom recommendations are submitted decides each year what particular act or achievement deserves the highest acclaim. The medal is usually presented at the annual convention of the National Association for the Advancement of Colored People. Listed below are the awards given for literary achievement.

1918
  William Stanley Braithwaite
1920
  W. E. B. Du Bois
1925
  James Weldon Johnson
1926
  Carter G. Woodson
1928
  Charles W. Chesnutt
1941
  Richard Wright

1955
  Carl Murphy
1960
  Langston Hughes
1966
  John H. Johnson
1972
  Gordon Alexander Buchanan Parks
1977
  Alex Haley

TSM Awards and R. R. Hawkins Award

The Technical, Scientific and Medical (TSM) Division of the Association of American Publishers established these annual awards in 1976 to honor those publishing companies who have published the year's most outstanding books and journal in the fields of science, medicine, technology, and business. In addition, the TSM Division presents the R. R. Hawkins Award to the publisher of the single most outstanding book of the year, selected from among the year's TSM Award winners. (R. R. Hawkins was the former head of the Science and Technology Division of the New York Public Library and the author of *Scientific, Medical and Technical Books Published in the U.S., 1930–1944* and its *Supplement, 1945–1948*.) Participation in the award selection process is a privilege of TSM Division membership. Each Division member-publisher may submit two books in each category, published during the previous calendar year with a printing of no more than 10,000 copies. Both hardcover and paperback books are eligible. If a book is published by joint venture, the primary publisher must be a TSM Division member. The judges are experienced publishers who are no longer affiliated with one particular publishing house. The awards are certificates—an enlarged, framed certificate for the R. R. Hawkins Award—which are presented during the TSM Division Annual Meeting in March or April. Inquiries may be sent to Patricia McLaughlin, Staff Director, TSM Division, Association of American Publishers, One Park Avenue, New York, New York 10016.

1977

Little, Brown & Company
Cleft Craft: The Evolution of Its Surgery, Vol. I, by D. Ralph Millard, Jr. (Medicine) R. R. Hawkins Award

M.I.T. Press
The Innovation Decision in Soviet Industry, by Joseph S. Berliner (Business/Management)

McGraw-Hill Book Company
McGraw-Hill Dictionary of the Life Sciences, by the McGraw-Hill Encyclopedia of Science and Technology staff (Technology/Science)

M.I.T. Press
Oppositions: A Journal for Ideas and Criticism in Architecture (Journal)

1978

M.I.T. Press
Encyclopedic Dictionary of Mathematics, Vols. I and II, by Shokichi Iyanaga and Yukiyoshi Kawada (Technology/Science) R. R. Hawkins Award

W. B. Saunders Company
Forensic Medicine: A Study in Trauma and Environmental Hazards, by C. G. T. Tedeschi, William G. Eckert, and Luke G. Tedeschi (Medicine)

Rutgers University Press
A History of Interest Rates, by Sidney Homer (Business/Management)

John Wiley & Sons
Journal of Graph Theory (Journal)

1979

McGraw-Hill Book Company
The Handbook of Optics, by The Optical Society of America (Science) R. R. Hawkins Award

Addison-Wesley Publishing Company
The Network Nation: Human Communication via Computer, by Starr Hiltz and Murray Turoff (Technology)

Little, Brown & Company
Pediatric Kidney Disease, by Chester M. Edelmann, Jr. (Medicine)

Johns Hopkins University Press
The Productivity Dilemma: Roadblock to Innovation in the Automobile Industry, by William J. Abernathy (Business)

Plenum Press
Grants Magazine (Journal)

Texas Institute of Letters

The Texas Institute of Letters, Box 7219, Austin, Texas 78712, gives several literary awards annually in February for books by Texas authors or on Texas subjects. Also given, but not listed here, are the Stanley Walker Journalism Award ($250) for the best piece of writing published in a Texas newspaper, the Texas Collectors' Institute Award ($250) for the best book design, and the Short Story Award ($250).

Carr P. Collins Award

Carr P. Collins of Dallas, under the auspices of the Institute, established in 1946 an award of $1,000 as a continuation of the Institute's Book Awards, begun in 1940, which had consisted of a plaque. The purpose of the award is to honor a book by a Texas author or on a Texas subject that, in the opinion of a committee of judges, is considered the most outstanding of the previous year's output.

1947
Green Peyton
San Antonio, City in the Sun (McGraw)

1948
John A. Lomax
Adventures of a Ballad Hunter (Macmillan)

1949
Herbert Gambrell
Anson Jones: The Last President of Texas (Doubleday)

1950
Tom Lea
The Brave Bulls (Little)

1951
Roy Bedichek
Karánkaway Country (Doubleday)

1952
Joe B. Frantz
Gail Borden, Dairyman to a Nation (Univ. of Oklahoma Press)

1953
J. Frank Dobie
The Mustangs (Little)

1954
Walter P. Webb
The Great Frontier (Houghton)

1955
Paul Horgan
The Great River: The Rio Grande in North American History, 2 vols. (Rinehart)

1956
John S. Spratt
The Road to Spindletop (Southern Methodist Univ. Press)

1957
Roy Bedichek
Educational Competition: The Story of the University Interscholastic League (Univ. of Texas Press)

1958
Frank Vandiver
Mighty Stonewall (McGraw)

1959
J. Lon Tinkle
Thirteen Days to Glory (McGraw)

1960
Lewis U. Hanke
Aristotle and the American Indian (Regnery)

1961
John Graves
Goodbye to a River (Knopf)

1962
Frances Sanger Mossiker
Queen's Necklace (Simon & Schuster)
1963
Rebecca Smith Lee
Mary Austin Holley (Univ. of Texas Press)
1964
Ellen Maury Slayden
Washington Wife (Harper)
1965
Frances Sanger Mossiker
Napoleon and Josephine (Simon & Schuster)
1966
Henry D. McCallum and Frances T. McCallum
The Wire That Fenced the West (Univ. of Oklahoma Press)
1967
William A. Owens
This Stubborn Soil (Scribner)
1968
Willie Morris
North toward Home (Houghton)
1969
Tom Lea
A Picture Gallery (Little)
1970
C. C. White and Ada Morehead Holland
No Quittin' Sense (Univ. of Texas Press)
1971
Gene Schulze
The Third Face of War (Jenkins)
1972
Charles W. Ferguson
Organizing to Beat the Devil: Methodists and the Making of America (Doubleday)
1973
Joseph C. Goulden
The Superlawyers (Weybright)
1974
Lewis L. Gould
Progressives and Prohibitionists: Texas Democrats in the Wilson Era (Univ. of Texas Press)
1975
John Graves
Hard Scrabble (Knopf)
1976
Paul Horgan
Lamy of Santa Fe (Farrar)
1977
Thomas Thompson
Blood and Money (Doubleday)
1978
William P. Humphrey
Farther Off from Heaven (Knopf)

Friends of the Dallas Public Library Award

In 1960 the Friends of the Dallas Public Library established this award of $500 to be given annually to the author of the book that constitutes the most important contribution to knowledge about Texas.

1960
David L. Miller
Modern Science and Human Freedom (Univ. of Texas Press)

1961
Robert Vines
Trees, Shrubs and Woody Vines (Univ. of Texas Press)

1962
W. W. Newcomb, Jr.
Indians of Texas (Univ. of Texas Press)
1963
Joseph S. Gallegly
Footlights on the Border: The Galveston and Houston Stage before 1900 (Humanities)
1964
Joseph Milton Nance
After San Jacinto (Univ. of Texas Press)
1965
Ramon Adams
Burrs under the Saddle (Univ. of Oklahoma Press)
1966
Lois Wood Burkhalter
Gideon Lincecum (Univ. of Texas Press)
1967
William H. Goetzmann
Exploration and Empire: The Explorer and the Scientist in the Winning of the American West (Knopf)
1968
W. W. Newcomb, Jr.
Rock Art of Texas Indians (Univ. of Texas Press)
1969
C. L. Sonnichsen
The Pass of the North: Four Centuries on the Rio Grande (Texas Western)
1970
Bill C. Malone
Country Music, USA: A Fifty-Year History (Univ. of Texas Press)

1971
Richard B. Henderson
Maury Maverick: A Political Biography (Univ. of Texas Press)
1972
Thomas Parke Hughes
Elmer Sperry: Inventor and Engineer (Johns Hopkins)
1973
A. C. Greene
The Last Captive (Encino)
1974
Donald E. Green
Land of the Underground Rain: Irrigation of the Texas High Plains, 1910–1970 (Univ. of Texas Press)
1975
Harry C. Oberholser
The Bird Life of Texas (Univ. of Texas Press)
1976
Elizabeth A. H. John
Storms Brewed in Other Men's Worlds (Texas A&M Univ. Press)
1977
Lawrence Goodwyn
Democratic Promise: The Populist Movement in America (Oxford Univ. Press)
1978
Frank E. Vandiver
Black Jack: The Life and Times of John J. Pershing, 2 vols. (Texas A&M Univ. Press)

Jesse H. Jones Award

Since 1960 the Jesse H. Jones Award has been given annually to the author of the best Texas book of fiction. The $1,000 award is given by Houston Endowment, Inc.

1961
   Walter Clemons
   The Poison Tree (Houghton)
1962
   Bill Casey
   A Shroud for a Journey (Houghton)
1963
   Larry McMurtry
   Horseman Pass By (Harper)
1964
   J. Y. Bryan
   Come to the Bower (Viking)
1965
   Tom Lea
   The Hands of Cantu (Little)
1966
   No award
1967
   William Humphrey
   The Ordways (Knopf)
1968
   Robert Flynn
   North to Yesterday (Knopf)
1969
   Tom Horn
   The Shallow Grass (Macmillan)

   Marshall Terry
   Tom Northway (Harcourt)
1970
   Willard Marsh
   Beachhead in Bohemia (Louisiana State Univ. Press)
1971
   Paul Horgan
   White Water (Farrar)
1972
   Nolan Porterfield
   A Way of Knowing (Harper's Magazine)
1973
   John Williams
   Augustus (Viking)
1974
   Shelby Hearon
   The Second Dune (Knopf)

   Chester L. Sullivan
   Alligator Gar (Crown)
1975
   Charles W. Smith
   Thin Men of Haddam (Grossman)
1976
   Donald Barthelme
   The Dead Father (Farrar)

Steck-Vaughn Award

The Steck-Vaughn Company of Austin offers this award for a children's book by a Texas writer or on a Texas subject. Formerly known as the Cokesbury Book Store Award, the $300 award is judged by a committee of three named by the Council of the Texas Institute of Letters.

1951
   Elizabeth Baker
   Sonny-Boy Jim (Rand McNally)
1952
   Carol Hoff
   Johnny Texas (Wilcox & Follett)
1953
   John Latham
   Lonesome Longhorn (Westminster)

1954
   Siddie Joe Johnson
   A Month of Christmases (Longmans)
1955
   Charlotte Baker Montgomery
   Magic for Mary M. (McKay)
1956
   Irmengarde Eberle
   Lone Star Fight (Dodd)

1957
Fred Gipson
The Trail Driving Rooster (Harper)
1958
Jessie Brewer McGaw
How Medicine Man Cured Paleface Woman (W. R. Scott)
1959
J. R. Williams
Tame the Wild Stallion (Prentice)
1960
Camilla Campbell
Coronado and His Captains (Follett)
1961
Byrd Hooper
Beef for Beauregard (Putnam)
1962
Edwin B. Sayles and M. E. Stevens
Throw Stones (Reilly & Lee)
1963
Myra Cohn Livingston
I'm Hiding (poetry) (Harcourt)

Lee McGiffin
Pony Soldier (Dutton)
1964
Wanda Jay Campbell
Ten Cousins (Dutton)
1965
Janette Sebring Lowrey
Love, Bid Me Welcome (Harper)
1966
No award
1967
Elizabeth Burleson
A Man of the Family (Follett)
1968
Michael Daves
Young Readers Book of Christian Symbolism (Abingdon)

1969
Gus Tavo
Ride the Pale Stallion (Knopf)
1970
Frances Alexander
Pebbles from a Broken Jar: Fables and Hero Stories from Old China (Bobbs)
1971
Betsy Warren
Indians Who Lived in Texas (Steck)
1972
Willie Morris
Good Old Boy (Harper)
1973
Byrd Baylor
When Clay Sings (Scribner)
1974
Loula Grace Erdman
A Bluebird Will Do (Dodd)
1975
Joan Lowry Nixon
The Alligator under the Bed (Putnam)
1976
Byrd Baylor
The Desert Is Theirs (Scribner)
1977
No award
1978
Byrd Baylor
Guess Who My Favorite Person Is (Scribner)
1979
No award

Voertman's Poetry Award

To be eligible for this award, a book must be a volume of poetry by a Texas writer or on a Texas subject. The first award in 1945 was known as the Daedalian Poetry

Award. Between 1945 and 1965 it was sponsored by various donors. In 1965 it was taken over by Paul Voertman of Denton. The award is $200.

1946
  David Russell
  Sing with Me Now (Kaleidograph)
1947
  Whitney Montgomery
  Joseph's Coat (Kaleidograph)
1948
  Arthur M. Sampley
  Of the Strong and the Fleet (Kaleidograph)
1949
  Vaida Montgomery
  Hail for Rain (Kaleidograph)
1950
  Frances Alexander
  Time at the Window (Kaleidograph)
1951
  Mary Poole
  Being in Night (Kaleidograph)
1952
  Arthur M. Sampley
  Furrow with Blackbirds (Kaleidograph)
1953
  William D. Barney
  Kneel to the Stone (Kaleidograph)
1954
  Robert Lee Brothers
  The Hidden Harp (Kaleidograph)
1955
  William Burford
  Man Now (Kaleidograph)
1956
  William D. Barney
  Permitted Proof (Kaleidograph)
1957
  Vassar Miller
  Adam's Footprint (Kaleidograph)
1958
  Eloise Roach, trans.
  Platero and I, by Juan Ramón Jiménez (Univ. of Texas Press)

1959
  No award
1960
  Ramsey Yelvington
  A Cloud of Witnesses (Univ. of Texas Press)
1961
  Vassar Miller
  Wage War on Silence (Wesleyan Univ. Press)
1962
  Conrad Pendleton [Walter E. Kidd]
  Time Turns West (American Weave)
1963
  Frederic Will
  A Wedge of Words (Univ. of Texas Press)
1964
  Vassar Miller
  My Bones Being Wiser (Wesleyan Univ. Press)
1965
  Thomas Whitbread
  Four Infinitives (Harper)
1966
  Roger Shattuck
  Half Tame (Univ. of Texas Press)
1967
  R. G. Vliet
  Events and Celebrations (Viking)
1968
  Frederic Will
  Planets (Golden Quill)
1969
  Edgar Simmons
  Driving to Biloxi and Other Poems (Louisiana State Univ. Press)
1970
  No award
1971
  R. G. Vliet
  The Man with the Black Mouth (Kayak)

1972
Arthur M. Samply
Selected Poems, 1937–1971 (North Texas State Univ. Press)
1973
Gene Shuford
Selected Poems, 1933–1971 (North Texas State Univ. Press)
1974
Fania Kruger
Selected Poems (American Universal Artforms)
1975
Michael Ryan
Threats Instead of Trees (Yale Univ. Press)

1976
Kurth Sprague
The Promise Kept (Encino)
1977
Walter McDonald
Caliban in Blue (Texas Tech Press)
1978
Glenn Hardin
Giants
Jack Myers
The Family War (L'Epervier)

Theatre Library Association

The Theatre Library Association, 111 Amsterdam Avenue, New York, New York 10023, offers two annual awards.

George Freedley Memorial Award

This award was established in 1968 in memory of the late theater historian, critic, author, and first curator of the New York Public Library Theatre Collection. A scroll is presented annually in the spring to an author of a book in the field of theater published in the United States and selected on the basis of scholarship, readability, and general contribution to knowledge.

1969
Louis Sheaffer
O'Neill, Son and Playwright (Little)
1970
Charles H. Shattuck
The Hamlet of Edwin Booth (Univ. of Illinois Press)
1971
Brooks Atkinson
Broadway (Macmillan)
1972
James M. Symons

Myerhold's Theatre of the Grotesque: The Post-Revolutionary Productions, 1920–1932 (Univ. of Miami Press)
1973
John Houseman
Run-Through (Simon & Schuster)
Lael Wertenbaker, coauthor with Jean Rosenthal
The Magic of Light: The Craft and Career of Jean Rosenthal, Pioneer in Lighting for the Modern Stage (Little/Theatre Arts Books)

1974

Stephen Orgel and Roy Strong
Inigo Jones: The Theatre of the Stuart Court (Sotheby Parke Bernet/Univ. of California Press)

1975

Robert C. Toll
Blacking Up: The Minstrel Show in Nineteenth-Century America (Oxford Univ. Press)

1976

Donald M. Oenslager
Stage Design: Four Centuries of Scenic Invention (Viking)

1977

Gerald Kahan
Jacques Callot: Artist of the Theatre (Univ. of Georgia Press)

1978

George C. Izenour
Theatre Design (McGraw)

1979

Richard D. Altick
The Shows of London (Belknap)

Theatre Library Association Award

This award was established in 1973 for the outstanding book dealing with recorded performance in films, television, and radio. A scroll is presented annually at the same time as the George Freedley Memorial Award.

1974

Donald Bogle
Toms, Coons, Mulattoes, Mammies, and Bucks: An Interpretive History of Blacks in American Films (Viking)

1975

Gerald S. Lesser
Children and Television: Lessons from Sesame Street (Random)

1976

Robert Sklar
Movie-Made America: A Social History of American Movies (Random)

1977

Fred W. Friendly
The Good Guys, the Bad Guys and the First Amendment: Free Speech and Fairness in Broadcasting (Random)

1978

Mira Liehm and Antonin Liehm
The Most Important Art: East European Film after 1945 (Univ. of California Press)

1979

Kevin Brownlow
The War, the West and the Wilderness (Knopf)

Irita Van Doren Book Award

Offered by the American Booksellers Association, the Publishers' Ad Club, and the Publishers' Publicity Association, this award is given in memory of one of the most influential and respected personalities in the publishing world. Formerly called the Irita Van Doren Literary Award, it is given for outstanding contributions to the cause of books and the popularity of book reading. The award, an engraved silver bowl, is presented annually during the convention of the American Booksellers Association. Further information may be obtained from American Booksellers Association, 122 East 42 Street, New York, New York 10017.

1967
William I. Nichols
Former editor, *This Week Magazine*, and former chairperson, National Book Committee
1968
Mildred Smith
Editor-in-Chief Emeritus, *Publishers Weekly*
1969
Robert Cromie
Literary Editor, *Chicago Tribune* and TV program "Book Beat"
1970
Edward A. Weeks
Consultant and Senior Editor, *Atlantic Monthly*
1971
Cass Canfield
Editor, Harper & Row
1972
Norman Cousins
Editor, *World Magazine, Inc.*
1973
Theodore Solotaroff
Editor, General Books Division, Bantam Books

1974
Kenneth D. McCormick
Consultant and Senior Editor, Doubleday & Co.
1975
"Today" (TV show)
1976
Judith F. Krug
Director, Office for Intellectual Freedom, American Library Association
1977
Digby Diehl
Former book editor, *Los Angeles Times*
1978
Barbara Bannon
Executive Editor, *Publishers Weekly*
1979
Louis Epstein
Former ABA president and founder of Pickwick Bookstores

Edward Lewis Wallant Book Award

This annual award was established in 1963 to perpetuate the memory of Edward Lewis Wallant (1926 –1962), the author of *The Human Season, The Pawnbroker, Children at the Gate*, and *The Tenants of Moonbloom*. The award is given to an American author of a work of creative fiction (novel or short story collection) of significance for American Jews. The award, $250 and a hand-lettered certificate, is presented in March at the Hartford (Connecticut) Jewish Community Center for a book published during the previous calendar year. The award is offered by Dr. and Mrs. Irving Waltman, 3 Brighton Road, West Hartford, Connecticut 06117. Books should be submitted to Dr. Lothar Kahn, Central Connecticut State College, New Britain, Connecticut 06150.

1964
  Norman Fruchter
  Coat upon a Stick (Simon & Schuster)
1965
  Seymour Epstein
  Leah (Little)
1966
  Hugh Nissenson
  A Pile of Stones: Short Stories (Scribner)
1967
  Gene Horowitz
  Home Is Where You Start From (Norton)
1968
  Chaim Potok
  The Chosen (Simon & Schuster)
1969
  No award
1970
  Leo E. Litwak
  Waiting for the News (Doubleday)
1971
  No award

1972
  Cynthia Ozick
  The Pagan Rabbi, and Other Stories (Knopf)
1973
  Robert Kotlowitz
  Somewhere Else (Charterhouse)
1974
  Arthur Allen Cohen
  In the Days of Simon Stern (Random)
1975
  Susan Fornberg Schaeffer
  Anya (Macmillan)
1976
  Anne Bernays
  Growing up Rich (Little)
1977
  No award
1978
  Curt Leviant
  The Yemenite Girl (Bobbs)
1979
  No award

The Washington Monthly Political Book Award

The Political Book Award was established in 1970 by *The Washington Monthly*, 1028 Connecticut Avenue N.W., Washington, D.C. 20036, to recognize the best of those books that explore the processes and values of the institutions that govern America, the books that share the *Monthly*'s purpose of identifying where the system breaks down, why it breaks down, and what can be done to make it work. Only books published in the year immediately preceding the announcement are eligible. Decision is made by the editors of *The Washington Monthly* from nominations by publishers, readers, and other interested parties. The annual Political Book Issue in March announces the winners and carries an article/review discussing the winning books.

1971
  Chester Cooper
  The Lost Crusade (Dodd)
  George Reedy

Twilight of the Presidency (World)
1972
  Ronald Glasser
  365 Days (Braziller)

Julian Prescott
A History of the Modern Age (Double-
day)
1973
Daniel Ellsberg
Papers on the War (Simon & Schus-
ter)
Frances FitzGerald
Fire in the Lake (Little)
1974
Ward Just
The Congressman Who Loved Flau-
bert (Little)
John Newhouse
Cold Dawn: The Story of SALT (Holt)
1975
Robert A. Caro
The Power Broker: Robert Moses
and the Fall of New York (Knopf)
David R. Mayhew
Congress: The Electoral Connection
(Yale Univ. Press)
1976
Martha Derthick
Uncontrollable Spending for Social

Services Grants (Brookings Institu-
tion)
1977
John Morton Blum
V Was for Victory (Harcourt)
John Dean
Blind Ambition (Simon & Schuster)
John Hollander
Reflections on Espionage (Athe-
neum)
1978
Morris P. Fiorina
Congress: Keystone of the Washing-
ton Establishment (Yale Univ. Press)
Simon Leys
Chinese Shadows (Viking)
1979
William Manchester
American Caesar: Douglas Mac-
Arthur (Little)
Theodore H. White
In Search of History (Harper)

William H. Welch Medal

This award, established in 1949 and first awarded in 1950, is for "particular contributions of outstanding scholarly merit in the field of medical history published during the
five years preceding the award." The medal is named for the great American physician William H. Welch, who was, among his many accomplishments, an outstanding
medical historian. Anyone is eligible, within the purposes for which the award is made.
Nominations for the annual award are made by a committee of the American Association for the History of Medicine, c/o Robert P. Hudson, Department of the History of
Medicine, Kansas University Medical Center, Kansas City, Kansas 66103, the final
decision being reserved to the Council of the Association. The winner is announced at
the annual meeting of the Association, usually held in April or May.

1950
Henry E. Sigerist
For scholarly contributions

1951
No award

1952
Owsei Temkin
For scholarly contributions
1953
Erwin H. Ackerknecht
For scholarly contributions
1954
Jerome Pierce Webster and Martha Teach Gnudi
The Life and Times of Gaspare Tagliacozzi (Herbert Reichner)
1955
No award
1956
Lyman Henry Butterfield
Letters of Benjamin Rush (Princeton Univ. Press)
1957
No award
1958
Charles F. Mullett
The Bubonic Plague and England: An Essay in the History of Preventive Medicine (Univ. of Kentucky Press)
1959
No award
1960
Richard Harrison Shryock
For scholarly contributions
1961
George Rosen
For contributions in the social history of medicine
1962
Genevieve Miller
The Adoption of Inoculation for Smallpox in England and France (Univ. of Pennsylvania Press)
1963
Saul Jarcho
For scholarly contributions
1964–1965
No awards
1966
Whitfield J. Bell, Jr.
John Morgan: Continental Doctor (Univ. of Pennsylvania Press)

1967
Howard B. Adelmann
Marcello Malpighi and the Evolution of Embryology (Cornell Univ. Press)
1968
Saul Benison
Tom Rivers: Reflections on a Life in Medicine and Science (M.I.T. Press)
1969
Charles Rosenberg
The Cholera Years (Univ. of Chicago Press)
1970
No award
1971
Charles Donald O'Malley (posthumous)
For scholarly contributions
1972
Erwin H. Ackerknecht
Medicine at the Paris Hospital, 1794–1848 (Johns Hopkins)
1973
Margaret Tallmadge May
Galen on the Usefulness of the Parts of the Body (Cornell Univ. Press)
1974
Walter Pagel
For extensive and most valuable publications
1975
George W. Corner
For invaluable contributions
1976
Lelland J. Rather
Addison and the White Corpuscles: An Aspect of Nineteenth-Century Biology and *Mind and Body in Eighteenth-Century Medicine: A Study Based on Jerome Gaub's De Regimine Mentis* (Univ. of California Press) and important continuing studies in the history of pathology
1977
Lester S. King
For scholarly contributions to the history of medicine

1978
Frederic Lawrence Holmes
Claude Bernard and Animal Chemistry: The Emergence of a Scientist
(Harvard Univ. Press)

1979
Charles Webster
The Great Instauration: Science, Medicine and Reform, 1626–1660
(Holmes & Meier)

Western Heritage Awards

The National Cowboy Hall of Fame and Western Heritage Center, 1700 N.E. 63 Street, Oklahoma City, Oklahoma 73111, established the Western Heritage Award in 1960. A Wrangler Trophy, a small replica of Charles M. Russell's bronze statue of "The Horse Wrangler," is presented for the "year's best efforts in preserving the image of the real American West and the people who were responsible for developing it." The award is given for motion pictures, musical compositions, television programs, documentary films, novels, nonfiction books, juvenile books, art books, and short story or magazine articles. Publishers or authors may enter books and articles published during the preceding calendar year and through January 15. Each category is judged by knowledgeable judges appointed by the Awards Committee. The Wrangler Trophies are presented at the Western Heritage Awards ceremony held each spring in Oklahoma City. Entries are due on January 15. Below are the winners for the literary prizes.

SHORT STORY, POETRY, OR MAGAZINE ARTICLE

1961
Steve Frazee
"All Legal and Proper," *Ellery Queen Magazine*
W. Bruce Bell
"The Old Chisholm Trail," *Kiwanis Magazine*
1962
Fred Grove
"Comanche Son," *Boys' Life*
Mari Sandoz
"The Look of the Last Frontier," *American Heritage*
1963
George Stewart
"The Prairie Schooner Got Them There," *American Heritage*

1964
Herman Lehmann
"Nine Years among the Indians," *Frontier Times*
1965
J. Frank Dobie
"Titans of Western Art," *The American Scene*
1966
Donald Jackson
"How Lost Was Zebulon Pike," *American Heritage*
1967
Jack Guinn
"The Red Man's Last Struggle," *Empire Magazine*
1968
Carolyn Woirhaye
"The Snows of Rimrock Ridge," *The Farm Quarterly*

SHORT STORY, POETRY, OR MAGAZINE ARTICLE (cont.)

1969
Donnie D. Good
"W. R. Leigh: The Artist's Studio Collection," *The American Scene*
1970
May Howell Dodson
"Bennett Howell's Cow Country," *Frontier Times*
1971
James E. Serven
"Cattle, Guns, and Cowboys," *Arizona Highways*
1972
David Humphreys Miller
"Echoes of the Little Bighorn," *American Heritage*
1973
George Keithley
The Donner Party (Braziller)
James E. Serven
"Horses of the West," *Arizona Highways*
1974
Spike Van Cleve
"Forty Years Gatherin's," *The Dude Rancher*
1975
Jim Jennings
"George Humphreys, Half Century with 6666," *Quarter Horse Journal*
1976
Patricia J. Broder
"The Pioneer Woman: Image in Bronze," *American Art Review*
1977
No award
1978
John Sinclair
"Where Cowboys Hunkered Down," *New Mexico Magazine*
1979
Richard Rhodes
"The Farther Continent of James Clyman," *American Heritage*

NONFICTION BOOK

1961
No award
1962
Alvin M. Josephy, Jr., ed.
The American Heritage Book of Indians (American Heritage)
1963
John Rolphe Burroughs
Where the Old West Stayed Young (Morrow)
1964
John Upton Terrell
Furs by Astor (Morrow)
1965
C. Gregory Crampton
Standing Up Country (Knopf)
1966
Alvin M. Josephy, Jr., ed.
American Heritage History of the Great West (American Heritage)
1967
George W. Groh
Gold Fever (Morrow)
1968
John A. Hawgood
America's Western Frontiers (Knopf)
1969
Robert Dykstra
The Cattle Towns (Knopf)
Laura Gilpin
The Enduring Navajo (Univ. of Texas Press)
1970
Merrill J. Mattes
The Great Platte River Road (Nebraska State Historical Society)
1971
Harry Sinclair Drago
The Great Range Wars (Dodd)
1972
Odie B. Faulk and Seymour V. Connor
North America Divided: The Mexican War (Oxford Univ. Press)

NONFICTION BOOK (cont.)

1973

Grace Dangberg
Carson Valley (Carson Valley Historical Society)

Tom McHugh
The Time of the Buffalo (Knopf)

S. L. A. Marshall
Crimsoned Prairie (Scribner)

1974

George Ellis
Bell Ranch as I Knew It (Lowell)

Richard Ketchum
Will Rogers: His Life and His Time (American Heritage)

Mike Hanley and Ellis Lucia
Owyhee Trails (Caxton)

David Muench, photos, and N. Scott Momaday, text
Colorado Summer/Fall/Winter/Spring (Rand McNally)

1975

Robert O. Beatty
Idaho: A Pictorial Overview (Idaho First National Bank, Boise)

Benjamin Capps
The Warren Wagontrain Raid (Dial)

Margaret Sanborn
The American: River of El Dorado (Holt)

C. L. Sonnichsen
Colonel Greene and the Copper Skyrocket (Univ. of Arizona Press)

Roy P. Stewart
Born Grown (Fidelity Bank; N.A., Oklahoma City)

1976

Jeff C. Dykes
Fifty Great Western Illustrators (Northland)

Turbesé Lummis Fiske and Keith Lummis
Charles F. Lummis: The Man and His West (Univ. of Oklahoma Press)

Don James
Butte's Memory Book (Caxton)

1977

No award

1978

Angie Debo
Geronimo: The Man, His Time, His Place (Univ. of Oklahoma Press)

Tim McCoy and Ronald McCoy
Tim McCoy Remembers the West (Doubleday)

1979

Nellie Snyder Yost
Buffalo Bill: His Family, Friends, Fame, Failures and Fortunes (Swallow)

NOVEL

1961

No award

1962

James D. Horan
The Shadow Catcher (Crown)

1963

Edward Abbey
Fire on the Mountain (Dial)

1964

Robert Roripaugh
Honor Thy Father (Morrow)

1965

Thomas Berger
Little Big Man (Dial)

1966

Vardis Fisher
Mountain Man (Morrow)

1967

Bill Gulick
They Came to a Valley (Doubleday)

1968

Robert Flynn
North to Yesterday (Knopf)

1969

Fred Grove
The Buffalo Runners (Doubleday)

NOVEL (cont.)

1970
   Benjamin Capps
   The White Man's Road (Harper)
1971
   A. B. Guthrie
   Arfive (Dodd)
1972
   Frank Waters
   Pike's Peak: A Family Saga (Swallow)
1973
   Will Henry
   Chiricahua (Lippincott)
1974
   Elmer Kelton
   The Time It Never Rained (Double-day)
1975
   James Michener
   Centennial (Random)
1976–1977
   No awards
1978
   Bill Brett
   The Stolen Steers: A Tale of the Big Thicket (Texas A&M Univ. Press)
   Dorothy M. Johnson
   Buffalo Woman (Dodd)
1979
   Elmer Kelton
   The Good Old Boys (Doubleday)

JUVENILE BOOK

1961
   No award
1962
   Gene Caesar
   King of the Mountain (Dutton)
1963
   Charles Clifton
   The Book of the West (Bobbs)
1964
   Betty Baker
   Killer-of-Death (Harper)

1965
   Paul Wellman
   The Greatest Cattle Drive (Houghton)
1966
   Carl G. Hodges
   Land Rush (Duell)
1967
   Marguerite Henry
   Mustang: Wild Spirit of the West (Rand McNally)
1968
   Eric Scott
   Down the Rivers, Westward Ho! (Meredith)
1969
   Weyman Jones
   Edge of Two Worlds (Dial)
1970
   Jessie Hosford
   An Awful Name to Live Up To (Meredith)
1971
   Betty Baker
   And One Was a Wooden Indian (Macmillan)
1972
   Richard Wormser
   The Black Mustanger (Morrow)
1973
   Bern Keating
   Famous American Explorers (Rand McNally)
1974
   No award
1975
   Harold Keith
   Susy's Scoundrel (Crowell)
1976–1978
   No awards
1979
   Harold Keith
   The Obstinate Land (Crowell)

ART BOOK

1961–1967
   No awards

ART BOOK (cont.)

1968
E. Maurice Bloch
George Caleb Bingham: The Evolution of an Artist (Univ. of California Press)
1969
Ed Ainsworth
The Cowboy in Art (World)
1970
William Reed
Olaf Wieghorst (Northland)
1971
Robert F. Karolevitz
Where Your Heart Is: The Story of Harvey Dunn (North Plains)
1972
Paul Rossi and David Hunt
The Art of the Old West (Knopf)
1973
Walt Reed
Harold Von Schmidt Draws and Paints the Old West (Knopf)
1974
Frank Getlein
The Lure of the Great West (Country Beautiful Corp.)

1975
Harold Davidson
Edward Borein Cowboy Artist (Doubleday)
1976
Emmie D. Mygatt and Roberta Cheney
Hans Kleiber: Artist of the Bighorn Mountains (Caxton)
1977
No award

1978
John K. Goodman
Ross Stefan: An Impressionistic Painter of the Contemporary Southwest (Northland)

1979
Searles R. Boynton
The Painter Lady: Grace Carpenter Hudson (Interface Corp.)

Susan Peterson
The Living Tradition of Maria Martinez (Kodansha)

Western Writers of America Awards

These awards were established in 1953 by the Western Writers of America, Inc., to encourage better craftsmanship in the writing of frontier fiction by giving recognition to meritorious work. Any writer of a Western novel, nonfiction book, historical or regional novel, juvenile, or short story is eligible. In 1964 the Best Western Short Story classification was changed to Best Western Short Material. Juvenile awards were divided into fiction and nonfiction categories during 1967–1975. Qualified and unbiased judges are appointed to select the best work from each of these categories. Requirements for submission vary from year to year. The award consists of a golden spur mounted on a W-shaped walnut plaque inscribed with the name of the recipient and the type of work for which it is awarded. It is presented in June at the Western Writers of America Spur Awards Dinner held the last night of the annual convention. For further information, write to Rex Bundy, Secretary-Treasurer, Western Writers of America, Inc., Route 1, Box 35H, Victor, Montana 59875.

NOVEL

1954
Wayne D. Overholser [Lee Leighton]
Law Man (Ballantine)
1955
Wayne D. Overholser [Lee Leighton]
The Violent Land (Macmillan)
1956
L. P. Holmes
Somewhere They Die (Little)
1957
Leslie Ernenwein
High Gun (Gold Medal)
1958
Elmer Kelton
Buffalo Wagon (Ballantine)
1959
Noel Loomis
Short Cut to Red River (Macmillan)
1960
Nelson Nye
Long Run (Macmillan)
1961
Will C. Brown
The Nameless Breed (Macmillan)
1962
Giles A. Lutz
The Honyocker (Doubleday)
1963
Fred Grove
Comanche Captives (Ballantine)
1964
Leigh Brackett
Follow the Free Wind (Doubleday)
1965
Benjamin Capps
The Trail to Ogallala (Duell)
1966
Benjamin Capps
Sam Chance (Duell)
1967
Herbert R. Purdom
My Brother John (Doubleday)
1968
Lee Hoffman
The Valdez Horses (Ace)

1969
Louis L'Amour
Down the Long Hills (Bantam)
1970
Clifton H. Adams
Tragg's Choice (Doubleday)
1971
Clifton H. Adams
The Last Days of Wolf Garnett (Doubleday)
1972
Elmer Kelton
The Day the Cowboys Quit (Doubleday)
1973
Cliff Farrell
Patch Saddle Drive (Doubleday)
1974
Elmer Kelton
The Time It Never Rained (Doubleday)
1975
Stephen Overholser
A Hanging at Sweetwater (Doubleday)
1976
Glendon Swarthout
The Shootist (Doubleday)
1977
Lou Cameron
Spirit Horses (Ballantine)

Douglas Jones
The Court Martial of George Armstrong Custer (Scribner)
1978
Fred Grove
The Great Horse Race (Doubleday)
1979
Norman Ballinger
Riders of Cibola (New Mexico Univ. Press)

HISTORICAL NOVEL

1954
Lucia Moore
The Wheel and the Hearth (Ballantine)

HISTORICAL NOVEL (cont.)

1955
John Prescott
Journey by the River (Random)
1956
No award
1957
John C. Hunt
Generations of Men (Little)
1958
Dan Cushman
The Silver Mountain (Appleton)
1959
Amelia Bean
The Fancher Train (Doubleday)
1960
John Prebble
The Buffalo Soldiers (Harcourt)
1961
Henry Allen [Will Henry]
From Where the Sun Now Stands (Random)
1962
William Wister Haines
The Winter War (Little)
1963
Don Berry
Moon Trap (Viking)
1964
Henry Allen [Will Henry]
The Gates of the Mountains (Random)
1965
E. E. Halleran
Indian Fighter (Ballantine)
1966
Todhunter Ballard
Gold in California (Doubleday)
Vardis Fisher
Man Mountain (Morrow)
1967
Garland Roark and Charles Thomas
Hellfire Jackson (Doubleday)
1968
Chad Oliver
The Wolf Is My Brother (New American Library)

1969
Lewis B. Patten
The Red Sabbath (Ace)
1970
Benjamin Capps
The White Man's Road (Harper)
1971–1972
No awards
1973
Lewis B. Patten
A Killing in Kiowa (New American Library)
1974–1976
No awards
1977
Matt Braun
The Kincaids (Putnam)
1978
Terrence Kilpatrick
Swimming Man Burning (Doubleday)
1979
No award

NONFICTION

1955
David Lavender
Bent's Fort (Doubleday)
1956
Paul F. Sharp
Whoop-up Country (Univ. of Minnesota Press)
1957
Irving Stone
Men to Match My Mountains (Doubleday)
1958
Robert West Howard
This Is the West (Rand McNally)
1959
Mabel Barbee Lee
Cripple Creek Days (Doubleday)
1960
Frank Tolbert
Day of San Jacinto (McGraw)

NONFICTION (cont.)

1961
Lola M. Homsher, ed.
James Chisholm's *South Pass, 1868* (Univ. of Nebraska Press)
1962
Don Russell
The Lives and Legends of Buffalo Bill (Univ. of Oklahoma Press)
1963
Richard A. Bartlett
Great Surveys of the American West (Univ. of Oklahoma Press)
1964
William S. Greever
The Bonanza West (Univ. of Oklahoma Press)
1965
Ernest Staples Osgood
The Field Notes of Captain William Clark (Yale Univ. Press)
1966
Alvin M. Josephy, Jr.
The Nez Percé Indians and the Opening of the Northwest (Yale Univ. Press)
1967
Ray Allen Billington
America's Frontier Heritage (Holt)
1968
John Hawgood
America's Western Frontiers (Knopf)
1969
Vardis Fisher and Opal Laurel Holmes
Gold Rushes and Mining Camps of the Early American West (Caxton)
1970
Nellie Snyder Yost
Boss Cowman (Univ. of Nebraska Press)
1971
Francis Haines
The Buffalo (Crowell)
1972
Elliott S. Barker
Western Life and Adventures (Horn)

1973
Tom McHugh
Time of the Buffalo (Knopf)
1974
Richard Dillon
Burnt Out Fires (Prentice)
1975
C. L. Sonnichsen
Colonel Green and the Copper Skyrocket (Univ. of Arizona Press)
1976
Paul Horgan
Lamy of Santa Fe (Farrar)
1977
Stan Steiner
The Vanishing Whiteman (Harper)
1978
Joyce Gibson Roach
The Cowgirls (Cordovan Corp.)
1979
Janet Lecompte
Pueblo, Hardscrabble & Greenhorn (Univ. of Oklahoma Press)

JUVENILE

1954
Frank C. Robertson
Sagebrush Sorrel (Thomas Nelson)
1955
Stephen Payne
Young Hero of the Range (Lantern)
1956
No award
1957
Charles C. Neihuis
Trapping the Silver Beaver (Dodd)
1958
Jim Kjelgaard
Wolf Brother (Holiday House)
1959
Dale White
Steamboat up the Missouri (Viking)
1960
Dale White
Hold Back the Hunter (John Day)

JUVENILE (cont.)

1961
   Ramona Maher
   Their Shining Hour (John Day)
1962
   J. R. Williams
   The Horse-Talker (Prentice)
1963
   Natlee Kenoyer
   The Western Horse (Meredith)
1964
   Sid Fleischman
   By the Great Horn Spoon (Little)

   Mari Sandoz
   The Story Catcher (Westminster)
1965
   Richard Wormser
   Ride a Northbound Horse (Morrow)
1966
   Rutherford Montgomery
   The Stubborn One (Duell)
1967–1975
   No awards
1976
   Bill Cleaver and Vera Cleaver
   Dust of the Earth (Lippincott)
1977
   Philip Ault
   All Aboard (Dodd)
1978
   Louis Irigarary and Theodore Taylor
   A Shepherd Watches, a Shepherd Sings (Doubleday)
1979
   Sonia Levitis
   The No-Return Trail (Harcourt)

JUVENILE FICTION

1967
   Annabel Johnson and Edgar Johnson
   The Burning-Glass (Harper)
1968
   Betty Baker
   The Dunderhead War (Harper)

Evelyn Lampman
Half Breed (Doubleday)
1969
   Elizabeth Burleson
   Middl'un (Follett)
1970
   Wayne D. Overholser and Lewis B. Patten
   The Meeker Massacre (Cowles)
1971
   Evelyn Lampman
   Cayuse Courage (Harcourt)
1972
   Richard Wormser
   The Black Mustanger (Morrow)
1973
   Nathaniel Benchley
   Only Earth and Sky Last Forever (Harper)
1974
   Jeanne Williams
   Freedom Trail (Putnam)
1975
   Harold Keith
   Susy's Scoundrel (Crowell)

JUVENILE NONFICTION

1967
   Aileen Fisher
   Valley of the Smallest (Crowell)
1968
   Ralph Andrist
   To the Pacific with Lewis and Clark (American Heritage)
1969
   Marian T. Place
   Rifles and Warbonnets (Washburn)
1970
   Olga Hall-Quest
   Conquistadores and Pueblos (Dutton)
1971
   Marian T. Place
   Retreat to the Bear Paw (Four Winds)

JUVENILE NONFICTION (cont.)

1972
  Jules Loh
  Lords of the Earth (Crowell/Collier)
1973
  Stan Steiner
  The Tiguas (Macmillan)
1974
  Franklin Folsom
  Red Power on the Rio Grande (Follett)
1975
  No award

SHORT MATERIAL

1954
  Thomas Thompson
  "Gun Job"
1955
  Thomas Thompson
  "Blood on the Sun"
1956
  S. Omar Barker
  "Bad Company"
1957
  Dorothy M. Johnson
  "Lost Sister"
1958
  Peggy Simpson Curry
  "The Brushoff"
1959
  Bill Gulick
  "Thief in Camp"
1960
  Noel Loomis
  "Grandfather out of the Past"
1961
  Bill Gulick
  "The Taming of Broken Bow"
1962
  John Prebble
  "A Town Named Hate"
1963
  Henry Allen [Will Henry]
  "Isley's Stranger"

1964
  Fred Grove
  "Comanche Woman"
1965
  Lola Shelton
  "Log Studio of C. M. Russell"
1966
  Henry Allen [Will Henry]
  "The Tallest Indian in Toltepec"
1967
  S. Omar Barker
  "Empty Saddles at Christmas"
1968
  Donald Hamilton
  "The Guns of William Longley"
1969
  Fred Grove
  "When the Caballos Came"
1970
  Cliff Farrell
  "Westward . . . To Blood and Glory"
1971
  Peggy Simson Curry
  "In the Silence"
1972
  Earl Clark
  "Shootout in Burke Canyon"
1973
  Harry Webb
  "Call of the Cow Country"
1974
  John Jarrell
  "The Comancheros"
1975
  Eve Ball
  "The Buried Treasure"
  Robert Laxalt
  "The Other Nevada"
1976
  Donald Worcester
  "Apaches in the History of the Southwest"
1977
  C. L. Sonnichsen
  "Jonathan Gilliam and the White Man's Burden"

SHORT MATERIAL (cont.)

1978
John L. Sinclair
"Where the Cowboys Hunkered Down"

1979
Carla Kelly
"Season for Heroes"

Woodrow Wilson Foundation Award

From 1947 to 1959, the Woodrow Wilson Foundation, Box 68, Princeton, New Jersey 08540, awarded $1,000 for the "best book of the year in the field of government and democracy." In 1956, the purpose of the award was clarified as follows: "To encourage significant research and reflection in the field of politics, government and international relations." In November 1959 the cash award was replaced by a specially designed medal. However, in 1964 the Foundation resumed the cash award of $1,000 in addition to the medal, with the stipulation that the $1,000 be shared if there were more than one winner.

1947
Robert M. MacIver
The Web of Government (Macmillan)
1948
Leonard D. White
The Federalists: A Study in Administrative History (Macmillan)
1949
V. O. Key, Jr.
Southern Politics in State and Nation (Knopf)
1950
Stephen K. Bailey
Congress Makes a Law (Columbia Univ. Press)
1951
John H. Herz
Political Realism and Political Idealism (Univ. of Chicago Press)
1952
Samuel Lubell
The Future of American Politics (Doubleday)
1953
Clinton Rossiter
Seedtime of the Republic (Harcourt)

1954
Merle Fainsod
How Russia Is Ruled (Harvard Univ. Press)
Bertram M. Gross
The Legislative Struggle (McGraw)
1955
Jacobus ten Broek and others
Prejudice, War, and the Constitution (Univ. of California Press)
1956
Louis Hartz
The Liberal Tradition in America (Harcourt)
1957
James MacGregor Burns
Roosevelt: The Lion and the Fox (Harcourt)
1958
Henry A. Kissinger
Nuclear Weapons and Foreign Policy (Harper)
Rexford Tugwell
The Democratic Roosevelt (Doubleday)

1959

Christian Bay
The Structure of Freedom (Stanford Univ. Press)

James S. Coleman
Nigeria: Background to Nationalism (Univ. of California Press)

1960

Arnold Brecht
Political Theory: The Foundations of Twentieth Century Thought (Princeton Univ. Press)

1961

Richard E. Neustadt
Presidential Power: The Politics of Leadership (Wiley)

1962

Robert A. Dahl
Who Governs? Democracy and Power in an American City (Yale Univ. Press)

1963

Inis L. Claude, Jr.
Power and International Relations (Random)

1964

Raymond A. Bauer, Ithiel de Sola Pool, and Lewis Dexter
American Business and Public Policy (Atherton)

1965

Robert E. Agger, Daniel Goldrich, and Bert E. Swanson
The Rulers and the Ruled (Wiley)

Samuel J. Eldersveld
Political Parties: A Behavioral Analysis (Rand McNally)

1966

Samuel H. Beer
British Politics in the Collectivist Age (Knopf)

1967

Barrington Moore, Jr.
Social Origins of Dictatorship and Democracy (Beacon)

1968

Duncan MacRae, Jr.
Parliament, Parties, and Society in France (St. Martins)

1969

Robert G. Dixon, Jr.
Democratic Representation (Oxford Univ. Press)

1970

David Butler and Donald Stokes
Political Change in Britain (St. Martins)

1971

Ted Robert Gurr
Why Men Rebel (Princeton Univ. Press)

1972

David E. Apter
Choice and the Politics of Allocation (Yale Univ. Press)

1973

Michael Brecher
The Foreign Policy System of Israel (Yale Univ. Press)

1974

Robert A. Scalapino and Chong-Sik Lee
Communism in Korea (Univ. of California Press)

1975

Hugh H. Heclo
Modern Social Politics in Britain and Sweden (Yale Univ. Press)

Discontinued

Thomas Wolfe Memorial Award

This trophy, established in 1954 by the Thomas Wolfe Memorial Association, Asheville, North Carolina, is awarded annually through a committee named by the Western

North Carolina Historical Association, Box 5456, Asheville, North Carolina. Any meritorious writing—book, article, poem, or drama—is eligible if its author is either a resident of western North Carolina or a native of western North Carolina now living elsewhere. Also eligible are works dealing with western North Carolina by anyone living in that territory. The award consists of a large silver trophy, retained by the recipient for one year, and a certificate. It is presented each year at the meeting of the Western North Carolina Historical Association, which takes place in October, the month of Wolfe's birth.

1955
  Wilma Dykeman
  French Broad (Rinehart)
1956
  Glenn Tucker
  Tecumseh: Vision of Glory (Bobbs)
1957
  Floyd Watkins
  Thomas Wolfe's Characters (Univ. of Oklahoma Press)
1958
  John Parris
  My Mountains, My People (Citizen-Times Press, Asheville)
1959
  Olive Tilford Dargan
  The Spotted Hawk (John F. Blair)
1960
  Luther Robinson
  We Made Peace with Polio (Broadman)
1961
  David English Camak
  Human Gold from Southern Hills (Human Gold)
1962
  Ina Van Noppen
  Stoneman's Last Raid (privately printed)
1963
  No award
1964
  Bruce R. McElderry, Jr.
  Thomas Wolfe (Twayne)
1965
  No award

1966
  Glenn Tucker
  Zeb Vance, Champion of Personal Freedom (Bobbs)
1967
  Michael Frome
  Strangers in High Places (Doubleday)
1968
  Neal F. Austin
  Biography of Thomas Wolfe (Beacham)
1969
  Harley E. Jolley
  A History of the Blue Ridge Parkway (Univ. of Tennessee Press)
1970
  Dell B. Wilson
  The Grandfather and the Globe (Puddingstone)
1971
  Rodney Leftwich
  Arts and Crafts of the Cherokees (Land of the Sky)
1972
  Moffitt Sinclair Henderson
  A Long, Long Day for November (Dorrance)
1973
  Ina Van Noppen and John Van Noppen
  Western North Carolina since the Civil War (Appalachian Consortium)
1974
  Ruby J. Lanier
  Blanford Barnard Dougherty: Mountain Educator (Duke Univ. Press)
1975
  Appalachian Consortium

1976
Francis Hulme
Mountain Measure (Appalachian Consortium)

1977
Frank L. FitzSimons
From the Banks of the Oklawaha, Vol. 1 (Golden Glow)

1978
Charlotte Young
Day of Miracles (Poetry Council of North Carolina)

1979
Theda Perdue
Slavery and the Evolution of Cherokee Society, 1540–1866 (Univ. of Tennessee Press)

Publishers' Prizes

American Heritage Publishing Company

Samuel Eliot Morison Award

An annual $5,000 prize in history was established in 1976 by the American Heritage Publishing Company, 10 Rockefeller Plaza, New York, New York 10020, in honor of the distinguished American historian Samuel Eliot Morison. The prize is given for the best book on American history by an American author that sustains the tradition that good history is literature as well as high scholarship, a tradition admirably exemplified by the many works by Morison. The prize is awarded by a panel of judges chaired by J. H. Plumb, Professor of Modern English History at the University of Cambridge, and Consulting Editor of the American Heritage Publishing Company. In 1979, the award was suspended until further notice.

1977
  Joseph P. Lash
  Roosevelt and Churchill, 1939–1941: The Partnership That Saved the West (Norton)
1978
  David McCullough
  The Path between the Seas: The Creation of the Panama Canal, 1870–1914 (Simon & Schuster)
Suspended

The Atlantic/The Atlantic Monthly Press/ Little, Brown and Company

Atlantic Grant

This grant, established in 1959, is jointly sponsored by *The Atlantic* and the Atlantic Monthly Press, both at 8 Arlington Street, Boston, Massachusetts 02116, and Little, Brown and Company, 34 Beacon Street, Boston, Massachusetts 02106. The grant, the amount of which varies, is designed to provide a young author with time in which to write and a contract with the Atlantic Monthly Press for publication of the completed manuscript. It is awarded at irregular intervals to young authors of special promise.

1959
Jesse Hill Ford
The Liberation of Lord Byron Jones
1965
Robert Coles
Children of Crisis, Vol. 1: A Study of Courage and Fear
1968
James Alan McPherson
Hue and Cry

1971
Sharon Curtin
Nobody Ever Died of Old Age
1974
M. F. Beal
Amazon One
1976
Andrew Ward
Fits and Starts: The Premature Memoirs of Andrew Ward

George Banta Company

Banta Award

The Banta Award was established in 1974 by the George Banta Company to recognize the work of authors who have worked and/or resided in Wisconsin. Selection of annual award winners is made by a committee of the Wisconsin Library Association on the basis "that it carry the marks which will contribute to the world of literature and ideas." The award, a medal, is presented at the Wisconsin Library Association's annual conference in late October or early November. Further information can be obtained from the George Banta Company, Inc., Menasha, Wisconsin 54952, or from Bonnie Robinson, Secretary, Wisconsin Library Association, 201 West Mifflin Street, Madison, Wisconsin 53703.

1974
Thornton Wilder
Theophilus North (Harper)
1975
Madeleine Doran
Time's Foot (privately published)
1976
Ben Logan
The Land Remembers (Viking)

1977
Richard N. Current
The Civil War Era, 1848–1873 (State Historical Society of Wisconsin)
1978
Reid A. Bryson and Thomas J. Murray
Climates of Hunger (Univ. of Wisconsin Press)

Coward, McCann & Geoghegan, Inc.

The Thomas R. Coward Memorial Award in Fiction

In 1966, Coward-McCann, Inc., 200 Madison Avenue, New York, New York 10016, announced this award, named for the company's founder. The award carried with it a

$15,000 prize—$10,000 as advance against royalties and the remaining $5,000 committed by the publisher as a minimum advertising budget for a campaign to run at least six weeks after publication. Manuscripts had a minimum of 50,000 words in length and came from all countries. Every manuscript submitted to Coward, McCann & Geoghegan was automatically considered as a candidate for the award.

1966
   Gavin Lambert
   Norman's Letter

1967
   Frank Elli
   The Riot

1968
   Charles Machardy
   Send Down a Dove

1969
   Brian Glanville
   The Olympian

1970
   Charles Flowers
   It Never Rains in Los Angeles
1974
   David Fletcher
   A Lovable Man
Discontinued

Dance Perspectives Foundation/ Wesleyan University Press

The de la Torre Bueno Prize

This prize, established in 1972 in honor of J. R. de la Torre Bueno, a former senior editor at Wesleyan University Press, is presented annually for the most distinguished unpublished book in the field of dance. It is jointly sponsored by the Dance Perspectives Foundation, 29 East Ninth Street, New York, New York 10003, and Wesleyan University Press, 356 Washington Street, Middletown, Connecticut 06457. The purpose of the award is to "find and to publish important, exciting works in dance, regardless of the period or the genre with which they deal." Manuscripts are judged on the quality of their research or depth of synthesis, literary style, originality, and significance. They may deal with any area of the dance—biographical, historical, critical, or esthetic—except that technical manuals and textbooks are ineligible. The deadline for submissions is December 31, but prospective applicants should first send an inquiry describing the work's purpose, length, unique features, and format, along with samples of the text, to the Dance Perspectives Foundation. Award winners are determined by a panel of three judges. The announcement of winners is made in April, with publication of the manuscript by Wesleyan University Press following as soon thereafter as is feasible. A certificate of honor is also presented to the winning author.

1973
   Mary Grace Swift
   A Loftier Flight: The Life and Accom- *plishments of Charles Louis Didelot*
   (Wesleyan Univ. Press)

1974
No award
1975
Jane Sherman
Soaring: The Diary and Letters of a Denishawn Dancer in the Far East, 1925–1926 (Wesleyan Univ. Press)
1976
David Vaughan
Frederick Ashton and His Ballets (Knopf)

1977
Nancy Reynolds
Repertory in Review: 40 Years of the New York City Ballet (Dial)
1978
No award
1979
Richard Ralph
The Life and Works of John Weaver (to be published by Dance Horizons)

The Dial Press

James Baldwin Prize

In early 1979, The Dial Press announced establishment of a new award, the James Baldwin Prize, to be given at irregular intervals to new or previously unrecognized black writers of unusual talent. The prize honors James Baldwin's "remarkable contributions to twentieth-century literature," including 16 works of fiction and nonfiction published by Dial. The award consists of a silver medal bearing the likeness of Baldwin, given at a presentation ceremony in New York City, and publication of the winning manuscript by The Dial Press. Further information can be obtained from The Dial Press, Publicity and Advertising Department, One Dag Hammarskjöld Plaza (245 East 47 Street), New York, New York 10017.

1979
Raymond Andrews
Appalachee Red

Doubleday & Company, Inc.

LeBaron R. Barker, Jr., Fiction Award

This award was established in 1974 to honor the memory of LeBaron R. Barker, Jr., editor-in-chief of Doubleday & Company, who at the time of his death in 1973 was senior editorial consultant for the firm. It is presented as recognition and encouragement for a Doubleday author whose current book represents a distinct advance in the author's craftsmanship. It is this sort of encouragement that Lee Barker gave during his many years of devotion to writers. The award of $2,500 is presented annually at Doubleday and is announced early in the calendar year. The judges are Margaret Cousins, Arthur Hailey, and Irving Stone. Doubleday also sponsors the O. Henry Awards, which are listed in the Short Story Prizes section.

1975
  Jane Gilmore Rushing
  Mary Dove
1976
  Shelby Hearen
  Now and Another Time

1977
  No award

E. P. Dutton & Company, Inc.

The Dutton Animal Book Award

Inspired by the great success of Gavin Maxwell's *Ring of Bright Water*, the story of two unforgettable otters, E. P. Dutton & Company, Inc., 201 Park Avenue South, New York, New York 10003, announced in 1962 an international literary prize that is now a $15,000 advance against all earnings, to be given to the author of the manuscript judged by the Dutton editors to be the best book-length work of adult fiction or non-fiction relating to animals. The contest is open to new authors and to previously published authors throughout the world, but manuscripts must be submitted in the English language. No manuscript of fewer than 35,000 words is eligible. The contest is annual, with an opening date of January 1 and a closing date of December 31. Dutton also sponsors the Dutton Best Sports Stories Awards, which are listed in the Short Story Prizes section.

1963
  Sterling North
  Rascal
1964
  Robert Murphy
  The Pond
1965
  No award
1966
  Faith McNulty
  The Whooping Crane: The Bird That Defies Extinction
1967
  Daniel P. Mannix
  The Fox and the Hound

1968
  No award
1969
  Sterling North
  The Wolfling
1970–1974
  No awards
1975
  Dayton O. Hyde
  Strange Companion
1976–1979
  No awards

The Man in His Environment Book Award

E. P. Dutton & Company, Inc., established this award in 1970 with the hope of stimulating the writing of outstanding books on ecological subjects. The only one of its kind given by any publisher, it is offered annually for the best manuscript dealing with the past, present, or future of man in his environment, natural or manmade. Dutton guarantees a minimum of $10,000 as an advance against all earnings to the author of the prize-winning manuscript, a single full-length work of adult nonfiction. The contest is open to new authors and to authors whose works have already been published, to authors in the United States, and to foreign authors. Manuscripts will be judged by the Dutton editors and may be submitted from January 1 to December 31. On the manuscript itself this statement should appear: Submitted for The Man in His Environment Book Award. Address manuscripts to the Man in His Environment Book Award, E. P. Dutton & Company, Inc., 201 Park Avenue South, New York, New York 10003.

1977
Richard A. Leakey and Roger Lewin
Origins

1978
Elliot Porter
Antarctica

Harvard University Press

Faculty Prize

The Faculty Prize of Harvard University Press, 79 Garden Street, Cambridge, Massachusetts 02138, was established during the academic year 1954–1955 to encourage the production of scholarly books by the faculty and to help Harvard University Press in its efforts to serve as the book publishing arm of the university. The winner of the first Faculty Prize was announced in April 1956. An annual award of $2,000 was given to the winner. Members of the teaching or research staff of Harvard University were eligible. A book-length manuscript was required, and decision was made by the Board of Syndics of the Press. The award was presented at Harvard University.

1956
Harry A. Wolfson
Faith, Trinity, Incarnation, The Philosophy of the Church Fathers, Vol. 1

1957
Mark DeWolfe Howe
Justice Holmes: The Shaping Years, 1841–1870

1958
Franklin L. Ford
Strasbourg in Transition, 1648–1789

1959
Merle Fainsod
Smolensk under Soviet Rule

1960
Renato Poggioli
The Poets of Russia, 1890–1930

1961
Sydney J. Freedberg
Painting of the High Renaissance in Rome and Florence, 1475–1521

1962
Herschel Baker
William Hazlitt
1963
Walter Kaiser
Praisers of Folly
Barry Dean Karl
Executive Reorganization and Reform
1964
Walter Jackson Bate
John Keats
1965
Bernard Bailyn
Pamphlets of the American Revolution, Vol. 1
1966
Don K. Price
The Scientific Estate
1967
Alfred B. Harbage
Conceptions of Shakespeare
1968
Giles Constable
The Letters of Peter the Venerable
1969
No award

1970
W. K. Jordan
Edward VI
Simon Kuznets
Economic Growth of Nations
1971
I. Bernard Cohen
Introduction to Newton's Principia
John Rawls
A Theory of Justice
1972
No award
1973
George M. A. Hanfmann
Letters from Sardis
1974
Stephan Thernstrom
The Other Bostonians: Poverty and Progress in the American Metropolis, 1880–1970
1975
Paul C. Mangelsdorf
Corn: Its Origin, Evolution, and Improvement
Discontinued

Robert Troup Paine Prize

The Robert Troup Paine Publication Fund was established under the will of Dr. Martyn Paine in memory of his son. A $3,000 prize, in addition to royalties, is awarded every four years to the author or authors of a manuscript chosen to be the best work on a specified subject in the natural and social sciences accepted by Harvard University Press during the preceding four years. The winning manuscript is designated a Robert Troup Paine Prize Treatise and is published by Harvard University Press. Eligible manuscripts must be original unpublished works of book length and may be of single or multiple authorship. The topics for the first four prizes are listed below. No award was given in 1978. The topic selected for the 1981 prize is materia medica and therapeutics. Manuscripts are welcome from the entire medical community on any relevant area of significant new research, clinical synthesis, expositions for the interested layperson, or innovative approaches to instruction. Submissions should be sent to the Editor for Science and Medicine, Harvard University Press, 79 Garden Street, Cambridge, Massachusetts 02138.

HISTORY OF RELIGION

1962
  Heiko A. Oberman
  The Harvest of Medieval Theology

ROLE OF COMMERCE IN SOCIETY

1966
  Raymond de Roover
  The Rise and Decline of the Medici Bank, 1397–1494

  Alasdair I. MacBean
  Export Instability and Economic Development

HISTORY AND PHILOSOPHY OF MEDICINE

1970
  Ralph C. Croizier
  Traditional Medicine in Modern China

LAW AND SOCIETY

1974
  John Rawls
  A Theory of Justice

Houghton Mifflin Company

Literary Fellowships

This is the oldest publisher-sponsored award of its kind, established in 1935. It is designed to encourage promising writers and to help authors complete literary projects of outstanding merit in fiction and nonfiction. There are no deadlines for applications or awards; an award may be granted at any time for a project that qualifies. The awards are $10,000 each, of which $2,500 is an outright payment and $7,500 an advance against royalties. The fellowships are open to all writers for a finished manuscript or a work in progress. At least fifty pages of the project and a description of its theme and intention must accompany each application, which may be obtained from Houghton Mifflin Company, 2 Park Street, Boston, Massachusetts 02107. Since some years may elapse between the granting of a fellowship, its official announcement, and the publication of a book, the dates in the list below indicate the years of publication. To commemorate the tenth anniversary of the fellowships, a special poetry fellowship of $1,000 was offered in 1944 and awarded to Elizabeth Bishop for *North and South*. In 1960, the twenty-fifth anniversary, Houghton Mifflin Company and the magazine *Esquire* gave a joint fellowship that was won by Ellen Douglas for her novel *A Family's Affairs*.

1936
  E. P. O'Donnell
  Green Margins
1937
  Jenny Ballou
  Spanish Prelude

  Clelie Benton Huggins
  Point Noir

1938
  Dorothy Baker
  Young Man with a Horn

David Cornel DeJong
Old Haven
1939
Robert Penn Warren
Night Rider
1940
Helen Todd
A Man Named Grant
1941
Mary King O'Donnell
Quincie Bolliver

Maurine Whipple
The Giant Joshua
1944
Elizabeth Bishop
North and South

A. Fleming MacLeish
Cone of Silence
1945
Joseph Wechsberg
Looking for a Bluebird
1946
Ann Petry
The Street
1947
Donald MacRae
Dwight Craig
1948
Beatrice Griffith
American Me

Helen Mears
Mirror for Americans, Japan
1950
Anthony West
The Vintage
1951
Arthur Mizener
The Far Side of Paradise

Rebecca Patterson
The Riddle of Emily Dickinson

Fred Ross
Jackson Mahaffey
1952
Madison Cooper
Sironia, Texas

1953
Charles Bracelen Flood
Love Is a Bridge
1954
Siegel Fleisher
The Lion and the Honeycomb

Harold Livingstone
The Coasts of the Earth

Milton Lott
The Last Hunt
1956
Eugene Burdick
The Ninth Wave

Edward Hoagland
Cat Man
1957
Herbert Simmons
Corner Boy
1959
Philip Roth
Goodbye Columbus
1960
Ellen Douglas
A Family's Affairs
1961
William Brammer
The Gay Place
1962
Clancy Sigal
Going Away
1965
John Stewart Certer
Full Fathom Five
1966
Berry Morgan
Pursuit

Margaret Walker
Jubilee
1967
Willie Morris
North toward Home

Robert Stone
A Hall of Mirrors
1969
Edward Hannibal
Chocolate Days, Popsicle Weeks

Georgia McKinley
Follow the Running Grass

1970
Elizabeth Cullinan
House of Gold

1972
Helen Yglesias
How She Died

1974
Henry Bromell
The Slightest Distance

1978
Julia Marcus
Uncle

Louisiana State University Press

Jules F. Landry Award

Offered by Louisiana State University Press, Baton Rouge, Louisiana 70803, this award was established in May 1968 with a gift of $10,000 from Jules F. Landry to stimulate scholarship and give recognition to the authors of scholarly books. A stipend of $1,000 is presented annually to the author of the book that adds the greatest distinction to the publication list of Louisiana State University Press in the fields of Southern history, Southern biography, or Southern literature submitted to the Press the previous year.

1968
George B. Tindall
The Emergence of the New South, 1913–1945
1969
David M. Potter
The South and the Sectional Conflict
1970
Dan T. Carter
Scottsboro
1971
Thomas Lawrence Connelly
Autumn of Glory
1972
Robert F. Durden
The Gray and the Black
1973
William C. Davis
Breckinridge

1974
John Pilkington
Stark Young: A Life in the Arts
1975
John Hope Franklin
A Southern Odyssey
1976
Thomas Daniel Young
Gentleman in a Dustcoat
1977
J. Mills Thornton III
Politics and Power in a Slave Society
1978
Louis D. Rubin, Jr.
The Wary Fugitives
1979
William Gillette
Retreat from Reconstruction, 1867–1878

McGraw-Hill Book Company

John Robert Gregg Award in Business Education

Offered by the Gregg Division of McGraw-Hill, Inc., 1221 Avenue of the Americas, New York, New York 10020, this award was established in 1953 in honor of the man who originated the widely used system of shorthand. Its purpose is to stimulate, encourage, and reward outstanding contributions to the advancement of business education. The recipient of the award must have made an outstanding, meritorious contribution to the development and advancement of business education. The contribution must be of current significance, i.e., a contribution that has come to be recognized or sustained in recognition within two calendar years preceding the year in which the award is made. The contribution may be a single achievement or a group of achievements, developments, or activities directly related to each other. The award consists of a citation and $1,000. It is presented at the annual convention of the National Business Education Association, usually held in April.

1953
  Frederick G. Nichols
1954
  Paul S. Lomax
1955
  David D. Lessenberry
1956
  Elvin S. Eyster
1957
  Hamden L. Forkner
1958
  Jessie Graham
1959
  Ann Brewington
1960
  Lloyd V. Douglas
1961
  Paul A. Carlson
1962
  Herbert A. Tonne
1963
  Paul F. Muse
1964
  Gladys Bahr
1965
  Ray G. Price

1966
  Russell J. Hosler
1967
  Samuel J. Wanous
1968
  McKee Fisk
1969
  Bernard A. Shilt
1970
  Alton B. Parker Liles
1971
  Ruth I. Anderson
1972
  J. Marshall Hanna
1973
  Warren G. Meyer
1974
  Lawrence W. Erickson
1975
  Estelle L. Popham
1976
  John L. Rowe
1977
  F. Kendrick Bangs
1978
  Louis C. Nanassy

Robert E. Slaughter Research Award

The Gregg Division of McGraw-Hill established the Robert E. Slaughter Research Award in order to stimulate, encourage, and reward outstanding contributions to the advancement of business, office, and distributive education through research. Each recipient of the award receives a citation and $1,000. A maximum of three recipients of the award may be selected in any one year. One of the three awards is reserved for research involving Gregg shorthand teaching methodology; the additional awards may be given for research in any other field of business, office, or distributive education. Studies may be doctoral dissertations, master's theses, or independent research. Each study must have been completed during the preceding twelve months prior to June 1 of the year in which the award is made. Though all studies will remain the property of the researchers, McGraw-Hill will have the right to publish and distribute free any part or all of the studies. The award is presented at the annual convention of the American Vocational Association, usually held in December.

1975
  L. Eugene Jones
  Gary N. McLean
1976
  M. Christine Gilmore
  Thomas O. Stanley
  Boyd G. Worthington

1977
  Thomas B. Duff
  Rita C. Kutie
1978
  Norma J. Olson

Pennsylvania State University Press

Louis H. Bell Memorial Award

The Pennsylvania State University Press, University Press Building, University Park, Pennsylvania 16802, established the Louis H. Bell Memorial Award in 1960 to recognize superior scholarly books. The recipient of the award must be a member of the teaching or research staff of Pennsylvania State University who has submitted the best book manuscript. The award of $1,000 is given annually in June at the university.

1960
  Helen Adolf
  Visio Pacis: Holy City and Grail
1961
  Philip Shriver Klein
  President James Buchanan: A Biography
1962
  Will Mason
  Clarification of the Monetary Standard

1963
  Jessie Bernard
  Academic Women

1964 –1979
  No awards

Playboy Magazine

Playboy Editorial Awards

The first *Playboy* award was presented in 1957 to pay tribute to the writers who participated in the young magazine's success. Through the years, the categories have changed and increased in number. Awards are currently presented to writers in six categories, as well as to artists and photographers, but the categories may well change in the future, depending upon the types of material published in the magazine. All free-lance contributors of written material to *Playboy* are eligible for awards. The magazine's editors choose winners from material published during the calendar year and announce them in *Playboy*'s January issue. The awards, $1,000 and an engraved medallion, are presented in New York City at a luncheon, cocktail party, or dinner, or they are mailed. During 1971–1978, awards of $500 and a medallion were also given to runners-up. Only first-prize award winners are listed below. Inquiries concerning these awards should be sent to *Playboy* Editorial Awards, *Playboy* Magazine, 919 North Michigan Avenue, Chicago, Illinois 60611.

1957
    Herbert Gold
    "The Right Kind of Pride" (Fiction)
1958
    George Langelaan
    "The Fly" (Fiction)
1959
    John Keats
    "Eros and Unreason in Detroit" (Nonfiction)

    Richard Matheson
    "The Distributor" (Fiction)
1960
    Ralph Ginzburg
    "Cult of the Aged Leader" (Nonfiction)
    John Wallace
    "I Love You, Miss Irvine" (Fiction)
1961
    Charles Beaumont
    "Chaplin" (Nonfiction)
    Ken Purdy
    "The Book of Tony" (Fiction)
1962
    Harvey Jacobs
    "The Lion's Share" (Fiction)
    Ken Purdy
    "Hypnosis" (Nonfiction)

1963
    James Jones
    "The Thin Red Line" (Fiction)
    Ken Purdy
    "Stirling Moss: A Nodding Acquaintance with Death" (Nonfiction)
1964
    William Iversen
    "Youth, Love, Death and the Hubby Image" (Nonfiction)
    Bernard Malamud
    "Naked Nude" (Fiction)
1965
    Romain Gary
    "A Bit of a Dreamer, a Bit of a Fool" (Fiction)
    Dan Greenburg
    "How to Be a Jewish Mother" (Humor/Satire)
    John Clellon Holmes
    "Revolution below the Belt" (Nonfiction)
    Irwin Shaw
    "Once in Aleppo" (Fiction)
1966
    Roald Dahl
    "The Visitor" (Fiction)

Jean Shepherd
"Leopold Doppler and the Orpheum Gravy Boat Ride" (Humor/Satire)

Kenneth Tynan
"Beatle in the Bull Ring" (Nonfiction)

1967

Nat Hentoff
"The Cold Society" (Nonfiction)

Tom Mayer
"The Eastern Sprints" (Best New Writer: Fiction)

Vladimir Nabokov
"Despair" (Fiction)

Jean Shepherd
"Daphne Bigelow and the Spine-Chilling Saga of the Snail-Encrusted Tinfoil Noose" (Humor/Satire)

1968

John Kenneth Galbraith
"Resolving Our Vietnam Problem" (Nonfiction)

Jean Shepherd
"Return of the Smiling Wimpy Doll" (Humor/Satire)

Isaac Bashevis Singer
"The Lecture" (Fiction)

Rafael Steinberg
"Day of Good Fortune" (Best New Writer: Fiction)

1969

John Cheever
"The Yellow Room" (Fiction)

Richard Duggin
"Gamma, Gamma, Gamma" (Best New Writer: Fiction)

Marvin Kitman
"How I Became a Renaissance Man in My Spare Time" (Humor/Satire)

Allan Watts
"Wealth versus Money" (Nonfiction)

1970

Woody Allen
"Snow White" (Satire)

Karl Hess
"The Death of Politics" (Best New Writer: Nonfiction)

Martin Luther King, Jr.
"Testament of Hope" (Essay)

Warner Law
"The Thousand Dollar Cup of Crazy German Coffee" (Best New Writer: Fiction)

James Leigh
"Yes It's Me and I'm Late Again" (Short Story)

Vladimir Nabokov
"Ada" (Fiction)

Eric Norden
"The Paramilitary Right" (Nonfiction)

Jean Shepherd
"Wanda Hickey's Night of Golden Memories" (Nonfiction)

1971

Hal Bennet
"Dotson Gerber Resurrected" (Best New Writer: Fiction)

Stanley Booth
"Furry's Blues" (Best New Writer: Nonfiction)

Richard Curtis
"The Giant Chicken-Eating Frog" (Satire)

David Halberstam
"The Americanization of Vietnam" (Essay)

Marvin Kitman
"George Washington's Expense Account" (Humor)

Joyce Carol Oates
"Saul Bird Says: Relate! Communicate! Liberate!" (Short Story)

Irwin Shaw
"Thomas in Elysium," "Rudolph in Money Land," and "Rich Man's Weather" (Fiction)

Alvin Toffler
"Future Shock" (Nonfiction)

1972

George Axelrod
"Where Am I Now When I Need Me?" (Fiction)

Arthur Hadley
"Goodbye to the Blind Slash Dead Kid's Hooch" (Best New Contributor: Nonfiction)

William Hjortsberg
"Gray Matters" (Best New Contributor: Fiction)

John Clellon Holmes
"Thanksgiving in Florence" (Essay)

Bruce McCall and Brock Yates
"Major Howdy Bixby's Album of Forgotten Warbirds" (Satire)

John McPhee
"Centre Court" (Nonfiction)

Robert Morley
"Morley Meets the Frogs" (Humor)

Sean O'Faolain
"Murder at Cobbler's Hulk" (Short Story)

1973

Herbert Gold
"In the Community of Girls and the Commerce of Culture" (Essay)

G. Barry Golson
"The People—Maybe!" (Satire)

Dan Greenburg
"My First Orgy" (Humor)

Dan Jenkins
"Semi-Tough" (Fiction)

Ed McClanahan
"Grateful Dead I Have Known" (Best New Contributor: Nonfiction)

James Alan McPherson
"The Silver Bullet" (Best New Contributor: Fiction)

Sean O'Faolain
"Falling Rocks, Narrowing Road, Cul-de-Sac, Stop" (Short Story)

Richard Rhodes
"The Killing of the Everglades" (Nonfiction)

1974

Anthony Austin
"When the Americans Came" (Short Story)

George MacDonald Fraser
"Flashman at the Charge" (Fiction)

Nadine Gordimer
"The Conservationist" (Best New Contributor: Fiction)

Germaine Greer
"Seduction Is a Four-Letter Word" (Essay)

John Clellon Holmes
"Gone in October" (Nonfiction)

Wayne McLoughlin and Scot Morris
"The Fallout Follies" (Satire)

William Neely and Bob Ottum
"I Lost It in the Second Turn by 'Stroker Ace' " (Humor)

Roger Rapoport
"It's Enough to Make You Sick" (Best New Contributor: Nonfiction)

1975

Saul Bellow
"Humboldt's Gift" (Fiction)

Carl Bernstein and Bob Woodward
"All the President's Men" (Nonfiction)

Richard Curtis
"Do Plants Have Orgasms?" (Satire)

O'Connell Driscoll
"Jerry Lewis, Birthday Boy" (Best New Contributor: Nonfiction)

Frederick Exley
"Saint Gloria and the Troll" (Essay)

Ed McClanahan
"Little Enis Purses His Muse" (Nonfiction)

Paul Reb
"The Legend of Step-and-a-Half" (Best New Contributor: Fiction)

Dick Tuck
"Watergate Wasn't All My Fault" (Humor)

John Updike
"Nevada" (Short Story)

1976

Harry Crews
"Going Down in Valdeez" (Best New Writer: Nonfiction)

Jay Cronley
"Houston" (Best New Contributor: Nonfiction)

George MacDonald Fraser
"Flashman in the Great Game" (Short Story)

Norman Mailer
"The Fight" (Nonfiction)

Larry McMurtry
"Dunlup Crashes In" (Best New Contributor: Fiction)

Robert S. Wieder
"Clarke Ghent's School Days" (Humor)

1977

Jim Davidson
"Punch Out the IRS" (Best New Contributor: Nonfiction)

Dan Greenburg
"Dominant Writer Seeks Submissive Miss" (Humor)

Alex Haley
"Roots" (Nonfiction)

Ron Kovic
"Born on the Fourth of July" (Essay)

Norman Mailer
"Trial of the Warlock" (Fiction)

Nicholas Meyer
"The West End Horror" (Best New Contributor: Fiction)

Robert Scheer
Jimmy Carter interview and "Jimmy, We Hardly Know Y'all" (Special Award)

Paul Theroux
"The Autumn Dog" (Fiction)

Kurt Vonnegut, Jr.
"Slapstick or Lonesome No More" (Fiction)

1978

Asa Baber
"Commodities Market" (Nonfiction)

Roy Blount, Jr.

"Chairman Billy" (Best New Contributor: Nonfiction)

Marshall Brickman
"The Book of Coasts" (Humor)

John le Carré
"The Honourable Schoolboy" (Fiction)

D. Keith Mano
"Rocky Mountain Hype" (Essay)

Paul Theroux
"Adulterer's Luck" (Short Story)

1979

Buck Henry
"My Night at Plato's" (Humor)

William Hjortsberg
"Falling Angel" (Fiction)

Trevanian
"Switching" (Best New Contributor: Fiction)

John Updike
"The Faint" (Short Story)

Craig Vetter
"Pushed to the Edge" (Nonfiction)

1980

Asa Baber
"The Condominium Conspiracy" (Nonfiction)

Christopher Cerf, Peter Elbling, et al.
"And That's the Way It Was, 1980–1989" (Humor)

Lynda Leidiger
"Snake Head" (Best New Contributor: Fiction)

Norman Mailer
"The Executioner's Song" (Best Major Work)

Richard Price
"Bear Bryant's Miracles" (Best New Contributor: Nonfiction)

Paul Theroux
"White Lies" (Short Story)

Publishers Weekly

Carey-Thomas Award

This award is named for two notable pioneers of American publishing, Mathew Carey of Philadelphia and Isaiah Thomas of Worcester, Massachusetts, who set standards of character, judgment, and vigor for later generations of publishing to emulate. The purpose of the award is to honor creative book publishing at its best, not editorial judgment alone but the exceptional display of initiative, imagination, cooperation with the author, appropriate manufacture, and successful promotion and marketing. Books are nominated for the award by the Bowker book review staff. A jury of three to five is selected annually by *Publishers Weekly*, 1180 Avenue of the Americas, New York, New York 10036, from the ranks of critics, authors, librarians, and booksellers. Every spring the jury names a winning publisher and usually one or two others for honor citations. The awards are in the form of bronze plaques with the names of the publisher, book, author, and members of the jury.

1943
Farrar & Rinehart
Rivers of America series
1944
University of Chicago Press
A Dictionary of American English on Historical Principles
1945
E. P. Dutton & Co., Inc.
The World of Washington Irving, by Van Wyck Brooks
1946
Alfred A. Knopf, Inc.
The American Language, by H. L. Mencken
1947
Duell, Sloan & Pearce, Inc.
The New World, by Stefan Lorant
1948
Oxford University Press
A Study of History, by Arnold Toynbee
1949
William Sloane Associates
American Men of Letters series
1950
Rand McNally & Co.
Cosmopolitan World Atlas

1951
Princeton University Press
The Papers of Thomas Jefferson, ed. by J. P. Boyd and others
1952
Houghton Mifflin Co.
Life in America, by Marshall B. Davidson
1953
The Macmillan Co.
The Diary of George Templeton Strong, 1835–1875, ed. by Allan Nevins and Milton H. Thomas
1954
Houghton Mifflin Co.
The Second World War, by Sir Winston Churchill
1955
Doubleday & Co.
Anchor Books series
1956
Belknap Press of Harvard University Press
The Poems of Emily Dickinson, ed. by T. H. Johnson

1957
Doubleday & Co.
Mainstream of America series
1958
Frederick A. Praeger, Inc.
The New Class, by Milovan Djilas
1959
New York Graphic Society
Complete Letters, by Vincent Van Gogh
1960
Oxford University Press
James Joyce, by Richard Ellmann
1961
Simon & Schuster
The Rise and Fall of the Third Reich, by William L. Shirer
1962
Belknap Press of Harvard University Press
The Adams Papers: Diary and Autobiography of John Adams
1963
Shorewood Publishers
Great Drawings of All Time
1964
Wesleyan University Press
New York Landmarks, ed. by Alan Burnham
1965
Sierra Club
Sierra Club Exhibit Format series, ed. by David Brower
1966
Doubleday & Co.
Anchor Bibles, ed. by William Foxwell Albright and David Noel Freedman
1967
George Braziller, Inc.
The Hours of Catherine of Cleves, introduction and commentaries by John Plummer
1968
Holt, Rinehart & Winston
Wilderness Kingdom: The Journals and Paintings of Father Nicolas Point, trans. and introduction by Joseph P. Donnelly

1969
W. W. Norton & Co.
The Norton Facsimile: The First Folio of Shakespeare, prep. by Charlton Hinman
1970
Alfred A. Knopf, Inc.
Huey Long, by T. Harry Williams
1971
Random House with Maecenas Press and Chanticleer Press
Picasso 347: Collected Drawings of Pablo Picasso
1972
Oxford University Press
The Compact Edition of the Oxford English Dictionary: Complete Text Micrographically Reproduced
1973
Yale University Press
The Children of Pride: A True Story of Georgia and the Civil War, ed. by Robert Manson Myers
1974
Princeton University Press
Bollingen series
1975
McGraw-Hill Book Co.
Madrid Codices of Leonardo da Vinci and *The Unknown Leonardo*, both ed. by Ladislao Reti
1976
Morgan Library/David R. Godine, Publisher
Early Children's Books and Their Illustration, by Gerald Gottlieb
1977
Basic Books
Berggasse 19: The Photographs of Edmund Engelman
1978
Horizon Press
An Autobiography, by Frank Lloyd Wright
1979
Pushcart Press
The Pushcart Prize, III: Best of the Small Presses, ed. by Bill Henderson

Roger Klein Award for Creative Editing

This award was established in 1970 in memory of Roger Klein, who died in 1968. Klein was recognized as one of the most gifted editors in New York City. The award is given to a trade book editor for work of at least five years. Qualifications for this award include the addition of important books and authors to a publishing house's list, developing ideas for books, working with authors, recognizing writing talent, and helping talented authors to realize their potential. Nominations can be made by publishers, editors, authors, or agents. The prize, consisting of a scroll and $1,000, is given biennially at a reception hosted by *Publishers Weekly*. Further information can be obtained from *Publishers Weekly*, 1180 Avenue of the Americas, New York, New York 10036.

1971
  Frances Monson McCullough, Harper & Row
1973
  James Landis, William Morrow
1975
  Michael di Capua, Farrar, Straus & Giroux

1977
  Robert D. Loomis, Random House
1979
  Joseph Kanon, Coward, McCann & Geoghegan

G. P. Putnam's Sons

Putnam Awards

Offered by G. P. Putnam's Sons, Inc., 200 Madison Avenue, New York, New York 10016, the Putnam Awards were given to manuscripts, fiction or nonfiction, by authors whose works had not previously been published by Putnam or associated companies. The award, consisting of a $7,500 advance against royalties and $7,500 to be spent for advertising and promotion, was given to no more than three fiction or nonfiction titles per year.

1960
  William Mulvihill
  The Sands of Kalahari
1961
  Ian Brook
  Jimmy Riddle
1962
  Sanche de Gramont
  The Secret War
1963
  Kay Martin
  All the Gods and Goddesses

1964
  Elliott Baker
  A Fine Madness
  H. R. Hays
  In the Beginnings
  Don Robertson
  A Flag Full of Stars

1965
  Gwyn Griffin
  A Last Lamp Burning

1966
  No award
1967
  Ronald Hardy
  The Savages

1968–1971
  No awards

1972
  Henry Carlisle
  Voyage to the First of December

1973
  Robert Coughlan
  Elizabeth and Catherine

William Turner Huggett
Body Count

1974
Thomas Gifford
The Wind Chill Factor

1975
Bari Wood
The Killing Gift
Discontinued

Syracuse University Press

John Ben Snow Prize

The John Ben Snow Prize, inaugurated in 1978, is given annually by Syracuse University Press for a nonfiction manuscript dealing with some aspect of New York State. The award is made to the author of the unpublished, book-length manuscript that, in the opinion of the selection committee, makes the most distinguished contribution to the study of the upstate area, with emphasis on central New York. The purpose of the award is to encourage the writing of books of genuine significance and literary distinction that will augment knowledge of New York State and appreciation for its unique physical, historical, and cultural characteristics. The award consists of $1,000 advance to the author against royalties and publication by Syracuse University Press. The award was made possible by a grant from the John Ben Snow Foundation. To be eligible, no substantial part of any manuscript can have been published previously, can be under submission for any other award, or can be under consideration simultaneously by any other publisher. Fiction, poetry, books written specifically for children, and unrevised theses are not eligible. December 31 is the final date for submission of manuscripts to be considered for the next year's prize, whose winner is announced in the spring. Inquiries to the Press are required before submission of manuscripts. They should be made to the Director, Syracuse University Press, 1011 East Water Street, Syracuse, New York 13210.

1978
  William H. Armstrong
  Warrior in Two Camps: Ely S. Parker,
  Union General and Seneca Chief

1979
Carleton Mabee
Black Education in New York State:
From Colonial to Modern Times

University of Michigan Press

University of Michigan Press Book Award

Established in 1965 by the University of Michigan Press, 839 Greene Street, Ann Arbor, Michigan 48106, this annual award is given "for the work, written or edited by a University of Michigan faculty member, which has added the greatest distinction to the Press's list." Members of the teaching and research staffs, including emeritus members, of the University of Michigan who have written or edited a book published by the University of Michigan Press within the two preceding calendar years are eligible. The Editorial Committee of the Press makes the selection. The award, $1,000, is given in late September at the annual faculty-staff convocation in the Lecture Hall, Horace H. Rackham School of Graduate Studies, the University of Michigan.

1965
Sidney Fine
The Automobile under the Blue Eagle: Labor, Management, and the Automobile Manufacturing Code

1966
R. H. Super, ed.
For the first five published volumes of his projected eleven-volume edition of *The Complete Prose Works of Matthew Arnold*

1967
Harold K. Jacobson and Eric Stein
Diplomats, Scientists, and Politicians: The United States and the Nuclear Test Ban Negotiations

1968
Austin Warren
The New England Conscience

1969
David Joel Steinberg
Philippine Collaboration in World War II

1970
Robert J. Niess
Zola, Cézanne, and Manet: A Study of "L'Oeuvre"

1971
Sidney Fine
Sit-Down: The General Motors Strike of 1936–1937

1972
Arthur R. Miller
The Assault on Privacy: Computers, Data Banks, and Dossiers

1973
Hans Kurath, Sherman M. Kuhn, and John Reidy
The Middle English Dictionary

1974
Jacob M. Price
France and the Chesapeake: A History of the Tobacco Monopoly, 2 vols.

1975
No award

1976
William Steinhoff
George Orwell and the Origins of 1984

1977
Peter O. Steiner
Mergers: Motives, Effects, Policies

1978
Gary Witherspoon
Language and Art in the Navajo Universe

1979
Rhoads Murphey
The Outsiders: The Western Experience in India and China

William E. Porter
Assault on the Media: The Nixon Years

Writer's Digest

Creative Writing Awards Contest
for Articles, Poetry, and Short Stories

In 1932, *Writer's Digest* announced its first annual short story contest; in subsequent years, article and poetry categories were added. In 1969, the first Creative Writing Awards Contest was held. There are no eligibility restrictions other than that entries be accompanied by an entry form. There are three categories—short story, article, and poetry. Entries are limited to one per category. Short stories are not to exceed 2,000 words; articles are not to exceed 2,500 words; and poetry is not to exceed sixteen lines. Entries are judged by the *Writer's Digest* staff. There is a $500 grand prize awarded to the winning entry, plus 100 merchandise prizes per category. Awards are given annually. The closing date for entries is June 30. Winners are announced in the November issue of *Writer's Digest*, and awards are officially presented at the offices of *Writer's Digest*, 9933 Alliance Road, Cincinnati, Ohio 45242.

Yale University Press

Chester Kerr Award

In 1979, Yale University Press announced the establishment of an annual $1,000 prize to honor Chester Kerr, who had recently retired from the Press after 20 years as its director. The award will be presented for a distinguished work of creative scholarship written by an author under 40 years of age and published by Yale University Press. The award will be made on the recommendation of a jury established by the Press's Governing Board and will be conferred by the board in October following the winning book's year of publication.

Juvenile Prizes

Jane Addams Children's Book Award

The Jane Addams Children's Book Award Committee, 5477 Cedonia Avenue, Baltimore, Maryland 21206, was created in 1953 by the United States Section of the Women's International League for Peace and Freedom, 1213 Race Street, Philadelphia, Pennsylvania 19107, in honor of Jane Addams, one of the founders of the League. The award is now sponsored jointly by the League and by the Jane Addams Peace Association, 777 United Nations Plaza, New York, New York 10017. The purpose of the award is twofold: to encourage publication of books for children that are of literary merit and contain constructive themes and to recognize and commend authors and publishers of such books. The committee sends an announcement of the award to publishers of children's books and invites their participation; then each member of the Award Committee reads and evaluates each book on the basis of the established criteria. Since 1972, honor books have also been chosen. The award is presented annually for a book published the previous year that best promotes peace, the dignity and equality of all peoples, and social justice. Announcement is made on Jane Addams's birthday, September 6. Authors receive hand-illuminated certificates, and publishers affix a silver seal to the book jacket of the award book.

1953
  Eva Knox Evans
  People Are Important (Capitol)
1954
  Jean Ketchum
  Stick-in-the-Mud (W. R. Scott)
1955
  Elizabeth Yates
  Rainbow round the World (Bobbs)
1956
  Arna Bontemps
  Story of the Negro (Knopf)
1957
  Margot Benary-Isbert
  Blue Mystery (Harcourt)
1958
  William O. Steele
  The Perilous Road (Harcourt)

1959
  No award
1960
  Edith Patterson Meyer
  Champions of Peace (Little)
1961
  Shirley L. Arora
  What Then, Raman? (Follett)
1962
  Aimée Sommerfelt
  The Road to Agra (Criterion)
1963
  Ryerson Johnson
  The Monkey and the Wild, Wild Wind
  (Abelard)
1964
  John F. Kennedy
  Profiles in Courage (Harper)

1965
  Duane Bradley
  Meeting with a Stranger (Lippincott)
1966
  Emily Cheney Neville
  Berries Goodman (Harper)
1967
  Robert Burch
  Queenie Peavy (Viking)
1968
  Eric Haugaard
  The Little Fishes (Houghton)
1969
  Esther Hautzig
  The Endless Steppe: Growing Up in Siberia (Crowell)
1970
  Theodore Taylor
  The Cay (Doubleday)
1971
  Cornelia Meigs
  Jane Addams: Pioneer of Social Justice (Little)

1972
  Betty Underwood
  · *The Tamarack Tree* (Houghton)
1973
  S. Carl Hirsch
  The Riddle of Racism (Viking)
1974
  Nicholasa Mohr
  Nilda (Harper)
1975
  Charlotte Pomerantz
  The Princess and the Admiral (Addison-Wesley)
1976
  Eloise Greenfield
  Paul Robeson (Crowell)
1977
  Milton Meltzer
  Never to Forget: The Jews of the Holocaust (Harper)
1978
  Laurence Yep
  Child of the Owl (Harper)

American Association of University Women, North Carolina Division, Award in Juvenile Literature

This award, established in 1952, is offered by the North Carolina Division of the American Association of University Women. The award, announced annually in November, is given to reward the creative activity involved in the writing of juvenile literature with the hope of stimulating throughout the state an interest in worthwhile children's literature. All works published and submitted to the Secretary of the North Carolina Literary and Historical Association, 109 East Jones Street, Raleigh, North Carolina 27611, are judged without regard to length, but each must have been published in book form. Both fiction and nonfiction books are eligible. Only one award is made each year, and in the case of multiple authorship, only one award is given. For a work to be eligible for the award, the author or authors shall have maintained either legal residence or actual physical residence, or a combination of both, in North Carolina for the three years immediately preceding the close of the contest period. The award, a cup, is officially presented at the annual meeting of the North Carolina Literary and Historical Association in Raleigh. Further information is available from Barbara Ann Hughes, 4208 Galax Drive, Raleigh, North Carolina 27612.

1953
Ruth Carroll and Latrobe Carroll
Peanut (Oxford Univ. Press)
1954
Mebane Holoman Burgwyn
Penny Rose (Oxford Univ. Press)
1955
Ruth Carroll and Latrobe Carroll
Digby, the Only Dog (Oxford Univ. Press)
1956
Julia Montgomery Street
Fiddler's Fancy (Follett)
1957
Nell Wise Wechter
Taffy of Torpedo Junction (Blair)
1958
Ina B. Forbus
The Secret Circle (Viking)
1959
Thelma Harrington Bell
Captain Ghost (Viking)
1960
Jonathan Daniels
Stonewall Jackson (Random)
1961
Glen Rounds
Beaver Business: An Almanac (Prentice)
1962
Manly Wade Wellman
Rifles at Ramsour's Mill: A Tale of the Revolutionary War (Washburn)
1963
Julia Montgomery Street
Dulcie's Whale (Bobbs)
1964
Randall Jarrell
The Bat-Poet (Macmillan)
1965
Alexander Key
The Forgotten Door (Westminster)
1966
Julia Montgomery Street and Richard Walser
North Carolina Parade (Univ. of North Carolina Press)

1967
Glen Rounds
The Snake Tree (World)
1968
Neal F. Austin
A Biography of Thomas Wolfe (Beacham)
1969
Mary B. Gillett
Bugles at the Border (Blair)
1970
Mebane Holoman Burgwyn
The Crackajack Pony (Lippincott)
1971
Suzanne Newton
Purro and the Prattleberries (Westminster)
1972
No award
1973
Barbara M. Parramore
The People of North Carolina (Sadlier)
1974
Suzanne Newton
c/o Arnold's Corner (Westminster)
1975
Alexander Key
The Magic Meadow (Westminster)
1976
Glen Rounds
Mr. Yowder and the Lion Roar Capsules (Holiday House)
1977
Ruth White Miller
The City Rose (McGraw)
1978
Suzanne Newton
What Are You Up To, William Thomas? (Westminster)
1979
Suzanne Newton
Rubella and the Old Focus Home (Westminster)

American Library Association

The American Library Association (ALA), Association for Library Service to Children (ALSC) Division, 50 East Huron Street, Chicago, Illinois 60611, administers the following awards in the field of children's literature. (The ALSC was formerly the Children's Services Division.)

Mildred L. Batchelder Award

Offered by the Association for Library Service to Children (ALSC), this award was established in 1966. It is presented to an American publisher for the most outstanding children's book originally published in a foreign language, in a foreign country, and subsequently published in the United States. Selection is made by a committee appointed annually by the ALSC president. The award is announced annually at the ALA midwinter meeting, and a citation is presented on April 2, International Children's Book Day, at an ALSC program presented at a library in the United States designated for the award presentation.

1968
Alfred A. Knopf, Inc.
The Little Man, by Erich Kastner, trans. by James Kirkup

1969
Charles S. Scribner's Sons
Don't Take Teddy, by Mrs. Friis-Baastad, trans. by Elisa Holt Somme McKinnon

1970
Holt, Rinehart and Winston, Inc.
Wildcat under Glass, trans. by Edward Fenton

1971
Pantheon Books
In the Land of Ur, by Hans Baumann, transcribed by Stella Humphries

1972
Holt, Rinehart and Winston, Inc.
Friedrich, by Hans Peter Richter, trans. by Edite Kroll

1973
William Morrow and Company
Pulgg, by S. R. Van Iterson, trans. by Alexander Gode and Alison Gode

1974
E. P. Dutton & Company, Inc.
Petros' War, by Alki Zei, trans. by Edward Fenton

1975
Crown Publishers, Inc.
An Old Tale Carved Out of Stone, by A. Linevski, trans. by Maria Polushkin

1976
Henry Z. Walck, Inc.
The Cat and Mouse Who Shared a House, retold by Ruth Hürlimann, trans. by Anthea Bell

1977
Atheneum Publishers
The Leopard, by Cecil Bødker, trans. by Gunnar Poulsen

1978
No award

1979
Harcourt Brace Jovanovich, Inc.
Rabbit Island, by Jörg Steiner, trans. by Ann Conrad Lammers
Franklin Watts, Inc.
Konrad, by Christine Nostlinger, trans. by Anthea Bell

Caldecott Medal

Offered by the Association for Library Service to Children, the Caldecott Medal, first awarded in 1938, is presented for the most distinguished American picture book for children. It was the first award established with the purpose of giving recognition to the illustrator of a book.

The award was named for the famous English illustrator Randolph Caldecott, who died in St. Augustine, Florida, in 1886. He, together with Kate Greenaway and Walter Crane, began a new era of picture books for children. The bronze medal is the gift of Daniel Melcher, son of the founder of the award. On the face of the medal is a reproduction of Caldecott's original illustration of John Gilpin on his famous ride. The reverse side carries an illustration of "four and twenty blackbirds baked in a pie" and the inscription "For the most distinguished American picture book for children." Presentation of the medal is made annually at the ALA summer conference.

1938
    Dorothy Lathrop
    Animals of the Bible. Text selected by Helen Dean Fish from the King James Bible (Stokes)
1939
    Thomas Handforth
    Mei Li (Doubleday)
1940
    Ingri d'Aulaire and Edgar d'Aulaire
    Abraham Lincoln (Doubleday)
1941
    Robert Lawson
    They Were Strong and Good (Viking)
1942
    Robert McCloskey
    Make Way for Ducklings (Viking)
1943
    Virginia Lee Burton
    The Little House (Houghton)
1944
    Louis Slobodkin
    Many Moons, by James Thurber (Harcourt)
1945
    Elizabeth Orton Jones
    Prayer for a Child, by Rachel Field (Macmillan)
1946
    Maud Petersham and Miska Petersham
    The Rooster Crows (Macmillan)

1947
    Leonard Weisgard
    The Little Island, by Golden MacDonald (Doubleday)
1948
    Roger Duvoisin
    White Snow, Bright Snow, by Alvin Tresselt (Lothrop)
1949
    Berta Hader and Elmer Hader
    The Big Snow (Macmillan)
1950
    Leo Politi
    Song of the Swallows (Scribner)
1951
    Katherine Milhous
    The Egg Tree (Scribner)
1952
    Nicolas Mordvinoff
    Finders Keepers, by Will Lipkind and Nicolas Mordvinoff (Harcourt)
1953
    Lynd Ward
    The Biggest Bear (Houghton)
1954
    Ludwig Bemelmans
    Madeline's Rescue (Viking)
1955
    Marcia Brown
    Cinderella (Scribner)

1956
Feodor Rojankovsky
Frog Went A-Courtin, by John Lang-
staff (Harcourt)
1957
Marc Simont
A Tree Is Nice, by Janice May Udry
(Harper)
1958
Robert McCloskey
Time of Wonder (Viking)
1959
Barbara Cooney
Chanticleer and the Fox (Crowell)
1960
Marie Hall Ets
Nine Days to Christmas (Viking)
1961
Nicolas Sidjakov
Baboushka and the Three Kings (Par-
nassus)
1962
Marcia Brown
Once a Mouse (Scribner)
1963
Ezra Jack Keats
The Snowy Day (Viking)
1964
Maurice Sendak
Where the Wild Things Are (Harper)
1965
Beni Montresor
May I Bring a Friend?, by Beatrice S.
de Regniers (Atheneum)
1966
Nonny Hogrogian
Always Room for One More (Holt)
1967
Evaline Ness
Sam, Bangs & Moonshine (Holt)
1968
Ed Emberley
Drummer Hoff (Prentice)

1969
Uri Shulevitz
*The Fool of the World and the Flying
Ship*, by Arthur Ransome (Farrar)
1970
William Steig
Sylvester and the Magic Pebble (Si-
mon & Schuster)
1971
Gail E. Haley
A Story-A Story (Atheneum)
1972
Nonny Hogrogian
One Fine Day (Macmillan)
1973
Blair Lent
The Funny Little Woman, retold by Ar-
lene Mosel (Dutton)
1974
Margot Zemach
Duffy and the Devil, retold by Harve
Zemach (Farrar)
1975
Gerald McDermott
*Arrow to the Sun: A Pueblo Indian
Tale* (Viking)

1976
Leo Dillon and Diane Dillon
*Why Mosquitoes Buzz in People's
Ears*, retold by Verna Aardema (Dial)
1977
Leo Dillon and Diane Dillon
Ashanti to Zulu, by Margaret Mus-
grove (Dial)

1978
Peter Spier
Noah's Ark (Doubleday)

1979
Paul Goble
The Girl Who Loved Wild Horses
(Bradbury)
1980
Ox- Cart Man
1981
Fables

1982
Chris Van Allsburg
Jumanji (Houghton Mifflin)

John Newbery Medal

The John Newbery Medal has been awarded annually since 1922 by the Association for Library Service to Children for the most distinguished contribution to American literature for children.

Presentation of this medal, which is for a book published during the preceding year, is made at the annual summer conference of ALA at the same time as the Caldecott Medal. The bronze medal, gift of Daniel Melcher, son of the founder of the award, was designed by the American sculptor, René Chambellan. The prize for the best juvenile book is named for John Newbery (1713–1767), a London bookseller, who first conceived the idea of publishing books especially for children.

1922
    Hendrik Willem Van Loon
    The Story of Mankind (Liveright)
1923
    Hugh Lofting
    The Voyages of Doctor Dolittle (Lippincott)
1924
    Charles Boardman Hawes
    The Dark Frigate (Little)
1925
    Charles J. Finger
    Tales from Silver Lands (Doubleday)
1926
    Arthur Bowie Chrisman
    Shen of the Sea (Dutton)
1927
    Will James
    Smoky, the Cowhorse (Scribner)
1928
    Dham Gopal Mukerji
    Gay-Neck, the Story of a Pigeon (Dutton)
1929
    Eric P. Kelly
    The Trumpeter of Krakow, a Tale of the Fifteenth Century (Macmillan)
1930
    Rachel Field
    Hitty, Her First Hundred Years (Macmillan)

1931
    Elizabeth Coatsworth
    The Cat Who Went to Heaven (Macmillan)
1932
    Laura Adams Armer
    Waterless Mountain (Longmans)
1933
    Elizabeth Foreman Lewis
    Young Fu of the Upper Yangtze (Winston)
1934
    Cornelia Meigs
    Invincible Louisa (Little)
1935
    Monica Shannon
    Dobry (Viking)
1936
    Carol Ryrie Brink
    Caddie Woodlawn (Macmillan)
1937
    Ruth Sawyer
    Roller Skates (Viking)
1938
    Kate Seredy
    The White Stag (Viking)
1939
    Elizabeth Enright
    Thimble Summer (Rinehart)
1940
    James Daugherty
    Daniel Boone (Viking)

1941
   Armstrong Sperry
   Call It Courage (Macmillan)
1942
   Walter D. Edmonds
   The Matchlock Gun (Dodd)
1943
   Elizabeth Janet Gray
   Adam of the Road (Viking)
1944
   Esther Forbes
   Johnny Tremain: A Novel for Old and Young (Houghton)
1945
   Robert Lawson
   Rabbit Hill (Viking)
1946
   Lois Lenski
   Strawberry Girl (Lippincott)
1947
   Carolyn Sherwin Bailey
   Miss Hickory (Viking)
1948
   William Pène du Bois
   The Twenty-One Balloons (Viking)
1949
   Marguerite Henry
   King of the Wind (Rand McNally)
1950
   Marguerite de Angeli
   The Door in the Wall (Doubleday)
1951
   Elizabeth Yates
   Amos Fortune, Free Man (Aladdin)
1952
   Eleanor Estes
   Ginger Pye (Harcourt)
1953
   Ann Nolan Clark
   Secret of the Andes (Viking)
1954
   Joseph Krumgold
   . . . And Now Miguel (Crowell)
1955
   Meindert DeJong
   The Wheel on the School (Harper)

1956
   Jean Lee Latham
   Carry On, Mr. Bowditch (Houghton)
1957
   Virginia Sorenson
   Miracles on Maple Hill (Harcourt)
1958
   Harold Keith
   Rifles for Watie (Crowell)
1959
   Elizabeth George Speare
   The Witch of Blackbird Pond (Houghton)
1960
   Joseph Krumgold
   Onion John (Crowell)
1961
   Scott O'Dell
   Island of the Blue Dolphins (Houghton)
1962
   Elizabeth George Speare
   The Bronze Bow (Houghton)
1963
   Madeleine L'Engle
   A Wrinkle in Time (Ariel/Farrar)
1964
   Emily Neville
   It's Like This, Cat (Harper)
1965
   Maia Wojciechowska
   Shadow of a Bull (Atheneum)
1966
   Elizabeth Borton de Treviño
   I, Juan de Pareja (Farrar)
1967
   Irene Hunt
   Up a Road Slowly (Follett)

1968
   Elaine Konigsburg
   From the Mixed-Up Files of Mrs. Basil E. Frankweiler (Atheneum)
1969
   Lloyd Alexander
   The High King (Holt)

1980
Joan Blos
A Gathering of Days

1981
Paterson, Katherine
Jacob Have & Loved

1970
  William H. Armstrong
  Sounder (Harper)
1971
  Betsy Byars
  Summer of the Swans (Viking)
1972
  Robert C. O'Brien
  Mrs. Frisby and the Rats of NIMH (Atheneum)
1973
  Jean Craighead George
  Julie of the Wolves (Harper)
1974
  Paula Fox
  The Slave Dancer (Bradbury)

1975
  Virginia Hamilton
  M. C. Higgins, the Great (Macmillan)
1976
  Susan Cooper
  The Grey King (Atheneum)
1977
  Mildred D. Taylor
  Roll of Thunder, Hear My Cry (Dial)
1978
  Katherine Paterson
  Bridge to Terabithia (Crowell)
1979
  Ellen Raskin
  The Westing Game (Dutton)

Laura Ingalls Wilder Award

1982
Nancy Willard
a Visit to William Blake's Inn
(Harcourt Brace Jovanovich)

This award, offered by the Association for Library Service to Children (ALSC), was established in 1954. Beginning in 1960, the award has been made every five years "to an author or illustrator whose books, published in the United States, have over a period of years made a substantial and lasting contribution to literature for children." In 1980, the award will be made every three years. A committee of six ALSC members receives nominations from ALSC members and selects a slate of nominees. The winner is chosen by mail ballot of the ALSC membership. The award is a medal designed by Garth Williams, who illustrated the Wilder Little House series, and it is presented at the ALA summer conference.

1954
  Laura Ingalls Wilder
1960
  Clara Ingram Judson
1965
  Ruth Sawyer Durand

1970
  E. B. White
1975
  Beverly Cleary

Hans Christian Andersen International Children's Book Medals

This award is offered by the International Board on Books for Young People (IBBY). Every two years a medal is presented to a living author and a living illustrator who, by the outstanding value of their complete works, have made a distinguished contribution to international literature for young people. (Until 1966 the prize was given only to an author for a specific book.) An international jury of members appointed by the Executive Committee of IBBY makes the decision from selections submitted from member countries throughout the world. Further information may be obtained from International Board on Books for Young People, Secretariat, Leonhardsgraben 38a, CH-4051, Basel, Switzerland.

1956
Eleanor Farjeon (United Kingdom)
1958
Astrid Lindgren (Sweden)
1960
Erich Kästner (Germany)
1962
Meindert DeJong (United States)
1964
Rene Guillot (France)
1966
Alois Carigiet, author (Switzerland)
Tove Jansson, illustrator (Finland)
1968
James Krüss, author (Germany)
José María Sánchez-Silva, author (Spain)
Jiri Trnka, illustrator (Czechoslovakia)

1970
Gianni Rodari, author (Italy)
Maurice Sendak, illustrator (United States)
1972
Scott O'Dell, author (United States)
Ib Spang Olsen, illustrator (Denmark)
1974
Maria Gripe, author (Sweden)
Farshid Mesghali, illustrator (Iran)
1976
Cecil Bødker, author (Denmark)
Tatjana Mawrina, illustrator (U.S.S.R.)
1978
Paula Fox, author (United States)
Svend Otto S., illustrator (Denmark)

Association of Jewish Libraries

AJL Book Award

The Association of Jewish Libraries (AJL) established its annual Book Award in 1968 to honor the book deemed to have made the most outstanding contribution during the previous year in the field of Jewish literature for children and young people. Any book of fiction or nonfiction for children age 16 or under that contains even marginal Jewish reference will be considered, whether from a trade publisher or a Jewish house. Books should have a "definite, positive Jewish focus," but it can be ethical Judaism rather than an explicitly religious view. The selection of winners is made by a committee of five Judaica librarians from the AJL Synagogue and Schools Division. The award, a framed scroll and gold seals for the book jackets, is presented at a banquet during the AJL national convention in June. Publishers or authors with suitable books to submit may write to Rita C. Frischer, AJL Book Award Chairperson, 9515 Gerald Avenue, Sepulveda, California 91343. Inquiries to the Association of Jewish Libraries should be sent to the National Foundation for Jewish Culture, 122 East 42 Street, Room 1512, New York, New York 10017.

1969
Esther Hautzig
The Endless Steppe: Growing Up in Siberia (Crowell)
1970
Sulamith Ish-Kishor
Our Eddie (Pantheon)
1971
Suzanna Lange
The Year (S. G. Phillips)
1972
Isaac Bashevis Singer
For general contributions
1973
Molly Cone
For general contributions
1974
Yuri Suhl
Uncle Misha's Partisans (Four Winds)

1975
No award
1976
Marietta Moskin
Waiting for Mama (Coward)
1977
Milton Meltzer
Never to Forget: The Jews of the Holocaust (Harper)
1978
Anita Heyman
Exit from Home (Crown)
1979
Doris Orgel
The Devil in Vienna (Dial)

Sydney Taylor Body of Work Award

Presented for the first time in 1979, this award will be given from time to time to an author whose entire body of work represents an outstanding contribution to Jewish literature for children and youth. The award winner is chosen by a committee of five Judaica librarians. The award is presented at a banquet during the AJL national convention in June. Inquiries should be directed to the Association of Jewish Libraries, c/o National Foundation for Jewish Culture, 122 East 42 Street, Room 1512, New York, New York 10017.

1979
Sydney Taylor
All-of-a-Kind Family books (Follett)

Irma Simonton Black Award

The Bank Street College of Education established this award in 1973 in memory of Irma Simonton Black, educator, author, and editor. Scrolls are presented annually in the spring to the author and illustrator of an outstanding book for young children published during the previous year. The award book carries a seal designed by Maurice Sendak. Entries are judged for a blend of excellence in story line, language, and illustrations. The Publications-Communications Division of the College, headed for many years by Irma Black, judges the entries. In recognition of the child's point of view, children participate in the judging. Further information can be obtained from the Book Award Committee, Publications Division, Bank Street College of Education, 610 West 112 Street, New York, New York 10025.

1973
  Arnold Lobel, author-illustrator
  Mouse Tales (Harper)
1974
  Remy Charlip and Burton Supree, authors-illustrators
  Harlequin and the Gift of Many Colors (Parents' Magazine)
  Berniece Freschet, author, and Donald Carrick, illustrator
  Bear Mouse (Scribner)
1975
  Eloise Greenfield, author, and John Steptoe, illustrator
  She Come Bringing Me That Little Baby Girl (Lippincott)
1976
  Irene Haas, author-illustrator
  The Maggie B (Atheneum)

Rosemary Wells, author-illustrator
Morris's Disappearing Bag (Dial)
1977
  Adrienne Adams, author-illustrator
  The Easter Egg Artists (Scribner)
  Jay Williams, author, and Mercer Mayer, illustrator
  Everyone Knows What a Dragon Looks Like (Four Winds)
1978
  Steven Kellogg, author-illustrator
  The Mysterious Tadpole (Dial)
1979
  Larry Bograd, author, and Dirk Zimmer, illustrator
  Felix in the Attic (Harvey House)

Boston Globe–Horn Book Awards

These awards are offered by the Boston Globe Newspaper Company, Boston, Massachusetts 02107, and the Horn Book, Inc., Park Square Building, St. James Avenue, Boston, Massachusetts 02116. The Boston Globe–Horn Book Awards were started in 1967 to foster and reward excellence in text and illustration in children's books. Children's books published in the United States between September 1 and August 31 of the following year are eligible; however, reprints or textbooks are not considered. There is no age limit. Three $200 awards are currently given: one for illustration; one for fiction or poetry; and one for nonfiction, the first award for which was given in 1976. Publishers may submit up to nine books each. Awards are made each autumn at the New England Library Association conference.

1967
  Erik Christian Haugaard, author
  The Little Fishes (Houghton)

  Peter Spier, illustrator
  London Bridge Is Falling Down (Doubleday)

1968
  John Lawson, author
  The Spring Rider (Crowell)

  Blair Lent, illustrator
  Tikki Tikki Tembo, by Arlene Mosel (Harcourt)

1969
Ursula K. LeGuin, author
A Wizard of Earthsea (Parnassus)

John S. Goodall, illustrator
The Adventures of Paddy Pork (Harcourt)

1970
John Rowe Townsend, author
The Intruder (Lippincott)

Ezra Jack Keats, illustrator
Hi, Cat! (Macmillan)

1971
Eleanor Cameron, author
A Room Made of Windows (Dell)

Kazue Mizumura, illustrator
If I Built a Village (Crowell)

1972
Rosemary Sutcliff, author
Tristan and Iseult (Dutton)

John Burningham, illustrator
Mr. Gumpy's Outing (Holt)

1973
Susan Cooper, author
The Dark Is Rising (Atheneum)

Trina S. Hyman, illustrator
King Stork, by Howard Pyle (Little)

1974
Virginia Hamilton, author
M. C. Higgins, the Great (Macmillan)

Tom Feelings, illustrator
Jambo Means Hello: Swahili Alphabet Book, by Muriel Feelings (Dial)

1975
T. Degens, author
Transport 7-41-R (Viking)

Mitsumasa Anno, illustrator
Anno's Alphabet (Crowell)

1976
Alfred Tamarin and Shirley Glubok, authors (nonfiction)
Voyaging to Cathay: Americans in the China Trade (Viking)

Jill Paton Walsh, author (fiction)
Unleaving (Farrar)

Remy Charlip and Jerry Joyner, illustrators
Thirteen (Parents' Magazine)

1977
Peter Dickinson, author (nonfiction)
Chance, Luck and Destiny (Atlantic-Little)

Laurence Yep, author (fiction)
Child of the Owl (Harper)

Wallace Tripp, compiler/illustrator
Granfa' Grig Had a Pig and Other Rhymes without Reason from Mother Goose (Little)

1978
Ilse Koehn, author (nonfiction)
Mischling, Second Degree: My Childhood in Nazi Germany (Greenwillow)

Ellen Raskin, author (fiction)
The Westing Game (Dutton)

Mitsumasa Anno, illustrator
Anno's Journey (Collins-World)

1979
David Kherdian, author (nonfiction)
The Road from Home: The Story of an Armenian Girl (Greenwillow)

Sid Fleischman, author (fiction)
Humbug Mountain (Atlantic-Little)

Raymond Briggs, illustrator
The Snowman (Random)

Lewis Carroll Shelf Award

The School of Education of the University of Wisconsin at Madison established this award in 1958 to honor juvenile books "worthy of sitting on the shelf with Alice." Approximately ten books are added to the shelf each year, chosen from nominees submitted annually by trade book publishers from their current lists. A reading committee composed of librarians and parents evaluates the nominees on the basis of eight factors, among them authenticity, insight, craftsmanship, impact, genre comparison, and the test of time. The winning titles are announced in July and are added to the Lewis Carroll Shelf. The books can be examined at the Cooperative Children's Book Center, Helen C. White Hall, Room 4290, University of Wisconsin, Madison, Wisconsin 53706, and at the Instructional Materials Center, Education Building, 225 North Mills, Madison, Wisconsin 53706. A cumulated list of the 212 winning books (1958–1979) is available from the University of Wisconsin, School of Education, Education Building, Box 66, 1000 Bascom Mall, Madison, Wisconsin 53706.

Child Study Children's Book Committee at Bank Street College Award

This award was established in 1943 by the Child Study Association of America/Wel-Met. It is currently awarded by the Child Study Children's Book Committee at Bank Street College, 610 West 112 Street, New York, New York 10025. It is given to a children's book that deals realistically with children's problems in order to make writers and publishers focus on the need of children and young people to find today's world honestly reflected in their literature in terms they can recognize and understand. Entries must have been previously published for a juvenile audience. The selection is made each year by the Children's Book Committee after careful reading and group discussion of all the year's books for children and young people.

1944
    John R. Tunis
    Keystone Kids (Harcourt)
1945
    Marjorie Hill Allee
    The House (Houghton)
1946
    Florence Crannell Means
    The Moved-Outers (Houghton)
1947
    Howard Pease
    Heart of Danger (Doubleday)
1948
    Lois Lenski
    Judy's Journey (Lippincott)
1949
    Pearl Buck
    The Big Wave (John Day)

1950
    Marie Gleit
    Paul Tiber (Scribner)
1951
    Eleanor Roosevelt and Helen Ferris
    The United Nations and Youth (Doubleday)
1952
    No award
1953
    Claire Huchet Bishop
    Twenty and Ten (Viking)
    Miriam Powell
    Jareb (Crowell)
1954
    Mary Stolz
    In a Mirror (Harper)

1955
  William Corbin
  High Road Home (Coward)

  Jonreed Lauritzen
  The Ordeal of the Young Hunter (Little)

1956
  Taro Yashima
  Crow Boy (Viking)

  Virginia Sorensen
  Plain Girl (Harcourt)

1957
  Meindert DeJong
  The House of Sixty Fathers (Harper)

1958
  Helen R. Sattley
  Shadow across the Campus (Dodd)

1959
  Lorenz Graham
  South Town (Follett)

1960
  Zoa Sherburne
  Jennifer (Morrow)

1961
  Robin McKown
  Janine (Messner)

1962
  Aimée Sommerfelt
  The Road to Agra (Criterion)

  Hila Colman
  The Girl from Puerto Rico (Morrow)

1963
  Joan Lexau
  The Trouble with Terry (Dial)

1964
  Mildred Lee
  The Rock and the Willow (Lothrop)

  Betty Schechter
  The Peaceable Revolution (Houghton)

1965
  Ruth Harnden
  The High Pasture (Houghton)

1966
  Natalie Savage Carlson
  The Empty Schoolhouse (Harper)

1967
  Robert Burch
  Queenie Peavy (Viking)

1968
  Robert Lipsyte
  The Contender (Harper)

1969
  Vadim Frolov
  What It's All About (Doubleday)

1970
  Margaretha Shemin
  The Empty Moat (Coward)

1971
  James Lincoln Collier
  Rock Star (Four Winds)

  Carli Laklan
  Migrant Girl (McGraw)

1972
  Lillie D. Chaffin
  John Henry McCoy (Macmillan)

1973
  Mollie Hunter
  A Sound of Chariots (Harper)

1974
  Doris Buchanan Smith
  A Taste of Blackberries (Crowell)

1975
  Eleanor Clymer
  Luke Was There (Holt)

1976
  Carol Farley
  The Garden Is Doing Fine (Atheneum)

1977
  Roberta Silman
  Somebody Else's Child (Warne)

1978
  Betsy Byars
  The Pinballs (Harper)

1979
  Doris Orgel
  The Devil in Vienna (Dial)

Children's Book Fair

Each year at the Children's Book Fair in Bologna, Italy, two international prizes are given by the Bologna Fairs Authorities for children's books: the Premio "Critici in Erba" ("Budding Critics" Prize) and the Premio Grafico Fiera di Bologna (Bologna Fair Graphic Prize). The prizes were established in 1966. Participation in the two competitions is open to all Italian and foreign publishers participating in the Fair. Each publisher may submit one or more books published in the twenty-five-month period (e.g., January 1, 1978–January 30, 1980) preceding the Fair, held in late March. The prizes consist of gold plates awarded to the publishers of the winning works. Further information is available from Ente Autonomo per le Fiere di Bologna, Piazza Constituzione 6, I-40128 Bologna, Italy.

Premio "Critici in Erba"

This prize is awarded for the best illustrated book, through the decision of a committee of nine children, ages 6 to 9, who are pupils in Bologna schools. The children are chosen by school authorities on the basis of their sensitivity to the esthetic values of illustrations.

1966
Bias (France)
L'Album de Bambi
1967
Diogenes Verlag (Switzerland)
Ich Schenck Dir einen Papagei
1968
Vallecchi (Italy)
Alla Scoperta dell'Africa
1969
Seymour Lawrence, Inc. (United States)
Pocahontas in London
1970
Stediv l'Aquila (Italy)
La Storia di Francesco e Chiara "Raccontata dai Bimbi di Groce"
1971
Gertrude Middelhauve Verlag (West Germany)
Alle Meine Blätter . . .
1972
Wílliam Collins Sons & Co., Ltd. (United Kingdom)
Waltzing Matilda

1973
Farrar, Straus & Giroux (United States)
Snow White and the Seven Dwarfs
1974
Detskaya Literatura (U.S.S.R.)
A Year in the Woods
1975
Paoline (Italy)
Il Principe Felice
1976
Carlsen Verlag (West Germany)
Das Gelbe Haus
1977
Diogenes Verlag (Switzerland)
Die Geschichte von Babar
1978
William Collins Publishers (Australia)
Nicholas and the Moon Eggs
1979
Diogenes Verlag (Switzerland)
Ein Tag im Leben der Dorothea Wutz

Premio Grafico Fiera di Bologna

This prize is awarded annually in each of two categories: Children and Youth. A committee of judges appointed from the Study Centre G. B. Bodoni, Parma, Italy, awards prizes for works having remarkable graphic, artistic, and technical value. A single prize was awarded in 1966 for children and youth.

CHILDREN

1966
  Rizzoli (Italy)
  Gesù Oggi
1967
  Otto Maier Verlag (West Germany)
  Drei Vögel
1968
  Atlantis Verlag (Switzerland)
  Die Wichtelmänner
1969
  Institute for the Intellectual Development of Children and Young Adults (Iran)
  The Little Black Fish
1970
  Stalling Verlag (West Germany)
  1, 2, 3, Ein Zug zum Zoo
1971
  Parents' Magazine Press (United States)
  Arm in Arm
1972
  Atlantis Verlag (Switzerland)
  Stadtmaus und Landmaus
1973
  Der Kinderbuchverlag (East Germany)
  Kopfblumen
1974
  Diogenes Verlag (Switzerland)
  Rotkäppchen
1975
  Grasset (France)
  Trois Petits Flocons
1976
  Kaisei-sha (Japan)
  Magic for Sale

1977
  Diogenes Verlag (Switzerland)
  Schorschi Schrumpft
1978
  Carl Überreuter (Austria)
  Grabianskis Stadtmusikanten
1979
  Gallimard (France)
  Histoire du Petit Stephen Girard

YOUTH

1966
  Rizzoli (Italy)
  Gesù Oggi
1967
  Sigbert Mohn (West Germany)
  Die Alte Linde Gondula
1968
  SNDK (Czechoslovakia)
  Příběhy
1969
  Casterman (France)
  La Cité de l'An 2000
1970
  Nederlandsche Zondags-School Vereniging (Netherlands)
  Vertel het Uw Kinderen
1971
  C. E. Giunti-Bemporad Marzocco (Italy)
  Tutto su Gerusalemme Biblica
1972
  Artia (Czechoslovakia)
  Slavische Märchen
1973
  Albatros (Czechoslovakia)
  Hodina Nachove Ruze

1974
 Felix Gluck (United Kingdom)
 The Last of the Mohicans
1975
 Jugend und Volk (Austria)
 Das Sprachbastelbuch
1976
 Detskaya Literatura (U.S.S.R.)
 Il Cavallo di Bronzo

1977
 Kaisei-sha (Japan)
 Takeru
1978
 Kodansha, Ltd. (Japan)
 Anno's Unique World
1979
 Dalla Parte delle Bambine (Italy)
 Aurora

Children's Literature Association Award for Literary Criticism

The Children's Literature Association established this award in 1976 to encourage the highest standards of scholarship and criticism in the study of children's literature. The award is given each year to the author of an outstanding paper published during the previous year. Occasionally a separate award will be given for an outstanding book. The award consists of $100 and a certificate, which are presented in March or April at the Association's annual conference, sponsored by a different university each year. Inquiries concerning the award should be sent to the Children's Literature Association, c/o Department of English, Villanova University, Villanova, Pennsylvania 19085, or to David L. Greene, Chairman, Department of English, Piedmont College, Demorest, Georgia 30535.

1978
 Aidan Chambers
 "The Reader in the Book,"
 Signal

1979
 Leonard Clark
 "Children and Poetry," *Children's Literature in Education*

Children's Reading Round Table Award

The Children's Reading Round Table Award was established in 1952. Between 1952 and 1960 the award was named the Midwest Award. The Round Table is an organization of authors, illustrators, editors, publishers, teachers, librarians, and others actively interested in the field of children's literature. The award, an engraved, framed scroll and $100, is presented each spring to a Midwesterner for outstanding contributions to children's literature over a period of years. The winner is chosen from a list of candidates submitted by members. Current officers of the Children's Reading Round Table can be contacted through Ellen Schweri, Program Chairperson, 5735 North Washtenaw, Chicago, Illinois 60659.

1953
Clara Ingram Judson, author
1954
Agatha Shea, head, Children's Division, Chicago Public Library
1955
Ada Whitcomb, head, Schools Division, Chicago Public Library
1956
Dilla McBean, author and Director of Libraries, Chicago Board of Education
1957
Ruth Harshaw, conductor of radio program *Carnival of Books*
1958
Martha Bennett King, author, folklore authority, and director of annual The Miracle of Books Fair
1959
Jene Barr, teacher-librarian, author
1960
Emily M. Hilsabeck, writer-reviewer
1961
Marguerite Henry, author
1962
Laura Bannon, author-illustrator
1963
Charlemae Rollins, author, librarian (retired)
1964
Polly Goodwin, children's book editor, *Chicago Tribune*
1965
Malinda R. Miller, editor

1966
Miriam E. Peterson, Director of Division of Libraries, Chicago Public School System
1967
Dorothy Aldis, poet (posthumous award)
1968
Isabelle Lawrence, author
1969
Rebecca Caudill and James Ayars, authors
1970
Mary Evans Andrews, author
1971
Dick Martin, illustrator
1972
Gladis Berry, teacher-librarian
1973
S. Carl Hirsch, author
1974
Sara Fenwick, Professor of Library Science, University of Chicago
1975
Caroline Rubin, editor
1976
Clementine Skinner, educator
1977
Elizabeth Vogenthaler, librarian
1978
Zena Sutherland, editor, *Bulletin of Children's Book Center*, University of Chicago, reviewer, lecturer
1979
Dorothy Haas, author, editor

Children's Science Book Awards

This award was established in 1971 by the New York Academy of Sciences to encourage the writing and publishing of high-quality science books for children. Two cash awards of $250, one for younger children and one for older children, are announced at a ceremony each March. Further information can be obtained from the New York Academy of Sciences, 2 East 63 Street, New York, New York 10021.

1972
  Robert S. Richardson
  The Stars and Serendipity (Pantheon)
1973
  Leonard Cottrell
  Reading the Past (Macmillan)
  Edward Gallob
  City Leaves, City Trees (Scribner)
1974
  Berniece Freschet
  The Web in the Grass (Scribner)
  Dorcas MacClintock and Ugo Mochi
  A Natural History of Giraffes (Scribner)
1975
  Roger Duvoisin
  See What I Am (Lothrop)
  Ruth Kirk and Richard D. Daugherty
  Hunters of the Whale (Morrow)
1976
  Bruce Buchenholz
  Doctor in the Zoo (Viking)

  Jean-Claude Deguine
  Emperor Penguin (Stephen Greene)
1977
  Aliki
  Corn Is Maize (Crowell)
  Bettyann Keules
  Watching the Wild Apes (Dutton)
1978
  Irene Brady
  Wild Mouse (Scribner)
  Elizabeth Burton Brown
  Grains (Prentice)
1979
  Lucia Anderson, author, and Leigh Grant, illustrator
  The Smallest Life around Us (Crown)
  Herman Schneider, author, and Radu Vevo, illustrator
  Laser Light (McGraw)

de Grummond Collection Medallion

Established in 1969, the award is given annually to an author or illustrator whose entire body of work constitutes an outstanding contribution to the field of children's literature. Winners are chosen by the Medallion Selection Committee, selected by the University of Southern Mississippi, School of Library Services, Hattiesburg, Mississippi 39401. The award, a silver medallion, is presented each spring at the University's Children's Book Festival.

1969
  Lois Lenski
1970
  Ernest H. Shepard
1971
  Roger Duvoisin
1972
  Marcia Brown
1973
  Lynd Ward
1974
  Taro Yashima

1975
  Barbara Cooney
1976
  Scott O'Dell
1977
  Adrienne Adams
1978
  Madeleine L'Engle
1979
  Leonard Everett Fisher

Ethical Culture School Book Award

The first Ethical Culture School Book Award was made in May 1976 by a Book Award Committee composed of three students, the school librarian, a children's book editor, and the assistant principal. The award was established to enable children to evaluate literature in a way that might constructively communicate to book publishers what kinds of books children truly appreciate, as well as to demonstrate that fourth- through sixth-graders can make valid judgments about excellence in children's books. The award is given for the best humorous book originally published during the previous calendar year. Books submitted by publishers are evaluated on the basis of seven criteria: overall impact, humor, characterization, plot, clarity, detail, and appropriateness of illustrations. Five finalists are chosen, and they are read by the more than 200 children in grades 4 to 6, who then vote for the best book. Each year in May, the children present a scroll in the School's library to the winning author. Inquiries can be sent to the Librarian, Ethical Culture School, 33 Central Park West, New York, New York 10023.

1976
Jean Van Leeuwen
The Great Christmas Kidnapping Caper (Dial)
1977
Roger Drury
Champion of Merrimack County (Little)

1978
Judie Angell
In Summertime It's Tuffy (Bradbury)
1979
Louis Sachar
Sideways Stories from Wayside School (Follett)

Dorothy Canfield Fisher Children's Book Award

The Vermont Department of Libraries and the Vermont Congress of Parents and Teachers sponsor this award, which is designed to encourage the state's children to read more and better books and to honor one of its most beloved and distinguished authors. Announced after May 1 each year, the winning book is chosen from a list of thirty books for children in grades 4 to 8. Picture books and foreign books are excluded. This list is compiled by a group of children's reading specialists and includes only books by living American authors published within two years before presentation of the award. Books on the list are voted upon by schoolchildren who have read the books; voting is carried out under classroom supervision. First given in 1957, the award, an illuminated scroll, is presented annually in June to the author of the winning book, alternately by the Vermont Department of Libraries and the Vermont Congress of Parents and Teachers. For further information contact Marjorie G. Lavalla, Chairperson, Dorothy Canfield Fisher Children's Book Award, c/o Vermont Congress of Parents and Teachers, 138 Main Street, Montpelier, Vermont 05602.

1957
Mildred Mastin Pace
Old Bones, the Wonder Horse
(McGraw)
1958
Beverly Cleary
Fifteen (Morrow)
1959
Margaret Leighton
Commanche of the Seventh (Farrar)
1960
Phoebe Erickson
Double or Nothing (Harper)
1961
Thelma Harrington Bell
Captain Ghost (Viking)
1962
Evelyn Sibley Lampman
The City under the Back Steps (Doubleday)
1963
Sheila Burnford
The Incredible Journey (Little)
1964
Zachary Ball
Bristle Face (Holiday House)
1965
Sterling North
Rascal (Dutton)
1966
Beverly Cleary
Ribsy (Morrow)
1967
Phillip Viereck
The Summer I Was Lost (John Day)
1968
Jacqueline Jackson
The Taste of Spruce Gum (Little)

1969
Mary Wolfe Thompson
Two in the Wilderness (McKay)
1970
Walt Morey
Kavik the Wolf Dog (Dutton)
1971
Betty Erwin
Go to the Room of the Eyes (Little)
1972
Mel Ellis
Flight of the White Wolf (Holt)
1973
Don Caufield and Joan Caufield
Never Steal a Magic Cat (Doubleday)
1974
George A. Woods
Catch a Killer (Harper)
1975
Betsy Byars
The 18th Emergency (Viking)
1976
Jean Merrill
The Toothpaste Millionaire (Houghton)
1977
Stella Pevsner
A Smart Kid Like You (Seabury)
1978
Lois Duncan
Summer of Fear (Little)
1979
Susan Beth Pfeffer
Kid Power (Franklin Watts)

Garden State Children's Book Awards

These awards were established in 1977 by the Children's Services Section of the New Jersey Library Association in order to encourage, stimulate, and captivate young readers with the printed word and good illustration. An awards committee composed of four children's librarians annually selects a book list based on literary merit and popularity. The nominated books must have been published at least three years prior to the award. Winners, both authors and illustrators, are then chosen by Children's Services Section members. The awards, framed certificates, are given in three categories: Easy-to-Read, Fiction (grades 2 to 5), and Nonfiction (grades 2 to 5). Winners are announced annually in March and receive the awards at the New Jersey Library Association spring conference at a banquet jointly sponsored by the New Jersey Educational Media Association. Further information is available from the New Jersey Library Association, Children's Services Section, 221 Boulevard, Passaic, New Jersey 07055.

1977

Peggy Parish, author, and Arnold Lobel, illustrator
Dinosaur Time (Harper) Easy-to-Read

Donald Sobol, author, and Leonard Shortall, illustrator
Encyclopedia Brown Lends a Hand (Thomas Nelson) Fiction

Marian T. Place
On the Track of Bigfoot (Dodd) Nonfiction

1978

Arnold Lobel
Owl at Home (Harper) Easy-to-Read

Marilyn Sachs, author, and Anne Sachs, illustrator
Dorrie's Book (Doubleday) Fiction

Millicent Selsam, author, and Esther Bubley, photographer
How Kittens Grow (Four Winds) Nonfiction

1979

Dick Gackenbach
Hattie Rabbit (Harper) Easy-to-Read

Leatie Weiss, author, and Ellen Weiss, illustrator
Heather's Feathers (Watts) Easy-to-Read

Hila Colman
Nobody Has to Be a Kid Forever (Crown) Fiction

Jill Krementz
A Very Young Dancer (Knopf) Nonfiction

The Golden Kite Award

The Society of Children's Book Writers, Box 296, Los Angeles, California 90066, established this award in 1973 to stimulate the creation of good books for children. The award was expanded in 1977 to give separate recognition to fiction and nonfiction books. The name of the award is derived from the kite that appears in the logo of all Society stationery, etc. The award recipient must be a member of the Society. Books must be original works published during the year for which the award is given; anthologies and translations are not eligible. A panel of five judges—three children's book authors, a children's book editor, and a librarian—selects the award winners. The works chosen are those that the judges believe exhibit excellence in writing and genuinely appeal to the interests and concerns of children. The awards are inscribed pewter statuettes on walnut bases; honor books, not listed here, are awarded certificates mounted on walnut bases. Books may be submitted by the author or publisher between February 1 and December 15 to the Society of Children's Book Writers, c/o Sue Alexander, 6846 McLaren, Canoga Park, California 91307.

1973
  Bette Greene
  Summer of My German Soldier (Dial)
1974
  Jane Yolen
  The Girl Who Cried Flowers (Crowell)
1975
  Carol Farley
  The Garden Is Doing Fine (Atheneum)
1976
  Eve Bunting
  One More Flight (Warne)
1977
  Berniece Raba
  The Girl Who Had No Name (Dutton)
  Fiction
  Robert McClung
  Peeper, First Voice of Spring (Morrow) Nonfiction
1978
  Stella Peysner
  And You Give Me a Pain, Elaine (Seabury) Fiction
  Phyllis Reynolds Naylor
  How I Came to Be a Writer (Atheneum) Nonfiction

Sue Hefley Award

The Louisiana Association of School Librarians established this award in 1970 to encourage Louisiana schoolchildren in grades 4 to 8 to read more and better books and to honor authors whose books are enjoyed by Louisiana children. The award honors Sue Hefley, who was a leader in the development of Louisiana libraries. An administrative committee reads and screens fiction and nonfiction books published in the United States during the previous two years and selects the best for a master list. Then Louisiana schoolchildren read the books and vote for their favorite. The award, a plaque, is announced in January and presented in March at the annual Louisiana Library Association convention. Inquiries should be addressed to the Louisiana Association of School Librarians, c/o Louisiana Library Association, Box 131, Baton Rouge, Louisiana 70821.

1973
  Beverly Cleary
  The Mouse and the Motorcycle (Morrow)
1974
  Rebecca Caudill
  Did You Carry the Flag Today, Charley? (Holt)
1975
  E. B. White
  The Trumpet of the Swan (Harper)
1976
  Richard Armstrong
  Sounder (Harper)
1977
  No award
1978
  Doris Buchanan Smith
  A Taste of Blackberries (Crowell)

International Reading Association Children's Book Award

The International Reading Association (IRA) established this award in 1974 for the purpose of encouraging promising beginning authors. It is given to an author whose first or second book, fiction or nonfiction, has been published in any country in the previous year. The award, $1,000 and a plaque, is sponsored by the Institute for Reading Research. Entry deadline is December 1. To submit a book for consideration by the IRA Children's Book Award Subcommittee, send seven copies to Dr. Bernice Cullinan, New York University, Department of Early Childhood and Elementary Education, 300 East Building, 239 Greene Street, New York, New York 10003. The International Reading Association is located at 800 Barksdale Road, Box 8139, Newark, Delaware 19711.

1975
   T. Degens
   Transport 7-41-R (Viking)
1976
   Laurence Yep
   Dragonwings (Harper)
1977
   Nancy Bond
   A String in the Harp (Atheneum)

1978
   Lois Lowry
   A Summer to Die (Houghton)
1979
   Alison Smith
   Reserved for Mark Anthony Crowder
   (Dutton)

Irvin Kerlan Award

Established in 1975 on the occasion of the twenty-fifth anniversary of the Kerlan Collection Committee, this annual award is given in recognition of "singular attainments in the creation of children's literature and in appreciation for generous donation of unique resources to the Kerlan Collection for the study of children's literature." The award winner, selected by the Kerlan Collection Committee, receives a laminated plaque in a ceremony at the University of Minnesota in the late spring. Inquiries should be sent to the Kerlan Collection, 109 Walter Library, University of Minnesota, Minneapolis, Minnesota 55455.

1975
   Elizabeth Coatsworth
   Marie Hall Ets
   Marguerite Henry
1976
   Roger Duvoisin

1977
   Wanda Gág (posthumous)
1978
   Carol Ryrie Brink
1979
   Margot Zemach

Massachusetts Children's Book Award

The Massachusetts Children's Book Award Program, founded and administered by Helen Constant, Education Department, Salem State College, Salem, Massachusetts 01970, is designed to encourage schoolchildren to read all types of books, both literary and popular, with a special emphasis on multiethnic books. Children, teachers, and librarians annually nominate books to be included in two reading lists, one for grades 4 to 6 (Elementary Division), the other for grades 7 to 9 (Young Adult Division). All Massachusetts schoolchildren in grades 4 to 9 who have read or have heard read at least five of the nominated books vote for their favorite book. Winners are selected for the Elementary Division and for the Young Adult Division. A Paul Revere bowl is given to the winning author(s) in each category, if he or she attends the Book Award Conference at Salem State College in June. If a winning author does not attend the conference, the prize is given to the runner-up who does attend.

ELEMENTARY

1976
   Thomas Rockwell
   How to Eat Fried Worms (Franklin Watts)
1977
   Judy Blume
   Tales of a Fourth Grade Nothing (Dutton)
1978
   Robert C. O'Brien
   Mrs. Frisby and the Rats of NIMH (Atheneum)

1979
   George Selden
   The Cricket in Times Square (Farrar)

YOUNG ADULT

1978
   Susie E. Hinton
   That Was Then, This Is Now (Viking)
1979
   Susie E. Hinton
   The Outsiders (Viking)
   Paula Danziger
   The Cat Ate My Gymsuit (Delacorte)

National Council of Teachers of English Award for Excellence in Poetry for Children

The National Council of Teachers of English (NCTE), 1111 Kenyon Road, Urbana, Illinois 61801, established this annual award in 1977 to honor the aggregate work of a living American author of poetry for children. The award, a plaque, is given by the NCTE Executive Committee at the NCTE convention in November.

1977
   David McCord
1978
   Aileen Fisher

1979
   Karla Kuskin

Nene Award

This award is sponsored by the Hawaii Association of School Librarians and the Children and Youth Section of the Hawaii Library Association. In 1958, a third-grade class at the University Elementary School started a contest to promote reading and to choose a book most enjoyed by the children in the group for the Nene Award. (The Nene goose is the official bird of Hawaii. Native to Hawaii and once nearly extinct, its numbers are gradually increasing due to conservation efforts.) The idea spread to several other schools, where librarians adopted the Nene Award too. In 1963, the Hawaii Association of School Librarians and the Children and Youth Section of the Hawaii Library Association decided to cosponsor the Nene Award as a statewide program. The award is a plaque of Hawaiian wood carved to represent the Nene goose. The winner is announced annually during National Library Week. To be eligible the book must be a work of fiction by a living author, suitable for children in grades 4 to 6, and written within the previous six years. The winning book is chosen by children in grades 4 to 8. A week of balloting is carried out in March in public and private schools. The winning author is invited to Hawaii to receive the award. Inquiries should be directed to Marsha Rapp, Children and Youth Section Head, Hawaii Library Association, 217 Forest Ridge Way, Honolulu, Hawaii 96822.

1964
    Scott O'Dell
    Island of the Blue Dolphins (Houghton)
1965
    Pamela Travers
    Mary Poppins (Harcourt)
1966
    Fred Gipson
    Old Yeller (Harper)
1967
    No award
1968
    Beverly Cleary
    Ribsy (Morrow)
1969
    Beverly Cleary
    The Mouse and the Motorcycle (Morrow)
1970
    Keith Robertson
    Henry Reed's Baby-Sitting Service (Grosset)
1971
    Beverly Cleary
    Ramona the Pest (Morrow)

1972
    Beverly Cleary
    Runaway Ralph (Morrow)
1973
    William H. Armstrong
    Sounder (Harper)
1974
    Richard Bach
    Jonathan Livingston Seagull (Macmillan)
1975
    Judy Blume
    Are You There, God? It's Me, Margaret (Bradbury)
1976
    Thomas Rockwell
    How to Eat Fried Worms (Franklin Watts)
1977
    Mary Rodgers
    Freaky Friday (Harper)
1978
    Roald Dahl
    Charlie and the Great Glass Elevator (Knopf)
1979
    Beverly Cleary
    Ramona and Her Father (Morrow)

The New York Times Best Illustrated Children's Book Awards

The New York Times, 229 West 43 Street, New York, New York 10036, established this annual award in 1952 to honor the highest quality illustration of children's books. All illustrated children's books published in the United States during the previous year are first screened by the Children's Book Editor of the *Times*, after which the editor and two other judges, usually an artist and an art critic, select the award-winning books. The winners are announced in mid-November in the special children's books supplement to the Sunday *Times Book Review*. A complete list of winners can be found in *Children's Books: Awards and Prizes*, published by the Children's Book Council, 67 Irving Place, New York, New York 10003.

Regina Medal

The Regina Medal was established in 1959 by the Catholic Library Association, 461 West Lancaster Avenue, Haverford, Pennsylvania 19041, to honor an individual whose continued distinguished dedication to children's literature exemplifies the words of Walter de la Mare, "Only the rarest kind of best in anything can be good enough for the young." Anyone, without restriction of religion or country of birth, whose life's work has been in the field of juvenile literature, is eligible for the award: authors, publishers, editors, illustrators, etc. The silver medal is presented annually at Easter time at the national convention of the Catholic Library Association.

1959
  Eleanor Farjeon
1960
  Anne Carroll Moore
1961
  Padraic Colum
1962
  Frederic G. Melcher
1963
  Ann Nolan Clark
1964
  May Hill Arbuthnot
1965
  Ruth Sawyer Durand
1966
  Leo Politi
1967
  Bertha Mahony Miller

1968
  Marguerite de Angeli
1969
  Lois Lenski
1970
  Ingri d'Aulaire and Edgar Parin d'Aulaire
1971
  Tasha Tudor
1972
  Meindert DeJong
1973
  Frances Clarke Sayers
1974
  Robert McCloskey
1975
  Mary McNeer and Lynd Ward

1976
  Virginia Haviland

1977
  Marcia Brown

1978
  Scott O'Dell
1979
  Morton Schindel

Charles and Bertie G. Schwartz Award

At its annual meeting in May, the JWB Jewish Book Council, 15 East 26 Street, New York, New York 10010, awards a citation and a prize of $500 to the author of a children's book on a Jewish theme published during the preceding year or for cumulative contributions to Jewish juvenile literature. A committee of judges makes the decision. The award was first given in 1952 and has borne various names in honor of donors of funds for the awards—the Isaac Siegel Memorial Juvenile Award; the Temple B'nai Jeshurun (Newark, New Jersey) Juvenile Award; the Fanny and Herman Rodman and Fanny and Abraham Bellsey Memorial Juvenile Award; and the Hayim Greenberg Memorial Juvenile Award of the Pioneer Women. It is now known as the Charles and Bertie G. Schwartz Award.

1952
  Sydney Taylor
  All-of-a-Kind Family (Follett)
1953
  Lillian S. Freehof
  Stories of King David (Jewish Publication Society) and *Star Light Stories* (Bloch)
1954
  Deborah Pessin
  The Jewish People: Book Three (United Synagogue Commission on Jewish Education)
1955
  Nora Benjamin Kubie
  King Solomon's Navy (Harper)
1956
  Sadie Rose Weilerstein
  For cumulative contributions to Jewish juvenile literature
1957
  Elma Ehrlich Levinger
  For cumulative contributions to Jewish juvenile literature

1958
  Naomi Ben-Asher and Hayim Leaf
  Junior Jewish Encyclopedia (Shengold)
1959
  Lloyd Alexander
  Border Hawk: August Bondi (Farrar)
1960
  Sylvia Rothchild
  Keys to a Magic Door: Isaac Leib Peretz (Jewish Publication Society/ Farrar)
1961
  Regina Tor
  Discovering Israel (Random)
1962
  Sadie Rose Weilerstein
  Ten and a Kid (Doubleday)
1963
  Josephine Kamm
  Return to Freedom (Abelard)
1964
  Sulamith Ish-Kishor
  A Boy of Old Prague (Pantheon)

1965
  Azriel Eisenberg and Dov Peretz Elkins
  Worlds Lost and Found (Abelard)
1966
  Betty Schechter
  The Dreyfus Affair (Houghton)
1967
  Meyer Levin
  The Story of Israel (Putnam)
1968-1969
  No awards
1970
  Gerald Gottlieb
  The Story of Masada by Yigael Yadin: Retold for Young Readers (Random)

  Charlie May Simon
  Martin Buber: Wisdom in Our Time (Dutton)
1971
  Sonia Levitin
  Journey to America (Atheneum)
1972
  Sulamith Ish-Kishor
  The Master of Miracle: A New Novel of the Golem (Harper)

1973
  Johanna Reiss
  The Upstairs Room (Crowell)
1974
  Yuri Suhl
  Uncle Misha's Partisans (Four Winds)
1975
  Bea Stadtler
  The Holocaust: A History of Courage and Resistance (Behrman House)
1976
  Shirley Milgrim
  Haym Salomon: Liberty's Son (Jewish Publication Society)
1977
  Chaya Burstein
  Rifka Grows Up (Hebrew Publishing)
1978
  Milton Meltzer
  Never to Forget: The Jews of the Holocaust (Harper)
1979
  Irena Norell
  Joshua: Fighter for Bar Kochba (Akiba)

Sequoyah Children's Book Award of Oklahoma

This program, sponsored by the Oklahoma Library Association, c/o Frances Kennedy, Executive Secretary, 1629 Camden Way, Oklahoma City, Oklahoma 73116, encourages Oklahoma boys and girls in grades 3 to 6 to read books of literary quality. A master list of notable books is compiled by the Sequoyah Children's Book Award Committee. To be eligible to vote for the best book, each student must have read at least two titles from the master list. The winning author is announced in February. In April, the Sequoyah Children's Book Award Luncheon is held as the final event of the annual Oklahoma Library Association conference. Two children, representing the boys and girls of Oklahoma, present the winning author with a plaque depicting Sequoyah and his "talking leaves."

1959
  Fred Gipson
  Old Yeller (Harper)

1960
  Marguerite Henry
  Black Gold (Rand McNally)

1961
  Robert A. Heinlein
  Have Space Suit–Will Travel (Scribner)
1962
  Catherine O. Peare
  The Helen Keller Story (Crowell)
1963
  Phyllis A. Whitney
  Mystery of the Haunted Pool (Westminster)
1964
  William Robinson
  Where the Panther Screams (World)
1965
  Madeleine L'Engle
  Wrinkle in Time (Farrar)
1966
  Sterling North
  Rascal (Dutton)
1967
  Louise Fitzhugh
  Harriet the Spy (Harper)
1968
  Walt Morey
  Gentle Ben (Dutton)
1969
  Ben Stahl
  Blackbeard's Ghost (Houghton)
1970
  Marguerite Henry
  Mustang (Rand McNally)

1971
  Beverly Cleary
  Ramona the Pest (Morrow)
1972
  Mary Lois Dunn
  Man in the Box: A Story from Vietnam (McGraw)
1973
  E. B. White
  Trumpet of the Swan (Harper)
1974
  Mel Ellis
  Flight of the White Wolf (Holt)
1975
  Judy Blume
  Tales of a Fourth Grade Nothing (Dutton)
1976
  Thomas Rockwell
  How to Eat Fried Worms (Franklin Watts)
1977
  Jean Merrill
  The Toothpaste Millionaire (Houghton)
1978
  Clyde R. Bulla
  Shoeshine Girl (Crowell)
1979
  Wilson Rawls
  Summer of the Monkeys (Doubleday)

Charlie May Simon Children's Book Award

This award, first given in 1971, is intended to promote reading and to honor the distinguished Arkansan Mrs. John Gould Fletcher, who wrote children's books under the pen name Charlie May Simon. Each year a book selection committee compiles a reading list of best books published during the preceding year. Then Arkansas children in grades 4 to 6 who have read at least two of the listed books vote for their favorite. A medallion is presented to the winning author at a banquet in Little Rock in September. Further information can be obtained from the Arkansas Elementary School Council, Arch Ford Education Building, Capitol Mall, Little Rock, Arkansas 72201.

1971
  Joan Lexau
  Striped Ice Cream (Lippincott)
1972
  David Harry Walker
  Big Ben (Houghton)
1973
  Beverly Cleary
  Runaway Ralph (Morrow)
1974
  Harold Keith
  The Runt of Rogers School (Lippincott)
1975
  Judy Blume
  Tales of a Fourth Grade Nothing (Dutton)

1976
  Hal Evarts
  Big Foot (Scribner)
1977
  Sid Fleischman
  The Ghost on Saturday Night (Little)

1978
  Clyde Robert Bulla
  Shoeshine Girl (Crowell)

1979
  Clifford Hicks
  Alvin's Swap Shop (Holt)

South Carolina Children's Book Award

The South Carolina Association of School Librarians has offered this award annually since 1976 to stimulate schoolchildren's interest in reading. Each year a committee of librarians, school administrators, teachers, parents, and consultants selects a list of twenty works of fiction from those published during the previous five years. From this list, South Carolina students in grades 4 to 8 who have read at least three of the nominated books vote for their favorite. The winner is announced in April at the spring meeting of the Association. The winning author receives a bronze medallion bearing the Children's Book Award logo. In the future, the award may be officially presented at a joint meeting with the Young Adult Book Award Program in November.

1976
  Thomas Rockwell
  How to Eat Fried Worms (Franklin Watts)
1977
  Judy Blume
  Tales of a Fourth Grade Nothing (Dutton)

1978
  Judy Blume
  Otherwise Known as Sheila the Great (Dutton)
1979
  Jean Van Leeuween
  Great Christmas Kidnapping Caper (Dial)

Southern California Council on Literature for Children and Young People Awards

The Southern California Council, located at California State College at Los Angeles, Room 200, Administration Building, 5151 State College Drive, Los Angeles, California

90032, established these awards in 1961. The awards are designed to give recognition for a distinguished contribution in the field of children's literature, but may also be given for contributions in the audiovisual field, teaching, and library service. Authors or illustrators residing in southern California are eligible if they have contributed to children's literature during the preceding calendar year either through a notable book published or a significant contribution in the field of illustration. Winners of the award, a plaque, are chosen by a committee of members that excludes authors or publishers' representatives. Presentations are made annually in November.

1961

Scott O'Dell
Island of the Blue Dolphins (Houghton) Notable book

Leo Politi
Moy Moy (Scribner) Significant contribution in the field of illustration

Conrad Buff and Mary Buff; Lucille Holling and Holling C. Holling
Comprehensive contributions of lasting value

1962

Jonreed Lauritzen
Legend of Billy Blue Sage (Little) Notable book

Don Freeman
Come Again, Pelican (Viking) Significant contribution in the field of illustration

Clyde Robert Bulla
Distinguished contribution in the field of children's literature

1963

Hildegarde Hoyt Swift
From the Eagle's Wing (Morrow) Notable book

W. W. Robinson and Irene Robinson
Distinguished contributions in the field of children's literature

1964

Robert B. Radnitz
Special citation for directing and producing the film *Island of the Blue Dolphins*

Sid Fleischman
By the Great Horn Spoon (Atlantic-Little) Notable book

Bernard Garbutt
Wild Wings over the Marshes (Golden Gate) Significant contribution in the field of illustration

Taro Yashima
Distinguished contribution in the field of illustration and writing

Dorothy C. McKenzie
Distinguished contribution to the field of literature for children and for outstanding community service

1965

Leonard Wibberley
A Dawn in the Trees: Thomas Jefferson, the Years 1776 to 1789 (Farrar) and *A Feast of Freedom* (Morrow) Notable books

Eleanor Cameron
Distinguished contribution to the field of children's literature

1966

Julia Cunningham
Dorp Dead (Pantheon) Notable book

Carol Ryrie Brink
Comprehensive contribution of lasting value in the field of children's literature

Mary Rogers Smith
Distinguished contribution in the field of children's literature

1967

Patricia Beatty and John Beatty
Royal Dirk (Morrow) Notable book

Bill Peet
Farewell to Shady Glade (Houghton) Significant contribution to the field of illustration

Margot Benary-Isbert
Comprehensive contribution of lasting value to the field of children's literature

Rosemary Livsey
Distinguished contribution to the field of children's literature

1968

Lorenz Graham
Significant contribution to the field of literature for young people

Taro Yashima
Seashore Story (Viking) Significant contribution to the field of illustration

Charles Coombs
Significant contribution to the field of informational books for children

Myra Cohn Livingston
Comprehensive contribution of lasting value in the field of literature for children and young people

1969

Robert Leslie
The Bears and I (Dutton) Notable book

Harriet Huntington
Comprehensive contribution of lasting value for children and young people

Frances Clarke Sayers
Distinguished contribution of lasting value for children and young people

1970

Theodore Taylor
The Cay (Doubleday) Notable book

Ann Atwood
New Moon Cove (Scribner) Significant contribution to the field of illustration

Richard Chase
Distinguished contribution to the field of folklore

Blanche Campbell
Outstanding community service

1971

Jane Louise Curry
The Daybreakers (Harcourt) Notable book

Graham Booth
Bobby Shafto's Gone to Sea, by Mark Taylor (Golden Gate) Comprehensive contribution to the field of illustration

Margaret Leighton
Comprehensive contribution of lasting value to the field of children's literature

Laramee Haynes
Distinguished contribution to the field of children's literature and outstanding community service

1972

Adrienne Jones
Another Place, Another Spring (Houghton) Notable book

Sid Fleischman
Comprehensive contribution of lasting value to the literature for children and young people

Lloyd Severe
Distinguished contribution for outstanding community service

Ann Atwood and Mark Pines
Distinguished contribution exhibiting the fusion of poetry and photography

1973

Myra Cohn Livingston
The Malibu and Other Poems (Atheneum) Notable book

Marguerite Henry
Comprehensive contribution of lasting value to the field of children's literature

Betty Kalagian
Distinguished contribution to the field of children's literature

1974

Patricia Beatty
Comprehensive contribution of lasting

value to the field of children's literature

Jean Rouverol
Juarez: A Son of the People (Macmillan) Distinguished work of nonfiction

Kin Platt
Chloris and the Creeps (Chilton) Distinguished work of fiction

Dr. Seuss
Special contribution to children's literature

1975

Adrienne Jones
So, Nothing Is Forever (Houghton) Distinguished work of fiction

Terry Dunnahoo
Before the Supreme Court: The Story of Belva Ann Lockwood (Houghton) Distinguished work of nonfiction

Ruth Bornstein
Son of Thunder, by Ethel McHale (Golden Gate) Significant contribution to the field of illustration

Edith Wynn Horton
Distinguished contribution for outstanding community service

1976

Clyde Robert Bulla
Shoeshine Girl (Crowell) Notable book

Don Freeman
Will's Quill (Viking) Significant contribution to the field of illustration

Diane Goode
Little Pieces of the West Wind (Bradbury) and *The Selchie's Seed* (Bradbury) Significant contribution to the field of illustration

Helen Hinckley Jones
Distinguished contribution to the field of children's literature

1977

Sonia Levitin
The Mark of Conte (Atheneum) Notable book

Ruth Bornstein
Little Gorilla (Seabury) Significant contribution to the field of illustration

Leonard Wibberley
Treegate series (Farrar) Significant contribution of excellence in a series

Sylvia Ziskind
Outstanding service in the field of children's literature

1978

Eve Bunting
Ghost of Summer (Warne) Notable book

Theodore Taylor
Distinguished body of work

Martin Tahse
Significant contribution for interpretation of literature through film

Helen Fuller
Dorothy C. McKenzie Award for distinguished contribution to the field of literature

George G. Stone Center for Children's Books Recognition of Merit

Established in 1965, this award is given annually to an author or illustrator for a single children's book, a series of books, or a body of work that makes teachers and children more aware of the human condition. It is offered by a committee of school district librarians from southern California, chaired by the director of the Stone Center. The committee chooses a single awardee from a list of about twenty nominees: books published during the period five to twenty years prior to the award. The award is a hand-lettered plaque, which is presented in January at the Claremont Reading Conference on the campus of one of the Claremont colleges. Inquiries should be sent to the George G. Stone Center for Children's Books, Claremont Graduate School, Claremont, California 91711.

1965
Harry Behn, translator
Cricket Songs (Harcourt)
1966
Natalia Belting, author, and Bernarda Bryson, illustrator
Calendar Moon (Holt)
1967
Frank Bonham, author, and Symeon Shimin, jacket illustrator
Durango Street (Dutton)
1968
Clyde Robert Bulla, author, and Leonard Weisgard, illustrator
White Bird (Crowell)
1969
Jean George, author and illustrator
My Side of the Mountain (Dutton)
1970
E. B. White, author, and Garth Williams, illustrator
Charlotte's Web (Harper)
1971
Norton Juster, author, and Jules Pfeiffer, illustrator
The Phantom Tollbooth (Random)
Scott O'Dell, author, and Evaline Ness, jacket illustrator
Island of the Blue Dolphins (Houghton)

1972
Sid Fleischman, author, and Eric von Schmidt, illustrator
By the Great Horn Spoon! (Atlantic-Little)
1973
Zilpha Snyder, author, and Alton Raible, illustrator
The Egypt Game (Atheneum)
1974
Robert Burch, author, and Jerry Lazare, illustrator
Queenie Peavy (Viking)
1975
Allan W. Eckert, author, and John Schoenherr, jacket illustrator
Incident at Hawk's Hill (Little)
1976
Leo Lionni, author and illustrator
Body of work
1977
John Christopher
White Mountains trilogy (Macmillan)
1978
Arnold Lobel
Frog and Toad series (Harper)
1979
Natalie Babbitt
Body of work (Farrar)

Mark Twain Award

The Mark Twain Award program was established in 1970 by the Missouri Association of School Librarians and the Missouri Library Association to encourage Missouri children in grades 3–8 to read the best contemporary literature. All children's books published in the previous year are examined, and a list of the 35 best is sent to Selectors representing ten organizations. They choose their 20 favorites, which then comprise a master list for Missouri school children. Children in the third through eighth grades who have read, or have heard read to them, four books on the master list vote for their favorite book in April. The winner of the award receives a bust of Mark Twain sculpted by Barbara Shanklin and engraved with the names of the winner and the sponsoring organizations. The bust is presented by a child representing all Missouri school children at a banquet during the Spring Conference of the Missouri Association of School Librarians held in April. Further information is available from the Missouri Library Association, 402 South Fifth Street, Columbia, Missouri 65201.

1972
  William H. Armstrong
  Sounder (Harper)
1973
  Robert C. O'Brien
  Mrs. Frisby and the Rats of NIMH (Atheneum)
1974
  Robert C. Lee
  It's a Mile from Here to Glory (Little)
1975
  Thomas Rockwell
  How to Eat Fried Worms (Watts)

1976
  Scott Corbett
  The Home Run Trick (Little)
1977
  Sid Fleischman
  The Ghost on Saturday Night (Little)
1978
  Beverly Cleary
  Ramona the Brave (Morrow)
1979
  Roger Drury
  The Champion of Merrimack County (Little)

University of Georgia, College of Education

Two children's book awards are offered annually by the University of Georgia, College of Education, Athens, Georgia. Each award recipient receives a plaque and $300 at the Annual Conference on Children's Literature in Elementary Education at the University in the spring. Inquiries should be sent to Shelton L. Root, Jr., Chair, Coordinating Committee, Georgia Children's Book Awards, University of Georgia, College of Education, 235 Aderhold Hall, Athens, Georgia 30602.

Georgia Children's Book Award

This award was established in 1968 to encourage the reading of trade books as a regular part of the school curriculum for grades 4 to 7. The author must be a U.S. resident. Twenty fiction nominees are selected from a list of books published in the United States during the preceding five years, excluding Newbery Medal winners.

Georgia schoolchildren who have read, or have heard read to them, at least three of the nominees vote for their favorite book.

1969
  Robert Burch
  Skinny (Viking)
1970
  Beverly Cleary
  Ramona the Pest (Morrow)
1971
  Robert Burch
  Queenie Peavy (Viking)
1972
  Jane Wagner
  J. T. (Van Nostrand)

1973
  Maia Wojciechowska
  Hey, What's Wrong with This One? (Harper)

1974
  Robert Burch
  Doodle and the Go-Cart (Viking)

1975
  Doris Buchanan Smith
  A Taste of Blackberries (Crowell)
1976
  Barbara Robinson
  The Best Christmas Pageant Ever (Harper)
1977
  Judy Blume
  Tales of a Fourth Grade Nothing (Dutton)
1978
  Mary Rodgers
  Freaky Friday (Harper)
1979
  Betsy Byars
  The Pinballs (Harper)

Georgia Children's Picture Storybook Award

This award was established in 1976 to encourage the reading of trade books as a regular part of the school curriculum for kindergarten through the third grade. Nominated authors and illustrators must be U.S. residents. Twenty nominees are selected from a list of picture storybooks published in the United States during the previous five years, excluding Caldecott Medal winners. Georgia schoolchildren who have read, or have heard read to them, at least ten of the nominated books vote for their favorite. If a winning book has both an author and an illustrator, each person receives a plaque and $300.

1977
  Judith Viorst, author, and Ray Cruz, illustrator
  Alexander and the Terrible, Horrible No Good, Very Bad Day (Atheneum)
1978
  Lorna Balian, author and illustrator
  The Sweet Touch (Abingdon)

1979
  Bill Peet, author and illustrator
  Big Bad Bruce (Houghton)

University of Wisconsin at Oshkosh, Department of Library Science

Marion Archer and Sally Teresinski, librarians in charge of the Educational Materials Center of the University of Wisconsin at Oshkosh Library, established two annual children's book awards: the Golden Archer Award and the Little Archer Award. Sponsorship of the awards was assumed by the University's Department of Library Science in 1978.

The winners of these awards each receive a handcrafted medal and a certificate at the annual librarians conference in September at the University. Inquiries should be sent to the University of Wisconsin at Oshkosh, Department of Library Science, Polk 112, Oshkosh, Wisconsin 54901.

Golden Archer Award

Established in 1974, the Golden Archer Award is given for a juvenile book published within the previous four years and selected by Wisconsin schoolchildren in grades 4 to 8 as the one giving them the greatest joy through theme, plot, style, and characterization.

1974
  Judy Blume
  Are You There God? It's Me Margaret (Bradbury)

1975
  Thomas Rockwell
  How to Eat Fried Worms (Franklin Watts)

1976
  Florence Parry Heide
  The Mystery of the Bewitched Bookmobile (Whitman)

1977
  Beverly Cleary
  Ramona the Brave (Morrow)

1978
  Scott Corbett
  The Home Run Trick (Little)

Little Archer Award

This award was established in 1976 for a picture book published within the previous four years and selected by Wisconsin schoolchildren in kindergarten through third grade as their favorite.

1976
Arlene Mosel, author, and Blair Lent, illustrator
The Funny Little Woman (Dutton)
1977
Bill Peet
Cyrus, the Unsinkable Sea Serpent (Houghton)

1978
Peter E. Spier
Oh, Were They Ever Happy (Doubleday)

Washington Children's Book Guild Nonfiction Award

Established in 1976 by the Washington (D.C.) Children's Book Guild, the award is given annually to an author of nonfiction in recognition of a total contribution of creatively written and produced books. The author must be a citizen or resident of the United States. Each winner receives $200 and a certificate at a Book Week luncheon in November sponsored by the Guild. Two honor award winners also receive monetary prizes and certificates. Further information is available from Virginia Haviland, Head, Children's Literature Center, Library of Congress, Washington, D.C. 20540.

1977
David Macaulay
1978
Millicent Selsam

1979
Jean Fritz

William Allen White Children's Book Award

The William Allen White Children's Book Award, established and directed by Emporia State University under the dedicated leadership of Ruth Gagliardo, honors the memory of one of the state's most distinguished citizens by encouraging the boys and girls of Kansas to read and enjoy good books. Each year a master list is chosen by the Book Selection Committee, which represents Kansas educational and professional organizations. Suggestions may also be submitted by other interested Kansans. Books must have been published in the United States during the previous year. Authors must reside in the United States, Canada, or Mexico. Translations, anthologies, and textbooks are not eligible. Schoolchildren in Kansas from the fourth through the eighth grade are encouraged to read as many books as possible from the master list and to vote for their favorite book. Voting takes place each year during March; announcement of the winner is made in April. The award, a bronze medal, is presented annually to the author of the winning book by the William Allen White Library, Emporia State University, Emporia, Kansas 66801.

1953
Elizabeth Yates
Amos Fortune: Free Man (Dutton)
1954
Doris Gates
Little Vic (Viking)
1955
Jean Bailey
Cherokee Bill: Oklahoma Pacer (Abingdon)
1956
Marguerite Henry
Brighty of the Grand Canyon (Rand McNally)
1957
Phoebe Erickson
Daniel Coon (Knopf)
1958
Elliott Arnold
White Falcon (Knopf)
1959
Fred Gipson
Old Yeller (Harper)
1960
William O. Steele
Flaming Arrows (Harcourt)
1961
Keith Robertson
Henry Reed, Inc. (Viking)
1962
Catherine O. Peare
The Helen Keller Story (Crowell)
1963
Scott O'Dell
Island of the Blue Dolphins (Houghton)
1964
Sheila Burnford
The Incredible Journey (Little)
1965
Zachary Ball
Bristle Face (Holiday House)
1966
Sterling North
Rascal (Dutton)

1967
Annabel Johnson and Edgar Johnson
The Grizzly (Harper)
1968
Beverly Cleary
The Mouse and the Motorcycle (Morrow)
1969
Keith Robertson
Henry Reed's Baby-Sitting Service (Viking)
1970
Elaine L. Konigsburg
From the Mixed-Up Files of Mrs. Basil E. Frankweiler (Atheneum)
1971
Walt Morey
Kavik, the Wolf Dog (Dutton)
1972
Barbara Corcoran
Sasha, My Friend (Atheneum)
1973
E. B. White
The Trumpet of the Swan (Harper)
1974
Robert O'Brien
Mrs. Frisby and the Rats of NIMH (Atheneum)
Zilpha K. Snyder
The Headless Cupid (Atheneum)
1975
William Steig
Dominic (Farrar)
1976
Beverly Cleary
Socks (Morrow)
1977
George Selden Thompson
Harry Cat's Pet Puppy (Farrar)
1978
Jean Van Leeuwen
The Great Christmas Kidnapping Caper (Dial)
1979
Wilson Rawls
Summer of the Monkeys (Doubleday)

Carter G. Woodson Book Award

In 1973 the National Council for the Social Studies (NCSS), 3615 Wisconsin Avenue N.W., Washington, D.C. 20016, established the Carter G. Woodson Book Award for the most distinguished social science book appropriate for young readers that depicts ethnicity in the United States. The Woodson Award is presented in honor of the distinguished black historian and educator, who wrote books for adults and young people, founded and edited the *Journal of Negro History*, and contributed in many significant ways to an understanding of black history. The purpose of the award is to encourage the writing, publishing, and dissemination of outstanding social science books for young readers that treat topics related to ethnic minorities and race relations sensitively and accurately. To be eligible the book must be a work of nonfiction, published in the United States during the preceding year and having a United States setting. Textbooks are not eligible. The winning book is chosen by the Selection Committee, which is appointed by the Board of Directors of the Council and includes representatives from the American Library Association, the Council on Interracial Books for Children, the Children's Book Council, the NCSS Board of Directors, and the NCSS Racism and Social Justice Committee. The Council presents the award, a plaque, each year at its annual convention and publishes an article about the author and the book in its official journal *Social Education*.

1974
Eloise Greenfield
Rosa Parks (Crowell)
1975
Jesse Jackson
Make a Joyful Noise unto the Lord: The Life of Mahalia Jackson, Queen of Gospel Singers (Crowell)
1976
Laurence Yep
Dragonwings (Harper)

1977
Dorothy Sterling
The Trouble They Seen (Doubleday)
1978
Jane Goodsell
The Biography of Daniel Inouye (Crowell)
1979
Peter Nabokov, ed.
Native American Testimony (Crowell)

Young Hoosier Book Award

The purpose of this award is to encourage students to read a variety of fiction books. A committee of Indiana teachers, librarians, and media specialists, selected by the Association for Indiana Media Educators (AIME) (the Indiana School Librarians Association, 1975–1978), prepares a list of 20 nominated books of fiction by living authors, residing in the United States, from those published during the preceding five years. Indiana students in grades 4 to 8 then select their favorite book from the list. The winning author receives a plaque at a luncheon during the annual AIME conference held in the spring, usually in March. Further information can be obtained from James Thompson, Executive Secretary, Association for Indiana Media Educators, Indiana State University, STW 1205, Terre Haute, Indiana 47802.

1975

E. B. White
Trumpet of the Swan (Harper)

1976

Judy Blume
Are You There, God? It's Me, Margaret (Bradbury)

1977

Thomas Rockwell
How to Eat Fried Worms (Franklin Watts)

1978

Barbara Robinson
The Best Christmas Pageant Ever (Harper)

1979

Sid Fleischman
The Ghost on Saturday Night (Atlantic-Little)

Young Reader Medal

The California Reading Association (CRA), through its Young Reader Medal, encourages California schoolchildren to become better acquainted with good literature and honors distinguished children's book authors. The program is an outgrowth of the International Reading Association's International Book Year Project (1972–1973), and it is currently sponsored by the California Librarians Association, the California Media and Library Educators Association, and the California Association of the Teachers of English, in addition to the founder, the California Reading Association. The Young Reader Medal is awarded annually in one or more of four categories: Primary (K–3), Intermediate (4–8), High School (9–12), and Young Adult. Nominated books must have been written by a living author and published within the previous five years. The winning titles are selected by a popular vote of California schoolchildren. Winners are announced in April and honored in November at the annual CRA conference. They each receive a bronze medal and a plaque. Inquiries should be directed to Ellis Vance, Chairperson, CRA Young Reader Medal Committee, California Reading Association, 3400 Irvine Avenue, Suite 118, Newport Beach, California 92660.

1975

Thomas Rockwell
How to Eat Fried Worms (Franklin Watts) Primary

1976

Bill Peet
How Droofus the Dragon Lost His Head (Houghton) Primary

1977

Mary Rodgers
Freaky Friday (Harper) Intermediate

Richard Adams
Watership Down (Macmillan) Young Adult

1978

Lucy Bate
Little Rabbit's Loose Tooth (Crown) Primary

1979

Roald Dahl
Danny, Champion of the World (Knopf) Intermediate

Sandra Scoppetone
The Late, Great Me (Putnam) High School

Young Readers' Choice Award

This award was established in 1940 upon the suggestion of Harry Hartman, a long-time bookseller in Seattle, Washington. It is given annually by the Children's and Young Adult Services Division of the Pacific Northwest Library Association. Representatives from each state and province within the Association serve as a committee to select ten to fifteen titles published during the preceding three years. Ballots are distributed to schools in Alaska, Idaho, Montana, Oregon, Washington, and British Columbia, and children in grades 4 to 8 vote for their favorite book during the first week of April each year. Eligible titles must have universal appeal and be recommended for purchase. The Young Readers' Choice Award is a handprinted parchment scroll, presented at the Authors' Breakfast at the Annual Pacific Northwest Library Association Conference in August. Further information may be obtained from the School of Librarianship, FM-30, University of Washington, Seattle, Washington 98195.

1940
Dell McCormick
Paul Bunyan Swings His Axe (Caxton)
1941
Florence Atwater and Richard Atwater
Mr. Popper's Penguins (Little)
1942
Laura Ingalls Wilder
By the Shores of Silver Lake (Harper)
1943
Eric Knight
Lassie Come Home (Winston)
1944
Walter Farley
Black Stallion (Random)
1945
Marie McSwigan
Snow Treasure (Dutton)
1946
John S. O'Brien
The Return of Silver Chief (Winston)
1947
Robert McCloskey
Homer Price (Viking)
1948
Walter Farley
Black Stallion Returns (Random)
1949
Shannon Garst
Cowboy Boots (Abingdon)

1950
Dr. Seuss
McElligot's Pool (Random)
1951
Marguerite Henry
King of the Wind (Rand McNally)
1952
Marguerite Henry
Sea Star (Rand McNally)
1953–1955
No awards
1956
Ellen MacGregor
Miss Pickerell Goes to Mars (McGraw)
1957
Beverly Cleary
Henry and Ribsy (Morrow)
1958
William Corbin
Golden Mare (McGraw)
1959
Fred Gipson
Old Yeller (Harper)
1960
Beverly Cleary
Henry and the Paper Route (Morrow)
1961
Jay Williams and Raymond Abrashkin
Danny Dunn and the Homework Machine (McGraw)

1962
Stewart H. Holbrook
Swamp Fox of the Revolution (Random)
1963
Jay Williams and Raymond Abrashkin
Danny Dunn and the Ocean Floor (Whittlesey)
1964
Sheila Burnford
Incredible Journey (Little)
1965
Richard Tregaskis
John F. Kennedy and P.T.-109 (Random)
1966
Sterling North
Rascal (Dutton)
1967
Ian Fleming
Chitty-Chitty-Bang-Bang (Random)
1968
Beverly Cleary
The Mouse and the Motorcycle (Morrow)
1969
Keith Robertson
Henry Reed's Baby-Sitting Service (Grosset)
1970
William Corbin
Smoke (Coward)

1971
Beverly Cleary
Ramona the Pest (Morrow)
1972
Donald J. Sobol
Encyclopedia Brown Keeps the Peace (Nelson)
1973
No award
1974
Robert C. O'Brien
Mrs. Frisby and the Rats of NIMH (Atheneum)
1975
Judy Blume
Tales of a Fourth Grade Nothing (Dutton)
1976
John D. Fitzgerald
Great Brain Reforms (Dial)
1977
Judy Blume
Blubber (Bradbury)
1978
John D. Fitzgerald
Great Brain Does It Again (Dial)
1979
Mildred Taylor
Roll of Thunder, Hear My Cry (Dial)

Poetry Prizes

Academy of American Poets

Academy of American Poets Fellowship

The Academy of American Poets, 1078 Madison Avenue, New York, New York 10028, was organized in 1934 to encourage the development of American poetry. A major activity of the Academy is to recognize and reward poets of proven merit with fellowship awards from the income of a permanent trust fund. Until 1969 these awards were $5,000, but they have recently been increased to $10,000. The number of such fellowships depends upon the size of the endowment. Two listings in one year indicates that two fellowships in the full amount were awarded. An eminent board of twelve chancellors, representing the different schools of poetry and the various geographical sections of the country, selects the poets to be honored. The fellowship is not open to application. In 1937, Edwin Markham was given a special award of $5,000 for great achievement in poetry. This was the Academy's first award. The first formal fellowship was awarded in 1946. Fellowships totaling over $200,000 have been awarded to date.

1946
Edgar Lee Masters
1947
Ridgely Torrence
1948
Percy MacKaye
1949
No award
1950
e. e. cummings
1951
No award
1952
Padraic Colum
1953
Robert Frost
1954
Oliver St. John Gogarty
Louise Townsend Nicholl

1955
Rolfe Humphries
1956
William Carlos Williams
1957
Conrad Aiken
1958
Robinson Jeffers
1959
Léonie Adams
Louise Bogan
1960
Jesse Stuart
1961
Horace Gregory
1962
John Crowe Ransom

1963
    Ezra Pound
    Allen Tate
1964
    Elizabeth Bishop
1965
    Marianne Moore
1966
    John Berryman
    Archibald MacLeish
1967
    Mark Van Doren
1968
    Stanley Kunitz
1969
    Richard Eberhart
    Anthony Hecht
1970
    Howard Nemerov

1971
    James Wright
1972
    W. D. Snodgrass
1973
    W. S. Merwin
1974
    Léonie Adams
1975
    Robert Hayden
1976
    J. V. Cunningham
1977
    Louis Coxe
1978
    Josephine Miles
1979
    May Swenson

The Copernicus Award

The Copernicus Award was first presented by the Academy of American Poets in 1974. The award honored the lifetime achievement of a living American poet, over 45 years of age, who preferably had published a book of poetry or a book about poetry within the two years preceding the year of the award. The Copernicus Award of $10,000 was supported by the Copernicus Society of America and was presented annually. A panel of three poets chose each year's winner.

1974
    Robert Lowell
1975
    Kenneth Rexroth
1976
    Robert Penn Warren

1977
    Muriel Rukeyser
Discontinued

Lamont Poetry Selection

In 1953, Mrs. Thomas W. Lamont made a bequest to the Academy of American Poets for the "discovery and encouragement of new poetic genius." This permitted the Academy to inaugurate an annual competition for the publication of a first book of poetry to be designated the Lamont Poetry Selection. In 1975, the Lamont Poetry Selection was awarded for the first time for a poet's second book. Only living Americans who have published one book of poetry in a standard edition are eligible. Manuscripts are submitted by publishers to the Academy for consideration. The decision is made by the majority vote of three judges. The winning poet receives a guaranteed purchase of 1,000 copies of his or her book by the Academy of American Poets for distribution to its membership.

1954
Constance Carrier
The Middle Voice (Swallow)
1955
Donald Hall
Exiles and Marriages (Viking)
1956
Philip Booth
Letter from a Distant Land (Viking)
1957
Daniel Berrigan
Time without Number (Macmillan)
1958
Ned O'Gorman
The Night of the Hammer (Harcourt)
1959
Donald Justice
The Summer Anniversaries (Wesleyan Univ. Press)
1960
Robert Mezey
The Lovemaker (Cummington)
1961
X. J. Kennedy
Nude Descending a Staircase (Doubleday)
1962
Edward Field
Stand up, Friend, with Me (Grove)
1963
No award
1964
Adrien Stoutenburg
Heroes, Advise Us (Scribner)
1965
Henri Coulette
The War of the Secret Agent and Other Poems (Scribner)
1966
Kenneth O. Hanson
The Distance Anywhere (Univ. of Washington Press)
1967
James Scully
The Marches (Holt)

1968
Jane Cooper
The Weather of Six Mornings (Macmillan)
1969
Marvin Bell
A Probable Volume of Dreams (Atheneum)
1970
William Harmon
Treasury Holiday (Wesleyan Univ. Press)
1971
Stephen Dobyns
Concurring Beasts (Atheneum)
1972
Peter Everwine
Collecting the Animals (Atheneum)
1973
Marilyn Hacker
Presentation Piece (Viking)
1974
John Balaban
After Our War (Univ. of Pittsburgh Press)
1975
Lisel Mueller
The Private Life (Louisiana State Univ. Press)
1976
Larry Levis
The Afterlife (Windhover)
1977
Gerald Stern
Lucky Life (Houghton)
1978
Ai
Killing Floor (Houghton)
1979
Frederick Seidel
Sunrise (Viking)

Harold Morton Landon Translation Award

The Harold Morton Landon Translation Award is given by the Academy of American Poets for a published translation of poetry from any language into English. The translation may be a book-length poem, a collection of poems, or a verse play translated into verse. The winning translator must be a living citizen of the United States. Published books (no manuscripts) should be sent to the Academy for consideration. A single judge, an eminent poet and translator, chooses the winner with the help of expert consultants. The biennial award of $1,000 was presented for the first time in February 1976.

1976
  Robert Fitzgerald
  The Iliad of Homer (Doubleday)
1978
  Galway Kinnell
  The Poems of François Villon (Houghton)

Howard Norman
The Wishing Bone Cycle (Stonehill)

Edgar Allan Poe Award

The Edgar Allan Poe Award was first presented in 1974. It recognized the continuing development of a living American poet, age 45 or under, on the occasion of the publication of a book of poems within the year preceding the year of the award. The award of $5,000 was offered annually in April by the Academy of American Poets and was supported by the Copernicus Society of America. A panel of three poets chose each year's winner.

1974
  Mark Strand
  The Story of Our Lives (Atheneum)
1975
  Charles Simic
  Return to a Place Lit by a Glass of Milk (Braziller)

1976
  Charles Wright
  Bloodlines (Wesleyan Univ. Press)
1977
  Stan Rice
  Whiteboy (Mudra)
Discontinued

Walt Whitman Award

The Walt Whitman Award was established in 1974 and first presented in 1975. Its purpose is to honor an American poet who has not yet published a book of poems and to ensure the publication of that poet's first book. The winning poet must be a living citizen of the United States. The Academy receives manuscript submissions between September 15 and November 15 of each year. One poet, serving as judge, makes the final selection of the winning manuscript. An entry form is required; potential contestants should write to the Academy during the summer before the contest for the rules brochure and entry form. The winning manuscript is published by a major publisher in a standard edition. The winning poet receives a cash award of $1,000. The Academy receives from the publisher 1,000 copies of the winning book and distributes them to members and friends. Presentation is made annually, usually in April.

1975
Reg Saner
Climbing into the Roots (Harper)
1976
Laura Gilpin
Hocus-Pocus of the Universe (Doubleday)
1977
Lauren Shakely
Guilty Bystander (Random)

1978
Karen Snow
Wonders (Viking)
1979
David Bottoms
Shooting Rats at the Bibb County Dump (Morrow)

Bollingen Prize in Poetry

The Bollingen Prize in Poetry, offered by the Yale University Library, New Haven, Connecticut 06520, was established in 1950. Funds for the period 1950–1973 were given by Bollingen Foundation, Inc. The award, based on published work and consisting of $5,000 ($1,000 from 1950 to 1959 and $2,500 from 1960 to 1963) is given to the American poet whose work in the opinion of the Committee of Award represents the highest achievement in the field of American poetry during the preceding two-year period. In 1949, when the award was under the sponsorship of the Library of Congress, Ezra Pound was the recipient. The Bollingen Prize was awarded annually from 1949 to 1963.

1950
Wallace Stevens
1951
John Crowe Ransom
1952
Archibald MacLeish
William Carlos Williams
1953
Marianne Moore
1954
W. H. Auden
1955
Léonie Adams
Louise Bogan
1956
Conrad Aiken
1957
Allen Tate

1958
e. e. cummings
1959
Theodore Roethke
1960
Delmore Schwartz
1961
Yvor Winters
1962
Richard Eberhart
John Hall Wheelock
1963
Robert Frost

1965
Horace Gregory
1967
Robert Penn Warren

1969
  John Berryman
  Karl Shapiro
1971
  Mona Van Duyn
  Richard Wilbur
1973
  James Merrill

1975
  A. R. Ammons
1977
  David Ignatow
1979
  W. S. Merwin

Robert Frost Fellowship in Poetry

The Bread Loaf Writers' Conference of Middlebury College, Middlebury, Vermont 05753, offers a fellowship in poetry made possible since 1956 by Holt, Rinehart and Winston, Inc., publishers of Robert Frost's works. Robert Frost helped to found the original American Writers' Conference in 1926 and was associated with it from the beginning. The award is given annually. The winner, announced each June, receives all expenses for tuition, room, and board for the Annual Bread Loaf Writers' Conference at Middlebury, Vermont. The fellowship is not open to general application; the winner is selected by the Bread Loaf staff upon nomination by distinguished writers and critics. Other awards given by the Bread Loaf Writers' Conference for prose or prose and poetry are described in the General Prizes section of this book.

1956
  Herbert A. Kenny
1957
  May Swenson
1958
  Anthony Ostroff
1959
  Anne Sexton
1960
  Claire McAllister
1961
  Milton Kessler
1962
  John Woods
1963
  Ruth Stone
1964
  David Ray (scholarship)
1965
  David Shapiro
1966
  Diane Wakoski
1967
  James Whitehead

1968
  Richard Braun
1969
  Mary Shumway
1970
  Gary Gildner
1971
  No award
1972
  Richard Allen
1973
  Lawrence Raab
1974
  Daniel Halpern
1975
  Carl Dennis
1976
  John Engels
1977
  Jane Shore
1978
  Greg Pape
1979
  Pamela Hadas

Golden Rose Trophy

Since 1925, the Golden Rose of the New England Poetry Club has been awarded annually to a poet for a notable contribution to the field of poetry, usually a recently published volume of verse. The Golden Rose, a naturalistic replica of silver gilt wrought by a French jeweler, is kept in a box on which the holders' names are inscribed. Passed to each new winner from year to year, the trophy was given to the club by the Reverend Eugene Shippen of the Second Unitarian Church, Boston, the originator of the Golden Rose Tournament in the United States. At that time the Rose was awarded to an annual winner in a poetry competition. This custom was patterned after the "Jeux Floreaux" which mimics the Provençal poetry tournaments of the Middle Ages. In recent years, the New England Poetry Club, c/o Diana Der Hovanessian, President, 2 Farrar Street, Cambridge, Massachusetts 02138, has awarded the trophy to a poet for outstanding "work in and service to poetry." Announcement of the new holder of the Golden Rose is made each May or June at the Golden Rose meeting in Boston. The winner is chosen by the Executive Board of the New England Poetry Club.

1925
   Earl Marlatt
1926
   Marshall Schacht
1927
   Katharine Lee Bates
1928
   Robert Frost
1929
   Joseph Auslander
1930
   Nancy Byrd Turner
1931
   Robert Hillyer
1932
   S. Foster Damon
1933
   Frances Frost
1934
   Archibald MacLeish
1935
   Gretchen Warren
1936
   Robert P. T. Coffin
1937
   John Hall Wheelock
1938
   John Holmes

1939
   Leonora Speyer
1940
   Kenneth Porter
1941
   David McCord
1942
   Robert Francis
1943
   Amos N. Wilder
1944
   Theodore Spencer
1945
   May Sarton
1946
   No award
1947
   David Morton
1948
   John Ciardi
1949
   William Rose Benét
1950
   Richard Eberhart
1951
   Richard Wilbur
1952
   No award

1953
Harry Elmore Hurd
1954
Harold Trowbridge Pulsifer
1956
Dorothy Burnham Eaton
1957
Samuel French Morse
1958
Norma Farber
1959
Morris Bishop
1960
Mark Van Doren
1961
Edwin Honig
1962
Howard Nemerov
1963
Dudley Fitts
1964
Robert Lowell
1965
Abbie Huston Evans
1966
Louis Untermeyer

1967
Elizabeth Coatsworth
1968
L. E. Sissman
1969
Allen Grossman
1970
Stanley Kunitz
1971
Constance Carrier
1972
Charles Edward Eaton
1973
Barbara Howes
1974
X. J. Kennedy
1975
Robert Penn Warren
1976
Robert Fitzgerald
1977
Maxine Kumin
1978
J. V. Cunningham
1979
John Updike

The Juniper Prize

The University of Massachusetts Press established the Juniper Prize in 1974 in honor of poet Robert Francis, who for many years has lived at Fort Juniper in Amherst, Massachusetts. The purpose of the award is to honor an outstanding manuscript of original English poetry. The award consists of $1,000 in lieu of royalties on the first print run. Manuscripts must be book length (approximately 64 printed pages), by a single author, and consist of poems not previously published in book form. Poems published in journals, chapbooks, and anthologies may be included but must be identified. Manuscripts should be sent to University of Massachusetts Press, Box 429, Amherst, Massachusetts 01002, together with a self-addressed stamped envelope and a $2 entry fee. Awards are announced annually in April.

1975
Eleanor Lerman
Come the Sweet By and By

1976
David Dwyer
Ariana Olisvos: Her Last Works and Days

1977
Jane Shore
Eye Level
1978
William Dickey
The Rainbow Grocery

1979
Eleanor Wilner
Maya

Lenore Marshall Memorial Poetry Award

This award was established in 1973 by the New Hope Foundation, Inc., in honor of Lenore Marshall, poet and author of "No Boundary," "Other Knowledge," and "Latest Will," who died in 1971. It is offered annually by the Book-of-the-Month Club, 485 Lexington Avenue, New York, New York 10017, in late spring or early summer. The award of $3,500 is presented for an outstanding new book of poems published in the United States by a living American poet. New editions of selected and collected works will be considered.

1974
Cid Corman
O/I (Elizabeth)
1975
Denise Levertov
The Freeing of the Dust (New Directions)

1976–1979
No awards

Harriet Monroe Poetry Award

The Harriet Monroe Poetry Award of $500 was established under the will of Harriet Monroe, founder and for more than twenty years editor of *Poetry*, for the "advancement and encouragement of poetry" in America. The Award Committee consists of three poets appointed by the president of the University of Chicago, Chicago, Illinois 60637. There is no competition for the award, and preference is given to poets of progressive, rather than academic, tendencies. The award is made from time to time, whenever sufficient income is available from the fund.

1941
Muriel Rukeyser
1944
Marianne Moore
1946
Wallace Stevens
1948
Louise Bogan

1950
e. e. cummings
1952
Robert Lowell
1954
Léonie Adams
1955
Richard Eberhart

1957
  John Berryman
1958
  Stanley Kunitz
1960-1961
  Hayden Carruth
  Yvor Winters

1974
  Elizabeth Bishop
1975
  John Ashbery
1976
  Richard Wilbur

Poetry Magazine

Poetry, published by the Modern Poetry Association, 601 South Morgan Street, Box 4348, Chicago, Illinois 60680, sponsors the following awards annually. The prizes are given for work that has appeared in the magazine during the preceding year and are announced in the November issue. A jury decides on the winning poems, giving consideration to each poet's general achievement or promise. Poems by members of the staff of Poetry or the Board of Trustees of the Modern Poetry Association are not eligible. No single prize can be given twice to the same poet. There is no official presentation of awards; checks are mailed to the winning poets. Many prominent American poets first achieved recognition in Poetry magazine. The George Dillon Memorial Prize (1968-1972), the Frank O'Hara Prize (1967-1972), and the Union League Civic and Arts Foundation Prize (1951-1972) have been discontinued. Lists of winners of these three awards can be found in the ninth edition of Literary and Library Prizes.

The Oscar Blumenthal Prize

The Oscar Blumenthal Prize of $100 is awarded for a poem or group of poems published in Poetry. It was established in 1936 by Charles Leviton, continued by Edward Blonder, and is now given annually through the generosity of Sol H. Morris.

1936
  Marion Strobel
1937
  Thomas Hornsby Ferril
1938
  Dylan Thomas
1939
  Maxwell Bodenheim
1940
  Muriel Rukeyser
1941
  Stanley Kunitz
1942
  E. L. Mayo

1943
  John Ciardi
1944
  P. K. Page
1945
  Yvor Winters
1946
  George Moor
1947
  James Merrill
1948
  Weldon Kees
1949
  Barbara Gibbs

1950
  Richard Wilbur
1951
  Randall Jarrell
1952
  Roy Marz
1953
  William Meredith
1954
  Anne Ridler
1955
  William Carlos Williams
1956
  Sydney Goodsir Smith
1957
  Ben Belitt
1958
  Howard Nemerov
1959
  Josephine Miles
1960
  Charles Tomlinson
1961
  Kathleen Raine
1962
  e. e. cummings
1963
  Karl Shapiro
1964
  Robert Creeley

1965
  Charles Olson
1966
  Louis Zukofsky
1967
  Guy Davenport
1968
  James Wright
1969
  Turner Cassity
1970
  Jon Anderson
1971
  Geoffrey Grigson
1972
  Douglas Le Pan
1973
  Brewster Ghiselin
1974
  David Wagoner
1975
  Sandra McPherson
1976
  David Bromwich
1977
  Alfred Corn
1978
  Robert Pinsky

Jacob Glatstein Memorial Prize

The Jacob Glatstein Memorial Prize of $100 for a poem or group of poems published in *Poetry* was established in 1972 in memory of the late Yiddish poet.

1972
  Rae Dalven
1973
  Marya Zaturenska
1974
  Raphael Rudnik
1975
  Jayanta Mahapatra

1976
  Martha Hollander
1977
  Robert Siegel
1978
  Daniel Weissbort

Bess Hokin Prize

This award of $100 was established in 1947 by the late Mrs. David Hokin of Chicago to be given annually in her memory for a poem or group of poems published in *Poetry* by a young poet. Mrs. Hokin was formerly a guarantor of *Poetry*.

1948
William Abrahams
1949
Barbara Howes
1950
Lloyd Frankenberg
1951
M. B. Tolson
1952
L. E. Hudgins
1953
Ruth Stone
1954
Hayden Carruth
1955
Philip Booth
1956
Charles Tomlinson
1957
Sylvia Plath
1958
Alan Neame
1959
Jean Clower
1960
Denise Levertov
1961
X. J. Kennedy
1962
W. S. Merwin
1963
Adrienne Rich

1964
Gary Snyder
1965
Galway Kinnell
1966
Thomas Clark
1967
Wendell Berry
1968
Michael Benedikt
1969
Marvin Bell
1970
Charles Martin
1971
Erica Jong
1972
Sandra McPherson
1973
Jane Shore
1974
Margaret Atwood
1975
Charles O. Hartman
1976
Norman Dubie
1977
Gary Soto
1978
Richard Kenney

Levinson Prize

The Levinson Prize of $100 was founded in 1914 and presented for twenty-seven years through the generosity of Salmon O. Levinson, internationally distinguished lawyer and publicist. It was continued by his family and is now permanently endowed, offering $300 each year. It is awarded for a poem or group of poems published in *Poetry*.

1914
Carl Sandburg
1915
Vachel Lindsay
1916
Edgar Lee Masters
1917
Cloyd Head
1918
O. C. Underwood
1919
H. L. Davis
1920
Wallace Stevens
1921
Lew Sarett
1922
Robert Frost
1923
Edwin Arlington Robinson
1924
Amy Lowell
1925
Ralph Cheever Dunning
1926
Mark Turbyfill
1927
Maurice Lesemann
1928
Elinor Wylie
1929
Marjorie Seiffert
1930
Hart Crane
1931
Edna St. Vincent Millay
1932
No award
1933
Marianne Moore
1934
Horace Gregory
1935
Mary Barnard
1936
Robert Penn Warren

1937
Louise Bogan
1938
Hilda Doolittle
["H.D."]
1939
e. e. cummings
1940
Robinson Jeffers
1941
Archibald MacLeish
1942
Karl J. Shapiro
1943
John Malcolm Brinnin
1944
John Frederick Nims
1945
Dylan Thomas
1946
John Ciardi
1947
Muriel Rukeyser
1948
Randall Jarrell
1949
James Merrill
1950
John Berryman
1951
Theodore Roethke
1952
Saint-John Perse
1953
Vernon Watkins
1954
William Carlos Williams
1955
Thom Gunn
1956
Stanley Kunitz
1957
Jay Macpherson
1958
Hayden Carruth
1959
Delmore Schwartz

1960
  Robert Creeley
1961
  David Jones
1962
  Anne Sexton
1963
  Robert Lowell
1964
  Robert Duncan
1965
  George Barker
1966
  Basil Bunting
1967
  Alan Dugan
1968
  Gary Snyder
1969
  A. D. Hope

1970
  A. R. Ammons
1971
  Turner Cassity
1972
  Michael Hamburger
1973
  Richard Howard
1974
  John Hollander
1975
  Howard Nemerov
1976
  Judith Moffett
1977
  John Ashbery
1978
  Brewster Ghiselin

Eunice Tietjens Memorial Prize

This award of $200 was established in 1944 by Cloyd Head as a memorial to Janet Tietjens Hart, a former associate editor of *Poetry,* and is continued by Marshal Head in memory of her and his father.

1944
  John Ciardi
1945
  Marie Borroff
1946
  Alfred Hayes
1947
  Theodore Roethke
1948
  Peter Viereck
1949
  Gwendolyn Brooks
1950
  Andrew Glaze
1951
  Robinson Jeffers
1952
  e. e. cummings

1953
  Elder Olson
1954
  Reuel Denney
1955
  James Wright
1956
  Mona Van Duyn
1957
  Kenneth Rexroth
1958
  James Merrill
1959
  Barbara Howes
1960
  Marie Ponsot
1961
  Karl Shapiro

1962
   Muriel Rukeyser
1963
   Helen Singer
1964
   Hayden Carruth
1965
   Pauline Hanson
1966
   Galway Kinnell
1967
   Robert Duncan
1968
   Adrienne Rich
1969
   Charles Wright
1970
   Jean Malley

1971
   Louise Glück
1972
   Maxine Kumin
1973
   Judith Moffett
1974
   Judith Minty
1975
   James McMichael
1976
   Richard Kenney
1977
   David Wagoner
1978
   William Heyen

Poetry Society of America

The Poetry Society of America, 15 Gramercy Park, New York, New York 10003, awards the following prizes, which are presented annually at the Poetry Society of America dinner in New York City in late January. Asterisks indicate years in which awards were made but for which the winners' names are not available. The James Joyce Award (1965 – 1975) and the William Marion Reedy Award (1965 – 1974) have been discontinued. Lists of winners are included in the ninth edition of *Literary and Library Prizes*.

Poetry Society of America Annual Prizes

Since its inception, the Poetry Society of America has read unpublished poems at its monthly meetings, with the identity of the authors remaining undisclosed until a vote was cast for the two favorite poems. All the monthly poems winning first and second place were printed in a poem ballot, which was mailed to all members, and the two receiving the highest score were declared winners of first and second annual awards. A Devil's Advocate's Award was also given, determined by a jury selecting one poem from those in the monthly contests that did *not* win prizes. The names of the winners listed below are taken from the Society's records. Only first-prize winners are listed below.

1916
   Jessie Rittenhouse

1917
   Sara Teasdale

1918
No award
1919
David Morton
1920
Amanda Benjamin Hall
*1921
*1922
1923
Roselle Mercier Montgomery
1924
Amanda Benjamin Hall
1925
Witter Bynner
1926
Grace Hazard Conkling
1927
Daniel Henderson
1928
Margaret Belle Houston
1929
Ernest Hartsock
1930
Roselle Mercier Montgomery
1931
Daniel Whitehead Hicky
William H. McCreary
1932
Gertrude B. Claytor
1933
Fay M. Yauger
1934
Dorothy C. Pinkney
1935
Leonora Speyer
1936
Leonora Speyer
1937
James Warren
1938
Helen Morrow
1939
Helen Morrow
1940
Clark Mills
1941
Frederick Wright

1942
Edith Henrich
1943
Edith Henrich
1944
Rosalie Moore
1945
Elda Tanasso
1946
Fania Kruger
1947
Inez Barclay Kirby
1948
Maureen Mabbott
1949
Laura Lourene LeGear
1950
Frances Minturn Howard
1951
Edna L. S. Barker
1952
Florence Ripley Mastin
1953
Ruth Forbes Sherry
1954
Constance Carrier
1955
Virginia Earle
1956
Joyce Horner
1957
I. L. Salomon
1958
Gustav Davidson
1959
Beren Van Slyke
1960
Ulrich Troubetzkoy
1961
Norma Farber
1962
Theodore Roethke
1963
Mary Oliver
1964
Frances Minturn Howard

1965
Christie Jeffries
1966
Hamilton Warren
1967
Lois Smith Hiers
1968
Charles A. Brady
1969
Beren Van Slyke
1970
Hamilton Warren
1971
Charles A. Wagner
1972
Frances Minturn Howard

1973
Larry Rubin
1974
Louise Gunn
1975
Sarah Singer
1976
Ryah Tumarkin Goodman
1977
Helen Adam
1978
Geraldine Little
1979
Alfred Dorn
Discontinued

Bernice Ames Memorial Award

This $100 award was established in 1978 for a poem of any length in any traditional form, excluding nonsyllabic free verse. It is given by friends of the late poet Bernice Ames. Deadline for entries is December 31.

Gordon Barber Memorial Award

Given by Melanie Barber in memory of her son Gordon, this annual $200 award is given for a poem of exceptional merit, of any length, style, or theme. The deadline is December 31.

Witter Bynner Poetry Translation Grant-in-Aid

A grant-in-aid of $1,000 was established in 1979 to be given for a book-in-progress by an American citizen or resident who has previously published at least one book of poetry translated into English in the United States. Applicants should submit before August 30 three copies of an outline of the translation-in-progress, a sample of the translation (under 20 pages), and a parallel sample of the original text.

Witter Bynner Poetry Translation Prize

This $1,000 prize will be awarded for a volume of poetry translated into English and published during the previous two years in the United States. It is open to works of single translators or to collaborations of two translators, at least one of whom must be a U.S. citizen or resident. Four copies of each entry should be submitted before August 30.

Melville Cane Award

This award for $500 was established by Harcourt Brace Jovanovich in 1960. It is given alternately for a book of poems and a book on poetry or a poet. Books should be submitted by publishers before December 31.

1962
Richard Wilbur
Advice to a Prophet and Other Poems (Harcourt)
1963
Clark Emery
The World of Dylan Thomas (Univ. of Miami Press)
1964
Joseph Langland
The Wheel of Summer (Dial)
1965
Jean Hagstrum
William Blake: Poet and Painter (Univ. of Chicago Press)
1966
James Dickey
Buckdancer's Choice (Wesleyan Univ. Press)
1967
Lawrance Thompson
Robert Frost: The Early Years (Holt)
1968
Jean Garrigue
New and Selected Poems (Macmillan)
1969
Ruth Miller
The Poetry of Emily Dickinson (Wesleyan Univ. Press)
1970
Rolfe Humphries
Coat on a Stick: Late Poems (Indiana Univ. Press)

1971
Harold Bloom
Yeats (Oxford Univ. Press)
1972
James Wright
Collected Poems (Wesleyan Univ. Press)
1973
Jerome J. McGann
Swinburne (Univ. of Chicago Press)
1974
William Stafford
Some Day, Maybe (Harper)
1975
Richard B. Sewall
The Life of Emily Dickinson (Farrar)
1976
Charles Wright
Bloodlines (Wesleyan Univ. Press)
1977
Donald R. Howard
The Idea of the Canterbury Tales (Univ. of California Press)
1978
Michael Harper
Image of Ki (Harcourt)
1979
Andrew Welsh
Roots of Lyric (Princeton Univ. Press)

Gertrude B. Claytor Memorial Award

This $250 award is for a poem in any form and of any length on the American scene or American character. Only members of the Poetry Society of America are eligible. The deadline is December 31.

1975
Charles A. Wagner
1976
Ulrich Troubetzkoy
1977
Gary Miranda

1978
Kathleen Spivack
L. L. Zeiger
1979
Isabel Nathaniel

Gustav Davidson Memorial Award

This $500 award is for an unpublished sonnet or a sonnet sequence, not to exceed three sonnets. Only members of the Poetry Society of America are eligible. The deadline is December 31.

1972
Lisa Grenelle
1973
Sallie W. Nixon
1974
Sarah Singer
1975
Florence Jacobs

1976
Peter Meinke
1977
Ulrich Troubetzkoy
1978
Norma Farber
1979
Richard Frost

Mary Carolyn Davies Award

This $250 award is for a poem, not to exceed thirty lines, that would be suitable for setting to music. The deadline is December 31. Only members of the Poetry Society of America are eligible.

1976
Catherine Hayden Jacobs
1977
Diana Der Hovanessian

1978
Cheri Fein
1979
Ulrich Troubetzkoy

Alice Fay di Castagnola Award

This $2,000 award is for a work-in-progress (prose, verse, or verse drama) in honor of a friend and benefactor of the Society. Contestants should send four copies of a brief résumé or outline (along with about 100 lines of verse if the project is poetry, a specimen chapter if prose, or a scene if verse drama) of a single, uncompleted but well-advanced original work, the prose work dealing with some aspect of poetry, either biographical or critical. Only members of the Poetry Society of America are eligible. The deadline is December 15.

1965
  Barbara Harr
  Paul Roche
1966
  Edsel Ford
1967
  Gustav Davidson
1968
  Joseph Tusiani
  Ruth Whitman
1969
  Wade Van Dore
1970
  Jenny Lind Porter
  Wallace Winchell
1971
  Cornel Lengyel
  Marcia Lee Masters

1972
  Erica Jong
  Myra Sklarew
1973
  Mary Oliver
  George Keithley
1974
  Charles Eaton
1975
  Philip Appleman
1976
  Ann Stanford
1977
  Naomi Lazard
  Linda Pastan
1978
  Carol Muske
1979
  No award

Emily Dickinson Award

This $100 award is for a poem, not to exceed thirty lines, inspired by the New England poet, although not necessarily in imitation of her style. Only members of the Poetry Society of America are eligible. The deadline is September 1.

1971
  Olga Cabral
  Ree Dragonette
1972
  Harold Witt
1973
  Sandra McPherson
*1974
1975
  Marjorie Hawksworth

1976
  Floyd Skloot
1977
  Siv Cedering Fox
1978
  Phyllis Janowitz
1979
  Mildred Nash

Consuelo Ford Award

This $250 award is for a lyric poem, not to exceed fifty lines. Only members of the Poetry Society of America are eligible. The deadline is December 31.

1972
  Frances Minturn Howard

1973
  Sarah Singer

1974
  Mary Ann Braunlin Coleman
  James Reiss
1975
  Florence Trefethen
  Ruth Whitman
1976
  Gary Miranda
  Nina Nyhart

1977
  Joan La Bombard
1978
  Gary Miranda
  Grace Morton
1979
  Joan La Bombard

Cecil Hemley Award

This $300 award is given annually for an unpublished lyric poem on a philosophical theme that does not exceed 100 lines. Donors are Ralynn Stadler and Jack Stadler. Only members of the Poetry Society of America are eligible. The deadline is September 1.

1969
  Willis Barnstone
1970
  Charles A. Brady
1971
  Bernice Ames
1972
  Ann Jonas
1973
  Helen Sorrells
1974
  Anne Marx

1975
  Ruth Lisa Schechter
1976
  No award
1977
  Isabel Nathaniel
1978
  Gary Miranda
1979
  Geraldine C. Little

Alfred Kreymborg Memorial Award

A $100 award is given for a poem of merit in any form, not to exceed 100 lines. Translations are ineligible. Only members of the Poetry Society of America are eligible. The deadline is December 31.

1973–1974
  No awards
1975
  Madeline Bass
1976
  Colette Inez

1977
  Geraldine C. Little
1978
  Phyllis Janowitz
1979
  Elizabeth Spires

Elias Lieberman Award

This $100 award is given for the best poem by a high school or preparatory school student in the United States, with no restriction as to subject, form, or length. The deadline is December 31.

1971
  Lyn Kelly
1972
  Alan Farago
1973
  Heidi Schmidt
1974
  Jean Sherrard
1975
  Psyche Anne Pascual

1976
  Edward Gaillard
1977
  Paul J. Davis
1978
  Marilyn Plastric
1979
  Catherine Talmadge

John Masefield Award

This $500 award was established by Dr. Corliss Lamont in memory of the late Poet Laureate. It is given for a narrative poem, written in English, which does not exceed 300 lines. The poet is not required to be a member of the Poetry Society of America. Translations are ineligible. The deadline is December 31.

1969
  Siv Cedering Fox
1970
  Alvin Reiss
1971
  Sallie Nixon
1972
  Donald Junkins
1973
  No award
1974
  Penelope Schott Starkey
1975
  Gail Trebbe

1976
  Burt Blume
  Ruth Whitman
  Jack Zucker
1977
  Frederick Feirstein
  Lynn Sukenick
1978
  Dorothy Foltz-Gray
1979
  G. N. Gabbard

Lucille Medwick Memorial Award

This $500 award was established by Maury Medwick in memory of his wife, the poet and editor, for an original poem of humanitarian theme, in any form or in free form, not to exceed 100 lines. Translations are ineligible. The deadline is December 31. Only members of the Poetry Society of America are eligible.

1974
   Joan La Bombard
1975
   Violette Newton
1976
   Olga Cabral

1977
   Peter Klappert
1978
   Willis Barnstone
1979
   Gary Miranda

Christopher Morley Award

This $500 award for light verse, not to exceed 100 lines, was given by Frances Steloff in honor of the late poet and satirist. It was open to members of the Poetry Society of America only.

1969
   David Ross
1970
   Philip Appleman
1971
   Sarah Lockwood
1972
   R. F. Armknecht
   Vinnie-Marie D'Ambrosio
1973
   Norma Farber

1974
   Milton Kaplan
   Gary Miranda
1975
   Philip Appleman
1976
   S. Gordden Link
   Ralph Robin
1977
   Darcy Gottlieb
Discontinued

Shelley Memorial Award

This annual prize in memory of Percy Bysshe Shelley was established in 1929 through a bequest by Mary P. Sears of Waltham, Massachusetts. The award, approximately $1,750, is given to the poet or poets judged most deserving on the basis of published work and financial need. All poets are eligible.

1930
   Conrad Aiken
1931
   Lizette Woodworth Reese
1932
   Archibald MacLeish
1933
   Stephen Vincent Benét
1934
   Frances Frost
   Lola Ridge
1935
   Lola Ridge
   Marya Zaturenska

1936
   Josephine Miles
1937
   Ben Belitt
   Charlotte Wilder
1938
   Lincoln Fitzell
1939
   Harry Brown
   Robert Francis
1940
   Herbert Brunchen
   Winfield Townley Scott

1941
Marianne Moore
1942
Ridgely Torrence
1943
Percy MacKaye
Robert Penn Warren
1944
Edgar Lee Masters
1945
e. e. cummings
1946
Karl Shapiro
1947
Rolfe Humphries
1948
Janet Lewis
1949
John Berryman
1950
Louis Kent
1951
Jeremy Ingalls
1952
Richard Eberhart
1953
Elizabeth Bishop
1954
Kenneth Patchen
1955
Léonie Adams
1956
Robert Fitzgerald
1957
George Abbe
1958
Kenneth Rexroth
1959
José García Villa
1960
Delmore Schwartz
1961
Robinson Jeffers

1962
Theodore Roethke
1963
Eric Barker
1964
William Stafford
1965
Ruth Stone
1966
David Ignatow
1967
Anne Sexton
1968
May Swenson
1969
Ann Stanford
1970
X. J. Kennedy
Mary Oliver
1971
Louise Townsend Nicholl
Adrienne Rich
1972
Galway Kinnell
1973
John Ashbery
Richard Wilbur
1974
W. S. Merwin
1975
Edward Field
1976
Gwendolyn Brooks
1977
Muriel Rukeyser
1978
Jane Cooper
William Everson
1979
Hayden Carruth

Celia B. Wagner Memorial Award

This annual $250 award is for the best poem worthy of the tradition of the art, in any style and of any length. It is given in recognition of the Executive Secretary of the Society and his late wife and is open to all poets. The deadline is December 31.

1976
  Sarah Singer
1977
  Joan La Bombard

1978
  Tony Weston
1979
  Ona Siporin

William Carlos Williams Award

This new award will be given for a book of poetry published by a small press, a nonprofit press, or a university press. Publishers should submit four copies of one original work (previously unpublished) by a poet who is a permanent U.S. resident. Translations, adaptations, and submissions by authors are ineligible. The Poetry Society of America will purchase 500 copies of the winning book at a discount of retail price to a total of $1,250 (1978). These copies will then be distributed free, upon request, to the Society's members. The book's author will receive a standard royalty from the publisher.

Roanoke – Chowan Poetry Cup

This award was established in 1953 by the Roanoke –Chowan Group in order to stimulate among the people of North Carolina an interest in their own literature. The cup is given each year at the annual meeting of the North Carolina Literary and Historical Association, 109 East Jones Street, Raleigh, North Carolina 27611, for the best work of poetry by a resident of North Carolina. For a work to be eligible it must have been published during the twelve-month period from July 1 to June 30; announcement is made in November. Authors of books considered must have maintained legal or actual residence in North Carolina for three years immediately preceding the close of the contest period.

1953
  Frank Borden Hanes
  Abel Anders (Farrar)
1954
  Thad Stem, Jr.
  The Jackknife Horse (Wolf's Head)
1955
  No award

1956
  Helen Bevington
  Change of Sky (Houghton)

1957
  Dorothy Edwards Summerrow
  Ten Angels Swearing
  (Exposition)

1958
Paul Bartlett
Moods and Memories (Heritage House)

1959
Olive Tilford Dargan
The Spotted Hawk (Blair)

1960
Carl Sandburg
Harvest Poems (Harcourt)

1961
Carl Sandburg
Wind Song (Harcourt)

1962
Helen Bevington
When Found, Make a Verse Of (Simon & Schuster)

1963
Herman Salinger
A Sigh Is the Sword (Heritage House)

1964
E. S. Gregg
Reap Silence (McNally & Loftin)

1965
Randall Jarrell
The Lost World (Macmillan)

1966
Thad Stem, Jr.
Spur Line (McNally & Loftin)

1967
Walter Blackstock
Leaves before the Wind (Methodist College Press)

1968
Paul Baker Newman
The Cheetah and the Fountain (South & West)

1969
Guy Owen
The White Stallion (Blair)

1970
Charles Edward Eaton
On the Edge of the Knife (Abelard)

1971
Paul Baker Newman
The Ladder of Love (Horizon)

1972
Fred Chappell
The World between the Eyes (Louisiana State Univ. Press)

1973
Ronald H. Bayes
The Casketmaker (Blair)

1974
Campbell Reeves
Coming Out Even (Moore)

1975
Marion Cannon
Another Light (Red Clay)

1976
Fred Chappell
River (Louisiana State Univ. Press)

1977
Norman Macleod
The Distance (Pembroke Univ. Press)

1978
Mary Louise Medley
Seasons and Days (St. Andrews)

The Swallow Press New Poetry Series Award

Anyone who has not previously published a book-length collection of poems is eligible for the New Poetry Series Award. Established in 1949, its purpose is to offer the most suitable publication for a first volume of poetry. The winning manuscript is published under royalty contract in the New Poetry series by the Swallow Press, Inc., 811 West Junior Terrace, Chicago, Illinois 60613. Except for juvenile verse, no subject is barred. Manuscript length varies, but is usually forty to sixty pages.

1949
  Donald F. Drummond
  No Moat No Castle
  John Pauker
  Yoked by Violence
  John Williams
  The Broken Landscape
1950
  Hanson Kellogg
  Attics Own Houses
1951
  Frona Lane
  The Third Eyelid
1952
  Carl Bode
  The Sacred Seasons
  Morris Weisenthal
  Walls of the Labyrinth
1953
  Harold Norse
  The Undersea Mountain
1954
  Harvey Shapiro
  The Eye
  Wesley Trimpi
  The Glass of Perseus
1955
  Katherine Bellamann
  Two Sides of a Poem
  Edgar Bowers
  The Form of Loss
  Robert Hutchinson
  The Kitchen Dance
1956
  Richard Lyons
  Men and Tin Kettles
  Marcia Nardi
  Poems
  Conrad Pendleton
  Slow Fire of Time
  Cynthia Pickard
  Woman in Apartment

1957
  Ellen Kay
  A Local Habitation
  Alan Stephens
  The Sum
1958
  Vi Gale
  Several Houses
1959
  Ronald Perry
  The Rock Harbor
1960
  Elma Wilkins Foster
  The Sound of Shadows
1961
  Elizabeth Harrod
  Seascape with Snow
  James L. Rosenberg
  A Primer of Kinetics
1962
  Charles Black
  Telescopes and Islands
  Maxine Cassin
  A Touch of Recognition
1963
  Carol Johnson
  Figure for Scamander and Other Poems
  Celeste Turner Wright
  Etruscan Princess and Other Poems
1964
  Joan Simpson Meyers
  Poetry and a Libretto
1965
  Richard Gillman
  Too Much Alone
  Lucien Stryk
  Notes for a Guidebook
  Joan Swift
  This Element
1966
  Nelson Bentley
  Sea Lion Caves and Other Poems

Ruby Fogel
Of Apes and Angels
Roger Hecht
27 Poems
1967–1968
No awards
1969
Charles Boer
The Odes
R. P. Dickey
Running Lucky
William Moebius
Elegies and Odes
Allen Planz
A Night for Rioting
1970
Michael Anania
The Color of Dust

Barbara Harr
The Mortgaged Wife
1971
James McMichael
Against the Falling Evil
John Matthias
Bucyrus
1972
Peter Michelson
The Eater
Linda Pastan
A Perfect Circle of Sun
1973
William Hunt
Of the Map That Changes
Temporarily suspended

United States Award

The International Poetry Forum and the University of Pittsburgh Press have presented this award annually since 1967. It is given for a manuscript of original poetry in English, which should be at least forty-eight manuscript pages long. U.S. citizens who have not previously published a volume of poetry are eligible. From 1967 through 1976, the award consisted of $2,000 and the publication of the manuscript by the University of Pittsburgh Press with standard royalties. Although after 1976 there has been no cash award and no formal "competition," the University of Pittsburgh Press will consider first manuscripts of poetry submitted between February 1 and April 1 and hope to publish at least one and perhaps more volumes from this consideration. Details may be obtained from Pitt Poetry Editor, University of Pittsburgh Press, 127 North Bellefield Avenue, Pittsburgh, Pennsylvania 15260.

1967
James Den Boer
Learning the Way
1968
David P. Young
Sweating out the Winter
1969
Shirley Kaufman
The Floor Keeps Turning
1970
Richard Shelton
The Tattooed Desert

1971
Larry Lewis
Wrecking Crew
1972
Marc Weber
48 Small Poems
1973
Judith Minty
Lake Songs and Other Fears
1974
Thomas Rabbitt
Exile

1975
   Mark Halperin
   Backroads

1976
   Gary Soto
   The Elements of San Joaquin

Yale Series of Younger Poets

Contests for publication in the Yale Series of Younger Poets were initiated in 1919 by Clarence Day, well-known author and brother of the founder of Yale University Press. The contests are intended to provide a medium for publication of a first volume of poetry for America's promising poets and are open to men and women under forty who have not previously published a volume of verse. Manuscripts must be submitted between February 1 and February 28. The choice of the winning manuscript is made by the editor of the Yale Series of Younger Poets. The award consists of publication by the Press and royalties on copies sold. For further information write to Yale Series of Younger Poets, Yale University Press, 92A Yale Station, New Haven, Connecticut 06520. During the editorship of Stephen Vincent Benét from 1933 to 1942 there was an additional award of $100 allocated to the winner from the editorial fee. From 1920 to 1923, four volumes were published each year as a result of semiannual contests held in the spring and fall. From 1926 to 1929, two volumes were issued semi-annually, and from 1930 on only one contest has been held each year.

1919
   Howard Buck
   The Tempering
   John Chipman Farrar
   Forgotten Shrines
1920
   Alfred Raymond Bellinger
   Spires and Poplars
   Darl Macleod Boyle
   Where Lilith Dances
   Thomas Caldecot Chubb
   The White God and Other Poems
   David Osborne Hamilton
   Four Gardens
1921
   Hervey Allen
   Wampum and Old Gold
   Theodore H. Banks, Jr.
   Wild Geese
   Viola C. White
   Horizons
   Oscar Williams
   The Golden Darkness

1922
   Medora C. Addison
   Dreams and a Sword
   Bernard Raymund
   Hidden Waters
   Paul Tanaquil
   Attitudes
   Harold Vinal
   White April

1923
   Marion M. Boyd
   Silver Wands
   Beatrice E. Harmon
   Mosaics
   Dean B. Lyman, Jr.
   The Last Lutanist
   Amos Niven Wilder
   Battle-Retrospect

1924
   Elizabeth Jessup Blake
   Up and Down

1925
Dorothy E. Reid
Coach into Pumpkin
1926
Thomas Hornsby Ferril
High Passage
Eleanor Slater
Quest
1927
Mildred Bowers
Twist o' Smoke
Lindley Williams Hubbell
Dark Pavilion
1928
Francis Claiborne Mason
This Unchanging Mask
Ted Olson
A Stranger and Afraid
1929
Henri Faust
Half-Light and Overtones
Frances M. Frost
Hemlock Wall
1930
Louise Owen
Virtuosa: A Book of Verse
1931
Dorothy Belle Flanagan
Dark Certainty
1932
Paul H. Engle
Worn Earth
1933
Shirley Barker
Dark Hills Under
1934
James Agee
Permit Me Voyage
1935
Muriel Rukeyser
Theory of Flight
1936
Edward Weismiller
The Deer Come Down
1937
Margaret Haley
The Gardener Mind

1938
Joy Davidman
Letter to a Comrade
1939
Reuel Denney
The Connecticut River and Other Poems
1940
Norman Rosten
Return Again, Traveler
1941
Jeremy Ingalls
The Metaphysical Sword
1942
Margaret Walker
For My People
1943
William Meredith
Love Letter from an Impossible Land
1944
Charles E. Butler
Cut Is the Branch
1945
Eve Merriam
Family Circle
1946
Joan Vincent Murray
Poems
1947
Robert Horan
A Beginning
1948
Rosalie Moore
The Grasshopper's Man and Other Poems
1949 –1950
No awards
1951
Adrienne Rich
A Change of World
1952
W. S. Merwin
A Mask for Janus
1953
Edgar Bogardus
Various Jangling Keys

1954
　Daniel G. Hoffman
　An Armada of Thirty Whales
1955
　No award
1956
　John L. Ashbery
　Some Trees
1957
　James Wright
　The Green Wall
1958
　John Hollander
　A Crackling of Thorns
1959
　William Dickey
　Of the Festivity
1960
　George Starbuck
　Bone Thoughts
1961
　Alan Dugan
　Poems
1962
　Jack Gilbert
　Views of Jeopardy
1963
　Sandra Hochman
　Manhattan Pastures
1964
　Peter Davison
　The Breaking of the Day: And Other Poems
1965
　Jean Valentine
　Dream Barker and Other Poems
1966
　James Tate
　The Lost Pilot

1967
　Helen Chasin
　Coming Close and Other Poems
1968
　Judith Johnson Sherwin
　Uranium Poems
1969
　Hugh Seidman
　Collecting Evidence
1970
　Peter Klappert
　Lugging Vegetables to Nantucket
1971
　Michael Casey
　Obscenities
1972
　Robert Hass
　Field Guide
1973
　Michael Ryan
　Threats Instead of Trees
1974
　Maura Stanton
　Snow on Snow

1975
　Carolyn Forché
　Gathering the Tribes

1976
　Olga Broumas
　Beginning with O

1977
　Bin Ramke
　The Difference between Night and Day

1978
　Leslie Ullman
　Natural Histories

Drama Prizes

New York Drama Critics Circle Award

In October 1935, the drama critics of New York, meeting in the Algonquin Hotel, established an organization known as the New York Drama Critics Circle. The Circle annually awards a scroll to an American playwright for the play that, in the Circle's opinion, was the best produced in New York City during the current season. This award was established to counterbalance the Pulitzer Prize for drama, with which the critics were rarely in agreement. In 1938 the Circle initiated an award for the best foreign play of the season, and since 1946 a citation has been given for the best musical. The Circle withholds the award if no play is deemed worthy of the distinction in any of the three categories.

The Circle decided in 1962 that in the future "There shall be one ballot cast for the best play—drama or musical—regardless of the country of its origin." The amendment also provides: "If a foreign work should win the award, the Circle may, if it chooses, name a best American play. If an American play wins, the Circle may also choose a best foreign play. The choice of a musical is, as always, left to the discretion of the Circle."

From 1966 to 1974, a cash award of $1,000 accompanied the critics' citation. This was provided by the Institute for Advanced Studies in the Theater Arts in conjunction with the Harry and Margery G. Kahn Foundation and was presented annually for five years. In 1978, theater owner and producer Lucille Lortiel donated a sum that ensures a permanent annual award of $1,000 for the best play presented in New York City during the previous year.

AMERICAN PLAY

1936
   Maxwell Anderson
   Winterset (Dodd)
1937
   Maxwell Anderson
   High Tor (Dodd)
1938
   John Steinbeck
   Of Mice and Men (Covici)
1939
   No award

1940
   William Saroyan
   The Time of Your Life (Harcourt)
1941
   Lillian Hellman
   The Watch on the Rhine (Random)
1942
   No award
1943
   Sidney Kingsley
   The Patriots (Random)
1944
   No award

AMERICAN PLAY (cont.)

1945
Tennessee Williams
The Glass Menagerie (Random)
1946
No award
1947
Arthur Miller
All My Sons (Reynal)
1948
Tennessee Williams
A Streetcar Named Desire (New Directions; New American Library)
1949
Arthur Miller
Death of a Salesman (Viking)
1950
Carson McCullers
The Member of the Wedding (Houghton)
1951
Sidney Kingsley
Darkness at Noon (Random)
1952
John Van Druten
I Am a Camera (Random)
1953
William Inge
Picnic (Random)
1954
John Patrick
The Teahouse of the August Moon (Putnam)
1955
Tennessee Williams
Cat on a Hot Tin Roof (New Directions; New American Library)
1956
Frances Goodrich and Albert Hackett
The Diary of Anne Frank (Random)
1957
Eugene O'Neill
Long Day's Journey into Night (Yale Univ. Press)
1958
Ketti Frings
Look Homeward, Angel (Scribner)

1959
Lorraine Hansberry
A Raisin in the Sun (Random)
1960
Lillian Hellman
Toys in the Attic (Random)
1961
Tad Mosel
All the Way Home (Obolensky)
1962
Tennessee Williams
The Night of the Iguana (New Directions)
1963 –1969
No awards
1970
Paul Zindel
The Effect of Gamma Rays on Man-in-the-Moon Marigolds (Bantam)
1971
John Guare
The House of Blue Leaves (Viking)
1972
No award
1973
Lanford Wilson
Hot l Baltimore (Hill & Wang)
1974
Miguel Piñero
Short Eyes (Hill & Wang)
1975
Ed Bullins
The Taking of Miss Janie (French)
1976
David Rabe
Streamers (Knopf)
1977
David Mamet
American Buffalo (Grove)
1978 –1979
No awards

FOREIGN PLAY

1938
Paul Vincent Carroll
Shadow and Substance (Random)

FOREIGN PLAY (cont.)

1939
  Paul Vincent Carroll
  The White Steed (Random)
1940
  No award
1941
  Emlyn Williams
  The Corn Is Green (Random)
1942
  Noel Coward
  Blithe Spirit (Doubleday)
1943
  No award
1944
  Franz Werfel and S. N. Behrman
  Jacobowsky and the Colonel (Random)
1945–1946
  No awards
1947
  Jean-Paul Sartre
  No Exit (Knopf)
1948
  Terence Rattigan
  The Winslow Boy (Dramatists)
1949
  Maurice Valency
  The Madwoman of Chaillot (Random)
1950
  T. S. Eliot
  The Cocktail Party (Harcourt)
1951
  Christopher Fry
  The Lady's Not for Burning (Oxford Univ. Press)
1952
  Christopher Fry
  Venus Observed (Oxford Univ. Press)
1953
  Peter Ustinov
  The Love of Four Colonels (Dramatists)
1954
  Maurice Valency
  Ondine (French)

1955
  Agatha Christie
  Witness for the Prosecution (Dell)
1956
  Christopher Fry
  Tiger at the Gates (Oxford Univ. Press)
1957
  Jean Anouilh
  Waltz of the Toreadors (Coward)
1958
  John Osborne
  Look Back in Anger (Criterion)
1959
  Friederich Duerrenmatt
  The Visit (Random)
1960
  Peter Shaffer
  Five Finger Exercise (Harcourt)
1961
  Shelagh Delaney
  A Taste of Honey (Grove)
1962
  Robert Bolt
  A Man for All Seasons (Random)

BEST PLAY

1963
  Edward Albee
  Who's Afraid of Virginia Woolf (Atheneum)
1964
  John Osborne
  Luther (New American Library)
1965
  Frank Gilroy
  The Subject Was Roses (Random)
1966
  Peter Weiss
  The Persecution and Assassination of Jean-Paul Marat as Performed by the Inmates of the Asylum of Charenton under the Direction of the Marquis de Sade (Harcourt)

BEST PLAY (cont.)

1967
Harold Pinter
The Homecoming (Evergreen)

1968
Tom Stoppard
Rosencrantz and Guildenstern Are Dead (Grove)

1969
Howard Sackler
The Great White Hope (Dial)

1970
Frank McMahon
Borstal Boy (Random)

1971
David Storey
Home (Random)

1972
Jason Miller
That Championship Season (Atheneum)

1973
David Storey
The Changing Room (Random)

1974
David Storey
The Contractor (Avon)

1975
Peter Shaffer
Equus (Avon)

1976
Tom Stoppard
Travesties (Grove)

1977
Simon Gray
Otherwise Engaged (Viking)

1978
Hugh Leonard
Da (Atheneum)

1979
Bernard Pomerance
The Elephant Man (Grove)

MUSICAL

1946
Oscar Hammerstein II, book and lyrics (Richard Rodgers, music)
Carousel (Knopf)

1947
Alan Jay Lerner, book and lyrics (Frederick Loewe, music)
Brigadoon (Coward)

1948
No award

1949
Joshua Logan and Oscar Hammerstein II, book (Oscar Hammerstein II, lyrics, and Richard Rodgers, music)
South Pacific (Random)

1950
Gian Carlo Menotti, libretto, music, and lyrics
The Consul

1951
Jo Swerling and Abe Burrows, book (Frank Loesser, music and lyrics)
Guys and Dolls

1952
John O'Hara, book (Richard Rodgers, music, and Lorenz Hart, lyrics)
Pal Joey (Random)

1953
Joseph Fields and Jerome Chodorov, book (Leonard Bernstein, music, and Betty Comden and Adolph Green, lyrics)
Wonderful Town (Random)

1954
John Latouche, book and lyrics (Jerome Moross, music)
The Golden Apple (Random)

1955
Gian Carlo Menotti, libretto, music, and lyrics
The Saint of Bleecker Street

MUSICAL (cont.)

1956
Alan Jay Lerner, book and lyrics
(Frederick Loewe, music)
My Fair Lady (Coward)

1957
Frank Loesser, libretto, music, and
lyrics
The Most Happy Fella (Frank Music)

1958
Meredith Willson, book, music, and
lyrics
The Music Man (Putnam)

1959
Robert Dhery, book (Gerald Calvi,
music, and Ross Parker, lyrics)
La Plume de Ma Tante

1960
Jerome Weidman and George Abbott,
book (Jerry Bock, music, and Sheldon
Harnick, lyrics)
Fiorello! (Random)

1961
Michael Stewart, book (Bob Merrill,
music and lyrics)
Carnival

1962
Abe Burrows, Jack Weinstock, and
Willie Gilbert, book (Frank Loesser,
music and lyrics)
*How to Succeed in Business without
Really Trying* (Frank Music)

1963
No award

1964
Michael Stewart, book (Jerry Herman,
music and lyrics)
Hello, Dolly! (D.B.S. Publications)

1965
Joseph Stein, book (Jerry Bock, mu-
sic, and Sheldon Harnick, lyrics)
Fiddler on the Roof (Crown)

1966
Dale Wasserman, book (Mitch Leigh,
music, and Joe Darion, lyrics)
Man of La Mancha

1967
Joe Masteroff, book (John Kander,
music, and Fred Ebb, lyrics)
Cabaret (Random)

1968
Donald Driver, book (Hal Hester and
Danny Apolinar, music and lyrics)
Your Own Thing

1969
Peter Stone, book (Sherman Edwards, music and lyrics)
1776 (Viking)

1970
George Furth, book (Stephen Sond-
heim, music and lyrics)
Company (Random)

1971
James Goldman, book (Stephen
Sondheim, music and lyrics)
Follies (Random)

1972
John Guare and Mel Shapiro, book
(Galt MacDermot, music, and John
Guare, lyrics)
Two Gentlemen of Verona (Holt)

1973
Hugh Wheeler, book (Stephen Sond-
heim, music and lyrics)
A Little Night Music (Dodd)

1974
Hugh Wheeler, book (Leonard Bernstein, music, and Richard Wilbur, lyrics)
Candide (Schirmer)

1975
James Kirkwood and Nicholas Dante,
book (Marvin Hamlisch, music, and
Edward Kleban, lyrics)
A Chorus Line

MUSICAL (cont.)

1976
John Weidman, book (Stephen Sond-
heim, music and lyrics)
Pacific Overtures (Dodd)
1977
Thomas Meehan, book (Charles
Strouse, music, and Martin Charnin,
lyrics)
Annie

1978
Murray Horvitz and Richard Maltby,
Jr., idea (Thomas "Fats" Waller, mu-
sic)
Ain't Misbehavin'
1979
Hugh Wheeler, book (Stephen Sond-
heim, music and lyrics)
*Sweeney Todd, the Demon Barber
of Fleet Street* (Dodd)

Charles H. Sergel Drama Prize

This award, first given in 1935, was established in 1930 by the late Mrs. Anne Meyers
Sergel in memory of her husband, Charles H. Sergel, founder of the Dramatic Publishing Company of Chicago. The contest, designed to encourage the writing of new
American plays, is administered by the University of Chicago, Faculty Exchange,
Chicago, Illinois 60637. Any U.S. citizen may enter the competition by submitting an
original, full-length play, not previously published or produced. Originally the annual
award was $500; however, the prize was increased to $1,000 and offered biennially
beginning 1942–1943. Since 1959, the competition has been held at three-year intervals, with a maximum of $3,000 divided among the winners. Prizes range from $500
to $1000. The judges reserve the right to withhold awards if, in their opinion, no plays
of sufficient merit have been submitted.

1935
Robert Ardrey
Emjo Basshe
1936
Alfred Kreymborg
1937
Marcus Bach
1938
Rosalie Moore
1939
Carl Allensworth
1940
Robert Whitehand
1942
Harry Kleiner
1944
Lewis Beach
1946
Bob S. McKnight

1948
Joseph Hayes
James Vincent McGee
Julia Ragir
1950
Bruce Brighton
Harry Granick
James Vincent McGee

1951
Mildred Kuner

1953
Sylvan Karchmer

1955
Bernard Reines
Anthony Terpiloff

1957
William J. Small

1959
　James Damice
　Barnard Sahlins
　Howard Stackler
1962
　Herbert Lieberman
　William Linahan
　Donald Spencer
1965
　Karl Eigsti
　Charles Notte
　J. J. Scott

1968
　Donald Capezzona
　Walter S. J. Swanson
1972
　Tim Kelly
　Doris H. Schwerin
　Wesley St. John
1973 –1979
　Winners unavailable

Stanley Drama Award

Wagner College, Staten Island, New York, New York 10301, established the Stanley Drama Award in 1957 as a memorial to Mrs. Robert C. Stanley. The award is $800 for an original full-length play or musical that has not been professionally produced or received trade book publication. Consideration is also given to a series of two or three thematically connected one-act plays. Plays must be recommended by a teacher of drama or creative writing, a critic, an agent, or another playwright or composer. Former Stanley Award winners are not eligible to compete.

1957
　William I. Oliver
　To Learn to Love
1958
　Josh Greenfeld
　Hear That Sweet Laughter
1959
　Gene Radano
　The Apple Doesn't Fall
1960
　George Hitchcock
　The Busy Martyr
1961
　Ernesto Fuentes
　La Loca
1962
　Terrence McNally
　This Side of the Door
1963
　Adrienne Kennedy
　Funnyhouse of a Negro and *The Owl Answers*

1964
　Joseph Baldwin
　Thompson
　Megan Terry
　Hothouse
1965
　Lonne Elder III
　Ceremonies in Dark Old Men
1966
　Albert Zuckerman
　To Become a Man
1967
　William Parchman
　The Prize in the Crackerjack Box
1968
　Venable Herndon
　Bag of Flies
1969
　Bernard Sabath
　A Happy New Year to the Whole World except Alexander Graham Bell

Yale Udoff
The Club

1970
Richard Lortz
Three Sons (of Sons and Brothers)

1971
Ben Rosa
Obtuse Triangle

1972
Marvin Denicoff
Fortune Teller Man

1973
C. Richard Gillespie
Carnivori

1974
Gus Weill
Son of the Last Mule Dealer

1975
Alan Riefe and Robert Haymes
Jonathan (musical)

1976
C. K. Mack
A Safe Place

1977
Jack Zeman
Past Tense

1978
Barry Knower
Cutting Away

Short Story Prizes

Atlantic "Firsts" Awards

In 1946 the *Atlantic Monthly*, 8 Arlington Street, Boston, Massachusetts 02116, announced an annual contest for *Atlantic* "firsts"—short stories by unestablished authors who were making their first appearance in the *Atlantic Monthly*. Until 1949, there were two awards a year over a six-month period, each with a first and second prize. Since 1949, the awards have been made annually, with $750 as the first prize and $250 as the second prize. This cash award is given in addition to payment for the story at regular rates. Only first-prize winners are listed below.

1946
  Alan R. Marcus
  "Ratachusky's Return"
  Cord Meyer, Jr.
  "Waves of Darkness"
1947
  Godfrey Blunden
  "The Indian Game"
  William R. Shelton
  "The Snow Girl"
1948
  Leon Wilson
  "Six Months Is No Long Time"
  Carl Moon
  "Victory"
1949
  Gudger Bart Leiper
  "The Magnolias"
1950
  Monty Culver
  "Black Water Blues"
1951
  Peter Mathiessen
  "Sadie"
1952
  George Green
  "The Orchard Ladder"

1953
  Richard Yates
  "Jody Rolled the Bones"
1954
  Richard Gill
  "The Secret"
1955
  Joseph Whitehill
  "Able Baker"
1956
  Winona McClintic
  "A Heart of Furious Fancies"
1957
  Harry Mark Petrakis
  "Pericles on 34th Street"
1958
  Esther Wagner
  "Beat Down Frigid Rome"
1959
  Jesse Hill Ford
  "The Surest Thing in Show Business"
1960
  Jack Ludwig
  "Requiem for Bibul"
1961
  Tom Cole
  "Familiar Usage in Leningrad"

1962
   Andrew Fetler
   "Longface"
1963
   Jordon Pecile
   "The Barrel Lifter"
1964
   H. L. Mountzoures
   "The Buoy"
1965
   Jack Cady
   "The Burning"
1966
   Rudolph Wurlitzer
   "The Boiler Room"
1967
   John Deck
   "Greased Samba"

1968
   James Alan McPherson
   "Gold Coast"
1969-1971
   No awards
1972
   Wallace Knight
   "The Way We Went"
1973
   James Polk
   "The Phrenology of Love"
1974-1975
   No awards
1976
   L. M. Rosenberg
   "Memory"
1977-1978
   No awards

Dutton Best Sports Stories Awards

A series of awards is offered annually by E. P. Dutton & Co., Inc., 201 Park Avenue South, New York, New York 10003, for outstanding sports writing and photographs published during the year in newspapers or magazines. Established in 1944, the contest originally included a prize of $500 for the best sports story and $100 for the best sports photograph. The present series awards $250 each for the best news coverage story, the best news feature story, and the best magazine story. Two prizes of $100 each are given for the best action photo and the best feature photo. In addition to the cash prizes, the award-winning stories and photographs are included in Dutton's yearly anthology *Best Sports Stories*, edited by Irving T. Marsh and Edward Ehre. The 1944 and 1945 anthologies were panoramas of those years. In 1946 the year in the title of the anthology was advanced to 1947, although it included a picture of sports in 1946. Later anthologies follow the same practice. Winners of the cash prizes are chosen by a panel of three judges. The closing date for entries is December 15 of the preceding year and submissions should be sent to Edward Ehre, 1315 Westport Lane, Sarasota, Florida 33580. Each newspaper story should be pasted on a backing of some sort and should have the name of publication. Photos should be 8 × 10 inch glossies and must be completely captioned. A biography of fifty words should be enclosed with the contestant's home address. Also included should be the name of the person who can grant permission to reprint. Clippings or photos cannot be returned.

NEWS FEATURE

1944
Al Laney
"A Dark Man Laughs," *New York Herald Tribune*
1945
Jerry Nason
"Wrecking Crew at Work," *Boston Globe*
1947
Red Smith
"A Sad Case of Malnutrition," *New York Herald Tribune*
1948
Red Smith
"Holy Sight," *New York Herald Tribune*
1949
Maxwell Stiles
"The Ghost of Wembley," *Long Beach* (Calif.) *Press-Telegram*
1950
Red Smith
"Happy Holiday," *New York Herald Tribune*
1951
Bill Rives
"Johnny Comes Home," *Dallas Morning News*
1952
Whitney Martin
"Little Giant," Associated Press
1953
Al Hirshberg
"That Forty-First Point," *Boston Post*
1954
Bill Corum
"Happy Anniversary," *New York Journal American*
1955
Jimmy Cannon
"The Beautiful Racket," *New York Post*
1956
Jim Gillooly
"Sox Apollo," *Boston Record*

Bob Goethals
"Locker Room," *San Francisco Chronicle*
1957
Milton Gross
"The Long Ride Home," *New York Post*
1958
Dick Young
"Obit On the Dodgers," New York *Daily News*
1959
Bob Collins
"The Falcons Win Their Wings," *Rocky Mountain News*
1960
John Steadman
"Another Day's Work," Baltimore *News-Post*
1961
Bill Clark
"It Ended in Silence," *Syracuse Herald-American*
1962
Howard M. Tuckner
"Man with Horse Sense," *New York Times Magazine*
1963
Bob Addie
"They Had Their Day," *Washington Post*
1964
Robert Lipsyte
"The Long Road to Broken Dreams," *New York Times*
1965
Red Smith
"Sweet Sioux," *New York Herald Tribune*
1966
Dick Young
"And What a Battler He Was," New York *Daily News*
1967
Robert Lipsyte
"Where the Stars of Tomorrow Shine Tonight," *New York Times*

NEWS FEATURE (cont.)

1968
  Lou O'Neill
  "A Study in Futility," *Long Island Star-Journal*
1969
  Joe Nichols
  "The Garden of Cheers and Tears," *New York Times*
1970
  Robert Lipsyte
  "The Medal," *New York Times*
1971
  Robert Lipsyte
  "Dempsey in the Window," *New York Times*
1972
  Dave Anderson
  "I'll Forgive, but I'll Never Forget," *New York Times*
1973
  Dan Lauck
  "Saturday's Hero; Saturday's Villain," *Topeka Capital-Journal*
1974
  Ray Didinger
  "Larry Brown: King of the Hill," *Philadelphia Bulletin*
1975
  Ross Thomas Runfola
  "A Model of Legalized Violence," *New York Times*
1976
  Wells Twombly
  "There Was Only One Casey," *San Francisco Examiner*
1977
  Jane Gross
  "Tennis Isn't the Only Issue," Long Island *Newsday*
1978
  David Klein
  "Wells Twombley-41; The Laughter Still Echoes," *Newark Star-Ledger*

1979
  Betty Cuniberti
  "Her Hands Were Made for Golf," *Washington Post*
  Tony Kornheiser
  "Reggie Jackson's Lonely World," *New York Times*

NEWS COVERAGE

1945
  Jimmy Powers
  "Tiger Triumph," New York *Daily News*
1947
  Jimmy Cannon
  "Lethal Lightning," *New York Post*
1948
  Stanley Woodward
  "One Strike Out," *New York Herald Tribune*
1949
  Jesse Abramson
  "Middie Miracle," *New York Herald Tribune*
1950
  Allison Danzig
  "The Semi-Final Is Final," *New York Times*
1951
  James P. Dawson
  "Bomber Bombed," *New York Times*
1952
  Art Rosenbaum
  "Defense Platoon," *San Francisco Chronicle*
1953
  Jesse Abramson
  "Melted Sugar," *New York Herald Tribune*
1954
  Ed Danforth
  "Late for the Dance," *Atlanta Journal*
1955
  Jim Gillooly
  "Golf by Braille," *Boston Record*

NEWS COVERAGE (cont.)

1956
Jesse Abramson
"The Checkered Flag," *New York Herald Tribune*
Joe Trimble
"Paradise at Last," New York *Daily News*
1957
Shirley Povich
"The Million-to-One Shot Comes In," *Washington Post Times Herald*
1958
Jesse Abramson
"The Tables Turn," *New York Herald Tribune*
1959
Jesse Abramson
"The Perils of Archie," *New York Herald Tribune*
1960
Dick Young
"From Bottom to Top," New York *Daily News*
1961
Dick Young
"It Isn't Over Yet," New York *Daily News*
1962
Stanley Woodward
"Baleful Light o'er the Hudson," *New York Herald Tribune*
1963
Jack Murphy
"When the World Stood Still," *San Diego Union*
1964
George Leonard
"The Forgotten Man," *Nashville Banner*
1965
Bill Conlin
"A Bad Day for Conservatives," *Philadelphia Bulletin*

Robert Lipsyte
"Incredible Cassius," *New York Times*
1966
Jesse Abramson
"Robinson's Pipedream," *New York Herald Tribune*
1967
Sandy Grady
"The Mob Hit .000," *Philadelphia Bulletin*
1968
Ray Grody
"The Torture Chamber," *Milwaukee Sentinel*
1969
Jerry Nason
"The 16-Point Minute," *Boston Sunday Globe*
1970
Wells Twombly
"The Impossible Dream," *Detroit Free Press*
1971
Art Spander
"They Were Singing 'God Save the Queen,' " *San Francisco Chronicle*
1972
Mickey Herskowitz
"The Stupor Bowl," *Houston Post*
1973
Jerry Nason
"Then Along Came Wottle," *Boston Globe*
1974
David Klein
"Peter Pan's Unexpected Birthday," *Newark Star-Ledger*

1975
Dwain Esper
"Davis Triggers the Explosion," *Pasadena Star-News*

1976
Maury Allen
" 'An Event for the Ages,' " *New York Post*

NEWS COVERAGE (cont.)

1977
Shirley Povich
"The Great Yankee Holdup," *Washington Post*
1978
Thomas Boswell
"The Sign Says Reggie-Reggie-Reggie," *Washington Post*
1979
Steven Jacobson
"Yankees Can Finally Say It," Long Island *Newsday*

David Klein
"Boxer Unseats Puncher," *Newark Star-Ledger*

MAGAZINE STORY

1945
Carol Hughes
"Heart of a Ballplayer," *Coronet*
1947
Kyle Crichton
"Hot Tamale Circuit," *Collier's*
1948
W. C. Heinz
"The Day of the Fight," *Cosmopolitan*
1949
Jimmy Cannon
"Club Fighter," *True*
1950
W. C. Heinz
"Fighter's Wife," *Cosmopolitan*
1951
Stanley Woodward
"The Pro Game Isn't Football," *Collier's*
1952
Ben East
"Frozen Terror," *Outdoor Life*
Bob Considine
"How Tennis Players Are Made," *Cosmopolitan*

W. C. Heinz
"Brownsville Bum," *True*
1953
Doug Kennedy
"She Skis for Fun," *Time*
1954
W. C. Heinz
"Punching Out a Living," *Collier's*
1955
Herman Hickman
"Rasslin' Was My Act," *Saturday Evening Post*
1956
Dick Young
"The Outlawed Spitball," *Saturday Evening Post*
1957
Joan Flynn
"Babe and George," *Sports Illustrated*
1958
Turnley Walker
"Fighting Man," *Pageant*
1959
W. C. Heinz
"The Rocky Road of Pistol Pete," *True*
1960
Roger Kahn
"The Real Babe Ruth," *Esquire*
1961
Jimmy Breslin
"Racing's Angriest Young Man," *True*
1962
Al Stump
"The Fight to Live," *True*
1963
Myron Cope
"Feats of Clay," *True*
1964
Gilbert Rogin
"Playing a Child's Game," *Sports Illustrated*
1965
Dave Anderson
"The Longest Day of Sugar Ray," *True*

MAGAZINE STORY (cont.)

1966
Gerald Astor
"Mickey Mantle: Oklahoma to Olympus," *Look*
1967
Gay Talese
"The Silent Season of a Hero," *Esquire*
1968
Leonard Shecter
"The Toughest Man in Pro Football," *Esquire*
1969
Roger Kahn
"An Hour or So of Hell" *Saturday Evening Post*
1970
Roger Kahn
"Willie Mays, Yesterday and Today," *Sport*
1971
Bill Bousfield
"The Housebreaker," *Outdoor Life*
1972
Roger Angell
"The Interior Stadium," *The New Yorker*

Lawrence Linderman
"The Tom McMillen Affair," *Playboy*
1973
Sandy Grady
"They Get a Glass of Beer . . . Maybe," *Philadelphia Bulletin Discover Magazine*
1974
Jim Hawkins
"Baseball's Wildest Owner," *True*
1975
John S. Radosta
"Stock-Car Streaking," *New York Times Magazine*
1976
Robert M. Lipsyte
"Pride of the Tiger," *Atlantic Monthly*
1977
Mark Jacobson
"Bound for Glory," *New York*
1978
A. Bartlett Giametti
"Tom Seaver's Farewell," *Harpers*
1979
Phil Berger
"Spinks," *Playboy*

Colin Campbell
"The Sharkers," *Sports Afield*

O. Henry Awards

Each year Doubleday & Company, Inc., Garden City, New York 11530, publishes *Prize Stories: The O. Henry Awards*, a collection of the year's best stories published by American authors in American periodicals. The three stories judged by the editor to be the best receive monetary prizes of $300, $200, and $100. For several years during the forties a special prize of $100 was given for the best "first published story." The O. Henry Memorial Awards were first given in 1919. No application may be made for the awards, since the eligible material is available to the editor in its published form. There is no presentation ceremony; checks are mailed to the winners at the time of the book's publication. Only first-prize winners are listed below.

1919
Margaret Prescott Montague
"England to America"

1920
Maxwell Struthers Burt
"Each in His Generation"

1921
  Edison Marshall
  "The Heart of Little Shikara"
1922
  Irvin S. Cobb
  "Snake Doctor"
1923
  Edgar Valentine Smith
  "Prelude"
1924
  Inez Irwin
  "The Spring Flight"
1925
  Julian Street
  "Mr. Bisbee's Princess"
1926
  Wilbur Daniel Steele
  "Bubbles"
1927
  Roark Bradford
  "Child of God"
1928
  Walter Duranty
  "The Parrot"
1929
  Dorothy Parker
  "Big Blonde"
1930
  W. R. Burnett
  "Dressing-Up"

  William M. John
  "Neither Jew nor Greek"
1931
  Wilbur Daniel Steele
  "Can't Cross Jordan by Myself"
1932
  Stephen Vincent Benét
  "An End to Dreams"
1933
  Marjorie Kinnan Rawlings
  "Gal Young Un"
1934
  Louis Paul
  "No More Trouble for Jedwick"
1935
  Kay Boyle
  "The White Horses of Vienna"

1936
  James Gould Cozzens
  "Total Stranger"
1937
  Stephen Vincent Benét
  "The Devil and Daniel Webster"
1938
  Albert Maltz
  "The Happiest Man on Earth"
1939
  William Faulkner
  "Barn Burning"
1940
  Stephen Vincent Benét
  "Freedom's a Hard-Bought Thing"
1941
  Kay Boyle
  "Defeat"
1942
  Eudora Welty
  "The Wide Net"
1943
  Eudora Welty
  "Livvie Is Back"
1944
  Irwin Shaw
  "Walking Wounded"
1945
  Walter Van Tilburg Clark
  "The Wind and the Snow of Winter"
1946
  John Mayo Goss
  "Bird Song"

1947
  John Bell Clayton
  "White Circle"

1948
  Truman Capote
  "Shut a Final Door"

1949
  William Faulkner
  "A Courtship"

1950
  Wallace Stegner
  "The Blue-Winged Teal"

1951
   Harris Downey
   "The Hunters"
1952–1953
   No awards
1954
   Thomas Mobry
   "The Indian Feather"
1955
   Jean Stafford
   "In the Zoo"
1956
   John Cheever
   "The Country Husband"
1957
   Flannery O'Connor
   "Greenleaf"
1958
   Martha Gelhorn
   "In Sickness As in Health"
1959
   Peter Taylor
   "Venus, Cupid, Folly and Time"
1960
   Lawrence Sargent Hall
   "The Ledge"
1961
   Tillie Olsen
   "Tell Me a Riddle"
1962
   Katherine Anne Porter
   "Holiday"
1963
   Flannery O'Connor
   "Everything That Rises Must Converge"
1964
   John Cheever
   "The Embarkment for Cythera"
1965
   Flannery O'Connor
   "Revelation"
1966
   John Updike
   "The Bulgarian Poetess"

1967
   Joyce Carol Oates
   "In the Region of Ice"
1968
   Eudora Welty
   "The Demonstrators"
1969
   Bernard Malamud
   "Man in the Drawer"
1970
   Robert Hemenway
   "The Girl Who Sang with the Beatles"
1971
   Florence M. Hecht
   "Twin Bed Bridge"
1972
   John Batki
   "Strange-Dreaming Charlie, Cow-Eyed Charlie"
1973
   Joyce Carol Oates
   "The Dead"
1974
   Renata Adler
   "Brownstone"
1975
   Harold Brodkey
   "A Story in an Almost Classical Mode"
   Cynthia Ozick
   "Usurpation (Other People's Stories)"
1976
   Harold Brodkey
   "His Son, in His Arms, in Light, Aloft"
1977
   Shirley Hazzard
   "A Long Short Story"
   Ella Leffland
   "Last Courtesies"
1978
   Woody Allen
   "The Kugelmass Episode"
1979
   Gordon Weaver
   "Getting Serious"

Iowa School of Letters Award for Short Fiction

This $1,000 award is given annually by the Iowa Arts Council, Writers Workshop, and University of Iowa Press for the best book-length collection of short stories by a writer who has not yet published a book. The winning work is published by the University of Iowa Press, which reserves the right to consider for publication any manuscript submitted. Entries should be sent to the Iowa School of Letters Award for Short Fiction, Department of English, English-Philosophy Building, University of Iowa, Iowa City, Iowa 52242. They must be postmarked no later than September 30. Return postage should be enclosed with all manuscripts. Finalist judges have included Vance Bourjaily, Kurt Vonnegut, Jr., George P. Elliott, Joyce Carol Oates, William Gass, Donald Barthelme, and John Gardner.

1970
   Cyrus Colter
   The Beach Umbrella
1971
   Philip F. O'Connor
   Old Morals, Small Continents, Darker Times
1972
   Jack Cady
   The Burning and Other Stories
1973
   H. E. Francis
   The Itinerary of Beggars
1974
   Natalie L. M. Petesch
   After the First Death, There Is No Other

1975
   Barry Targan
   Harry Belten and the Mendelssohn Violin Concerto
1976
   Charles Poverman
   The Black Velvet Girl
1977
   Pat M. Carr
   The Women in the Mirror
1978
   Lon Otto
   A Nest of Hooks
1979
   Mary Hedin
   Fly Away Home

John H. McGinnis Memorial Award

This award is offered by the *Southwest Review*, Southern Methodist University, Dallas, Texas 75222. It was established in 1960 through the generosity of Robert F. Ritchie of Dallas in memory of the man who served as editor of the *Southwest Review* from 1927 to 1943. Choices are made from material published in the *Southwest Review* after decision by its editors and publishers. The $500 award is given in alternate years for fiction and nonfiction short stories, covering in each case publication during the two previous years. Winners are announced annually in the Winter issue of the *Southwest Review*, issued in January.

1961
  Paul F. Boller, Jr.
  "Jefferson's Dreams of the Future"
1962
  Julian Silva
  "With Laughter"
1963
  John Houghton Allen
  "Little Pinto"
1964
  Cecil Dawkins
  "A Simple Case"
1965
  Levi A. Olan
  "The University and Man's Condition"
1966
  Victor White
  "The Hotel"
1967
  Borden Deal
  "The Function of the Artist: Creativity and the Collective Unconscious"
1968
  H. E. Francis
  "One of the Boys"
1969
  Dorothy I. Height
  "A Time to Listen: Civil Rights and the Mass Media"
1970
  Abraham Rothberg
  "The Sand Dunes"
1971
  George Anastapolo
  "Greece Today and the Limits of American Power"
1972
  Jack Canson
  "Friday Night Smith"
1973
  Bill D. Schul
  "Exploration of Inner Space"
1974
  Charles Oliver
  "Drunk and Singing on a Southern Mountain"
1975
  Abraham Rothberg
  "What Time Is It Now?"
1976
  Charles S. Drum
  "El Gusano Durc de Xachtomel"
1977
  Joan Myers Weimer
  "The Belly Dancer and the Virgin: Mythic Women in Modern Egypt"
1978
  C. W. Smith
  "The Plantation Club"
1979
  Jo Brans
  "Common Needs, Common Preoccupations: An Interview with Saul Bellow"

St. Lawrence Award for Fiction

This annual award was established in 1972 by Joe David Bellamy, editor and publisher of *Fiction International*, with the financial support of St. Lawrence University. Its purpose is to recognize the author of an outstanding first collection of short fiction published by a North American press in the preceding calendar year. Nominations may be submitted by editors, writers, literary agents, or publishers before January 31. The award, $1,000 and a leather-bound certificate, is presented at the *Fiction International*/St. Lawrence University Writers' Conference in June. Further information is available from the St. Lawrence Award for Fiction, St. Lawrence University, Canton, New York 13617.

1972
Gordon Weaver
The Entombed Man of Thule (Louisiana State Univ. Press)

1973
Mark Costello
The Murphy Stories (Univ. of Illinois Press)

1974
Clark Blaise
Tribal Justice (Doubleday)

1975
Russell Banks
Searching for Survivors (Fiction Collective)

1976
Gail Godwin
Dream Children (Knopf)

1977
Margaret Atwood
Dancing Girls (McClelland & Stewart)

1978
William Kittredge
The Van Gogh Field and Other Stories (Univ. of Missouri Press)

Jayne Anne Phillips
Counting (Vehicle Editions)

Seventeen Magazine Short Story Contest

This annual award encourages young people to develop skill in the writing of the short story. *Seventeen*, 850 Third Avenue, New York, New York 10022, accepts entries between April 1 and July 1. Teenagers between thirteen- and nineteen-years-old on the closing date of the contest may submit previously unpublished stories of approximately 2,500 to 3,000 words, which are judged for literary worth and convincing characterization. Entries must be typed double-spaced and must be accompanied by a signed statement, certified by a notary public, attesting to the writer's birthdate and to the fact that no part of the story has been published before and that the entire story is original work. There are nine annual prizes of $500, $300, $200, and six $50 honorable mentions. Winners are announced and the top three stories are printed in *Seventeen*.

Library Prizes

American Library Association

The American Library Association (ALA), 50 East Huron Street, Chicago, Illinois 60611, presents a number of awards, citations, and scholarships, usually at the annual conference. They are given in recognition of service and accomplishment or to further education and projects in various fields of library work. Individual juries for each award make their choices from nominations received from membership recommendations.

ASCLA Exceptional Service Award

This award was established in 1957 by the ALA Association of Hospital and Institution Libraries, later called the ALA Health and Rehabilitative Library Services Division, which then merged in 1977 with the Association of State Library Agencies to form the Association of Specialized and Cooperative Library Agencies (ASCLA). The award is given annually (biennially from 1959 to 1963) to recognize exceptional service to the Association or to the clientele of or the professional and nonprofessional staffs in hospitals, institutions, communities, and in health, rehabilitative, and special education agencies, as well as to the homebound. The winners are chosen by the Exceptional Service Award Jury, working with the ASCLA Awards Committee, with the final choice approved by the Board of Directors. The award, a citation, is presented at the ALA annual conference each summer.

1959
   Margaret L. Wallace
   Hospital Librarian, Gary (Indiana) Public Library (retired)
1961
   Clara E. Lucioli
   Head, Hospital and Institutions Department, Cleveland Public Library
1963
   No award
1964
   Charlotte Mitchell
   Librarian, Miles Laboratories, Elkhart, Indiana

1965
   Perrie Jones
   Librarian, St. Paul Public Library (retired)
1966
   Marion Vedder
   New York State Library, Albany
1967
   Helen T. Yast
   Librarian, American Hospital Association, Chicago, Illinois
1968
   Bertha K. Wilson
   Ashmore, Illinois (retired)

1969
    Vera S. Flandorf
    Chief Librarian, Children's Memorial
    Hospital, Chicago, Illinois
1970
    No award
1971
    Margaret C. Hannigan
    Coordinator, Library Services for the
    Handicapped, U.S. Office of Educa-
    tion
1972
    Hilda K. Limper
    Specialist, Exceptional Children, Pub-
    lic Library of Cincinnati and Hamilton
    County
1973
    Robert S. Bray
    Chief, Division for the Blind and Phys-
    ically Handicapped, Library of Con-
    gress
1974
    Eleanor Phinney
    Former Executive Secretary, Associa-
    tion of Hospital and Institution Librar-
ies and of the Adult Services Division
of ALA
1975
    Mildred T. Moody
    Former Librarian, Glen Lake Sanitar-
    ium and Oak Terrace Nursing Home
    Ruth Marie Tews
    Former Head, Mayo Clinic Hospital Li-
    brary Service
1976
    Earl C. Graham
    Former Librarian, National Easter
    Seal Society
1977
    Grace J. Lyons
    District of Columbia Public Library
1978
    Katherine Prescott
    Former Head, Braille and Talking
    Book Department, Cleveland Public
    Library
1979
    Genevieve Casey
    Wayne State University

Academic/Research Librarian of the Year

Established in 1977, this annual award is given by the Association of College and Research Libraries (ACRL) and the Baker and Taylor Company for outstanding national or international contributions to academic or research librarianship. The award of $2,000 is presented at the ACRL annual conference, held at the time of the ALA annual conference in the summer.

1978
    Robert B. Downs
    Keyes D. Metcalf

1979
    Henriette Avram
    Frederick G. Kilgour

Armed Forces Librarians Achievement Citation

This award was established in 1964 to recognize members of the Armed Forces Librarians Section, Public Library Association, who have made significant contributions to the development of armed forces library service and to organizations encouraging an interest in libraries and reading.

1965
  Helen E. Fry
  Fourth U.S. Army, Fort Sam Houston,
  San Antonio
1966
  Harry F. Cook
  Air Forces Library Bureau
1967
  Ruth Sheahan Howard
  Director, Army Library Program,
  U.S. Army Tago, Washington, D.C.
1968
  Agnes Crawford
  Director, Army Library Program (re-
  tired)
1969
  Mary J. Carter
  Command Librarian, U.S. Air Force
  Headquarters Pacific Dpsr., APO
  96553 San Francisco, California
1970
  Frances M. O'Halloran
  Director, USARPAC Library Program
  Headquarters, USARPAC

1971
  Dorothy Fayne
  District Director of Libraries, Third
  Naval District
1972
  Lucia Gordon
  Command Libraries, CINCPACAF
1973
  No award
1974
  Josephine Neil
  Robert W. Severance
1975
  No award
1976
  Mariana J. Thurber
1977–1979
  No awards

Beta Phi Mu Award

In 1954, Beta Phi Mu, the national library science honorary fraternity, established the Beta Phi Mu Award for a library school faculty member or anyone who makes a distinguished contribution to education for librarianship. Only persons nominated by an American Library Association member are considered. Since the 1977 award, the ALA Awards Committee has administered the nominations and selection of the winner. The award consists of a citation, $500, and an invitation to join Beta Phi Mu.

1954
  Rudolph H. Gjelsness
  Head, Department of Librarianship,
  University of Michigan

1955
  Gretchen Knief Schenk
  Library consultant and author, Sum-
  merdale, Alabama

1956
  Margaret I. Rufsvold
  Director, Division of Library Science,
  Indiana University

1957
  Lucy Crissey
  Assistant to the Dean, School of Li-
  brary Service, Columbia University

1958
Florence Van Hoesen
Associate Professor of Library Science, Syracuse University
1959
Anita Hostetter
Formerly Secretary, Board of Education for Librarianship, American Library Association, and Secretary, Committee on Accreditation, American Library Association
1960
Louis Round Wilson
Formerly Dean, Graduate School of Librarianship, University of Chicago
1961
Robert L. Gitler
Formerly Executive Secretary, Library Education Division, and Secretary, ALA Committee on Accreditation
1962
Florrinell F. Morton
Director, Library School, Louisiana State University
1963
Ernest J. Reece
Professor Emeritus, School of Library Service, Columbia University
1964
Charles C. Williamson
Director of Libraries Emeritus, School of Library Service, Columbia University
1965
Jesse H. Shera
Dean, School of Library Science, and Director, Center for Documentation and Communication Research, Western Reserve University
1966
James J. Kortendiek
Head, Department of Library Science, Catholic University of America
1967
Louis Shores
Dean, School of Library Science, Florida State University

1968
Sarah Rebecca Reed
Director, School of Library Science, University of Alberta
1969
Ethel M. Fair
3025 North Second Street, Harrisburg, Pennsylvania
1970
Raynard C. Swank
Dean, School of Librarianship, University of California, Berkeley
1971
Leon Carnovsky
Professor, Graduate Library School, University of Chicago
1972
Margaret E. Monroe
Professor and formerly Director, Library School, University of Wisconsin, Madison
1973
Lester E. Asheim
Director, ALA International Relations Office and Office for Library Education
1974
Martha Boaz
Dean, School of Library Science, University of Southern California
1975
Kenneth R. Shaffer
Formerly Director, School of Library Science, Simmons College
1976
Carolyn Whitenack
Chairperson, Media Sciences, Department of Education, Purdue University
1977
Russell E. Bidlack
Dean, School of Library Science, University of Michigan
1978
Frances Henne
1979
Conrad H. Rawski
Dean, School of Library Science, Case Western Reserve University

Francis Joseph Campbell Citation

Offered by the Library Service to the Blind and Physically Handicapped Section of the Association of Specialized and Cooperative Library Agencies, this award was first presented in 1966. It is given annually to a person who has made an outstanding contribution to the advancement of library service for the blind. The contribution may be an imaginative and constructive program in a particular library; a recognized contribution to the national library program for blind persons; creative participation in library associations or organizations that advance reading for the blind; a significant publication or writing in the field; imaginative contribution to library administration, reference, circulation, acquisitions, or technical services; or any activity of recognized importance. The award consists of a citation and bronze medal designed by the sculptor Bruce Moore.

1966
  Howard Haycraft
  The H. W. Wilson Company
1967
  Kenneth Jernigan
1968
  Robert Stuart Bray
  Library of Congress
1969
  Alexander J. Skrzypek
  Public Library, Chicago, Illinois
1970
  Alexander Scourby
1971
  Mrs. Ronald H. Macdonald
  Founder and honorary Chairman, Recording for the Blind, Inc.
1972
  Keith Jennison
  Publisher, Keith Jennison Large Print Books
  Frederick A. Thorpe
  Publisher, Ulverscroft Large Print Books

1973
  Marjorie S. Hooper
  American Printing House for the Blind, Louisville, Kentucky
1974
  Jennings Randolph
  U.S. Senator
1975
  Arthur Helms
  Rowayton, Connecticut
1976
  Charles Gallozzi
  Library of Congress, Division for the Blind and Physically Handicapped
1977
  Adeline Franzel
  Former Coordinator, New Jersey State Library, Programs for the Handicapped and Institutionalized
1978
  Richard Kinney
  Hadley School for the Blind
1979
  Jenny M. Beck
  Volunteer, Services for the Blind, Inc.

John Cotton Dana Library Public Relations Awards

The Council of the American Library Association established the John Cotton Dana Library Public Relations Awards in 1942. The annual awards are sponsored by the Public Relations Section of the ALA's Library Administration and Management Association and are administered by the H. W. Wilson Company, 950 University Avenue,

Bronx, New York 10452. Their purpose is to encourage library publicity. Any library, including libraries overseas, may submit a scrapbook showing a cross section of the year's publicity or promotion of one special project. Citations are given to winning libraries, which are listed each year in *The Bowker Annual of Library and Book Trade Information*.

Clarence Day Award

The American Education Publishers Institute donated this annual $1,000 award to a librarian or other individual for outstanding work in encouraging a love of books and reading. This award was established in 1959 and was presented for the first time in 1960. It recognized a distinctive book, essay, or series of lectures published within the preceding five years.

1960
  Lawrence Clark Powell
1961
  William B. Ready
1962
  Lillian H. Smith
1963
  Robert B. Downs
1964
  No award
1965
  Elizabeth Nesbitt
1966
  Frances Clarke Sayers
1967
  No award
1968
  Granville Hicks

1969
  Clifton Fadiman
1970
  No award
1971
  Dee Alexander Brown
1972
  Robert Cromie
1973
  Sol M. Malkin and Mary Ann O'Brien Malkin
1974
  Augusta Baker
1975
  Margaret McNamara
Discontinued

Melvil Dewey Medal

The Melvil Dewey Medal, donated by Forest Press, Inc., is given annually to an individual or group for recent creative professional achievement of a high order, particularly in those fields in which Melvil Dewey was so actively interested—library management, library training, cataloging and classification, and the tools and techniques of librarianship. The award, established in 1952, consists of the medal and a citation.

1953
  Ralph R. Shaw
1954
  Herman H. Fussler

1955
  Maurice F. Tauber
1956
  Norah Albanell MacCall

1957
Wyllis E. Wright
1958
Janet S. Dickson
1959
Benjamin A. Custer
1960
Harriet E. Howe
1961
Julia C. Pressey
1962
Leon Carnovsky
1963
Frank B. Rogers
1964
John W. Cronin
1965
Bertha Margaret Frick
1966
Lucile Morsch
1967
Walter H. Kaiser
1968
Jesse H. Shera

1969
William S. Dix
1970
Joseph Treys
1971
William J. Welsh
1972
Jerrold Orne
1973
Virginia Lacy Jones
1974
Robert B. Downs
1975
No award
1976
Louis Round Wilson
1977
Seymour Lubetzky
1978
Frederick G. Kilgour
1979
Russell E. Bidlack

Distinguished Library Service Award for School Administrators

This award, offered by the American Association of School Librarians, was established at the annual conference of the American Library Association in 1967. The award is made annually to honor a person who is directly responsible for a school or a group of schools and who has made a unique and sustained contribution toward furthering the role of the library and its development in elementary and/or secondary education. Eligible individuals are state, county, or district school superintendents and building principals currently in administrative office and directly responsible for a school or group of schools at the elementary and/or secondary level. A jury selects one, two, or three recipients from nominees selected by a committee. A citation is presented to the winner at the ALA annual conference.

1968
M. G. Bowden
Professor of Education
Wesley Gibbs
Superintendent

James A. Sensenbaugh
Superintendent
1969
Paul W. Briggs
Superintendent

Everette B. Stanley
Division Superintendent
E. C. Stimbert
Superintendent
1970
Edward Kruse
Superintendent
1971
Paul Douglass West
Superintendent, Fulton County
Schools, Georgia
1972
James H. Broughton
Whitfield County Public Schools, Dalton, Georgia
John W. Letson
Superintendent, Atlanta Public
Schools, Georgia
1973
John F. Powers
Superintendent, Walpole, Massachusetts
1974
George N. Smith
Superintendent, Mesa Public
Schools, Arizona

1975
Burton C. Tiffany
Superintendent, Chula Vista City
School District, California
1976
Wilmer S. Cody
Superintendent, City School System,
Birmingham, Alabama
1977
John M. Franco
Superintendent, City School District,
Rochester, New York
1978
Nolan Estes
General Superintendent, Dallas Independent School District, Dallas, Texas
Alvin E. Morris
Superintendent, Wichita Public
Schools, Wichita, Kansas
1979
Richard C. Hunter
Superintendent, Richmond Public
Schools, Richmond, Virginia

Robert B. Downs Award

The University of Illinois, Graduate School of Library Science, Urbana, Illinois 61801, sponsors this award, which was created to honor Dean Robert B. Downs for his defense of intellectual freedom and to mark his twenty-five years at the University. The award may be made to a librarian, a library board member, or a group that has contributed to furthering intellectual freedom in any type of library.

1969
LeRoy Charles Merritt
Dean, School of Librarianship, University of Oregon, and editor, *Newsletter on Intellectual Freedom*
1970
Orrin B. Dow
Librarian, Farmingdale Public Library,
New York

1971
The President's Commission on Obscenity and Pornography

1972
John Carey
Formerly Director, Groton Public Library, Connecticut

1973
  Alex P. Allain
  Attorney and President of St. Mary
  Parish Library Board of Trustees,
  Jeanerette, Louisiana
1974
  Everett T. Moore
  Associate University Librarian for
  Public Services, University of Califor-
  nia, Los Angeles
1975
  No award
1976
  Eli M. Oboler
  University Librarian, Idaho State Uni-
  versity

1977
  Irene Turin
  District Chairperson of Libraries, Is-
  land Trees High School, Levittown,
  New York
1978
  Judith F. Krug
  Director, Office of Intellectual Free-
  dom, American Library Association
1979
  Ralph E. McCoy
  Dean Emeritus of Library Affairs,
  Southern Illinois University, Carbon-
  dale

Facts on File Award

The ALA Reference and Adult Services Division established this award in 1979 to honor an individual librarian who has made current affairs more meaningful to an adult audience. This award of $1,000 is presented annually by Facts on File, Inc., to promote wider public knowledge of and involvement in current affairs. The first presentation will be made during the 1980 ALA annual conference to a recipient selected by a committee of the ALA Reference and Adult Services Division.

Grolier Foundation Award

The annual Grolier Foundation Award was established in 1953. It is given for outstanding work with children and young people through high school age and recognizes either continued service or a single contribution of lasting value. The nominee must be an employed librarian who works most with children and young people. The award consists of $1,000 and a certificate.

1954
  Miss Siddie Joe Johnson
  Children's Librarian, Dallas Public Li-
  brary
1955
  Charlemae Rollins
  Children's Librarian, Hall Branch, Chi-
  cago Public Library

1956
  Georgia Sealoff
  Librarian, West Seattle High School,
  Seattle

1957
  Margaret Alexander Edwards
  Coordinator of Work with Young

People, Enoch Pratt Free Library, Baltimore

1958
Mary Peacock Douglas
Supervisor, Public School Libraries, Raleigh, North Carolina

1959
Evelyn Sickels
Formerly Coordinator, Children's Services, Indianapolis Public Library

1960
Margaret C. Scoggin
Librarian and Coordinator, Young Adult Services, New York Public Library

1961
Della Louise McGregor
Chief, Youth Service, St. Paul Public Library

1962
Alice Brooks McGuire
Librarian, Casis Elementary School, Austin, Texas

1963
Carolyn W. Field
Coordinator, Work with Children, Free Library of Philadelphia

1964
Inger Boye
Children's Librarian, Public Library, Highland Park, Illinois

1965
Sarah Lewis Jones
Chief Library Consultant, Georgia State Department of Education, Atlanta

1966
Mildred L. Batchelder
Formerly Executive Secretary of the CSD and YASD, ALA

1967
Lura E. Crawford
Head, Library Service, Oak Park-River Forest High School, Oak Park, Illinois

1968
Augusta Baker
Coordinator, Children's Services, New York Public Library

1969
Anne Rebecca Izard
Children's Consultant, Westchester Library System, Mt. Vernon, New York

1970
Julia Losinski
Young Adult Services, Prince George's County Memorial Library, Maryland

1971
Sara Siebert
Coordinator, Work with Young Adults, Enoch Pratt Free Library, Baltimore

1972
Ronald W. McCracken
Librarian, Keswick Public School, Ontario, Canada

1973
Eleanor Kidder
Former Superintendent of Work with Young Adults, Seattle Public Library

1974
Regina U. Minudri
Director, Professional Services, Alameda County Library, California

1975
Jane B. Wilson
Chapel Hill, North Carolina

1976
Virginia Haviland
Library of Congress

1977
Elizabeth Fast
Groton, Connecticut

1978
Dorothy C. McKenzie
Santa Barbara, California

1979
Anne Pellowski
UNICEF, New York City

Grolier National Library Week Grant

The American Library Association has offered this award since 1975 to the state library association that submits the best plans for a public relations program. The goal of the award is to stimulate public relations activities in order to increase the visibility of libraries and to extend and strengthen the library's relationships throughout the target area. The award is also intended to provide assistance for the development of effective programs, while stimulating interest in National Library Week activities. The grant of $1,000 is awarded annually during the ALA's midwinter meeting in January. Applications may be submitted by state library associations; they must be brief and must describe how the state association plans to use $1,000 for a public relations program to increase the visibility of libraries within the state. A specific budget should be included. The ALA National Library Week Committee selects the recipient on the basis of the proposal's potential for an effective use of media or personal contacts to reach a specific audience with a specific message about library services.

1975
  West Virginia Library Association
1976
  Illinois Library Association
1977
  New Jersey Library Association

1978
  Mississippi Library Association
1979
  Utah Library Association

Hammond, Incorporated, Library Award

This award was established in 1962 and donated by Hammond, Incorporated. It was given annually to a librarian or library in a community or school for contributing to effective use of or increased interest in maps, atlases, and globes by children and young people through high school age. The award, $500 and a citation, was given for either continued service or a single contribution of lasting value.

1963
  Clara E. Le Gear
  Consultant in historical cartography,
  Library of Congress
1964
  No award
1965
  James M. Day
  Director of the State Archives, Texas
  State Library
1966–1967
  No awards

1968
  Ellen Freeman
  Geology Librarian, Indiana University
  and Indiana Geological Survey,
  Bloomington
1969–1970
  No awards
1971
  University of Chicago Laboratory
  Schools, High School Library
1972
  Patterson Library, Westfield, New
  York

1973	1974–1975
Betty Ryder	No awards
Pasadena Public Library, California	Discontinued

J. Morris Jones and Bailey K. Howard–World Book Encyclopedia–ALA Goal Awards

These awards were established by World Book–Childcraft International and the American Library Association. The awards commemorate two outstanding leaders in publishing: J. Morris Jones, former editor-in-chief of the World Book Encyclopedia, and Bailey K. Howard, former chairman of the board of Field Enterprises Educational Corporation. Two $5,000 grants are provided annually by World Book to support the ALA's programs in public, academic, and school library service and to further the goals and objectives of the Association. The Association announces the availability and terms of the awards to all units of the Association, including its chapters, accepts applications for the awards from those units, evaluates the programs proposed in the applications, and selects the program or programs to be supported in that year. The recipients of the awards are announced at the annual conference of the ALA. Application forms are available from the Awards Committee, American Library Association, 50 East Huron Street, Chicago, Illinois 60611.

Library Buildings Award Program

This award was established by the American Institute of Architects, the American Library Association, and the National Book Committee to encourage excellence in the architectural design and planning of libraries. The award consists of a citation and a plaque to be placed in each winning classification: school libraries (up to and including secondary schools), college and university libraries, and public libraries (including county and state). Winners are announced during National Library Week and are listed in the *American Libraries* issue announcing winners of the annual ALA awards. ALA participation was authorized by the ALA Council in 1962.

Joseph W. Lippincott Award

A special certificate, medal, and $1,000 are given each year to a librarian for distinguished service in the profession of librarianship. Service includes outstanding participation in the activities of professional library associations, notable published professional writing, or other significant activity related to librarianship and its aims. Beginning in 1938, except for 1940–1947, the awards have been presented annually by the J. B. Lippincott Company.

1938	1939
Mary U. Rothrock	Herbert Putnam

1948
  Carl H. Milam
1949
  Harry M. Lydenberg
1950
  Halsey W. Wilson
1951
  Helen E. Haines
1952
  Carl Vitz
1953
  Marian C. Manley
1954
  Jack Dalton
1955
  Emerson Greenaway
1956
  Ralph A. Ulveling
1957
  Flora Belle Ludington
1958
  Carleton B. Joeckel
1959
  Essae Martha Culver
1960
  Verner W. Clapp
1961
  Joseph L. Wheeler
1962
  David H. Clift
1963
  Frances W. Henne

1964
  Robert B. Downs
1965
  Frances Clarke Sayers
1966
  Keyes DeWitt Metcalf
1967
  Edmon Low
1968
  Lucile Nix
1969
  Germaine Krettek
1970
  Paul Howard
1971
  William S. Dix
1972
  Guy Lyle
1973
  Jesse H. Shera
1974
  Jerrold Orne
1975
  Leon Carnovsky
1976
  Lester Asheim
1977
  Virginia Lacy Adams
1978
  Henry T. Drennan
1979
  Helen H. Lyman

Margaret Mann Citation

This award was named in honor of Margaret Mann for her outstanding contributions to the field of cataloging and classification. The award was established in 1950 by the former Division of Cataloging and Classification and was given for the first time in 1951. It is presented to a librarian for significant professional achievement in the field of cataloging and classification in one of the following areas: (1) notable publication, such as an article, pamphlet, or book; (2) outstanding contribution to the activities of professional cataloging associations; (3) outstanding contributions to the technical improvements of cataloging and classification and/or the introduction of new techniques of recognized importance; or (4) outstanding contribution in the area of teaching cataloging and classification. Individuals may be nominated without regard to membership in either the Cataloging and Classification Section of the Resources and

Technical Services Division or any other section or division of the American Library Association and without regard to nationality. The award is administered by the Cataloging and Classification Section, Resources and Technical Services Division of the ALA. It consists of a citation of achievement.

1951
Lucile M. Morsch
Chief, Descriptive Cataloging Division, Library of Congress, Washington, D.C.
1952
Marie Louise Prevost
Newark Public Library, Newark, New Jersey
1953
Maurice F. Tauber
Professor, School of Library Service, Columbia University, New York, New York
1954
Pauline A. Seely
Head, Cataloging Department, Denver Public Library, Denver, Colorado
1955
Seymour Lubetzky
Consultant, Bibliographic and Cataloging Policy, Processing Department, Library of Congress, Washington, D.C.
1956
Susan Grey Akers
Professor and Dean, School of Library Science, University of North Carolina, Chapel Hill, North Carolina
1957
David Judson Haykin
Specialist in Subject Cataloging and Classification, Library of Congress, Washington, D.C.
1958
Esther J. Piercy
Chief, Processing Division, Enoch Pratt Free Library, Baltimore, Maryland
1959
Andrew D. Osborn
Librarian, Fisher Library, University of Sydney, Sydney, Australia

1960
M. Ruth MacDonald
Assistant to the Director, National Library of Medicine, Washington, D.C.
1961
John W. Cronin
Director, Processing Department, Library of Congress, Washington, D.C.
1962
Wyllis E. Wright
Librarian, Williams College, Williamstown, Massachusetts
1963
Arthur Hugh Chaplin
Keeper of the Department of Printed Books, British Museum, London, England
1964
Catherine MacQuarrie
Chief, Technical Services Division, Los Angeles County Public Library, Los Angeles, California
1965
Laura C. Colvin
Professor, Simmons College School of Library Science, Boston, Massachusetts
1966
F. Bernice Field
Yale University Library, New Haven, Connecticut
1967
C. Sumner Spalding
Assistant Director, Processing Department, Library of Congress, Washington, D.C.
1968
Paul S. Dunkin
Professor, Rutgers University Graduate School of Library Service, New Brunswick, New Jersey

1969

Katharine L. Ball
Professor, University of Toronto
School of Library Science, Toronto,
Ontario, Canada

1970

S. R. Ranganathan
President and Head of Documentation Research and Training Centre,
Bangalore, India

1971

Henriette D. Avram
Chief, MARC Development Office,
Processing Department, Library of
Congress, Washington, D.C.

1972

Edmund Lewis Applebaum
Assistant Director, Acquisitions and
Overseas Operations, Processing Department, Library of Congress, Washington, D.C.

1973

Doralyn J. Hickey
Associate Professor, School of Library Science, University of North
Carolina, Chapel Hill, North Carolina

1974

Frederick G. Kilgour
Director, Ohio College Library Center,
Columbus, Ohio

1975

Margaret Webster Ayrault
Professor, Graduate School of Library
Studies, University of Hawaii, Honolulu, Hawaii

1976

Eva Verona
Gundulićeva 61, YU-41000 Zagreb,
Yugoslavia

1977

Phyllis Allen Richmond
Case Western Reserve University,
Cleveland, Ohio

1978

Derek Austin
Head, Subject Systems Office, The
British Library, London, England

1979

Michael Gorman
University of Illinois, Urbana, Illinois

Paul W. Winkler
Library of Congress, Washington,
D.C.

Frederic G. Melcher Scholarship

This award was established in 1956 by the Children's Library Association, now known as the Association for Library Service to Children, now a division of the American Library Association. Currently, a $4,000 award is presented annually to each of two prospective librarians for basic graduate education in library service to children in public and school libraries. Open to candidates of the United States and Canada, the scholarship is named in honor of the late Frederic G. Melcher for his contribution to children's librarianship.

1957

Celia Louise Barker

1958

Margaret D. Petter

1959

Thusnelda Schmidt

1960

Judith Rose Hursch

1961

James F. Walz

1962

Mary E. Bogan

1963

Diana A. DeRollin

1964

Mrs. Dallas D. Shaffer

1965
    Mary Ann Stevenson
1966
    Maureen H. Davis
    Carol Senda
1967
    Forence Willson
1968
    Carol Lynn Gabriel
1969
    Linda Joan Brass
1970
    Gloria H. Woodward
1971
    E. Relleen Smith
1972
    Marjorie Ann Knoedel

1973
    James Bray
1974
    Jennifer Bobbit
1975
    Esta Anderson
1976
    Nancy Snyder
1977
    Lynn Joy Melton
1978
    Elizabeth Horner
1979
    Dianne Albers
    Linda Halas Papajcik

Isadore Gilbert Mudge Citation

The first presentation of this annual award was made at the American Library Association conference in 1959. It is given to a person who has made a distinguished contribution to reference librarianship. This contribution may be an imaginative and constructive program in a particular library, a significant book or articles in the reference field, creative and inspirational teaching of reference service, active participation in professional associations devoted to reference services, or activities that stimulate reference librarians to more distinguished performance. The Reference and Adult Services Division of the ALA administers the award.

1959
    Mary Neill Barton
    Formerly Head, General Reference Department, Enoch Pratt Free Library, Baltimore, Maryland
1960
    Constance M. Winchell
    Reference Librarian, Columbia University Libraries, New York, New York
1961
    Edith M. Coulter
    Formerly Professor, School of Librarianship, University of California, Berkeley, California
1962
    Frances Neel Cheney
    Associate Director, Peabody Library

School, George Peabody College for Teachers, Nashville, Tennessee
1963
    Mabel Conat
    Executive Secretary, Friends of the Detroit Public Library, and formerly Director, Reference Services, Detroit Public Library, Detroit, Michigan
1964
    Ruth Walling
    Associate University Librarian and Head of Reference, Emory University Library, Atlanta, Georgia
1965
    Katharine G. Harris
    Director, Reference Services, Detroit Public Library, Detroit, Michigan

1966
Frances B. Jenkins
Graduate School of Library Science, University of Illinois, Urbana, Illinois
1967
Louis Shores
Florida State University School of Library Science, Tallahassee, Florida
1968
Thomas S. Shaw
Louisiana State University Library School, Baton Rouge, Louisiana
1969
No award
1970
Theodore Besterman
1971
James Bennet Childs
Honorary Consultant, Library of Congress, Washington, D.C.
1972
Thomas J. Galvin
Associate Professor of Library Science, Simmons College, Boston, Massachusetts
1973
William A. Katz
School of Library Science, State University of New York at Albany, Albany, New York

1974
Florence E. Blakely
Head, Reference Department, Perkins Library, Duke University, Durham, North Carolina
1975
Jean L. Connor
Former Director, Division of Library Development, New York State Library, Albany, New York
1976
John Neal Waddell (awarded posthumously)
School of Library Service, Columbia University, New York, New York
1977
Bohdan S. Wynar
President, Libraries Unlimited, Inc., Littleton, Colorado
1978
C. Edward Wall
Head Librarian, University of Michigan at Dearborn, and Publisher and Editorial Director, Pierian Press, Ann Arbor, Michigan
1979
Henry J. Dubester
Formerly at the College of Library and Information Services, University of Maryland, College Park, Maryland

Eunice Rockwell Oberly Memorial Award

The Eunice Rockwell Oberly Memorial Award is presented in odd-numbered years to an American citizen who compiles the best bibliography in agriculture or related sciences in the preceding two-year period. The award consists of a citation and cash. It is administered by the Science and Technology Section of the Association of College and Research Libraries of the American Library Association.

1925
Max Meisel
"Bibliography of American Natural History," vol. 1
1927
Mary G. Lacy, Annie M. Hannay, and Emily L. Day

"Price Fixing by Governments, 424 B.C.–1926 A.D."
1929
Annie M. Hannay
"Control of Agricultural Products by Government; A Selected Bibliography"

1931
Everett E. Edwards
"A Bibliography of the History of Agriculture in the United States"
1933
Louise O. Bercaw and Esther M. Colvin
"Bibliography on the Marketing of Agricultural Products"
1935
Louise O. Bercaw, Annie M. Hannay, and Esther M. Colvin
"Bibliography of Land Settlement"
1937
Victor A. Schaefer
"Survey of Current Bibliographies on Agriculture and Allied Subjects"
1939
Louise O. Bercaw and Annie M. Hannay
"Bibliography on Land Utilization, 1918-1936"
1941
Elmer D. Merrill and Egbert H. Walker
"A Bibliography of Eastern Asiatic Botany"
1945
Sidney F. Blake and Alice C. Atwood
"Geographical Guide to the Floras of the World," pt. 1
Jules C. Cunningham
"Maize Bibliography for the Years 1917-1936"
1947
Burch H. Schneider
"Feeds of the World; Their Digestibility and Composition"
1949
Ina L. Hawes and Rose Eisenberg
"Bibliography on Aviation and Economic Entomology"
1951
Richard Wiebe and Janina Nowakowska
"The Technical Literature of Agricultural Motor Fuels"

1953
Ralph W. Planck, Frank C. Pack, and Dorothy B. Skau
"Abstract Bibliography of the Chemistry and Technology of Tung Products"
1955
Arthur Rose and Elizabeth Rose
"Distillation Literature, Index and Abstracts, 1946-1952"
1957
Ira J. Condit and Julius Enderud
"A Bibliography of the Fig"
1959
J. Richard Blanchard and Harald Ostvold
"Literature of Agriculture Research"
1961
Egbert H. Walker
"A Bibliography of Eastern Asiatic Botany"
1963
Allan Stevenson
"Catalogue of Botanical Books in the Collection of Rachel McMasters Miller Hunt"
1965
Ida Kaplan Langman
"A Selected Guide to the Literature of the Flowering Plants of Mexico"
1967
George Neville Jones
"Annotated Bibliography of Mexican Ferns"
1969
No award
1971
John T. Schlebecker
"Bibliography of Books and Pamphlets on the History of Agriculture in the United States, 1607-1967"
1973
Olga Lendway
"Bibliography of Wheat" and "Bibliography of Corn"
1975
Henry T. Murphy, Jr., and Ann E. Kerker

"Comparative and Veterinary Medicine: A Bibliography of Resource Literature"
1977
  Helen Purdy Beale
  "Bibliography of Plant Viruses and Index to Research"

1979
  James B. Beard, Harriet Beard, and D. P. Martin
  "Turfgrass: A Bibliography from 1672 to 1972"

PLA Allie Beth Martin Award

This annual award, established in 1978, has been donated by the Baker and Taylor Company and is administered by the Public Library Association (PLA). It is given in honor of the late Allie Beth Martin, who was the director of the Tulsa City–County Library and a president of the American Library Association. The award is presented to a librarian who, in a public library setting, has demonstrated an extraordinary range and depth of knowledge about books or other library materials and has exhibited a distinguished ability to share that knowledge. The award consists of a $2,000 stipend, a citation, and the opportunity to select the author of his or her choice to speak at the PLA's annual meeting, held concurrently with the ALA annual conference in the summer.

1979
  Harriett Bard
  Head Librarian, Morrisson–Reeves
  Public Library, Richmond, Indiana

Esther J. Piercy Award

This award was established in 1968 by the Resources and Technical Services Division, American Library Association, to recognize contributions in the field of technical services by younger members of the profession. It is for a librarian with no more than ten years of professional experience who has shown outstanding promise for continuing contributions and leadership in any of the fields comprising technical services by such means as (1) leadership in professional associations at the local, state, regional, or national level; (2) contributions to the development, application, or utilization of new or improved methods, techniques, and routines; (3) a significant contribution to professional literature; or (4) studies or research in the technical services. The award is given each year in which the jury finds a qualified recipient. The winner is announced and a citation is given at the annual membership and business meeting of the Resources and Technical Services Division during the ALA annual conference.

1969
  Richard M. Dougherty
1970
  John B. Corbin

1971
  John Phillip Immroth
1972
  Carol A. Nemeyer

1973
  Glen A. Zimmerman
1974
  No award
1975
  John D. Byrum, Jr.
1976
  Ruth L. Tighe

1977
  No award
1978
  S. Michael Malinconico
1979
  Pamela Darling

President's Award

This annual award was established in 1977 by the Baker and Taylor Company, the donor, and the American Association of School Librarians (AASL), which administers the award. It is given to recognize a school librarian who has made outstanding national or international contributions to school librarianship or to school library development. The award, a $2,000 stipend, is announced in January and presented at the ALA annual conference in the summer.

1978
  Jean Lowrey
1979
  Frances Henne
  Professor Emeritus, School of Library Service, Columbia University, New York, New York

Herbert Putnam Honor Fund

The Herbert Putnam Honor Fund was created and presented to the American Library Association by friends and associates of Dr. Herbert Putnam, Librarian of Congress from 1899 to 1939 and two-term president of the ALA. It was established to honor Dr. Putnam by remembering his services to librarianship and by inspiring future generations to emulate the qualities and accomplishments that distinguished his career. A grant-in-aid, presented when the income from the fund accumulates to $500, is given to an American librarian of outstanding ability for travel, writing, or other use that might improve his or her service to the library profession or to society.

1949
  Carleton B. Joeckel
  For a projected study on "Libraries in the American Federal System"
1954
  Louis R. Wilson
  For notable contributions to librarianship, particularly through his surveys and writings, including the revision of *The University Library: Its Organization, Administration and Functions*
1963
  Mary V. Gaver
  For outstanding and significant contributions and leadership in library development and organization, research

and children's and school library work, library education, and professional writing

1972

Michael H. Harris

For inventive and scholarly approach to a long-term research project based on his personal concern with the investigation of the influence of reading on human behavior

1975

Wayne A. Wiegund

1979

Isabel Schon

To study the effects of selected books on students' perceptions of Mexican-American people

John R. Rowe Memorial Award

The John R. Rowe Memorial Award of the American Library Association, formerly the Exhibits Round Table Award, is an annual award for an individual or group for the aid or improvement of a specific aspect of librarianship or library service. The award, established in 1957, consists of a $500 grant, given on the basis of need within the profession or within the operation of a professional library association. After consulting with the ALA executive director and other ALA officials to determine the areas of greatest need, a committee of the Exhibits Round Table (ERT) makes the award.

1957

ALA Public Relations Office

1958

American Association of School Librarians

1959

No award

1960

$1,000 for display cases in the new ALA headquarters building

1961

Public Library Association for expenses incident to committee meeting for completion of report "Interim Standards for Small Public Libraries"

1962

ALA Public Relations Office for brochure on advisory and consultative services of headquarters staff

1963

ALA Public Relations Office for production of a pamphlet on ALA services to be distributed at the Chicago conference

1964

The 1964 ERT Award was made in the form of the printing and distribution of a humorously illustrated instruction booklet on the most effective manner of spending one's time visiting the exhibits. It was mailed to the home address of everyone who had registered for a hotel room in St. Louis for the ALA conference

1965

To honor memory of John R. Rowe with a John R. Rowe memorial award

1966

PLA Committee on Public Library Service to the Functionally Illiterate

1967

Intellectual Freedom Committee, California Library Association

1968

ALA Committee on Economic Opportunity Programs

1969
ERT: Special Project to Coordinate and Improve Local, State, and Regional Library Meetings through Exhibits
1970
Freedom to Read Foundation

1971-1973
No awards
1974
Freedom to Read Foundation
1975-1978
No awards

School Library Media Program of the Year Award

The annual School Library Media Program of the Year Award is cosponsored by the American Association of School Librarians (AASL) and the Encyclopaedia Britannica, Inc. Inaugurated in 1973, the program succeeds the Encyclopaedia Britannica School Library Awards given during 1963-1972, with the advisory assistance of the AASL. The awards recognize school systems for achievement in providing exemplary library media programs at the elementary level. One $5,000 cash prize is awarded each spring to the one school system with the most outstanding school library media program, and as many as five National Finalist Citations may be awarded upon recommendation of the AASL Selection Committee. Any public, independent, or parochial school system may apply. All applications are judged on the basis of the quality of the program (systemwide) and the degree to which the program meets the needs of its own school community. Detailed information and application forms are available each July from AASL, 50 East Huron Street, Chicago, Illinois 60611, or Encyclopaedia Britannica, Inc., 425 North Michigan Avenue, Chicago, Illinois 60611.

1973
First place
Duneland Community Schools, Chesterton, Indiana
National finalists
Palm Beach County Schools, West Palm Beach, Florida
Jefferson County Public Schools, Louisville, Kentucky
West Linn Public Schools, West Linn, Oregon
Hampton City Schools, Hampton, Virginia
Oconomowoc Public Schools, Oconomowoc, Wisconsin
1974
First place
Cedar Rapids Community Schools, Cedar Rapids, Iowa

National finalists
Urbana Community Schools, Urbana, Illinois
Fort Knox Dependent Schools, Fort Knox, Kentucky
Beaverton Public Schools, Beaverton, Oregon
Arlington Public Schools, Arlington, Virginia
1975
First place
Rochester City Schools, Rochester, New York
National finalists
Missoula Public Schools, Missoula, Montana
Shelby County Schools, Memphis, Tennessee

LaCrosse Area Public Schools, La-Crosse, Wisconsin
1976
First place
Littleton Public Schools, Littleton, Colorado
National finalists
Chula Vista City School District, Chula Vista, California
St. Helena Unified School District, St. Helena, California
Stamford Public Schools, Stamford, Connecticut
1977
First place
Los Alamitos School District, Los Alamitos, California
National finalists
Brittan School District, Sutter, California
DeKalb County School System, Decatur, Georgia

Community Unit School District 200, Wheaton, Illinois
Portage Public Schools, Portage, Michigan
1978
First Place
Cobb County Public Schools, Marietta, Georgia
National finalist
Punahou School, Honolulu, Hawaii
1979
First place
Greenwich Public Schools, Greenwich, Connecticut
National finalists
Irvine Unified School District, Irvine, California
Community Consolidated School District 64, Park Ridge, Illinois
Shaker Heights City School District, Shaker Heights, Ohio

Ralph R. Shaw Award for Library Literature

In 1959 this award was established as the Scarecrow Press Award for Library Literature, to be presented to an American librarian in recognition of an outstanding contribution to library literature during the three preceding calendar years. The name of the award was changed in 1976. It is made only when a title merits recognition. The donor of the $500 prize and citation is the Scarecrow Press.

1960
Marjorie Fiske Lowenthal
Book Selection and Censorship: A Study of School and Public Libraries in California (Univ. of California Press)
1961
No award
1962
Sarah K. Vann
Training for Librarianship before 1923 (ALA)
1963
Joseph L. Wheeler and Herbert Goldhor

Practical Administration of Public Libraries (Harper)
1964
Edward G. Holley
Charles Evans, American Bibliographer (Univ. of Illinois Press)
1965
Roberta Bowler
Local Public Library Administration (International City Managers)
1966
Keyes DeWitt Metcalf
Planning Academic and Research Library Buildings (McGraw)

1967
No award
1968
Lester E. Asheim
Librarianship in the Developing Countries (Univ. of Illinois Press)
1969
Ralph E. McCoy
Freedom of the Press: An Annotated Bibliography (Southern Illinois Univ. Press)
1970
Lowell A. Martin
Library Response to Urban Change: A Study of the Chicago Public Library (ALA)
1971
Irene A. Braden (Hoadley)
The Undergraduate Library (ALA)
1972–1973
No awards
1974
Jesse L. Shera
Foundations of Education for Librarianship (Becker & Hayes)

1975
No award
1976
Herman H. Fussler
Research Libraries and Technology (Univ. of Chicago Press)
1977
Redmond Kathleen Molz
Federal Policy and Library Support (M.I.T. Press)
1978
Frederick W. Lancaster
The Measurement and Evaluation of Library Services (Information Resources)
1979
Joan K. Marshall
On Equal Terms: A Thesaurus for Non-Sexist Indexing and Cataloging (Neal-Schuman)

Trustee Citations

The American Library Association announced in 1940 the establishment of the ALA Trustee Citations to honor some 30,000 library trustees throughout the country who voluntarily give their time and thought to library service. Illuminated citations are presented to two trustees for distinguished service to library development on the local, state, or regional level recommended to the Jury on Citation of Trustees by any library board, state library extension agency, state library association, or state trustee association. The following are recent winners.

1952
Harold J. Baily
Trustee, Brooklyn Public Library
Josephine M. Quigley
Trustee, Seattle Public Library
1953
Jacob M. Lashly
Board of Directors, St. Louis Public Library

Frank Adams Smith
Ordinary of Rabun County, Georgia
1954
Joseph B. Fleming
Board of Directors, Chicago Public Library
Mrs. Merlin M. Moore
Chairman, Arkansas Library Commission, Little Rock

1955
Ralph D. Remley
Trustee, Montgomery County Library Board, Maryland

Mrs. George R. Wallace
Trustee, Fitchburg Public Library, Massachusetts

1956
Judge Eugene A. Burdick
Trustee, James Memorial Library, Williston, South Dakota

Mrs. Otis G. Wilson
West Virginia Library Commission

1957
J. N. Heiskell
President, Board of Trustees, Little Rock Public Library, Arkansas

Stephen Pronko
Past president, Brentwood Public Library, Missouri

1958
Cecil U. Edmonds
President, Trustee Division, Arkansas Library Association, West Memphis, Arkansas

Mrs. J. Henry Mohr
San Francisco Public Library Commission

1959
Francis Bergan
Trustee, Albany Public Library, New York

Alan Neil Schneider
Trustee, Louisville Free Public Library, Kentucky

1960
Mrs. Emil G. Bloedow
Trustee, Edgeley Public Library, North Dakota

Thomas Dreier
Florida State Library Board

1961
Paul D. Brown
Trustee, Charles County Public Library Board, Maryland

Walter L. Varner
Trustee, Yuma City-County Library, Arizona

1962
S. L. Townsend
Trustee, Suwanee River Regional Library, Live Oak, Florida

1963
Kenneth U. Blass
Trustee, Pathfinder Community Library, Baldwin, Michigan

John E. Fogarty
Trustee, Harmony Public Library, Harmony, Rhode Island

1964
Mrs. Samuel Berg
Trustee, Public Libraries of Lake County, Crown Point-Merrillville, Indiana

Mrs. Weldon Lynch
Trustee, Allen Parish Library, Oberlin, Louisiana

1965
Jacob A. Meckstroth
Trustee, Public Library, Columbus, Ohio

Mrs. Henry Steffens
Trustee, Herrick Public Library, Holland, Michigan

1966
Mrs. Bruce Coombs
Washington State Library Commission

Charles Reid
Paramus Public Library, Paramus, New Jersey

1967
James L. Love
Trustee, Temple Memorial Library, Diboll, Texas

Mrs. J. R. Sweasy
Trustee, Carnegie-Lawther Library, Red Wing, Minnesota

1968
Raymond Holden
Trustee, Richards Free Library, Newport, New Hampshire
John Bennett Shaw
Trustee, Oklahoma State Library, Oklahoma City, Oklahoma

1969
Alex P. Allain
Trustee, St. Mary Parish Library, Franklin, Louisiana
Rachael Gross
Trustee, Public Library, Huntingdon Valley, Pennsylvania

1970
George Coen
Chairperson, Ohio State Library Board
John Veblen
Washington State Library Commission

1971
Jacquelin Enochs
Trustee, Pike County Library System, Mississippi
Jean Smith
Trustee, Burbank Public Library, California

1972
Story Birdseye
Superior Court, Washington, formerly Trustee, King County Public Library, Washington
Mary M. Carlson
Chairperson, Board of Trustees, Weld County Library, Greeley, Colorado

1973
Alice Ihrig
Past President, American Library Trustee Association, and Illinois Library Trustee Association
Carroll K. Shakelford

1974
R. A. Cox
Eldred G. Wolzien
Retired Physical Science Administrator of the National Bureau of Standards, Boulder, Colorado

1975
Marie Cole
Greenwich, Connecticut
Dorothy Engstrom Rosen
New Mexico State Library Commission

1976
James A. Hess
Trustee, East Brunswick Public Library, New Jersey
Elizabeth F. Ruffner
White House Conference on Library and Information Services, Prescott, Arizona

1977
C. E. Campbell Beal
Trustee, Public Library, Martinsburg, West Virginia
Daniel W. Casey
Trustee, Public Library, Syracuse, New York

1978
Barbara D. Cooper
Trustee, Broward County Division of Libraries, Fort Lauderdale, Florida
Albert I. Mayer
Trustee, Ocean County Library, Toms River, New Jersey

1979
Jean M. Coleman
Trustee, Dayton and Montgomery County Public Library, Dayton, Ohio
Ella Pretty
Trustee, Fraser Valley Regional Library, British Columbia, Canada

H. W. Wilson Company Library Periodical Award

This award was established in 1960 by the H. W. Wilson Company for an outstanding contribution to the library profession. A prize of $250 and a certificate is awarded to a periodical published by a local, state, or regional library, library group, or library association in the United States and Canada. Issues published in the preceding calendar year are judged on the basis of sustained excellence in both content and format with consideration given to size of budget and staff.

1961
California Librarian
California Library Association, William R. Eshelman, editor

1962
North Country Libraries
New Hampshire State Library and the Vermont Free Public Library, Louise Hazelton, editor

1963
Bay State Librarian
Massachusetts Library Association, John Berry, editor

1964
California Librarian
California Library Association, Henry M. Madden, editor

1965
PNLA Quarterly
Pacific Northwest Library Association, Eli M. Oboler, editor

1966
Ohio Library Association Bulletin
Dayton and Montgomery County Public Library, Gerald R. Shields, editor

1967
British Columbia Library Quarterly
Alan Woodland, editor

1968
California Librarian
California Library Association, Richard D. Johnson, editor

1969
Missouri Library Association Quarterly
John Gordon Burke, editor

1970
Synergy
Bay Area Reference Center, San Francisco Public Library, Celeste West, editor

1971
Texas Library Journal
Texas Library Association, Mary Pound, editor

1972
Synergy
Bay Area Reference Center, San Francisco Public Library, Celeste West, editor

1973
Illinois Libraries
Illinois State Library, Springfield, Irma Bostian, editor

1974
Ohio Library Association Bulletin
Robert F. Cayton, editor

1975
PNLA Quarterly
Pacific Northwest Library Association, Richard Moore, editor

1976
Hennepin County Library Cataloging Bulletin
Sanford Berman, editor

1977
Utah Libraries
Blaine H. Hall, editor

1978
Documentation et Bibliothèques (Montreal)
Hubert Perron, editor

1979
The Southeastern Librarian
Leland M. Park, editor

Women's Information Service Award

The Business and Professional Women's Foundation announced in 1979 that this award will be presented for the first time at the ALA Annual Conference in New York City in June 1980. The award is given to honor the best plan or design to improve information services for women through libraries, library schools, or other nonprofit information agencies. The award can recognize any aspect of information services, including but not limited to the development of materials, collection organization, bibliographic instruction, the provision of service, or the dissemination of information. Individuals, groups, or nonprofit information agencies may apply for the $1,000 award. The deadline for application is February 1. The judging will be undertaken by the BPW Foundation and representatives of the ALA Committee on the Status of Women, the ALA Social Responsibilities Round Table Task Force on Women, and the Women Library Workers. For an application or more information, contact the Business and Professional Women's Foundation, Library, 2012 Massachusetts Avenue N.W., Washington, D.C. 20036.

Council on Library Resources.

Academic Library Management Intern Program

In 1974, the Council began to offer academic library management internships to mid-career librarians of outstanding leadership potential. Librarians spend an academic year working closely with the director and top administrative staff of one of the country's academic libraries, selected for its administrative excellence. While the individual programs vary, interns spend an intensive period observing and participating in management activities, reading, and undertaking special assignments. The result for each individual is a well-rounded picture of the techniques and skills required of directors as they fulfill their responsibilities on a daily basis.

The internship covers ten months. The interns receive an amount equal to their normal basic salary and benefits (up to a total of $22,000), some assistance for moving costs, and approved travel expenses.

To qualify, applicants must be librarians who are citizens or permanent residents of the United States or Canada. A selection committee composed of eminent librarians chooses the final candidates after carefully reviewing their applications and conducting personal interviews. The selection committee considers professional library experience, administrative skills, academic record, and the intellectual and personal qualities that are important in academic library leadership.

Interested librarians may receive applications by writing to the Academic Library, Management Intern Committee, Council on Library Resources, One Dupont Circle, Suite 620, Washington, D.C. 20036. Completed applications must be received no later than October 15. The awards are announced on or about April 1.

1974

Barbara Brown
Head, Reference and Public Services, Washington and Lee University Library

Ralph Edwards
Assistant Director, School of Librarianship, Western Michigan University

Judy Fair
Director, Urban Institute Library, Washington, D.C.

Thomas J. Michalak
Librarian, Economics and Political Science, Indiana University

Barbara von Wahlde
Associate Director, Technical Processing, University of West Florida Library

1975

Linda Beaupré
Coordinator of Public Services, Undergraduate Library, University of California, Berkeley

Jean W. Boyer
Chief, Collection Development, Temple University Library

George C. Grant
Associate Director of Public Services, Southern Illinois University (Edwardsville) Library

Robert Koester
Head, Undergraduate Reference Library, University of Tennessee

Lee Ann Putnam
Associate Librarian, Gallaudet College

1976

Stanton F. Biddle
Associate Director, Research and Planning, Howard University Library

William Joseph Crowe, Jr.
Coordinator, Processing and Order Librarian, Indiana University, Regional Campus Libraries

Peter C. Haskell
Associate University Librarian, Colgate University

Wilson Luquire
Associate Librarian and Senior Cataloger, Indiana University

Merrily E. Taylor
Collection Development Librarian, University of South Florida

1977

Graham R. Hill
Director, Division of Archives and Special Collections, McMaster University, Hamilton, Ontario

Jo Nell Hintner
Head, Humanities Research Center Cataloging Department, University of Texas at Austin

Shelley E. Phipps
Orientation Librarian, University of Arizona

Jordan M. Scepanski
Assistant Director, Library, University of North Carolina at Charlotte

J. Daniel Vann III
Deputy Chief Librarian, College of Staten Island, City University of New York

1978

Joan L. Chambers
Head, Government Publications Department, Library, University of Nevada, Reno

Sandra S. Coleman
Head, Reference Department, University of New Mexico General Library

Sara C. Heitshu
Assistant Head, Book Purchasing and Business Operations, University of Michigan Library

1979

Rebecca D. Dixon
Director, Library Services Division, Center for the Study of Youth Development, Boys Town, Nebraska

Susan K. Nutter
Associate Head, Engineering Libraries, Massachusetts Institute of Technology

Fellowship Program

Since 1969 the Council on Library Resources (CLR) has offered a limited number of fellowships each year to mid-career librarians of the United States and Canada who have demonstrated a strong potential for leadership in the profession. Similar to the traditional sabbaticals enjoyed by college and university faculty, the fellowships enable successful applicants to pursue a self-developed study or research project aimed at improving their competence in the substantive, administrative, and/or technical aspects of librarianship. In the eleven years of the program, 215 fellowships have been awarded. Fellowship holders have published nearly eighty journal articles and at least fifteen books or occasional papers. Some fellows have used the opportunity to improve their technical and administrative skills through short-term internships or work experiences. Others have shared their research in conference programs or applied new skills to the improvement of their current work situations.

In the fall of 1978, the CLR Board of Directors decided to suspend the Fellowship Program. Proposals for research projects will still be considered for funding on an individual basis. Preliminary letters of inquiry should be addressed to Warren J. Haas, President, Council on Library Resources, One Dupont Circle, Suite 620, Washington, D.C. 20036.

The recipients of CLR fellowships for 1969–1979 follow. The positions listed below are those held at the time the fellowship was announced.

1969

Florence Blakely
Head, Reference Department, Duke University

Warren Boes
Director of Libraries, Syracuse University

John M. Dawson
Director of Libraries, University of Delaware

Richard M. Dougherty
Associate Director of Libraries, University of Colorado

Andrew J. Eaton
Director of Libraries, Washington University

James F. Govan
Librarian, Swarthmore College

Tyrus G. Harmsen
Librarian, Occidental College

Miles M. Jackson, Jr.
Librarian, Atlanta University

Irving Lieberman
Director, School of Librarianship, University of Washington

Ellsworth Mason
Director of Library Services, Hofstra University

Luella R. Pollock
Librarian, Reed College

Eldred Smith
Head, Loan Department, University of California, Berkeley

Jessie Carney Smith
University Librarian, Fisk University

David Weber
Associate Director of Libraries, Stanford University

Robert Wedgeworth
Assistant Chief Order Librarian, Brown University

1970

Kenneth S. Allen
Associate Director of Libraries, University of Washington

Donald C. Anthony
Associate Director of Libraries, Columbia University

Richard W. Boss
Associate Director of Libraries, University of Utah

Maynard J. Brichford
University Archivist, University of Illinois

John C. Broderick
Assistant Chief, Manuscript Division, Library of Congress

Richard De Gennaro
Senior Associate University Librarian, Harvard University

Richard H. Dillon
Sutro Librarian, San Francisco

Robin N. Downes
Associate Head, Technical Services

Department, University of Michigan Library

Johnnie E. Givens
Librarian, Austin Peay State University

Joan I. Gotwals
Head, Reference and Bibliographic Service Division, University of Pennsylvania Library

David M. Henington
Director, Houston Public Library

David R. Hoffman
Deputy State Librarian, Montana State Library

Edward G. Holley
Director of Libraries, University of Houston

Henry C. Koch
Assistant Director of Libraries, Michigan State University

Jay K. Lucker
Associate University Librarian, Princeton University

John McGowan
Associate University Librarian, Northwestern University

Elvin E. Strowd
Head, Circulation Department, Duke University

Allen B. Veaner
Assistant Director of University Libraries for Automation, Stanford University

Theodore Welch
Assistant University Librarian for Public Service, Northwestern University

1971

Albert G. Anderson, Jr.
Librarian, Worcester Polytechnic Institute

Howard L. Applegate
Director, George Arents Research Library, Syracuse University

Clifton Brock
Associate University Librarian, University of North Carolina

Betty Duvall
Assistant Dean for Instructional Resources, Florissant Valley Community College

Jane G. Flener
Assistant Director of Libraries, Indiana University

Yates M. Forbis
Librarian, Dickinson College

Clyde L. Haselden
Librarian, Lafayette College

Donald D. Hendricks
Director, South Central Regional Medical Library Program, Dallas, Texas

Carol F. Ishimoto
Senior Cataloger, Harvard College Library

David A. Kronick
Librarian, Medical School at San Antonio, University of Texas

John Lubans, Jr.
Assistant Director for Public Services, University of Colorado Libraries

Howard Messman
Mathematics Librarian, University of Illinois Library

T. H. Milby
Science Librarian, University of Oklahoma

Theodore P. Peck
Chief, Reference Services Department, University Libraries, University of Minnesota

James A. Riddles
Director of Libraries, University of the Pacific

Frederick E. Smith
Law Librarian, University of California at Los Angeles

Morton Snowhite
Librarian, Newark College of Engineering

Richard L. Snyder
Director of Libraries, Drexel University

1972

Patricia Andrews
Chief Librarian, National Archives Library, Washington, D.C.

John M. Bruer
Head of Acquisitions, University of Kentucky Library

Lois Nabrit Clark
Head Librarian, Knoxville College

John Y. Cole, Jr.
Technical Officer, Reference Department, Library of Congress

Richard E. Combs
Head Librarian, Northbrook, Illinois, Public Library

Andrea Claire Dragon
Librarian, Minneapolis Institute of Arts, Minnesota

Ralph E. Ehrenberg
Assistant Director, Cartographic Archives, National Archives, Washington, D.C.

Katherine T. Emerson
Assistant to Director of Libraries, University of Massachusetts, Amherst

Elizabeth T. Fast
Director of Media Services, Groton, Connecticut, Public Schools

Gordon E. Fretwell
Associate Director of the University Library, University of Massachusetts, Amherst

Guy G. Garrison
Professor and Dean, Graduate School of Library Science, Drexel University

J. Myron Jacobstein
Law Librarian, Stanford University School of Law

Richard D. Johnson
Director of Libraries, Claremont Colleges, California

W. David Laird, Jr.
Associate Director of Libraries, University of Utah

Karl Lo
Head of Asiatic Collection, University of Washington

Nolan Lushington
Director of Greenwich, Connecticut, Public Library

Maurice Marchant
Associate Professor of Library and Information Sciences, Brigham Young University

Susan K. Martin
Systems Librarian, Harvard University

Ellis Mount
Science and Engineering Librarian, Columbia University

Richard L. O'Keefe
Librarian, Fondren Library, Rice University

Margaret A. Otto
Assistant Director of Reader Services, Massachusetts Institute of Technology

Robert E. Pfeiffer
Head, Graduate Social Sciences Library, University of California, Berkeley

Harold T. Pinkett
Chief, Natural Resources Branch, National Archives, Washington, D.C.

George Piternick
Professor, School of Librarianship, University of British Columbia

Donald L. Roberts
Head Music Librarian, Northwestern University

Priscilla R. Scott
Head, Circulation Division, University of Victoria Library, British Columbia

Ernest Siegel
Director, Central Library, Los Angeles Public Library

Alva W. Stewart
Associate Librarian, College of William and Mary

Dorothy G. Whittemore
Head, Social Sciences Division, Tulane University Library

Fay Zipkowitz
Head, Information Processing Department, University of Massachusetts, Amherst

Martin J. Zonligt
Head of Extension and Outreach Services, Stanislaus County, California Free Library

1973

Shelah Bell-Cragin
Assistant Director of Libraries, El Paso Public Library

George S. Bobinski
Dean, School of Information and Library Studies, State University of New York at Buffalo

Mary B. Cassata
Assistant Director of University Libraries for Public Service, State University of New York at Buffalo

Charles Kwang Hsiang Chen
Far East Specialist, Dartmouth College Library

Phyllis Dain
Associate Professor of Library Service, Columbia University

Richard James Dionne
Head, Science and Technology Libraries, Syracuse University

James Beaupré Dodd
Associate Professor and Information Consultant, Georgia Institute of Technology Library

Herbert Paul Dove, Jr.
Librarian, Erskine College, South Carolina

Allan Judge Dyson
Head, Undergraduate Library, University of California, Berkeley

Fern L. Edwards
Reference Librarian and Associate Professor of Library Science, Gallaudet College

G. Edward Evans
Assistant Professor, School of Library Service, University of California at Los Angeles

Esther Greenberg
Chief Cataloger and Assistant Head, Technical Services, Case Western Reserve University

Theodore Godfrey Grieder, Jr.
Curator, Division of Special Collections, New York University Libraries

Ira Whitney Harris
Assistant Dean, Graduate School of Library Studies, University of Hawaii

Helen Arlene Howard
University Librarian, Sir George Williams University, Canada

Brigitte L. Kenney
Assistant Professor, Graduate School of Library Science, Drexel University

Donald M. Koslow
Executive Officer, Library and Information Systems, University of Massachusetts, Amherst

Robert French Lewis
Biomedical Librarian, University of California, San Diego

Avinash C. Maheshwary
South Asia Librarian, Duke University

John A. McCrossan
Coordinator of Interlibrary Cooperation, Pennsylvania

Robert S. McGee
Assistant Systems Development Librarian, University of Chicago

John B. McTaggart
Director of Library Services, Methodist Theological School, Delaware, Ohio

Robert Carl Miller
Associate Director for Reader Services, University of Chicago

Dorothy May Schmidt Obi
Sublibrarian, Enugu Campus Library, University of Nigeria

Hal B. Schell
Associate Director of Libraries, University of Cincinnati

Russell Shank
Director of Libraries, Smithsonian Institution

Thomas Shaughnessy
Director, Dana Library, Rutgers University

Barbara Eggleston Smith
Documents Librarian, Skidmore College

Francis F. Spreitzer
Head, Micrographics and Reprography Department, University of Southern California

Sarah Katharine Thomson
Chairman, Library and Learning Resources Department, Bergen Community College, New Jersey

John W. Weatherford
Director of Libraries, Central Michigan University

1974

John David Amend
Library Consultant, California State Library

Richard J. Beck
Associate Director of Libraries, University of Idaho

Herbert Biblo
Assistant Librarian for Reader Services, John Crerar Library, Chicago

Kenneth John Bierman
Systems Librarian, Virginia Polytechnic Institute and State University

Larry Earl Bone
Assistant Director of Libraries for Public Services, Memphis Public Library and Information Center

Robert Keady Bruce
Librarian, Carleton College

Robert Whitehall Burns, Jr.
Librarian for Research and Development, Colorado State University

John Donald Byrum, Jr.
Catalog Librarian, Princeton University

Susan Thach Dean
Reference Librarian, University of Wisconsin-Parkside, Kenosha

Sue Fontaine
Information Officer, Tulsa, Oklahoma, City-County Library

Eileen Elizabeth Hitchingham
Science Librarian, Oakland University, Michigan

Herbert Frederick Johnson
Librarian, Oberlin College

Anne Whaley LeClercq
Nonprint Librarian, University of Tennessee

Robert S. McGee
Assistant Systems Development Librarian, University of Chicago

Jerold Arthur Nelson
Assistant Professor, School of Librarianship, University of Washington

Harriet Keiko Rebuldela
Head, Acquisitions Department, University of Colorado

Marion Taylor Reid
Head, Order Department, Louisiana State University

Harry Robinson, Jr.
Dean of Learning Resources, Alabama State University

Charles William Sargent
Director, Health Sciences Information Center and Professor of Health Communications

James S. Sokoloski
Library Systems Manager, University of Massachusetts

Thomas Gregory Czetong Song
Associate Director of Libraries and Lecturer in Philosophy, Bryn Mawr College

Roderick G. Swartz
Deputy Director, National Commission on Libraries and Information Science

Herman Lavon Totten
Associate Dean and Associate Professor, College of Library Science, University of Kentucky

Rose Vainstein
Professor, School of Library Science, University of Michigan

Larry N. Yarbrough
Reference Librarian, Northwestern University

1975

Judith Armstrong
Director of the Library, Drury College

Pauline Atherton
Professor, School of Information Studies, Syracuse University

Martha J. Bailey
Physics Librarian, Purdue University

Boyd M. Bolvin
Associate Dean of Instruction, Bellevue Community College

Keith M. Cottam
Assistant Director for the Undergraduate Library, University of Tennessee at Knoxville

Doris C. Dale
Associate Professor, Department of Instructional Materials, Southern Illinois University at Carbondale

Lynn C. Dennison
Professional Assistant, Association of College and Research Libraries, American Library Association

Barbar L. Feret
Director of the Library, Culinary Institute of America

Thelma Freides
Associate Professor, School of Library Service, Atlanta University

Wolfgang M. Freitag
Fine Arts Librarian, Harvard College Library, Harvard University

Jane C. Henning
Head, Howe Architecture Library, Arizona State University at Tempe

Judith Holliday
Librarian, Fine Arts Library, Cornell University

Richard G. Landon
Assistant Head, Thomas Fisher Rare Book Library, University of Toronto

Alan H. MacDonald
Health Science Librarian, Dalhousie University

James W. McGregor
Head of the Library's Technical Services, Northeastern Illinois University

Joan K. Marshall
Chief of the Library's Catalog Division, Brooklyn College

Ann F. Painter
Professor, Graduate School of Library Science, Drexel University

James F. Parks, Jr.
Head Librarian, Millsaps College

Stephen L. Peterson
Librarian, Divinity School, Yale University

Eugene E. Petriwsky
Assistant Director for Technical Services, University of Colorado Library

Hannelore B. Rader
Orientation Librarian, Eastern Michigan University

Donald L. Roberts
Audiovisual Librarian, Hennepin County Library, Minnesota

Earl R. Schwass
Library Director, Naval War College

Patricia H. Shoyinka
Cataloger, Ibadan University Library, Nigeria

Mildred C. Tietjen
Director of Library Services, Georgia Southwestern College

Joyce L. White
Librarian, Penniman Library of Education, University of Pennsylvania

1976

Mae Benne
Professor, School of Librarianship, University of Washington

Elizabeth Beyerly
Chief, Reference and Loan, UNESCO Library, Paris

Susan D. Csaky
Head, Department of Government Publications, University of Kentucky Libraries

Shirley A. Edsall
Assistant Professor, School of Information and Library Studies, State University of New York at Buffalo

Richard D. Hershcopf
Assistant Director for Public Services, Colorado State University Libraries

Paul Jonan Ho
Catalog Librarian, East Asian Library, University of Pittsburgh

Orlyn B. LaBrake
Assistant Director of Libraries, Rensselaer Polytechnic Institute, New York

Isaac T. Littleton
Director of Libraries, North Carolina State University

William M. McClellan
Music Librarian, University of Illinois at Urbana

Robert L. Mowery
Humanities Librarian, Illinois Wesleyan University

Katherine Anne Peters
Head Librarian, Kauai Community College, Hawaii

Elspeth Pope
Associate Professor, College of Librarianship, University of South Carolina

Catherine J. Reynolds
Head, Government Documents Division, University of Colorado Libraries

Katherine M. Rottsolk
Reference Librarian, St. Olaf College, Minnesota

Anita R. Schiller
Reference Librarian/Bibliographer, University of California, San Diego

Philip Schwarz
Automation Development Librarian, University of Wisconsin

1977

Walter C. Allen
Associate Professor, Graduate School of Library Science, University of Illinois

Wilmer H. Baatz
Assistant Director, Indiana University Libraries

Elsie Lilias Bell
Chief of Main Library, Oklahoma County Libraries System

Carolyn P. Brown
Chief, Information Services, National Bureau of Standards

Lois Mai Chan
Associate Professor, College of Library Science, University of Kentucky

Josephine Riss Fang
Professor, School of Library Science, Simmons College

Robert W. Karrow, Jr.
Curator of Maps, Newberry Library, Chicago

Mark Kovacic
Gifts and Exchange Librarian, Pennsylvania State University Libraries

Frederick C. Lynden
Assistant Chief, Acquisitions Department, Stanford University Library

Kathryn J. Owens
Catalog Librarian, Indiana State University Library

Theodore P. Peck
Head of Public Services and Assistant Professor of Library Science, University of Minnesota at St. Paul

Alvis H. Price
Associate Personnel Officer, Library, University of California, Los Angeles

Phyllis A. Richmond
Professor, School of Library Science, Case Western Reserve University

Anne Roberts
Associate Librarian Library, State University of New York, Albany

Shiro Saito
Associate University Librarian for Public Services, Library, University of Hawaii

Margaret F. Steig
Assistant Professor, School of Library Service, Columbia University

Sheh Wong
Head, East Asian Library, University of Minnesota

1978

Virginia M. Bowden
Assistant to the Library Director, Li-

brary, University of Texas Health Science Center at San Antonio

Jay B. Clark
Chief of Technical Services, Houston Public Library

Florence Kell Doksansky
Assistant Librarian, Rotch Library, Massachusetts Institute of Technology

Wayne Gossage
Director, Library, Bank Street College of Education, New York

Hugo Kunoff
Subject Librarian for Modern Languages, Indiana University Library

Mary Drake McFeely
Head, Reference Department, Smith College Library

Dorothy A. Pearson
Serials Librarian, Princeton University Library

W. Boyd Rayward
Assistant Professor, Graduate Library School, University of Chicago

Jean F. Trumbore
Associate Reference Librarian, University of Delaware Library

1979
Rao Aluri
Research Assistant, OCLC, Inc.

Judith S. Braunagel
Assistant Professor, Library School, State University of New York, Buffalo

Boyd Childress
Periodicals Librarian, Western Kentucky University Library

Sheila D. Creth
Assistant Director, University of Connecticut Library

George S. Grossman
Director of Law Library, University of Minnesota

William E. Hannaford, Jr.
Acquisitions Librarian, Middlebury College Library

Mary E. Pensyl
Head, Northeast Academic Scientific Information Center, Massachusetts Institute of Technology

Anne G. Piternick
Professor, School of Librarianship, University of British Columbia

Patricia Ann Polansky
Russian Bibliographer, Library, University of Hawaii

Suzanne Striedieck
Chief, Serials Department, Library, Pennsylvania State University

Discontinued

Distinguished Achievement Award

This award was presented from 1959 to 1976 to a person who had made a substantial contribution to the development of librarianship as a profession or to the growth, promotion, or endowment of libraries. The contribution was financial, political, scholarly, or professional. The recipient was chosen by the Awards Committee of the Executive Board of the Library School Alumni Association. The award was sponsored jointly by the Library School Alumni Association and the Graduate School of Library Science of Drexel University, 32 and Chestnut Streets, Philadelphia, Pennsylvania 19104. A citation was presented annually at the Distinguished Achievement Awards Dinner in Philadelphia.

1959
  Luther E. Evans
1960
  John E. Fogarty
1961
  John Dos Passos
1962
  Harry Golden
1963
  James Bryan
1964
  Elizabeth Gray Vining
1965
  Emerson Greenaway
1966
  Joseph L. Wheeler
1967
  Germaine Krettek

1968
  Lawrence Clark Powell
1969
  Catherine Drinker Bowen
1970
  L. Quincy Mumford
1971
  Jesse H. Shera
1972
  Norman Cousins
1973
  Frank B. Rogers
1974
  John Updike
1975
  Alfred A. Knopf
1976
  Daniel J. Boorstin
Discontinued

Drexel Award

The School of Library and Information Science, Drexel University, Philadelphia, Pennsylvania 19104, in cooperation with the Free Library of Philadelphia, established the Drexel Award in 1963. It is given irregularly to Philadelphia-area authors, illustrators, and publishers who have made outstanding contributions to literature for children. The award is a hand-lettered citation, which is presented at the annual conference on children's literature in March, cosponsored by Drexel and the Free Library.

1963
  Marguerite de Angeli
1964–1966
  No awards
1967
  Katherine Milhous
1968–1969
  No awards
1970
  Carolyn Haywood
1971
  No award
1972
  Lloyd Alexander
1973–1974
  No awards

1975
  J. B. Lippincott Company
1976
  Elizabeth Gray Vining
1977   .
  Nancy G. Larrick
1978
  Catherine Crook de Camp
  L. Sprague de Camp
1979
  Suzanne Hilton
1980
  Beth Krush
  Joe Krush

Donald F. Hyde Award

Friends of the Princeton University Library established this award in 1967 to recognize a distinguished private book collector. The recipient is chosen by an anonymous jury of three appointed by the Executive Committee of the Friends. In making the selection, the jury looks for the collector who has acquired his or her collection for the most part by individual items rather than entire libraries, has penetrated new fields, and has willingly made the collection available to scholars. A citation is presented at intervals determined by the sponsors of the award. Further inquiries may be obtained from the Friends of the Princeton University Library, Princeton University, Princeton, New Jersey 08544.

1967
  Lessing J. Rosenwald
1968
  Wilmarth S. Lewis
1969
  Philip Hofer
1970
  Sinclair Hamilton
1972
  C. Waller Barrett

1973
  Mary Hyde
1975
  Robert H. Taylor
1977
  William H. Scheide
1979
  Gordon N. Ray

Landau Award

The biennial Landau Award was established in 1975 by the University of Utah, School of Education, and the Salt Lake County Library System to honor Elliott Landau, who founded the Intermountain Conference on Literature for Children and Young Adults. The award is presented to a living American instructor of children's or young adult literature, noted for excellence in teaching and an inspirational impact upon the lives of students. Staff members of the sponsoring institutions select the winner, who receives an inscribed sterling silver plaque during a general session of the Intermountain Conference held at the University of Utah. Further information can be obtained from the University of Utah, School of Education, Milton Bennion Hall, Salt Lake City, Utah 84112, or the Salt Lake County Library System, 2197 East 7000 South, Salt Lake City, Utah 84121.

1975
  Virginia Westerberg
  University of Colorado, School of Education
1977
  M. Jerry Weiss
  Distinguished Service Professor of Communication, Jersey City State College
1979
  Charlotte S. Huck
  Ohio State University

Medical Library Association

The Medical Library Association, Inc., 919 North Michigan Avenue, Chicago, Illinois 60611, annually offers the following awards.

Ida and George Eliot Prize Essay Award

A prize of $100 is awarded for the essay published in any journal during the past year that, in the opinion of the committee, has done most to further medical librarianship.

1962
Seymour I. Taine
"Planning the Library for the Librarian"

1963
Frank B. Rogers and Thelma Charen
"Abbreviations for Medical Journal Titles"

1964
Scott Adams
"Medical Library Resources and Their Development"

1965
Paul J. Sanazaro
"Guidelines for Medical School Librarians"

1966
MLA Subcommittee on Recruitment
"Medical Library Careers"

1967
Elizabeth Keenan
In recognition of her personal efforts, which were instrumental in the establishment of the MLA Committee on Surveys and Statistics

1968
John B. Blake and Charles Roos
"Medical Reference Works, 1679–1966; A Selected Bibliography"

1969
No award

1970
Thomas C. Meyer
"Communications—A Supplement to Medical Library Service"

1971
Jane Fulcher
"Medical Librarian Examination Review Book," Vol. 1

1972
Alfred N. Brandon
"Selected List of Books and Journals for the Small Medical Library"

1973
William K. Beatty
In recognition of his long and distinguished editorship of "Vital Notes on Medical Periodicals"

1974
John A. Timour and William P. Koughan
"Are Hospital Libraries Meeting Physicians' Information Needs?"

1975
Joan Titley Adams
In recognition of her excellent job in editing and coordinating the July 1974 issue of *Library Trends*

1976
Susan Crawford
"Health Sciences Libraries in the U.S.; A Five-Year Perspective"

1977
Winifred Sewell
"Guide to Drug Information"

1978
Sylvia Feuer
"Circuit Rider Librarian"

1979
Ursula H. Poland
"The Medical Library Association's International Fellowship Program"

Murray Gottlieb Prize Essay Award

Johanna Gottlieb originated this award in memory of her husband, who was an associate member of the Medical Library Association and had planned to establish a similar award. The annual prize, which is intended to stimulate the writing of American medical history, is offered by the Medical Library Association. It has been presented at the Association's annual banquet since 1956. It includes a cash award of $100 and publication of the essay in the *Bulletin* of the Medical Library Association. Three medical librarians, well known for their contributions in the field of medical history, serve as judges for selection of the winning essay.

1956
Dorothy Long
"Medical Care among the North Carolina Moravians"
1957
Marian A. Patterson
"The Cholera Epidemic of 1832 in York, Upper Canada"
1958
Bernice Hetzner
"The Development of the Omaha Medical College"
1959
Robert T. Divett
"The Medical College of Utah at Morgan"
1960
Janet Doe
"The Development of Medical Practice in Bedford Township, New York, Particularly in the Area of Katonah"
1961
Martha Benjamin
"The McGill Medical Librarians, 1829–1929"
1962
Robert T. Divett
"Medicine and the Mormons"
1963
Joan Titley
"The Library of the Louisville Medical Institute, 1837–47"
1964
Irwin H. Pizer
"Medical Aspects of the Westward Migrations, 1830–60"

1965
Philip J. Weirmerskirch
"Benjamin Rush and John Minson Galt II: Pioneers of Bibliotherapy in America"
1966
No award
1967
Marjorie Wannarka
"Medical Collections in Public Libraries in the United States"
1968
No award
1969
Katherine T. Barkely
"Samuel Nichles, Dry and Quaint, a Landmark of Western Medicine"
1970
Kay Olschner
"Pre-Civil War Journals in Louisiana"
1971
Violet M. Baird
"Nineteenth Century Medical Journalism in Texas"
1972–1975
No awards
1976
Joan Campbell
"The Library of M. Richard Meade"
1977
Estelle Brodman
"Pediatrics in an 18th Century Remedy Book"

1978

Mary Lynette Ryan
"Historical Journal Resources of the Rudolf Matas Library, Tulane University"

1979

Georgia Walter
"Osteopathic Medicine: Past and Present"

Marcia C. Noyes Award

The Medical Library Association established this award in 1948 to honor outstanding contributions to medical librarianship. The award, an engraved silver tray, is usually given every other year, but this is not a rigid condition. The Selection Committee presents the award only for exceptional achievement. Presentation is made at the Association's annual meeting, usually held in May or June.

1949

Eileen R. Cunningham
Librarian, Vanderbilt University School of Medicine

1951

James F. Ballard
Director, Boston Medical Library

1953

Mary Louise Marshall
Librarian, Tulane University School of Medicine

1954

Janet Doe
Librarian, New York Academy of Medicine

1956

Harold Wellington Jones
Librarian, Army Medical Library

1958

William Dosite Postell
Librarian, Louisiana State University School of Medicine

1960

Leslie Thomas Morton
Librarian, National Institute of Medical Research, London

1961

Frank B. Rogers
Director, National Library of Medicine

1963

Stanislaw Konopka
Director, Central Medical Library, Warsaw

1965

Mildred Jordan
Librarian, Emory University School of Medicine

1966

Thomas E. Keys
Librarian, Mayo Clinic Library

1968

Gertrude L. Annan
Librarian, New York Academy of Medicine

1969

Scott Adams
Deputy Director, National Library of Medicine

1971

Estelle Brodman
Librarian, Washington University School of Medicine

1972

Thomas P. Fleming
Librarian, Columbia University School of Medicine

1973
  Martin M. Cummings
  Director, National Library of Medicine
1974
  Louise Darling
  Librarian, Biomedical Library, University of California, Los Angeles
1976
  Mildred C. Langner
  Librarian, Louis Calder Memorial Library, University of Miami School of Medicine
1977
  Alfred N. Brandon
  Librarian, New York Academy of Medicine
1978
  Emilie V. Wiggins
  Head, Catalog Section, National Library of Medicine

Rittenhouse Award

This award was established in 1968 by the Medical Library Association and is presented by Rittenhouse Book Distributors, Inc., Philadelphia. It is given to a student for a paper that is applicable to medical librarianship and constitutes an outstanding original contribution. The recipient must be in an Association-approved medical library course or a trainee in an Association-approved internship program. The $100 award is presented annually in May or June at the Association's annual meeting.

1968
  Nancy C. Lorenzi
  "Role of the Library within the Hospital System"
1969
  Mary Jordan Coe
  "Mechanization of Library Procedures in the Medium-Sized Library: X. Uniqueness of Compression Codes for Bibliographic Retrieval"
1970
  No award
1971
  James R. Reed
  "The Case for Public Health Librarianship"
1972
  Vicki Glasgow
  "Contributions of Eileen R. Cunningham to Medical Librarianship"
1973
  Linda Smith
  "The Medical Librarian and Computer Assisted Instruction"
1974
  No award

1975
  Faye Zucker
  "English Abstracts and the Language Barrier in Biomedical Research"
1976
  Bonnie J. Fridley
  "The Patient's Need for Medical Information: An Emergent Responsibility"
1977
  Theresa Strasser
  "The Information Needs of Registered Nurses in Northeastern New York State"
1978
  Ronald Rader
  "Bibliographic Analysis of the Literature of Government Regulated Chemical Carcinogens"
1979
  Lonnie J. Spotts
  "Independent Study-Guidelines for Conversion of Subject Headings for the FDA Medical Library: Methodology Using Drug Class Terms as a Model"

Modisette Awards

The Louisiana Library Association, Baton Rouge, Louisiana, offers four annual awards in honor of the late James Oliver Modisette, who was president of the Louisiana Library Association in 1934 and 1935. The Modisette Award for Public Libraries and the Modisette Award for School Libraries, established in 1944, are given to recognize improvement and development during the preceding year. A similar award honoring elementary school libraries was established in 1964. The Modisette Award for Library Trustees was established in 1953 to recognize outstanding individual service, based on recommendations submitted by librarians or other interested individuals. The awards consist of citations of merit, presented during the annual meeting of the Louisiana Library Association.

LIBRARY TRUSTEES

1955
Ovey Trahan
Winn Parish Library Board, Winnfield
1956
Edith Steckler
St. Martin Parish Library Board, St. Martinville
1957
Mary Mims
Louisiana State Library Board, Baton Rouge
1958
Mrs. B. W. Biedenharn
Ouachita Parish Public Library Board, West Monroe
1959
Mrs. O. N. Reynolds
Caldwell Parish Public Library, Columbia
1960
James Madison
Morehouse Parish Library Board, Bastrop
1961
Mrs. Weldon Lynch
Allen Parish Library Board, Oberlin
1962
Mrs. Robert R. Rhymes
Richland Parish Library Board, Rayville

1963
Warren E. Dietrich
Webster Parish Library Board, Minden
1964
Mrs. W. B. MacMillan
Vermilion Parish Public Library Board, Abbeville
1965
Alex P. Allain
St. Mary Parish Library Board, Franklin
1966
Don T. Caffery
St. Mary Parish Library Board, Franklin
1967
Helen S. Smith
Terrebonne Parish Library Board, Houma
1968
George T. Lallande
Iberia Parish Library Board, New Iberia
1969
Mrs. Clifford M. Strauss
Ouachita Parish Public Library, Monroe
1970
Mrs. Charles Keller, Jr.
New Orleans Public Library Board, New Orleans

LIBRARY TRUSTEES (cont.)

1971
Robert C. Snyder
Lincoln Parish Library Board, Ruston; Trail Blazer Pilot Library System Board, Monroe; Louisiana State Library Board, Baton Rouge
1972
L. H. Coltharp
Beauregard Parish Library Board, De Ridder
1973
W. P. Cotton
Richland Parish Library Board, Rayville
1974
Clifton E. Hester
Madison Parish Library Board, Tallulah
1975
Matt Vernon
Opelousas-Eunice Public Library Board, Eunice
1976
Murphy Tannehill
LaSalle Parish Library Board, Olla
1977
Jacob S. Landry
Iberia Parish Library Board, New Iberia
1978
W. R. Alexander
Union Parish Library Board, Farmerville
1979
James E. Abadie
Ascension Parish Library Board, Donaldsonville

HIGH SCHOOL AND JUNIOR HIGH SCHOOL LIBRARIES

1949
Many High School Library

1950
Terrebonne High School Library
1951
Natchitoches High School Library
1952
Natchitoches High School Library
1953
Hall Summit High School Library
1954
Kinder High School Library
1955
No award
1956
Lake Charles High School Library
1957
Opelousas High School Library
1958
Eunice High School Library
1959
W. T. Henning Elementary School Library, Sulphur
1960
W. W. Lewis Junior High School Library, Sulphur
1961
Westside Elementary School Library, Winnfield
1962
Lakeshore Elementary School Library, Monroe
1963
North Bayou Elementary School Library, Alexandria
1964
Ouachita Parish High School Library
1965
Wesdale Junior High School Library, Baton Rouge
1966
Homer High School Library
1967
No award, criteria revised
1968
Covington High School Library
1969
Walnut Hill High School Library, Shreveport

HIGH SCHOOL AND JUNIOR HIGH SCHOOL LIBRARIES (cont.)

1970
Eunice High School Library
1971
Bastrop High School Library
1972
De Ridder Junior High School Library
1973
Alfred M. Barbe High School Library, Lake Charles
1974
Southwood High School, Shreveport
1975
Landry Library of St. Louis High School, Lake Charles
1976
Byrd High School, Shreveport
1977
St. Mary's Dominican High School, New Orleans
1978
Carenco High School
1979
Airline High School, Bossier City

PUBLIC LIBRARIES

1948
East Baton Rouge Parish Public Library, Baton Rouge
1949
Ouachita Parish Public Library, Monroe
1950
Iberia Parish Library, New Iberia
1951
Vermilion Parish Public Library, Abbeville
1952
Winn Parish Library, Winnfield
1953
Jefferson Parish Library, Gretna

1954
Iberville Parish Public Library, Plaquemine
1955
Morehouse Parish Library, Bastrop
1956
Lafourche Parish Library, Thibodaux
1957
Webster Parish Library, Minden
1958
St. Martin Parish Library, St. Martinville
1959
Vernon Parish Library, Leesville
1960
Vernon Parish Library, Leesville
1961
Allen Parish Library, Oberlin
1962
Morehouse Parish Library, Bastrop
1963
Pointe Coupee Parish Library, New Roads
1964
Union Parish Library, Farmerville
1965
Ouachita Parish Public Library, Monroe
1966
Franklin Parish Library, Winnsboro
1967
Calcasieu Parish Library, Lake Charles
1968
Shreve Memorial Library, Shreveport
1969
La Salle Parish Library, Jena
1970
Union Parish Library, Farmerville
1971
Assumption Parish Library, Napoleonville
1972
Opelousas-Eunice Public Library, Opelousas
1973
No award

PUBLIC LIBRARIES (cont.)

1974
  Iberville Parish Library, Plaquemine
1975
  No award
1976
  Concordia Parish Library, Ferriday
1977
  No award
1978
  Ouachita Parish Public Library, Monroe
1979
  No award

ELEMENTARY SCHOOL LIBRARIES

1965
  Samuel J. Montgomery Elementary School Library, Lafayette
1966
  No award
1967
  No award, criteria revised

1968
  University Terrace Elementary School Library, Baton Rouge
1969
  Sherwood Forest Elementary School Library, Baton Rouge
1970
  Kaplan Elementary School Library
1971
  Hillsdale Elementary School Library, Shreveport
1972
  L. J. Alleman Elementary School Library, Lafayette
1973–1975
  No awards
1976
  St. Martinville Primary School
1977
  DeQuincy Elementary School
1978
  No award
1979
  Leesville State School

New York Library Association, School Library Media Section

The School Library Media Section (SLMS) of the New York Library Association (NYLA), 60 East 42 Street, Suite 1242, New York, New York 10017, offers three annual awards concerning school library media personnel, programs, and materials. Since 1963, the SLMS has offered awards for school library media centers throughout the state to recognize achievement in various categories: from 1963 to 1972, the Architects Award for design excellence; from 1968 to 1972, the Outstanding School Library Program of the Year; and, in 1973 only, these two awards combined into the Outstanding School Library Media Center of the Year Award. The NYLA, SLMS currently offers the Administrator's Elementary School Media Program Award, the Elliot Rabner Cultural Award, and the John T. Short/SLMS Award.

Administrator's Elementary School Media Program Award

This annual award was established to recognize an administrator who has effectively supported the improvement of an elementary library media program in a New York

State school district during the preceding three to five years. Applications are accepted by members of the NYLA School Library Media Section. The Awards Committee chooses the winner based on information gained from the applications and visits to the nominated school districts. The winner receives a plaque at the SLMS spring conference. The awards chairperson changes annually; the chairperson for 1979–1980 is Helen Flowers, 401 East Main Street, Bay Shore, New York 11706.

Elliot Rabner Cultural Media Award

The NYLA School Library Media Section (SLMS) and Elliot Rabner, a school librarian and a lecturer in adult education in the Great Neck, New York, school system, established this annual award to encourage the acquisition of humanistic nonbook materials that will enrich the media collection and the school curriculum. The award was originally called the Elliot Rabner Asian Media Award. Members of the SLMS are eligible for the award by submitting a selection list of humanistic nonbook materials to the Awards Committee, which selects the best list. The winner receives $100 to purchase listed materials. The award is presented at the SLMS spring conference. The awards chairperson changes annually; the chairperson for 1979–1980 is Helen Flowers, 401 East Main Street, Bay Shore, New York 11706.

John T. Short/SLMS Award

This award was established in 1974 in conjunction with the School Library Media Day in New York State, officially proclaimed to highlight school library media centers' educational contributions. The award is currently cosponsored by the School Library Media Section (SLMS) of the New York Library Association (NYLA), based on a contribution by John Short. The award is given in recognition of a school library media specialist who conducts an outstanding publicity program aimed at the school and community that effectively emphasizes the importance of the school library media center. Entries are accepted from New York State school library media specialists on behalf of their building or district program. They should consist of a typed description of the current year's publicity program, with such supporting evidence as newspaper clippings, photographs, slides, posters, and the like. Entries, due in June, are screened by the School Library Media Day Committee of SLMS/NYLA. Each winner receives $250 and a certificate, each honorable mention a certificate, at the NYLA annual conference in the fall.

1974
  Barbara Dugman
  Horseheads Central School District
1975
  Rouletta Gasparin
  Wantagh Union Free School District

1976
  Joy Casadonte
  Lewiston-Porter Central Schools

1977
  Irene Johnson
  Circleville Middle School and Pine
  Bush Central School
1978
  Falconer Central School District

1979
  Cathy Wellner and Steve Nash
  Greece Athena Junior-Senior High
  School and Greece Central School
  District

Special Libraries Association

The Special Libraries Association (SLA), 235 Park Avenue South, New York, New York 10003, offers two annual awards, one for a specific contribution to the profession of library and information science and one for continuing contributions over a period of years. Both awards are presented at the SLA annual conference in June.

Professional Award

The Special Libraries Association annually presents an appropriate silver award to an individual or group, who may or may not hold membership in the Association, in recognition of a specific major achievement in, or a specific significant contribution to, the field of librarianship or information science that advances the stated objectives of the Special Libraries Association. The timing of the award follows, as soon as practicable, the recognized fruition of the contribution.

1949
  Edwin T. Coman, Jr.
1950
  Anne L. Nicholson
1951
  No award
1952
  Mortimer Taube
1953
  Rose L. Vormelker
1954
  Eleanor S. Cavanaugh
  Ruth M. Savord
1955
  Jolan M. Fertig
1956
  Irene M. Strieby Shreve
1957
  Elizabeth W. Owens
1958
  Marion E. Wells

1959
  No award
1960
  Rose Boots
1961
  No award
1962
  Cyril W. Cleverdon
1963–1964
  No awards
1965
  Ruth S. Leonard
1966
  No award
1967
  Illinois Chapter, SLA
1968
  No award
1969
  Beatrice V. Simon

1970-1971
  No awards
1972
  James B. Adler
1973
  Marjorie R. Hyslop
1974
  Loretta J. Kiersky
1975
  No award

1976
  Jacqueline Sisson
1977
  Audrey N. Grosch
1978
  Lorna Daniells
1979
  No award

SLA Hall of Fame

This award was established in 1959 to recognize individuals who have made outstanding contributions to the growth and development of the Special Libraries Association. The award is given for work done over a period of years, rather than for an individual achievement. It is awarded to a member or former member of SLA near or following the completion of an active career. The award is an engraved silver bowl and a certificate.

1959
  William K. Alcott
  Sarah B. Ball
  Herbert O. Brigham
  Marguerite D. Burnett
  Eleanor S. Cavanaugh
  Alta B. Claflin
  John Cotton Dana
  Daniel N. Handy
  Josephine B. Hollingsworth
  Dorsey W. Hyde
  John A. Lapp
  Guy E. Marion
  Alma Clarvoe Mitchell
  Linda H. Morley
  Rebecca B. Rankin
  Anna B. Sears
  Lura Shorb
  Irene M. Strieby Shreve
  Marian Manley Winser
  Laura B. Woodward
1960
  Dorothy Bemis
  Florence Bradley
  Pauline M. Hutchinson
  Ruth Savord

1961
  Alberta L. Brown
  Thelma Hoffman
1962
  Rose Boots
  Margaret Miller Rocq
  Fannie Simon
1963
  Betty Joy Cole
  Josephine I. Greenwood
  Lucile L. Keck
  Kathleen Brown Stebbins
  Rose L. Vormelker
1964
  Jolan M. Fertig
  Margaret Hatch
  Mary Jane Henderson
  Marion E. Wells
1965
  Marie Simon Goff
  Ruth H. Hooker
1966
  Mary Louise Alexander
  Elizabeth W. Owens
  Howard L. Stebbins

1967
  No award
1968
  Eleanor B. Gibson
  Anne L. Nicholson
1969
  Margaret H. Fuller
1970
  Elizabeth Ferguson
  W. Roy Holleman
1971
  Herman H. Henkle
  Ruth S. Leonard
1972
  Janet Bogardus
1973
  Sara Aull
1974
  Agnes O. Hanson
  Ethel S. Klahre

1975
  Safford Harris
  Katharine L. Kinder
1976
  Phoebe Hayes (posthumous)
  Ruth M. Nielander
1977
  Grieg G. Aspnes
  Rocco Crachi
  Sam Sass

1978
  Chester M. Lewis

1979
  Gretchen D. Little
  Frank E. McKenna

Wisconsin School Library Media Association

The Wisconsin School Library Media Association (WSLMA) gives annual awards for distinguished library service to a school administrator and to a school librarian, each of whom has made a unique, sustained contribution toward furthering the role of the library or media center and its development in elementary and/or secondary education. Nominations for the awards may be made by any WSLMA member. The award, a citation, is presented at the Wisconsin Library Association convention during the WSLMA annual meeting in late October. Nomination forms and other information can be obtained from Lois Nelson, Chairperson, Awards Committee, Emerson Elementary IMC, 21 and Campbell Road, La Crosse, Wisconsin 54601.

WSLMA Service Award for School Administrator

This award is given to a school superintendent, building principal, curriculum supervisor, or administrator currently in office and directly responsible for a Wisconsin school or group of schools. It is awarded for effective interpretation of the school library role and leadership in instituting library policies and practices that result in the improvement of classroom instruction.

1973
Eugene C. Balts
Superintendent, La Crosse Area Public Schools
1974
C. Richard Nelson
Superintendent, Unified School District, Racine
1975
Clifford Fisher
Principal, Jacob Shapiro Elementary School, Oshkosh

1976
Gavin Strand
Superintendent, Black River Falls School District
1977
James J. Koehn
Principal, J. R. Gerritts Junior High School, Kimberly
1978
Fred R. Holt
Superintendent (retired), Janesville Public Schools

WSLMA Service Award for a School Librarian

This award is given to a school librarian or a school library media specialist at any level in a Wisconsin school system who effectively interprets the school library role to the staff, students, and community, and who shows leadership in instituting library policies and practices that improve curriculum and instruction.

1973
Alice Haase
Eau Claire Memorial High School
1974
Sally Davis
Oconomowoc Public Schools
1975
Iris Glidden
West Bend Public Schools

1976
No award
1977
Patricia McCarthy
Eisenhower High School, New Berlin
1978
Eliza T. Dresang
Lapham Elementary School, Madison

British Prizes

British Prizes

James Tait Black Memorial Prizes

These literary prizes, the most valuable in Great Britain, were founded by the late Janet Coats Black in memory of her husband, a partner in the publishing house of A. and C. Black, Ltd., London. Mrs. Black set aside £11,000 to be used for two prizes of whatever income the fund would produce after paying expenses. The prizes now amount annually to approximately £1,000 each and are given by the trustees of the fund at the University of Edinburgh, Old College, Edinburgh, with a supplement from the Scottish Arts Council. One prize is given to the author of the best biography in the English language published in the United Kingdom during the year and the other to the author of the best novel. The choice is made in the spring for books of the preceding year by the regius professor of English literature at the University of Edinburgh, preferably, or the professor of English at the University of Glasgow.

BIOGRAPHY

1920
H. Festing Jones
Samuel Butler (Macmillan)
1921
G. M. Trevelyan
Lord Grey of the Reform Bill (Longmans)
1922
Lytton Strachey
Queen Victoria (Harcourt)
1923
Percy Lubbock
Earlham (Scribner)
1924
Ronald Ross
Memoirs (Dutton)
1925
William Wilson
The House of Airlie (Murray)

1926
Geoffrey Scott
The Portrait of Zelide (Scribner)
1927
H. B. Workman
John Wycliff (Oxford Univ. Press)

1928
H. A. L. Fisher
James Bryce (Macmillan)

1929
John Buchan
Montrose (Houghton)

1930
David Cecil
The Stricken Deer, or The Life of Cowper (Bobbs)

1931
Francis Yeats-Brown
Lives of a Bengal Lancer (Viking)

465

BIOGRAPHY (cont.)

1932
J. Y. T. Greig
David Hume (Oxford Univ. Press)
1933
Stephen Gwynn
The Life of Mary Kingsley (Macmillan)
1934
Violet Clifton
The Book of Talbot (Harcourt)
1935
J. A. Neale
Queen Elizabeth (Harcourt)
1936
R. W. Chambers
Thomas More (Harcourt)
1937
Edward Sackville-West
A Flame in Sunlight: The Life and Work of Thomas de Quincey (Yale Univ. Press)
1938
Eustace Percy
John Knox (Hodder)
1939
Edmund Chambers
Samuel Taylor Coleridge (Oxford Univ. Press)
1940
David C. Douglas
English Scholars (Transatlantic)
1941
Hilda F. M. Prescott
Spanish Tudor (Columbia)
1942
John Gore
King George V (Scribner)
1943
Lord Ponsonby of Shulbrede
Henry Ponsonby: Queen Victoria's Private Secretary (Macmillan)
1944
G. G. Coulton
Fourscore Years (Macmillan)
1945
C. V. Wedgwood
William the Silent (Yale Univ. Press)

1946
D. S. McColl
Philip Wilson Steer (Faber)
1947
Richard Aldington   •
The Duke (Viking) (English title: *Wellington*)
1948
C. E. Raven
English Naturalists (Macmillan)
1949
Percy A. Scholes
The Great Dr. Burney (Oxford Univ. Press)
1950
John Connell
W. E. Henley (Constable)
1951
Mrs. Cecil Woodham-Smith
Florence Nightingale (McGraw)
1952
Noel G. Annan
Leslie Stephen (Harvard Univ. Press)
1953
G. M. Young
Stanley Baldwin (Hart-Davis)
1954
Carola Oman
Sir John Moore (Verry)
1955
Keith Feiling
Warren Hastings (Macmillan)

1956
R. W. Ketton-Cremer
Thomas Gray (Cambridge Univ. Press)

1957
St. John Ervine
George Bernard Shaw (Morrow)

1958
Maurice Cranston
John Locke (Longmans)

1959
Joyce Hemlow
History of Fanny Burney (Oxford Univ. Press)

BIOGRAPHY (cont.)

1960
Christopher Hassall
Edward Marsh (Harcourt)
1961
Adam Fox
Dean Inge (Transatlantic) (English title: *Life of Dean Inge*)
1962
M. K. Ashby
Joseph Ashby of Tysoe (Cambridge Univ. Press)
1963
Meriol Trevor
Newman, Vol. 1: The Pillar and the Cloud; Vol. 2: Light in Winter (Doubleday)
1964
Georgina Battiscombe
John Keble: A Study in Limitations (Knopf)
1965
Elizabeth Longford
Queen Victoria (Harper)
1966
Mary Moorman
William Wordsworth: The Later Years 1803-1850 (Oxford Univ. Press)
1967
Geoffrey Keynes
The Life of William Harvey (Oxford Univ. Press)
1968
Winifred Gérin
Charlotte Brontë (Oxford Univ. Press)
1969
Gordon S. Haight
George Eliot (Oxford Univ. Press)
1970
Antonia Fraser
Mary Queen of Scots (Weidenfeld)
1971
Jasper Ridley
Lord Palmerston (Constable)
1972
Julia Namier
Lewis Namier (Oxford Univ. Press)

1973
Quentin Bell
Virginia Woolf (Hogarth)
1974
Robin Lane Fox
Alexander the Great (Dial)
1975
John Wain
Samuel Johnson (Macmillan)
1976
Karl Miller
Cockburn's Millennium (Duckworth)
1977
Ronald Hingley
A New Life of Chekhov (Oxford Univ. Press)
1978
George Painter
Chateaubriand, Vol. 1: The Longed-for Tempests (Chatto)
1979
Robert Gittings
The Older Hardy (Heinemann)

NOVEL

1920
Hugh Walpole
The Secret City (Doran)
1921
D. H. Lawrence
The Lost Girl (Viking)
1922
Walter de la Mare
Memoirs of a Midget (Knopf)
1923
David Garnett
Lady into Fox (Knopf)
1924
Arnold Bennett
Riceyman Steps (Doran)
1925
E. M. Forster
A Passage to India (Harcourt)
1926
Liam O'Flaherty
The Informer (Knopf)

NOVEL (cont.)

1927
Radclyffe Hall
Adam's Breed (Houghton)
1928
Francis Brett Young
Love Is Enough (Knopf) (English title:
Portrait of Clare)
1929
Siegfried Sassoon
Memoirs of a Fox-Hunting Man (Coward)
1930
J. B. Priestley
The Good Companions (Harper)
1931
E. H. Young
Miss Mole (Harcourt)
1932
Kate O'Brien
Without My Cloak (Doubleday)
1933
Helen Simpson
Boomerang (Doubleday)
1934
A. G. Macdonell
England, Their England (Macmillan)
1935
Robert Graves
I, Claudius and *Claudius the God*
(Smith & Haas)
1936
L. H. Myers
The Root and the Flower (Harcourt)
1937
Winifred Holtby
South Riding (Macmillan)
1938
Neil M. Gunn
Highland River (Lippincott)
1939
C. S. Forester
A Ship of the Line and *Flying Colours*
(Little)

1940
Aldous Huxley
After Many a Summer Dies the Swan
(Harper)
1941
Charles Morgan
The Voyage (Macmillan)
1942
Joyce Cary
A House of Children (Harper)
1943
Arthur Waley, trans.
Monkey, by Wu Ch'êng-ên (John
Day)
1944
Mary Lavin
Tales from Bective Bridge (Little)
1945
Forrest Reid
Young Tom (Faber)
1946
L. A. G. Strong
Travellers (Methuen)
1947
Oliver Onions
Poor Man's Tapestry (Michael Joseph)
1948
L. P. Hartley
Eustace and Hilda (Putnam)
1949
Graham Greene
The Heart of the Matter (Viking)
1950
Emma Smith
The Far Cry (Random)
1951
Robert Henriques
Too Little Love (Viking) (English title:
Through the Valley)
1952
W. C. Chapman-Mortimer
Father Goose (Hart-Davis)
1953
Evelyn Waugh
Men at Arms (Little)

NOVEL (cont.)

1954
Margaret Kennedy
Troy Chimneys (Rinehart)
1955
C. P. Snow
The New Men and *The Masters*
(Scribner)
1956
Ivy Compton-Burnett
Mother and Son (Messner)
1957
Rose Macaulay
The Towers of Trebizond (Farrar)
1958
Anthony Powell
At Lady Molly's (Little)
1959
Angus Wilson
The Middle Age of Mrs. Eliot (Viking)
1960
Morris West
The Devil's Advocate (Morrow)
1961
Rex Warner
Imperial Caesar (Little)
1962
Jennifer Dawson
The Ha-Ha (Little)
1963
Ronald Hardy
Act of Destruction (Doubleday)
1964
Gerda Charles
A Slanting Light (Knopf)
1965
Frank Tuohy
The Ice Saints (Scribner)

1966
Muriel Spark
The Mandelbaum Gate (Knopf)

1967
Christine Brooke-Rose
Such (Michael Joseph)

Aidan Higgins
Langrishe, Go Down (Calder)
1968
Margaret Drabble
Jerusalem the Golden (Weidenfeld)
1969
Maggie Ross
The Gasteropod (Barrie)
1970
Elizabeth Bowen
Eva Trout (Cape)
1971
Lily Powell
The Bird of Paradise (Bodley)
1972
Nadine Gordimer
A Guest of Honour (Jonathan Cape)
1973
John Berger
G (Weidenfeld)
1974
Iris Murdoch
The Black Prince (Viking)
1975
Lawrence Durrell
Monsieur, or The Prince of Darkness
(Viking)
1976
Brian Moore
The Great Victorian Collection (Farrar)
1977
John Banville
Doctor Copernicus (Secker)

1978
John le Carré
The Honourable Schoolboy (Hodder)

1979
Maurice Gee
Plumb (Faber)

Jock Campbell *New Statesman* Award

In 1965, Lord Campbell of Eskan, Chairman of the *New Statesman* Board, endowed a literary prize to encourage Caribbean and African writers by an award for a work of literary merit. Writers born in Africa or the Caribbean were eligible for the award. The cash award of £1,000 was first made in 1965, thereafter at three-year intervals. The panel of three or four judges that made the selection included the literary editor of the *New Statesman*, 10 Great Turnstile, London WC1V 7HJ, England.

1965
  Chinua Achebe
  Arrow of God (Heinemann)

1968
  Wole Soyinka
  The Interpreters (Heinemann)

1971
  Shiva Naipaul
  Fireflies (Penguin)
1974
  Derek Walcott
  Another Life (Jonathan Cape)
Discontinued

Children's Book Circle
Eleanor Farjeon Award

The Eleanor Farjeon Award was established in 1965 to commemorate the work of the late children's author. The Children's Book Circle makes an annual award in May of £75 to a librarian, teacher, author, artist, publisher, reviewer, or television producer who, in the judgment of the Awards Committee, is considered to have done outstanding work for children's books. Further details are available from Diana Syrat, The Bodley Head, 9 Bow Street, London WC2E 7AL, England.

1966
  Margery Fisher
1967
  Jessica Jenkins
1968
  Brian Alderson
1969
  Anne Wood
1970
  Kaye Webb
1971
  Margaret Meek
1972
  Janet Hill
1973
  Eleanor Graham

1974
  Leila Berg
1975
  Naomi Lewis
1976
  Joyce Oldmeadow and Court Oldmeadow
1977
  Elaine Moss
1978
  Peter Kennerley
1979
  Joy Whitby

Commonwealth Poetry Prize

The Commonwealth Institute, Kensington High Street, London W8 6NQ, England, has offered this award since 1972. The prize of £500 is awarded annually for a first published book of poetry in English by an author from a Commonwealth country other than Britain. Joint winners share the prize money, which is donated by the Diamond Trading Company, Ltd. The prize is administered by the Commonwealth Institute. Inquiries should be addressed to the Librarian of the Institute. Entries must be submitted before June 30 of each year. Announcement of the prize winner is made at the opening of the Commonwealth Book Fair in the autumn.

1972
Chinua Achebe (Nigeria)
Beware Soul Brothers (Heinemann)
George McWhirter (Canada)
Catalan Poems (Oberon, Toronto)
1973
Wayne Brown (Trinidad)
On the Coast (André Deutsch)
1974
Dennis Scott (Jamaica)
Uncle Time (Univ. of Pittsburgh Press)
1975
No award
1976
Michael Jackson (New Zealand)
Latitudes of Exile (John McIndoe)

1977
Arun Kolatkar (India)
Jejuri (Clearing House of Bombay/ Peppercorn)
1978
Timoshenko Aslanides (Australia)
The Greek Connection (privately printed)
1979
Gabriel Okara (Nigeria)
The Fisherman's Invocation (Heinemann Educational)
Brian Turner (New Zealand)
Ladders of Rain (McIndoe)

The Duff Cooper Memorial Prize

The Duff Cooper Memorial Prize was established in 1956 in memory of Alfred Duff Cooper, Viscount Norwich (1890–1954). Money contributed by friends and admirers has been placed in a trust fund, and the interest from the fund comprises an annual prize for a literary work published in English or French during the previous two years. Two permanent judges (the present Lord Norwich and the Warden of New College, Oxford) and three others, who change every five years, make the decision.

1956
Alan Moorehead
Gallipoli (Harper)

1957
Lawrence Durrell
Bitter Lemons (Dutton)

1958
  John Betjeman
  Collected Poems (Houghton)
1959
  Patrick Leigh Fermor
  Mani (Harper)
1960
  Andrew Young
  Collected Poems (Dufour)
1961
  Jocelyn Baines
  Joseph Conrad (Dufour)
1962
  Michael Howard
  The Franco-Prussian War (Macmillan)
1963
  Aileen Ward
  John Keats: The Making of a Poet (Viking)
1964
  Ivan Morris
  The World of the Shining Prince: Court Life in Ancient Japan (Knopf)
1965
  George Painter
  Marcel Proust (Atlantic-Little)
1966
  Nirad C. Chaudhuri
  The Continent of Circe (Chatto)
1967
  J. A. Baker
  The Peregrine (Harper)
1968
  Roy Fuller
  New Poems (Dufour)

1969
  John Gross
  The Rise and Fall of the Man of Letters (Macmillan)
1970
  Enid McLeod
  Charles of Orleans: Prince and Poet (Chatto)
1971
  Geoffrey Grigson
  Discoveries of Bores and Stores (Macmillan)
1972
  Quentin Bell
  Virginia Woolf (Hogarth)
1973
  Robin Lane Fox
  Alexander the Great (Dial)
1974
  Jon Stallworthy
  Wilfred Owen (Oxford Univ. Press)
1975
  Seamus Heaney
  North (Faber)
1976
  Denis Mack Smith
  Mussolini's Roman Empire (Longmans)
1977
  E. R. Dodds
  Missing Persons (Oxford Univ. Press)
1978
  Mark Girouard
  Life in the English Country House (Yale Univ. Press)

Rose Mary Crawshay Prizes for English Literature

The prize fund for these awards originates from an 1888 bequest by Rose Mary Crawshay. The prizes may be awarded annually by the fund's trustees to a woman of any nationality who, in the judgment of the Council of the British Academy, Burlington House, Piccadilly, London W1V 0NS, England, has written or published within the preceding three years an outstanding historical or critical work on any subject connected with English literature. Preference is given to works on Byron, Shelley, or Keats. In the earlier years, only works about these poets were considered. Listed below are the recipients of the prizes since the scope was widened in 1915.

1916

Mrs. C. C. Stopes
Shakespeare's Environment and her other contributions to Shakespearean literature

1917

M. Stawell
"Shelley's Triumph of Life" (published in Vol. 5 of *Essays and Studies* by members of the English Association)

Léonie Villard
"Jane Austen: Sa Vie et Son Oeuvre" (published in the *Annales* of the University of Lyon, 1915)

1918

Grace Dulais Davies
Historical Fiction of the Eighteenth Century

1919

Mary Paton Ramsay
Les Doctrines Médiévales Chez Donne

1920

Jessie L. Weston
From Ritual to Romance

1921

M. E. Seaton
A Study of the Relations between England and the Scandinavian Countries in the Seventeenth Century

1922

E. C. Batho
James Hogg, the Ettrick Shepherd

1923

Joyce J. S. Tompkins
Works of Mrs. Radcliffe

1924

Madeleine L. Cazamian
Le Roman et les Idées en Angleterre —Influence de la Science, 1860–1890

1925

No award

1926

Mrs. E. R. Dodds [A. E. Powell]
The Romantic Theory of Poetry: An Examination in the Light of Croce's Aesthetic

1927

Alice Galimberti
L'Aèdo d'Italia, by A. C. Swinburne (Biblioteca Sandron)

1928

Enid Welsford
The Court Masque: A Study in the Relationship between Poetry and the Revels (Cambridge Univ. Press)

1929

Hope Emily Allen
The Writings Ascribed to Richard Rolle, Hermit of Hampole, and Materials for His Biography (Modern Language Association of America)

1930

U. M. Ellis-Fermor
For her work on Christopher Marlowe and her edition of Marlowe's *Tamburlaine*

1931

Janet G. Scott
Les Sonnets Elizabéthains (Champion, Paris)

1932

Helen Darbishire
The Manuscript of Paradise Lost, Book I (Oxford Univ. Press/Clarendon Press)

1933

Eleanore Boswell
The Restoration Court Stage, 1660–1702 (Harvard Univ. Press)

1934

Dottore Giovanna Foá
Lord Byron, Poèta e Carbonaro

1935
Hildegarde Schumann
The Romantic Elements in John Keats' Writings
1936
Caroline Spurgeon
Shakespeare's Imagery (Macmillan)
1937
Frances A. Yates
John Florio (Cambridge Univ. Press)
1938
Dorothy Hewlett
Adonais (Bobbs)
1939
No award
1940
M. M. Lascelles
Jane Austen (Oxford Univ. Press)
1941
Julia Power
Shelley in America in the Nineteenth Century (Univ. of Nebraska Press)
1942
Sybil Rosenfeld
Strolling Players and Drama in the Provinces, 1660-1765 (Cambridge Univ. Press)
1943
Kathleen Tillotson
Edition of the *Poems of Michael Drayton* (Blackwell)
1944
Katharine Balderston
Thraliana (Oxford Univ. Press/Clarendon Press)
1945
Rae Blanchard
The Correspondence of Richard Steele (Oxford Univ. Press)
1946
No award
1947
M. H. Nicolson
Newton Demands the Muse: Newton's "Opticks" and the Eighteenth Century Poets (Princeton Univ. Press)

1948
No award
1949
Rosamond Tuve
Elizabethan and Metaphysical Imagery (Univ. of Chicago Press)
1950
Helen Darbishire
For her Clark Lectures and collaboration in an edition of *Wordsworth's Poetical Works* (Oxford Univ. Press)
1951
Rosemary Freeman
For her work on *Emblem Books* (Chatto)
1952
M. E. Seaton
Abraham Fraunce's Arcadian Rhetorike (Blackwell)
1953
Helen Gardner
Divine Poems of John Donne (Oxford Univ. Press)
1954
Alice Walker
Textual Problems of the First Folio (Cambridge Univ. Press)
1955
Evelyn M. Simpson
The Sermons of John Donne (Univ. of California Press)
1956
Helen Estabrook Sandison
Sir Arthur Gorges: Poems (Oxford Univ. Press)
1957
J. E. Norton
The Letters of Edward Gibbon (Cassell)
1958
Mary Moorman
William Wordsworth: A Biography (Oxford Univ. Press)
1959
Kathleen Coburn
The Notebooks of S. T. Coleridge, Vol. 1, 1794-1804 (Pantheon)

1960
Joyce Hemlow
The History of Fanny Burney (Oxford Univ. Press)

1961
Vittoria Sanna
Sir Thomas Browne's *Religio Medici*

1962
Barbara G. Hardy
The Novels of George Eliot (Oxford Univ. Press)

1963
Joan Bennett
Sir Thomas Browne: His Life and Achievement (Cambridge Univ. Press)

1964
Aileen Ward
John Keats: The Making of a Poet (Viking)

1965
Madeline House
The Letters of Charles Dickens (Oxford Univ. Press/Clarendon)

1966
Margaret Crum
Poems of Henry King (Oxford Univ. Press/Clarendon)

1967
Enid Welsford
Salisbury Plain, a Study in the Development of Wordsworth's Mind and Art (Blackwell)

1968
Winifred Gérin
Charlotte Brontë (Oxford Univ. Press/Clarendon)

1969
Alethea Hayter
Opium and the Romantic Imagination (Faber)

1970
Barbara Rooke
Coleridge's "The Friend" (Princeton Univ. Press)

1971
No award

1972
Valerie Eliot, ed.
Facsimiles of the Original Drafts of "The Waste Land" (Faber)

1973
Marilyn Butler
Maria Edgeworth: A Literary Biography (Oxford Univ. Press/Clarendon)
Christina Colvin
Maria Edgeworth: Letters from England, 1830–1844 (Oxford Univ. Press/Clarendon)

1974
Jean Robertson, ed.
Old Arcadia by Sir Philip Sidney (Oxford Univ. Press/Clarendon)

1975
Doris Langley Moore
Lord Byron —Accounts Rendered (Murray)

1976
Hilary Spurling
Ivy When Young (Gollancz)

1977
Harriett Hawkins
Poetic Freedom and Poetic Truth (Oxford Univ. Press)

1978
Lyndall Gordon
Eliot's Early Years (Oxford Univ. Press)

[The Academy wished to award a second prize to Miriam Leranbaum for *Alexander Pope's Magnum Opus* (Clarendon), but her death restricted the prizes to one.]

1979
Elizabeth Murray
Caught in the Web of Words (Yale Univ. Press)
Joan Rees
Shakespeare and the Story (Athlone)

Mary Elgin Prize

This award is offered by Hodder and Stoughton, Ltd., 47 Bedford Square, London WC1, England. It was made possible through a trust fund established in 1969 by Colonel Walter Stewart in memory of his wife, who died suddenly in 1966. Writing as Mary Elgin, she made a notable beginning as a novelist with *Visibility Nil, Return to Glenshael* (American title *Highland Masquerade*), and *The Wood and the Trees*, published posthumously. The aim of the award is to encourage gifted new writers of fiction. There are no restrictions of sex, age, or nationality. Writers need not be first novelists but must be on the Hodder and Stoughton publishing list with work published or submitted during the preceding twelve months. The winner is chosen by three trustees and is announced annually on March 31. The £50 award is sent to the winner with an accompanying letter.

1969
  Helena Osborne
  The Arcadian Affair
1970
  Gillian Tindall
  Someone Else
1971
  Jay Gilbert
  An Edge to the Laughter
1972
  M. O'Donoghue
  Wild Honey Tree
1973
  Phyllis Gamp
  Islands

1974
  Frances Murray
  The Burning Lamp
1975
  Anne Worboys
  Lion of Delos
1976
  Sarah Neilan
  The Braganza Pursuit
1977
  Roseleen Milne
  Borrowed Plumes

English Centre of International P.E.N.

The English Centre of International P.E.N., 7 Dilke Street, Chelsea, London SW3 4JE, England, instituted the Silver Pen Award in 1969. It was suspended in 1973, but it was revived in 1974 with different conditions under the new name of P.E.N. Awards, which in turn has been discontinued. In 1980, the Silver Pen Award will be reinstated.

P.E.N. Awards

Known originally as the annual Silver Pen Award, the prizes of £50 in book tokens and an illuminated scroll went to the author of the novel adjudged best of those published in the preceding two years and to the author of a book in another literary category.

1974
Christopher Leach
The Send Off (Chatto) Fiction
Storm Jameson
There Will Be a Short Interval (Collins)
Fiction

V. S. Pritchett
Balzac (Chatto) Biography/Autobiog-
raphy
Discontinued

Silver Pen Award

This award was instituted in 1969 to encourage writers and, through the annual awards dinner at which they are presented, to add an event to the literary calendar of London. The award was offered in three categories during 1969–1971: fiction, non-fiction, and books by authors under the age of twenty-five. The Novel was always one winner, and the other two prize categories varied each year. The awards were presented annually in November at a dinner held at the Cafe Royal in London, where a silver pen and emblem were given to each winner. The award was suspended during the years 1972–1979, replaced briefly by the P.E.N. Awards, and reinstated in 1980, at which time a Silver Pen will be awarded for the best novel of 1979 by a British author. Novels will be nominated by the Executive Committee of the English Centre of International P.E.N. and by the three judges who make the final selection.

1969
Steven Runciman
The Great Church in Captivity (Cambridge Univ. Press) Nonfiction
John Fowles
The French Lieutenant's Woman (Jonathan Cape) Fiction
Mary Teresa Reynolds
Myself My Sepulchre (Macdonald) Author under 25
1970
Melvyn Bragg
The Hired Man (Secker) Novel
Brian Fothergill
Sir William Hamilton (Faber) Biography/Autobiography

John Rowe Townsend
The Intruder (Oxford Univ. Press) Children's Book
1971
Iain Crichton Smith
Selected Poems (Gollancz) Poetry
Mary Renault
Fire from Heaven (Longmans) Novel
F. D. Ommaney
Lost Leviathan (Hutchinson) Science for the General Reader
1972–1979
No awards

Evening Standard Drama Awards

The first *Evening Standard* Drama Awards were made in 1955 by the *Evening Standard*, 47 Shoe Lane, London EC4P 4DD England. They were established to focus attention on the arts in London. Statues are presented to the winners at a luncheon in one of London's leading hotels annually in January following the year of presentation of the drama. All major West End productions, writers, actors, and actresses are eligible. Winners are chosen by a panel of judges composed of critics from London's newspapers.

1955

Richard Adler and Jerry Ross
The Pajama Game (Random) Best Musical

Jean Giraudoux
Tiger at the Gates (Oxford Univ. Press) Best New Play

Samuel Beckett
Waiting for Godot (Grove) Most Controversial Play

1956

Cranks Best Musical Entertainment

Peter Ustinov
Romanoff and Juliet (Random) Best New Play

John Osborne
Most Promising British Playwright

1957

Ray Lawler
Summer of the Seventeenth Doll (Random) Best Play of the Year

Robert Bolt
Most Promising British Playwright

1958

Leonard Bernstein
West Side Story (Random) Best Musical

Tennessee Williams
Cat on a Hot Tin Roof (New American Library) Best Play of the Year

Peter Shaffer
Most Promising British Playwright

1959

William Mankowitz
Make Me an Offer (André Deutsch) Best Musical

C. Shurr
The Long and the Short and the Tall (Vanguard) Best Play of the Year

John Arden
Most Promising British Playwright

Arnold Walker
Most Promising British Playwright

1960

F. Norman
Fings Ain't Wot They Used T'Be (Grove) Best Musical

Harold Pinter
The Caretaker (Grove) Best Play of the Year

J. P. Donleavy
Most Promising Playwright

1961

Alan Bennett
Beyond the Fringe (Random) Best Musical

Jean Anouilh
Becket (New American Library) Best Play of the Year

Gwyn Thomas
Most Promising Playwright

Henry Livings
Most Promising Playwright

1962

Bertolt Brecht
The Caucasian Chalk Circle (Grove) Best Play of the Year

David Rudkin
Most Promising Playwright

1963

Theater Workshop
Oh What a Lovely War (Methuen) Best Musical

Jean Anouilh
Poor Bitos (Coward) Best Play of the Year

Charles Wood
Most Promising Playwright

James Saunders
Most Promising Playwright

1964

Patrick Dennis
Little Me (Fawcett) Best Musical

Edward Albee
Who's Afraid of Virginia Woolf? (Atheneum) Best Play of the Year

1965

John Osborne
A Patriot for Me (Faber) Best Play

F. Marcus
The Killing of Sister George (Random) Best Play

David Mercer
Most Promising Playwright

1966

Jule Styne
Funny Girl (Random) Best Musical of the Year

Joe Orton
Loot (Grove) Best Play of the Year

David Halliwell
Most Promising Playwright

1967

Neil Simon
Sweet Charity (Random) Best Musical of the Year

Peter Nichols
A Day in the Death of Joe Egg (Grove) Best Play of the Year

Tom Stoppard
Most Promising Playwright

David Storey
Most Promising Playwright

1968

Fred Ebb
Cabaret (Random) Best Musical

John Osborne
Hotel in Amsterdam (Faber) Best New Play

Alan Bennett
Forty Years On. Special Award

1969

Burt Bacharach
Promises, Promises (Random) Best Musical of the Year

Peter Nichols
National Health. Best Play of the Year

Peter Barnes
Most Promising Playwright

1970

David Storey
Home (Jonathan Cape) Best Play of the Year

Christopher Hampton
The Philanthropist (Faber) Best Comedy of the Year

David Hare
Most Promising Playwright

Heathcote Williams
Most Promising Playwright

1971

Simon Gray
Butley (Methuen) Best Play of the Year

Alan Bennett
Getting On (Faber) Best Comedy of the Year

E. A. Whitehead
Most Promising Playwright

1972

Tom Stoppard
Jumpers (Faber) Best Play of the Year

Charles Wood
Veterans (Methuen) Best Comedy of the Year

Wilson John Haire
Most Promising Playwright

1973

Eduardo de Filippo
Saturday, Sunday, Monday (Heinemann) Best Play of the Year

Rocky Horror Show. Best Musical of the Year

Alan Ayckbourn
Absurd Person Singular (French)
Best Comedy of the Year

David Williamson
Most Promising Playwright

Laurence Olivier
Special Award

1974

Alan Ayckbourn
Norman Conquests. Best Play of the Year

Tom Stoppard
Travesties. Best Comedy of the Year

John, Paul, George, Ringo and Bert. Best Musical of the Year

Mustapha Matura
Most Promising Playwright

1975

A Little Night Music. Best Musical of the Year

Michael Frayn
Alphabetical Order. Best Comedy of the Year

Simon Gray
Otherwise Engaged. Best Play of the Year

Stephen Poliakoff
Most Promising Playwright

Ben Travers
Special Award

1976

Howard Brenton
Weapons of Happiness. Best Play of the Year

Johnny Speight
The Thoughts of Chairman Alf. Best Comedy of the Year

A Chorus Line. Best Musical of the Year

Peggy Ashcroft
Special Award

Stewart Parker
Most Promising Playwright (for *Spokesong*)

1977

Alan Ayckbourn
Just between Ourselves. Best Play of the Year

Peter Nichols
Privates on Parade. Best Comedy of the Year

Elvis. Best Musical of the Year

Hampstead Theatre
Special Award for Outstanding Achievement

Mary O'Malley
Most Promising Playwright (for *Once a Catholic*)

1978

Tom Stoppard
Night and Day. Best Play of the Year

Michael Hastings
Gloo-Joo. Best Comedy of the Year

Annie. Best Musical of the Year

Brian Clark
Most Promising Playwright (for *Whose Life Is It Anyway?*)

Geoffrey Faber Memorial Prize

The Geoffrey Faber Memorial Prize was established in 1964 by Faber and Faber, Ltd., 3 Queen Square, London WC1N 3AU, England, as a memorial to the founder and first chairman of the firm. The annual award of £500 is given in alternate years for a volume of verse and for a novel that, in the opinion of the judges, are of the greatest literary merit. The writer must not be more than forty years old at the date of publication of the book and must be a citizen of the United Kingdom and colonies, of any

Commonwealth state, Ireland, or South Africa. Three judges are nominated each year by the editors or literary editors of newspapers and magazines that regularly publish literary reviews. The award is usually given in the spring.

1964
George Macbeth
The Broken Places (Scorpion)
Christopher Middleton
Torse Three (Longmans)
1965
Frank Tuohy
The Ice Saints (Scribner)
1966
Jon Silkin
Nature with Man (Chatto)
1967
William McIlvanney
Remedy Is None (Eyre)
John Noone
The Man with the Chocolate Egg (Hamilton)
1968
Seamus Heaney
Death of a Naturalist (Faber)
1969
Piers Paul Read
The Junkers (Alison/Secker)
1970
Geoffrey Hill
King Log (Deutsch)
1971
J. G. Farrell
Troubles (Jonathan Cape)
1972
Tony Harrison
The Loiners (London Magazine Editions)

1973
David Storey
Pasmore (Longmans)
1974
John Fuller
Cannibals and Missionaries: Epistles to Several Persons (Secker)
1975
Richard Wright
The Middle of a Life (Macmillan)
1976
Douglas Dunn
Love or Nothing (Chilmark)
1977
Carolyn Slaughter
The Story of the Weasel (Hart-Davis/ MacGibbon)
1978
David Harsent
Dreams of the Dead (Oxford Univ. Press)
Kit Wright
The Bear Looked over the Mountain (Salamander)
1979
Timothy Mo
The Monkey King (Deutsch)

Guardian Fiction Prize

This annual prize, offered by the *Guardian*, 164 Deansgate, Manchester M6O 2RR, England, was founded in 1965 by the *Guardian*'s present literary editor, W. L. Webb, to acknowledge each year a novel of originality and promise by a British or Commonwealth writer. On four occasions the prize has been awarded for a first novel. Writers from Britain, Ireland, or any of the Commonwealth countries whose novels are published in Britain are eligible. The judges are the *Guardian*'s literary editor and regular reviewers throughout the year. The novel is chosen from among those reviewed in the *Guardian* in the previous year. The award, £300, is presented at the annual Christmas books luncheon for reviewers and publishers, held on the last Thursday in November in London.

1965
 Clive Barry
 Crumb Borne (Faber)
1966
 Archie Hind
 The Dear Green Place (Hutchinson)
1967
 Eva Figes
 Winter Journey (Faber)
1968
 P. J. Kavanagh
 A Song and Dance (Chatto)
1969
 Maurice Leitch
 Poor Lazarus (MacGibbon)
1970
 Margaret Blount
 When Did You Last See Your Father? (Hutchinson)
1971
 Thomas Kilroy
 The Big Chapel (Faber)

1972
 John Berger
 G (Weidenfeld)
1973
 Peter Redgrove
 In the Country of the Skin (Routledge)
1974
 Beryl Bainbridge
 The Bottle Factory Outing (Duckworth)
1975
 Sylvia Clayton
 Friends and Romans (Faber)
1976
 Robert Nye
 Falstaff (Hamilton)
1977
 Michael Moorcock
 The Condition of Muzak (Allison & Busby)
1978
 Roy A. K. Heath
 The Murderer (Allison & Busby)

Historical Novel Prize in Memory of Georgette Heyer

Bodley Head and Corgi Books established this £1,500 award in 1977 in memory of the late Georgette Heyer for an outstanding full-length historical novel. Submissions must be in English, unpublished in any form, and must be received by September 30. The winning manuscript is published by Bodley Head/Corgi, and the winning author receives the cash award at a reception in London in March or April. Inquiries should be sent to Bodley Head, Ltd., 9 Bow Street, London WC2E 7AL, England.

1978
 Rhona Martin
 Gallow's Wedding

1979
 Norah Lofts
 Day of the Butterfly

Martin Luther King Memorial Prize

This prize is awarded for a literary work reflecting the ideals to which Martin Luther King, Jr., dedicated his life. It may be given for a novel, story, poem, play, or TV, radio, or motion picture script published or performed in the United Kingdom during the preceding calendar year. The £100 prize is usually presented at the offices of the publishers of winning items. Inquiries and works to be considered should be sent with a self-addressed stamped envelope to John Brunner, Martin Luther King Memorial Prize, NatWest Bank, 7 Fore Street, Chard, Somerset TA20 1PJ, England.

1969
    No award
1970
    Eldridge Cleaver
    Soul on Ice (Jonathan Cape)
1971
    Bobby Seale
    Seize the Time (Hutchinson)
1972
    Derek Humphry and Gus John
    Because They're Black (Penguin)
1973
    Chris Searle
    The Forsaken Lover (Routledge)

1974
    James Walvin
    Black and White (Lane/Penguin)
1975
    No award
1976
    Evan Jones
    The Fight against Slavery (BBC-TV and Time/Life-TV)
1977
    No award
1978
    Amrit Wilson
    Finding a Voice (Virago)

Library Association

Inquiries concerning the six medals awarded by the Library Association should be directed to the Publishing Manager, Library Association, 7 Ridgmount Street, London WC1E 7AE, England.

Besterman Medal

The Library Association awards this medal annually for an outstanding bibliography or guide to the literature first published in the United Kingdom during the preceding year. Recommendations for the award are invited from members of the Library Association. Among criteria for the award are the authority of the work, quality of articles and entries, accessibility of information, scope and coverage, up-to-dateness, and originality.

1971
    James F. Arnott and John W. Robinson

English Theatrical Literature, 1559–1900 (Society for Theatre Research)

1972
   Brenda White
   *Sourcebook of Planning Information:
   A Discussion of Sources of Informa-
   tion for Use in Urban and Regional
   Planning, and in Allied Fields* (Bing-
   ley)
1973
   Geoffrey H. Martin and Sylvia MacIn-
   tyre
   *A Bibliography of British and Irish
   Municipal History, Vol. 1: General
   Works* (Leicester Univ. Press)
1974
   No award
1975
   Ernest A. R. Bush
   Agriculture: A Bibliographical Guide,
   2 vols. (Macdonald and Jane's)

1976
   Ralph Hyde
   Printed Maps of Victorian London
   (Dawson)
1977
   Central Statistical Office
   Guide to Official Statistics, no. 1,
   1976 (HMSO)
1978
   E. W. Padwick, comp.
   A Bibliography of Cricket (Library As-
   sociation)

Carnegie Medal

The Library Association Carnegie Medal, the English equivalent of the Newbery Medal in America, is awarded annually for an outstanding book for children written in
English and first published in the United Kingdom during the preceding year. At the
end of each year, recommendations for the award are invited from members of the
Library Association. They are asked to submit a preliminary list of no more than three
titles from which a committee makes the final selection. The contest is open to works
of nonfiction as well as fiction.

1937
   Arthur Ransome
   Pigeon Post (Jonathan Cape)
1938
   Eve Garnett
   The Family from One End Street (Mul-
   ler)
1939
   Noel Streatfield
   The Circus Is Coming (Dent)
1940
   Eleanor Doorly
   Radium Woman (Heinemann)
1941
   Kitty Barne
   Visitors from London (Dent)

1942
   Mary Treadgold
   We Couldn't Leave Dinah (Jonathan
   Cape)
1943
   "B.B." [D. J. Watkins-Pitchford]
   The Little Grey Men (Eyre)
1944
   No award
1945
   Eric Linklater
   The Wind on the Moon (Macmillan)
1946
   No award

1947
Elizabeth Goudge
The Little White Horse (Univ. of London Press)

1948
Walter de la Mare
Collected Stories for Children (Faber)

1949
Richard Armstrong
Sea Change (Dent)

1950
Agnes Allen
The Story of Your Home (Faber)

1951
Elfrida Vipont Foulds
The Lark on the Wing (Oxford Univ. Press)

1952
Cynthia Harnett
The Wool-Pack (Methuen)

1953
Mary Norton
The Borrowers (Dent)

1954
Edward Osmond
A Valley Grows Up (Oxford Univ. Press)

1955
Ronald Welch [Ronald Oliver Felton]
Knight Crusader (Oxford Univ. Press)

1956
Eleanor Farjeon
The Little Bookroom (Oxford Univ. Press)

1957
C. S. Lewis
The Last Battle (Bodley)

1958
William Mayne
A Grass Rope (Oxford Univ. Press)

1959
A. Philippa Pearce
Tom's Midnight Garden (Oxford Univ. Press)

1960
Rosemary Sutcliff
The Lantern Bearers (Oxford Univ. Press)

1961
I. W. Cornwall
The Making of Man (Phoenix)

1962
Lucy M. Boston
A Stranger of Green Knowe (Faber)

1963
Pauline Clarke
The Twelve and the Genii (Faber)

1964
Hester Burton
Time of Trial (Oxford Univ. Press)

1965
Sheena Porter
Nordy Bank (Oxford Univ. Press)

1966
Philip Turner
The Grange at High Force (Oxford Univ. Press)

1967
No award

1968
Alan Garner
The Owl Service (Collins)

1969
Rosemary Harris
The Moon in the Cloud (Faber)

1970
Kathleen Peyton
The Edge of the Cloud (Oxford Univ. Press)

1971
Leon Garfield and Edward Blishen
The God beneath the Sea (Longmans)

1972
Ivan Southall
Josh (Angus & Robertson)

1973
Richard Adams
Watership Down (Rex Collings)

1974
Penelope Lively
The Ghost of Thomas Kempe (Heinemann)
1975
Mollie Hunter
The Stronghold (Hamilton)
1976
Robert Westall
The Machine Gunners (Macmillan)

1977
Jan Mark
Thunder and Lightning (Kestrel)
1978
Gene Kemp
The Turbulent Term of Tyke Tiler (Faber)
1979
D. Rees
The Exeter Blitz (Hamilton)

Kate Greenaway Medal

The Library Association Kate Greenaway Medal recognizes the importance of illustrations in children's books. It is awarded to the artist who, in the opinion of the Library Association, has produced the most distinguished work in the illustration of children's books first published in the United Kingdom during the preceding year. Books intended for older as well as younger children are eligible, and the quality of reproduction is taken into account. Recommendations for the award come from members of the Library Association.

1956
No award
1957
Edward Ardizzone
Tim All Alone (Oxford Univ. Press)
1958
V. H. Drummond
Mrs. Easter and the Storks (Faber)
1959
No award
1960
William Stobbs
Kashtanka and *A Bundle of Ballads* (Oxford Univ. Press)
1961
Gerald Rose
Old Winkle and the Seagulls (Faber)
1962
Antony Maitland
Mrs. Cockle's Cat (Constable)
1963
Brian Wildsmith
A.B.C. (Oxford Univ. Press)

1964
John Burningham
Borka: The Adventures of a Goose with No Feathers (Jonathan Cape)
1965
C. Walter Hodges
Shakespeare's Theatre (Oxford Univ. Press)
1966
Victor G. Ambrus
The Three Poor Tailors (Oxford Univ. Press)
1967
Raymond Briggs
The Mother Goose Treasury (Hamilton)
1968
Charles Keeping
Charley, Charlotte and the Golden Canary (Oxford Univ. Press)
1969
Pauline Baynes
A Dictionary of Chivalry (Longmans)

1970
   Helen Oxenbury
   The Quangle Wangle's Hut and *The Dragon of an Ordinary Family* (Heinemann)
1971
   John Burmingham
   Mr. Gumpy's Outing (Jonathan Cape)
1972
   Jan Pienkowski
   The Kingdom under the Sea (Jonathan Cape)
1973
   Krystyna Turska
   The Woodcutter's Duck (Hamilton)
1974
   Raymond Briggs
   Father Christmas (Hamilton)

1975
   Pat Hutchins
   The Wind Blew (Bodley)
1976
   Victor G. Ambrus
   Horses in Battle and *Mishka* (Oxford Univ. Press)
1977
   Gaile E. Haley
   The Post Office Cat (Bodley)
1978
   Shirley Hughes
   Dogger (Bodley)
1979
   Janet Ahlberg
   Each Peach Pear Plum (Kestrel)

McColvin Medal

This annual award is given for an outstanding reference book first published in the United Kingdom. Encyclopedias, dictionaries, biographical dictionaries, annuals, yearbooks, directories, handbooks, compendia of data, and atlases are eligible. Recommendations are invited from members of the Library Association, who are asked to submit a preliminary list of not more than three titles.

1971
   Ian G. Anderson, ed.
   Councils, Commmittees and Boards: A Handbook of Advisory, Consultative, Executive and Similar Bodies in British Public Life (CBD Research)
1972
   Walter Shepherd
   Shepherd's Glossary of Graphic Signs and Symbols (Dent)
1973
   Arthur Jacobs, ed.
   Music Yearbook, 1972/1973 (Macmillan)
1974
   No award
1975
   W. F. Maunder, ed.
   Reviews of United Kingdom Statistical Sources, Vols. 1–3 (Heinemann Educational Books, published by the Royal Statistical Society and the Social Science Research Council)
1976
   Peter Kennedy
   Folksongs of Britain and Ireland (Cassell)
1977
   C. G. Allen
   A Manual of European Languages for Librarians (Bowker)
1978
   No award

Robinson Medal

This medal is awarded every two years to reward the originality and inventive ability of librarians and other individuals or firms who have devised new and improved methods in library technology or library administration. Methods or inventions submitted for the award must be designed or adapted primarily for use in the field of library technology or library administration. At the discretion of the Adjudicating Committee, a sum of money up to £200 may be awarded with the medal.

1968
   Mansell Information/Publishing, Ltd., of London, for their development of an automatic abstracting camera for use in producing book catalogs from library cards or other sequential material
1970
   Frank Gurney of Automated Library Systems, for computer bookcharging

1972
   University of Lancaster Library, Research Unit for the Development of Simulation Games in Education for Library Management
1974–1976
   No awards

Wheatley Medal

The Library Association Wheatley Medal is awarded annually for an outstanding index published in the United Kingdom during the preceding three years. Recommendations are invited from members of the Library Association, the Society of Indexers, publishers, and other individuals.

1963
/   Michael Maclagan
   Clemency Canning (Macmillan)
1964
   J. M. Dickie
   How to Catch Trout, 3rd ed. (Chambers)
1965
   Guy Parsloe, ed.
   Wardens' Accounts of the Worshipful Company of Founders of the City of London, 1497-1681 (Athlone)
1966
   Alison Quinn
   "Modern Index" to *The Principall Navigations, voiages and discoveries of the English Nation*, by Richard Hakluyt (Oxford Univ. Press for the Hakluyt Society)

1967
   No award
1968
   G. Norman Knight
   Index to *Winston S. Churchill*, Vol. 2 (Heinemann)
1969
   Doreen Blake and Ruth E. M. Bowden
   Journal of Anatomy: Index to the First 100 Years, 1866-1966 (Cambridge Univ. Press)
1970
   E. L. C. Mullins
   Index to *A Guide to the Historical and Archaeological Publications of Societies in England and Wales, 1901-1933* (Athlone Press)
1971–1973
   No awards

1974
Kenneth Boodson
Index to *Non-ferrous Metals: A Biblio-graphical Guide* (Macdonald)
L. M. Harrod
Index to *History of the King's Works*, Vol. 6 (HMSO)
1975
C. C. Banwell
Index to *Encyclopaedia of Forms and Precedents*, 4th ed. (Butterworths)
1976
M. D. Anderson
Index to *Copy-Editing* (Cambridge Univ. Press)

1977
John A. Vickers
Index to *The Works of John Wesley: The Appeals to Men of Reason and Religion and Certain Related Open Letters*, Vol. 11 (Clarendon)
1978
T. Rowland Pavel
Index to *Archaeologia Cambrensis, 1901-60* (Cambrian Archaeological Association)

National Book League

The National Book League (NBL), 7 Albemarle St., London W1X 4BB, England, administers the following six prizes. Requests for information should be addressed to Marianna Googan, Publicity Officer of the NBL.

Booker McConnell Prize

This annual award, which is sponsored by Booker McConnell, Ltd., is given to the best novel published between January 1 and November 30 of the year of the award, as judged by a three- to five-member jury. The prize is open to novels written in English by citizens of the British Commonwealth, Ireland, and South Africa, published for the first time by a British publisher in the United Kingdom. Entries are submitted *only* by United Kingdom publishers, who may each submit not more than four novels. The judges may also call in novels. A shorter list of up to six titles is announced in October, and the winner is announced in November. There is no fixed place for official presentation. The prize is £10,000 and the Booker Trophy.

1969
P. H. Newby
Something to Answer For (Faber)
1970
Bernice Rubens
The Elected Member (Eyre)
1971
V. S. Naipaul
In a Free State (Deutsch)

1972
John Berger
G (Weidenfeld)
1973
J. G. Farrell
The Siege of Krishnapur (Weidenfeld)
1974
Nadine Gordimer
The Conservationist (Jonathan Cape)

Stanley Middleton
Holiday (Hutchinson)

1975

Ruth Prawer Jhabvala
Heat and Dust (Murray)

1976

David Storey
Saville (Jonathan Cape)

1977

Paul Scott
Staying On (Heinemann)

1978

Iris Murdoch
The Sea, the Sea (Chatto)

1979

Penelope Fitzgerald
Offshore (Collins)

Christopher Ewart-Biggs Memorial Prize

This annual prize of £1,500 was inaugurated in 1977 in memory of Britain's ambassador to Eire, killed there on July 21, 1976. It is awarded to the writer, of any nationality, whose work is considered by the judges to have contributed most to peace and understanding in Ireland, closer ties between the peoples of Britain and Ireland, and cooperation between the members of the European Economic Community. Entries, consisting of books or other writings (such as a series of press articles), should have been published between June 1 of the previous year and May 31 of the year of award presentation. The closing date for submissions is July 1.

1977

Michael MacGreil
Prejudice and Tolerance in Ireland (College of Industrial Relations)

Anthony Stewart
The Narrow Ground (Faber)

1978

Dervla Murphy
A Place Apart (Murray)

David Higham Prize for Fiction

To celebrate David Higham's eightieth birthday in November 1975, the author's agents, David Higham Associates, established the David Higham Prize for Fiction. The prize of £500 is awarded annually for any first novel written in English by a citizen of the British Commonwealth, Eire, or South Africa that shows promise for the author's future.

1975

Jane Gardam
Black Faces, White Faces (Hamilton)

Matthew Vaughan
Chalky (Secker)

1976

Caroline Blackwood
The Stepdaughter (Duckworth)

1977

Patricia Finney
A Shadow of Gulls (Collins)

1978

Leslie Norris
Sliding (Dent)

Jewish Chronicle/Harold H. Wingate Book Awards

The National Book League administers two annual book prizes of £1,000 each, one for fiction and one for nonfiction, aimed at stimulating an interest in and awareness of Jewish themes, as well as giving tangible reward to writers and scholars. It replaces the *Jewish Chronicle* Award. Eligible books must have been published between April 1 of the previous year and March 31 of the year of the award. Works of fiction or nonfiction published in English in the United Kingdom and written by a resident of Great Britain, the British Commonwealth, Eire, South Africa, or Israel are eligible. The award winners are announced in December, and the awards are presented at Stationer's Hall, London.

1977
　Chaim Bermant
　Coming Home (Allen & Unwin) Non-fiction
　David Markish
　The Beginning (Hodder) Fiction
1978
　Lionel Kochan
　The Jew and His History (Macmillan) Nonfiction

Dan Jacobson
Confessions of Josef Baisz (Secker) Fiction

Manchester Odd Fellows Social Concern Book Awards

The National Book League offers two annual prizes of £500 each (£200 each in 1977) for books, or pamphlets of over 10,000 words, that make the most useful contribution to finding solutions to, increasing public awareness of, or providing impetus for improvement of social problems that concern the community. Entries are requested from works published between August 1 of the previous year and July 31 of the year of the award. Citizens of the United Kingdom, the British Commonwealth, Eire, South Africa, and Pakistan are eligible, provided that their entries have been published first in England. Four copies of each book should be submitted to arrive no later than August 10.

1977
　Susan Hooker
　Caring for Elderly People (Routledge)
　Valerie Karn
　Retiring to the Seaside (Routledge)
1978
　Gill Brason
　The Ungreen Park (Bodley)

Ruth Lister and Frank Field, eds.
Wasted Labour (Child Poverty Action Group)
1979
Merren Parker and David Mauger
Children with Cancer: A Handbook for Families and Helpers (Cassell)

John Llewelyn Rhys Memorial Prize

John Llewelyn Rhys, a young Englishman killed in active service with the Royal Air Force in 1940, was awarded the Hawthornden Prize posthumously in 1942 for his book of short stories *England Is My Village*. As a fitting memorial to him, his widow established this prize for a "memorable work" by a writer who is under thirty at the time of the book's publication and a citizen of the British Commonwealth. Entries must be received by the end of the year in which they are published. The prize of £100 is officially presented at the National Book League, through the John Llewelyn Rhys Memorial Trust.

1942
Michael Richey
"Sunk by a Mine," *New York Times Magazine*
1943
Morwenna Donelly
Beauty for Ashes (Routledge)
1944
Alun Lewis
The Last Inspection (Macmillan)
1945
James Aldridge
The Sea Eagle (Little)
1946
Oriel Malet
My Bird Sings (Doubleday)
1947
Anne-Marie Walters
Moondrop to Gascony (Macmillan)
1948
Richard Mason
The Wind Cannot Read (Putnam)
1949
Emma Smith
Maidens' Trip (Putnam)
1950
Kenneth Allsop
Adventure Lit Their Star (Latimer)
1951
E. J. Howard
The Beautiful Visit (Random)
1952
No award
1953
Rachel Trickett
The Return Home (Constable)

1954
Tom Stacey
The Hostile Sun (Duckworth)
1955
John Wiles
The Moon to Play With (John Day)
1956
John Hearne
Voices under the Window (Faber)
1957
Ruskin Bond
The Room on the Roof (Deutsch)
1958
V. S. Naipaul
The Mystic Masseur (Vanguard)
1959
Dan Jacobson
A Long Way from London (Weidenfeld)
1960
David Caute
At Fever Pitch (Pantheon)
1961
David Storey
Flight into Camden (Longmans)
1962
Robert Rhodes James
An Introduction to the House of Commons (Collins)

Edward Lucie-Smith
A Tropical Childhood and Other Poems (Oxford Univ. Press)
1963
Peter Marshall
Two Lives (Stein)

1964
Nell Dunn
Up the Junction (Lippincott)
1965
Julian Mitchell
The White Father (Farrar)
1966
Margaret Drabble
The Millstone (Morrow)
1967
Anthony Masters
The Seahorse (Secker)
1968
Angela Carter
The Magic Toyshop (Simon & Schuster)
1969
Melvyn Bragg
Without a City Wall (Knopf)
1970
Angus Calder
The People's War (Jonathan Cape)
1971
Shiva Naipaul
Fireflies (Deutsch)

1972
Susan Hill
The Albatross (Hamilton)
1973
Peter Smalley
A Warm Gun (Deutsch)
1974
Hugh Fleetwood
The Girl Who Passed for Normal (Hamilton)
1975
David Hare
Knuckle (Faber)
Tim Jeal
Cushing's Crusade (Heinemann)
1976
No award
1977
Richard Cork
Vorticism and Abstract Art in the First Machine Age (Fraser)
1978
Andrew Wilson
The Sweets of Pimlico (Secker)

Sir Roger Newdigate Prize for English Verse

The Newdigate Prize Foundation was established in 1806 by Sir Roger Newdigate, who had been a member of Parliament for Oxford University from 1750 to 1780. This foundation was the first one founded solely to award a literary prize. The sum of £1,000 was bequeathed by Sir Roger with the stipulation that £21 of the income should be awarded each year to a member of Oxford University for "a copy of English verse of fifty lines and no more, in recommendation of the study of the ancient Greek and Roman remains of architecture, and painting." Later, with the consent of the Newdigate heirs, these restrictions were modified. The award, increased to about £80, is now open to members of Oxford University who have not exceeded four years from their matriculation. It is given for a poem of no more than 300 lines on a given subject. Three judges award the prize. Announcement is made by Oxford University annually in May or early June; the winner recites part of the poem at commemoration in June. The award was not given during the war, but was resumed again in 1947. Listed on the following page are recent winners.

1935
A. W. Plowman
Canterbury
1936
D. M. de R. Winser
Rain
1937
M. Stanley-Wrench
The Man in the Moon
1938
M. Thwaites
Milton Blind
1939
K. S. Kitchin
Dr. Newman Revisits Oxford
1947
M. G. de St. V. Atkins
Nemesis
1948
P. D. L. Way
Caesarion
1949
P. Weitsman
The Black Death
1950
J. O. Bayley
Eldorado
1951
M. Hornyansky
The Queen of Sheba
1952
D. A. Hall
Exile
1953–1954
No awards
1955
E. S. Gomer-Evans
Elegy for a Dead Clown
1956
D. L. Posner
The Deserted Altar
1957
R. J. Maxwell
Leviathan

1958
J. H. Stallworthy
The Earthly Paradise

1959
No award
1960
J. L. Fuller
A Dialogue between Caliban and Ariel
1961
No award
1962
S. P. Johnson
May Morning
1963
No award
1964
J. D. Hamilton Paterson
Disease
1965
P. A. C. Jay
Fear
1966
No award

1967
No award
1968
J. M. Fenton
Japan Opened, 1853–4
1969
No award
1970
C. W. Radice
Instructions to a Painter
1971
No award

1972
N. P. P. Rhodes
The Ancestral Face

1973
C. M. Mann
The Wife's Tale

1974
A. J. Hollinghurst
Death of a Poet

1975
A. P. Motion
The Tides

1976
D. L. Winzar
Hostages
1977
M. A. King
The Fool

1978–1979
No awards

The Frederick Niven Literary Award

Pauline Niven established this award in 1950 in memory of her husband, the Scottish novelist, who died in Canada during World War II. The Scottish Centre of International P.E.N. administers the award. A prize of £500 is awarded triennially for the best novel by a Scotsman or Scotswoman published during the preceding three years. The prize, £50 from 1950 to 1974, was increased to £500 in 1977 with the assistance of the Scottish Arts Council. The novels, which must be submitted by the publishers, are considered by a panel of experts and a final independent judge. Inquiries should be made to Mary Baxter, Hon. Secretary, P.E.N. Scottish Centre, 18 Crown Terrace, Glasgow G12 9E5S, Scotland.

1950
N. Brysson Morrison
The Winnowing Years (Hogarth)
1953
Edwin Muir (special award)
Collected Poems (Oxford Univ. Press)
1956
Robin Jenkins
The Cone-Gatherers (MacDonald)
1959
No award
1962
Allan Campbell McLean
The Islander (Collins)
Alistair Mair
The Devil's Minister (Hale)

1965
James Allan Ford
Season of Escape (Hodder)
1968
Archie Hind
The Dear Green Place (Hutchinson)
1971
Mary Stewart
The Crystal Cave (Hodder)
1974
Maureen O'Donoghue
Wild Honey Time (Hodder)
1977
John Quigley
King's Royal and *Queen's Royal* (Hamilton)

Poetry Society

The Poetry Society, 21 Earls Court Square, London SW 5, England, offers several awards for poetry. The Arnold Vincent Bowen Competition awards £10 for a single poem no more than thirty lines in length. Only one poem may be submitted. Authors should adopt a nom-de-plume and send their real name and address in a sealed envelope with the nom-de-plume on the outside. The winning poem will be published in the *Newsletter,* and the prize winner will be informed by post. The annual deadline for each competition is February 28. Address entries to the Arnold Vincent Bowen Competition. The Shirley Carter Greenwood Prize and the Premium Competition have been discontinued. The Alice Hunt Bartlett Prize, described below, is for published books of poetry.

Alice Hunt Bartlett Prize

This prize of £200 has been offered annually since 1966 by the Poetry Society to a poet the Society wishes to honor and encourage. The prize is awarded for a book of poetry published in English and presented in duplicate to the Society's Library in the year of publication. The closing date is December 31. Special consideration will be shown to newly emerged poets and to first published collections of their work. In the event of poems being translated into English, the original poet must be alive and the prize will be divided equally between that poet and the translator.

1966
  Gavin Bantock
  Christ (Parsons)
  Paul Roche
  All Things Considered (Duckworth)
1967
  Ted Walker
  The Solitaries (Jonathan Cape)
1968
  Gael Turnbull
  A Trampoline (Cape Goliard)
1969
  Tom Raworth
  The Relation Ship (Cape Goliard)
1970
  Leslie Norris
  Ransoms (Chatto)
1971
  Geoffrey Hill
  Mercian Hymns (Deutsch)
1972
  Paul Evans
  February (Fulcrum)

1973
  Rodney Pybus
  In Memoriam Milena (Chatto/Hogarth)
1974
  Allen Fisher
  Place (Aloes)
  Bill Griffiths
  War with Windsor (Pirate/Writers' Forum)
1975
  Elizabeth Ashworth
  A New Confusion (Outposts)
1976
  Andrew Crozier
  Pleats (Great Works)
  Lee Harwood
  H.M.S. Little Fox (Oasis)
1977
  Kit Wright
  The Bear Looked over the Mountain (Salamander)

Queen's Gold Medal for Poetry

This award was instituted in 1933 by King George V, at the suggestion of the poet laureate John Masefield. The medal is given for a book of verse, on the recommendation of a committee of eminent men and women of letters. The medal is usually given to a book by an English subject writing in English, but an exceptional translation may also be considered. The medal is not necessarily awarded each year.

1934
Laurence Whistler
1937
W. H. Auden
1940
Michael Thwaites
1952
Andrew Young
1953
Arthur Waley
1954
Ralph Hodgson
1955
Ruth Pitter
1956
Edmund Blunden
1957
Siegfried Sassoon
1959
Frances Cornford
1960
John Betjeman
1962
Christopher Fry

1963
William Plomer
1964
R. S. Thomas
1965
Philip Larkin
1967
Charles Causley
1968
Robert Graves
1969
Stevie Smith
1970
Roy Fuller
1971
Stephen Spender
1973
John Heath-Stubbs
1974
Ted Hughes
1977
Norman Nicholson

Romantic Novelists Association

The Romantic Novelists Association (RNA), Hillfoot, Brookfield Crescent, Ramsey, Isle of Man, offers the following two awards to romantic novelists. The RNA Historical Award was discontinued in 1974.

Netta Muskett Award

Netta Muskett, for whom this award is named, was a former vice-president of the RNA and was recognized as a distinguished romantic novelist. The award was established in 1960 to help unpublished writers of romantic novels. The submitted manuscript must be written specially for this award, and the author must be unpublished in the field of the romantic novel. The award, a trophy, is presented at a luncheon or dinner each April. The winning manuscript is also guaranteed publication.

1966
  Anne Rundle
1967
  Frances Stevens
1968
  Alannah Knight
1969
  No award
1970
  Catherine Fellows
1971
  No award

1972
  Barbara Carr
1973
  Sheila Walsh
1974
  Freda Michel
1975
  Hester Rowan
1976–1977
  No awards
1978
  Margery Goulden

RNA Major Award

The RNA established this award in 1960 to honor the best romantic novel (modern or historical) published during the year. Since 1974 the RNA Historical Award has been combined with this award. Both members and nonmembers are eligible. A trophy is awarded annually for each category at a luncheon or dinner in April.

1960
  Mary Howard
  More than Friendship (Collins)
1961
  Paula Allardyce
  The Witches Sabbath (Hodder)
1962
  Margaret Maddocks
  Larksbrook (Hurst)
1963
  Dorothy Cray
  House Divided (Hurst)
1964
  Suzanne Ebel
  Journey from Yesterday (Collins)
1965
  Margaret Maddocks
  The Silver Answer (Hurst)
1966
  Anne Betteridge
  The Truth Game (Hurst)
1967
  Maynah Lewis
  The Future Is Forever (Hurst)

1968
  Doris E. Smith
  Comfort & Keep (Ward)
1969
  Margaret Maddocks
  Thea (Hurst)
  Joanne Marshall
  Cat on a Broomstick (Jenkins)
  Rona Randall
  Broken Tapestry (Hurst)
1970
  Joanne Marshall
  Flower of Silence (Mills)
1971
  Maynah Lewis
  The Pride of Innocence (Hurst)
1972
  Constance Heaven
  The House of Kuragin (Heinemann)
1973
  Frances Murray
  The Burning Lamp (Hodder)

1974
  Jay Allerton
  Vote for a Silk Gown (Troubadour)
1975
  Anna Gilbert
  The Look of Innocence (Hodder)
1976
  Anne Worboys
  Every Man a King (Hodder)

1977
  Catherine MacArthur
  It Was the Lark (Hodder)
1978
  Josephine Edgar
  Countess (MacDonald & Jane's)

The Royal Society of Literature

Benson Medal

In 1916, Dr. A. C. Benson presented the Royal Society of Literature of the United Kingdom, 1 Hyde Park Gardens, London W2 2LT, England, with an endowment for the Award of Silver Medals. The award is given by the Council for meritorious work in poetry, fiction, history, biography, and belles lettres. Applications are not invited. The medal is given at the discretion of the Council of the Royal Society of Literature.

1917
  Gabrielle D'Annunzio
  Maurice Barrès
  Benito Perez Galdós
1923
  Lytton Strachey
1925
  Gordon Bottomley
1926
  Percy Lubbock
  Robert Lynd
  Harold Nicolson
1927
  F. A. Simpson
  Helen Waddell
1928
  George Santayana
1930
  Edmund Blunden
1932
  Stella Benson
1933
  Edith Sitwell

1937
  E. M. Forster
  G. M. Young
1939
  John Gawsworth
  Christopher Hassall
1940
  F. L. Lucas
  Andrew Young
1942
  Christopher La Farge
1952
  Frederick S. Boas
1966
  J. R. R. Tolkien
  Rebecca West
1968
  E. V. Rieu
1969
  C. Woodham-Smith
1975
  Philip Larkin

Heinemann Award for Literature

A foundation was established in 1944 through a bequest in the will of William Heinemann, eminent British publisher. The Royal Society of Literature administers the annual foundation award, which is "primarily to reward those classes of literature which are less remunerative, namely, poetry, criticism, biography, history, etc." and "to encourage the production of works of real merit." The amount of the award is not definitely specified, but is now £200 each to two winners. Submitted works must have been written originally in English. A reading committee decides on the winner, whose name is announced in April or May; the prize is presented at a meeting of the Royal Society of Literature in June or July.

1945
  Norman Nicholson
  Five Rivers (Dutton)
1946
  D. Colston-Baynes
  In Search of Two Characters (Scribner)
  Andrew Young
  Prospect of Flowers (Jonathan Cape)
1947
  Bertrand Russell
  History of Western Philosophy (Simon & Schuster)
  Victoria Sackville-West
  The Garden (Doubleday)
1948
  J. Stuart Collis
  Down to Earth (Clarke)
  Martyn Skinner
  Letters to Malaya (Putnam)
1949
  John Betjeman
  Selected Poems (Murray)
  Frances Cornford
  Travelling Home (Cresset)
1950
  John Guest
  Broken Images (Longmans)
  Peter Quennell
  John Ruskin (Collins)
1951
  Patrick Leigh-Fermor
  Travellers Tree (Harper)

Mervyn Peake
Glassblowers and Gormanghast (Eyre)
1952
  Nicholas Monsarrat
  The Cruel Sea (Knopf)
  G. Winthrop Young
  Mountains with a Difference (British Book Centre)
1953
  Edwin Muir
  Collected Poems (Grove)
  Reginald Pound
  Arnold Bennett (Harcourt)
1954
  L. P. Hartley
  The Go-Between (Knopf)
  Ruth Pitter
  The Ermine (Cresset)
1955
  Robert Gittings
  John Keats: The Living Years (Harvard Univ. Press)
  R. S. Thomas
  Song at the Years Turning (Hart-Davis)
1956
  Vincent Cronin
  Wise Man from the West (Dutton)
  R. W. Ketton-Cremer
  Thomas Gray (Cambridge Univ. Press)

1957
  Harold Acton
  The Bourbons of Naples (Humanities)
  James Lees-Milne
  Roman Mornings (British Book Centre)
1958
  Peter Green
  Sword of Pleasure (World)
  Gavin Maxwell
  A Reed Shaken by the Wind (Longmans)
1959
  Hester Chapman
  The Last Tudor King (Macmillan)
  John Press
  The Chequer'd Shade (Oxford Univ. Press)
1960
  C. A. Trypanis
  The Cocks of Hades (Faber)
  Morris West
  The Devil's Advocate (Morrow)
1961
  James Morris
  World of Venice (Pantheon) (English title: *Venice*)
  Vernon Scannell
  The Masks of Love (Putnam)
1962
  Christopher Fry
  Curtmantle (Oxford Univ. Press)
  Christopher Hibbert
  The Destruction of Lord Raglan (Little)
1963
  Alethea Hayter
  Mrs. Browning (Barnes & Noble)
1964
  Robert Rhodes James
  Rosebery (Weidenfeld)
  Alan Moorehead
  Cooper's Creek (Harper)

1965
  Harold Owen
  Journey from Obscurity, II, Youth (Oxford Univ. Press)
  Wilfred Thesiger
  The Marsh Arabs (Dutton)
1966
  Nigel Dennis
  Jonathan Swift (Macmillan)
  Derek Walcott
  The Castaway (Jonathan Cape)
1967
  John Bayley
  Tolstoy and the Novel (Viking)
  Norman MacCaig
  Surroundings (Wesleyan Univ. Press)
  Jean Rhys
  Wide Sargasso Sea (Deutsch)
1968
  Michael Ayrton
  The Maze Maker (Holt)
  Winifred Gérin
  Charlotte Brontë (Oxford Univ. Press)
1969
  Gordon S. Haight
  George Eliot (Oxford Univ. Press)
  Jasmine Rose Innes
  Writing in the Dust (Deutsch)
  V. S. Pritchett
  A Cab at the Door (Chatto)
1970
  Ronald Blythe
  Akenfield: Portrait of an English Village (Lane)
  Brian Fothergill
  Sir William Hamilton (Faber)
  Nicolas Wollaston
  Pharaoh's Chicken (Lippincott)
1971
  Corelli Barnett
  Britain and Her Army (Lane)
  R. W. Southern
  Medieval Humanism (Blackwell)

1972

Dorothy Carrington
Granite Islands: Portrait of Corsica (Longmans)

Geoffrey Hill
Mercian Hymns (Deutsch)

Thomas Kilroy
The Big Chapel (Faber)

1973

Thomas Keneally
The Chant of Jimmy Blacksmith (Angus & Robertson)

William St. Clair
That Greece Might Still Be Free (Oxford Univ. Press)

1974

Robin Lane Fox
Alexander the Great (Dial)

Alasdair Maclean
From the Wilderness (Harper)

Barry Unsworth
Mooncranker's Gift (Houghton)

1975

Robin Furneaux
William Wilberforce (Hamilton)

John Wain
Samuel Johnson (Macmillan)

1976

Malcolm Bradbury
The History Man (Oxford Univ. Press)

William Trevor
Angels at the Ritz (Bodley)

1977

Edward Crankshaw
Shadow of the Winter Palace (Macmillan)

Philip Ziegler
Melbourne (Collins)

1978

Christopher Hill
Milton and the English Revolution (Faber)

F. S. L. Lyons
Charles Stewart Parnell (Collins)

Norman Mackenzie and Jeanne Mackenzie
The First Fabians (Weidenfeld)

1979

Robert Gittings
The Older Hardy (Heinemann)

Frank Tuohy
Live Bait (Macmillan)

Winifred Holtby Memorial Prize

In 1966, this annual award of £100 was instituted by Vera Brittain in memory of Winifred Holtby, who died at the age of thirty-seven. The Royal Society of Literature administers the prize, which is given for the best regional novel of the year.

1967

David Bean
The Big Meeting (Secker)

1968

Catherine Cookson
The Round Tower (Macdonald)

1969

Ian MacDonald
The Humming Bird Tree (Heinemann)

1970

Shiva Naipaul
Fireflies (Deutsch)

1971

John Stewart
Last Cove Days (Deutsch)

1972–1973

No awards

1974
　Ronald Harwood
　Articles of Faith (Secker)
　Peter Tinniswood
　I Didn't Know You Cared (Hodder)
1975
　Graham King
　The Pandora Valley (Heinemann)
1976
　Jane Gardam
　Black Faces, White Faces (Hamilton)

1977
　Eugene McCabe
　Victims (Gollancz)
1978
　Anita Desai
　Fire on the Mountain (Heinemann)
1979
　Richard Herley
　The Stone Arrow (Davies)

Scottish Arts Council Book Awards

A limited number of awards of £500 each are made each year by the Scottish Arts Council to published books of literary merit written by Scots or writers resident in Scotland. The awards fall into two categories: Scottish Arts Council New Writing Awards for first books and Scottish Arts Council Book Awards for established authors. Most types of books are eligible for consideration. Books must be submitted by the author's publisher. Further information is available from the Literature Department, Scottish Arts Council, 19 Charlotte Square, Edinburgh EH2 4DF, Scotland.

W. H. Smith & Son Literary Award

An annual literary prize was started in 1959 to encourage and bring international esteem to authors of the British Commonwealth. The £2,500 award, offered by W. H. Smith & Son, Ltd., Strand House, 10 New Fetter Lane, London EC4A 1AD, England, is given to an author whose book, written in English and published in the United Kingdom, makes the most significant contribution to literature. Eligible books must be published during the preceding year ending on December 31. A panel of three judges chooses the prize-winning work. An award may be made to two or more joint authors but may not be given more than once to the same author.

1959
　Patrick White
　Voss (Viking)
1960
　Laurie Lee
　Cider with Rosie (Hogarth)
1961
　Nadine Gordimer
　Friday's Footprints (Viking)

1962
　J. R. Ackerley
　We Think the World of You (Obolensky)

1963
　Gabriel Fielding
　The Birthday King (Morrow)

1964
Ernst H. Gombrich
Meditations on a Hobby Horse (Phaidon) (New York Graphic)
1965
Leonard Woolf
Beginning Again (Harcourt)
1966
R. C. Hutchinson
A Child Possessed (Harper)
1967
Jean Rhys
Wide Sargasso Sea (Deutsch)
1968
V. S. Naipaul
The Mimic Men (Macmillan)
1969
Robert Gittings
John Keats (Little)
1970
John Fowles
The French Lieutenant's Woman (Jonathan Cape)
1971
Nan Fairbrother
New Lives, New Landscapes (Architecture Press)

1972
Kathleen Raine
The Lost Country (Humanities)
1973
Brian Moore
Catholics (Jonathan Cape)
1974
Anthony Powell
Temporary Kings (Heinemann)
1975
Jon Stallworthy
Wilfred Owen: A Biography (Oxford Univ. Press/Chatto)
1976
Seamus Heaney
North (Faber)
1977
Ronald Lewin
Slim: The Standardbearer (Cooper)
1978
Patrick Leigh-Fermor
A Time of Gifts (Murray)
1979
Mark Girouard
Life in the English Country House (Yale Univ. Press)

The Society of Authors

The five awards listed below are administered by the Society of Authors, 84 Drayton Gardens, London SW10 9SD, England.

Cholmondeley Award for Poets

This award was established by the Marchioness of Cholmondeley in 1965 for "the benefit and encouragement of poets of any age, sex, or nationality." The award is for work generally, rather than for a specific book, and no entries are requested. The winners are selected by a panel of judges and are announced annually, usually in the summer, at a Society of Authors presentation party. The award of £2,000 is divided among the winners.

1966
Stevie Smith
Ted Walker
1967
Seamus Heaney
Brian Jones
Norman Nicholson
1968
Harold Massingham
Edwin Morgan
1969
Tony Harrison
Derek Walcott
1970
Edward R. Braithwaite
Douglas Livingstone
Kathleen Raine
1971
Charles Causley
Gavin Ewart
Hugo Williams
1972
Molly Holden
Tom Raworth
Patricia Whittaker
1973
Patric Dickinson
Philip Larkin

1974
D. J. Enright
Alasdair Maclean
Vernon Scannell
1975
Jenny Joseph
Norman MacCaig
John Ormond
1976
Fleur Adcock
Peter Porter
1977
Peter Bland
George Macbeth
James Simmons
Andrew Waterman
1978
Christopher Hope
Leslie Norris
Peter Reading
D. M. Thomas
R. S. Thomas
1979
Alan Brownjohn
Andrew Motion
Charles Tomlinson

The Eric Gregory Trust Fund Award

The Society of Authors annually makes awards from this fund for the encouragement of young poets. Candidates for awards must be British subjects by birth, but not "nationals of Eire or any of the British Dominions or Colonies," and resident in the United Kingdom; be under the age of thirty on March 31 in the year of the award; and submit for the judges' consideration a published or unpublished volume of belles lettres, poetry, or drama poems (not more than thirty). The closing date for submission of entries is October 31; awards will be made before March 31. The sum paid out in awards varies from year to year, but in 1979 there were eight awards amounting to a total of £7,000.

1960
Christopher Levenson
1961
Geoffrey Hill
Adrian Mitchell

1962
Brian Johnson
Jenny Joseph
James Simmons
Donald Thomas

1963
   Stewart Conn
   Peter Griffith
   Ian Hamilton
   David Wevill
1964
   Robert Nye
   Ken Smith
   Jean Symons
   Ted Walker
1965
   John Fuller
   Michael Longley
   Derek Mahon
   Normal Talbot
1966
   Robin Fulton
   Seamus Heaney
   Hugo Williams
1967
   Angus Calder
   Marcus Cumberlege
   David Harsent
   Brian Patten
   David Selzer
1968
   James Aitchison
   Douglas Dunn
   Brian Jones
1969
   Gavin Bantock
   Jeremy Hooker
   Jenny King
   Neil Powell
   Landeg E. White
1970
   Helen Frye
   Paul Mills
   John Mole
   Brian Morse
   Alan Perry
   Richard Tibbitts
1971
   Martin Booth
   Florence Bull
   John Pook

D. M. Warman
John Welch
1972
   Richard Burns
   Tony Curtis
   Andrew Greig
   Robin Lee
   Paul Muldoon
   Brian Oxley
1973
   John Beynon
   Ian Caws
   James Fenton
   Keith Harris
   David Howarth
   Philip Pacey
1974
   Duncan Forbes
   Roger Garfitt
   Robin Hamilton
   Frank Ormsby
   Penelope Shuttle
1975
   John Birtwhistle
   Duncan Bush
   Peter Cash
   Philip Holmes
   Alasdair Paterson
   Val Warner
1976
   Stewart Brown
   Valerie Gillies
   Paul Groves
   Paul Hyland
   Nigel Jenkins
   Andrew Motion
   Tom Paulin
   William Peskett
1977
   David Cooke
   Tony Flynn
   Douglas Marshall
   Melissa Murray
   Michael Vince
1978
   Ciaran Carson
   Peter Denman

Martyn A. Ford
Christopher Reid
James Sutherland-Smith
Paul Wilkins
1979
  Stuart Henson
  Alan Hollinghurst

Michael Jenkins
Peter Thabit Jones
James Lindesay
Brian Moses
Sean O'Brien
Walter Perrie

Hawthornden Prize

The Hawthornden Prize, the oldest of the famous British literary prizes, was founded in 1919 by Alice Warrender. The award, £100 until 1978, was increased to £500 in 1979 through the generosity of the Arts Council of Great Britain. It is awarded annually in June to an English writer under forty-one years old for the best work of imaginative literature. It is especially designed to encourage young authors, and the word "imaginative" is given a broad interpretation. Biographies are not excluded. Books do not have to be submitted for the prize; it is awarded without competition. A panel of judges chooses the winner.

1919
  Edward Shanks
  The Queen of China (Knopf)
1920
  John Freeman
  Poems New and Old (Harcourt)
1921
  Romer Wilson
  The Death of Society (Doubleday)
1922
  Edmund Blunden
  The Shepherd (Knopf)
1923
  David Garnett
  Lady into Fox (Knopf)
1924
  Ralph Hale Mottram
  The Spanish Farm (Dial)
1926
  Sean O'Casey
  Juno and the Paycock (Macmillan)
1927
  Victoria Sackville-West
  The Land (Doubleday)
1928
  Henry Williamson
  Tarka the Otter (Dutton)

1929
  Siegfried Sassoon
  Memoirs of a Fox-Hunting Man (Coward)
1930
  David Cecil
  The Stricken Deer (Bobbs)
1931
  Geoffrey Dennis
  The End of the World (Simon & Schuster)
1932
  Kate O'Brien
  Without My Cloak (Doubleday)
1933
  Charles Morgan
  The Fountain (Knopf)
1934
  James Hilton
  Lost Horizon (Morrow)
1935
  Robert Graves
  I, Claudius (Harrison Smith)
1936
  Evelyn Waugh
  Edmund Campion (Little)

1937
Ruth Pitter
A Trophy of Arms (Macmillan)
1938
David Jones
In Parenthesis (Faber)
1939
Christopher Hassall
Penthesperon (Heinemann)
1940
James Pope-Hennessy
London Fabric (Scribner)
1941
Graham Greene
The Labyrinthine Ways (Viking) (English title: *The Power and the Glory*)
1942
John Llewelyn Rhys
England Is My Village (Reynal)
1943
Sidney Keyes
The Cruel Solstice and *The Iron Laurel* (Routledge)
1944
Martyn Skinner
Letters to Malaya (Putnam)
1945–1957
No awards
1958
Dom Moraes
A Beginning (Parton)
1959
Emyr Humphreys
A Top Epic (McClelland and Stewart)
1960
Alan Sillitoe
The Loneliness of the Long Distance Runner (Knopf)
1961
Ted Hughes
Lupercal (Harper)
1962
Robert Shaw
The Sun Doctor (Harcourt)

1963
Alistair Horne
The Price of Glory (Macmillan)
1964
V. S. Naipaul
Mr. Stone and the Knight's Companion (Deutsch)
1965
William Trevor
The Old Boys (Viking)
1966
No award
1967
Michael Frayn
The Russian Interpreter (Collins)
1968
Michael Levey
Early Renaissance (Penguin)
1969
Geoffrey Hill
King Log (Dufour)
1970
Piers Paul Read
Monk Dawson (Lippincott)
1971–1973
No awards
1974
Oliver Sacks
Awakenings (Doubleday)

1975
David Lodge
Changing Places (Secker)

1976
Robert Nye
Falstaff (Hamilton)

1977
Bruce Chatwin
In Patagonia (Jonathan Cape)

1978
David Cook
Walter (Secker)

Somerset Maugham Awards

The Society of Authors administers these awards, which were founded in 1946 by Somerset Maugham in order to encourage young writers to travel abroad. They are given to a promising author of a published work in fields of poetry, fiction, criticism, biography, history, philosophy, belles lettres, and travel. Dramatic works are not eligible. Candidates for the awards must be British subjects by birth ordinarily residing in the United Kingdom and under the age of thirty-five. Works must be submitted to the Society of Authors by December 31 each year; awards are announced the following March. The books submitted may have been published in any previous year. The winners must use the prizes of approximately £500 each for traveling abroad.

1947
   A. L. Barker
   Innocents (Scribner)
1948
   P. H. Newby
   Journey to the Interior (Doubleday)
1949
   Hamish Henderson
   Elegies for the Dead in Cyrenaica (Macdonald)
1950
   Nigel Kneale
   Tomato Cain and Other Stories (Knopf)
1951
   Roland Camberton
   Scamp (Lehman & Longmans)
1952
   Francis King
   The Dividing Stream (Morrow)
1953
   Emyr Humphreys
   Hear and Forgive (Putnam)
1954
   Doris Lessing
   Five Short Novels (Michael Joseph)
1955
   Kingsley Amis
   Lucky Jim (Doubleday)
1956
   Elizabeth Jennings
   A Way of Looking (Rinehart)
1957
   George Lamming
   In the Castle of My Skin (McGraw)

1958
   John Wain
   Preliminary Essays (Macmillan)
1959
   Thom Gunn
   A Sense of Movement (Univ. of Chicago Press)
1960
   Ted Hughes
   The Hawk in the Rain (Harper)
1961
   V. S. Naipaul
   Miguel Street (Vanguard)
1962
   Hugh Thomas
   The Spanish Civil War (Harper)
1963
   David Storey
   Flight into Camden (Macmillan)
1964
   Dan Jacobson
   Time of Arrival (Macmillan)

   John le Carré
   The Spy Who Came In from the Cold (Coward)
1965
   Peter Everett
   Negatives (Simon & Schuster)
1966
   Michael Frayn
   The Tin Men (Collins)

   Julian Mitchell
   The White Father (Farrar)

1967
  B. S. Johnson
  Trawl (Secker)
  Andrew Sinclair
  The Better Half (Harper)
1968
  Paul Bailey
  At the Jerusalem (Atheneum)
  Seamus Heaney
  Death of a Naturalist (Oxford Univ. Press)
1969
  Angela Carter
  Several Perceptions (Simon & Schuster)
1970
  Jane Gaskell
  A Sweet Sweet Summer (Hodder)
  Piers Paul Read
  Monk Dawson (Secker)
1971
  Richard Barber
  The Knight and Chivalry (Longmans)
  Michael Hastings
  Tussy Is Me (Weidenfeld)
  Susan Hill
  I'm the King of the Castle (Hamilton)
1972
  Douglas Dunn
  Terry Street (Faber)
  Gillian Tindall
  Fly Away Home (Hodder)

1973
  Peter Prince
  Play Things (Gollancz)
  Paul Strathern
  A Season in Abyssinia (Macmillan)
  Jonathan Street
  Prudence Dictates (Hart-Davis)
1974
  Martin Amis
  The Rachel Papers (Knopf)
1975
  No award
1976
  Dominic Cooper
  The Dead of Winter (Chatto)
  Ian McEwan
  First Love, Last Rites (Jonathan Cape)
1977
  Richard Holmes
  Shelley: The Pursuit (Quartet)
1978
  Tom Paulin
  A State of Justice (Faber)
  Nigel Williams
  My Life Closed Twice (Secker)
1979
  Helen Hodgman
  Jack and Jill (Duckworth)
  Sara Maitland
  Daughter of Jerusalem (Blond & Briggs)

Tom-Gallon Trust Award

The Tom-Gallon Trust was founded by Nellie Tom-Gallon in 1943 and is administered by the Society of Authors. The award is given to short-story writers of limited means. Entrants must submit a list of already published fiction, one published or unpublished short story, and a brief statement of their financial position and willingness to devote substantial time to writing fiction as soon as they are financially able. The biennial award has been increased from £100 to £500 through the generosity of the Arts Council of Great Britain.

1943
  Elizabeth Myers

1945
  Jack Aistrop

1947
   Dorothy K. Haynes
1949
   Olivia Manning
1951
   Fred Urquhart
1953
   Maurice Cranston
1955
   Robert Roberts
1957
   E. W. Hildick
1959
   Harold Elvin
1961–1963
   No awards
1965
   Peter Greave
   Jean Stubbs

1966
   Gillian Edwards
1968
   No award
1970
   A. Craig Bell
   Aileen Pennington
1972
   Kathleen Julian
1974
   Neilson Graham
1976
   Jackson Webb
1978
   Michael Morrissey

TES Information Book Awards

The Times Educational Supplement, New Printing House Square, Grays Inn Road, Box 7, London WC1X 8E2, England, offers two awards, one for children up to ten years, the other for children aged eleven to sixteen. The books must be published either in Britain or the Commonwealth. Further information may be obtained from Michael Church, Literary Editor, *The Times Educational Supplement.*

1972
   Magnus Magnusson
   Introducing Archaeology (Bodley)

1973
   David Hay
   Human Populations (Penguin) Senior award
   No Junior award

1974
   F. D. Ommanney
   Frogs, Toads and Newts (Bodley) Junior award

   Betty Churcher
   Understanding Art (Holmes McDougall) Senior award

1975
   Ralph Whitlock
   Spiders (Priory) Junior award
   Geraldine Lux-Flanagan and Sean Morris
   Window into a Nest (Kestrel) Senior award

1976
   Eleanor Allen
   Wash and Brush Up (Black) Junior award
   Macdonald's Encyclopedia of Africa (Macdonald) Senior award

1977
   Richard Mabey
   Street Flowers (Kestrel) Junior award

Man and Machines (Mitchell Beazley) Senior award

1978

Richard Barber

Tournaments (Kestrel) Junior award

Dulcie Gray

Butterflies on My Mind (Angus & Robertson)

Amaury Talbot Prize

Established in 1955, the Amaury Talbot Prize is awarded annually to the author(s) of the work that, in the opinion of the judges, is the most valuable work of anthropological research relating to Africa published in the previous year. Preference is given to works relating to Nigeria, then to any other part of West Africa, and finally to other regions of Africa. Applications, along with two copies of the book, should be submitted to be received by January 31 by the Trustees, Amaury Talbot Prize, Barclays Bank Trust Company, Ltd., Central Administration Trustee Office, Radbroke Hall, Knutsford, Cheshire WA16 9EU, England. Award winners from 1969 on are listed below.

1969

Abner Cohen

Custom and Politics in Urban Africa: A Study of Hausa Migrants in Yoruba Towns (Routledge)

1970

Thurstan Shaw

Igbo-Ukwu: An Account of Archaeological Discoveries in Eastern Nigeria, 2 vols. (Faber)

1971

John R. Goody

Technology, Tradition, and the State in Africa (Oxford Univ. Press)

1972

Richard N. Henderson

The King in Every Man: Evolutionary Trends in Onitsha Ibo Society and Culture (Yale Univ. Press)

1973

No award

1974

P. C. Lloyd

Power and Independence: Urban Africans' Perception of Social Inequality (Routledge)

1975

Simon Ottenberg

Masked Rituals of Afikpo: The Context of an African Art (Univ. of Washington Press)

1976

No award

1977

Polly Hill

Population, Prosperity and Poverty: Rural Kano, 1900 and 1970 (Cambridge Univ. Press)

1978

Thurstan Shaw

Nigeria: Its Archaeology and Early History (Thames)

The Translators Association

The three annual awards for translations described below are administered by the Translators Association, 84 Drayton Gardens, London SW10 9SD, England.

John Florio Prize

Established in 1963 under the auspices of the Italian Institute and the British-Italian Society, the John Florio Prize is awarded for the best translation into English of a twentieth-century Italian work of literary merit and general interest published in Great Britain during the preceding year. The prize, originally £200, was increased to £500 in 1976.

1963

Eric Mosbacher
Hekura: The Diving Girls' Island, by Fosco Maraini (Hamilton)

Donata Origo
The Deserter, by Giuseppe Dessi (Harvill)

1964

Angus Davidson
More Roman Tales, by Alberto Moravia (Secker)

H. S. Vere-Hodge
The Odes, by Dante Alighieri (Oxford Univ. Press)

E. R. Vincent
The Diary of One of Garibaldi's Thousand, by Giuseppe C. Abba (Oxford Univ. Press)

1965

W. C. Darwell
Dongo, the Last Act, by Pier Luigi Bellini delle Stelle and Urbano Lazzaro (Macdonald)

1966

Kenelm Foster and Jane Grigson
The Column of Infamy, by Alessandro Manzoni, prefaced by *Of Crimes and Punishments,* by Cesare Beccaria (Oxford Univ. Press)

Stuart Woolf
The Truce: A Survivor's Journey Home from Auschwitz, by Primo Levi (Bodley)

1967

Isabel Quigly
The Transfer, by Silvano Ceccherini (Eyre)

1968

Muriel Grindrod
The Popes in the Twentieth Century: From Pius X to John XXIII, by Carlo Falconi (Weidenfeld)

Raleigh Trevelyan
The Outlaws, by Luigi Meneghello (Michael Joseph)

1969

Sacha Rabinovitch
Francis Bacon: From Magic to Science, by Paolo Rossi (Routledge)

William Weaver
A Violent Life, by Pier Paolo Pasolini (Jonathan Cape)

1970

Angus Davidson
On Neoclassicism, by Mario Praz (Thames)

1971

William Weaver
The Heron, by Giorgio Bassani (Weidenfeld), and *Time and the Hunter,* by Italo Calvino (Jonathan Cape)

1972

Patrick Creagh
Selected Poems, by Giuseppe Ungaretti (Penguin)

1973

Bernard Wall
Wrestling with Christ, by Luigi Santucci (Collins)

1974

Stephen M. Hellman
Letters from Inside the Italian Communist Party, by Maria Antonietta Macciocchi (New Left Books)

1975
    Cormac O'Cuilleanain
    Cagliostro, by Roberto Gervaso (Gollancz)
1976
    Frances Frenaye
    The Forests of Norbio, by Giuseppe Dessi

1977
    Ruth Feldman and Brian Swann
    Shema: Collected Poems of Primo Levi, by Primo Levi (Menard)

Schlegel-Tieck Prize

This prize is offered annually for the best translation published in the United Kingdom by a British publisher of a twentieth-century German work of literary merit and general interest. The translator may be of any nationality. A panel of three judges is appointed annually to select the winner(s). The award, £500, is presented in the spring at the London Embassy of the Federal Republic of Germany.

1965
    Michael Bullock
    The Thirtieth Year, by Ingeborg Bachmann (Deutsch), and *Report on Bruno*, by Joseph Breitbach (Jonathan Cape)
1966
    Ralph Manheim
    Dog Years, by Günter Grass (Secker)
1967
    James Strachey
    Works of Sigmund Freud (Hogarth)
1968
    Henry Collins
    History of the International, by J. Braunthal (Thomas Nelson)
1969
    Leila Vennewitz
    The End of a Mission, by Heinrich Böll (Weidenfeld)
1970
    Eric Mosbacher
    Society without the Father, by Alexander Mitscherlich (Tavistock)
1971
    Ewald Osers
    The Scorched Earth, by Paul Carell (Harrap)

1972
    Richard Barry
    The Brutal Takeover, by Kurt von Schuschnigg (Weidenfeld)
1973
    Geoffrey Strachan
    Love and Hate, by Irenaus Eibl-Eibesfeldt (Methuen)
1974
    Geoffrey Skelton
    Frieda Lawrence, by Robert Lucas (Secker)
1975
    John Bowden
    Judaism and Hellenism, by Martin Hengel (SCM)
1976
    Marian Jackson (posthumous)
    War of Illusions, by Fritz Fischer (Chatto)
1977
    Charles Kessler
    Wallenstein: His Life Narrated, by Golo Mann (Deutsch)
    Ralph Manheim
    The Resistible Rise of Arturo Ui, by Bertolt Brecht (Eyre Methuen)

1978
Michael Hamburger
German Poetry, 1910–1975 (Carcanet New Press)

1979
Ralph Manheim
The Flounder, by Günter Grass (Secker)

Scott-Moncrieff Prize

This prize is awarded annually by a panel of three judges to the best translation of a twentieth-century French work of literary merit and general interest. Entries must be works published in the United Kingdom by a British publisher. The prize of £1,000 (£800 until 1978) is awarded at a reception at the French ambassador's residence in London.

1965
Edward Hyams
Joan of Arc, by Herself and Her Witnesses, by Régine Pernoud (Macdonald)
1966
Barbara Bray
Laurence Sterne: From Tristram to Yorick, by Henri Fluchère (Oxford Univ. Press)
1967
John Weightman and Doreen Weightman
Jean-Jacques Rousseau, by Jean Guéhenno (Routledge)
1968
Jean Stewart
French North Africa, by Jacques Berque (Faber)
1969
Terence Kilmartin
Antimemoirs, by André Malraux (Hamilton), and *The Girls*, 2 vols., by Henry de Montherlant (Weidenfeld)
1970
Richard Barry
The Suez Expedition, 1956, by André Beaufre (Faber)
William G. Corp
The Spaniard, by Bernard Clavel (Harrap)

Elaine P. Halperin
The Other Side of the Mountain, by Michel Bernanos (Gollancz)
1971
Maria Jolas
Between Life and Death, by Nathalie Sarraute (Calder)
Jean Stewart
Maltaverne, by François Mauriac (Eyre)

1972
Joanna Kilmartin
Sunlight on Cold Water, by Françoise Sagan (Weidenfeld)
Paul Stevenson
Germany in Our Time (Pall Mall)
Elizabeth Walter
A Scent of Lilies, by Claire Gallois (Collins)

1973
Barbara Bray
The Erl-King, by Michel Tournier (Collins)

1974
John Weightman and Doreen Weightman
Tristes Tropiques and *From Honey to Ashes*, by Claude Lévi-Strauss (Jonathan Cape)

1975
> Douglas Parmée
> *The Second World War*, by Henri Michel (Deutsch)
>
> Brian Pearce
> *Leninism under Lenin*, by Marcel Liebman (Jonathan Cape)

1976
> Peter Wait
> *French Society, 1789–1970*, by Georges Dupeux (Methuen)

1977
> David Hapgood
> *The Totalitarian Temptation*, by Jean François Revel (Secker)

> Janet Lloyd
> *The Gardens of Adonis: Spices in Greek Mythology*, by Marcel Detienne (Harvester)

1978
> Richard Mayne
> *Memoirs*, by Jean Monnet (Collins)
>
> John Weightman and Doreen Weightman
> *Introduction to a Science of Mythology, Vol. 3: The Origin of Table Manners*, by Claude Lévi-Strauss (Jonathan Cape)

Welsh Arts Council

Awards to Writers

Since 1968 the Welsh Arts Council has given awards to authors whose books are of exceptional literary merit or which make an important contribution to the literature of Wales. The prize is awarded to recognize achievement, to draw attention to writers of promise, and to encourage the writing of creative literature in English and Welsh. The cash prizes of £300–£500 are presented annually in March. Two major prizes (Honours) are also given annually to Welsh or Anglo-Welsh writers who have made distinguished contributions over the years. Further inquiries should be sent to the Welsh Arts Council (Cyngor Celfyddydau Cymru), Museum Place, Cardiff CF1 3NX, Wales.

1969
> Pennar Davies
> *Meibion Darogan* (Llyfrau'r Dryw)
>
> Raymond Garlick
> *A Sense of Europe* (Gomerian)
>
> Glyn Jones
> *The Dragon Has Two Tongues* (Dent)
>
> Gwilym R. Jones
> *Cerddi*

1970
> Marion Eames
> *Y Stafell Ddirgel* (Llyfrau'r Dryw)

> Tudor Wilson Evans
> *Iwan Tudur* (Cyhoeddiadau Modern Cymreig)
>
> John Gwyn Griffiths
> *Cerddi Cairo* (Y Lolfa)
>
> John Ormond
> *Requiem and Celebration* (Davies)
>
> Sally Roberts
> *Turning Away* (Gwasg Gomer)
>
> Harri Webb
> *The Green Desert: Collected Poems, 1950–1969* (Gwasg Gomer)

Gwynne Williams
Rhwng Gewyn ac Asgwrn (Llyfrau'r Dryw)

1971

Dannie Abse
Selected Poems (Hutchinson)

Euros Bowen
Achlysuron (Gwasg Gomer)

Joseph Clancy
The Earliest Welsh Poetry (Macmillan)

David Tecwyn Lloyd
Safle'r Gerbydres, ac Ysgrifau Eraill (Gwasg Gomer)

Derec Llwyd Morgan
Pryderi (Gwasg Gomer)

John Stuart Williams
Dic Penderyn and Other Poems (Gwasg Gomer)

1972

Pennar Davies
Y Tlws yn y Lotws (Llyfrau'r Dryw)

Emyr Humphreys
National Winner (MacDonald & Co.)

Bobi Jones
Allor Wydn (Llyfrau'r Dryw)

Richard Jones
The Tower Is Everywhere (Macmillan)

David Tecwyn Lloyd
Lady Gwladys a Phobl Eraill

Roland Mathias
Absalom in the Tree, and Other Poems (Gwasg Gomer)

1973

Raymond Garlick
A Sense of Time: Poems and Anti-poems, 1969–1972 (Gwasg Gomer)

Harri Pritchard Jones
Dychwelyd (Gwasg Gomer)

Alison Morgan
Pete (Chatto)

Gerallt Lloyd Owen
Cerddi'r Cywilydd

Iorwerth Peate
Tradition and Folk Life: A Welsh View (Faber)

Kate Roberts
Gobaith a Storïau Eraill (Gwasg Gee)

Gwyn Thomas
Enw'r Gair (Gwasg Gee)

Ronald S. Thomas
H'm: Poems (Macmillan)

R. Bryn Williams
O'r Tir Pell

1974

David Jenkins
Thomas Gwynn Jones: Cofiant (Gwasg Gee)

John Ormond
Definition of a Waterfall (Oxford Univ. Press)

Alun Richards
Dai Country: Short Stories (Joseph)

1975

J. Eirian Davies
Cân Galed (Gwasg Gomer)

Thomas Glynne Davies
Marged (Gwasg Gomer)

Jeremy Hooker
Soliloquies of a Chalk Giant

Emyr Humphreys
Flesh and Blood (Hodder)

Leslie Norris
Mountains, Polecats, Pheasants and Other Elegies (Chatto)

Peter Tinniswood
Except You're a Bird (Hodder)

John G. Williams
Maes Mihangel (Gwasg Gee)

1976

Ruth Bidgood
Not without Homage (Davies)

J. M. Edwards
Cerddi Ddoe a Heddiw (Gwasg Gee)

Gwilym R. Jones
Y Syrcas a Cerddi Eraill (Llyfrau'r Faner)

Alan Llwyd
Edrych trwy Wydrau Lledrith

Alun Llywelyn-Williams
Gwanwyn yn y Ddinas: Darn o Hun-angofiant (Gwasg Gee)

Kenneth Morgan
Keir Hardie: Radical and Socialist (Weidenfeld)

Marged Pritchard
Gwylanod yn y Mynydd

Bernice Rubens
I Sent a Letter to My Love (W. H. Allen)

R. S. Thomas
Laboratories of the Spirit (Macmillan)

1977

Jane Edwards
Dros Fryniau Bro Afallon (Gwasg Gomer)

Donald Evans
Egin (Gwasg Gomer)

Raymond Garlick
Incense: Poems, 1972–1975 (Gwasg Gomer)

Owain Owain
Mical, 1780–1849: Cofiant Dych-mygus (Gwasg Gomer)

R. J. Rowlands
Cerddi R. J. Rowlands y Bala

Gwyn Thomas
Cadwynau yn y Meddwl (Gwasg Gee)

Gwyn A. Williams
Goya and the Impossible Revolution (Lane)

1978

Aled Islwyn
Lleuwen (Llyfrau'r Faner)

Jane Edwards
Miriam (Gwasg Gomer)

Alice Thomas Ellis
The Sin Eater (Duckworth)

Dyfed Evans
Bywyd Bob Owen (Gwasg Gwynedd)

Stuart Evans
The Caves of Alienation (Hutchinson)

Paul Ferris
Dylan Thomas (Hodder)

Rhiannon Davies Jones
Llys Aberffraw (Gwasg Gomer)

Gwyn Thomas
Y Traddodiad Barddol (Gwasg Prifysgol Cymru)

1979

Gillian Clarke
The Sundial (Gomer)

Marion Eames
I Hela Cnau (Gwasg Gomer)

James Hanley
A Kingdom (Deutsch)

Emyr Humphreys
The Best of Friends (Hodder)

Dic Jones
Storom Awst: Trydedd Cyfrol o Gerddi Dic Jones (Gwasg Gomer)

Tristan Jones
The Incredible Voyage: A Personal Odyssey (Bodley)

Leslie Norris
Sliding: Short Stories (Dent)

John Rowlands
Tician, Tician

Gwyn A. Williams
The Merthyr Rising (Croom Helm)

J. G. Williams
Betws Hirfaen (Gwasg Gee)

HONOURS

1968
Kate Roberts
R. S. Thomas

1969
David Jones
Waldo Williams

1970
Jack Jones
Saunders Lewis

HONOURS (cont.)

1971
   Rhys Davies
   T. H. Parry-Williams
1972
   Glyn Jones
   John Gwilym Jones
1973
   Aneirin Talfan Davies
   Gwyn Jones
1974
   Euros Bowen
   Richard Hughes

1975
   No awards
1976
   T. J. Morgan
   Gwyn Thomas
1977
   Iorwerth Peate
   Gwyn Williams
1978 –1979
   No awards

International Writer's Prize

The Welsh Arts Council (Cyngor Celfyddydau Cymru), Museum Place, Cardiff CF1 3NX, Wales, established the International Writer's Prize in 1974 to recognize international achievement in literature. The £1,000 prize is awarded biennially.

1974
   Eugene Ionesco, French playwright
1976
   Friedrich Dürrenmatt, Swiss author and playwright
1978
   Astrid Lindgren, Swedish author of children's books

1980
   Derek Walcott, Trinidadian poet and playwright

Whitbread Literary Awards

Whitbread & Company, Ltd., Brewers, offers annual awards of £1,500 each for outstanding books in several categories. The awards are administered by the Booksellers Association, 154 Buckingham Palace Road, London SW1W 9TZ, England. Authors domiciled for at least five years in the United Kingdom or Ireland who have published a book in the previous twelve months are eligible. Works to be considered eligible must be in book form, published no later than November 3, and may be submitted only by the publishers. Page proofs for books published after September 1 are acceptable only with prior permission from the Booksellers Association. The recipients are chosen by a panel of judges appointed by the donors and the administrators, and presentation is made annually at The Brewery, Chiswell Street, London EC1.

FICTION

1971
   Gerda Charles
   The Destiny Waltz (Scribner)
1972
   Susan Hill
   The Bird of Night (Saturday Review)
1973
   Shiva Naipaul
   The Chip Chip Gatherers (Knopf)
1974
   Iris Murdoch
   The Sacred and Profane Love Machine (Viking)
1975
   William McIlvanney
   Docherty (G. Allen)
1976
   William Trevor
   The Children of Dynmouth (Bodley)
1977
   Beryl Bainbridge
   Injury Time (Duckworth)
1978
   Paul Theroux
   Picture Palace (Hamilton)

BEST FIRST BOOK

1974
   Clair Tomalin
   The Life and Death of Mary Wollstonecraft (Harcourt)
1975
   Ruth Spalding
   The Improbable Puritan: A Life of Bulstrode Whitelocke (Faber)
Discontinued

CHILDREN'S BOOK

1972
   Rumer Godden
   The Diddakoi (Viking)

1973
   Alan Aldridge and William Plomer
   The Butterfly Ball and the Grasshopper's Feast (Jonathan Cape)
1974
   Russell Hoban and Quentin Blake
   How Tom Beat Captain Najork and His Hired Sportsmen (Jonathan Cape)
   Jill Paton Walsh
   The Emperor's Winding Sheet (Macmillan)
1976
   Penelope Lively
   A Stitch in Time (Heinemann)
1977
   Shelagh Macdonald
   No End to Yesterday (Deutsch)
1978
   Philippa Pearce
   The Battle of Bubble and Squeak (Deutsch)

BIOGRAPHY/AUTOBIOGRAPHY

1971
   Michael Meyer
   Henrik Ibsen (Doubleday)
1972
   James Pope-Hennessy
   Trollope (Little)
1973
   John Wilson
   C.B.: A Life of Sir Henry Campbell-Bannerman (St. Martin's)
1974
   Andrew Boyle
   Poor Dear Brendan (Hutchinson)
1975
   Helen Corke
   In Our Infancy: An Autobiography, 1882-1912 (Cambridge Univ. Press)
1976
   Winifred Gérin
   Elizabeth Gaskell (Clarendon)

BIOGRAPHY/AUTOBIOGRAPHY
(cont.)

1977
  Nigel Nicholson
  Mary Curzon (Weidenfeld)

1978
  John Grigg
  Lloyd George: The People's Champion, 1902-1911 (Eyre Methuen)

Wolfson History Awards

These awards were established in 1972 to honor authors of published works in history. A first prize of £5,000 is given in recognition of the author's published body of work, culminating with the particular work for which the award is given. A second prize of £3,000 is also presented. The awards, sponsored by the Wolfson Foundation, are presented annually in November. For information write to M. D. Paisner, Paisner and Company, Bouverie House, 154 Fleet Street, London EC4A 2DQ, England.

1972
  Michael Howard (First)
  Keith Thomas (Second)
1973
  Frances A. Yates (First)
  W. L. Warren (Second)
1974
  M. I. Finley (First)
  Theodore Zeldin (Second)
1975
  Frances Donaldson (First)
  Olwen Hofton (Second)

1976
  Nikolaus Pevsner (First)
  Norman Stone (Second)
1977
  Denis Mack Smith (First)
  Simon Schama (Second)
1978
  H. M. Colvin (First)
  Alistair Horne (Second)

Yorkshire Arts Association Awards

These awards were established in 1973 as a means of stimulating public interest in Yorkshire authors and books about the region. They are offered biennially for books published in Britain during the previous two years that have strong literary connections with Yorkshire. In 1979, prizes totaling £2,000 were awarded: Premier Award, £700; two Established Writers Awards, £450 each; Best First Novel Award, £200; and Judges' Special Award, £200. The awards are usually presented during the Ilkley Literature Festival. Inquiries should be sent to the Director, Yorkshire Arts Association, Glyde Ho, Glydegate, Bradford BD5 OBQ, West Yorkshire, England.

1975
  Philip Larkin
  High Windows (Faber)

  Pamela Haines
  Tea at Gunter's (Heinemann)

Nick Toczek
Book of Numbers (Aquila)
1977
Lynne Reid Banks
Dark Quartet (Weidenfeld)
Barry Collins
Judgement (Faber)
David Brett
Black Folder (Harrap)
Glenda George
Slit Here (Pressed Curtains)
Ted Burford
Cranefly Incident (Ealing)
1979
R. C. Scriven
Edge of Darkness, Edge of Light
(Souvenir) Premier Award

Elizabeth North
Everything in the Garden (Gollancz)
Established Writers Award
Elizabeth Gunn
Ella's Dream (Hamilton) Established
Writers Award
Brian Thompson
Buddy Boy (Gollancz) Best First Novel Award
George Moor
Fox Gold (Calder) Judges' Special Award

Yorkshire Post

Yorkshire Post Newspapers Ltd., Box 168, Wellington Street, Leeds LS1 1RF, England, offers the following awards for best books in various categories. Prize money is donated by patrons and subscribers to the *Yorkshire Post* literary luncheons, and in the case of the Art and Music Awards, also by some leading Yorkshire-based companies. Requests for information should be addressed to Richard Douro, Yorkshire Post Newspapers.

Art and Music Awards

In 1973, the *Yorkshire Post* established two new awards to reward those authors whose works, in the opinion of the judges, have made the greatest contribution to the understanding and appreciation of art and music. The awards, presented at a *Yorkshire Post* literary luncheon, consist of £275 and a scroll for the winner in each category.

1975
Hans Hess (award made posthumously to his widow)
George Grosz (Studio Vista) Art
Hans Gal
Franz Schubert and the Essence of Melody (Gollancz) Music

1976–1977
Winners unavailable
1978
Frank Whitford
Japanese Prints and Western Painters (Studio Vista) Art

Michael Evans
Janacek's Tragic Operas. Music
1979
Winner of Art Award unavailable

Julian Budden
The Operas of Verdi, Vol. 2 (Cassell)
Music

Book of the Year Awards

The *Yorkshire Post* offers two annual awards for the best books of the year in fiction and nonfiction. A first prize of £400 and a runner-up prize of £250 are presented each year in January. If the first prize goes to a nonfiction work, the runner-up goes to a work of fiction, and vice versa. In addition, the *Yorkshire Post* offers a first prize of £300 and a runner-up prize of £200 for the best first work by a new author published in the previous year.

BOOK OF THE YEAR

1965
George Malcolm Thomson
The Twelve Days (Hutchinson) First prize
Elizabeth Berridge
Across the Common (Heinemann) Runner-up

1966
Frederick W. F. Smith [Earl of Birkenhead]
Halifax (Hamilton) First Prize
Muriel Spark
The Mandelbaum Gate (Macmillan) Finest fiction

1967
Rebecca West
The Birds Fall Down (Macmillan) First prize
Robert Blake
Disraeli (Eyre & Spottiswoode) Runner-up

1968
Harold Nicolson
Diaries and Letters, 1939–1945 (Collins) First prize
Laurens van der Post
The Hunter and the Whale (Hogarth) Finest fiction

1969
Michael Holroyd
Lytton Strachey (Heinemann) First prize
P. H. Newby
Something to Answer For (Faber) Finest fiction

1970
Elizabeth Longford
Wellington, the Years of the Sword (Weidenfeld) First prize
Iris Murdoch
Bruno's Dream (Chatto & Windus) Finest fiction

1971
Angus Wilson
The World of Charles Dickens (Secker) First prize
Edna O'Brien
A Pagan Place (Faber) Finest fiction

1972
Richard Austen Butler
The Art of the Possible (Hamilton) First prize
Paul Scott
The Towers of Silence (Heinemann) Finest fiction

BOOK OF THE YEAR (cont.)

1973
Quentin Bell
Virginia Woolf, Vols. 1-2 (Hogarth)
First prize
Margaret Drabble
The Needle's Eye (Weidenfeld) Finest
fiction
1974
David Cecil
The Cecils of Hatfield House (Constable) First prize
Evelyn Anthony
The Occupying Power (Hutchinson)
Finest fiction
1975
Philip Mason
A Matter of Honour (Cape) First prize
Kingsley Amis
Ending Up (Cape) Finest fiction
Elizabeth Longford (Special award)
For *The Royal House of Windsor*
(Weidenfeld) and *Churchill* (Sidgewick & Jackson), and for her outstanding services to literature as an
author and biographer during the past
ten years
1976
Paul Johnson
Pope John XXIII (Little) First prize
David Lodge
Changing Places (Secker) Finest fiction
1977
Winners unavailable
1978
Alistair Horne
*A Savage War of Peace: Algeria,
1954-1962* (Macmillan) First prize
Olivia Manning
The Danger Tree (Weidenfeld) Finest
fiction
1979
Gavin Kennedy
Bligh (Duckworth) First prize

Siân James
Yesterday (Collins) Finest fiction

BEST FIRST BOOK

1966
Terry Coleman
The Railway Navvies (Hutchinson)
1967
Archie Hind
The Dear Green Place (Nelson Foster
& Scott)
1968
Catherine Dupré
The Chickencoop (Collins)
1969
J. J. Scarisbrick
Henry VIII (Eyre & Spottiswoode)
Sally Trench
Bury Me in My Boots (Hodder) Runner-up
1970
Spike Mays
Reuben's Corner (Eyre & Spottiswoode)
Eithne Wilkins
The Rose-Garden Game (Gollancz)
Runner-up
1971
Patrick Davis
A Child at Arms (Hutchinson)
John M. Carter
The Battle of Actium (Hamilton) Runner-up
1972
James Douglas-Hamilton
Motive for a Mission (Macmilian)
Stewart Edwards
The Paris Commune, 1871 (Eyre
Methuen) Runner-up
1973
Jennifer Johnston
The Captains and the Kings (Hamilton)

BEST FIRST BOOK (cont.)

Michael Davie
In the Future Now (Hamilton) Runner-up
1974
Robin Lane Fox
Alexander the Great (Allen Lane)
Arianna Stassinopoulos
The Female Woman (Davis-Poynter)
1975
Anne Redmon
Emily Stone (Secker)
John MacKinnon
In Search of the Red Ape (Collins)
1976
Iain Douglas-Hamilton and Oria Douglas-Hamilton
Among the Elephants (Harvill) First prize
Siân James
One Afternoon (Davies) Runner-up
Jonathan Sumption
Pilgrimage: An Image of Mediaeval Religion (Faber) Special award

1977
Winners unavailable

1978
Max Egremont
The Cousins: The Friendship, Opinions and Activities of Wilfred S. Blunt and George Wyndham (Collins) First prize
John Campbell
Lloyd George: The Goat in the Wilderness, 1922–1931 (Cape) Runner-up

1979
Edna Healey
Lady Unknown: The Life of Angela Burdett-Coutts (Sidgwick) First prize
Jane Dunn
Moon in Eclipse: A Life of Mary Shelley (Weidenfeld) Runner-up
Lord Hailsham [Quintin Hogg Hailsham]
The Case for Conservatism, The Door Wherein I Went (Collins), and *The Dilemma of Democracy* (Collins) Special award

Canadian Prizes

Canadian Prizes

Canada Council

The Canada Council, 255 Albert Street, Box 1047, Ottawa, Ontario K1P 5V8, Canada, administers or finances the following six prizes.

Canada-Australia Literary Prize

Cosponsored by the governments of Canada and Australia, the $2,500 Canada-Australia Literary Prize is awarded in alternate years to an English-language Canadian or Australian writer. The award is made on the basis of a writer's complete works. Canadian participation is financed by the Department of External Affairs, and the prize is administered by the Canada Council.

1976
John Romeril, Australian playwright
1977
Alice Munro, Canadian writer

1978
Thomas Shapcott, Australian poet

Canada-Belgium Literary Prize

Cosponsored by the governments of Canada and Belgium, the Canada-Belgium Literary Prize is awarded annually in alternate years to a French-language Belgian or Canadian writer. Canadian participation is financed by the Department of External Affairs, and the prize is administered by the Canada Council. The award is made on the basis of the complete works of a writer, who receives a $2,500 prize.

1971
Géo Norge, Belgian poet
1972
Gaston Miron, Canadian poet
1973
Suzanne Lilar, Belgian author
1974
Réjean Ducharme, Canadian novelist
1975
Pierre Mertens, Belgian writer

1976
Marie-Claire Blais, Canadian novelist and playwright
1977
Marcel Moreau, Belgian novelist
1978
Jacques Godbout, Canadian author

Canada Council Translation Prizes

Instituted in 1974, the Translation Prizes of the Canada Council are awarded in recognition of the increasingly important role played by this discipline in communications, arts, and culture in Canada. The Council annually awards the prizes to the two works (one in English and one in French) that are judged to be the best of the translations published in the preceding year. With the exception of school texts and manuals, books in all categories are eligible, providing that they have been written and translated by Canadians or by landed immigrants with at least twelve months' residence in Canada.

1974
  Alan Brown
  The Antiphonary, by Hubert Aquin (Anansi)
  Jean Paré
  Docteur Bethune, by Ted Allan and Sydney Gordon
1975
  Sheila Fischman
  They Won't Demolish Me, by Roch Carrier (Anansi)
  Michelle Tisseyre
  Telle Est Ma Bien-Aimée and L'Hiver, by Morley Callaghan (Cercle du Livre de France), and *Les Saisons de l'Eskimo*, by Fred Bruemmer
1976
  John Glassco
  Complete Poems of Saint-Denys Garneau (Oberon)
  Jean Simard
  Mon Père, Ce Héros, by Mordecai Richler

1977
  Joyce Marshall
  Enchanted Summer, by Gabrielle Roy (McClelland & Stewart)
  No award for translation from English to French
1978
  Jean Paré
  Un Homme de Week-End, by Richard B. Wright
  Frank Scott
  Poems of French Canada, 3 vols., by 11 Quebec poets (Blackfish)
1979
  Michael Bullock
  Stories for Late Night Drinkers, by Michel Tremblay (Intermedia)
  Gilles Hénault
  Sans Parachute, by David Fennario

Children's Literature Prizes

Two prizes in children's literature, one for an English-language work and one for a French-language work, were established by the Canada Council in 1975. These prizes, worth $5,000 each, are awarded annually to a writer or illustrator. A single prize may be shared by a writer and an illustrator of the same or different books. All Canadian books intended for young people are eligible, whether published in Canada or abroad.

1976

Louise Aylwin
Raminagradu (Editions du Jour)

Bill Freeman
Shantymen of Cache Lake (Lorimer)

1977

Myra Paperny
The Wooden People, illus. by Ken Strampnick (Little)

Bernadette Renaud
Emilie, la Baignoire à Pattes, illus. by France Bédard (Editions Héritage)

1978

Denise Houle
Lune de Neige (Maheux)

Claude Lafortune, illustrator
L'Evangile en Papier, by Henriette Major (Editions Fides)

Jean Little
Listen for the Singing (Dutton/Clarke, Irwin)

1979

Ginette Anfousse
La Varicelle and *La Chicane* (Courte Echelle)

Ann Blades, illustrator
A Salmon for Simon, by Betty Waterton (Douglas & McIntyre)

Kevin Major
Hold Fast (Clarke, Irwin)

Governor General's Literary Awards

The Governor General's Literary Awards were instituted in 1937 by the Canadian Authors Association and were named with the agreement of the Governor General of Canada, Lord Tweedsmuir, widely known as John Buchan, novelist and historian. Originally, the awards were only for works in English. In 1944, the Canadian Authors Association created the Governor General's Awards Board to supervise the selection process. In 1954, the Board became an autonomous self-perpetuating body of five members appointed for a three-year term. In 1959, at the request of the Awards Board, the Canada Council agreed to finance the administration of the awards and to provide a cash prize of $1,000 to each winner. The rules were amended to provide for six prizes each year, three for works in English and three for works in French, published in Canada during the preceding year. The Awards Board was reorganized into a bilingual Awards Committee divided into two three-member juries, one for each language.

In 1965, the Canada Council increased the cash prize to $2,500 for each winner. In 1972, the Selection Committee was reorganized and expanded to eighteen people. The reading task of the nine-person jury for each language was divided among three subcommittees—one for Fiction, Nonfiction, and Poetry and Drama. Since 1973, each winner receives $5,000 and a specially bound copy of his or her book. The awards are usually announced in April.

1937

Bertram Brooker
Think of the Earth (Thomas Nelson)

T. B. Roberton
T.B.R.—Newspaper Pieces (Macmillan)

1938

Stephen Leacock
My Discovery of the West (Hale)

E. J. Pratt
The Fable of the Goats (Macmillan)

Laura G. Salverson
The Dark Weaver (Ryerson)

1939

John Murray Gibbon
Canadian Mosaic (Dodd)

Gwethalyn Graham
Swiss Sonata (Thomas Nelson)

Kenneth Leslie
By Stubborn Stars (Humphries)

1940

Arthur S. Bourinot
Under the Sun (Macmillan)

Franklin D. McDowell
The Champlain Road (Macmillan)

Laura G. Salverson
Confessions of an Immigrant's Daughter (Ryerson)

1941

E. J. Pratt
Brébeuf and His Brethren (Macmillan)

Ringuet [Philippe Panneton]
Thirty Acres (Macmillan)

J. F. C. Wright
Slava Bohu (Thomas Nelson)

1942

Emily Carr
Klee Wyck (Farrar)

Anne Marriott
Calling Adventurers (Ryerson)

Alan Sullivan
Three Came to Ville Marie (Coward)

1943

Earle Birney
David and Other Poems (Ryerson)

Bruce Hutchison
The Unknown Country (Coward)

Edgar McInnes
The Unguarded Frontier (Doubleday)

G. Herbert Sallans
Little Man (Humphries)

1944

E. K. Brown
On Canadian Poetry (Ryerson)

Thomas H. Raddall
The Pied Piper of Dipper Creek (McClelland & Stewart)

John D. Robins
The Incomplete Anglers (Duell)

A. J. M. Smith
News of the Phoenix (Coward)

1945

Dorothy Duncan
Partner in Three Worlds (Harper)

Gwethalyn Graham
Earth and High Heaven (Lippincott)

Dorothy Livesay
Day and Night (Ryerson)

Edgar McInnes
The War: Fourth Year (Oxford Univ. Press)

1946

Earle Birney
Now Is Time (Ryerson)

Hugh MacLennan
Two Solitudes (Duell)

Ross Munro
Gauntlet to Overlord (Macmillan)

Evelyn M. Richardson
We Keep a Light (Ryerson)

1947

Winifred Bambrick
Continental Revue (Ryerson)

Robert Finch
Poems (Oxford Univ. Press)

Frederick Philip Grove
In Search of Myself (Macmillan)

A. R. M. Lower
Colony to Nation (Longmans)

1948

R. MacGregor Dawson
The Government of Canada (Univ. of Toronto Press)

Dorothy Livesay
Poems for People (Ryerson)

Gabrielle Roy
The Tin Flute (Harcourt)

William Sclater
Haida (Oxford Univ. Press)

1949

A. M. Klein
The Rocking Chair and Other Poems
(Ryerson)

Hugh MacLennan
The Precipice (Duell)

Thomas H. Raddall
Halifax, Warden of the North (McClelland & Stewart)

C. P. Stacey
The Canadian Army, 1939–1945
(King's Printer)

1950

Philip Child
Mr. Ames against Time (Ryerson)

R. MacGregor Dawson
Democratic Government in Canada
(Univ. of Toronto Press)

R. S. Lambert
Franklin of the Arctic (McClelland & Stewart)

Hugh MacLennan
Cross-Country (Collins)

James Reaney
The Red Heart (McClelland & Stewart)

1951

Marjorie Wilkins Campbell
The Saskatchewan (Rinehart)

Donalda Dickie
The Great Adventure (Dent)

Germaine Guèvremont
The Outlander (McGraw)

W. L. Morton
The Progressive Party in Canada
(Univ. of Toronto Press)

James Wreford Watson
Of Time and the Lover (McClelland & Stewart)

1952

Charles Bruce
The Mulgrave Road (Macmillan)

Morley Callaghan
The Loved and the Lost (Macmillan)

John F. Hayes
A Land Divided (Copp)

Frank MacKinnon
The Government of Prince Edward Island (Univ. of Toronto Press)

Josephine Phelan
The Ardent Exile (Macmillan)

1953

Donald G. Creighton
John A. Macdonald, the Young Politician (Macmillan)

Bruce Hutchison
The Incredible Canadian (Longmans)

Marie McPhedran
Cargoes on the Great Lakes (Bobbs)

E. J. Pratt
Towards the Last Spike (Macmillan)

David Walker
The Pillar (Houghton)

1954

N. J. Berrill
Sex and the Nature of Things (Dodd)

J. M. S. Careless
Canada, A Story of Challenge (Macmillan)

John F. Hayes
Rebels Ride at Night (Copp)

Douglas Le Pan
The Net and the Sword (Clarke, Irwin)

David Walker
Digby (Houghton)

1955

Marjorie Wilkins Campbell
The Nor'westers (Macmillan)

Igor Gouzenko
The Fall of a Titan (Norton)

A. R. M. Lower
The Most Famous Stream (Ryerson)

Hugh MacLennan
Thirty and Three (Macmillan)

P. K. Page
The Metal and the Flower (McClelland & Stewart)

1956

N. J. Berrill
Man's Emerging Mind (Dodd)

Donald G. Creighton
John A. Macdonald, the Old Chieftain (Houghton)

Lionel Shapiro
The Sixth of June (Doubleday)

Wilfred Watson
Friday's Child (Faber)

Kerry Wood
The Map-Maker (Macmillan)

1957

Pierre Berton
The Mysterious North (Knopf)

Robert A. D. Ford
A Window on the North (Ryerson)

Farley Mowat
Lost in the Barrens (Little)

Joseph Lister Rutledge
Century of Conflict (Doubleday)

Adele Wiseman
The Sacrifice (Viking)

1958

Bruce Hutchison
Canada: Tomorrow's Giant (Knopf)

Jay Macpherson
The Boatman (Oxford Univ. Press)

Thomas H. Raddall
The Path of Destiny (Doubleday)

Gabrielle Roy
Street of Riches (Harcourt)

Kerry Wood
The Great Chief (St. Martin's)

1959

Pierre Berton
Klondike (Knopf)

Joyce Hemlow
The History of Fanny Burney (Oxford Univ. Press)

Colin McDougall
Execution (St. Martin's)

James Reaney
A Suit of Nettles (St. Martin's)

Edith Lambert Sharp
Nkwala (Little)

1960

André Giroux
Malgré Tout, la Joie (Institut Litéraire du Québec)

Irving Layton
Red Carpet for the Sun (McClelland & Stewart)

Hugh MacLennan
The Watch That Ends the Night (Scribner)

Félix-Antoine Savard
Le Barachois (Editions Fides)

1961

Margaret Avison
Winter Sun (Univ. of Toronto Press)

Anne Hébert
Poèmes (Editions du Seuil)

Brian Moore
The Luck of Ginger Coffey (Little)

Paul Toupin
Souvenirs pour Demain (Cercle du Livre de France)

Frank Underhill
In Search of Canadian Liberalism (St. Martin's)

1962

Robert Finch
Acis in Oxford (Univ. of Toronto Press)

T. A. Goudge
The Ascent of Life (Univ. of Toronto Press)

Jean Le Moyne
Convergences (HMH)

Malcolm Lowry
Hear Us O Lord from Heaven Thy Dwelling Place (Lippincott)

Yves Thériault
Ashini (Fides)

1963

Kildare Dobbs
Running to Paradise (Oxford Univ. Press)

Jacques Ferron
Contes du Pays Incertain (Orphée)

Jacques Languirand
Les Insolites et les Violons de l'Automne (Cercle du Livre de France)

Marshall McLuhan
The Gutenberg Galaxy (Univ. of Toronto Press)

Gilles Marcotte
Une Littérature qui se Fait (HMH)

James Reaney
Twelve Letters to a Small Town (Ryerson) and *The Killdeer and Other Plays* (Macmillan)

1964

J. M. S. Careless
Brown of the Globe (St. Martin's)

Hugh Garner
Hugh Garner's Best Stories (Ryerson)

Gustave Lanctot
Histoire du Canada (Beauchemin)

Gatien Lapointe
Ode au Saint-Laurent (Editions du Jour)

1965

Phyliss Grosskurth
John Addington Symonds (Longmans)

Douglas Le Pan
The Deserter (McClelland & Stewart)

Pierre Perrault
Au Coeur de la Rose (Beauchemin)

Jean-Paul Pinsonneault
Les Terres Sèches (Beauchemin)

Réjean Robidoux
Roger Martin du Gard et la Religion (Aubier)

Raymond Souster
The Colour of the Times (Ryerson)

1966

Gérard Bessette
L'Incubation (Déom)

James Eayrs
In Defence of Canada (Univ. of Toronto Press)

Alfred Purdy
The Cariboo Horses (McClelland & Stewart)

André S. Vachon
Le Temps et l'Espace dans l'Oeuvre de Paul Claudel (Editions du Seuil)

Gilles Vigneault
Quand les Bateaux s'en Vont (Arc)

1967

Margaret Atwood
The Circle Game (Contact)

Réjean Ducharme
L'Avalée des Avalés (Gallimard)

Margaret Laurence
A Jest of God (McClelland & Stewart)

Claire Martin
La Joue Droite (Cercle du Livre de France)

Marcel Trudel
Le Comptoir, 1604–1627 (2nd vol. of his *Histoire de la Nouvelle France*) (Fides)

George Woodcock
The Crystal Spirit: A Study of George Orwell (Little)

1968

Jacques Godbout
Salut Galarneau (Editions du Seuil)

Françoise Loranger
Encore Cinq Minutes (Cercle du Livre de France)

Eli Mandel
An Idiot Joy (Hurtig)

Alden Nowlan
Bread, Wine and Salt (Clarke, Irwin)

Robert-Lionel Séguin
La Civilisation Traditionnelle de l' "Habitant" aux XVIIe et XVIIIe Siècles (Editions Fides)

Norah Story
The Oxford Companion to Canadian History and Literature (Oxford Univ. Press)

1969

Marie-Claire Blais
Manuscrits de Pauline Archange (Editions du Jour)

Fernand Dumont
Le Lieu de l'Homme (HMH)

Alice Munro
Dance of the Happy Shades (Ryerson)

Mordecai Richler
Cocksure and Hunting Tigers under Glass (McClelland & Stewart)

1970

George Bowering
Rocky Mountain Foot (McClelland & Stewart) and *The Gangs of Kosmos* (Anansi)

Michel Brunet
Les Canadiens après la Conquête (Editions Fides)

Robert Kroetsch
The Studhorse Man (Macmillan)

Gwendolyn MacEwen
The Shadow-Maker (Macmillan)

Louis Maheux-Forcier
Une Forêt pour Zoé (Cercle du Livre de France)

Jean-Guy Pilon
Comme Eau Retenue (Hexagone)

1971

Monique Bosco
La Femme de Loth (HMH)

Jacques Brault
Quand Nous Serons Heureux (Ecrits du Canada Français)

Dave Godfrey
The New Ancestors (New Press)

B. P. Nichol
Still Water (Talonbooks); *The True Eventual Story of Billy the Kid* (Weed/Flower Press); *Beach Head* (Runcible Spoon Press); and *The Cosmic Chef: An Evening of Concrete* (Oberon)

Michael Ondaatje
The Collected Works of Billy the Kid (Anansi)

1972

Pierre Berton
The Last Spike (McClelland & Stewart)

Gérard Bessette
Le Cycle (Editions du Jour)

Gérald Fortin
La Fin d'un Règne (Editions Hurtubise HMH)

John Glassco
Selected Poems (Oxford Univ. Press)

Paul-Marie Lapointe
Le Réel Absolu (Hexagone)

Mordecai Richler
St. Urbain's Horseman (McClelland & Stewart)

1973

Robertson Davies
The Manticore (Macmillan)

Jean Hamelin and Yves Roby
Histoire Économique du Québec 1851–1896 (Editions Fides)

Gilles Hénault
Signaux pour les Voyants (Hexagone)

Dennis Lee
Civil Elegies and Other Poems (Anansi)

Antonine Maillet
Don l'Orignal (Leméac)

John Newlove
Lies (McClelland & Stewart)

1974

Victor-Lévy Beaulieu
Don Quichotte de la Démanche (Editions de l'Aurore)

Nicole Brossard
Mécanique Jongleuse suivi de Masculin Grammaticale (Hexagone)

Louise Dechêne
*Habitants et Marchands de Montreal au XVII*e *Siècle* (Plon)

Ralph Gustafson
Fire on Stone (McClelland & Stewart)

Margaret Laurence
The Diviners (McClelland & Stewart)

Charles Ritchie
The Siren Years (Macmillan)

1975

Milton Acorn
The Island Means Minago (NC Press)

Louis-Emond Hamelin
Nordicité Canadienne (Hurtubise)

Anne Hébert
Les Enfants du Sabbat (Editions du Seuil)

Marion MacRae and Anthony Adamson
Hallowed Walls (Clarke, Irwin)

Brian Moore
The Great Victorian Collection (McClelland & Stewart)

Pierre Perrault
Chouennes (Hexagone)

1976

Carl Berger
The Writing of Canadian History (Oxford Univ. Press)

Marian Engel
Bear (McClelland & Stewart)

André Major
Les Rescapés (Editions Quinze)

Fernand Ouellet
Le Bas Canada, 1791–1840: Changements Structuraux et Crise (Editions de l'Univ. d'Ottawa)

Alphonse Piché
Poèmes, 1946–1968 (Hexagone)

Joe Rosenblatt
Top Soil (Porcepic)

1977

Timothy Findley
The Wars (Clarke, Irwin)

Michel Garneau
Les Célébrations suivi de Adidou Adidouce (VLB)

D. G. Jones
Under the Thunder the Flowers Light Up the Earth (Coach House)

Denis Monière
Le Développement des Idéologies au Québec des Origines à Nos Jours (Editions Québec/Amérique)

Gabrielle Roy
Ces Enfants de Ma Vie (Stanké)

Frank Scott
Essays on the Constitution (Univ. of Toronto Press)

1978

Roger Caron
Go Boy (McGraw)

François-Marc Gagnon
Paul-Emile Borduas: Biographie Critique et Analyse de l'Oeuvre (Editions Fides)

Patrick Lane
Poems New and Selected (Oxford Univ. Press)

Gilbert Langevin
Mon Refuge Est un Volcan (Hexagone)

Alice Munro
Who Do You Think You Are? (Macmillan)

Jacques Poulin
Les Grandes Marées (Leméac)

The Molson Prizes

The Canada Council's Molson Prizes are given annually to recognize and encourage outstanding contributions to the arts, humanities, and social sciences. These $20,000 prizes are among Canada's highest tokens of recognition for cultural achievement. They are financed from the interest on a $900,000 gift to the Canada Council from the Molson Foundation.

1963
Donald Creighton
Alain Grandbois
1965
Jean Gascon
Frank Scott
1966
Georges-Henri Lévesque
Hugh MacLennan
1967
Arthur Erickson
Anne Hébert
Marshall McLuhan
1968
Glenn Gould
Jean Le Moyne
1969
Jean-Paul Audet
Morley Callaghan
Arnold Spohr
1970
Northrop Frye
Duncan Macpherson
Yves Thériault
1971
Maureen Forrester
Rina Lasnier
Norman McLaren

1972
John James Deutsch
Alfred Pellan
George Woodcock
1973
Celia Franca
W. A. C. H. Dobson
Jean-Paul Lemieux
1974
Alex Colville
Pierre Dansereau
Margaret Laurence
1975
Orford String Quartet
Denise Pelletier
Jon Vickers
1976
John Hirsch
Bill Reid
Jean-Louis Roux
1977
Gabrielle Roy
Jack Shadbolt
George Story
1978
Jean Duceppe
Betty Oliphant
Michael Snow

Canadian Authors Association

Information concerning the awards described below can be obtained from the Canadian Authors Association, 24 Ryerson Avenue, Toronto M5T 2P3, Ontario, Canada.

Vicky Metcalf Award for Children

This award of $1,000, donated by Vicky Metcalf, is awarded annually for the body of work of a children's book author. The prize is given to stimulate writing for children—fiction, nonfiction, and picture books—by Canadian authors. Nominations are accepted from an individual or association before March 31 each year.

1963
  Kerry Wood
1964
  John F. Hayes
1965
  Roderick Haig-Brown
1966
  Fred Swayze
1967
  John Patrick Gillese
1968
  Lorrie McLaughlin
1969
  Audrey McKim
1970
  Farley Mowat
1971
  Kay Hill

1972
  William E. Toye
1973
  Christie Harris
1974
  Jean Little
1975
  Lyn Harrington
1976
  Suzanne Martel
1977
  James Houston
1978
  Lyn Cook
1979
  Cliff Faulknor

Vicky Metcalf Short Story Award for Children

In 1979, the Canadian Authors Association established this $500 award for an outstanding published short story for children.

1979
  Marina McDougall
  "The Kingdom of Riddles"

Rothmans Merit Award for Literature

This award, established in 1974, was offered by Rothmans of Pall Mall Canada, Ltd., and administered by the Canadian Authors Association. Its purpose was to honor a writer who had made a significant contribution to Canadian letters. It was awarded for one book only or for a body of work, either prose or poetry. The Judging Committee included the immediate past president of the Association and two other members coopted at his discretion. The award was presented at the annual awards dinner of the Canadian Authors Association, held in June in a different province each year.

1974
  Fred Bodsworth
  For a body of work

1975
  John Patrick Gillese
  For a body of work
  Discontinued

Canadian Children's Book Award

In 1956, this award was jointly established by Little, Brown & Company, Inc., 34 Beacon Street, Boston, Massachusetts 02106, and Little, Brown & Company (Canada), Ltd., 25 Hollinger Road, Toronto M4B 3G2, Ontario, Canada. It is given intermittently, but no more than every two years, to encourage the writing of original children's books by Canadian authors. Any unpublished manuscript by a resident of Canada is eligible. The award is $4,500 in prize and royalty advances. The winner is selected by the combined editorial boards of Little, Brown in Boston and Toronto. Announcement is made at the annual meeting of the Canadian Library Association.

1958
  Edith Lambert Sharp
  Nkwala
1961
  Jean Little
  Mine for Keeps
1965
  Clifford V. Faulknor
  The White Calf

1967
  Norah A. Perez
  Strange Summer in Stratford
1975
  Myra Paperny
  The Wooden People
1977
  Brenda Sivers
  The Snailman

Canadian Library Association

The Canadian Library Association (CLA), 151 Sparks Street, Ottawa K1P 5E3, Ontario, Canada, currently offers three scholarships, two awards sponsored by the Canadian Association of Children's Librarians, and two awards sponsored by the Canadian School Library Association.

CLA Book of the Year for Children

This annual award was established in 1946 for a children's book by a Canadian citizen or resident. The award's former name was the English Medal Award of the Canadian Association of Children's Librarians. From its establishment until 1950, the award was given for a book written in English. For a number of years after 1950, awards were made for both English and French books. Awards could be made to both in the same year, or one could be given without the other. Currently the award is given only for books in English. The award, a silver medal, is presented at the June conference of the Canadian Library Association. Inquiries may be addressed to the Canadian Association of Children's Librarians c/o the CLA.

1947
  Roderick Haig-Brown
  Starbuck Valley Winter (Morrow)

1948
  No award

1949
Mabel Dunham
Kristli's Trees (McClelland & Stewart)
1950
Richard S. Lambert
Franklin of the Arctic (Bobbs)
1951
No award
1952
Catherine A. Clark
The Sun Horse (Macmillan)
1953
No award
1954
Emile Gervais
Mgr. de Laval (Comité des Fondateurs de l'Église)
1955
No award
1956
Louise Riley
Train for Tiger Lily (Viking)
1957
Cyrus Macmillan
Glooscaps's Country and Other Indian Tales (Oxford Univ. Press)
1958
Béatrice Clément
Le Chevalier du Roi (Editions l'Atelier)
Farley Mowat
Lost in the Barrens (Little)
1959
Hélène Flamme
Un Drôle Petit Cheval (Leméac)
John F. Hayes
The Dangerous Cove (Messner)
1960
Marius Barbeau and Michael Hornyansky
The Golden Phoenix and Other French Canadian Fairy Tales (Walck)
Paule Daveluy
L'Été Enchanté (Jeunesse)
1961
Marcelle Gauvreau
Plantes Vagabondes (Centre de Psychologie et de Pédagogie)

William Toye
The St. Lawrence (Walck)
1962
Claude Aubry
Les Isles du Roi Maha-Maha II (Editions du Pélican)
1963
Sheila Burnford
The Incredible Journey (Little)
Paule Daveluy
Drôle d'Automne (Editions du Pélican)
1964
Cécile Chabot
Féerie (Beauchemin)
Roderick Haig-Brown
The Whale People (Collins)
1965
Claude Aubry
Le Loup de Noël (Centre de Psychologie et de Pédagogie)
Dorothy M. Reid
Tales of Nanabozho (Oxford Univ. Press)
1966
James Houston
Tikta'liktak: An Eskimo Legend (Longmans)
Monique Corriveau
Le Wapiti (Jeunesse)
James McNeill
The Double Knights (Oxford Univ. Press)
Andrée Maillet
Le Chêne des Tempêtes (Editions Fides)
1967
Christie Harris
Raven's Cry (McClelland & Stewart)
1968
James Houston
The White Archer: An Eskimo Legend (Longmans)
Claude Mélançon
Légendes Indiennes du Canada (Editions du Jour)

1969
   Kay Hill
   And Tomorrow the Stars: The Story of John Cabot (Dodd)
1970
   Edith Fowke
   Sally Go Round the Sun: 300 Songs, Rhymes and Games of Canadian Children (McClelland & Stewart)
1971
   William Toye
   Cartier Sails the St. Lawrence (Oxford Univ. Press)
1972
   Ann Blades
   Mary of Mile 18 (Tundra)
1973
   Ruth Nichols
   The Marrow of the World (Atheneum)

1974
   Elizabeth Cleaver
   The Miraculous Hind (Holt)
1975
   Dennis Lee
   Alligator Pie (Houghton)
1976
   Mordecai Richler
   Jacob Two Two Meets the Hooded Fang (McClelland & Stewart)
1977
   Christie Harris
   Mouse Woman and the Vanished Princesses (McClelland & Stewart)
1978
   Dennis Lee
   Garbage Delight (Macmillan
1979
   Kevin Major
   Hold Fast (Clarke, Irwin)

CLA Scholarship

This scholarship for work at an accredited Canadian library school, granted to a Canadian citizen or landed immigrant, has recently been combined with the Elizabeth Dafoe Scholarship. The CLA Scholarship was formerly $1,000, the Dafoe Scholarship $250; the value of the new combined scholarship will be increased. Inquiries concerning details of the new CLA Scholarship should be sent to the Scholarship Awards Committee of the Canadian Library Association.

Distinguished Service Award for School Administrators

This award was instituted in 1976 to recognize the responsible and influential role that school administrators perform in developing successful resource center programs and to honor those who have made outstanding contributions to that end. Nominees may be a school principal, superintendent, or director, directly responsible for a school or group of schools; learning resource program coordinators are not eligible. The award is given annually in June, if a suitable candidate is nominated. Each recipient is awarded an engraved work of Canadian art. Inquiries should be directed to the Canadian School Library Association, c/o the Canadian Library Association.

1977
   L. P. Rogers
1978
   M. J. Kindrachuk

1979
   B. J. Webber

Amelia Frances Howard-Gibbon Medal

This award was established to commemorate the illustrator of *An Illustrated Alphabet*, published in 1859 and considered Canada's first picture book. The manuscript is in the Osborne Collection in the Toronto Public Library. The medal is awarded by the Canadian Association of Children's Librarians for outstanding illustrations of children's books published in Canada. First given in 1971, the award is made only when an entry is judged to be worthy in quality.

1971
    Elizabeth Cleaver
    The Wind Has Wings (Oxford Univ. Press)
1972
    Shizuye Takashima
    A Child in Prison Camp (Tundra)
1973
    Jacques de Roussan
    Au-delà du Soleil/Beyond the Sun (Tundra)
1974
    William Kurelek
    A Prairie Boy's Winter (Tundra)
1975
    Carlo Italiano
    The Sleighs of My Childhood/Les Traîneaux de Mon Enfance (Tundra)

1976
    William Kurelek
    A Prairie Boy's Summer (Tundra)
1977
    Pam Hall
    Down by Jim Long's Stage (Breakwater)
1978
    Elizabeth Cleaver
    The Loon's Necklace (Oxford Univ. Press)
1979
    Ann Blades
    A Salmon for Simon, by Betty Waterton (Douglas & McIntyre)

Howard V. Phalin–World Book Graduate Scholarship

This is a one-year scholarship of up to $5,000 for study at an accredited library school in either Canada or the United States. The award must be used for a program of study or series of courses either leading to a further library degree or relating to library work in which the candidate is currently engaged or will be undertaking upon completion of the program or courses. Candidates must be Canadian citizens or have landed immigrant status. The award is presented at the annual conference of the CLA in June.

Margaret B. Scott Award of Merit

This award, instituted in 1972, recognizes individuals who by their leadership and sustained effort have made outstanding contributions to school librarianship in Canada. In 1976, it was named after the late Margaret B. Scott, an award recipient and a former president of the Canadian School Library Association. Nominations are open to all individuals. The final choice is based on evidence of outstanding and sustained national leadership resulting in the establishment of resource center policies and practices leading to improved teaching and learning. The award, an engraved work of Canadian art, is given annually in June, if a suitable candidate is nominated. Inquiries should be directed to the Canadian School Library Association, c/o the Canadian Library Association.

1972
  M. Allison Vaness
1973
  No award
1974
  Margaret B. Scott
1975
  Agnes Florence
  Margaret Gayfer

1976
  John Wright
1977
  No award
1978
  Lyle Evans King
1979
  Ken Haycock

H. W. Wilson Education Foundation Scholarship

This $1,000 award is for one year at an accredited Canadian library school. Consideration is given to financial need and academic standing. Candidates must be Canadian citizens or have landed immigrant status. The award is presented annually at the annual conference of the CLA in June.

Leacock Medal for Humour

This medal was established in 1946 by Leacock Associates, Orillia, Ontario, in memory of Stephen Leacock, Canadian humorist. It is awarded to the Canadian author of the best humorous book published in the preceding year. The medal is presented annually, usually in July, at a dinner in Orillia sponsored by Leacock Associates at the beginning of the Stephen Leacock Festival of Humour Week.

1947
  Harry L. Symons
  Ojibway Melody (Ambassador)

1948
  Paul G. Hiebert
  Sarah Binks (Oxford Univ. Press)

1949
  Angeline Hango
  Truthfully Yours (Oxford Univ. Press)

1950
  Earle Birney
  Turvey (McClelland & Stewart)

1951
  Eric Nicol
  The Roving 1 (Ryerson)
1952
  Jan Hilliard
  The Salt-Box (McLeod)
1953
  Lawrence Earl
  The Battle of Baltinglass (Clarke, Irwin)
1954
  Joan Walker
  Pardon My Parka (McClelland & Stewart)

1955
Robertson Davies
Leaven of Malice (Clarke, Irwin)

1956
Eric Nicol
Shall We Join the Ladies? (Ryerson)

1957
Robert Thomas Allen
The Grass Is Never Greener (McClelland & Stewart)

1958
Eric Nicol
Girdle Me a Globe (Ryerson)

1959
No award

1960
Pierre Berton
Just Add Water and Stir (McClelland & Stewart)

1961
Norman Ward
Mice in the Beer (Longmans)

1962
William O. Mitchell
Jake and the Kid (Macmillan)

1963
Donald Jack
Three Cheers for Me (Collier-Macmillan)

1964
Harry J. Boyle
Homebrew and Patches (Clarke, Irwin)

1965
Gregory Clark
Gregory Clark War Stories (Ryerson)

1966
George Bain
Nursery Rhymes to Be Read Aloud by Young Parents and Old Children (Clarke, Irwin)

1967
Richard J. Needham
Needham's Inferno (Macmillan)

1968
Max Ferguson
And Now . . . Here's Max (McGraw)

1969
Stuart Trueman
You're Only as Old as You Act (McClelland & Stewart)

1970
Farley Mowat
The Boat Who Wouldn't Float (McClelland & Stewart)

1971
Robert Thomas Allen
Children, Wives and Other Wildlife (Doubleday)

1972
Max Braithwaite
The Night They Stole the Mounties Car (McClelland & Stewart)

1973
Donald Bell
Saturday Night at the Bagel Factory (McClelland & Stewart)

1974
Donald Jack
That's Me in the Middle (Doubleday)

1975
Morley Torgov
A Good Place to Come From (Lester & Orpen)

1976
Harry J. Boyle
The Luck of the Irish (Macmillan)

1977
Ray Guy
That Far Greater Bay (Breakwater)

1978
Ernest Buckler
Whirligig (McClelland & Stewart)

1979
Sondra Gotlieb
True Confections (Musson)

President's Medals

The President's Medals have been awarded since 1951 to complement the Governor General's awards for literature by giving recognition to periodical publication. They are awarded to the best works submitted in four categories: a poem or short story in English; an article in English in a learned journal; an article in English in a general-interest magazine; and an article in French in a general-interest magazine. Previously there were separate awards for a poem and a short story, and the award for an article in French in a general-interest magazine was recently established. To be eligible a work must be done by a citizen or resident of Canada and must have been published in Canada in the preceding calendar year. The entries are judged by special committees drawn from the faculty of the University of Western Ontario. A cash award of $1,000 accompanies each medal. For further details, contact J. G. Rowe, The Faculty of Arts, The University of Western Ontario, London N6A 3K7, Ontario, Canada.

SINGLE POEM

1952
Earle Birney
"Northwest Star"
1953
No award
1954
Dorothy Livesay
"Lament"
1955
James Reaney
"The Horn"
1956
Louis Dudek
"Keewaydin Poems"
1957
Jay Macpherson
"The Fisherman—A Book of Riddles"
1958
James Reaney
"The April and May Eclogues"
1959
F. E. Sparshott
"By the Canal"
1960
No award
1961
Irving Layton
"Keine Lazarovitch"

1962
Wilfred Watson
"The Necklace"
1963
Eli Mandel
"On the Death of Dr. Tom Dooley"
1964
Alfred Purdy
"The Country North of Belleville"
1965
Richard Emil Braun
"Niagara"
1966
Margaret Atwood
"The Settlers"
1967
Raymond Souster
"The Farm Out the Sydenham Road"
1968
Michael Ondaatje
"Paris"
1969
Joan Finnigan
"Death of a Psychiatrist"
1970
Glen Siebrasse
"The Human Being Who Wished He Were a Flag"
1971
Paulette Jiles
"A Letter to Grandad on the Occasion

SINGLE POEM (cont.)

of a Letter from My Mother Saying
Grandad Is Too Infirm to Feed the
Cows and Is Not Long for This World"
1972
Don Gutteridge
"Death at Quebec"
1973
No award

GENERAL ARTICLE

1951
Blair Fraser
"The Secret Life of Mackenzie King,
Spiritualist"
1953
Robert Thomas Allen
"I Am Looking for the Man We Cele-
brate"
1954
Bruce Hutchison
"The Dangerous Luxury of Hating
Americans"
1955
Bill Stephenson
"There'll Never Be Another Model T"
1956
Ralph Allen
"The Land of Eternal Change"
1957
Sidney Katz
"The Seven Who Survived"
1958
Sidney Katz
"What Kind of Man Was Herbert Nor-
man?"
1959
Mordecai Richler
"Confessions of a Fellow Traveler"
1960
McKenzie Porter
"Varley"

1961
Blair Fraser
"Free Asia's Revolt Against Western
Ways"
1962
Barbara Moon
"The Nuclear Death of a Nuclear Sci-
entist"
1963
Wynne Francis
"Montreal Poets of the Forties"
1964
Peter Gzowski
"Conversations with Quebec Revolu-
tionaries"
1965
Mollie Gillen
"The Masseys"
1966
William French
"The Cultural Guerillas of Quebec"
1967
Dave Godfrey
"Letter from Africa to an American Ne-
gro"
1968
Hugh Hood
"It's a Small World"
1969
Sylvia Fraser
"The Thousand-Year Week"
1970
Christina Newman
"Mr. McKasey Goes to Ottawa"
1971
Michael Macklem
"A Book a Mile"
1972
Michele Landsberg
"How Trade Unions Let Women
Down"
1973
Peter C. Newman
"Reflections on a Fall from Grace"

SHORT STORY

1952
  Farley Mowat
  "Lost in the Barren Lands"
1953
  W. O. Mitchell
  "The Princess and the Wild Ones"
1954
  Colin McDougall
  "The Firing Squad"
1955
  P. B. Hughes
  "Catherine and the Winter Wheat"
1956
  Eva Lis Wuorio
  "Call Off Your Cats"
1957
  Ernest Buckler
  "The Dream and the Triumph"
1958
  Ernest Buckler
  "Anything Can Happen at Christmas"
1959
  Howard O'Hagan
  "Trees Are Lonely Company"
1960
  Henry Kreisel
  "The Travelling Nude"
1961
  Margaret Laurence
  "A Gourdful of Glory"
1962
  Margaret Laurence
  "The Tomorrow-Maker"
1963
  Hugh Hood
  "The End of It"
1964
  Margaret Laurence
  "Mask of Beaten Gold"
1965
  Dave Godfrey
  "Gossip: The Birds That Flew, the Birds That Fell"
1966
  Austin C. Clarke

  "Four Stations to His Circle"
1967
  Dave Godfrey
  "The Hard-Headed Collector"
1968
  Clark L. Blaise
  "The Mayor"
1969
  J. Metcalf
  "The Estuary"
1970
  Alden Nowlan
  "There Was an Old Woman from Wexford"
1971
  W. D. Valgardson
  "Bloodflowers"
1972
  Alden Nowlan
  "Life and Times"
1973
  Jack Hodgins
  "After the Season"

SCHOLARLY ARTICLE

1953
  Norman Ward
  "The Formative Years of the Canadian House of Commons"

1954
  Northrop Frye
  "Towards a Theory of Cultural History"

1955
  Emil L. Fackenheim
  "Kant and Radical Evil"

1956
  D. M. Stanley
  "Kingdom to Church"

1957
  Blair Neatby and John T. Saywell
  "Chapleau and the Conservative Party in Quebec"

SCHOLARLY ARTICLE (cont.)

1958
J. E. Hodgetts
"The Civil Service and Policy Formation"
1959
Pierre-Elliott Trudeau
"Some Obstacles to Democracy in Quebec"
1960
A. S. P. Woodhouse
"Tragic Effect in Samson Agonistes"
1961
Hubert Guindon
"The Social Evolution of Quebec Reconsidered"
1962
F. E. Sparshott
"The Central Problem of Philosophy"
1963
R. Morton Smith
"Tradition and Modernization in India"
1964
R. B. Parker
"Dramaturgy in Shakespeare and Brecht"
1965
Philip Stratford
"Chalk and Cheese: A Comparative Study of *A Kiss for the Leper* and *A Burnt-Out Case*"

1966
Ramsay Cook
"The Historian and French-Canadian Nationalism"
1967
F. E. Sparshott
"Philosophy and the 'Creative Process' "
1968
Ramsay Cook
"French Canadian Interpretations of Canadian History"
1969
Andrew Brink
"Sylvia Plath and the Art of Redemption"
1970
A. I. Silver
"French Canada and the Prairie Frontier, 1870 –1890"
1971
J. W. Graham
"Point of View in the Waves: Some Services of the Style"
1972
Grazia Merler
"La Réalité dans la Prose d'Anne Hébert"
1973
No award
1974 –1979
Winners unavailable

Prix Littéraire Esso du Cercle du Livre de France

This annual award is given for a French-Canadian novel of outstanding merit. It was inaugurated in 1949 by Le Cercle du Livre de France (French Book Guild). In 1977, the Compagnie Pétrolière Impériale, Ltee., became the sponsor and changed the award's name from Prix du Cercle du Livre de France to its present form. Winning authors received $1,000 until 1975, when the prize was increased to $5,000. The prize-winning book is published by Le Cercle du Livre and distributed to its Canadian and American members. A jury of writers and critics from both France and Canada chooses the winning manuscript.

1949
  Françoise Loranger
  Mathieu
1950
  Bertrand Vac
  Louis Genest
1951
  André Langevin
  Evadé de la Nuit
1952
  Bertrand Vac
  Deux Portes, Une Adresse
1953
  André Langevin
  Poussière sur la Ville (Dust over the
  City, Putnam)
1954
  Jean Vaillancourt
  Les Canadiens Errants
1955
  Jean Filiatrault
  Chaînes
1956
  Eugène Cloutier
  Les Inutiles

  Maurice Gagnon
  L'Ehéance

  Jean Simard
  Mon Fils Pourtant Heureux
1957
  J. Marie Poirier
  Le Prix du Souvenir
1958
  Claire Martin
  Avec ou sans Amour
1959
  Pierre Gélinas
  Les Vivants, les Morts et les Autres
1960
  Claude Jasmin
  La Corde au Cou
1961
  Diane Giguère
  Le Temps des Jeux
1962
  No award

1963
  Louis Maheux-Forcier
  Amadou
1964
  Georges Cartier
  Le Poisson Péché
1965
  Bertrand Vac
  Histories Galantes
1966
  André Berthiaume
  La Fugue
1967
  Anne Bernard
  Cancer
1968
  Yvette Naubert
  L'Eté de la Cigale
1969
  Josette Bernier
  Non Monsieur
1970
  No award
1971
  Lise Parent
  Les Iles Flottantes
1972
  No award
1973
  Huguette Légaré
  La Conversation entre Hommes
1974
  Jean-Pierre Guay
  Mise en Liberté
1975
  Pierre Stewart
  L'Amour d'une Autre
1976
  No award
1977
  Simone Piuze
  Les Cercles Concentriques
1978
  Négovan Rajie
  Les Hommes Taupes

Royal Society of Canada

The Royal Society of Canada, 344 Wellington Street, Ottawa K1A ON4, Ontario, Canada, awards a number of medals for literary accomplishment and scientific research. They are given to authors who have published or, having completed outstanding research, intend to publish works in the fields of literature, history, and the sciences. The medals are awarded and presented each June at the annual meeting of the Society. Medals given for literary accomplishment in the fields of literature and history are listed below.

Pierre Chauveau Medal

This award, a silver medal and $1,000, was established in 1952 to honor outstanding contributions in the humanities other than Canadian history and Canadian literature. The award is named for the nineteenth-century Quebec statesman, writer, and historian Pierre Chauveau. The award was given annually from 1952 to 1966 and biennially since then.

1952
  Pierre Daviault
1953
  B. K. Sandwell
1954
  Gérard Morisset
1955
  Jean-Marie Gauvreau
1956
  Victor Morin
1957
  Claude Melançon
1958
  No award
1959
  Harry Bernard
1960
  F. C. A. Jeanneret
1961
  Gérard Malchelosse
1962
  Maurice Lebel

1963
  Arthur Maheux
1964
  Rosaire Dion-Lévesque
1965
  Robert Charbonneau
1966
  Louis-Philippe Audet
1968
  B. Wilkinson
1970
  H. N. Frye
1972
  Louis-Edmond Hamelin
1974
  Wilfred Cantwell Smith
1976
  Edward Togo Salmon
1979
  Kathleen Coburn

Jason A. Hannah Medal

This award was established in 1976 by the Royal Society of Canada and the Associated Medical Services, Inc., to honor their late president by recognizing research in the history of Canadian medicine. The award consists of a bronze medal and $1,000, to be awarded annually if there is a suitable candidate. The medal is awarded for an important publication on the history of Canadian medicine published in the preceding ten years. The medal's recipient is chosen by a committee of six members of the Royal Society and a representative of Associated Medical Services.

1978
  Henri Ellenberger

1979
  John Farley

Innis-Gérin Medal

The Innis-Gérin Medal, founded in 1967 by the Royal Society of Canada, is named in memory of Harold Innis and Léon Gérin. It is awarded biennially to a citizen or resident of Canada for a distinguished and sustained contribution to the literature of the social sciences including human geography and social psychology. The award consists of a bronze medal and $1,000.

1967
  W. A. Mackintosh
1968
  Esdras Minville
1969
  Alexander Brady
1971
  Jacques Henripin

1973
  Jean-Charles Falardeau
1975
  Noel Mailloux
1977
  H. G. Johnson
1979
  Marc-Adélard Tremblay

Lorne Pierce Medal

This gold medal, first awarded in 1926, is the gift of Dr. Lorne Pierce of Toronto; the Society has added $1,000 to the award. It honors fellows of the Royal Society of Canada, or other Canadian citizens, for significant achievements in imaginative or critical literature. Literary criticism dealing with Canadian subjects receives primary consideration. Originally an annual award, the medal has been given biennially since 1964.

1926
  Charles G. D. Roberts
1927
  Duncan C. Scott
1928
  Bliss Carman
1929
  Camille Roy
1930
  Andrew Macphail

1931
  Adjutor Rivard
1932
  Archibald MacMechan
1933
  No award
1934
  Frederick Philip Grove
1935
  Edouard Monpetit

1936
  Pelham Edgar
1937
  Stephen Leacock
1938
  Mazo de la Roche
1939
  Wilfrid Bovey
1940
  E. J. Pratt
1941
  Léon Gérin
1942
  Watson Kirkconnell
1943
  George H. Clark
1944
  Audrey Alexandra Brown
1945
  Félix Antoine Savard
1946
  Charles N. Cochrane (posthumously)
1947
  Dorothy Livesay [Mrs. Duncan Macnair]
1948
  Gabrielle Roy [Mrs. Carbotte]
1949
  John Murray Gibbon
1950
  Marius Barbeau
1951
  E. K. Brown
1952
  Hugh MacLennan
1953
  Earle Birney

1954
  Alain Grandbois
1955
  William Bruce Hutchison
1956
  T. H. Raddall
1957
  A. M. Klein
1958
  Northrop Frye
1959
  Philippe Panneton
1960
  Morley Callaghan
1961
  Robertson Davies
1962
  F. R. Scott
1963
  Léo-Paul Desrosiers
1964
  Ethel Wilson
1966
  A. J. M. Smith
1968
  R. D. C. Finch
1970
  Roy Daniells
1972
  Desmond Pacey
1974
  Rina Lasnier
1976
  Douglas Le Pan
1978
  Carl F. Klinck

Tyrrell Medal

This award, a gold medal and $1,000, was founded in 1928 and named for its donor, the late Dr. J. B. Tyrrell of Toronto. It gives recognition to outstanding work on the history of Canada. The contribution may be published or unpublished research, biography, or a collection of historical material in French or English. The medal is intended not only as a citation for past accomplishment but as an incentive toward further effort.

The recipient is to be preferably, but not necessarily, a Canadian. The award was presented annually until 1966, irregularly thereafter.

1928
John Chapais
1929
George M. Wrong
1930
Adam Shortt
1931
Lawrence J. Burpee
1932
Pierre Georges Roy
1933
F. W. Howay
1934
J. C. Webster
1935
E. A. Cruikshank
1936
W. Stewart Wallace
1937
Aegidius Fauteux
1938
William Wood
1939
E. Z. Massicotte
1940
Chester Martin
1941
Arthur S. Morton
1942
D. C. Harvey
1943
Gustave Lanctôt
1944
Harold A. Innis
1945
Fred Landon
1946
A. L. Burt
1947
A. R. M. Lower
1948
Lionel Groulx
1949
Reginald G. Trotter

1950
John Bartlet Brebner
1951
Jean Bruchési
1952
C. B. Sissons
1953
Séraphin Marion
1954
G. de T. Glazebrook
1955
C. P. Stacey
1956
Olivier Maurault
1957
George F. G. Stanley
1958
W. L. Morton
1959
Arthur Maheux
1960
S. D. Clark
1961
Guy Frégault
1962
J. M. S. Careless
1963
F. H. Underhill
1964
Marcel Trudel
1965
W. Kaye Lamb
1966
Edgar McInnis
1968
G. W. L. Nicholson
1970
Fernand Ouellet
1972
Jean Hamelin
1975
Ramsay Cook
1979
W. J. Eccles

U.B.C. Medal for Popular Biography

Since 1951, the University of British Columbia, Vancouver 8, British Columbia, Canada, has annually offered the U.B.C. Medal for Popular Biography for the best book in this category written by a Canadian author and published during the preceding year.

1952
Josephine Phelan
The Ardent Exile (Macmillan)
1953
Bruce Hutchison
The Incredible Canadian (Longmans)
1954
Grace MacInnis
J. S. Woodsworth (Macmillan)
1955
Robert Tyre
Saddlebag Surgeon (Dent)
1956
D. G. Creighton
John A. Macdonald, the Old Chieftain (Houghton)
1957
William Kilbourn
The Firebrand (Clarke, Irwin)
1958
Elisabeth Wallace
Goldwin Smith, Victorian Liberal (Univ. of Toronto Press)
1959
R. MacGregor Dawson
William Lyon Mackenzie King, Vol. I (Univ. of Toronto Press)
1960
J. M. S. Careless
Brown of the Globe (St. Martin's)
1961
Dale C. Thompson
Alexander MacKenzie (Macmillan)
1962
No award
1963
W. H. Graham
The Tiger of Canada West (Clarke, Irwin)

1964
John M. Gray
Lord Selkirk of Red River (Macmillan)
1965
Phyllis Grosskurth
John Addington Symonds (Longmans)
1966
Joseph Schull
Laurier (Macmillan)
1967
D. J. Goodspeed
Ludendorff: Genius of World War One (Houghton)
1968
Neil McKenty
Mitch Hepburn (McClelland & Stewart)
1969
No award
1970
William Rodney
Kootenai Brown (Gray's)
1971
James H. Gray
The Boy from Winnipeg (Macmillan)
1972
No award

1973
George Woodcock
Gandhi

1974
Denis Smith
Gentle Patriot: A Political Biography of Walter Gordon (Hurtig)
Douglas Spettigue
F P G: The European Years (Oberon)

1975
Lena Newman
The John A. Macdonald Album (Tundra)

1976
Margaret E. Prang
N. W. Rowell: Ontario Nationalist (Univ. of Toronto Press)

George Woodcock
Gabriel Dumont: The Métis Chief and His Lost World (Hurtig)

1977
James M. Minifie
Expatriate (Macmillan)

1978
David R. Williams
The Man for a New Country: Sir Matthew Baillie Begbie (Gray)

1979
Michael Bliss
A Canadian Millionaire: The Life and Business Times of Sir Joseph Flavelle, Bart., 1858–1939 (Macmillan)

Index

This index lists the names of all active and discontinued awards described in the first ten editions of this book. The index also lists, for the current edition only, the names of all award sponsors and award winners, i.e., authors, editors, illustrators, translators, and, for a few awards, the names of publishers or the titles of books, dramas, or periodicals.

Names of awards that are no longer active are indicated with the notation "disc." If awards were discontinued prior to the 1959 edition, the notation "disc." without a date is used. Discontinued awards that appeared in the last six editions are given with the notation "disc. 1959 ed.," "disc. 1963 ed.," "disc. 1967 ed.," "disc. 1970 ed.," "disc. 1973 ed.," or "disc. 1976 ed."

Index users should note that while an individual author may have won an award more than one time and his or her name may appear more than once on a single page of text, this fact is not indicated in the index. For example, John Steinbeck is listed in this index with a reference to page 84, though his name appears on that page three times as a winner of the California Literature Medal Award.

Ihrig, Alice, 434
Iko, Momoko, 194
Ilkley Literature Festival, 521
Illinois Chapter, SLA, 458
Illinois Libraries, 435
Illinois Library Association, 419
Illinois Sesquicentennial Literary Awards—disc. 1973 ed.
Immroth, John Phillip, 427
Indiana Authors' Day Awards—disc. 1973 ed.
Indiana School Librarians Association, 352
Inez, Colette, 377
Infeld, Leopold, 56
Ingalls, Jeremy, 22, 132, 380, 386
Inge, William, 233, 390
Inkeles, Alex, 181
Innaurato, Albert F., 137
Inner Sanctum Mystery Contest—disc. 1967 ed.
Innes, Jasmine Rose, 501
Innis-Gérin Medal, 552
Innis, Harold, 552, 554
Institute for Advanced Studies in the Theater Arts, 389
Institute for Reading Research, 335
Institute for the Intellectual Development of Children and Young Adults, 327
Institute Manuscript Award—disc. 1976 ed.
Institute of Early American History and Culture, 154
Institute of Early American History and Culture, Institute Manuscript Award—disc. 1976 ed.
Intermountain Conference on Literature for Children and Young Adults, 448
International African Institute, 3
International Board on Books for Young People, 319
International Book Award, 6
International Book Committee, 6
International Children's Book Day, 314
International League of Antiquarian Booksellers, 6
International Literary Prize (Prix International de Littérature)—disc. 1973 ed.
International Novel Award—disc. 1967 ed.
International Poetry Forum, 384
International Reading Association Children's Book Award, 335
International Reading Association, International Book Year Project, 353
International Wildlife Federation, 128
International Writer's Prize, 519
Ionesco, Eugene, 8, 519
Iowa Arts Council, Writers Workshop, 406
Iowa School of Letters Award for Short Fiction, 406

Iowa State University Press Award—disc. 1970 ed.
Ippolito, Felice, 5
Ireland, Marion P., 90
Irigaray, Louis, 92, 283
Irish-American Cultural Institute Literary Awards, 7
Irschick, Eugene F., 48
Irvine Unified School District, California, 431
Irvine, William, 86
Irving, John W., 137
Irwin, Inez, 404
Isaacs, Harold R., 58
Ish-Kishor, Sulamith, 321, 339, 340
Isherwood, Christopher, 26, 69
Ishimoto, Carol F., 440
Islwyn, Aled. *See* Aled Islwyn
Israel, Fred, 252
Italian Institute, 513
Italiano, Carlo, 543
Ivens, Dorothy, 113
Iversen, William, 301
Iyanaga, Shokichi, 262
Izard, Anne Rebecca, 418
Izenour, George C., 270

JWB Jewish Book Council, 145, 339
Jack, Donald, 545
Jackson, Charles, 23
Jackson, Donald, 275
Jackson, Edith B1
Jackson, Gabriel, 38
Jackson, Jacqueline, 332
Jackson, Jesse, 352
Jackson, Joseph Henry, 84, 226
Jackson, Joseph Henry, Award, 153
Jackson, Marian, 514
Jackson, Michael, 471
Jackson, Miles M., Jr., 439
Jacobs, Arthur, 487
Jacobs, Bernard, 120
Jacobs, Catherine Hayden, 375
Jacobs, Florence, 375
Jacobs, Harvey, 195, 301
Jacobs, Jane, 141
Jacobs, Rita, 120
Jacobson, Dan, 491, 492, 509
Jacobson, Harold K., 309
Jacobson, Jon, 40
Jacobson, Mark, 403
Jacobson, Steven, 402
Jacobstein, J. Myron, 440
Jacques, Florence P., 82
Jaffa, Harry V., 206
Jaffe, Mordicai, 152